PLIMSOLLS ON, EYEB.
The Rise and Horrenc
of Marathon Legend J.

AWARD-WINNING ATHLETICS BIOGRAPHIES BY ROB HADGRAFT:

The Little Wonder: The Untold Story of Alfred Shrubb - World Champion Runner
ISBN 978-1-874287-81-0

'Only now, in the centenary of his finest year, has the tiny Englishman Alf Shrubb been given due recognition in this delightful and finely-crafted biography, which brings alive a fascinating sporting era.' (*Athletics Weekly*)

'This is a story richly evocative of the heyday of Edwardian athletics.' (*The Guardian*) The great thing about this book is how it takes something forgotten by everybody and brings it back to vivid life. This book is begging for a nibble from a film producer. (BBC London)

Beer and Brine: The Making of Walter George - Athletics First Superstar
ISBN 978-1-905328-20-8

'This is one of the finest sporting biographies you will ever read. Not only is the text illuminated with stirring reportage of the record-breaking races in which George took part, but it also provides the reader with as good a picture of mid-to late-Victorian England and the growth of sport as any book has ever done. Gripping from start to finish, it is meticulously researched and vividly encapsulates what sporting biography is all about. George was born in 1858 in the small town of Calne and the story of his early life in the idyllic Wiltshire countryside is beautifully told with plenty of social and political background, a feature which underpins the narrative throughout.' (*Birmingham Post*)

Deerfoot: Athletics' Noble Savage - From Indian Reservation to Champion of the World
ISBN 978-1-905328-52-9

'The first biography of this extraordinary American athlete, who dominated English professional running from 1861-63, written by the assiduous Rob Hadgraft, an enthusiast who already gave us fascinating books on Shrubb and George. Hadgraft's usual thoroughness brings to life the noisy, rough-edged vigour of 19th century running. It also gives insight into matters as important as racism, Victorian popular culture and the colourful early history of advertising and promotion. Hadgraft is also commendably forthright about the prevalence of race-fixing and show-boating.' (*Running Times USA*).

'Hadgraft is a meticulous researcher, a freelance journalist, who consults every available source: other athletics historians, contemporary newspapers, magazines and books. He even managed to find family members and thus accessed family papers. Deerfoot's British tour saw him run 130 events in 87 weeks and Hadgraft documents each.' (*Cool Running Australia*).

Tea with Mr Newton: 100,000 Miles - The Longest Protest March in History
ISBN 978-1-905328-85-7 (Long-listed for 2010 William Hill Sports Book of the Year)

'Who better to write the long-awaited biography of Arthur Newton than Rob Hadgraft, author of a trilogy of beautifully written books on the lives of Alf Shrubb, Walter George and Deerfoot. Once again, Hadgraft has succeeded in crafting a meticulously researched and highly entertaining biography, his subject this time being the founding father of ultra-distance running. This is a truly fascinating story of an aging English gentleman who, against all odds, goes from complete obscurity to international acclaim as a long-distance runner and later as a writer. Newton broke world records in addition to inventing 'LSD' (Long Slow Distance) running, and is credited with being the inspirational figure behind the Comrades, the world's leading ultra-marathon, and the legendary London to Brighton race.' (Amazon)

PLIMSOLLS ON, EYEBALLS OUT
The Rise and Horrendous Fall
of Marathon Legend Jim Peters

Series editor: Clive Leatherdale

Rob Hadgraft

DESERT ISLAND BOOKS

First published in 2011
by
DESERT ISLAND BOOKS LIMITED
Unit 1, 36 Clifftown Parade, Southend-on-Sea, Essex SS1 1DL
United Kingdom
www.desertislandbooks.com

© 2011 Rob Hadgraft

The right of Rob Hadgraft to be identified as author of this work has
been asserted under The Copyright Designs and Patents Act 1988

British Library Cataloguing-in-Publication Data
A catalogue record for this book is available from the British Library

ISBN 978-1-905328-96-3

Printed in Great Britain

Contents

AUTHOR'S NOTE

This study of maverick marathon legend Jim Peters follows my four earlier biographies of long-distance runners, published by Desert Island Books. All five subjects were chosen for being runners who became the world's best at their chosen distances. In chronological order, Deerfoot, Walter George, Alf Shrubb and Arthur Newton were all champion runners spanning the period between the American Civil War and the start of World War Two. Then, after Nazi Germany was defeated, Jim Peters emerged to become a true athletics icon of the 1950s.

I am indebted to a number of people for their help during my research into Jim's life and career. Some are historians, fans or contemporaries who watched him in awe from the sidelines, while others have fond memories of actually running with or against him – their sense of wonder no less pronounced, I suspect.

I would like to thank: Alex Wilson, Jackie Mekler, Geoff Warren, Don Macgregor, Trevor Vincent, Dave Bedford, Nigel Wingate, Bob Phillips, Andy Milroy, Allan Lawrence, John Landy, Frank Sando, Sir Roger Bannister, Colin Young, Ted Baverstock, Dave Green, Colin Kirkham, Neil Robbins, Kevan Gosper, Peter Lovesey, David Thurlow, George Knight, Kevin Kelly, Peter Matthews, Charles Baker, Keith Morbey, Wilf Morgan, Dave Terry, Bob Smith, Tony Benton, Alan Mead, Nicola Oakey, Len Johnson, Rob de Castella, Mel Watman, Peter Radford, Barrie Almond, Ian Champion, Timothy Noakes, Roger Robinson, Ian Tempest, Ian Linton, Jack Miller, Malcolm Bailey, Norman Harris Tony Maxwell, Brian Ecott, Louise Abbott and Jacqui Ramsden.

The above-named provided, or helped me obtain, original source material. I also gleaned much from publications spanning the last 90 years or so, including: *Athletics Weekly, Athletics World, Athletics Review, Scots Athlete, World Sports, The Beagle* newsletter, RRC newsletter, *Marathon & Distance Runner, Track Stats, Dagenham Digest, The Times, News of the World, Sunday People, Daily and Sunday Express, Daily Mirror, News Chronicle, Evening Standard, Vancouver Sun, Newcastle Journal, Ilford Guardian, Dagenham Post, Essex Chronicle, East Essex Gazette* and *Barking Advertiser*.

I also acknowledge the help of staff at the Essex Record Office, British Newspaper Library at Colindale, British Library St Pancras, and the Valence House Museum in Dagenham. Newham & Essex Beagles kindly loaned me a stash of yellowing minute books, and some of the quotes I have attributed to Jim came from these – and others from his own book *In the Long Run*. Of the illustrations used, some are my own and others were kindly contributed from private collections.

SELECT BIBLIOGRAPHY

A Clean Pair of Heels (Halberg, 1963)
Age is No Distance (Jones, 1988)
An Olympic Life (Gosper & Korporal, 2000)
Austerity Britain 1945-51 (Kynaston, 2007)
Boston Marathon (Derderian, 1994)
Essex Beagles Centenary History (Benton, 1987)
First Four Minutes (Bannister, 1956)
Gordon Pirie: The Impossible Hero (Booth, 1999)
Honour of Empire, Glory of Sport (Phillips, 2000)
How London Rescued the Games (Phillips, 2007)
In The Long Run (Peters & Edmundson, 1955)
Wally Hayward: Just Call Me Wally (Jamieson, 1999)
Long Spikes, Short Rations: GB Athletics 1950 (Sheridan, 2004)
Lore of Running (Noakes, 2003)
Marathon Kings (Giller, 1983)
Masters of the Marathon (Benyo, 1983)
Modern Middle and Long-Distance Running (Peters, Johnston & Edmundson, 1957)
Official Centenary History of the AAA (Lovesey, 1979)
Running My Life (Macgregor, 2010)
Running Round the World (Crump, 1966)
Sunset of the Golden Years: GB Athletics 1951-59 (Sheridan, 2008)
Sydney Wooderson: Forgotten Champion (Thurlow, 1989)
The Austerity Olympics (Hampton, 2008)
The Landy Era (Johnson, 2009)
The Lonely Breed (Clarke & Harris, 1967)
The Long Hard Road (Hill, 1981)
Who's Who of GB International Athletes 1945-60 (Sheridan, 2010)
Why Die? The Extraordinary Percy Cerutty (Sims, 2003)
Woodford Green AC: From Tiny Acorns (Maxwell, 2008)

NOTE ON TIMINGS: For readers unfamiliar with running statistics, this book gives race timings thus: 2:17.24 indicates a run of 2 hours, 17 minutes and 24 seconds. In some of Jim Peters' races, tenths of a second were also included in published times – this is denoted as 2:17.24.4, meaning 2 hours 17 minutes, 24.4 seconds.

ROB HADGRAFT
Chelmsford, Essex
September 2011

Foreword

by Dave Bedford

He might not have won major international titles, but Jim Peters will always be remembered as one of the most distinguished figures in the annals of British athletics. He was the man who revolutionised the world of marathon running.

Jim was just months away from his 30th birthday when he competed in the London Olympics of 1948. To represent your country at an Olympics is every athlete's ambition, and having achieved that, but deeply disappointed at being lapped in the 10,000 metres, he considered retirement. He had won a couple of AAA track titles but his times fell well short of world class and it seemed unlikely at his age that he would make any significant improvement.

Happily, he was prevailed upon by his coach, former Olympic 5000 metres runner 'Johnny' Johnston, not only to continue running, but to switch to the marathon. Jim needed plenty of persuasion, realising the extra demands of marathon training, but he relented ... and the rest is history.

There were no half measures with Jim. He trained at an intensity unlike any marathoner before him and in June 1951 made a notable marathon debut at the age of 32 by smashing the long-standing British record with a time of 2:29.24. A year later, over the same Windsor to Chiswick course, he produced what at the time was considered an absolutely phenomenal performance. The world best stood at 2:25.39 – and Jim ran 2:20.43!

He would have finished almost a mile ahead of any previous marathon runner. A front-runner unafraid to push out the boundaries of what had been thought possible, he improved the record to 2:17.40 in 1954.

His uncompromising approach to racing would unfortunately prove to be his undoing. At the 1954 Empire Games in Vancouver he failed to take full account of the extreme heat and humidity and, literally miles ahead of his nearest opponent as he entered the stadium, he repeatedly fell while groggily attempting to cover the last few hundred yards. Within sight of the finish, Jim was carried off by anxious officials and never raced again. Seriously dehydrated, he was lucky to escape with his life. In fact he lived to celebrate his 80th birthday.

All these years later the name of Jim Peters is still revered by marathon runners the world over. He showed them that by dint of hard work, dedication and guts, anything is possible.

Following his passing in January 1999, we at the London Marathon instigated the Jim Peters Trophy as a lasting memory and tribute to him. This trophy is awarded to the first British athlete to finish each London Marathon, regardless of gender, and has since been awarded to many notable British runners, one of whom was Paula Radcliffe in 2003.

Jim Peters Trophy winners: 1999 – Jon Brown; 2000, 2001 and 2002 Mark Steinle; 2003 Paula Radcliffe; 2004 and 2005 Jon Brown; 2006 Peter Riley; 2007 and 2008 Dan Robinson; 2009 Andi Jones; 2010 Andrew Lemoncello; 2011 Lee Merrien.

DAVE BEDFORD
London
July 2011

FOOTNOTE: Born in December 1949, Dave Bedford is one of the most colourful characters in distance-running history. With his long hair, splendid moustache and red socks, he smashed the world record for 10,000 metres in dramatic style in 1973. Earlier he'd won national cross-country titles, a series of AAA championships, and appeared at the 1972 Munich Olympics. Much-loved by the fans but not the authorities, typical of his legendary stunts was the day in 1970 he put his name down for both senior and junior races at a major championship on his beloved Hampstead Heath. He did, of course, win both titles! Like Jim Peters he was renowned for his heavy training mileage and brave front-running approach to racing. This 'poacher-turned-gamekeeper' later became race director of the hugely successful London Marathon for many years.

Where Have All the Distance Runners Gone?

Peters, Pirie, Chataway, Ibbotson, Tulloh, Heatley, Hill, Batty, Kilby, Adcocks, Alder, McCafferty, Macgregor, Foster, Stewart, Bedford, Thompson, Simmons, Rose, Moorcroft, Jones, Spedding. For 35 years or so after the Second World War, Britain was truly a force to be reckoned with in distance running, admired for its strength in depth and its harrier traditions, if not its championship medals tally.

But in more recent times the great names listed above have become mere reminders of a halcyon age long since vanished. Little did we know back then that over the first decade of the 21st century Britain would only have one true distance hero – a female, Paula Radcliffe.

Defying post-war austerity, a slew of talented British runners emerged in the early 1950s, chasing world records and championship medals, training in their spare time after work, and firing the imagination of an entertainment-starved nation. They blazed a trail that saw the UK become a running hotbed, in turn paving the way for the golden track and field era of the 1980s and the citizen running/fitness boom of the same decade.

At the very vanguard of all this was a working-class enthusiast in his thirties from gritty Dagenham. His name was James Henry Peters and he worked in an optician's shop. He'd been an only child, his early years in London's East End dogged by ill-health. He was small, skinny and frail-looking, but possessed a mysterious hidden quality that drove him to run harder, faster and further than all his mates. Mild-mannered and companionable, when he pulled on his Woolworths plimsolls he turned into a man possessed.

Jim Peters was certainly no stylist, and never an athlete lauded by the purists. He was no master tactician either, nor a runner of grace and poise, but he had the guts, motivation and sheer bloody-mindedness to grind out very fast times no matter how stiff the task.

He took on unprecedented training loads that would break lesser men, and never jogged along or took things easy. He always 'bashed it' night after night. When he ran, his head wagged from side to side, his upper body driving him forward in a sort of lurching motion. He got nervous before races, and often shot away recklessly, anxious to leave all opposition behind in the early stages, whatever the conditions or length of the race. Taking on fluids before, during or after an event upset his stomach, so he simply didn't bother.

For several years this *modus operandi* saw Jim Peters reign supreme as the world's fastest marathon runner, blasting all opposition out of sight. But then, in a Vancouver heatwave in August 1954, his world came crashing down. Jim Peters paid, and paid dearly, for his uncompromising 'kill or be killed' outlook.

What happened to Peters that fateful afternoon 'made women weep and grown men lose their lunch'. And that wasn't just glib hyperbole from the Canadian press either. Grown men did indeed throw up at the awful sight that Peters presented on the track in front of them. Women certainly did weep and faint, and even the normally inscrutable Duke of Edinburgh turned his head away, unable to look.

Cockney Jim Peters was a likeable, ordinary bloke whose rise to sporting greatness was little short of miraculous. His fall was simply horrible. This is his story.

CHAPTER 1

Heaven With the Gates Off

OCTOBER 1918 – OCTOBER 1933

Destiny only ever had one thing in mind for little Jimmy Peters. He would be a runner.

He was on the run from the moment he was born in poverty-stricken East London. On the run from ill-health, on the run from hardship. In both life and in sport, he would face a series of long and arduous battles. He was far from being a natural-born athlete, but an astonishing work ethic and bucketloads of determination would see him through. When Jim Peters ran, he ran hard.

Born in October 1918, a few days before the Great War ended, Jim was the only child of 23-year-old railway worker Percy Henry Peters and his wife Emma. The couple eked out a living amid the tightly packed Victorian streets of Hackney and Homerton, at the heart of an area soon to be the subject of major slum clearance.

These were distinctly unpromising beginnings in London's grimy East End, but Jim was not just another of the scrawny, unhealthy little kids that were ten-a-penny in Georgian London. Many of them died tragically young, many survived to have unremarkable working-class lives, whereas Jim Peters' journey would be long and strenuous and would make him world famous.

It was largely for the boy's sake, but also to beat the arrival of London County Council's demolition wrecking ball, that Percy Peters upped sticks during the economic crisis of 1926 and headed out of Church Street in Homerton for good. He and Emma sought sanctuary and a brand new start a mile or two away in the Bow district. Their upheaval was hastened by stern warnings from doctors about the condition of little Jimmy, by now aged around seven and still a frail little specimen. In his own words: 'I was weak and ill, small, underweight and anaemic.' Infant mortality rates were relatively high at the time, and Jim's failure to achieve normal weight and strength levels meant Percy and Emma were told his best chance of a normal life would be to move him away from their sooty surroundings.

The boy had needed several bouts of hospital treatment by now and his poor health must have been a matter of some concern to his parents, for Percy had been one of a robust family of eleven siblings, while Emma was one of ten. Both had been raised in the Hackney district, Emma growing up on the same street as a boy called Budd, who subsequently emigrated to South Africa. Budd's London birthplace would later be responsible for his granddaughter Zola being entitled to run for Britain in the 1980s.

And so, shortly after the 1926 General Strike, the Peters family pitched up in Bow. Railway workers like Percy Peters had been condemned by Prime Minister Stanley Baldwin for pushing the nation towards anarchy, but it seems all Percy really wanted was fresh air and healthier surroundings for his boy. Bow was hardly a rural nirvana, but it was certainly an improvement, the air cleaner and surroundings a little less oppressive.

However, barely twelve months on and the family would be packing their few modest bags once again. This time the move would prove thrilling and truly life-changing. One can only imagine the rush of excitement of Percy and Emma when told they'd been granted one of the newly built council cottages springing up on the posh Becontree housing estate a few miles away, close to Dagenham. This huge estate was a ground-breaking post-war initiative in the wake of former Prime Minister Lloyd George's promise to provide 'Homes for Heroes'. Building had got underway in 1921, and although barely 50 per cent finished when the Peters family arrived, Becontree was already hailed as the biggest public housing provision in the world. It was barely six miles out from Bow, yet represented a completely different world. It looked out on miles of green, open farmland, and, to its wide-eyed incomers, was nothing less than bucolic bliss.

Although Becontree would later grow into a London suburb in its own right, at this point it was surrounded by its own green belt. It suited Percy Peters well and maybe there were genetic reasons for him gravitating towards this patch of Eastern England countryside ... after all, his own father Simeon had been a bricklayer from Gamlingay, a small farming village in Cambridgeshire.

Jim was nine when his parents moved 'to the country', proudly picking up their house keys and tenants' handbook, and crossing the threshold of 199 Grafton Road for the first time. It felt like the lap of luxury and Becontree felt like the promised land. Each cottage had little gardens at front and back, and a privet hedge bordering the pavement outside. Inside there was electric light, running water, a toilet and a bath, and a smart scullery with a big window right next to the kitchen sink. Not bad after two rooms in the East End where you shared a tap and WC with other families. Excitingly, there were farms and market gardeners nearby, from where you could fetch eggs, milk and other staples.

Jim recalled how the family thought Becontree was truly 'a grand spot' even though they had to shiver through their early days during the severe winter of 1927-28. Blizzards raged in the December, providing a picture-postcard white Christmas, and there was more of the same in March 1928. Although people loved their new homes, they did find the sash windows very draughty, there was no insulation in the attics, and few could afford coal to heat the bedrooms upstairs. The toilet, bath and copper boiler were all fed from a reservoir tank in the attic which tended to freeze on winter mornings, leaving toilets unusable. However, these were relatively minor issues for families used to much worse. Looking back, Jim had only good memories: 'I remember playing about in the snow and having a really wonderful time going round the local farms. I think it was from that time onwards my health really started to pick up [even though] I was still very thin and never really looked well.'

Even the rather frightening prospect of having to start at a new school didn't hang over Jim – for the best part of a year at least – for there were simply no places available for the many incoming children at that point. He and hundreds like him were told they must wait until the building of schools and other services were completed. In Jim's case, his parents could keep close tabs on the situation, for the building of Grafton Road Boys School took place just across from their new home. At first it was a temporary wooden edifice, but around nine months after their arrival it was ready, and Jim was able to venture inside and resume his education. Scores of kids from neighbouring streets arrived on that first day in late 1928, the first wave at a school that over the years would grow considerably from its humble beginnings.

Having to wait for a school place was a minor drawback for the awestruck newcomers. Although council estates would later be regarded by the better-off with a degree of scorn and disdain, during the 1920s and 1930s Becontree was viewed as an innovative marvel. It followed in the wake of Letchworth, Hertfordshire, the world's first 'garden city', a privately funded project that introduced the idea of individual houses with gardens, specifically for the working classes.

Letchworth's architect Raymond Unwin became known as the founding father of the British council house and his ideas were copied at Becontree. Unwin's aims and philosophies underpinned the Housing Act of 1919, and his 'garden cottage' was the prototype for these so-called Homes for Heroes. Around 27,000 homes went up over four square miles at Becontree between 1921 and 1932, making it bigger than many London boroughs. The area was described by the thrilled incomers as 'Heaven with the gates off'. In poured more than 100,000 residents, many of them refugees of East End slum clearance, but relatively prosperous working class types nevertheless. Those who successfully settled at Becontree tended to be hard-working factory staff or bus and railway workers, and not feckless 'slum people' with no money to pay the rent. Occasionally, there would be the sad sight of newcomers having to return whence they came: one local history tells of a hapless caravan of around 50 families trekking all the way back to Islington with their belongings, unable to afford the rents at Becontree. New tenants who had steady jobs, like Percy Peters, were often only just keeping their heads above water: years later Jim would be told by his parents that the reason he'd been an only child was because they couldn't afford more children on a 'starvation level' railwayman's wages.

The construction of Becontree and creation nearby of the Ford Motor Company's 500-acre plant, the biggest of its kind in Europe, certainly gave the Dagenham district an atmosphere of prosperity, even if few local families considered themselves comfortably off. Ford cut the first sod at their new complex in 1929 and two years later the first vehicle rolled off the production line. The plant replaced their Manchester factory and saw 2,000 workers decamp south on special trains over a single weekend for a new life in Dagenham. Becontree and the Ford plant had bravely surfaced together in the depths of the depression, prompting the press to marvel at 'magnificent gestures of faith' in Britain's economic future. They were lighthouses of hope for the people of the Essex-East London border. Becontree was recognised as the largest municipal housing estate ever seen, a status it had maintained even 50 years later.

The relationship between Becontree newcomers and their LCC 'landlord' represented new and uncharted territory. The grateful new keyholders obediently toed the line and weren't inclined to question the rules and regulations in their little tenancy handbooks – especially as failure to comply could result in instant eviction. Percy Peters and the rest were warned to clean their windows at least once a week, sweep their chimneys once a year and use only the rear garden to hang out washing. Some were dismayed to find the planners were apparently aiming at a teetotal community, for pubs were notable by their absence. There was no town centre as such, and Becontree would soon become cast as a town without a heart – a situation that exists to this day. Having given the working-classes these 'ideal homes', the authorities were soon fretting over how to replace the culture and sense of neighbourhood they had erased.

Instead of kicking his prized football around on his own (the ball had cost his dad ten times his normal pocket money allowance), shy Jim

Peters was now able to enjoy organised games at school, and soon became obsessed with sport. He recalled: 'I wanted, more than anything, to play for the school under-11 team. I struggled and struggled, trying to learn the proper way to kick a ball, but I don't think I would have got very far if it hadn't been for the enthusiasm and interest of one of the teachers, Mr E J Kingdon. He encouraged me every way he could.'

Jim remained tiny, much smaller than most boys his age, but had bags of enthusiasm and this impressed Mr Kingdon, who picked him for the second-string football team. By the time he'd reached eleven, still well under six stones, Jim was tried at left-wing in the first team. He used his uncle's football boots, stuffing paper into the toe-caps and wearing two thick pairs of socks to ensure a snug fit. Usually the smallest boy on the field, his sheer guts saw him win regular opportunities and he graduated to half-back, his favourite position, and even scraped into the cricket team too, to become a useful left-arm bowler. He was less effective with the bat, which, oddly, he used right-handed. One sport he avoided like the plague was cross-country running, not taking part in a single race during his schooldays, convinced his weedy frame would mean he was bound to come last.

His devotion to football and cricket saw him pal up with classmates Harry Orbell and Charlie Fuller: 'We three were just sports crazy and had ambitions to be footballers when we left school,' Jim later told *Dagenham Digest* magazine. Orbell was a talented player who lost his life to a chest condition in his late teens. Fuller, however, would make Erith & Belvedere's first team aged seventeen before joining Walthamstow Avenue, one of the country's top amateur sides. He guested for Luton Town in wartime football and later blossomed into an England amateur international, captaining Bromley in the Amateur Cup final at Wembley in front of 95,000 and leading the GB team at the 1952 Helsinki Olympics. Coincidentally, Fuller's glittering career would end through injury in 1954, within weeks of the same fate befalling classmate Jim.

Another local lad making headlines was Alfred Ramsey, known widely by the nickname 'Darkie'. Jim knew him as a talented boy from an old cottage situated in Halbutt Street, which had been completely surrounded by all the new-builds. Jim recalled with pride bowling Ramsey middle stump when Grafton Road played Becontree Heath school cricket team. Ramsey would, of course, later concentrate on football and achieve fame as captain of Tottenham and England, before managing Ipswich Town to the 1962 League title and England to 1966 World Cup glory.

Like the majority of local lads and fellow 'Graftonians', Jim was a West Ham United fan: 'Jim Barrett the famous centre-half was one of our idols – he weighed somewhere between 16 and 18 stone and had a kick like a mule,' recalled Jim, who, because of his own lack of inches, desperately wanted to emulate more diminutive Hammers stars like wing-halves Charlie Cox, Joe Cockcroft and Jimmy Collins. More than anything else in life, Jim wanted to be a footballer: this was not the casual pipedream of many boys of his age, but an obsession he carried around for years, and something he would often refer to later in life. It was to widespread local dismay that the beloved Hammers were relegated from Division One in 1932 (not to return for 26 years) but the enthusiasm of Jim and his pals remained undiminished.

Jim established himself as an energetic and regular member of the school team between 1930 and 1933, during which time its results improved hugely, having earlier been one of the region's weaker outfits, regularly trounced by double-figure scores. 'I was all energy when I played. I never used to stop,' Jim said.

In his final year at Grafton Road school, a general medical inspection took place, with headmaster F J May announcing afterwards the most common ailment was flat feet, found to be extremely common. Flat feet or not, the kickabouts in the playground with a tennis ball were fast, furious and highly popular.

One day, near the end of his final term, a daydreaming Jim was rapped on the knuckles and told he must miss one of these enjoyable kickabouts to stay behind and see Mr Kingdon. Sick with nerves, Jim soon found this was not a punishment but a thinly disguised pep talk from a man genuinely interested in the future prospects of the wiry, bright-eyed lad before him.

Their little chat had a profound effect on Jim and he later recalled almost word-for-word what he was told: 'You've had to struggle hard here at Grafton Road, but you've made a lot of progress. You've got over your nervousness and you've been a prominent member of the school football and cricket teams. You haven't been the best player Jim, by any means, but let me tell you that it's not always the most outstanding players at school who make great champions. It's my experience that the boys and girls who climb slowly towards the top often turn out to be the best of all. You've got to get a job, Jim. I know we're in the middle of a great slump, but when you do find a job no matter how poor the prospects may seem you must do your utmost to work with enthusiasm. When you come home [from work] you must join a decent club that has a football and cricket team. That's very important as far as you are concerned. Don't wish your life away, get on with whatever job you're doing, and as soon as you can, join a good club.'

With Mr Kingdon's advice ringing in his ears, Jim left school in 1933 with Britain still in the grip of the great economic slump and found himself joining the ranks of the unemployed. Putting his football dreams on hold, he told the local Labour Exchange he fancied work as a carpenter ('I enjoyed woodwork at school, but was no good at it'). Along with around 300 other local lads, Jim found little on offer in the Dagenham area, and several months went by without any success at all. Eventually he was advised to try Snow Hill Labour Exchange to see if there were vacancies in the City of London financial district, which was reasonably easy to reach from Dagenham and Becontree by train. This proved a good move and he was soon fixed up with a junior office boy's job at a printing firm in Great Tower Street, taking home a princely 12 shillings (60p) a week.

From this sum a half-rate season ticket from Chadwell Heath station had to be bought, a further chunk had to be given to mum to pay for keep, thus leaving the new working man with about a shilling a week for himself. He was disappointed to only have 12 pennies for his own use, but certainly didn't begrudge two of them disappearing as his weekly membership subs to a new club that opened near his home that summer of 1933.

Heeding Mr Kingdon's advice, Jim had been quick to apply for membership when the Dagenham Boys' and Girls' Club in St George's Road was launched on 6 July 1933, its opening ceremony conducted by HRH the Duchess of York (later Queen Elizabeth, the Queen Mother). The club cost £2,000 to build and represented a boon for local teenagers, with its splendid main hall and stage, separate changing rooms for boys and girls and an activity list that included football, boxing, gymnastics, carpentry, table-tennis, chess, draughts and more. It was managed by a talented hockey-playing Oxford graduate from New Zealand called Reynolds, and within months had filled to capacity with 100 members of each sex on its books, Jim among the eager new recruits.

Its opening was attended by a huge and enthusiastic crowd, and was for many the most exciting and glamorous thing they'd ever seen: the 32-year-old Duchess of York swept into St George's Road accompanied by Lady Helen Graham (Lady-in-Waiting and Woman of the Bedchamber) to declare the club open. The Duchess charmed onlookers by 'breaking ranks' to hurry over and congratulate a choirmaster on the singing of the 500 children under his charge. Her commitment to helping the working classes continued into the evening, for she headed off to support the Dockland Settlements charity at a gala function alongside her husband, the soon-to-be-crowned King George VI.

These were exciting times in the Dagenham area. Less than 24 hours after the royal visit, the local courthouse was the focus of great interest when local man Robert Kirby was charged with the notorious 'Becontree Murder', the strangling of his seventeen-year-old girlfriend Grace Newing at her home in Stevens Road. And as if this wasn't enough, an aircraft on its way to Margate encountered problems over Dagenham and crash-landed just inside the main gates of Central Park, the place where Jim and his mates regularly had their kickabouts.

Meanwhile, the Boys and Girls' Club manager Reynolds (a man of 'blazing enthusiasm', according to Jim) garnered help in his valuable work from local volunteers, notable among these being John O'Leary, a flamboyant and eccentric character whose day job was running a pioneering public library service for the area. As the first chief librarian for the Borough of Dagenham (1929-65) he developed a service for the working-class population that not only supplied books but supported culture and learning. O'Leary recalled being impressed with little Jim Peters' general enthusiasm and often gave him lifts to and from the various local sporting events he attended.

Joining the club changed Jim's life forever. It not only helped banish his shyness, but was an outlet for his boundless energy. It satisfied a thirst for regular sporting action that Grafton Road School had only partly satisfied. The club dominated his waking hours and he got full value for his tuppence a week. Up early to catch the train into work in London, he would return at dusk and most evenings go straight to the St George's Road premises. There was something going on at the club every night, and the regime mapped out for Jim involved an hour's PE on a Monday evening, a road run on Wednesdays, the choice of boxing, PE or running on Thursdays, an organised football match on Saturdays and a kickabout on Sundays. Like most kids he had the energy and motivation to handle this programme with ease, but admitted later it had been a real shock when Mr Reynolds insisted he would have to do running and PE training if he wanted to play organised football. He'd initially expected they would simply play match after match with nothing in between.

Jim grew to love every minute and even the prospect of being made redundant at work failed to dampen his new enthusiasm for life. He was savvy enough to know that if his employers were to keep him past the age of eighteen, they would be obliged to raise his salary, which meant they would probably ditch him and replace him with a younger boy: 'Not that I really thought much about this gloomy prospect, for by now I had become really infected with Mr Reynolds' enthusiasm about the club,' he reflected later.

The very first week of Mr Reynolds' programme of training kindled the spark that set Jim Peters' on the road to sporting greatness. On a Wednesday evening a raggle-taggle group of around 50 boys headed out of the club and onto the streets of Dagenham for their first road run. Excited chatter soon faded as the effort of jogging steadily along for more than three miles took its toll on their breathing. But for Jim it felt comfortable and he had no trouble keeping pace, even with the many bigger and stronger-looking boys. It gave him confidence and no doubt a broad smile soon plastered his face.

As they were heading back, around 300 yards from the entrance to the club, one of the boys suddenly began sprinting for home. It was Bill Roberts, winner of the West Ham Boys Sprint Championship a year earlier. Immediately, others took up the impromptu challenge and hared after Roberts. Jim, to his own surprise, found himself one of them, flying along as fast as his skinny legs would go. The boys skittered down the final stretch of road and clattered into the club noisily, eyes ablaze, chests heaving and cackling with laughter.

As they recovered, hands on knees and breathing heavily, Jim looked around and counted out that he'd been the sixth boy to reach the club. There were dozens behind him, many looking white-faced and on the verge of collapse after the effort of it all. Most had been far too tired to even attempt the late sprint. Jim was thrilled with himself. This felt wonderful: 'Something suddenly struck me rather forcibly. I seemed to be less out of breath and much fresher than those around me. If I'd run just a little faster throughout that 3½ miles, I might possibly have finished first instead of sixth.'

In that moment, the seeds of fierce ambition were planted. He didn't really know it, but little Jim Peters was now a runner.

CHAPTER 2

The Simple Pleasure of Running Fast

NOVEMBER 1933 – JULY 1945

The source of every great river is a gentle trickle. For James Henry Peters the route to sporting greatness started with those low-key football training runs around the Becontree estate. Jogging around the block was probably a dull chore for most Boys' Club members, but for Jim it ignited a competitive instinct he never realised he had.

Having sampled the exhilaration of flying along in the cool evening air of that first outing from St George's Road – leaving most of his mates labouring in his wake – Jim was instantly hooked on the simple pleasure of running fast. He would confess later: 'The whole idea of wanting to finish first in a football training run was just ridiculous, but the idea stuck and by the next Wednesday evening I had worked out a plan to realise this stupid ambition.'

Jim's cunning plan involved persuading a friend with a bike, Bill Robinson, to ride just ahead and act as a pacemaker. The rest of the pack saw what was happening when Jim steamed off after the bike but could do little about it as he opened up a big lead on the rest of them. Despite feeling exhausted after completing a mile, a seemingly in-built ability to ignore pain and drive onwards, which would serve him so well later, soon took effect. Bike and runner arrived back at the clubhouse way ahead of the rest, leading to euphoria for Jim, but resentment and anger among the also-rans. Roberts, football captain, and the sprint-finish man from the previous Wednesday, was particularly vociferous and told Jim there would be no more cycle-paced solo runs, merely steady running as a group. Jim was suitably chastened but secretly delighted, knowing the grumpy Roberts was only miffed because he'd been beaten. It was exciting to find he could run faster than many of his contemporaries, although the idea of tackling athletics seriously remained a long way from his thoughts.

By the time he turned fifteen, Jim was a working man, small in stature but growing fast in self-confidence and losing the shyness born of a childhood bereft of siblings. Club leader Reynolds watched his progress with interest and made a special note of Jim's determination in the Wednesday road runs. Towards the end of a very successful 1933-34 football season, Reynolds told the boys he was entering them for the London Federation of Working Boys Clubs junior cross-country championships, to be staged on the edge of Epping Forest.

The response was initially less than enthusiastic. Jim and pals thought they were the bee's knees, having just won the local football league, and failed to see the point of switching to a new sport. It would take a mass cycle ride to the race venue at Chingford, for an experimental trial run, for the boys to become a little more comfortable with the idea. They tackled the daunting steep hill beside the Royal Forest Hotel, and the muddy bridal path known locally as 'Easy Street' and got familiar with what awaited them.

Jim admitted to getting highly nervous as the race drew closer, but never had an inkling this was to be the launching pad for a twenty-year career of racing over similarly tricky terrain. The contest was on a Saturday, which meant he had to be up at 5.30 as usual to report for work in Great Tower Street by 8am. By around 11, he was relieved to get a nod and a wink from his immediate superior, meaning the coast was clear to quietly slip away.

Back in Becontree by lunchtime, he bumped into clubmate Chris Freeman, also due to run at Chingford that afternoon. Before reporting to the clubhouse, the pair decided sustenance was required and pooled the contents of their pockets for fish and chips. Of course, comic book hero Alf Tupper ('Tough of the Track' in *Rover*), would always beat the toffs after a meal of fish and chips, but in the real world these two nervous lads would find such pre-race 'fuel' a serious misjudgement.

Six boys and Mr Reynolds squeezed into an ancient little borrowed car for the journey to Epping Forest and Jim Peters' racing debut. The sight of 500 people milling around the Jubilee Retreat hall added to pre-race nerves, and the uncomfortable journey on a grease-filled stomach didn't help matters either. The very last thing Jim felt like doing at that moment was running up and down muddy hills against bigger and stronger boys, struggling in wholly unsuitable plimsolls and baggy shorts.

'I always felt nervous even before cricket or football matches, but never before had I felt as I was feeling then ... Mr Reynolds elbowed his way through the competitors and gave me my number. He had to pin it on for me. At that moment, a safety pin in my hands would have been a menace to everyone around me.'

Nearly 250 boys contested the junior race, started by a pistol held aloft by London Federation of Boys' Clubs President Sir Charles Wrench. Jim was now fifteen, but the junior category included runners as old as eighteen, meaning he faced bigger and stronger lads on the verge of joining the senior ranks. Mr Reynolds knew this and didn't expect miracles, but the little debutant from Becontree still felt under pressure in this strange new environment. His knees knocked, his stomach felt bloated, his mouth tinder-dry, but he ignored it all and sped off like a madman at the gun. He established himself in fourth place after around a mile of running. Mr Reynolds couldn't believe his eyes.

Disadvantaged by having no spikes, Jim slithered around on the muddy patches but maintained a place in the top ten throughout, and through his pain recalled one glorious passage where he got 'a second wind' and began to feel better. Sadly the euphoria didn't last. His fellow diner from earlier, Chris Freeman, had spectacularly deposited his fish and chips high on the Royal Forest hill during the race, and Jim was to do likewise – his own stomach evacuation coming moments after he staggered across the finish line in a remarkably impressive ninth place.

Mr Reynolds was jubilant, but a retching Jim was rather more concerned with his queasy stomach, and panicking over how he would explain the state of his running kit to his mum. A top-ten finish against all odds was all very well, but at that moment he could only curse himself for not sticking to football – this cross-country lark was even harder than it looked. Mr Reynolds brushed this aside, assuring Jim that because he had three more years in this age group, doing so well today indicated he stood a great chance of becoming champion soon. Achieving ninth place at his tender age, with no experience and little training, was a sensational result against older boys and indicated he was a bright prospect indeed. It would take a while for this to sink in and in the immediate aftermath a nauseous Jim could only repeat his vow to concentrate on football in future and leave competitive running well alone.

He had reckoned without Mr Reynolds' determination, ambition and what Jim later called a 'benevolent dictatorship'. A month or two afterwards the lads were entered for the London Federation of Boys Club sports, an annual track and field meeting with heats in Deptford Park and finals at the famous Herne Hill track. Mr Reynolds was in no mood to let a lad of Jim's potential get away, and ensured he was included when the time came to train on the rough-and-ready shale track in Dagenham. Non-attendance was not an option, and any reluctance on Jim's part soon crumbled. Before long he even found himself saving up for a pair of track spikes.

By now Jim's wages had risen to 14 shillings week, but spikes cost 12s 6d which meant several weeks of scrimping and saving before they could be obtained. But once he'd introduced them in place of his Woolworths plimsolls he knew it was money well spent. A few weeks before his sixteenth birthday came his competitive track debut in the half-mile heat at Deptford Park, against some of London's fastest youths. A nervous Jim showed well, and was only beaten in a frantic late sprint down the home

straight, coming third in a highly respectable time of 2 mins 12 secs. The
two boys who beat him also secured first and second place in the subsequent final in record time, meaning Jim had been unlucky to draw this
pair in his heat.

As he would recount later, this race provided some important pointers: 'There and then, as a result of that first race, I decided that I just
couldn't do a finishing sprint, and that coloured my running tactics for
several years ahead.'

Despite these promising beginnings, Jim was happy to let running
take a back seat again, returning to his football and cricket for the next
nine months or so and using running as merely a means of keeping fit. It
would only be in early 1935, pushed into a return to the turmoil of cross-
country racing, that the idea of taking running seriously began to unfold.

Just as Mr Reynolds had predicted, a Jim Peters twelve months older
fared much better than his impressive debut at the Boys Clubs cross-
country. Wearing spikes, avoiding fish and chips, and somewhat better
prepared, Jim led for much of the race, only to be pipped at the post by
a fast-finisher called Mann, who turned out to be a distant cousin.

Jim would pinpoint this as the day 'the athletics germ' infected his system in a major and irreversible way: 'Despite my still relatively frail
physique, I could run. It was quite unskilled and natural running, just one
of those things that one can or can't do in spite of oneself – and despite
my lack of knowledge and technique, I managed to win that cross-country race for the next two years in succession; in one of them I won in a
time that was actually three seconds faster than that which won the senior race for boys over 18.'

The only blot on his landscape around this time was the likelihood of
losing his office boy's job in the city. As he'd anticipated, his employers
didn't fancy paying him the required 17s 6d a week once he'd reached the
age of eighteen, and took the opportunity to give his lowly position to
somebody younger and cheaper. It was not a good time to be traipsing
back to the Labour Exchange. Unemployment had soared to unprecedented levels in recent years and finding a good position was no easy matter for ordinary, unskilled working class lads like Jim.

Although the worst of the great depression seemed to be over, Britain
continued to lurch from crisis to crisis. This was the year three different
men sat on the throne, thanks to Edward VIII's abdication, not to mention major problems in our overseas territories like India and Palestine.
Worst of all, the rise of Hitler and Nazi Germany cast an ever deepening shadow over Europe, and Whitehall was pushed into rearmament,
just twenty years after the 'war to end all wars' had ended.

But Jim's luck was in. Before long they were celebrating in the Peters household in Grafton Road after the boy secured an apprenticeship with a Dagenham firm of opticians, a position that eliminated his need to commute into London, and which also guaranteed him work for several years – provided he passed exams along the way – and would lead to qualifications to set him up for life. It is thought the company he joined was the family business Arthur Hawes & Son, who had a workshop and several branches in the area. The good news about the job arrived around the same time as his first running victory, in the London Federation of Boys Clubs one-mile track race in an excellent time. It was recorded by various sources as either 4:36 or 4:43, but either way it was not bad for a raw seventeen-year-old. It was a performance that certainly caught the eye of Essex Beagles, a senior athletics club whose members also trained at the Dagenham track.

The Beagles had been recruiting young talent from the Becontree estate since about 1925, and vice-president Sam Filer reckoned Jim Peters was one of the most outstanding prospects he'd ever found. Jim was soon persuaded to join the Beagles' ranks, and on Monday, 30 November 1936 his membership was formally approved at a committee meeting at the Pigeons Hotel in Romford Road, Stratford. Along with Frank Edward Purcell and Colin Macaulay Campbell, Jim was voted in as an active first-claim member, having paid his first year's subscription of six shillings (30p).

His horizons as a sportsman were considerably widened from this point. The Beagles were affiliated to the Essex amateur athletics body, the oldest and arguably strongest of the county associations, its annual championships long established as a major social and sporting event. Coinciding with Jim's arrival, Essex also began taking road running more seriously, and staged their first road promotion, a twenty-mile race, and would a year later put on the inaugural Essex Marathon championships. The latter did not prove an instant success and they quickly reverted to annual twenty-milers (not reintroducing the marathon until 1967).

The Beagles hierarchy was proud to be congratulated by Essex officials on entering their 50th year of athletics in 1936, but not so pleased when told Essex's prestigious county cross-country championships for 1936-37 would be held adjacent to the Beagles' winter headquarters at Riggs Retreat in Buckhurst Hill. It had been arranged without consultation, which Beagles committee-men saw as a snub, firing off a letter of protest. This was all part of the cut-and-thrust of local sporting politics, and must have had an impact on new member Jim, for the minute books show that before long he was contributing his views at meetings, too.

Jim had enjoyed his three years at the Boys' Club, and found the more grown-up world of the Beagles very much to his liking too: 'Through the encouragement of the older club members, I began to get more and more interested in athletics, and my training, if not concentrated, was at least proceeding on the right lines.'

Essex Beagles had started life many years earlier as Beaumont Harriers, an offshoot of the People's Palace in the Mile End Road, which was a unique philanthropic entertainment complex completed in 1892, with library, swimming pool, gymnasium, winter garden and much more. After Beaumont changed their name to Essex Beagles, the club's first star athlete was James Kibblewhite, who held the world best time for three miles (14 mins 34 secs) for thirteen years around the turn of the century. By the time Jim Peters joined up in 1936, membership exceeded 200 and the club had adopted a white vest with gold and black bands as its official colours. By now it had a Dagenham section, to cater for new members who found it difficult to travel to the club's meeting places in the Stratford and Forest Gate areas.

The outstanding Beagle runner when Jim arrived was probably Eddie Sears, a county half-mile champion five times in the 1930s, who would continue to run well into the 1950s. Sears and his colleagues toiled in vain during the inter-war years to regain former glories for the Beagles, but better times were now ahead, and Jim Peters would be playing a central role in that renaissance.

The club's runners, many of whom proudly wore special Beagles lapel badges on their overcoats, were looked after assiduously by trainer Nobby Clarke, however humble their ability. Nobby (a nickname given to most people called Clarke in those days) was paid six shillings week as a retainer for his efforts, plus expenses. As the 1937-38 winter season approached, Nobby successfully fought off a challenge for his job, and into the bargain saw his money increased to 7s 6d a week, as long as he attended both Saturday and midweek training sessions.

Having sometimes used the local Victoria Park to train, the Beagles were by now settled at Dagenham Old Park, but it was far from an ideal home. Not only did they have to share with Dagenham Football Club, but the facilities were poor and the track not well maintained. The club drummed up interest by publicising its activities on a noticeboard, and worked hard at getting write-ups in the local papers. One member, J W Pocock, made headlines around this time for doggedly walking all the way from London to Brighton in plimsolls, but he blotted his copybook soon afterwards – the Beagles committee censured him for what was mysteriously described as 'unusual conduct' at certain sporting gatherings.

Jim Peters' first full summer season with the Beagles was his last as a junior athlete, for his nineteenth birthday was by now on the horizon. His past successes in Boys' Club cross-countries and county junior miles counted for little as he began competing against experienced adults who knew all the tricks and tactics of track and distance-running. The season began in a promising manner on the evening of Wednesday, 5 May 1937 at Victoria Park, although club minutes record it as being a poorly supported meeting. The 100 yards handicap only had three starters, but there were a dozen in the two-miles handicap, and this was won by Jim, with Ken Richardson second and Charlie Rixon third. All three had started from the 275 yards mark, and Peters' winning time was recorded as 9:26. The committee noted: 'This was a very pleasing result as all three were new members, the winner [Peters] being only 18 years of age.'

These were halcyon days for Jim, enjoying his football, cricket and athletics in equal measure, all his spare time devoted to sport after his daily shift learning the ropes as an assistant optician. He was one of the brightest sparks at Essex Beagles, and soon made many new friends. The club as a whole, however, experienced a winter of discontent, some of its senior officials becoming concerned that they were now in a rut as far as the southern athletics scene was concerned.

This unrest came to a head in January 1938, once the cross-country season had got underway. The club was rocked by a radical proposal from committee member Ted Copley, who felt that following its golden jubilee year, the club was showing no signs of progress and needed drastic reform. Beagles had become something of a peripatetic club, moving around between different summer and winter training HQs, often having to use poor facilities into the bargain, while attempting the tricky job of catering for a membership spread all over East London and the Essex borders. This lack of focus frustrated Copley, and others backed him up. Copley proposed the club should change its name and attach itself to a single district in which it would be better placed to lobby for a new track, and also able to canvas local talent to make it a truly 'local' club. After much discussion there was general agreement and the district of neighbouring Barking was agreed upon as the prospective new home. The committee duly met in Barking the following month, at Westbury School in Ripple Road, and it was agreed to ask Barking Council to provide a new track. These talks would kick-start a long process which would ultimately see Beagles move into Mayesbrook Park in 1951.

Jim continued to develop as a useful half-miler and miler, but his training remained relatively light at this point. As he passed his twentieth birthday his increasing strength saw him slowly improve on the track, and in the summer of 1939 he completed a mile in 4:28. He may never have guessed it at the time, but this would remain his lifetime personal best for the distance. It was a fine effort, but nowhere near Sydney Wooderson's world record of 4:06.4, achieved by 'the Mighty Atom' at Motspur Park in south London two years earlier.

As he headed towards the end of his apprenticeship, Jim was required to attend the Northampton Polytechnic in Islington (later City University) for lectures and exams on the road to qualifying as a dispensing optician. If all went well he could expect to be fully qualified by the autumn of 1939, but as time went by the increasing likelihood of war with Germany threatened to disrupt such plans.

Jim would admit that the Munich crisis of 1938 and its implications completely passed him by, and it wasn't until the spring of 1939 when it dawned on him that Adolf Hitler and his expansionist plans might impact seriously on his life. He recalled that in May 1939, along with other young men in their 21st year, he had to sign up for six months National Service plus three-and-a-half years as an unpaid reserve: 'I suddenly realised that my life of football and cricket and athletics might possibly be interrupted. It was a nuisance, but there it was.'

As the end of his apprenticeship was so close, the authorities allowed him to complete his exams and his National Service was deferred until November 1939, by which time, of course, the Second World War was underway – albeit still as a 'phoney war' at this stage. It meant that immediately after qualifying as a dispensing optician he found himself on a train to Waterloo, and then to Aldershot, about to become '7366379, Private J Peters of the Royal Army Medical Corps' initially based at Boyce Barracks, Crookham.

Basic training, first aid training, and the chance to run a couple of Army cross-country races came along in his first few months as a soldier, and after an overseas posting was cancelled at the eleventh hour, he was allowed home on leave. By now his parents had moved from Grafton Road into 104 Keppel Road on the Becontree estate, and it was here he repaired for a happy reunion. An important facet of his return would be discussions with his attractive dark-haired young girlfriend Frieda, which culminated in their engagement. By the time Jim returned to barracks their decision had been made to wed very soon – hopefully during his next leave.

Naturally his wedding plans were not high on the Army's priority list and Jim had a few angst-ridden weeks waiting to find out when he could return to Dagenham to tie the knot. One particularly stressful episode came on the day he expected to collect a leave pass, but was instead told to report to Netley, near Southampton, to join up with the No 4 company, RAMC. Already bitter at this unexpected turn of events, things got worse when he arrived to find a shortage of sleeping accommodation and had to spend an uncomfortable first night in a damp tent. Cursing the Army, he rose early the next day to report to his new sergeant-major for instructions.

All the resentment drained quickly away when he was given stunning news. Not only was Private Peters promoted to the rank of sergeant, he was to take the important job of Dispensing Optician in the RAMC's Opthalmic Department. He would be working at the Royal Victoria Hospital, a very grand building which, it was rumoured, should have been built in India, but due to a War Office mix-up with the plans had been put up here in Hampshire instead. Bursting with pride, it was a happy Jim Peters who finally got back to Essex in the summer of 1940, and was able to marry fiancée Frieda, who at nineteen was two years his junior.

The new job meant Jim's part in the war effort would ultimately be to supply around 35,000 pairs of spectacles to fellow soldiers based far and near. Mostly they were of the austere 'steel-rimmed, Mark 3' variety, which he later described as 'horrible monstrosities'. But it was vital work, safer than heading for foreign battlefields, and, crucially for him, meant sport remained a big part of his weekly routine. Jim soon emerged as one of the Army's best runners in the south. He raced in plenty of inter-service events during wartime, mainly half-miles, miles, and some cross country, even winning three medals in Hampshire civilian championship events. He loved the cut-and-thrust of the track mile, but the extensive RAMC grounds provided ideal training routes to test his stamina over something a little longer. He still played football and cricket once a week, and on occasions played alongside fellow Dagenham lad Alf Ramsey, the future England manager then serving with the Duke of Cornwall's Light Infantry.

Speaking of these wartime days, Jim would reflect later: 'There was nothing exciting, and no feats of bravery about my job. I was just one of many backroom technicians, but I enjoyed it and I felt that at least I was doing a job I knew, and one for which I had been trained.'

A constant worry during wartime must have been the well-being of his new young wife back in Essex. One can only imagine the horror he must have felt when news reached him in the autumn of 1940 that Dagenham had been severely bombed by the Germans. Bill Riddiford, a milkman who was a near neighbour of the Peters family, was an ARP warden on Becontree at the time, who kept a detailed wartime diary. On Sunday, 29 September 1940 Riddiford wrote:

'One of the largest bombs dropped in Grafton Road [the Peters' had earlier lived in this street] at 11.15pm. Went out on job: terrible sight, three Anderson shelters blew 80-100 yards away. Also parts of bodies 60-80 yards away. Bomb crater about 30 feet deep and about 45 yards round. Four people killed. Shelter blew off one family, and they finished up sliding down the crater, unhurt, marvellous escape. About 150 houses damaged, gas leaking water running etc, raid still on overhead and heavy gun firing. Went out at daybreak picking up pieces of flesh with shovel and sack.'

Although he stayed fit and enjoyed his running, Jim's progress and potential as a serious athlete was of course hampered by the intervention of the war. Like most sports, athletics was able to continue in Britain, albeit in a low-key manner. Jack Crump, who would later get to know Jim well, held important administrative posts in British athletics before, during and after the war, and described how the sport was affected:

'Although the declaration of war brought an immediate and almost complete shutdown of international and domestic athletics, this did not last long. The absence of expected air raids during the early "phoney war" period encouraged enthusiasts to keep the sport alive on a limited basis. Championships were obviously out, but special cross-country and walking races in winter were arranged and track meets in summer.'

Crump and other officials were often to be found doing their bit as air-raid wardens in 'Dad's Army' but most were anxious to maintain some continuity, so that when war finished and athletes returned from active service, the clubs and associations would be in good shape to resume normal service quickly. The authorities and services approved of this attitude, and as a result 'Holidays at Home' programmes for servicemen were devised, featuring sporting promotions – and from 1940 onwards there was a resurgence of activity and interest in all sections of athletics. Commonwealth and overseas athletes based in the UK added strength and variety to the turnouts, taking part in competitions in aid of the Red Cross and other war-related charities. Popular Sydney Wooderson may have been a super-fit champion miler, but his poor eyesight had precluded active service, so he was able to race regularly, along with exotic foreign stars like Arthur Wint (Jamaica) and Emmanuel McDonald Bailey (Trinidad), both RAF men. Jack Crump recalled that once the threat of invasion had receded, the British programme of wartime athletics increased. On mainland Europe it was only Sweden who were able to run a near-normal athletics programme, which allowed their star milers Arne Andersson and Gunder Hagg to cash in and lower the world mile record a number of times.

During the war Jim and Frieda had a son, but sadly the baby did not live long, a tragedy that left the couple anxious to start a family once hostilities were over. By the time it was clear the conflict might soon be at an end, Jim was posted in the winter of 1943-44 by the RAMC to a hospital opposite Hampshire Cricket Ground – where again he found good facilities nearby for running training. At this point he was running four or five times a week, often alongside well-known athletes like Reg Gosney and Ron Bryan, and it appears he guested for local club Eastleigh AC during this period.

Meanwhile, Essex Beagles had continued to operate in bomb-damaged Essex and East London, even though many key members were in the forces and unavailable to compete. Committee meetings were reduced in number, but the club survived the war due to donations and voluntary subscriptions. People still needed entertainment and activity during these grim times, and occasional events were put on, some very well supported. In September 1944, a few months after the D-Day landings, the Beagles committee began discussing arrangements for resuming normal operations once war was over – but as it turned out, it would be a full year before these plans could be implemented.

Following Germany's surrender in May 1945, demobilisation could begin. Having served since 1939, Jim would not have long to wait and by August he was back home, 'civilian suit in a cardboard box, and all my army possessions in a kit-bag.'

The end of the war brought a widespread desire in Europe to re-establish international sport as quickly as possible, and this was particularly evident in athletics. Although clearly Germany was in no position to participate, there were determined moves to restart the European Championships and Olympic Games. Jack Crump was among those who confessed to be 'staggered' by news that Britain would not only support the rapid resuscitation of the Olympics in 1948, but was applying for them to be staged in war-torn London.

Jim Peters was by now nearly 27, clearly a better-than-average club runner, but had still achieved relatively little in the sport thus far. He must have had an inkling he could be among the nation's better performers at the established distances of three and six miles – but after six years of war it was impossible to say for sure whether he was currently up there with the very best of British. As he headed home from his Southampton war posting, a new life as a married man needing to find work beckoned – and that would have dominated his thoughts. But the news that the next Olympic Games might be held in London – and before his 30th birthday too – must have caused a frisson of excitement.

CHAPTER 3

The 'Unknown' who Stunned White City

AUGUST 1945 – JULY 1946

Monday, 6 August 1945 was the most remarkable Bank Holiday of all time. With the war in Europe over, Londoners went on a frenzied search for leisure and pleasure. Around 52,000 filled White City Stadium to the brim for the athletics, thousands more rushing a barrier to join them. In Regent's Park more than 31,000 visited London Zoo, while just up the road at Lord's Cricket Ground, around 10,000 were locked out of the fourth 'Victory' test match. To the west, thunderstorms encouraged nearly 5,000 people to crowd inside the Victoria & Albert Museum for some indoor entertainment. Meanwhile, countless others had already left this mayhem behind, boarding 35 special 'relief trains' exiting Liverpool Street for the east coast seaside resorts.

Amid all this fuss, there was startling news on the BBC Home Service's teatime bulletin. US President Harry S Truman confirmed that an atomic bomb had that day landed on a Japanese army base. His statement didn't mention the horrific detail that 80,000 had been killed directly, and that tens of thousands deaths would follow due to the effects of injury and radiation.

On that sunny morning, the American B-29 bomber Enola Gay had veered ten miles clear by the time its deadly cargo obliterated the best part of Hiroshima. It meant world peace was on the way. Dads, brothers and boyfriends were already coming home and life would soon resemble something like normality again. The British sporting scene was emerging from hibernation, attendance records set to tumble in the face of the public's desperate need for entertainment and fun.

But adjusting to this new world order wouldn't be easy for everyone. With the danger and misery now over, returning soldiers like Sgt Jim Peters would, commonly, find themselves feeling strangely restless and anxious. In his book *Austerity Britain*, David Kynaston points out: 'The returnees were seldom seen as heroes by a deeply war-weary society, and the prosaic realities of peace frequently came to seem less attractive than the relative glamour, and male bonding, of war.'

Thanks to the hospitality of his mother-in-law, Jim and wife Frieda were given somewhere to live for the time being, and his pre-war employers found him a job again, this time at their Leadenhall Street branch in the City. Jim was one of the fortunate ones, but it was still not enough.

In a frank confession later on, he would reflect: 'I suppose I ought to have considered myself lucky, at least I'd got somewhere to live and I was earning a living. But I was restless. Six years of army life and shifting around had made me very unsettled … I was also dissatisfied with my physical condition and felt that my stomach was getting much too big for a man of 27. The only answer to me was to do some training again. Perhaps subconsciously, I realised the expenditure of some physical energy would also act as a safety valve for my restlessness.'

Jim made contact with the Beagles again. His wartime athletics experiences had shown he was a capable three and six-miler and cross-country exponent, and it was clear that continuing with the half-mile and mile was inadvisable now he was nearing his thirties. The Swedes Andersson and Hagg were showing how it should be done over four laps, the likes of Sydney Wooderson, Bill Nankeville and Doug Wilson dominating the mile as far as Brits were concerned. Jim had never been near the 4:10 mark now needed to compete at world level, and must have known if he had a future in the sport it would have to be over longer distances.

At this point there was one major hurdle in his path. A certain Mrs Frieda Peters did not think that taking up running again was a good idea for her husband. She insisted he was too old at 27 to be playing around with athletics and football when they should be concentrating on getting a home of their own and starting a family. Times were hard, and thousands of women in her position would no doubt have agreed with her. After what Jim called 'lots of friendly arguments', she was persuaded to allow him back to the Dagenham track a few times a week – but only so he could see his old pals again, and to lose the excess weight around his midriff. He was under orders not to proceed with any fanciful idea of rebuilding an athletics career, or recapturing his lost youth.

Frieda's concessions were clearly a matter of great relief to Jim. For a man of such energy, running was the perfect antidote to the strains of the daily commute into London, and life in a single room at his mother-in-law's house. Sure enough, after a couple of weeks back with the Beagle boys, he could report that his strange restlessness was disappearing, as was the size of his waistline.

During that early autumn of 1945, Jim put his name down for a three-mile club race, treating it as a time-trial in which he could check the effectiveness of his recent training. Frieda, still sceptical, came to the track to watch proceedings and was put on stop-watch duty. Jim's time of around sixteen minutes didn't particularly impress either of them, but his gift of the gab won the day again, and Frieda was persuaded to let him continue for a few more weeks, so that he could dabble in a bit of cross-country.

'I must confess she nearly convinced me that perhaps I was too old for competitive athletics,' he commented later. 'After all, you can't argue with a stop-watch, but at the back of my mind was the feeling that if only I could get in some more training and get really fit again, perhaps I could go on for another two or three seasons. Besides, I didn't like to think that at 27 I was an old man – even if only in relation to athletics. I must have had a very persuasive manner, for in the end she did agree I could go training, but was still unconvinced that I would get anywhere in athletics.'

For their part, Essex Beagles were glad to have him back, the club's elders anxious to re-establish themselves as a force in local athletics. In September, the day after Japanese forces formally surrendered, the Beagles conducted their first Annual General Meeting for seven years. In the convivial surroundings of the Rabbits Hotel in Manor Park, club stalwarts Arthur Dove and Fred Fullalove were elected as the club's first post-war secretary and treasurer respectively, under the continued presidency of Frank Saunders, a Woodford businessman whose benevolence had kept the club afloat in recent times. The meeting promised a determined attempt to 'gather together various trophies and other belongings in order to get going again'. Most trophies were subsequently rescued from their wartime resting places, but items that would never be found included 'spoons, cups, a megaphone and a stopwatch.'

The club's assets, after six years of reduced wartime activity, added up to £113 0s 9d, with no liabilities. This healthy state of affairs was attributed to secretary Phil Everard's sterling efforts, plus donations and some members continuing to pay subs voluntarily. Annual subscriptions were set at 7s 6d (37.5p) for over-nineteens, 3s (15p) for sixteen-eighteen year olds, and 2s (10p) for the under-sixteens, with no charge for members still serving with the armed forces. A room at the sixteenth century Retreat pub at Chigwell Row, beside Hainault Forest, was identified as the club's winter training HQ, while Howards sportsground would be the midweek venue. The Retreat was a fine facility, believed to be the same 'delicious old inn opposite the church' described by Charles Dickens in *Barnaby Rudge*. Dickens loved this district and frequently stayed in local pubs like The Retreat, and called Chigwell 'the greatest place in the world'.

Having decided to knuckle down to some serious training, Jim Peters enjoyed following in Dickens' footsteps as he prepared for a tough November fixture, his first serious race since the war. It was the North of the Thames cross-country championship, over a tricky five-mile course at Ruislip. Race day dawned chilly and windy, and a team of six Beagles journeyed into Middlesex. Elsewhere that same afternoon the touring Moscow Dynamo football team thrashed Cardiff City 10-1, but over the muddy fields of Ruislip, a 22-year-old insurance broker representing Hampstead Harriers, Harry Hicks, was the class act, winning in 29:06. He beat a seventeen-year-old from Finchley Harriers called Raven (29:34) and third was Jim Peters (29:38), just ahead of Woodford Green rival Ron Manley. It was a good start to this new phase of Jim's running career, even though he was miffed to have been beaten by two lads so much younger than he, a fact he would surely have kept from Frieda later that evening!

A week or so later, Jim's renewed commitment to his club saw him invited to join the committee, which he agreed to do. He was back in the swing of club life and thoroughly enjoying it. Frieda may have had her doubts, but Jim could at least point to the fact that his chosen sport was not an expensive one in these times of continued rationing and general austerity. You didn't need to spend a fortune to be a serious runner in post-war Britain, but if you did feel like splashing out, it was possible to buy jars of Elliman's Athletic Rub and Aero-Ped treatment for athlete's foot for 2s 3d apiece (11.5p), Simpkins' Vita-glucose energy tablets were 7d (3p) for a packet of ten, while the latest track spikes with leather uppers, plated soles and steel spikes were 39s 6d a pair (£1 97.5p). Regulation training shoes with canvas uppers (i.e. plimsolls or tennis shoes) were roughly 10s (50p) a pair.

On the first day of December 1945, Beagles took on Woodford Green AC and the Royal Army Pay Corps in a triangular six-mile match over the country. Jim powered to victory in 33:28 without serious opposition, an impressive second lap ensuring first place. It was good to be back to winning ways, but a week later came a more severe test. The Southern Counties cross-country championship featured 170 of the best runners in the south, 24 of whom failed to finish this gruelling race over five miles. Affected by a leg muscle problem, Jim came twelfth in 27:02, more than a minute behind winner Reg Gosney, his wartime friend from Southampton.

With no Beagles clubmates racing, Jim wore the same Eastleigh colours as winner Gosney for the day, and helped them into fourth place in the team competition. Marathon man and Sussex cross-country champion Cecil Ballard came second and Belgrave Harriers ace Tom Carter was third. It had been a decent showing by Jim, particularly given the leg problem which would trouble him for a number of weeks, and it left him in optimistic mood. His battling run in adversity was a lesson for young Finchley runner Johnny Hovell, who had been doing well in second place at halfway, but then lost both shoes in the mud, and ended up walking disconsolately for the rest of the race.

Things were going according to plan with his running, but as far as earning a living was concerned, it was time to ring the changes. Exact dates are unknown, but it seems Jim was unhappy at the Leadenhall Street opticians Arthur Hawes & Son, and sought a change of scene. At some point he got the move he desired and was recruited by another family firm of opticians, Melson Wingate Ltd. This company was managed by fellow runner Douglas Wingate, a talented member of Bournemouth AC, who also enjoyed cross-country and three and six-milers on the track. With Jim having taken part in a number of south-coast meetings in recent years, it is reasonable to assume he'd landed this job thanks to their connection through athletics. Melson Wingate had more than a dozen branches in the south, and Jim began work at their Monarch Parade premises in Mitcham, Surrey. Although it meant a fairly lengthy commute from his East London home, no doubt he was relieved to at least avoid the hurly-burly of heading into the City each day.

By the end of 1945 it was beginning to look sure that the Olympic Games of three years hence would be staged in London, despite all the post-war problems the city and its people were confronted with. The three leading figures in the British Olympic Association (BOA) – Lord Aberdare, Lord Burghley and Sir Noel Curtis-Bennett – had always been convinced London was the ideal venue, and International Olympic Committee (IOC) delegates from elsewhere seemed to agree. Lausanne was put up as an alternative choice, but when the Lord Mayor of London formally applied for the Games, he quickly received a letter confirming acceptance of the bid. The war had cost Britain £7,000 million – a quarter of the nation's wealth – so it was perhaps inevitable these would become known as the Austerity Games. Their staging wasn't welcomed in all quarters, but it certainly gave British athletes something exciting to aim for. The bid was formally accepted in February 1946, meaning the nation had less than 30 months to get ready.

As far as Jim Peters was concerned, December's leg problem had failed to heal completely over Christmas and into early 1946, but wasn't bad enough to seriously curtail training. With a squad of clubmates, he made the short journey to Bancroft's School on Saturday, 12 January, where Woodford Green AC hosted the Essex cross-country championships. The afternoon's events ended in farce: high winds played havoc with the trail that had been laid, and caused confused runners to go badly off course. Officials called a halt, and ordered the race to be re-run three weeks later.

The second attempt was held at Woodford Green Men's Club over a tough 7½-mile course. Jim set off hard and held his lead, winning by a comfortable 200 yards and 40 seconds from reigning champion Brown of Chelmsford, the modest time of 51:05 reflecting the gruelling conditions that day. The host club packed their leading men well and took the team prize, but Jim came away proud to have lifted the individual title for the Beagles. He dedicated the win as a repayment to the club for 'friendliness and encouragement' given to him. The club reciprocated, writing him a letter of congratulations on a 'grand effort' which had enhanced the Beagles' reputation. They diplomatically added sincere thanks to Mrs Peters for supporting her husband's return to athletics. Jim later said the latter remark pleased Frieda no end, and the win left him feeling he was proving her wrong about his being 'over the hill'.

For the remainder of the winter season Jim concentrated on maintaining a consistent training load and raced mostly in relatively low-key cross-country fixtures. Beagles didn't enter any runners in the English National cross-country championship in March, staged in Leamington, an event won in grand style by veteran marathon man Jack Holden. The popular Tipton Harrier was eleven years older than Jim, who must have been vastly encouraged to see success coming the way of one of the sport's elder statesman. Holden had been AAA champion at six and ten miles, and cross-country champion twice before the war, during which he served as an RAF PT instructor. Now 38, he was a cult hero in the Midlands.

Essex Beagles were by now back on their feet in the wake of the war, and secretary Arthur Dove placed an announcement in the monthly magazine *Athletics* (predecessor of *Athletics Weekly*) to confirm the fact: 'We are going again,' it read simply. During March 1946, Jim Peters went along to his first committee meeting as a club official, and was welcomed with the news that he would be receiving an overdue trophy which he'd won before the war, but had never been handed over.

Having committed himself fully to distance work, Jim began studying the training advice offered by the likes of Armour Milne and others in *Athletics*. During April, the retired ultra-runner Arthur Newton began contributing coaching articles to the magazine, which stirred up much controversy. Vastly experienced, but something of an outsider since turning pro between the wars, Newton was deliberately provocative with his views, and some embarrassed editor Green, who would frequently backtrack and apologise in the wake of the articles. Newton's opening salvo was to suggest that sprinters generally trained badly, and should never hit top speed in training, instead saving themselves for races. Going flat out in training would only cause damage, he postulated. Newton's books and articles certainly divided opinion, but before long many of the distance men in the London area would swear by the old chap's coaching ideas, and he helped devise many a training schedule.

As winter 1946 turned into spring, road racing dominated the athletics calendar and Jim decided to get experience at racing over ten miles against good opposition, and travelled across London for the Walton AC ten-miler on Saturday, 13 April. A small field of 59 started, and Jim held his own, finishing runner-up to Polytechnic Harriers' R V Hughes, a runner who had finished fourth in the recent English National cross-country. Jim's 53:13 was encouraging, and only ten seconds adrift of Hughes. The proud Beagles committee formally recorded in their minutes their great appreciation of this splendid effort.

Jim was brimming with confidence by now, happy to have proved he could hold his own in good company. The local press in the Dagenham area began taking notice too, calling him 'much improved'. He began making plans for the summer track season, and showed little interest in the longer road events taking place.

He was in good shape by the time of the Essex AAA track and field champs at a soggy Castle Park in Colchester on Saturday, 22 June. The track was heavy in many places, but Jim felt light on his feet and had no trouble keeping pace with reigning three-mile champion, Squadron Leader Peter Dainty, as they set off in pursuit of the Atalanta Trophy. Dainty, representing Southend, took an early lead, but as they approached halfway Jim sensed he was trying to slow the pace down, perhaps to engineer a late sprint for the line. Instinctively Jim grabbed the lead, intent on doing things his way, and attempted to open a gap. Cheered on by a crowd of 4,000, Jim increased the pace as they tackled the final half-dozen laps, and the demoralised Dainty even lost his grip on second place, passed by Southend teammate Philip Morgan, a nineteen-year-old Oxford student.

'I was in really first class condition,' Jim reflected later, his strong finish impressing the crowd and seeing him hit the tape around 130 yards clear of Morgan. Given the state of this waterlogged riverside track, his time of 15:05.6 was very respectable. The performance was seen as a high spot of the meeting, Essex's first since the war, with several other events falling below the standard of years gone by. It won Jim the Atalanta Trophy, the county's most valuable athletics cup, which had been presented to the association 46 years earlier and bore a reproduction of Sir Edward Poynter's celebrated painting 'Atalanta's Race'.

Previously won by legendary figures like Alf Shrubb, the trophy was so large that Mayoress of Colchester Mrs H G Thompson needed assistance to hand it over to its beaming new owner. The victory prompted another letter of congratulation from the Beagles committee to plop on to Jim's doormat.

There was no danger of Jim getting carried away by his win, for the next day the Sunday papers revealed that evergreen Sydney Wooderson had won a three-miler at Rotherham around 33 seconds quicker than he – the best time recorded anywhere thus far in 1946. Jim reacted by immediately cancelling plans to run the three miles at the AAA championships at White City in just under a month's time, fearing he would be obliterated by Wooderson. He decided to try his luck at the AAA six-mile title instead. There was speculation that Dutch champion Willy Slykhuis might run the three-miler too, another reason to concentrate on the more open longer distance.

1946 was proving a pivotal summer in all sorts of ways. Following the Labour Party's landslide victory at the polls a year earlier, Britain's new Welfare State was now well on course. The passing of the National Insurance Act facilitated introduction of a National Health Service, to be launched in 1948. In the meantime, citizens of all classes and backgrounds struggled to maintain a healthy diet, with many foods still rationed and others not available at all. Athletes, who needed to take particular care over nutritional needs, were having to make do and mend like anybody else.

These were days of austerity, days when even a mug of Oxo felt like a treat. Its manufacturers reckoned Oxo was ideal for distance runners, as it contained 'sustaining value' and, furthermore: 'What Oxo can do in the athletic world it can do as effectively in every other walk in life. It should be taken by all to whom health and strength are valued assets!'

A fortnight before the big AAA meeting, Jim had a chance to sample the atmosphere at White City stadium when the Southern AAA championships were staged at the huge West London edifice on Saturday, 6 July. Built for the 1908 Franco-British Exhibition and used for that year's Olympic Games, the venue had a chequered history. It fell into disrepair between the wars until greyhound racing began there in 1927, and then athletics in 1932 following the AAA's move from Stamford Bridge. Now bigger-than-ever crowds were beginning to descend on this part of Shepherd's Bush, giving the old place another new lease of life.

Jim didn't record his thoughts when he arrived to run at White City, but the surroundings must have seemed intimidating to someone more used to the Dagenham parks. The place was cavernous. The seven-lane cinder running track had been built inside the greyhound track, and tiered and covered seating all the way round produced a great atmosphere when it filled up. Before competing, athletes were asked to disappear underneath the stadium and then, just prior to their event, were led up a stair-case to emerge into the main arena near the long-jump pit. There were no proper warm-up facilities, and many runners loosened up by jogging under the stands, where they could run a complete circuit as long as they didn't mind dodging spectators. It didn't suit everyone, of course, and Gordon Pirie was one star who preferred to go outside and jog along local streets to warm up, a habit that astounded some of his less-demonstrative contemporaries.

These early post-war meetings at White City heralded a golden era at the stadium, in which bank holiday and floodlit meetings would become particularly popular, generating a 'cup final' atmosphere to rival that at Wembley. In 1947 London Underground would move the Wood Lane tube station close to the stadium and rename it White City, a convenient move for competitors like Jim Peters who had to rush there from work on a Friday evening, along with the spectators.

Dick Booth, who ran there himself, and later penned Gordon Pirie's biography, says athletes loved White City's atmosphere because it was a great place to meet friends in the sport. By the standards of the day it had a good track, although this often cut up badly in wet weather. There were good sight lines from the huge stands and a restaurant allowed diners a view of the finishing straight. The only drawback was that spectators were a long way back from the track. Before long *The News of the World* would begin sponsoring major White City meetings and would pay athletes' expenses. Gate money would go to the AAA or, in the case of floodlit meetings (usually arranged by *The Evening News*), to a group of London athletic clubs who helped with organisation.

The Southern championships came to White City for the first time in seven years on a beautiful July afternoon in 1946. Jim was pleased to comfortably improve on his recent Colchester winning time, coming fourth in the three miles. Winner was 31-year-old accountant Maurice Bingham of Finchley in 14:35.6, who just pipped Len Herbert (Belgrave). Then came a gap of around 60 yards before Stan Cox (Southgate) was closely followed by Jim (14:48). Typically, Jim had run hard from the gun, showing well near the front for long periods, before being eclipsed. In the final lap of the twelve he made a desperate but vain attempt to catch the wiry figure of Cox, a runner who would soon become a good friend and regular adversary.

It was an entertaining race, although the event that grabbed all the headlines that day would be sprinter McDonald Bailey, with wind assistance, equalling Eric Liddell's 23-year-old British 100 yards record of 9.7 seconds.

Jim's fourth place at White City was barely noticed in the great scheme of things, but it proved a useful warm-up prior to his return to the same stadium thirteen days later – for what would be the biggest day of his career so far. The evening of Friday, 19 July saw the opening of the two-day AAA championships – the first to be held since before the war. There were over 400 entries in all and interest was bigger than usual, now that Britain was preparing to host the 1948 Olympics. A good crowd assembled for the opening on the Friday night, when the two-mile walk, tug-of-war, six miles, and hop, step and jump were held. The main glamour events were the following day, but highlight of the opening night was undoubtedly the six miles, in which Jim Peters emphatically announced his arrival on the national stage.

Ace Belgian runner Jean Chapelle was hot favourite, being the reigning AAA steeplechase and ten miles champion, having done this 'double' back in 1939, a feat that won him the coveted Harvey Cup that year. Reg Draper of Hinckley Technical College, an experienced cross-country man who had also been a ten-mile champion before the war, was also running and seen as a bigger threat to the Belgian than 'unknown' Jim Peters. Chapelle shot into an early lead, but Jim refused to be cowed and stayed on his heels. If Chapelle thought retaining his title would be straightforward, he was in for a shock. Jim stuck to his task over the early laps, not allowing much daylight between them. The first real drama came when Draper suddenly dropped out before halfway, by which time Jim had experienced a surge of confidence and taken the lead for the first time.

Jim's characteristic rolling gait, his head rocking from side to side, had barely been noticed outside of Essex before, and must have given the White City crowd the false impression he was beginning to tire. Was this just another club grafter, out of his depth and with no chance of hanging on against the classy Belgian? Nothing could have been further from the truth.

During the middle part of the 24-lap race, the two men became locked in a see-saw struggle, passing and re-passing each other regularly. Surely Jim would crack soon? By now it had become an absorbing contest and clear that the star from the Continent had a major fight on his hands. The crowd noise slowly increased as the lead swapped hands continuously and they completed 22 laps.

With half a mile left, Jim, who admitted he'd been inspired by the excitement in the stands, took the lead again, and this time piled on the pressure like never before. He said afterwards: 'I could hear him coming up close behind me so I further increased my pace and gradually drew clear of him. Though I could no longer hear the pad of his feet, I didn't slacken up at all.'

The gap between them grew bigger, as did the cheers for this British underdog. AAA team manager Jack Crump looked on in amazement as an Englishman he'd never heard of stole the show at the nation's most important domestic athletics event. To great roars Jim breasted the tape around 140 yards clear of Chapelle in 30:50.4, becoming the new national champion, 25 seconds ahead of the man he'd dethroned. Amid all the fuss, few noticed that the man trailing in third was none other than Jim's company boss at the optician's practice, Douglas Wingate of Bournemouth AC, someone with personal ambitions of running the Olympics himself.

Jim's winning time was below Olympic qualifying standard, but this didn't unduly bother him as his immediate thought was whether he'd done enough to be picked for the forthcoming European Championships in Oslo. He'd come from nowhere to lift the AAA crown, even though nearly 28, and *Athletics* raved over how he'd finished in such good shape and was therefore: 'A distinct find, with great possibilities, and what he now needs is some international competition.'

Jack Crump congratulated him afterwards, admitting he'd not heard of him before tonight, and seemed surprised to be told Jim had won junior titles before the war. The nature of the victory, combined with Crump's reaction, left Jim feeling 'reasonably certain' he would be on the plane to Oslo later that summer.

Looking on from the stands was Jim's dad Percy, who told *The Dagenham Post* how proud he was: 'It was a thrilling race and the spectators loudly cheered our boy from Dagenham.' Commenting on the view that Jim was a surprise latecomer to top athletics, Percy pointed out there was only one more honour his boy now coveted – an international vest. 'With a bit of luck he may even do this before he retires.'

Jim's triumph came a little late in the evening to get much coverage in the following day's papers, and by the end of the weekend had been overshadowed anyway by events on the second day. Bespectacled Wooderson won a real thriller on his three-mile debut in a GB record of 13:53.2, trouncing the talented Dutchman Slykhuis. The crowd of 25,000 saw more fun and games when grey-haired 40-year-old Squire Yarrow (Polytechnic Harriers) won the marathon in a dramatic sprint finish with Scotsman Donald McNab Robertson. The pair entered the stadium while the steeplechase was still in progress on the track, causing major confusion and chaos for runners, officials and spectators alike.

CHAPTER 4

Feeling the Pinch

London, even a year after war ended, was a gloom-ridden city. J G Ballard returned from years abroad and noticed how 'everyone looked small and tired and white-faced and badly nourished'. Fellow writer Christopher Isherwood flew in from America to remark: 'Londoners' faces were still wartime faces, lined and tired' and several friends told him the city was dying and would never recover.

Jim Peters at least had the security of a good job, but he and Frieda still didn't have a home of their own, and rationing continued to make day-to-day shopping a tricky task. Providing her husband with sufficient nourishment to cope with a nine or ten-hour working day, plus his racing and training, must have been tough. During the summer of 1946 house-wives like Mrs Peters were shocked to be told that even bread would now be rationed. This was condemned by a furious Winston Churchill and described by *The Daily Mail* as 'The most hated measure ever to have been presented to the people of this country'.

A blossoming athletics career provided a convenient escape from the austerity for Jim – although not everything went according to plan that summer. The amazing high of winning the AAA six-mile title as an underdog would be followed by shock and bafflement when he was left out of the British team for the European Championships in Oslo. Normally his White City victory would have guaranteed a place in the team, but in their wisdom the selectors decided the new champion was too inexperienced for international competition – and they didn't bother to fill any of the three places available in the 10,000 metres event. To compound the controversy, popular marathon man Jack Holden was also left out – apparently punishment for his missing the AAA marathon so he could take his family on holiday following demob from the RAF.

'I was completely at a loss to know why I was not selected,' recalled Jim. 'So much for ambition and pride of achievement. I was bitterly disappointed [but I] received a considerable amount of sympathetic and sometimes indignant comment from the national press and from athletes.'

The implication was that Jim's six-mile win had been a flash in the pan. Jimmy Green, editor of *Athletics*, condemned the snub, saying the manner of his AAA win should have assured his place: 'He had so much in hand that we have clearly not seen the best of him yet. We talk about the supremacy of the Finns and Swedes, yet here is a boy who has won a national title at the first time of asking and we fail to give him the chance or encouragement to go further. No wonder people find it difficult to understand.'

Jim's summer on the track fell a little flat after this blow, but fellow victim Holden gave an emphatic response to the contrary selectors, going out and thrashing all opposition at the Salisbury fifteen-mile race, winning by more than four minutes in 1:22.05. He followed this by winning the South London Harriers 30-miler, a unique event that was first staged during wartime. Holden had trained specifically for Oslo and let people know he was unhappy, unlike Jim, whose natural modesty meant he didn't create anywhere near as many headlines. In Oslo, the undersized GB team would enjoy only moderate success, the highlight being Sydney Wooderson's brilliant victory with a late kick in the three miles to beat continental stars like Slykhuis, Zatopek, Nyberg and Reiff in 14:08.6. The marathon, minus Holden and over a course that was two kilometres short, saw Britons Squire Yarrow come seventh and Horace Oliver drop out mid-race.

By now it was becoming clear to Jim that if he wanted to make a mark on the international scene it would probably have to be in six-mile races (10,000 metres in Europe), and not at three-milers (5,000) – as competition in the latter seemed much hotter, with good youngsters coming through. Runners generally move up to longer distances as they get older, and although he could still punch out a good three miles, it was over 24 or 25 laps where his strength and consistency looked likelier to bring rewards.

His stated goal at this point was simple. He wanted an international vest, and the sooner the better, as the window of opportunity might not remain open for long.

One of the handful of contemporaries he knew he must at least match to achieve that goal was Stan Cox of Southgate Harriers. Cox was the same age, of similar small build to Jim, and had re-emerged in the summer having first made his name before the war. In 1939, just days before turning 21, Cox had a sensational debut at three miles (14:13.6), beating the previous GB record, and a few weeks later clocked a lifetime best in the mile (4:22.4). After serving the RAF during the war, Cox had joined an elite squad of service athletes who trained virtually full-time at the RAF track at Uxbridge. This paid off with some fine 1946 displays, including winning a strong 5,000 metres in Antwerp in a lifetime best of 15:02.2, an event that was generously restarted after he turned up late.

Cox's career was beginning to follow a similar path to Jim's and he would soon become a major player in the Jim Peters story.

Jim was not in contention to represent Britain when the team jubilantly trounced France in the first post-war international match at White City, in front of a bumper bank holiday crowd of 50,000, for there was no six-mile event on the schedule. However, he was invited to represent the AAA in a meeting in Belfast a few days later – a fixture which, it appears, was subsequently cancelled, for reasons unknown.

There followed the start of a busy period for Essex Beagles. First up was a committee meeting at the Barclay Hall in Forest Gate, attended by Jim, who was greeted by much back-slapping from club officials delighted by his recent AAA title win. Treasurer Fred Fullalove stood up and proposed: 'The heartiest congratulations from the committee and club members be extended to J H Peters on his wonderful performance in winning the AAA six-miles title on Friday, 19 July, a performance not equalled by an Essex Beagle for 30 years or more.' It was also agreed Jim's victory be rewarded by a special presentation from the club. Later the same month the committee gathered again at the Barclay Hall, Jim himself proposing the club get its club magazine *The Beagle* up and running again, an idea that was heartily approved, and he and two others were tasked with assembling editorial content for each issue. Once again, the meeting heaped praise on Jim, awarding him the annual H W Gray Cup and F W Gilkes Cup, in honour of his AAA title win. His heavy involvement in committee meetings was certainly a far cry from the days of the shy young lad who saved up his pocket money in 1936 to join the club.

On the August afternoon originally scheduled for Belfast, Jim instead raced on the dusty Dagenham track over three miles in a club challenge with Chelmsford AC, winning in an unspectacular 15:42. The match ended in a big win for the home side, although Chelmsford claimed many of their top men were away on holiday.

Later the same month, the nation's favourite, Wooderson, ran what would prove his last appearance on the track, and very nearly went out in a blaze of glory. In front of a good-sized crowd, he attacked the two miles world record in a Blackheath Harriers meeting at Motspur Park. He was well on course until things went badly awry with around three laps remaining. The crowd gasped as the little figure clad in black suddenly slowed and begin hobbling. He ignored pleas from officials to give up and minimise the damage, continuing so as not to harm his team's chances. Finishing in some distress, he was inevitably well outside the record of 9:03.4. It was a sad way to bid farewell, but the 'Mighty Atom' would at least bounce back in cross-country events later.

As the 1946 track season gave way to the delights of ploughing across muddy fields, Essex Beagles invited their star runner Jim Peters to become 'captain of running' (for track and road), with a separate captain for the walkers section. This was welcomed by members, but a little more controversial was an issue involving Jim's colleague Eddie Sears, criticised in the local press for his performance in a recent relay. The report was written by Beagles secretary Arthur Dove, and led to angry correspondence between the two men, with Sears quitting the club. The majority thought Sears had been harshly treated in the write-up, and condemned 'washing dirty linen in public' in this way. Dove apologised and the runner subsequently withdrew his resignation. Jim was keen for peace to be restored after this petty affair, and formally asked to be 'dissociated' from it at the annual meeting. On a more positive note, the club announced it was back on its feet after the war, and now in a 'very sound' financial position. They'd even been able to splash out on new footbaths and a first-aid box.

During the autumn, AAA official Crump drew up a GB rankings list for 1946, published in *Athletics*. Jim was not in the top ten for the three-miles, but was second at six miles, behind top dog Steve McCooke of East Antrim Harriers, and one place ahead of Jack Holden. Holden's strength was really at longer distances, and he emphasised the point by smashing the world best 30-mile time in October at White City. He ran a mind-numbing 120 laps (all between 83 and 98 seconds each) in 3:00.16.4 secs, obliterating long-standing amateur and professional records that had been set in the 1880s.

During the early part of what would prove a severe winter, Jim showed his cross-country mettle with some solid running for his club, including the fastest time of the day (24:26) in a Beagles 4½-mile handicap at Chigwell Row. Another significant event for the club was the arrival of a promising young runner called Reg Robins, of Weston Green, Dagenham. Reg would become a long-standing training partner and friend to Jim, and a more-than-useful performer in his own right.

With the London Olympics barely eighteen months away, it was reported in Essex that the Butlin's holiday camp in Clacton-on-Sea had been put forward as a ready-made Olympic village. Boss Billy Butlin saw the chance to promote Clacton as a resort, as well as promote his own business. The camp had opened eight years earlier, but lost six of those years to requisition by the government during wartime. It had cost £100,000 to build and could accommodate 2,000, and had been packed to the gills over the recent summer. The national press took up the story, accusing the non-committal British Olympic Association of dithering and being secretive over its pre-Games plans. *The Sunday Dispatch* reckoned that if the BOA attitude was indicative of what was to come, the 1948 Olympics would turn into one huge GNMU ('Grand national mess-up').

The calendar year of 1947 got underway in great style for Jim as he shrugged off pre-race injury worries to successfully defend his Essex cross-country title over a very heavy 7½-mile course at Chelmsford. Twelve teams, amounting to 100 of the county's top runners, assembled at the Essex Home Approved School in Rainsford Road, and set off into Admiral's Park just before 3pm. Jim led from start to finish and was never in serious trouble, coming home in 44:17, nine seconds clear of Woodford Green's Ron Manley, with Peter Dainty of Southend a further twelve seconds down. Coached by marathon record-holder Harry Payne, Woodford Green took the team prize, with Beagles third.

Fifty-three-year-old Payne had set a GB marathon best of 2:30.57 in 1929, at which point it was also a world best. Payne was well known locally, having dominated Essex cross-country and road-running through the 1920s. He remained active in the sport despite his first-class career being terminated in 1930 when he was hit by a vehicle on the Niagara highway, while out training prior to the inaugural Empire Games in Hamilton, Ontario.

The top twelve finishers at Chelmsford were sent to represent Essex at the inter-counties championship at Bestwood Colliery, Nottingham on Saturday, 18 January 1947 – just days before Britain was brought to its knees by the worst spell of wintry weather for 200 years or more. It was a seven-mile battle for *The Daily Telegraph* Trophy, over an undulating course with many obstacles and sections where runners were forced to go single file. The start was delayed by 45 minutes due to the late arrival of two Midlands teams, which did not amuse others who'd travelled from further away and didn't appreciate hanging around in the cold. This late start would subsequently lead to Sussex runners missing rail connections later and having to sleep on the platform at Victoria station as a result.

The delayed start, the nature of the course, and problems with the finish funnels, led to much irritation in the bitter cold, but frayed tempers disappeared when everyone was ushered in to enjoy hot showers and canteen facilities normally used by the coalminers. It was a rare luxury in the spartan world of cross-country running. Kent recorded a rousing victory, with Jim's wartime pal Reg Gosney of Hampshire the individual winner in 40:41.

Jim ran well on the open stretches, but didn't enjoy tackling the various obstacles, and ended up 33rd in 42:29. He was disappointed not to end up Essex's top scorer, having finished eight seconds behind Dainty, and Essex were declared the eighth team. Although never short of strength or determination in this type of race, Jim was clearly not the most elegant or agile of runners, and found the stiles, gates and other fences a real problem. Clubmate Colin Young confirmed this to me: 'One thing Jim detested were the cross-country obstacles – the quite fearsome wooden and steel gates we often encountered in those days. He used to laboriously climb over them, losing time and distance on the more agile of his opponents, such as Peter Dainty, Harry Hicks and Alec Olney and the like.'

It wasn't an enjoyable afternoon, but Jim was pleased for his friend Gosney, a quiet and modest athlete who was eight years older, and who worked for Ordnance Survey in Southampton as a lithographic draughtsman. Gosney was one of the very few runners in the late 1940s still gripping corks in his hands to aid his running. However, it emerged after the inter-counties race that he had recently decided to abandon the habit, so his fine victory at Nottingham suggests he was better off without them! The carrying of corks by runners was a curious practice, apparently done to benefit posture and eliminate tension. A cork would be carried in each hand, thumb and forefinger pressing firmly on either end, a technique that would in theory shape the runner's hands and lower arms into the optimum position for running. All these years later it sounds like a bizarre idea – so for further enlightenment your author asked a range of experts what the cork craze of yesteryear was all about. Their replies were fascinating:

Former marathon world record holder Rob de Castella says his grandfather, Sir William Hall, trained with corks with a pin pushed through them in each hand, held between finger and thumb, to aid hand, arm and upper-body relaxation. Any unnecessary tension would result in a sharp jab from the pin. 'I never tried it,' says de Castella, 'but visualising doing it was enough to keep me relaxed, and I did that often.' 1960 Olympic medallist Peter Radford confirms corks were a sort of aide-memoire, with athletes told to hold them firmly enough not to drop them, but not so tightly as to produce tension in hands and arms, which might spread to the shoulders. 1972 Olympic marathoner Colin Kirkham says he was told sprinters of the past gripped them hard at the finish line to help them dip more effectively. Some corks even came with elastic or leather bands, for securing around the wrist. They weren't just for sprinters, as distance legend Alf Shrubb used them on occasion in the 1900s, as did Ken McArthur of South Africa when winning the 1912 Olympic marathon. Coach Harry Andrews published the following 'useful hint' for runners in 1904: 'Some men carry circular pieces of cork just about as long as the hand is broad and about 1¼ inches in diameter. The gripping of them during a run calls for an exertion of will-power which is most beneficial in any feat of strength or endurance.' Historian Alex Wilson says early marathon men used them to help concentration, to maintain cadence and form, and possibly as a way of dealing with pain. In the 1950s and 60s, celebrated Australian coach Percy Cerutty taught his runners to pinch the tips of their fingers together instead of using corks, to improve posture and relaxation and prevent tension in the upper body.

By early February 1947, the weather across Britain and most of Europe had deteriorated so badly that even cross-country races were being called off, a rare event before or since. Among those that fell victim was the Orion ten-miler at Chingford, at which Jim and the Beagles were to have raced, but which was put back to March because of drifting snow and the terrible state of roads nearby.

Road and rail transport was seriously affected across the UK and with coal supplies, already low after the war, not getting through, the government introduced power-saving restrictions. This included cutting domestic electricity to nineteen hours a day and some industrial supplies completely. Radio and TV broadcasts were limited or suspended, newspapers reduced in size, and a nation battered by war and the resultant austerity had its fragile morale badly dented again. Minister of Fuel Manny Shinwell was public enemy No 1, even receiving death threats. Prisoners of war were put to work clearing snow off the railways, and food rations were cut to levels below that of the war years. The government brought in supplies of a cheap South African fish called snoek to nourish the nation, but people hated it, and stocks would eventually be used as cat food.

The main cause of the freeze-up was an anti-cyclone over Scandinavia which refused to budge. Temperatures as low as minus 20 centigrade were recorded in Essex, a few miles north of Jim's home. February turned into one of the coldest months on record and in much of London there was no recorded temperature above 5°C for the entire month and no sunshine whatever for twenty successive days. Ferry services were cancelled when coastal waters of the North Sea froze.

Organisers of the North of Thames cross-country championship somehow got their race on in early February, but only 127 men, the smallest field in the race's history, were able to get there. Jim didn't feature in the leading places over a very slippery 7½ miles course at Enfield Lock, and Beagles finished with an incomplete team. Many runners suffered painful falls, but the nimble Harry Hicks (Hampstead) won, thanks to a brave late surge on the icy surface. Second was Alec Olney, an up-and-coming Chiswick motor mechanic representing Thames Valley Harriers, who put in his best performance to date.

On Saturday, 22 February there was thick snow on Ascot Heath, but the Southern cross-country championship went ahead regardless, 276 runners tackling four laps of a 2½-mile route. Len Herbert of Belgrave won in 54.04, pipping Olney by just 25 yards, with Wooderson, making his first high-profile appearance since last summer's track retirement, coming in fifth. Jim could only manage 25th, a huge margin of 2:49 behind the winner, but still the first Beagles scorer. The club was eleventh in the team competition, won by Aylesford Paper Mills.

More heavy snow blanketed the nation on 4 and 5 March, in what was later confirmed as the worst blizzards over Britain during the entire twentieth century. Parts of Scotland reported drifts of 23 feet deep. Food supplies were hit so badly that in some areas police broke into abandoned delivery lorries to feed local communities. Distance runners are nothing if not resilient, however, and the decision to press ahead with the diamond jubilee English National cross-country champs in Hertfordshire on Saturday, 8 March was welcomed, it seems, for organisers reported a record entry of 1,193 runners.

Staged in Shendish Park, Apsley, adjacent to the paper mills and canal, the ten-mile race would be over laps of 2½ miles, meaning a very tricky 200 yards of plough had to be tackled four times. Of an unprecedented entry of 49 teams, seventeen failed to show on the day, the majority of these reportedly having set out, only to be foiled by blocked and treacherous roads, or problems with trains. A number of Britain's leading runners were among the missing. Tipton Harriers, including marathoner Holden, arrived too late to compete, while the talented Birchfield outfit didn't make it at all. Sutton Harriers set out the evening before the race, and ended up getting barely two hours sleep as a result. It was astonishing the championship went ahead at all: *The Times* of that morning reported that even the historic Wilson Run at Sedbergh School in Cumbria had been cancelled due to bad weather for the first time since inauguration in the nineteenth century – and this was a fell race in which participants actually preferred dreadful conditions.

Undaunted by the deep snow, a big crowd of well-wrapped spectators cheered the hardy National runners on their way, but fewer than 230 men would finish from the initial entry of more than 1,000. Bertie Robertson, a Maltese-born schoolteacher representing Reading AC, won by a comfortable 67 seconds (59:18), from Matt Smith of Blaydon, then dashed off to get his cricket sweater before agreeing to be being interviewed and photographed. Sydney Wooderson, spectacles misted and black shirt shimmering with frost, was cheered home in seventh. Jim Peters came in an unhappy 62nd (66:19), well beaten by his employer Douglas Wingate (63:12), and the Beagles were the eleventh team.

The selectors picked the England team for the forthcoming international championships purely from those who turned out here at Apsley, a decision which attracted criticism in view of the number of leading runners who had been unable to get there. This particularly rankled with the Midlanders, who felt they were once again being discriminated against by officials with a southern bias.

Two days after the National, milder air briefly moved in, leading to widespread flooding as the snow melted and ice thawed. The River Lea – not far from Jim at Dagenham – burst its banks spectacularly on 14 March.

It seemed like one crisis after another for beleaguered Britain, and at one point even the people of Canada, who knew a thing or two about severe winters, began sending food parcels to villages in eastern England. Toward the end of March, with things getting back to near normal, road runners could get back into proper training to try and make up for lost time. Essex Beagles staged a 5½-mile yacht handicap on the roads on Saturday, 22 March, and Jim recorded the fastest time of the day (29:45). Although he enjoyed the hurly-burly and camaraderie of cross-country, it seemed that here, back on the roads, he was in his natural habitat.

By now, his name was well known within the hallowed walls of the AAA and, as the 1947 track season loomed, he found himself with a number of invitations to run in representative matches, by dint of being the reigning six-mile champion. Unfortunately the state of his feet prevented him accepting: 'I got badly blistered feet through wearing rather poorly made spikes,' he recalled. 'At this time I was still not in a position to buy a really expensive hand-made pair – even though I was the national six miles champion.'

By the time the AAA ten-mile track championship was held at White City in early April, the blisters had largely healed, and he was able to make the start line, no doubt heartened by news that favourite Chapelle of Belgium had withdrawn. And there was a further boost to his chances when Bertie Robertson, reigning cross-country champion, was denied a place after turning up without having pre-registered. The remaining ten runners didn't constitute a particularly strong line-up for a championship race, meaning this was a great opportunity for Jim to add to his growing reputation. Wearing a large No 8 on his vest, Jim surged into an early lead and ran the first mile in 4:52, and from there had things his own way for the entire race.

His bullish attitude at the start frightened off any serious challengers, and before long he was lapping opponents. By halfway, 'Peters only had to keep on his feet to win,' according to one report. As a contest, it was a less-than-entertaining spectacle, Jim cruising home in 53:21, a comfortable 37 seconds ahead of Reg Draper, the 34-year-old Hinckley stalwart, who didn't have one his best days. Third was Dick Towndrow of Polytechnic Harriers nearly two minutes further back (55:46), and the remainder of the field were nowhere, all lapped twice by Jim during his 40-lap journey.

Writing in *Athletics*, Jack Crump hinted that the disappointing standard of the field might lead to a championship race at ten miles being scrapped in future years – and so it would prove, meaning Jim Peters was the last ever of Britain's ten-mile track champions. Crump was nevertheless full of praise for Jim (whom he erroneously called 'John'), describing him as 'a great runner whose best performances look yet to come'. Commentator Harold Abrahams, the former champion sprinter, was less diplomatic than Crump: 'Not one of the starters was able to give J H Peters a race and some of them ought never to have been allowed to enter a championship event. One runner who carried a stopwatch [Paavo Nurmi-style] finished over ten minutes behind the winner. He might have found a calendar more useful.'

The mutterings about a poor field didn't discourage Jim, who could only beat what was put in front of him, and was immensely proud to have carried off his second AAA title, less than two years after misgivings over whether he was too old and unfit to relaunch an athletics career. It greatly amused him how the various newspaper reports of the race differed, both from each other and from his own views. He pointed out that one report said he ran 'well within himself', another talked of his 'impressive confidence' while a third said he paid the penalty for a fast start by finishing a very tired man. Of the three, the first was the most accurate, he reflected.

It was certainly a good time to make a mark as a national champion, for athletics was on the cusp of a new era as far as popularity and interest was concerned. The huge increase in crowds at big meetings since the war, plus the excitement surrounding the forthcoming Olympics, led in 1947 to newspapers discussing the idea of ploughing cash into the sport via sponsorship deals. Not surprisingly, the prime mover was the top-selling *News of the World*, which had three athletics enthusiasts (Sir William Carr, Ernest Riley and Joe Binks) among its bigwigs.

CHAPTER 5

A Long Chat Over a Cup of Tea

If the Fleet Street hacks were right, patriotic Jim Peters would achieve the ambition of a lifetime in his 30th year. He badly wanted an international vest, and was thrilled to find the press describing him as a genuine Olympic prospect a year ahead of the 1948 Games. If they were right and he were to be selected for Britain, he could retire a happy man.

But for this modest, unassuming fellow it felt strange to be getting media attention. At least two national papers named him as a very serious candidate for London 1948, and the most knowledgeable athletics correspondent of them all – Joe Binks of *The News of the World* – simply stated: 'I fancy we have a good 'un here, coming along fast.'

Jim wasn't the type to get carried away by praise, but if any complacency were creeping in, fate would soon bring him tumbling back to earth. The month of May 1947 ended in one of the worst ways possible as far as his pride was concerned – he was forced to quit midway through a big race, embarrassed and humiliated in front of 50,000 people.

The calamity occurred at White City on Whit Monday afternoon, during a lively six-mile invitation race staged alongside the British Games. The meeting was organised by *The News of the World* on a scale never seen before in Britain. In glorious weather, the gates opened at midday and the stadium filled well before the start. The graceful Finn Viljo Heino was to attempt the fastest six miles on British soil (previously Nurmi's 29:36.2 in 1930), and was up against the best of Britain: Holden, Gosney, Towndrow, Wingate, Draper and Jim Peters.

Thirty-three-year-old Heino, fit again after being shot in the leg during the war, was in impressive form and he dished out a salutary lesson to the still relatively inexperienced Jim. From the start, Jim had surged away in typical fashion, leading through the first mile in 4:46.4, with Heino close behind, the others, led by Gosney, working hard to keep pace. In domestic events, Jim could break opponents early with his front running, but today he was badly exposed. Heino kept pace easily and after six laps cruised past. Instead of being able to relax at this stage of the race and take stock, Jim had to fight hard to simply keep within reach of the Finn. He couldn't do it.

After two miles it was clear he'd badly misjudged things. Before long Draper passed him and gave chase to Heino, while Jim's race went from bad to worse and by halfway his form and posture had gone completely. He stumbled to a complete halt and shuffled crestfallen off the track. There seemed to be no specific physical injury, it was simply a case of overdoing things early, getting into serious oxygen debt and then being hit psychologically. For a runner with serious Olympic ambitions, it was a disastrous display.

'It was an astonishing and almost fantastic race,' he recalled later. 'I have always done my utmost to put up a good show and tried to finish every race I have entered – but there are times when owing to all sorts of circumstances you just can't finish. At three miles, I was feeling so bad I just couldn't keep going any more and dropped out.'

The home fans' groans redoubled as they spotted more trouble further down the field. Holden had developed blisters and slowed down, kicking off his spikes before attempting to continue barefoot. The discomfort was too much and he too quit. By the end Heino was lapping opponents and in complete command, his final lap of around 60 seconds bringing the huge crowd to its feet. He fell short of his own world record of 28:38.6 but still won by a 750-yard margin (in 29:22.4) and looked a class apart, Gosney trailing in second in 31:48. Heino beat Nurmi's GB allcomers record by around fourteen seconds, and caused a rumpus by not stopping at the finish line, choosing to slow down gradually and not leaving the track for some time. Medical staff misread this and dashed after him, believing he was disorientated, but there was no cause for alarm, and within a minute or two Heino was happily signing autographs.

It had been a wonderful day for British athletics, the huge crowd and generous sponsorship of *The News of the World* heralding a new era for the sport. The afternoon was slightly tarnished by organisational blunders, with far too few programmes being printed, and a badly drawn-up events schedule. The tail end of the meeting had to be abandoned altogether, which upset athletes who had hung around all day waiting for their events. And in one heat of the 880 yards, around 40 juniors were shoved on the track to run together, simply to save time.

Jim left White City that day feeling gloomier than ever before. The embarrassment at being forced to give up was compounded by the fact that Heino's winning time was 90 seconds quicker than his own six-mile best, leaving his pretensions at being world-class in tatters. Not only was it clear he needed better tactical awareness, he would also have to step up his training.

By now Jim and Frieda were keener than ever to secure a home of their own, especially as she was expecting a baby that summer, so thoughts of quitting, or at least reducing, his athletics commitments must have crossed his mind. But with the AAA championships six weeks away, he resolved to plough on for now and at least attempt a defence of his six-mile title. Enough had happened earlier in 1947 to convince him it was worth pressing on. The ups just about outweighed the downs, and the evidence that the sport itself was going from strength to strength must have helped.

A few weeks earlier the first London-to-Brighton relay since the war was won by Belgrave Harriers, the event's revival once again thanks to funds from *The News of the World*. Essex Beagles were among the many absent clubs who took note, vowing to take part in future stagings.

Just days before his disaster against Heino, Jim had the boost of winning representative honours, albeit not quite the international vest he craved, when he was picked for the AAA team to take on London University at Motspur Park on the Wednesday evening. That night he won a thrilling three-miler in which there was the rare sight of someone else tearing away at the gun. This time it was Alec Olney, the 25-year-old from Thames Valley Harriers, who ran the first lap in 62 seconds, only to be gradually worn down and then pipped by Jim by the narrowest of margins in a dramatic late sprint. Had Olney not made the fatal mistake of looking over his shoulder as the tape loomed it might have been a dead-heat. The students couldn't live with Peters and Olney that night, and their best-placed man was a lap and a half behind Jim's winning time of 14:34.

Jim certainly needed a psychological boost after the depressing events of Whit Monday, and it would come five days later when he scored a resounding win to lift the Essex AAA six-miles track title. Chelmsford was proving a happy hunting ground, and he stormed home at the Marconi Annual Athletic Sports in front of a large crowd in 32:45, not a sensational time, but still more than a lap clear of Southend's Dainty. A week later he completed an Essex 'double', successfully defending his three-mile title despite painful blisters, on home ground in Dagenham. These 56th annual track and field championships were held at the SE Essex Technical College grounds and were difficult for spectators to follow, for runners wore no numbers due to them getting lost in the post (according to an embarrassed official). Jim won in 15:24.0, leaving Dainty to again settle for second 100 yards or more adrift, with a late sprint from Ilford's Jimmy Catton grabbing third. Peters thus retained his Atalanta Trophy. This, added to his cross-country and six-mile titles, meant he now had the 'triple crown' as far as Essex distance running was concerned. These were days of renaissance for the Beagles, whose members won a total of five Essex AAA titles that summer.

Jim's modest winning time in the three miles was partly down to strong winds and partly to painful feet. Although heavy rain had fallen prior to the race, the fierce winds dried out the track to the extent that Jim suffered bad blisters. He told *The Dagenham Post* afterwards he must now take a good rest, recover fully, and spend time with his heavily pregnant wife. To this end, he had already refused several invitations to run for the AAA, at least two of which were to races overseas.

While he was quietly preparing for the AAA championships, a month hence, the historic Polytechnic Marathon took place on a rainy Saturday afternoon west of London, Cecil Ballard of Surrey AC first of the soggy runners to arrive in Chiswick. His time of 2:36.52.4 was the quickest in this 38-year-old event since 1932. Two more events Jim missed that summer were the Southern AAA championships in Motspur Park and then the triangular match at Edinburgh, in which England beat Scotland and Ireland. For the latter, many thousands tuned their radios to the special BBC Light Programme commentary to hear Jim's three-mile rival Alec Olney score a tremendous win in 14:32, beating Scotland's Alec Forbes by inches.

Away from the action that summer, the Beagles' committee made loud and frustrated noises about the 'deplorable' state of the Dagenham cinder track – and issued an urgent appeal to the Borough Engineer to have it put right. They also fired off letters to the AAA and their local MP about it. It badly needed work to restore it to a decent condition following the severe winter. The club must have been casting envious eyes at local rivals Woodford Green, who welcomed the Duke of Gloucester to Ashton Playing Fields to formally open their new cinder track. Winston Churchill had also been due to attend but sent his wife instead. Jim Peters was one of the first to try the new track for size, toeing the line in a special star-studded two-mile race, along with Sydney Wooderson, the feature race in a triangular match between the AAA, Combined Universities and Essex & Kent.

It was a useful warm-up for the AAA championships, and was followed a week later by an Essex Beagles evening meeting, back on the rough-and-ready track at Dagenham, where Jim won the three-mile club title in 15:16. Barely 24 hours later he was celebrating the joys of fatherhood, as Frieda presented him with a son, Robin.

Naturally the arrival of Robin led to a week unlike any other in the Peters household, but Jim refused to use this as an excuse for another disappointing result at White City at the AAA championships. The event kicked off on Friday, 18 July, when the evening's highlight was his six-mile race. Strangely there appeared to be plenty of empty seats in the stands, despite tickets having sold out weeks earlier. This was blamed on fans steering clear of an anticipated crush on what was a humid and uncomfortable day in the London area.

Maybe the humidity played a part in Jim being unable to impose himself on proceedings as he normally would, for it was soon clear he was in grave danger of losing his title. Tony Chivers of Reading AC turned on the power at the right moments and ultimately came home eighteen seconds clear of Jim, whose gait suggested he was struggling badly, even though he managed to beat his winning time of the previous year with 30:49. He would be one of thirteen reigning AAA champions who would be toppled during the course of the weekend. Twenty-seven-year-old Chivers, who hailed from the west country, was a well-educated man who'd returned to his studies after the war and was now recapturing the form of his youth as a public schools' mile champion.

It could have been worse for Jim, who very nearly lost second place right at the finish to J C Smart, the Belgrave runner. Smart did remarkably well in the circumstances, for he was tired, under-nourished and short of sleep after a laborious trip to London by road, rail and boat from Germany, where he worked for the Allied Control Commission. He'd been unable to get a flight as expected, but persevered in his keenness to take part in the championships. Without the effects of having travelled during the night, Smart would surely have passed Jim, who looked very unhappy in those final few yards.

Assessing what had happened, the *Athletics* correspondent was pessimistic over whether Britain would be able to challenge the likes of Heino or Zatopek over six miles or 10,000 metres in the near future. Thirteen Hungarians had competed at White City, along with many other foreigners, but none from the USA, who were said to be staying at home as part of long-term preparations for the London Olympics. A star of the show had been Prince Adegboyega Adedoyin, son of the royal house of Ijabu-Remo in Nigeria, while only Captain Harry Whittle was able to warm British hearts, carrying off a brilliant long jump and 440 yards hurdles double. Sandor Garay (Hungary) won the mile in a championship best of 4:10.6.

Less than three weeks later, Jim was back at the home of British athletics, this time for the big August Bank Holiday meeting, this year featuring the inter-counties championships instead of the traditional international meeting. British athletics was learning fast how to entertain its crowds and put on a real spectacle, matters getting underway with a lunchtime march-past of the 22 counties. BBC radio's Light Programme featured a fifteen-minute live broadcast from the event, which was squeezed in between a brass band competition and a variety show from Newquay. Virtually all the nation's top athletes were present, and Jim opted to represent Essex in the three miles.

His indifferent summer continued with a disappointing fifth place, finishing a long way behind in-form Olney, who won in an event record of 14:27.8. Surrey lifted the overall title, with Essex down in equal-seventh. Fifth for Jim meant he missed out on an invitation to represent the BAAB in a match against Combined Services at White City later that month. All in all, it had not been the summer season Jim Peters had wanted, or foreseen.

Reflecting on his major races of the season, he found it highly ironic he should have run faster at six miles than in the previous year, yet still lost his champion's crown. He deduced from this that other elite athletes must be improving at a quicker rate than he, and recognized he was now at something of a crossroads as far as his Olympic prospects went.

Jim didn't know it, but help was soon to be at hand. The answer to his angst was just over the horizon. It presented itself a few weeks later, in the unlikely form of an invitation to a local tennis club's social evening. Here, a talk was to be given by a pre-war runner called Herbert 'Johnny' Johnston, a man who had represented Britain at the 1924 and 1928 Olympics, and who nowadays lived not far from Jim in Upminster.

Johnston, as it turned out, was familiar with Jim's recent progress as an Olympic 'possible' and thought it would be a good idea to invite him along to the tennis club event as a means of making it more topical, rather than focusing things entirely on his own pre-war achievements. Jim, ever polite and glad to help, accepted the invitation, and the two men immediately hit it off. Thus began a fruitful relationship that would, in time, transform Jim's life as an athlete.

Johnston, now in his forties and working in the insurance business, had joined Herne Hill Harriers as a youngster and after close guidance from renowned coach Bill Thomas became a regular international and double Olympian. Achilles tendon damage ended his career in 1929, but he was an intelligent man who had absorbed Thomas' wisdom and formed his own careful theories about running and training. He was, to all intents and purposes, a coach without an athlete.

Directly after the tennis club talk, Jim and Johnny sat down for a long chat over a cup of tea. Jim was fascinated by what he heard. Life with the Beagles in the past two years had seen him enjoy great banter and comradeship with fellow runners, but what his running lacked was the serious advice, planning and guidance that Johnny seemed to know about. To modern ears, what Johnny told him would sound obvious and logical, but to Jim Peters that night it was revelatory stuff and he couldn't get enough of it. One pearl of wisdom that had particular impact was Johnny's theory that, in a race, a runner could not take out of himself more than he'd put in during training: 'Your body is just like a bank book; the more money you put in, the greater the interest you will draw all the time, and the more you can take out when you really need it.'

Uncoached and naive in running terms, Jim was clearly ripe for the attentions of a good coach. Johnny, of course, could see this, and he suggested he take Jim to south London to meet his former mentor Bill Thomas, whom he knew would be happy to take Jim on. This was all very well, but Jim knew he couldn't afford the expense and time required to make regular trips across London, for he had precious little spare time as it was. He responded with his own idea: forget Bill Thomas, why didn't Johnny become his coach? It made perfect sense: He liked the cut of Johnny's jib, the man knew all about Thomas' methodology anyway, and – best of all – they lived fairly near to each other.

With little hesitation, it seems, Johnston agreed. The role of preparing Jim Peters, ten-mile and former six-mile champion, for the 1948 Olympic Games was his. Moments earlier such a vacancy hadn't even existed, but now both men were committed and enthusiastic about the task. They arranged to meet at the Dagenham track so that Johnny could assess Jim's running style at close quarters.

Jim went home that night in a state of high excitement. Meeting Johnny Johnston had been just what the doctor ordered. The self-doubt that had plagued him lately was already beginning to disappear, and he confessed later: 'As I got undressed that night, I could almost see and feel that coveted Union Jack on my vest!'

With hindsight, it is crystal clear Jim needed the guidance of a coach and expert confidant at this point in his career. The Olympics were nine months away and 1947 had not been a huge success in his admittedly short career. Other top runners, meanwhile, looked more likely to peak at exactly the right time – ie, the summer of 1948. Take Jack Holden, for example, who, after lying low for a while, had won the recent AAA marathon championship at Loughborough in a comfortable 2:33.20.2. And, with an eye on his Olympic preparations, Holden would soon be devouring food parcels sent secretly to him by runner Hardy Ballington and his wife from South Africa. Ballington would be one of several athletes based around the globe to generously donate food parcels to help fellow athletes in under-nourished ration-book Britain. When these unsolicited offers came in, the authorities would send off a list of the British Olympic 'possibles' so the donor could choose who to help.

Looking further down the rankings at the late-emerging talent, an interesting 'personal best' was chalked up in the Loughborough AAA marathon by a relative unknown called Dr Alan Turing (Walton AC) who came fifth in 2:46.03. Turing would make enough progress this year to be ranked in the GB top ten, although ultimately would become more famous as the founder of computer science, mathematician, philosopher, and Bletchley Park 'Enigma' war-time codebreaker. Turing, recruited by the Walton club when they spotted him out running alone, would not last long as an Olympics prospect however. Ultimately he would commit suicide, two years after prosecution for homosexuality offences.

Jim may have studied the national rankings lists with some anxiety after the close of the 1947 season, but as far as his club was concerned, he was still very much the bee's knees. They not only unanimously re-elected him as their running captain, but made him a life member of the club, and also handed over the H W Gray trophy to recognise his AAA ten-mile title-winning performance back in April. Another of their gestures, much appreciated in the Peters household, came when they elected his 52-year-old father Percy as an honorary member.

With Jim now moving in high circles as an athlete, the club's committee made good use of this by formally requesting he speak to Joe Binks at *The News of the World*, to ensure the Beagles name was put forward for inclusion in the next London-to-Brighton relay event. Jim was only too happy to take on this sort of job, and also showed he was prepared to 'muck in' with minor tasks too, including taking on the voluntary task of maintaining a photo album of club members in action. He may have been a national champion, but he remained a true club man.

The key development during autumn 1947 for Jim was undoubtedly his link-up with Johnny Johnston. It was a relationship which got properly underway when Johnny stood trackside at Dagenham, studying Jim as he jogged around on his own, injecting the occasional hard lap and burst of speed. Although he'd seen Jim in action before, this was Johnny's first chance to study closely the mechanics of his running. Jim knew full well he wasn't the most elegant of movers, and wasn't surprised to hear Johnny's verdict, which he recalled later:

'You've got an unusual sort of gait, Jim, but quite honestly I don't think that's anything to worry about at all. Your head roll's a little peculiar, too, but again I'm not unduly bothered about that. If it doesn't cause you any discomfort I think we'll leave it alone. You run absolutely straight and true down a line and you carry your arms quite normally.'

Establishing that Jim currently did no proper speedwork, and did not run every day, Johnny began devising a brand new regime for the winter.

Jim had never been a slacker, and liked to run hard in all his workouts, but nevertheless his training to that point had lacked focus and direction. Under Johnny all this would change and he would now be training virtually every evening, and the runs would generally be high quality sessions at shorter than race distance. At least once a week he was to race or carry out a time-trial. Early on, this weekly 'test' would involve sessions of six 440-yard laps at 70 seconds each, or three laps at 65 seconds each, or one-and-a-half laps at 60 seconds pace. This would develop good pace judgement and acclimatise him to race pace. Johnny also added stretching and warming up to his schedule.

Jim would now find himself out running more frequently than before, and each session would be accompanied by a sense of purpose, rather than just chugging along aimlessly. He launched into his schedule that autumn, remotivated and full of enthusiasm. He began training for an hour most evenings after getting home from work and at weekends there was usually a Beagles event in which to test himself. Prominent among these was the club's five-mile handicap at the beginning of November in which he set off from scratch and powered past clubmates to record the fastest time of the day – an excellent 23:01.

Jim wasn't involved a fortnight later when the North of Thames five-mile cross country race at the Metropolitan Police Sports Ground in Chigwell saw the leading runners go badly off course. Wilkins of Wycombe, leading by 200 yards, and Phillips of Southend both became hopelessly lost, which allowed third-placed Reg Robins of the Beagles to chalk up an encouraging if lucky victory. The course had been well marked and mystery surrounded the reason for the leaders' problems.

Feeling fit and strong, Jim fancied his chances in the revived road contest between Ipswich Harriers and Essex Beagles on the afternoon of Saturday, 22 November. As in years gone by, the race was staged from near Ipswich town centre, this time 48 hours after the nation had ground to a halt for the royal wedding of Princess Elizabeth and Lt Philip Mountbatten. The lavish ceremonials in London had provided quite an antidote for a make-do-and-mend nation, still rationed to 1oz bacon and 2oz butter a week, and the resultant feelgood factor lasted for days. The crowd who came out to watch the Ipswich race was certainly full of smiles and good cheer.

The host club was delighted to have Jim Peters in their event, and announced beforehand there would be an attempt to break the 4½-mile course record (23:32.4). It had been set over 50 years earlier by Peter Thurlow, who came along to watch proceedings himself. Jim, wearing No 159, dominated the race as it headed off from outside St Margaret's

Church, up Tuddenham Road, towards Westerfield and back again. Knowing the record was within his reach, he powered home to win comfortably, but missed the long-standing mark by 22.6 seconds. Bert Gorringe of the home club was second and the bespectacled and moustachioed Jim Culver of the Beagles third. Across town a crowd of over 12,000 was watching Ipswich beat Crystal Palace in a Division Three (South) football match, but this didn't prevent good numbers turning out for the race. They saw the elderly Thurlow congratulate Jim on his efforts, and the latter promised he would return for another attack on the old man's record.

Jim's new training regime seemed to be paying off, and December featured two fine victories, firstly in the Beagles cross-country handicap race over 7½ miles, where he won in 42:55, having set off from scratch. A fortnight later at Chingford, he was first home in a seven-mile cross-country triangular match between the Beagles, Victoria Park Harriers and North London Harriers. His time of 37:12 saw him hold off the challenge of Geoff Iden (Victoria Park) by nine seconds and spark great Beagles celebrations as they won the team prize. Iden, a fellow East-ender who worked in the rag trade as a tailor's finisher, was four years older than Jim, and a talented latecomer to the road-running scene, training under the expert eye of former marathon champion Sam Ferris.

A junior Beagles member of the time, Colin Young, remembers this period well. He told me: 'My clearest memory of Jim Peters is that period between 1947 and 1949, training on the Central Park cinder track in Dagenham, with Jim always at the head of the bunch, pushing the pace and urging the others on. The regulars were Eddie Sears, Jim Culver, Herbie Bull, George Lenney, Reg Robins and Tom Hoskins. I was merely a young lad keen to help, who would take Jim's heavy sweater in the changing room after the Sunday morning long run, while he unbuttoned his grey flannels. No fancy tracksuits in those days!'

Christmas 1947 found Jim Peters in optimistic mood, happy with his new training regime and his general fitness, and pleased to have been officially placed in the published list of 'possibles' for Britain's 1948 Olympic team. The BAAB list of 196 athletes was published in *The Times* and in *Athletics*, with Jim one of eight men included in the 10,000 metres category, but not mentioned at three miles. Equally desperate to win a place in the final squad for London was Jim's employer Douglas Wingate, and he too was pleased to be listed at 10,000 metres. Oxford student Roger Bannister, a highly promising miler, was also named, but would subsequently withdraw, feeling he was not ready for competition at this level – a decision he would later regret.

The BAAB explained that the list was not definitive and had been made public purely to 'encourage' those named to try and peak for the following summer. Jim was the only male Essex club athlete to be named. Shortly afterwards the AAA secretary and team manager Jack Crump prompted yet more discussion and speculation when he announced his British 'rankings' for 1947 and joked: 'No doubt this will cause a storm of disagreement around the country!' He placed Jim at No 3 in the six-mile list and at No 6 for the three miles. With Britain entitled to enter three men for the Olympic 10,000 metres, it appeared that Jim Peters was on course for selection. Now all he had to do was prove it.

CHAPTER 6

Five Rings and a Very Special Vest

DECEMBER 1947 – JULY 1948

New Year's Day 1948 was a grey Thursday which dawned misty and mild in the London area, a thaw well underway following a bitterly cold Christmas. The simple act of turning over the new calendar that day will surely have given Jim Peters palpitations. Olympic year had arrived.

All roads led to Wembley for the staging of the fourteenth Olympiad in mid-summer 1948, but this make-or-break year got started for Essex's top runners in rather less glamorous surroundings. The venue was the Bungalow Tea Rooms and Retreat Inn at Chigwell Row – or at least that's how *The Times* sports columns described it. Locals knew the place as simply 'The Retreat', winter HQ of Essex Beagles and where the Essex cross-country championships were staged on the first Saturday afternoon of the new year.

Jim's recent training, now being monitored closely by Johnny Johnston, had gone well and although cross-country was not his top priority, he was keen retain his county title, especially over this 7½-mile route he knew so well. Squadron Leader Peter Dainty had other ideas and was able to exploit the one well-known weakness in Jim Peters' running – his dislike of fences and obstacles. There were twelve of them, and Jim hated the way they slowed him almost to a standstill and disrupted his rhythm. He and Dainty contested the lead throughout, but the stop-start nature of the course favoured the Southend man and he romped in 100 yards clear, looking fresh, to regain a title he'd won eleven years earlier. Jim's valiant late sprint came too late to matter, leaving him fifteen seconds adrift of Dainty's 41:52. Welshman Jim Alford, another senior RAF man, and an Empire Games gold medallist, was third.

Beagles managed to pack all their scorers into the first fourteen to chalk up a notable team victory, thus ending a Woodford Green stranglehold on this event. The beer tasted good in Dagenham later that evening. On the same weekend, old campaigner Sydney Wooderson delighted his fans by regaining the Kent title he'd won before the war. Everyone's favourite solicitor's clerk could still show the young 'uns a thing or two.

Jim's new training load, much heavier than for previous cross-country campaigns, was giving him extra strength and confidence, but often meant he wasn't particularly fresh or rested before his weekend racing. But the races were part of the schedule, however, a means to an end, and not crucially important in themselves. Therefore, coming fifteenth at the seven-mile inter-counties championship at Horsham a fortnight later was certainly not seen as disappointing. His time of 43:22 saw him second, 46 seconds adrift of Bert Swindells of Staffordshire. Wooderson raced in third to lead holders Kent to victory in the team competition, and they lifted the coveted *Daily Telegraph* Trophy. A record 21 teams (183 runners) took part, with extra interest this time from the north. The course was a real test on a wet and windy day, some heavy plough to get through but fast sections too, and only one fence. Jim was part of a group of six who finished clustered together.

In late January, on the weekend of the assassination of Indian political and spiritual leader Mahatma Gandhi, Essex Beagles staged its own ten miles championships, run on a handicap basis, and Jim got back to winning ways. His 56:26 was fastest by some distance, although club stalwart F Almond took advantage of a generous start to actually cross the line first. Buried beneath the shock news from India on this day was the announcement that athletics had lost one of its own best-known names, tuberculosis claiming the life of 47-year-old Evelyn Aubrey Montague. He was London editor of the *Manchester Guardian* as well as an Olympian and former cross-country and steeplechase champion, and would later be immortalised by Nicholas Farrell in the feature film *Chariots of Fire*.

Jim and colleagues were pleased to hear that North of Thames CCA officials had recently visited the disused horse-racing circuit at Galleywood, just outside Chelmsford, and had been pleasantly surprised by what they found, giving the go-ahead for Essex to host the North of Thames championships for 1948 here in mid-February. Chelmsford AC had first suggested the idea of using Galleywood Common, with its old racecourse and grandstands, for human instead of equine racing.

It proved a big success, competitors and supporters turning out in droves, many arriving by motor coach, and bringing the old venue to life again. The picturesque racecourse, the only one in Britain to go around a church, had last been used properly in 1935. The old stands proved popular although many preferred to line the course itself. An unknown ex-guardsman, Doug Thompson of Shaftesbury Harriers, upset the home crowd by holding off the challenge of Jim Peters and two other Essex men to win the title handsomely in 42:47. Behind him, just a few seconds separated Southend pair Roy McCalla and Peter Dainty from Jim in fourth, before the remaining 225 runners trailed in.

Jim maintained his hectic schedule, racing on most Saturdays, and headed across to Kent in late February for the prestigious Southern Counties championships at Aylesford. Here, in bright sunshine, Sydney

Wooderson proved a popular winner over the ten miles. Reg Gosney of Eastleigh was runner-up, and Jim bagged fifth place, just failing to overhaul title-holder Len Herbert of Belgrave at the end. A fortnight later a record field assembled for the 1948 National in Graves Park, Sheffield, an event the Beagles chose to miss this year. Wooderson ended his wonderful fourteen-year career in sensational style, blasting away from Vic Blowfield of Belgrave in the latter stages to win by twenty yards.

By the time spring arrived, Jim's thoughts had turned to road and track. In training he was churning out the miles after work, and testing himself on Saturdays. It left little time for more conventional leisure pursuits, and he only followed West Ham and the other football news via the papers and radio. His was certainly not a typical working man's lifestyle of the time: most of his ilk could be found queuing for the cinema, going to dog racing, the pub, doing the pools, all with a fag hanging from their lips. Not Jim Peters.

Attendance at football soared everywhere, and early in the year nearly 84,000 turned out to see Manchester United tackle Arsenal, the biggest Football League crowd on record. The need to be entertained had become more important since the war, and whatever was on, it seemed, people would turn out and queue for. Established variety acts like Sid Field did a roaring trade, and new young stars like Peters Sellars and Norman Wisdom filled the musty theatres.

But Jim and his pals got their kicks from pursuits in the fresh air, bright-eyed and ruddy cheeked from the exhilarating camaraderie of events like the London-to-Brighton relay. The responsibility of ferrying a baton to a waiting clubmate up ahead seemed to bring out the best in many runners, a breed more used to plodding along in a world of their own. On Saturday, 10 April, Beagles were one of the 21 southern clubs snaking their way down a 46-mile route from the capital to the sea, and they finished a creditable seventh, less than nine minutes behind Belgrave who retained their title. The ten Belgrave men were carrying a special baton conveying a goodwill message from Sir Frederick Wells, Lord Mayor of London, to his Brighton counterpart.

Just after the Easter weekend that followed, Jim and nearly 200 other British Olympic hopefuls enjoyed a break of sorts when invited to Butlin's holiday camp in Clacton-on-Sea for a get-together, some pep talks and light training. The capricious British weather did its worst to spoil the occasion. After a week of glorious sunshine, the athletes' arrival coincided with a day of torrential showers. Their daily twelve-hour programme involved lectures and film shows on training and preparation from BAAB director M C Nokes, team manager Jack Crump, and chief coach Geoff Dyson. A new device was unveiled which allowed film footage to be played in slow-motion, and this caused a great stir.

Although the rain truncated some sessions under public gaze on the Recreation Ground in Vista Road, there was pole-vaulting and high-jumping in full swing for the passers-by to observe, and well-known athletes could be stopped for autographs as they tried their skills on the putting green. On the Sunday, holidaymakers sat quietly on the greensward to watch handsome mile champion Doug Wilson training under the watchful eye of Sydney Wooderson, as well as top female stars Maureen Gardner and Muriel Cornell. Newsreel cameras and a large posse of reporters followed the athletes around and Wooderson told the man from the *East Essex Gazette* how invaluable such a get-together was for Britain's medal chances. Protected from the sea breezes by his large over-coat, Sydney was then coaxed by photographers into an awkward-looking pose with sprinters Sylvia Cheeseman and Winnie Jordan.

The athletes were welcomed to Butlin's by PE supervisor Captain Bond, and by Gladys Painter, Butlin's first 'Red Coat', whose motto was 'Our true intent is all for your delight'. At times there was a definite 'school trip' atmosphere to the event, with some athletes behaving better than others, and plenty of giggling from the back of the ranks. After training there was entertainment on offer, including beauty contests and the communal singing of the Butlin's Buddies theme song. Clacton was delighted by the publicity generated by the athletes' presence, although its local paper castigated civic leaders for not laying on a more grander official welcome for the famous faces. Using the camp this week had been some consolation to Billy Butlin after his original offer of the premises for an Olympic Village was rejected due to it being too far (70 miles) from Wembley.

Meanwhile, further down the coast at Southend-on-Sea, Britain's biggest sporting summer for years kicked off in mid-May when the touring Australian cricketers amassed 721 runs in a single day's play at Southchurch Park in front of a record 16,000 crowd. Later that weekend, cricket fan Jim Peters headed across London to White City to represent Essex at the inter-counties three-miles championship, which was taking place alongside an international *News of the World* promotion, 'The British Games.' These Whit Monday events were effectively the first of the Olympic trials, and many of the 'possibles' who had fun at Butlin's were here today in more serious mode.

Under the gaze of television cameras (by now around 60,000 TV sets were in use across the country), and the BBC radio commentators, there were some very nervous athletes in attendance, few more so than Jim, who still fancied his chances at three miles as well as six, despite the rankings indicating otherwise. After roughly eight laps of his twelve-lap race, Jim hit a bad spell, lost ground, and found he couldn't get going again. His time was respectable but he was well beaten. He came in a disappointed fifth, thirteen seconds adrift of winner Alec Olney who chalked up 14:26.6 and looked comfortable. At the time it felt to Jim like a major setback to his Games hopes, and he needed reassuring words from Johnny Johnston to convince him he was still a contender, and there was plenty of time left to impress the selectors.

Also on trial that day at White City were the team of smartly blazered officials, vying for jobs at the Olympics. Their tension and anxiety was as palpable as that of the athletes, and the lack of communication about a bewildering number of heats and finals meant most of the crowd must have spent the day wondering what on earth was happening. 'This fiasco must never happen again, least of all at Wembley,' castigated *The Times* correspondent. To add to the stress and strain, a new device was making its trackside debut, whereby a microphone relayed the starter's instructions to small loudspeakers near the runners, the aim of which was to eliminate the normal delay of a tenth of a second before his starting pistol was heard.

Jim's defeat at White City saw him step up training even more, but a fortnight later he was beaten again, this time in the Essex three-mile championship on a soggy track at Prittlewell, Southend. Teammate Reg Robins lifted the title, four seconds ahead of Jim in 14:50, but it was clear the heavy track had slowed everybody. It was flooded in parts and conditions were so bad that three events were abandoned altogether. Jim, a natural worrier, again came away feeling miserable, even though he'd given a good display in awful conditions and Johnny had to convince him that by 'sticking with it' rewards would follow.

By the following midweek, on the first Wednesday evening in June, Jim was smiling again. On a far better track, at Motspur Park in south London, he was victorious over three miles in 14:43.6, running on behalf of the AAA against a London University line-up. It was the first three-miler he'd actually enjoyed for some time, and Johnny seemed to be right about his hard training starting to pay off. There was a further morale boost ten days down the line when he was third in the Southern Counties three-mile championship at Uxbridge, the stopwatches giving him a personal best time of 14:30. With the Olympics now just seven weeks away, he was getting quicker and appeared to be peaking just at the right time. The in-form Olney was again winner, with Rowe of Herne Hill nipping into second place.

Then followed what would prove the real red-letter day in Jim's build-up to the Olympics. Stepping back up to six-mile racing, he made the short journey to the smart new track at Woodford to defend his Essex title on the evening of Wednesday, 23 June. What unfolded delighted and surprised both runner and coach in equal measure, Jim powering through the 24 laps without serious opposition and recording the best six-mile time by anybody in the UK for more than ten years. His 30:07 smashed the all-time Essex record and was, of course, a personal best by a good margin. He had never dreamed he was currently this close to breaking the 30-minute barrier for six miles.

The victory margin was a massive two minutes, meaning it was virtually a solo run against the clock, and he improved on the previous year's winning time by 43 seconds: 'Just the tonic I needed,' he reflected later. 'I had no pace help at all, and at the end felt I could go and do it again because I was so fit at the time.' The nature and impact of the win meant for several years he would often describe this as the most satisfying performance of his career to date. It proved emphatically that Johnny's training regime was paying off. And, in timely fashion, it had come barely ten days before the selectors sat down to consider their Olympic squad.

Such a fine performance naturally brought pressure to repeat the feat, to underline it had been no flash in the pan. The opportunity to do just that came along on Friday, 2 July, the opening night of the crucial AAA championships. The White City programme for that evening included the hop, step and jump, the tug of war, and the six miles – the opening exchanges of what was seen as the most important single athletics meeting anywhere since 1936.

After a nervous day at work, Jim arrived at White City with the other hopefuls, battled through the Shepherd's Bush crowds and began his preparations under the cavernous stands. He now had the fastest six-mile time on paper, but the opposition looked mean and hungry, with everyone knowing a place in tonight's first three would mean a great chance of inclusion in the Olympic team. Despite his great show at Woodford, Jim was convinced that winning the right to wear the Union Jack on his vest depended chiefly on a good run tonight. His desire to gain that vest had become almost obsessive, and he certainly won't have needed too many words from Johnny to emphasise the race's importance.

He set off hard as usual and maintained a place at, or close to, the front of the pack throughout. Stan Cox was up there alongside him and looking in good shape, Irishman Steve McCooke was another contender, and also in the mix was his employer Douglas Wingate. With Jim unable to open a significant gap, and not known for his late sprinting ability, it looked anybody's race. In the final couple of laps Cox made his move, drew away and did so purposefully enough to maintain a gap. Jim was rolling from side to side with the effort of trying to catch him, but it was no use, Cox was away. He crossed the line in 30:08.4 to virtually guarantee his own place at the Olympics, with Jim giving everything to finish second (30:16) around 50 yards down. McCooke came in next, with Wingate unable to make an impression on the first three. Poor Wingate's Olympic dream had all but died in the cinders and he was devastated.

Jim was left to stew over his chances, worrying as usual, even though it seemed certain the selectors would back the first three. For Wingate it was hopeless and, now in his thirties and plagued by back trouble, his career was almost over. After a decent pre-war running career, Wingate had resumed in 1945 aged 30, his pre-war trophies among the Bournemouth AC silverware rescued from an underground 'ice house' on a large estate in the Dorset countryside where they'd been stored for the duration of the war. He did well over the country in Hampshire races and in the 1947 National had finished ahead of Jim, who worked for him, but was based at a different branch of the company.

As athletes and supporters readied themselves for announcement of the GB Olympic team in early July, the international political situation began to dominate newspaper headlines. The USSR, which already had close control of Poland and Romania since 1945, began to seal what Churchill called the 'Iron Curtain' and access to Berlin was closed off. It was a worrying situation that led to a large amount of Olympic ticket bookings being cancelled, particularly from potential American visitors. Around half the 2¼ million tickets had already gone overseas and the Berlin crisis was one of a series of tricky situations facing the organisers, who saw off a prolonged campaign by one newspaper to have the Games called off altogether.

The GB team was named on Wednesday, 7 July and there were no big surprises. The first three home in the AAA six miles – Cox, Peters and McCooke – got the nod for the Olympic 10,000 metres. It was entirely predictable, but Jim was nevertheless hugely relieved and proud: 'An international at last!' he recalled as his first thoughts on hearing the news. Veteran 400 metres man Bill Roberts, 36, from Salford Harriers, was named team captain in this his swansong season.

It was too much to expect the selection process to pass entirely without controversy. The old professional/amateur debate rose its troublesome head again. The Olympics were still considered the sporting pinnacle for the principled amateur sportsperson, and the British administrators still set standards of almost absurd purity. A classic example of their inflexibility featured AAA champion Denis Watts, selected for the team in both the long jump and hop, step and jump, but subsequently kicked out because of a technicality which, in the eyes of officials, cast doubts on his amateur credentials. Watts' mistake had been to recently apply for a job involving athletics coaching; had he delayed this career move just a few weeks, he would have been free to take part. Marathon runner Jack Holden must have looked at Watts and thought: 'There but for the grace of God go I.' Holden was caretaker of a sausage factory sportsground, but in case that was seen as earning money from sport, he described himself as a 'labourer'.

There were three weeks from the day the team was announced to the start of the Games proper, and Jim Peters' preparations during this period largely involved sharpening his speed. He tackled a couple of two-mile track races to get his legs familiar with sustained running at below five-minute-mile pace. In Victoria Park he held off the challenge of the host club's Geoff Iden to win in 9:34, and at Motspur Park came in second, but clocked an improved 9:29.

He was happy with these performances, but noticed at Motspur Park he was beginning to develop a chesty cough. Just a week before the Olympics opened the cough had got worse, and he admitted this led to feelings of 'near panic' as the problem threatened to sideline him. He wasn't the only one in trouble: British team manager Crump collapsed at an event in Manchester, apparently due to overwork and exhaustion, and was briefly hospitalised. As the nervous days crept by, Jim found his running was not affected by the cough, and to his great relief it soon subsided.

Unlike some members of the GB team, Jim was granted time off work for the duration of the Games. Excitedly, he travelled across London to check in at the men's Olympic village at RAF Uxbridge on Tuesday, 26 July, three days before the opening ceremony, and four before his own event on the track. He was 29, a qualified optician married with a son, but on this day felt like a small boy at Christmas. At Uxbridge the athletes were cut off from the drabness of everyday life, and all they did was eat, read and chat about the Olympic Games. Jim Peters was at the very centre of it all and he'd never known anything quite as thrilling.

CHAPTER 7

Food Parcels, Flags and a Flaming Torch

July – August 1948

Although the global significance of the Olympics was appreciated, the British media didn't get carried away beforehand in 1948 and much of the coverage was perfunctory and restrained. Members of the home team were, of course, proud and thrilled to be involved, but few appeared under intense pressure to pocket medals. They were just expected to do their best and not let down crown and country.

Jim Peters was fortunate to have an understanding employer and amenable wife, and grabbed the chance to hunker down at RAF Uxbridge athletes' village for the duration. He was one of the fortunate ones. Those unable to take time off work had to pitch up at Wembley along-side the fans, having lugged their kit-bags on public transport.

The likes of 5,000 metres runner Jack Braughton must have envied Jim. Braughton, a building site manager from south London had no time to absorb the grandeur of the occasion. He popped briefly into Uxbridge one day to collect his GB tracksuit, found someone had stolen it and replaced it with a smaller one, cursed his luck and then returned home. On the day of his race he jumped aboard a No 12 red bus from Peckham Rye to Wembley (fare: 2½ old pence), ran his event and was back home in time for tea – losing a day's wages into the bargain.

Not only did the likes of Jack Braughton and others miss out on the benefits of team-bonding and a relaxed preparation, they missed out on food supplies that were good and plentiful at Uxbridge. The much-pub-licised shortages and rationing across Britain had seen foreign food parcels arriving for team members, and, in addition, the American ath-letes at Uxbridge were generously sharing their own supplies with the wide-eyed Brits. Allies indeed.

Large quantities of fresh fruit, vegetables, eggs and bottled water had been sent over for the Brits from Holland, Denmark and Czechoslovakia, prompting many to ask why things had got so bad in Britain in the wake of war, when these smaller nations apparently had goodies to spare? Traditional British reserve was put to one side, and these luxuries were gratefully snapped up by people worn down by years of austerity and two appalling winters.

Without this type of handout, each British track and field star would have had to survive, like anyone else, on the following weekly rations at the time: one ounce of bacon, eight of sugar, two of tea, two of cheese, thirteen of meat, seven of butter or margarine, four of preserves, four of sweets, 63 of bread, one egg and 2½ pints of milk.

The coming Olympics allowed a temporary shaft of sunlight on London life, even though the weather didn't always behave itself. Athletics historian David Thurlow was a schoolboy at the time, and told *Track Stats* magazine the Games were a wonderful antidote to the hard times: 'There was tremendous excitement in the air at Wembley. It was a terrific thrill for me to be there and I'm sure that everyone there felt the same. The war was only just over. England was a mess. There was rationing and no money and the winter of 1947 had been awful. It was so cold that at boarding school we wore overcoats under the blankets when we went to bed. People today really have no idea what it was like. So the Olympics were something marvellous. There was colour and pageantry and the buzz each day would grow bigger and better and no amount of rain – and, oh, how it rained – could spoil it.'

Olympic historian Ernest A Bland gave a broader view: '[London] stands now, stained and untidy, having gone through two major wars and several economic crises, but her voice, as personified in Big Ben, has not been silenced. And it calls with courage a gallant welcome to some 5,000 athletes and maybe a quarter of a million of their followers. They may not see her in festival dress. They may have to scrum for their food. They may find a tight pack in their hotels. But they will come!'

Jim and his colleagues at RAF Uxbridge were issued with their GB uniform of blazer, tie and beret and spent the daytime hours doing gentle training and wandering around the camp watching others in action and making new friends. If you visited the canteen for a mug of Horlicks before bedtime, you could even sit down and listen to the GB football manager Matt Busby chatting with his players. Many of the Brits had not experienced training camps and suchlike before, and found it all highly exciting and stimulating. Some found it hard to sleep, particularly miler Bill Nankeville, who shared a room with Tom Richards, the Welsh marathon runner. Richards was a psychiatric nurse in south London, fond of telling gruesome tales about his patients, and these reportedly gave poor Nankeville nightmares.

Some female British athletes had to resort to needle-and-cotton to either make or adapt their own competition kit, but the men had no such trouble, helped by corporate sponsors Coopers' outfitters, who provided every male competitor with free 'Y-front' underpants. Other sponsors who invested in the Games were Coca-Cola, Craven 'A' cigarettes, Guinness and Brylcreem. Considerable help from abroad was needed, and Finland came forward to donate timber for the basketball flooring, while Switzerland generously provided gymnastic equipment. Germany, of course, took no active part, but her prisoners of war had been put to work on building the Olympic Way road to the front of the stadium – a landmark that in future years would often be mistakenly referred to as 'Wembley Way' by generations of football fans.

The opening ceremony coincided with the hottest day in London for 37 years, temperatures soaring to 34 degrees centigrade. The sultry heat inside a stadium packed with 80,000 spectators even caused a number of athletes to faint during the colourful parade of 59 participating nations and around 4,000 competitors. Jim remembered the day as a 'wonderful and stirring experience'. The crowd looked happy in summer clothes, but in the stiflingly hot VIP area and royal box, King George VI looked thin, pale and unwell, and the teenage Princess Margaret had only just recovered from a reported bout of measles.

As host nation, Britain were last to enter the arena. They marched in 313 strong and six abreast, berets correctly worn one inch above the eyebrows – apart from flag bearer John Emrys-Lloyd who had mislaid his. The 40-year-old's *faux pas* was overlooked when it emerged that not only was he missing a hat, he very nearly didn't have a flag to carry either: the Union Jack had mysteriously gone missing and it was left to a resourceful young man called Roger Bannister – working as aide to the *chef de mission* – to dash into the car park and break into a locked car where a spare flag was stowed. Nineteen-year-old Bannister's sprinting ability saved the day.

One aspect of this gala left a sour taste in many mouths. The role of the all-important Olympic torch bearer would surely have been a fitting tribute to popular Sydney Wooderson at the end of his wonderful career, but the job was surprisingly given to blond-haired and well-toned John Mark, a Cambridge University half-miler. Six-footer Mark was clearly chosen for his looks, physique and background, ahead of the more deserving but scrawny, bespectacled Sydney. Having believed earlier that he had got the job, solicitor's clerk Sydney was only replaced at a late stage in proceedings and, even worse, not properly informed of this decision (the whole disgraceful episode would be exposed four years later at the Helsinki Olympics, when Finnish hero Paavo Nurmi carried the torch before his adoring fans, even though he was now 55 years old, bald and rotund).

Even in the absence of 'The People's Choice', few could deny the spine-tingling impact of the scene as John Mark strode gracefully around the track, ran smoothly up a ramp and lit the huge Olympic flame. The crowd went wild, and Roger Bannister was certainly not the only onlook-er to have his breath taken away: 'I had the feeling we were witnessing sacred rites being performed in an open air cathedral.'

The weather remained very hot and humid for the start of the action and crowds again streamed in great numbers along Olympic Way. Admission cost between 3s 6d and 10s 6d for a day, and around £3 for the week. The unaccustomed colour and spectacle of the opening cere-mony ensured the Games got off to a good start, and the public was fur-ther buoyed by the fact this was the start of a Bank Holiday weekend. The feelgood factor had returned to London for the first time since the VE and VJ day celebrations.

The gossip that first day surrounded the Wooderson torch controver-sy, how the King had got through his sixteen-word opening speech with-out stuttering, and the matter of if and when Britain might win its first gold medal. One controversial talking point that didn't make the papers, however, involved Jack Dearlove, cox of the British rowing eight, who had lost a leg as a boy and who was barred from the parade as it was felt an amputee would look 'inappropriate'.

The heat and humidity of Friday, 30 July was bad news for the dis-tance runners, especially the Brits, unused to such conditions. They had all poured with sweat in their blazers for several hours before and during Thursday's opening parade, and Jim Peters was not the only man to approach the 10,000 metres final feeling drained and apprehensive. One of his opponents, New Zealand's Harold Nelson, had endured the extra burden of being his team's flag bearer at the ceremony. Another who pre-pared badly was the talented but still relatively unknown Czech Emil Zatopek, who sneaked into the sweltering ceremony even though his team doctor had banned him from doing so.

The 10,000 metres was due to start at 6pm, the climax and only final on the programme on the first day. But it was far from being the cool, pleasant summer's evening that British runners Jim Peters, Steve McCooke and Stan Cox would have chosen. Jim recalled their nerves as they were ferried to Wembley from Uxbridge: 'As we drove to the stadi-um, we felt sticky and almost listless. Our only consolation was that everyone else had exactly the same weather.'

The heat wasn't the only problem. Soon after arrival it was evident that officials had encountered problems identifying the start and finish lines. Ten thousand metres equates to roughly six miles and 378 yards, a fact which apparently caused headaches for harassed officials evidently unfamiliar with the metric system. According to Jim's recollection, this problem led to a delay of nearly two hours. The 27 competitors had more time than they needed to jog around and keep loose along the underground concourse. There wasn't much else to do except sit around and study the official programme. The best-known names on the list were world record holder Viljo Heino of Finland and the French Algerian Alain Mimoun, plus up-and-coming prospect Zatopek.

The British trio were almost cripplingly nervous. McCooke, a father of six and a cash-strapped farm labourer, was worried about a nagging Achilles tendon injury that threatened to ruin his big day. The unexpected delay to the start meant the effects of his pain-killing injection were wearing off. Meanwhile, Jim and Stan Cox both fretted over not letting their family and country down, knowing that because of their age this might be their final chance of real glory. Cox was a storeman with the Standard Telephone & Cable Company and often struggled to get time off work to compete. He had taken unpaid leave to be at Wembley and had to be back at work directly afterwards if he didn't want his young family to starve.

When the race finally got underway, poor McCooke's heel soon gave him serious grief and he quit after just two laps. By now Heino had shot into the lead, his first two kilometres at world record pace, chased gamely by fellow countryman Heinstrom, and Albertsson of Sweden. During the third mile, Zatopek moved ominously through the field, going from seventeenth to fourth in less than two laps. Jim and compatriot Cox were holding their place in the top ten, still not completely out of the picture, but finding the pace as hot as the thermometer.

Things were suddenly shaken up by Zatopek, the 25-year-old who boasted the second fastest 10,000 metres time in history. He surged to the front, looking immensely strong albeit far from graceful. His surge provided an unexpected wake-up call for Heino, who had previously looked untroubled. Heino responded, and even briefly re-took the lead around halfway when the pace momentarily slowed a little. But Zatopek was in no mood to hang around for long and lifted the tempo once again.

By now, the massed crowd could see Britain fading out of contention. They seemed almost to switch allegiance and urged on the brave front running of Zatopek. Could he really overcome the brilliant Heino? Had he ploughed past him far too early? Were they about to see the duel of the century? With around nine laps remaining, the answer came in sensational and unexpected fashion: Heino suddenly gave up the chase and walked grim-faced off the track. Nobody could quite believe it. The flying Finn had caved in, destroyed by the relentless machine in front of him. Apparently, he would rather walk away than stay in contention for one of the minor medals.

The chant 'Za-to-pek, Za-to-pek' swelled around the stadium, people of all nations willing the Czech soldier on as he pounded the track relentlessly. His head lolled around, his shoulders rolled and he grimaced, but these were not signs of weakening, it was simply the way he ran. It was reminiscent of the Jim Peters style (or lack of it), but on this day there was little chance of the two men running side by side for the purposes of comparison.

Jim and Stan continued to work hard and maintained places in the top ten or so, although as Zatopek and Mimoun both began lapping opponents, it became hard to fathom who was placed where. New Zealander Nelson was one of a number to drop out through the heat, collapsing unconscious on the track. Zatopek stormed home alone in an Olympic record of 29:59.6, with Mimoun around 47 seconds behind. Bertil Albertsson of Sweden took the bronze medal in 30:53.6. After this, utter confusion reigned.

The excitement generated by Zatopek and the boisterous crowd only added to the mayhem caused by men being lapped. It seemed to faze the poor officials completely. The bell signalling the final lap was sounded at the wrong point for a number of runners, it seems, and the race disintegrated into chaos. Officials were unable to record any of the finish times after eighth place, nor even the finishing positions beyond eleventh (although it was generally agreed the last man home was a Frenchman called Paris). Stan Cox was given seventh place in 31:08.0, but later revealed he'd run one lap too many, a theory backed by the watching Harold Abrahams who announced as much in his radio broadcast. If correct, Cox could have possibly placed anywhere between third and fifth. One theory behind the problems was that the official ringing the bell thought he was on six-mile duty (24 laps), and forgot about the extra distance dictated by the metric system.

This was 1948, so there were no digital clocks or large video screens to assist the runners. Few of them can have known for sure where they stood in those final laps, except of course Zatopek. Jim Peters came home, according to officialdom, one place behind Cox, in eighth place in 31:16.0. It has been suggested that he also fell foul of the blundering officials and did an extra lap, but his time seems to suggest the correct distance was run, based on current form, race conditions and his own description of how he felt.

For Zatopek it was the first of many gold medals and the first major win by an athlete from a Communist-led Eastern European regime. But for the two Englishmen, who had run decent enough times in very trying conditions, it was a day of anti-climax. Both came away from

Wembley despondent at the way they had been lapped and outclassed on home territory. Said Jim: 'Not to have been in the first six was bad enough, but to have been lapped [by both Zatopek and Mimoun] was indeed a bitter blow.'

The British fans, however, had been determined to enjoy themselves and weren't at all deflated about the result, for they had taken Zatopek to their hearts. One teenage boy in the stands that day was Gordon Pirie, a young member of South London Harriers who would within a few years go on to become one of Europe's top runners. Pirie admitted he went to Wembley to cheer Peters and Cox, but as the race unfolded became 'awestruck' by the surges and control of Zatopek, and couldn't stop talking about him afterwards. Zatopek's bursts and then his slowing down to destroy the tempo of others had not been seen before in a major track race. Pirie later said: 'Zatopek inspired me to do something different. From that moment I wanted to run like Zatopek, like a machine. I wanted to run every day.'

The Czech, having already defied instructions at the opening ceremony, played the rebel again, bunking off that night for a forbidden visit to the London hotel of his javelin thrower girlfriend Dana Ingrova. As she appeared at an upstairs window, he is said to have waved his 10,000 metres gold medal at her, only for it to fly out of his grasp and plop into an adjacent swimming pool. He immediately stripped to his underwear and dived in to recover it.

Zatopek had the 5,000 metres to aim at later in the week, but for the likes of Jim Peters it was time to depart Uxbridge and return to normality. Jim did return to the stadium twice in order to watch some events – he saw Belgian Gaston Rieff pip Zatopek in a thrilling 5,000 on a rain-flooded track on the Bank Holiday Monday.

He also witnessed the dramatic finish to the marathon on the final day of the Games, Saturday, 7 August. Britain's big hope for marathon gold, Jack Holden, came to grief with severe blisters and had to quit mid-race (he 'over-pickled' his feet when bathing them pre-race, he would later confess), but the real drama came in the final few yards when leader Etienne Gailly of Belgium – a former member of Belgrave Harriers – entered the stadium first, but began to falter badly.

To the dismay of a sympathetic crowd, Gailly slowed to a virtual crawl and Delfo Cabrera of Argentina entered the stadium in far better shape and quickly passed him. Worse was to follow – though it was good news for medal-hungry Britain – when veteran Tom Richards arrived, and also overtook the distressed Gailly, who had been reduced to little more than a tottering walk.

It was a dramatic and compelling scene, the gallant Gailly losing gold and silver in awful circumstances after all his hard work outside on the roads of north-west London. Jim admitted he got caught up in the emotion of it all and wrote: 'It was the first time I had seen the finish of a marathon and I was considerably moved by both the drama and the excitement of the race. [Gailly] was almost completely exhausted and could hardly drag one foot after the other. Less than 500 yards away was the finishing post.' Little did Jim know the heart-rending scene in front of him would be replayed on a far worse scale six years hence, and he would be cast in the role of victim.

As he left the stadium alongside coach Johnny to hurry for their train, Jim couldn't help feeling sad. He was now a few weeks short of his 30th birthday, he'd achieved his ambition of gaining an international vest, but the pinnacle of his career had ended in great disappointment. Despite chalking up a personal-best time and finishing in the first ten, he couldn't come to terms with the humiliation of being so outclassed by opposition from abroad. 'Crushing' was the word he used, his mind haunted by the vision of being lapped. He was being harsh on himself, for his time of 31:16 was the fourth best 10,000 metres ever run by a Briton (only Alec Burns in 1936, Alf Shrubb in 1904 and Stan Cox at Wembley had clocked better).

In the three years since the war ended, Jim knew he'd done well as a runner, but there remained a nagging feeling he hadn't achieved enough for his own peace of mind. He was also only too well aware that all the time-consuming training had been leaving him tired at work, disrupting his domestic life generally, and that he, Frieda and Robin still didn't have a home of their own. Deep down he knew he ought to quit top class athletics now and reprioritise his life, but it was a desperately hard decision to make.

The Underground journey that Saturday night, away from Wembley and across towards East London, saw Jim in untypical non-talkative mood. As he brooded, his coach must have sensed what was coming. There was a strong sense of anti-climax in the air: 'For quite a distance neither of us said a word,' said Jim later. 'We were both sitting staring into space busy with our own thoughts.'

Then, as the Tube rattled homeward along the Metropolitan Line, came the bombshell: 'Johnny,' he said firmly. 'I'm going to retire.'

CHAPTER 8

Out With a Whimper?

For many people – sportsmen and women in particular – the arrival of a 30th birthday is hugely significant. It's a milestone, more than any other, which underlines the disappearance of youth. At best, it's a somewhat dispiriting anniversary, and at worst can trigger a huge crisis of confidence. The sudden fear of being 'over the hill' can feel even more intense if ambitions or targets remain unfulfilled.

The anti-climax of the Olympic Games, added to the normal pressures facing a young working man with a family, certainly took its toll on Jim Peters over his final few weeks as a 29-year-old.

After his grim conversation with his coach on the train home from the Games, Jim stayed true to his word and spent the three months of autumn 1948 in self-imposed retirement from athletics. But Johnny steadfastly kept faith in him, and urged him to think seriously about coming back as a marathon runner. It was a career change that had been successful for the likes of Jack Holden, Ernie Harper and Harry Payne at the end of their track careers.

Holden, in fact, had reacted to his disastrous Olympic marathon by emulating Jim and hanging up his running shoes. Both men seem to have found life without running difficult, becoming restless and unhappy. Holden was eventually ordered to get back into training by his exasperated wife Millie, while Jim also emerged again in November 1948 to help out Essex Beagles at cross-country events.

The winter season effectively got underway at the end of October when Beagles staged their annual 4½ miles cross-country race from Chigwell Row, but interest in this was eclipsed by a brand new event in Chelmsford the following week. Beagles joined around a dozen other clubs for a road relay starting from outside the Corn Exchange in Tindal Square, competing for the Sidney C Taylor Memorial Trophy. Chelmsford AC had recently opened a new HQ and track in the town and this new race was to honour late club president Taylor, a long-serving Mayor of Chelmsford, president of the county athletic association and local newspaper proprietor. The impressive trophy weighed in at more than twelve pounds, was three feet high and worth £250 (£7,000 in modern terms). Each team of six men had to cover twenty miles, the 150 runners doing a 3.7-mile lap each. Jim, a little heavier around his middle following the lay-off, completed his duties in 15:45 and then stood at the roadside to encourage teammates. Beagles took the lead on the fourth leg and, despite a brilliant final stage by Williams of Mitcham, just kept their noses in front to win the cup by seven seconds. Jim felt pleased to be back.

A fortnight later, the annual tussle on Ipswich's roads took place between the Beagles and the local Harriers. Invigorated by the Chelmsford relay success, Jim showed he was back and firing on all cylinders, one of three runners to go inside Peter Thurlow's ancient record for this 4½-mile undulating course. The presence of the two Olympians, Peters and Cox, ensured a good crowd, but they failed to inspire a home win, Beagles packing four men into the top five places. Cox completed a blistering run in Ipswich colours to win in 22:55.8, while Jim and teammate Reg Robins crossed the line together behind him in 23:15.0, all three well inside the 23:32.4 course record of 1896.

Shortly before Christmas 1948 it was announced the next Empire Games would be staged in Auckland, New Zealand in just over a year's time. Jim was currently second-fastest Englishman at 10,000 metres, but these Games held no interest. His immediate plans didn't go beyond helping out the Beagles from time to time over the winter. He even admitted that, compared to a year earlier, he was now merely 'playing with athletics'. Johnny Johnston, meanwhile, was speaking privately to various contacts, men with good marathon experience, to arm himself with the best knowledge and advice should Jim ever come to a positive decision about tackling the 26.2-mile event. Throughout the first half of 1949, however, it looked like Johnny was wasting his time.

Jim had mulled things over and a typical marathon training schedule of four or five runs a week, some of them twenty miles or more, filled him with horror: 'I couldn't think of anything more monotonous than plodding along for twenty miles, particularly in winter, and as I didn't get home until well after six o'clock such a programme would only enable me to have a meal, go out for a run – and then go to bed.'

On New Year's Day 1949 the Essex cross-country championships from Chelmsford AC's new base in Waterhouse Lane proved a typical mud-and-guts affair over 7½ miles. The course resembled a quagmire, so bad it was almost laughable, with torrential rain throughout. A significant number of runners lost footwear, their shoes sucked off by the deep mud. Ray Fullerton, secretary of the host club, was an early victim, running most of the race in just one shoe, eventually finishing a plucky eighteenth. Third-placed Reg Robins fared best for Beagles, whose defence of the team title failed after Dellow of Woodford Green won a thrilling three-man sprint for the line. Jim is thought to have finished ninth, narrowly winning himself a place on the Essex team for the inter-counties race later on.

On the same day, Jack Holden made his much heralded comeback from retirement to win the annual Morpeth to Newcastle 13½-mile road race in a record time. England's favourite marathoner would turn 42 in a few weeks' time, but was clearly far from finished, a fact that will have registered with Johnny Johnston as he continued to sketch out his ideas for Jim's future.

For the first time in the event's history, the inter-counties championship was staged in the north of England on Saturday, 15 January 1949, and hosts Lancashire marked the occasion with victory, their first of many over the next quarter-century. The seven-mile course at Grange Farm, Worsley, Manchester, was heavy throughout and continuous rain worsened matters. Essex came fifth and nobody had an answer to the fine running of Lancs' new sensation Williams – a champion after just twelve months in the sport. Jim finished well down the pecking order, but his form was slowly returning and a fortnight later he romped to victory in the Essex Beagles ten-mile championship at Chigwell Row in 57:20, more than a full minute clear of Reg Robins.

Beagles went on to celebrate an excellent February, Jim continuing to play an important part, and they won the team prize at the North of Thames cross-country and were runners-up in the Southern Counties event. The former was over a three-lap course at Hutton School in Shenfield, where Jim was sixteenth in 45:50, the third Beagles scorer of six who made the top 30. Douglas Thompson of Shaftesbury won in 43:12, seven seconds clear of Thames Valley Harriers' Alec Olney. In the 'Southern' at Camberley, Beagles were second behind Belgrave in a lively race won by Olney, Jim 28th, one of half-a-dozen Beagles in the top 50.

Jim obliged again when Beagles urged him to lead their team at the 62nd staging of the English national championships at Bromford Bridge racecourse, Birmingham, over ten miles on a chilly, rainy day in March. Sutton Harriers took the team honours, and the new individual champion was 28-year-old pathologist at the Royal Halifax infirmary, Dr Frank Aaron of Leeds St Marks Harriers, who beat Olney by less than eight seconds. Len Eyre, a Yorkshire-based civil servant, was third. Beagles were eighth team, and Jim led them home in 46th, a few places ahead of Sydney Wooderson, in his final year as a competitive runner.

For an athlete supposedly in semi-retirement, Jim was running a lot of races and next it was back to the roads for the relay season. After being pipped by Surrey AC at the annual Ilford Road relays, Beagles sent a team to join the star-studded line-up at the London to Brighton relay on Saturday, 2 April. This was one of Jim's favourite events. He took the baton for the six-mile stage from Handcross and recorded a strong 31:42, finding he was competing directly with some of the best GB distance-runners of the era – alongside him in the holding area were Holden (Tipton) who would run 30:34, Bertie Robertson (Reading) 30:56, Bobby Reid (Birchfield) 30:50, Tom Richards (South London) 31:54 and Wooderson (Blackheath) 31:29. Also running was the Government code-breaking 'boffin' Alan Turing of Walton (33:52). A record 25 teams took part and Belgrave completed a hat-trick of wins, Beagles tenth.

This *News of the World*-promoted event was establishing itself as one of the most popular events on the athletics calendar. Its format promot-ed team spirit and camaraderie, and responsibility to the team ethic seemed to bring out the best in most men. George Knight of the Beagles would confirm this later: 'I think the London to Brighton really held a lot of clubs together – it seemed to unite a whole club. Track people would come along in the coach. The half-milers would train hard and aspire to do the short leg. It was a great social occasion as well as a hugely exciting athletic event.' On Jim's contribution, he adds: 'He was always a reliable team member, particularly on road relays such as these, and always active in suggesting team selection and strategies.'

The great day out at the relays reminded Jim what he would be miss-ing if he retired too soon. Another Beagles colleague, Dave Green, con-firms Jim's enthusiasm for such events: 'He was a great team man and inspired others, particularly in this type of club race. He was always will-ing to give advice and was extremely proud to wear the club vest, what-ever the occasion.' Beagle Colin Young adds: 'Jim absolutely loved [the relay format]. He was always out to run the fastest time on his stage, no matter where he took over or who he was up against.'

Jim later described this period as one of 'half-hearted' running, but it included winning the Essex AAA six-mile track title in 31:47 and coming second in the three-mile version, both during June 1949. The latter, at the Crittall Sports Ground in Cressing Road, Braintree, saw him pipped by inches by clubmate Jim Culver in 15:04.4. Heavy showers made the going tough at these 58th anniversary championships and kept the crowd down to around 1,000, who spent most of the afternoon running for cover. The tall, barrel-chested Culver lifted the Atalanta Cup, having led from early on, but one report described Jim's late effort to overhaul him as 'magnificent'. Reg Robins was next home to make it a clean sweep for Beagles. Politician and businessman Lord Braintree, president of the county association and recently elevated to the House of Lords, was an enthralled spectator. His daughter, the Hon Mary Crittall, handed over the prizes at the conclusion.

The summer of 1949 was notable in British athletics for the emergence of young talent like eighteen-year-olds Walter Hesketh and Gordon Pirie. Mancunian Hesketh won the Northern three and six-mile titles in record times, as well as the Army championships, while in the RAF version at Uxbridge, Corporal Pirie was three miles champion in 14:48.4. Meanwhile, another 40,000-plus Bank Holiday crowd filled White City to see the USA win *The News of the World*'s British Games, while Jack Holden retained his crown at the Polytechnic Marathon (known widely as 'the Poly') in a modest 2:42.52.4.

Jim accepted an invitation to run for the AAA in a match against a combined Lancashire and Yorkshire team, a showpiece that was part of the Longwood Harriers Diamond Jubilee Sports, held at Fartown Cricket Ground in Huddersfield. Jim ran hard but could do no better than fifth in the three miles, clocking 14:50. His best days as three-miler were clearly over, a point emphasised when one of the new guard – Tony Chivers of Somerset – won the inter-counties three-mile title that summer in a championship best of 14:20.2, a shock victory over the more-fancied Olney and Aaron. It was a glum Jim Peters who headed south from Huddersfield, and he recorded his thoughts in his training diary: 'Another poor, struggling race. Is it my feet? Is anything wrong? Am I finished with top stuff? Hope not.'

His morale was low but at least the Huddersfield test served as a warm-up for his appearance in the six miles on the first day of the AAA track and field championships at White City on Friday, 15 July. The crowd here was boosted by thousands of free-entry schoolchildren, admission on this first day costing adults between 1s 3d and 5s. It was a warm and sultry day and things went badly again for Jim, the heat leading to bad blisters. In terms of outcome, time and position, the race was a near-carbon copy of the Olympic 10,000 metres, as he came home a very unhappy eighth in 31:16. He was never in serious contention, with title-holder Stan Cox leading almost all the way until the Estonian Valdu Lillikas (Polytechnic Harriers) stormed past on the final lap and won in 30:15. The exciting finish saw Cox runner-up, just 1.4 seconds adrift, youngster Hesketh third a further 2.8 seconds down, and only the width of a vest in front of Leeds' student Des Birch, whose heroic personal best was not quite enough.

For the second time in less than twelve months a relative failure on a hot, humid day at White City prompted the same response from Jim Peters: it was time to get out of top-level athletics. We can only guess what emotions flooded his mind, for the entry in his diary was brief and matter-of-fact: 'My last AAA run. Heat blisters. Lack of training. Decided to retire from top class. Busy with optician's business.'

Standards were seen to be rising generally – two men went under 14:15 in the three-mile race, and Bill Nankeville created a championship record in the mile (4:08.8) – despite the cloudbursts on day two. But it was a particularly inglorious weekend as far as Jim was concerned. He was no longer among the top-ranked men at any distance and felt it was clearly time to leave the stage.

Having made the decision to quit, he had one more fixture he was obliged to fulfil, a three-mile race at the Ponders End AC Sports & Fete the following Saturday on what would prove another very hot day. Not surprisingly, he put in another lack-lustre performance in North London, and trailed in eighth in only 15:15. His diary entry says it all: 'Felt lousy. No hard training. Too hot and tired of the sport. Rest.'

He'd threatened to quit before, but this time it seemed like he really meant it. As he pencilled the Ponders End result in his book, it must have felt like the final entry he would make, for he literally drew a thick line under things. He would later recall the exact thought that ran through his mind at that moment: 'And that is definitely the end of Jim Peters' athletic career!'

A miserable eighth at a summer fete in Ponders End? Could he really stomach going out like this – with a whimper instead of a bang?

CHAPTER 9

Mad Whales and Englishmen

Jim Peters abandoned running in the autumn of 1949, but it didn't abandon him. He stopped pounding the roads and tracks, focused his energies on his work at the opticians in Mitcham, and saw his fitness levels drop and the weight pile on. Johnny Johnston was aware of this, but bided his time and never gave up on his plan to make Jim a marathon champion.

Several times the two men bumped into each other and each time Johnny chipped away a little more. Initially Jim had absolutely no inclination to tackle marathons, but Johnny's was a persuasive voice that he'd always respected and listened to. There would soon be signs he was weakening. As he recalled later:

'At first I was dead against it, but very gradually Johnny's propaganda began to work. I began to think more and more of the possibilities of having a shot at it. I realised of course just what it was going to require, what the training and hours and hours of dreary preparation it would require – and for what result? I might not even be fairly successful. It was possible I might even be an utter failure.'

Early in Jim's inactive period, Britain's leading marathoner Jack Holden hit the headlines by winning the Enschede race in a remarkable 2:20.52, but, as immediately suspected, the course was found to be well short of the proper distance – to the tune of a massive 2,630 metres (1½ miles plus) in fact. Nevertheless it was a fast run by the Tipton veteran and he deserved the post-race ritual in which he was ceremoniously robed in a special blanket and kissed on each cheek by a beautiful Dutch maiden, who then placed a colossal wreath on his head. The embarrassed Holden then had to walk up and down acknowledging the crowd before he could persuade someone to help him remove his flowery headgear so he could escape to the dressing rooms. Holden's time was roughly equivalent to a world best time for the marathon, which indicated Jim would have his work cut if he fancied a shot at becoming the best Briton.

By early November Jim had made a complete U-turn following his earlier rejection of the marathon idea. Perhaps it was itchy feet at seeing clubmates embarking on their new cross-country season, or simply a desperate inability to give up old habits, but the net result was a sheepish phone call to Johnny in which he asked for a meeting to discuss possibly taking the plunge.

Johnny was pleased, for he already knew Jim possessed characteristics that would stand him in good stead for the task ahead. He had an ability to push himself very hard in a race, beyond the point where many men would weaken or cave in. He was inclined to train in a disciplined way and follow instructions closely, and also had a stubborn streak born of a need not to let himself or others down. If he could cope with the training and steer clear of injury, Jim Peters certainly seemed to be made of the right stuff to become a top marathoner. There were only two major problems in his path: firstly he was not prepared at this stage to commit to very long training runs (excursions in the region of twenty miles) and, secondly, his wife was firmly against the whole idea.

Mrs Peters presumably had health and lifestyle factors in mind when she raised objections to a man of his age and commitments embarking on long distance work. Knowing him better than anyone else, she was probably concerned over Jim's propensity not to do anything by halves, and this marathon lark was already littered with tales of men suffering badly and coming a cropper very publicly. Jim would go on the record later to confirm this delicate domestic impasse: 'She was much more concerned that we should get a house, and that I should do my utmost to improve my position in the firm for which I worked.'

It was clear to Jim and Johnny that a bit of care and diplomacy would be required. They would have to convince Mrs P there would be no harm in him returning to his old routine of attending club training nights and doing a few races at weekends – but only they would know the long-term aim was marathons. They would have to be discreet, and in the early months the training load would have to be relatively light. Johnny was happy to go along with this, and the two men agreed on a regime involving regular runs of around four miles that would get his body used to the routine of running nearly every day. In addition Jim would tackle the usual club events on a Saturday and on most Sundays attempt something a little longer – say seven or eight miles. According to Jim: 'If, as quite frequently happened, I got involved in taking out my son Robin in his pram on Sunday mornings, then I would do my run in the evening.' This would be Phase One of his programme and it would be carried out for the best part of six months.

Naturally his three-month lay-off caused rustiness and a lack of sharpness, so his comeback in late 1949 on the local club scene was quiet and steady. It seems he was slipped quietly into the Beagles line-up that travelled a few miles north to Chelmsford for the annual Sidney C Taylor Memorial Relays, one of a record entry of twenty teams. Leading clubs came from far and wide, and delighted organisers boasted they could now consider this a true national event. Sadly the race was marred by appalling weather as the batons were ferried six times around the 3½-mile lap of the Boarded Barns council housing estate. Aylesford Paper Mills from Kent won in a swift 1:38.03, despite only arriving at the start line at King Edward Grammar School with seconds to spare, following delays catching the Tilbury Ferry into Essex.

Jim's fitness slowly returned as he carried out Johnny's instructions and pounded out fast four-milers during the week. He would usually arrive home from work on the train from Mitcham just after 6pm, get changed and head straight out, not sitting down for his evening meal until later. Having gone up to more than 11½ stones during his lay-off, his weight was now returning to previous levels: 'My stomach began to look more steamlined again,' he reported.

A club colleague who could usually keep pace, and consequently accompanied Jim on many a training run, was Reg Robins, who was now emerging as a consistent racer in his own right. In December, Jim and Reg came home side by side to win Beagles' cross-country match against Chelmsford AC at Chigwell Row, the pair both given 37:43 for the tough three-lap course of 6¼ miles. With teammate Jim Culver snatching third, some 130 yards behind them, Beagles completed a clean sweep and won the match.

As Jim toiled away quietly over the winter of 1949-50, there were significant developments in the wider world of athletics. The sport got its very first weekly magazine when the monthly *Athletics* morphed into *Athletics Weekly* under Jimmy Green's editorship. Runners loved the new format and the little periodical would soon become established as the sport's 'bible'. It was a triumph for Green, who had been told his publication would never succeed in cash-strapped post-war Britain. Interestingly, the first issue in the new format carried an article that will have been of interest to Jim, given his recent experiences: it was penned by Sir Adolphe Abrahams, medical officer to the international athletic board and British Olympic team, and discussed the phenomenon of the 'burnt-out athlete'.

There was plenty of news for the new *AW* to cover. Shortly after Christmas the athletics community mourned the death of former world mile record holder and Olympic gold medallist Jack Lovelock, tragically killed by a train in New York, aged just 39. Attracting attention with his fast mile times was a young Roger Bannister, who showed he certainly had the guts and determination to reach the top when winning a race after being struck by a lorry just before the start. Anyone who doubted whether university athletes had true grit had to eat humble pie when

Bannister won the five-mile cross-country near Oxford with blood pouring from a head wound inflicted by the truck's wing mirror.

The war had been over for more than four years now, but Britain was still rebuilding and rationing still in force. The 1950s represented a new decade of hope, but the decade began with another General Election looming, the Cold War raging, India becoming a republic, and 64 men lost when submarine *HMS Truculent* sank in the Thames estuary. But at least there was sport. Humble Portsmouth FC were reigning Football League champions and the English national team was set for a first-ever tilt at the World Cup.

On a bitterly cold January day at Chigwell Row, Jim Peters' first competitive run of the 1950s saw him concede his Essex Beagles ten-mile title, beaten comfortably through the trees and pathways of Hainault Forest by George Lenney and Jim Culver. A few weeks later, what *The Times* called the greatest gathering of cross-country runners ever seen in the south of England assembled at windswept Eastbourne for the Southern Counties event, a total of nearly 900 men and boys racing in the various categories. A hard day's running saw Jim come in 38th, some five minutes down on winner Harry Hicks. Those bare facts might look somewhat underwhelming for a former champion, but Jim was happy to be holding his own in good company and knew these races were simply part of a schedule and not important in themselves. Johnny's master-plan involved building strength and stamina before trying him out at twenty miles later in 1950, with the long-term aim of a marathon in the spring of 1951.

Experienced Jack Holden showed how it was done at the fourth staging of the Empire Games in early 1950, in New Zealand's City of Sails, Auckland. Just a few weeks short of his 43rd birthday, Holden won marathon gold for England in 2:32.57, finishing more than four minutes clear of the rest. True to form, however, it was not a straightforward run, for not only did he have to fend off an over-enthusiastic dog en route, he had to discard his plimsolls near the fifteen-mile mark after they disintegrated, forcing him to run around nine miles barefoot, his feet a bloody mess by the end.

Blood was also spilled at the English National cross-country a week or two later, a tricky course posing some unusual problems for runners who set out from the Hazell sportsground in Aylesbury. The ten-mile route in the Buckinghamshire countryside contained all the disruptive hazards Jim hated: ditches full of water, an awkward bridge and fences. The 493 men in the senior event were warned what to expect after the earlier junior race became badly congested at a narrow part of the course.

Some of the youngsters tried to avoid the problem by hurdling barbed wire, a number of nasty injuries the inevitable result. Officials reacted quickly and re-routed the course before the stampede of the main race came along. Jim's solid but unspectacular display saw him finish 53rd, the third Beagles scorer, a long way behind the impressive Frank Aaron (Leeds St Marks) who retained his title in 50:32, coming home in splendid isolation. Visitors from the north dominated proceedings and Sutton Harriers won the team prize, with Beagles down in eleventh.

After the barbed wire and mud of the Aylesbury Vale, the running community then enjoyed a complete change of scene. The leading southern clubs booked their single-decker buses and headed en masse for the twentieth London to Brighton road relay on April Fool's Day. This year Jim opted to run the second leg, a five-mile section, during which he was passed by the Reading AC schoolmaster Bertie Robertson, but still stormed in with the baton to keep Beagles in third place overall. Their position slipped in the latter stages and the club was ultimately seventh, around seven minutes down on winners Thames Valley Harriers.

Easter 1950 marked six months since Jim's comeback, and his semi-secret early preparations for the marathon had gone well so far. It was time for a serious chat with Johnny Johnston over the next phase.

Jim felt fit and ready to move on to longer training runs and suggested to Johnny the time was right to step things up. The coach didn't want him to overdo it at this stage and urged caution, reminding him there was a full year at least before he might make his competitive marathon debut. Jim's natural eagerness and impatience saw him lengthen some of his runs anyway, and occasionally what used to be a midweek four-mile spin would now be extended into something nearer ten miles. Johnny accepted this, and eventually gave Jim his head a little more, even agreeing that, if he felt confident, he could put his name down for the Essex twenty-mile road championship that was to be held in Chelmsford in May.

The two men were still keeping their marathon plans under wraps, and Jim confessed later that even his wife had still not been told at this stage. He knew she would only worry about him over-doing things. Spouses often know more than they let on, however, and Frieda probably had a shrewd suspicion something was afoot. The night before the Essex 20 – double the length of the longest race Jim had ever attempted before – Frieda apparently noticed her husband was taking extra time and care over packing his kit for Chelmsford. Their ensuing discussion concluded with him being told he could go ahead as long as he wasn't doing anything silly like running a marathon. 'No, it's definitely not a marathon, my dear!' smiled Jim, truthfully.

Perhaps it's not so surprising that Mrs Peters should have been worried about her husband's well-being at this point. There had been scare stories in the newspapers that April, in which a heart specialist named cross-country running as potentially a 'dangerous' sport. Although he acknowledged that endurance sports didn't harm a healthy heart, he felt that excessive strain – as witnessed in the toughest XC races — led to impairment of the whole physiological reaction to exercise. The effect of sport on the heart had long worried medical experts and lay people alike, said the reports, and endurance athletes often possessed unusually large hearts.

The long distance fraternity will have sneered and dismissed such talk as 'tosh and piffle'. And their number will surely have included the small band of enthusiasts who gathered for the Essex 20 on Saturday, 13 May, on a strength-sappingly hot afternoon. Their main worry as they gathered in the shade of the Chelmsford AC clubhouse in Waterhouse Lane will have been the possibility of blisters, not heart problems. Jim had certainly chosen highly unsuitable weather for his long-distance debut, for there was brilliant sunshine all day and by the time of the 3.30pm start, the mercury had risen to over 80 degrees Fahrenheit. It was a heatwave that caught the whole UK on the hop that day, including a school of 164 whales who got so confused they became stranded on a Scottish beach, most sadly perishing in view of thousands of curious onlookers.

The Essex 20 had been inaugurated fourteen years earlier when it was the first county championship promotion of its sort. Long distance races were not easy to find back then, and this one went down well; a year later in 1937 it was decided to increase its length and lay on the first marathon championship to be promoted at county level. Stan Worboys of Woodford Green won, but the rest of the field seemed ill-prepared for the ordeal, the second man coming in a full half-hour later and most of the rest quitting altogether. The event was quickly shortened back to twenty miles and soon became a well-established annual event.

As far as is known, at this point Jim's sturdy legs had only ever taken him beyond ten miles in a single outing on two occasions. Once was an experimental 22-miler and the other a fifteen-miler – both relatively unpressurised training spins ('jog trots' as he liked to call them). It meant today's twenty-mile race represented unknown territory and he will have been as nervous as anyone as he chatted with members of the Chelmsford host club beforehand. Despite his track and cross-country running of recent times, some of the others only remembered Jim from his half-mile and one-mile exploits before the war. They told him how surprised they were to see him tackling twenty-mile racing – normally the preserve of an exclusive minority. Jim told them about his recent training and how he had dropped his weight by 21 pounds in just six months to its present level of 10st 2lbs. These were startling statistics and the diligent reporter from the *Essex Chronicle* pencilled them into his notebook and used them in his report later.

Just 25 men toed the line, heading off during the hottest part of the day, an unforgiving sun baking the figure-of-eight route of two laps. It took them along Writtle Road, narrow Lawford Lane, Rainsford Road, Broomfield Road, Patching Hall Lane, Chignal Road, Rainsford Road and back to Waterhouse Lane. A pack of eight formed at the head of the field, with Jim just in front at the five-mile point in 28:05. Making steady progress, he maintained his lead and clocked 59:34 at the halfway point, still looking strong. Ken Cook, representing the newly formed Hadleigh club, was nearest challenger, but finding the going tough and soon afterwards decided to quit. Between ten and fifteen miles Jim sped up slightly and seemed to be enjoying himself. He passed fifteen in 1:27.40, a good distance ahead of Wally Nicholson of Woodford Green, who had been touted as pre-race favourite.

Jim remained in firm control as the men behind began to fade, and although there was a slowing in the latter stages, his overall pace remained at below six-minutes-per-mile and he came in to win in 1:59.50, a fine achievement in these difficult conditions. The more-fancied Nicholson had been burned off and crossed the line three-and-a-half minutes later. Jim's Beagles teammate J Carroll was third in 2:06.52. They were well strung out further back, and the tenth finisher didn't arrive until a good half-hour after Jim.

The effort took a lot out of him, his feet covered in blisters and he felt 'decidedly groggy', but it had been a stunning victory for a debutant at this distance, and he was quietly jubilant. Although exhausted, he now knew for sure he would be capable of putting up a good show at marathon level. Today represented a great double victory for the Beagles, who won the team prize by a single point from Woodford Green. Jim would look back on this red-letter day and identify it as the occasion when the 'marathon bug' really took a hold of him in earnest.

As he returned home and staggered through the door, Mrs Peters wondered if the tiny winner's medal he produced from his bag was worth all the exhaustion. But after a light meal and short rest, Jim was bubbling again. He phoned Johnny Johnston who was ecstatic to hear the result, and quizzed him about how he'd felt during the race, and how he felt he would cope with racing a distance six miles longer than today's effort. Jim's excited responses told him all he needed to know. The two men arranged to meet to discuss their next moves, and Jim went to bed knowing the die was cast. Marathons were his future.

Shortly after the Essex 20 victory, a major life-change occurred that helped Jim's marathon aspirations – he and Frieda were at last able to move into a house of their own. It was in Chadwell Heath, a short distance north of Dagenham and closer to the highly attractive training routes around Hainault Forest. This change of circumstances helped free up more time in which Jim could fit his training. It was very reassuring for Johnny, who had worried his highly active protege might struggle to fit in all the mileage.

Jim attacked his training with a vengeance that summer, putting quantity ahead of quality to a large extent. Although he ran strongly in just about every outing, the frequency of running and the mileage were of a higher priority than taking part in races. In fact his only serious competition of the entire summer season would be the Essex three-mile championship race for the Atalanta Trophy in June. For this, a bumper crowd of 4,000 packed into the Chelmsford cricket ground in Rainsford Road and saw championship records fall in the 440 yards hurdles, the javelin and the hop, step and jump. Beagles filled all three leading positions in the three miles, Jim settling for third place behind Tommy Hoskins and George Lenney.

Just as athletics was thriving nationally, bigger crowds and new heroes emerging, so the sport flourished in Essex. The county association's profile was boosted when Jim's fellow East Ender-made-good, the film actress Anna Neagle, was made president of the Essex Women's AAA. Currently Britain's top box-office actress, she took her athletics' role very seriously. She declared it was one of the most important jobs she had ever secured and promised to participate fully, despite currently filming *Odette* with Trevor Howard and Peter Ustinov. Born just up the road from Jim in Forest Gate in 1904, Anna would become a CBE in 1952, and a Dame in 1969.

Jack Holden won his third successive Poly Marathon this summer, his 2:33.07 placing him a massive five-and-a-half minutes clear of all opposition. It won't have escaped Jim's attention that the popular Holden was now aged 43 and surely in the latter stages of his career. His marathon crown would be there for the taking soon. Another man said to be considering a switch to the marathon was Stan Cox, Jim's old track adversary, who had also taken a step back from competitive running lately and was mostly just doing club events for fun. Cox passed on some training advice in an article in *Athletics Weekly* and found himself at the heart of a great debate with the legendary ultra-distance runner and writer Arthur

Newton, over whether distance men actually needed to do 'speedwork' or not. Newton was convinced time spent on the feet was far more important than trying to develop speed. The way Jim Peters attacked some of his training runs made it clear which side of the fence he was on. Nevertheless, Jim was curious about Newton's views and it is thought the two men exchanged cordial correspondence.

Such debates filled many column inches of *AW* around this time, which was a healthy development in a sport still partly stuck in the dark ages. Johnny Johnston was certainly a deep thinker with his own views on how to tackle marathons, and Jim himself would recall this as a period when conventional practice began to change in a big way. He would write: 'The accepted marathon training methods [up to 1950 or so] were to run long distances at a slow pace. The whole object seemed to be to make absolutely sure that you stayed the course; the pace at which you travelled seemed to be of secondary importance.' He was critical of the many marathon runners of the era who seemed to spend all their Sundays on very long walks, a training technique he felt was probably a complete waste of time.

By now, six-milers on the track were no longer on Jim's radar, which is just as well, for he probably wouldn't have lived with Dr Frank Aaron at the AAA championships at White City in July. The modest and quietly spoken pathologist from Yorkshire held off the former Belgian resistance member, Marcel Van de Wattyne, to smash the British record in 29:33.6. Shortly after this, Holden, barely a month after the Poly, became the first man to lift the AAA marathon title four times in a row, winning at Reading in 2:31.34 from a field of more than 100. Again Holden was utterly dominant, nearly a full mile clear of runner-up Edward Denison (Milocarians AC), a 41-year-old army officer who clocked 2:37.00 in only the second marathon he'd ever tackled. The first two men were picked for the forthcoming European championships despite having a combined age of 84. It underlined again how the GB marathon crown would soon be there for the taking by any promising newcomers.

The displays at shorter distances by the likes of Pirie, Hesketh and Bannister suggested the future was bright for English athletics, although failure to dominate one or two international meets saw the sport unexpectedly discussed in the House of Commons. High Wycombe MP John Haire asked Prime Minister Clement Attlee if, following the poor performances of Britain in certain recent matches, he would back provision of new post-school training opportunities for youngsters in athletics as well as team games, physical culture and sports generally. He demanded that promising athletes should be identified early on and then sponsored, but Attlee – to loud cheers – responded by saying it would be better to encourage a raising of standards generally rather than cultivate individuals.

As far as Essex Beagles was concerned, all the club really wished for was an improvement to the shabby track facilities it was having to use in Dagenham. The local council currently saw fit to charge individuals 3d per hour, or 7s 6d per season, for casual use of the track, but it fell below the standard of many other London tracks and the council dragged their heels over improving it, despite Beagles regularly imploring them to do so. Finding somewhere to train away from the track wasn't a problem though, for by 1950 Dagenham had ten parks or recreation grounds to serve its booming population. This amounted to 330 acres, and on top of this was the 530 acres nearby of Hainault Forest, now being well used by Jim Peters, and the 107 acres at Parsloes Park.

As the summer drew to a close Jim and his coach began discussing how he would train during the coming winter, ahead of his all-important marathon debut. The final hurrahs of an interesting but mixed summer season came in Brussels at the four-day European championships at the end of August, the British taking six men's titles and two women's. The consistent Holden won the marathon in 2:32.13.2 (Denison eleventh in 2.44.31.0), despite a tricky course featuring a concrete bicycle track and cobbled sections and humid weather. Alec Olney had no answer to Emil Zatopek who created a championship record with 14:03.0 in the 5,000 metres, and then did even better by setting a world record in the 10,000 (29:12) leaving the likes of Frank Aaron in his wake. South Londoner Derek Pugh won double gold for Britain in the 400 metres and 400 relay, proving he was fully recovered from the horrendous incident a while earlier at Antwerp when he was speared in the head by a stray javelin.

The GB team that performed in Brussels was described by at least one commentator as the best that had ever left these shores in search of athletics glory. Back in Hainault Forest, a small, Brylcreemed chap in a Beagles vest was toiling away alone, dreaming of the day he could join them on their travels.

CHAPTER 10

Jack has been stalked!

SEPTEMBER 1950 – JUNE 1951

Friday, 1 September 1950. The sun came up shortly after 6am on a cloudy, showery day in the London suburbs. Radios crackled into life to serenade breakfasts with the morning news: a plane crash in the desert near Cairo with all passengers and crew lost; printers on strike in London preventing publication of many weekly papers; a worrying increase in food poisoning cases in England; nationalised airlines BOAC and BEA reporting worst ever losses. It was all pretty grim stuff as Jim Peters headed out of the front door to catch his train for work at Mitcham.

But this was no ordinary day: something new and exciting was on his mind. Today was the day Jim Peters would become a serious marathon runner. For this was day one of what he called a 'full marathon training programme' and his run this evening would be the start of a concerted attempt to win the prestigious Polytechnic Marathon from Windsor to Chiswick in June 1951. During the past year he'd done his basic conditioning work, preparing legs and lungs for the regular, almost daily running that would start today and have him in shape for the big race in nine months' time.

Coach Johnny Johnston was determined to do this thing properly and not let Jim loose at 26 miles before he was ready, and Jim concurred. Hence the careful planning and steady progress which had all sprung from that little chat back in November 1949. Runner and coach were in full agreement about the need for caution, with Jim telling Johnny: 'I'm not going in before I'm prepared, and, when I do go, I want to win.'

His training log shows that he ran most evenings throughout September 1951 as he launched his new programme. He would usually set off at around 6.30pm, immediately after getting home from work. It was a physically and mentally draining schedule, for he was setting off having not had a break after at least ten hours of travelling and working, and was deliberately running on what he called 'a more or less empty stomach'.

Some of these early runs from his Chadwell Heath home were what he called 'jog trots' up nearby Billet Road, Mawney Road and to the landmark known locally as Soldier's Fort. The latter was a large purpose-built anti-aircraft site that protected London in the war, and was the last line of defence against enemy bombers heading to Dagenham and the

London Docks during the 1940-41 Blitz. These runs entailed Jim crossing the main arterial road from London into East Anglia (now the A12 Eastern Avenue, a dual carriageway) and heading out of the urban surroundings. The early efforts were not fast or long by Jim's standards, but by the end of September virtually every run had become a 'fast trot', many of them blistering four-milers north of his home.

The same week that his new schedule began, *Athletics Weekly* published the best performances for the season just ended, revealing that only seven British men had run a marathon in under 2:40, which must have been highly encouraging for Jim in view of the fact that he'd already run twenty miles in under two hours on very little specific training. Leading the rankings for the year was, of course, Jack Holden, whose best was just a few seconds slower than the all-time GB best of Harry Payne (2:30.57.8). It was around now Jim decided to write to Holden, seeking advice about marathon training. Holden is said to have replied by extolling the virtues of attempting more than 100 miles a week in order to reach the top. It was a mileage that could only be sensibly achieved by training more than once a day. Jim listened and absorbed, but knew he was not ready for that kind of commitment just yet.

Some autumnal cross-country runs on Saturday afternoons with the Beagles spiced up the monotony of his road training, and there was also the entertaining Sidney C Taylor Memorial Trophy road relays at Chelmsford in early November, which attracted top runners from around the country, including miler Bill Nankeville. Belgrave won this twenty-mile race in 1:35.48, with Aylesford Paper Mills second and the Beagles third. More than 125 runners enjoyed favourable weather as they sped around the residential streets of Fox Crescent, Langton Avenue, Melbourne Avenue, Chignal Road, Rainsford Road, Cedar Avenue, Broomfield Road, Swiss Avenue and Christy Avenue.

Jim was careful to pick and choose which races to do at weekends, mindful of his relatively heavy midweek mileage. He opted not to run the annual 4½-mile road match in Ipswich, which left the way clear for club-mate Tommy Hoskins to roar to victory in 23:48. But Jim did pull on the club vest for a seven-mile cross-country match with Victoria Park Harriers in December, pipped by just two seconds by winner Geoff Iden of the host club.

By the end of the year Jim had clocked up 302.5 miles over the first three months of his new marathon-specific training era. It had gone well, this modest tally providing a good base from which to increase the intensity in the new year. By February 1951 most of the four-mile burn-ups had become six-milers, some very tough cross-country had been mixed in, and then by April there were nine and ten-mile runs being regularly added. This increase naturally took its toll and some of the remarks in Jim's training log tell the story, with frequent mention of stiffness, blisters and some rueful remarks about the weather. On Saturday, 7 April, for example, he completed a rare excursion over fifteen miles in 1:36.00, his only comment being 'Nasty day'.

His willingness to work hard and carry out these runs at a good pace, as opposed to just cruising along, showed an impressive level of commitment. There were no 'jog trots' any more, and his average speed represented a new, unprecedentedly aggressive approach to marathon training. On paper it looked a highly risky strategy, but he seems to have largely avoided the clutches of those twin imposters, illness and injury. Sam Ferris, an Olympic and Empire games medallist of yesteryear, sensed the change that was in the air that winter, and wrote that marathons were becoming a more popular pursuit than ever, and were no longer 'the old man's game and only for plodders'. He added: 'The modern athlete no longer regards the marathon as an ordeal – remember, it's the pace that kills, not the distance.'

Although Jim had almost disappeared from view for the best part of eighteen months as far as the national athletics scene was concerned, his clubmates at Essex Beagles were well aware of his workload and his performances in local cross-country events. A recent teenage recruit to the club at that point, George Knight, recalled the period for me:

'My first encounter with Jim was in only my second cross-country race – a club 4½-miler in the winter of 1950 – I believe. When the field settled down about half-a-mile after the start, we were on a long climb called Foxburrows when suddenly this old boy I had not seen before was visible twenty yards up ahead of me. He looked like he was rolling all over the place with his head lolling from side to side. I already knew I could not climb hills well and assumed that at the top of the hill it would be no problem to pass this fellow. But, amazingly, I pretty well ran myself into the ground for the rest of the race and didn't make an inch on him. I believe we finished third and fourth. I later found out this period was the start of Jim's comeback for the marathon.'

Ilford-born Knight, an architect's assistant, would go on to become good friends with Jim and learn much from him, and would enjoy a good career himself in the 1950s, culminating in an AAA title at six miles (28:50.4), followed by a British record at 10,000 metres (29:06.4) achieved on a golden day in Warsaw in 1957.

After Christmas, Jim set his sights on the Wigmore fifteen-mile road race to be held in March, followed by the Finchley 20, three weeks later, two serious tests of his training and progress to date. They were competitive, well-established events, and would be an interesting challenge following all those quiet, routine training runs and the slogs over muddy fields. In the lead-up to these two races, he kept his taste for competition in check, entering only occasional events when the Beagles needed him. This included the club's ten-mile cross-country contest at the end of January, in which he was runner up in 59:16, narrowly beaten over the final few yards by his sometime training partner Reg Robins.

A month later the club sent a team to Cockfosters in London's northern suburbs for the Southern Counties championships. Over a heavy and undulating course the surprise winner was moustachioed RAF man J W Stone of Dorking St Paul's, from a huge field of 431 competitors. Favourites Alec Olney and Harry Hicks had led early on, but Stone won a well-judged race (64:36) by sixteen seconds from Olney. Jim put in a solid show in 34th (68:21), Beagles only finishing tenth team, well adrift of winners Aylesford Paper Mills.

By now Jim had found that running almost every single day had become part and parcel of his routine and he and Frieda organised their lives around it: 'It never became a task or a trial … once Frieda had become reconciled to the fact that I was determined to run a marathon, she co-operated with me to the utmost and in doing so involved herself in a considerable amount of extra work to further my new ambition. Daily running in all sorts of weather automatically caused her lots of extra washing and cleaning, for every night she had ready for me a clean pair of socks, shorts and vest. This, by the way, was necessary, not only because she liked to see me go out looking fresh and tidy, but also to prevent any chance of my developing any form of skin trouble.'

The last day of March saw Jim take on the highest profile road race since the decision to commit to the marathon, the Wigmore 15. Most of the athletics fraternity had no idea about his plans, so a good run today would be something of a public statement of intent. Wearing No 43 on his red vest, he lined up with 138 others on Parliament Hill Fields, Hampstead Heath, in appalling weather.

The host club, Wigmore Harriers, was so named as its founder members had worked in central London's Wigmore Street, although their HQ was near Hampstead Heath, and was currently the Freemason's Arms on Downshire Hill. Road closures meant the race's usual route had to be amended. Reward for the winner would be the Harman Memorial Cup, headlines in the athletics press, and, in Jim's case, a major boost to confidence. They started on the Parliament Hill running track and headed over a tough hilly course, battered by heavy rain and high winds.

Early on Jim pushed through to take the lead and for long periods had Stone, the Southern cross-country champion, on his heels or by his side. Also featuring strongly was Edward Denison, ranked Britain's No 2 marathon runner. Twice Jim misjudged the course and headed off in the wrong direction, but on both occasions was called back immediately and rectified the errors without losing too much ground. He worked hard to keep his lead, but was never able to pull significantly clear. Returning to the track in the final stages, he accelerated in a desperate bid to shake Stone off and, to his surprise, did so quite comfortably and won by about 30 yards in 1:26.55. Denison was third, 41 seconds behind Jim, and Charlie Busby of Blackheath fourth.

It was an important milestone victory and, as he had felt strong throughout, Jim knew it meant his training was bang on course and producing results. It pleased him and his coach immensely – particularly when told he'd smashed the event record by seven seconds. He rested the following day, a Sunday, no doubt taking son Robin for a long walk in the pram, before returning to training on the Monday with a hard nine-miler in the evening. He recorded a decent time of 50:30. 'Terribly stiff, but made it,' he wrote happily in his training log.

He'd beaten Denison by some distance at the Wigmore event, and in the forthcoming Finchley 20 knew he would now get the chance to test himself against the country's No 1, Jack Holden. He would later recall: 'We had one main objective in view [at Finchley] and that was to watch Jack, for he was entered for the Polytechnic Marathon which he had won for the last three years, and the more I could learn from first hand about him, the better we hoped I would be able to counter his moves on the full distance course. He was a ruthless runner, full of confidence and always starting with an absolute determination to kill the opposition right from the start by setting off at such a pace that no one else could stay with him for very long.'

Holden's well-known tactics worried Jim's coach, who was confident Jim could cope with the twenty miles at Finchley, and was capable of a good time, but didn't know how he would react to the aggressive running of Holden. Meanwhile, in the aftermath of the Wigmore victory, it would take around ten days before Jim felt he was running well again, having reported stiffness and blisters on more than one occasion.

During this recovery period, the annual 45-mile relay from London to Brighton was staged for the first time as a proper 'national road relay' and Beagles were one of several clubs controversially not deemed strong enough to be invited. The event would be marred by tragedy when winning team Belgrave's starting official Mr A Fell collapsed and died. Back in Essex, Jim slogged out a fifteen-mile training run in bad weather, returning home exhausted in 1:36.00.

Citizens of the UK were told during April that all roads led to the 1951 Festival of Britain exhibition on London's South Bank, but for Jim a more pressing matter was preparing properly for what awaited him at the Finchley 20. On the Tuesday evening before the big race he headed up Whalebone Lane and into Hainault Forest for a steady ten-mile run, completed in 62:45, and then eased off until race day, noting with relief that he felt strong and his blisters were healing. Across London that same evening, dreams that a British runner might be capable of smashing the four-minute-mile barrier were strengthened when Roger Bannister broke the twelve-year GB record for the three-quarter mile, clocking 2:56.8 at Motspur Park in a match between Walton AC and Imperial College.

Saturday, 21 April was a sunny day, not too hot, good conditions for distance running. Finchley Harriers welcomed 211 runners for the nineteenth annual staging of Britain's premier twenty-mile road race, a four-lap affair starting from Ruislip. A large crowd assembled and there were worrying moments for officials when spectators ignored requests to keep the course clear for traffic, which led to police threatening to discontinue the race. There was congestion caused by people parking on verges and the general mayhem was worsened by the large number of cyclists who turned up, most intent on following the runners around the course. The star attraction was of course Holden, and by now Jim had made his mind up to stick with the Tipton champion for as long as possible to study how he tried to burn off the opposition. Jim knew this would be a harder race than the Essex 20, and wasn't sure he was capable of hanging on to Holden's coat-tails for the full distance. However, the idea of copying Holden's tactics for his own use appealed to him, and there was no better way of studying them than by placing himself in the firing line.

The favourite, shadowed closely by Jim, hit the front from the start and completed the first five-mile lap in the same time (27:28), with another long-distance novice, Stan Cox, going well in third. Over the course of the second circuit, Holden applied occasional bursts of pressure at well-chosen moments to try and shake Jim off. This gradually won him a lead of around 50 yards, but Jim continued to work hard and the clock showed that both men were inside the pace required for a new course record. It was turning into an intriguing battle.

Just when he thought he was pegging Holden back a little on their third lap, the Midlander pulled off what Jim described as 'another heartbreaking spurt' which ensured he was in total command, and after fifteen miles his lead increased to about 30 seconds. Chasing Holden meant Jim had pulled away from his own challenger, Cox, and it was clear that only an unforeseen disaster would prevent him finishing in the first two. Holden came home in 1:50.48 to break his own course record by almost three minutes, with Jim chugging over the line with a smile, his 1:52.24 also well inside the old mark: 'I was tired, I had some blisters, but I was happy. And so was Johnny. I'd seen Jack Holden in action at the closest possible quarters, I'd seen his method of jumping and I knew what to expect when we met again,' he said.

Naturally Holden got most of the plaudits, but Jim was praised in the press for 'a most courageous run' and Cox's debut at a major distance race was not ignored either. The general standard had improved compared to previous stagings, for nineteen men beat the two-hour barrier, and 154 in all lasted the distance. After lengthy shenanigans over a Blackheath runner's eligibility, the organisers announced that Woodford Green had won the team prize.

Athletics Weekly pointed out that had it not been for Holden's sensational record time, everybody would have been noting the phenomenal display by the inexperienced Peters – although the praise was cheapened slightly when they repeated a previous *faux pas* and referred to him as 'Johnny'. Their editorial praised Peters and Cox for stepping up from track and cross-country, and for bravely 'having a go' one last time before hanging up their running shoes: 'No one can begrudge these chaps any success which comes their way. Though many of our track men still don't know what real hard work is, the long distance road men certainly know, and they know they have to put it in to get anywhere. Good luck to them!' The five-mile splits of the first three men at the Finchley 20 were as follows: Holden – 27:28, 26:51, 27:37, 28:52. Peters – 27:28, 27:01, 28:00, 29:55 and Cox – 27:32, 27:59, 29:02, 29:49. Holden had been the most even-paced, Jim the least so.

Old-timers Sam Ferris and Arthur Newton both watched the race, and Ferris was astounded by the performance of the first three men home, and reckoned it was clear evidence that GB now possessed a bunch of distance men who could hold their own at world level. He was particularly enamoured of the way 44-year-old Holden held off Jim's dogged challenge, and then broke his own record and wrote: 'No superlatives of mine could do adequate justice to the magnificent performance of our own Jack Holden … the meagre publicity given to this particular feat in the daily press does not worry Jack one iota and similarly, time, in respect of age and athletic records, means little to him – it's just another race to Jack – but let it be voiced from the house-tops that Jack's latest triumph is amazing and compares favourably with world track records over similar distances. Comparison between track and road records may be unfair, not to mention unsporting, but to serve as a guide, take George Crosland's twenty miles British record of 1:51.54, made at Stamford Bridge [track] in 1894.'

Third-placed Cox lifted the Middlesex twenty-mile title on his debut, but confessed he was only training three times a week and knew this was not really sufficient for his ambitions. He said he was 'a normal working class chap', so training had to be done at about 8pm after a full day's work, meaning he was out half the night and couldn't do that sort of thing six times a week. He said it was unfair to expect working men to compete on equal terms with the runners whose jobs allowed them far greater freedom for training, for example Zatopek in the Czech army.

Jim wisely rested after his Ruislip heroics and returned to training three days later, having visited a chiropodist with his troublesome blisters. Basking in the memory of Saturday's great run, he cruised around Hainault Forest and then scribbled 'Lovely night, well satisfied' in his training log. By the middle of May he had run 1,000 miles since starting marathon training 36 weeks earlier, with the weekly totals steadily increasing over that period. His daily run was by now regularly ten or more miles – and on Saturday, 5 May he ventured out for a strength-sapping 22 miles, which he covered in a highly satisfactory time of 2:19.00. By now he and Johnny had agreed things were going so well that there would be no harm in attempting a defence of his Essex 20 title on Saturday, 19 May. In fact the Essex event fitted perfectly with his preparations for the Poly Marathon, for it came exactly one month before his big date with destiny.

So to Chelmsford once again. Here Jim was starting a twenty-miler as favourite for the first time, and he showed just why by hitting the front immediately, opening up a 600-yard lead before they'd even reached the five-mile point. Jack Fenn of Woodford Green remained in second place throughout, but endured the miserable sight of Jim disappearing slowly into the distance until he was no longer visible by halfway. At ten miles the lead was at least three-and-a-half minutes, a huge gulf, but the absence of a challenge from behind didn't seem to bother Jim in the slightest. He even managed to speed up, completing the second half in a quicker time despite being under no pressure whatsoever. The clock stopped at 1:47:08 as he crossed the line feeling fresh and happy, and astonished onlookers wondered out loud if they had witnessed a new world record. Jack Fenn was runner-up in 1:56.47 and Jimmy Catton of Ilford third in 1.57.52.

Jim's time was easily a course and county record, but was it really a world best too? Initially there was confusion. Doubts began to arise about the length of the course, and when re-measuring finally took place it was found to be 620 yards short of twenty miles. Nevertheless the time remained a brilliant effort for nineteen miles and 1,140 yards, and attracted great publicity in the ensuing days. Jim recalled: 'My time was said to be a phenomenal one … I was now considered to be a definite danger to Jack Holden in the marathon.' Reporter Stan Tomlin raved about Jim in *The People*, warning Holden to watch his step, as the optician from Chadwell Heath had his heels in focus.

By the end of May, Jim was by now running every day except Sundays and there had been no let-up for months. Runner and coach were both delighted with how this 'conditioning' had gone. Everything was nicely on course, but Jim wasn't getting carried away as he knew there was much more work to be done in June.

His schedule over the final two weeks before the Poly would see him continue with daily running. In fact, there was hardly a winding-down period at all, for in this period he ran ten times, averaging over twelve miles per outing. Even more startling, the final five days before the race involved four runs of more than ten miles each – and they were fast too, each well under six-minute-mile pace.

Had the rest of the athletic world known what he was up to, many would have questioned Jim's sanity. 'Tapering off' was clearly not in his vocabulary. Few, if anybody, had ever prepared for the ordeal of a marathon in such a bullish manner. Not only this, but Jim and Johnny had also cooked up a plan to give the great Jack Holden problems: Jim would set off in the race at a very fast pace, a deliberate bid to surprise Holden, put him off his stride and disrupt his normal race-plan.

Amazingly, Jim appeared to be breaking all the rules of conventional marathon wisdom – and on his debut too. Not only was he piling in the miles in the days before the ordeal, he was now planning to start the race at breakneck speed.

Had Jim Peters and his coach gone completely mad?

CHAPTER 11

The King is Dead, Long Live the King

The Polytechnic Marathon ('The Poly') had been launched in direct response to Britain's poor showing in the 1908 London Olympic Marathon. Our best man had only managed twelfth in a mediocre 3:16 and there was an enormous outcry. *The Sporting Life* put up a huge, expensive trophy with the intention that the new Poly should be a high-class annual race that would help prevent repetition of the 'foolish tactics and lack of judgement' by British runners in the Olympics.

Forty-three years later, anybody looking at Jim Peters' preparations and tactics for his debut at the 1951 Poly would have been tempted to think this novice was about to commit the errors of yesteryear all over again.

As he packed his kit-bag on the evening of Friday, 15 June, Jim could reflect on a preparation programme of around 40 weeks that had seen him complete 1,340 miles in 187 separate runs. It didn't sound excessive, but what these facts tended to hide was that the schedule started off gently and the bulk of the mileage had come recently, nearly all of it at a fast pace. Nevertheless, Jim had reached this point feeling strong and fit, and had largely steered clear of illness and injury despite the repeated pressure of a long working day followed by a demanding training run.

To be testing himself at 26.2 miles for the first time in a very public manner was all very nerve-racking for this unprepossessing man, now well into his 33rd year. After his trio of superb runs in 1951 (Wigmore 15, Finchley 20 and Essex 20) all eyes were fixed on him as the most likely pretender to Holden's crown, and as a potential star at the following year's Olympics in Helsinki. To add to the sense of occasion, this weekend's marathon from Windsor to Chiswick was an event steeped in history and an awe-inspiring choice for a debut.

The race took its name from its organisers, the Polytechnic Harriers, who in turn were named after the Regent Street Polytechnic in London (later the University of Westminster). In the early days there was no set distance for a marathon – it was merely a long race of roughly 25 miles – and when Polytechnic Harriers devised the Olympic course from outside the Royal apartments at Windsor Castle to the Royal Box inside White City stadium, their route just happened to end up being measured 26 miles and 385 yards. This distance was copied by the first 'Poly' a year later, even though the route was slightly different, and 26.2 miles subsequently became established as 'official' all across the globe.

Since 1909 The Poly witnessed several world records, eight victories by RAF man Sam Ferris (who was here again in 1951 as a reporter and coach), plus of course the more recent hat-trick by Jack Holden. What it had probably never witnessed, however, was a performance by a single runner that would prompt the normally restrained sub-editors of *The Times* to call 'truly astonishing'. That single runner would be debutant Jim Peters.

Race-day dawned warm and sunny and with an afternoon start for the marathon there was plenty of time for temperatures to soar into the 70s F. The morning papers had Holden down as favourite, although the experts reckoned he wouldn't get things all his own way. People lined the streets of Windsor outside the Castle, while over at the finish, a record crowd assembled at Chiswick Stadium for the Kinnaird Trophy meeting, a key feature of which was the arrival of the Poly runners during the late afternoon.

The field was sent on its way by Wing Commander 'Laddie' Lucas, international golfer, war hero and MP for the Chiswick area. Jim Peters stuck with his plan to power away fast from the gun. Holden must have been startled as he watched Jim adopt this killing pace so early, especially in the warm weather. The experienced old hand kept close tabs on his impetuous little rival from Essex, but allowed him a lead that extended as far as 200 yards when they passed an early landmark, the Slough Training Centre. From here to the five-mile point, Holden upped his workrate and pulled Jim in little by little, finally drawing alongside. The effort, however, left him breathing hard, something which Jim immediately noticed and took heed of.

'He was breathing rather heavily … which made me think perhaps I had taken quite a bit out of him, which of course was what I had planned to do. I increased the pace again, and immediately Jack responded. For several miles we ran side by side, almost step for step, grunting and groaning, neither of us saying a word, but watching each other like a cat watches a mouse.'

The five-mile point was passed in 27:50, which was almost a minute quicker than GB record pace for a marathon, and inside the world mark too. Those who recognised this shook their heads in disbelief, especially when the two men began going even quicker and reached ten miles in 54:45. If they were to keep this up, even the world's best time (2:25.39 by Korean Suh Yun-Bok at Boston in 1947) might be in danger. On the other hand, a far more likely outcome would surely be of one of them blowing up, allowing the other to slow, recover, and cruise to victory. Would it be Jim or would it be Jack?

Holden's propensity to suddenly spurt for a few yards in a bid to shake off opposition was much in evidence, but Jim was ready for it every time. Having discussed the tactic thoroughly with Johnny Johnston, Jim was able to respond to each little surge by not panicking, allowing a small gap to open and then closing it steadily before creeping back alongside. It wasn't easy, but it was taking less out of him than the spurts were taking out of Holden. The so-called marathon novice was winning this battle of wills.

Jim recalled this crucial period of the race clearly later, confirming he was desperately hoping Holden would get rattled and might over-reach himself when trying to shake him off. The little surges had come earlier and with more frequency than he'd expected, but he covered them all successfully – until, that is, at the halfway point when Holden opened up a bigger gap of 200 yards and maintained it for a while. Pessimism temporarily gripped Jim and he even admitted to himself: 'How pleasant it would be just to give up and lie down in the road.'

Fortunately, such thoughts soon passed and as the village of Heston loomed, and the fifteen-mile point was passed, the gap between the men no longer looked as substantial and this filled Jim with new hope.

Fifteen had been completed in 1:22.10, still remarkably fast on paper, and inside record pace, and Jim was telling himself he might now be the stronger man. He slowly reeled Holden back in and as they went through Heston itself he regained the lead. He pushed onwards hard, and resisted the temptation to look around and check on Holden. It would prove a defining moment in the careers of both men.

A spectator called out that there were less than seven miles to go and joyous visions of reaching Chiswick first flashed through Jim's mind. Moments later came stunning news, by way of a cyclist following the race, who pedalled vigorously to Jim's side and bellowed in his ear that Holden had given up (near the twenty-mile point) and urged Jim to take it easy for he was miles ahead of the next man, who happened to be fellow debutant Stan Cox.

The urgency and enthusiasm in the cyclist's voice convinced Jim the words were true, and he was at once gripped by excitement, bewilderment and fear. Should he relax and slow down? Maintain the same pace? Attempt to speed up? Keep checking over his shoulder? It was the 'frightened rabbit' syndrome that many a race-leader will be familiar with. To the untrained eye, however, nothing changed, for he motored on, ploughing relentlessly forward in his characteristic rough-and-ready style. The split times show this was his slowest part of the race, but there was no conscious easing up at all, and he recalled the only coherent thought in his head had been: 'I must get there at all costs.'

It was a highly uncomfortable final few miles, but there was a moment of minor relief near the 23-mile point when suddenly coach Johnny appeared at the roadside. Telling Jim he was 'quite entitled' to feel exhausted, Johnny urged him to hold things together for another fifteen minutes and all would be well. It was basic stuff, but those words felt strangely comforting, and there was a further boost to Jim's spirits when the numbers watching from the roadside began increasing tenfold, applauding and cheering him on with great enthusiasm. He grinned at them, but behind the smile he was worried that he was only 'plodding' along and his head was 'wagging from side to side' too much. Indeed, he had slowed to above six-minute-mile pace, but he refused to go easy on himself, unconvinced by the shouts that he was so far ahead he couldn't possibly lose now.

Only when he spotted the grandstand at the Polytechnic Stadium in Cavendish Road up ahead did he fully acknowledge the idea of victory. As he went through the gap under the stand and burst back into the sunshine on the track, the crowd's huge roar brought a smile to his face and a new spring in his step. Although he didn't know it, the clock was still well short of 2:30.00. The crowd cheered him around the final lap of the track, prompting a 50-yard sprint to break the tape and fly past the animated timekeepers sitting at their wooden trestle table.

There were no other runners in sight as Jim staggered to a stop, but there were a few moments of mayhem, as people ran to and fro around him. *News of the World* reporter Joe Binks was waving his arms about and chattering wildly, and Sam Ferris was in hysterics, screaming that it was the greatest performance he'd ever seen. Soon Johnny was at Jim's side, and as photographers rushed up, the loudspeaker finally gave the stunning announcement. The winning time was two hours, 29 minutes and 24 seconds. It was not only a Poly record, but Jim was the first Briton ever to break the 2:30 barrier, and he'd smashed Harry Payne's 22-year-old national record by more than a minute and a half.

Coincidentally, Payne himself was race referee, and came over to pump Jim's hand, later signing the certificate of authentication that passed his own record over to Jim. It had been an astonishing debut, and Jim had only fallen short of Kitei Son's 1936 Olympic record by less than five seconds.

Stan Cox came in second in 2:34.34, also a remarkable debut, and Geoff Iden (VPH) was third in a solid 2:35.49. Jim enquired about

Holden's whereabouts, wanting to commiserate with him, but was told that after quitting he'd been brought in by car, and had quickly dressed and disappeared. Holden told *The Sunday Express* he'd been in agony with a stitch, something he'd never suffered before, and once Peters passed him, knew he was done for. He said his marathon career was now over, thus living up to an earlier promise that as soon as he was beaten by another Brit he would retire and let the younger men get on with it. This was all manna from heaven for the press boys and headlines like 'The Old Fox is beaten' covered the sports pages the next day.

Statistician and writer Norris McWhirter called Jim's victory 'one of the most dramatic moments in the history of the sport'. Alan Hoby of *The Sunday Express* wrote: 'You wouldn't have thought it possible for any British runner to beat Holden … but yesterday he found himself up against a steel wire, a pale little man who went on and on as remorselessly and ruthlessly as a Crusader tank. I passed Peters time and again from Windsor to Chiswick [in a press car] and always he looked ill, but not even when Holden turned on the heat between the 13th and 18th mile did Peters quit.'

Harold Abrahams, star sprinter-turned-writer, gave a more considered analysis in *World Sports* magazine, but even he couldn't resist touting Jim as a candidate for Olympic gold: 'The performance of Holden's conqueror, J H Peters, was so astonishing as to make many people ask – have we not a potential Olympic champion over the distance in this 32-year-old runner? Now I am much too cautious or timid an individual to start predicting twelve months ahead that any man will win an Olympic title, but I will say at once that I am enormously impressed with the potentialities of Peters.' He added that if Jim's luck and training went well, and if he could make his pace a little more even, he would be a contender: 'If Peters gets to Helsinki, and is lying handy within a minute or so of the leaders at 10 or even 15 miles, I shall feel pretty happy.'

The morning after the race was not the normal peaceful suburban Sunday in Havering Gardens, Chadwell Heath. Reporters and cameramen descended in great numbers on Jim's home, desperate for the lowdown on Britain's newest potential gold medal man. Smiling broadly, Jim was keen to maintain his usual Sunday routine and emerged from No 47 with young Robin in his pram, ready to set off for a seven-mile walk. The photographers loved it. And although his training log doesn't record it, Jim apparently headed out again that evening for a few more miles, presumably a steady run to get rid of any lingering stiffness. He told the reporters he felt great and would be back to 'normal' training – i.e. fast runs of ten miles or more – by Tuesday or Wednesday. True to his word,

he had fitted in four ten-mile runs by the following Saturday, all of them
knocked off in well under an hour, and – apart from slight foot soreness
– he felt good.

Jim Peters' name was on everybody's lips for a while and he was pic-
tured on the front cover of *Athletics Weekly*, crossing the finish line at
Chiswick. His head was cocked characteristically to one side, the number
51 on his vest had somehow slipped down to hip level, but he looked in
good shape and his white Dunlop regulation plimsolls from Woolworths
seemed pristine even after 26.2 gruelling miles. Looking so untroubled
was not a trick of the camera, for he did indeed recover quickly, as evi-
denced by his fast return to normal training, and within a few days he was
even mulling over whether to have a crack at the AAA marathon at the
end of July, which was to be held just 42 days after the Poly.

Overshadowed by all the headlines for Jim, North Londoner Stan Cox
perhaps received less publicity than his own marathon debut deserved.
Although he ended up five minutes behind Jim in second, it was still an
exceptional first effort for a man whose career mirrored Jim's in many
ways. The two men were roughly the same age, weight and height, and the
similarities didn't end there. Having achieved success on the track either
side of the war, Cox had also decided to move up to marathoning, going
into semi-secret heavy training, reportedly covering 100 miles per week
on occasion. But, unlike Jim, Cox experienced occasional difficulties getting time off work to assist his athletics, and found that doing a full-time
job, bringing up a young family, and attempting to be a top-class
marathoner was a difficult juggling act. Cox pulled a muscle during the
Poly which slowed him towards the end, and without which he would
surely have reduced the five-minute winning margin. Nevertheless he had
emerged as another genuine Olympic prospect, thanks largely to what he
called his 'secret commando training'. Cox had often beaten Jim back in
their track days, but from now would find it hard to match the Essex man
on the roads.

Three weeks after the Poly sensation, Jack Holden made an appearance at the Mitcham fifteen-mile road race, coming third behind Cerou
of France (1:23.03) and Stone of Dorking. He confirmed he was winding his long career down, and that he would definitely not return to the
marathon following his beating by Jim. There would be no comeback this
time, he promised. It was not sour grapes, merely acceptance by a hugely popular figure that his days at the top of the tree were over. The King
(or 'Old Fox' as the papers liked to call him) was dead, long live the King.
With a year to go before the Olympics, the columnists began to chatter
optimistically about Britain's medal chances in a number of events. Fuel

was added to the fire on a Friday evening in July when Gordon Pirie – still only twenty – smashed the British six-mile record on the first day of the AAA champs in front of 40,000 at White City. His magnificent 29:32 saw him 100 yards clear of Walter Hesketh and only a handful of seconds adrift of the fastest six miles ever run in Britain. Reg Robins flew the flag for Essex Beagles with sixth place in 30:25.2.

The following afternoon saw the thrills continue with a championship-best mile from Roger Bannister (Achilles) in 4:07.8 and a sensational three-mile race in which Roy Beckett (Hythe) edged out Chris Chataway (Walton) by the width of a vest, both given the time of 14:02.6. The press were jubilant about the form of runners like Peters and Pirie, with Doug Wilson of *The News of the World* calling the latter 'our very own Emil Zatopek'. *The Times* said the record crowd at White City underlined the continued advance of GB athletics.

Jim and Johnny's original plan had been just the one marathon during 1951, but his fast and trouble-free recovery from the effects of the Poly led to a long chat about the forthcoming AAA marathon on an out-and-back course in Birmingham. On paper it seemed far too close for comfort, and Johnny was very dubious, but Jim's enthusiasm and the evidence of his training log won him over. It looked a highly risky venture, but Jim was confident he would lift the AAA crown – especially as Holden and Cox would be absent – and would therefore complete a double victory that would virtually guarantee his passage to Helsinki.

A further marathon opportunity cropped up when he was invited to the Enschede event in Holland. This sounded even more attractive than the Birmingham race, and Jim was in favour, but Johnny convinced him he was not yet ready for international competition and they settled for the Alexander Stadium, Perry Barr, Birmingham instead.

Not aware that he was now entitled to apply for automatic entry at Birmingham, complete with overnight accommodation, Jim did as he always did and dutifully filled in an entry form and sent it off with five shillings. It meant instead of relaxing in a nearby hotel, he found himself getting up on race day at the crack of dawn to head for Euston station with coach Johnny. Sandwiches on the train provided his pre-race meal. Arriving at the stadium, the runners and their aides were dismayed to find certain rule changes would affect the provision of help during the race. Runners could only use four official aid stations, where there would be water and personal drinks dropped off earlier – but the AAA couldn't afford to lay on sponges.

A moist sponge was the only thing Jim actually wanted, and when Johnny found out, tempers became frayed. Johnny was allegedly told by one official that his man would have to do without sponges and dunk his head in a bucket if he wanted to cool down.

Johnny kept all this bad news from Jim to avoid him getting stressed, and hoped for the best. The only good news was being offered a lift around the course in a timekeeper's car, which would enable him to keep a close eye on Jim, plus the loan from photographer Guy Butler of a cine-camera with which he could film Jim's running style for analysis afterwards.

The runners were set off in the early afternoon and Jim quickly established himself at the front. It was quite hilly early on and he covered five miles in 29:00, 25 seconds clear of the rest, and hit ten miles in 55:54, nearly a minute up on nearest challenger Jack Winfield. Insurance agent Winfield, who helped train the footballers at Derby County in his spare time, was a veteran international in his mid-40s making his debut at the distance, a full twenty years after winning the international cross-country title. Winfield was beginning to fade by now and Jim looked in little danger. Johnny passed him a flimsy wet handkerchief in the absence of the expected sponge, and Jim didn't seem to miss his sponge too much. He was so far ahead at this point that Johnny even began to fret that they might have gone off course.

Jim passed fifteen miles in 1:20.13, now more than three minutes ahead of Winfield and increased this further by the time he hit twenty miles in 1:51.12. It was a superb time, but surely he couldn't keep this up? He received the sodden handkerchief again as he passed Johnny at an aid station, and noticed nearby the hotel owned by 1924 Olympian Charlie Blewitt, a famous Birchfield Harrier. Blewitt is said to have cried out: 'By God, Johnny, you've got a boy there!'

A small but noisy crowd welcomed Jim back into the Alexander Stadium and he crossed the line victorious in 2:31.42, a new course record. Welshman Tom Richards left the flagging Winfield well behind in the closing stages and took second, still a massive five minutes and twenty seconds behind Jim. Winfield clocked 2:41.42. It would be fair to say Jim had been pretty much in a class of his own on this day – for twenty minutes after he crossed the finish line, still only fifteen others had come home, the rest toiling away out on the road.

Despite having felt better during this race than on his debut six weeks earlier, Jim suddenly began feeling unwell afterwards. After presentation of his trophy by the Lord Mayor of Birmingham, Johnny hustled him away to the dressing rooms just as the crowd cheered home runner-up Richards. Jim craved water, but Johnny felt it unwise to allow him to drink copiously and only permitted a few sips. This was immediately vomited back up, which happened repeatedly, reducing the meagre fluid intake even further. Johnny had put salt in the water to compensate for that lost by sweating, and Jim simply couldn't keep it down. Instead of recovering from his run, he was slowly getting worse. It was worrying for Johnny, who was desperately trying to do the right thing, but clearly unsure about the correct quantity and content of the drinks he should be providing.

For an hour or two Jim was in a bad way, craving water but not getting it – partly because of the reaction it caused, and partly because Johnny felt it was wrong to drink too much before taking food. In his desperation he even fed Jim a tot of brandy, but this also made him vomit. In a semi-daze the new AAA champion managed to autograph a programme for former rival Jack Holden, before slowly getting changed and being ferried to the railway station. He'd accomplished his mission on the day, but at that moment looked anything but a potential Olympic champion.

After a struggle to find the train seat reserved for him, poor Jim then had to endure the sight of runner-up Richards jovially enjoying a beer, while unable to partake himself. He would recall later: 'Johnny kept on trying to make me have a biscuit. He was still convinced that too much liquid was the cause of my trouble. I did eventually manage to eat a little of one – and gradually began to feel my old self again … about half-an-hour from London I was sufficiently improved to be able to sit up and take notice – much to the great relief of Johnny, who'd had visions of ambulances and hospitals and breaking the news to Frieda.'

By the time he was at his breakfast table and reading the Sunday papers the next morning, all was well again with the Peters digestive system. He was certainly getting to know the demands and quirks of marathon running intimately. Although distressed for several hours the previous evening, he had now twice shown the ability to apply himself brilliantly to the task in hand when out on the road. Others were beginning to question how this inelegant and unsophisticated chap had somehow transformed himself from a moderately good track runner into the country's top marathoner in just a few weeks. One little tip that Jim did let loose was a technique he had developed to break any mid-race monotony: if things got tough in these long races he would began humming Al Jolson tunes to himself. He didn't reveal which of the Jolson classics were most helpful, but it is presumed *Leaning on a Lampost* wasn't one of them.

The summer of 1951 had so far been memorable for British athletics and there was more to come in August when 30,000 ignored the rain to cheer another GB record at six miles. It was set in the GB-versus-France bank holiday contest by mud-spattered Walter Hesketh (29:13.8) despite the puddles on the White City track. The season ended a week or two later with the staging of Britain's first floodlit athletics meetings, both at White City – the 'City Charity Festival' sponsored by *The Financial Times* and watched by more than 10,000, and then a match between London and Gothenburg, at which nearly 30,000 roared the home team to victory. All were agreed that sport under lights was even more exciting and atmospheric, but there was much debate over whether it was better to light the track from overhead, as they did in greyhound racing, or to use surrounding floodlights to spread light across the entire arena.

Although he had largely abandoned track running himself, Jim was as pleased as anyone at the Beagles when the club's brand new cinder track was officially opened in Mayesbrook Park, Barking, on the first day of September. Around 2,000 gathered to see Mayor of Barking W G Wermerling declare the track open for business and then summon Jim to the microphone. Dressed proudly in his GB international vest, Jim then did a two-lap solo run around the new track to huge cheers from the crowd. The afternoon's events were somewhat spoiled by incessant rain, but included the revival after 56 years of an event known as 'The Flying Squadron', a three-stage relay of distances at quarter, three-quarters and a mile. As in its last staging in 1895, a lead gained on the first leg proved decisive, with host club Beagles beating Blackheath, Finchley and Ranelagh in a time of 8:39. There was also a world record attempt by a women's 4x220 yards relay team (Joan Penn, Margaret Brian, Jean Desforges and Dorothy Hall), the downpours proving less than helpful as they missed out by less than one second.

The new facilities looked impressive and were long overdue for the district, and the building of a grandstand beside the track was to follow. Under the care of groundsman Jim Patient, the Beagles' home track would subsequently become one of the premier tracks in the south during the 1950s. Beagle Colin Young recalls: 'The new track was excellent compared with the unkempt cinders at Dagenham's Central Park, where it had been like a dustbowl in hot weather and a swamp when it rained. The new dressing rooms were like the Ritz compared with the old ones, where the remnants from the football season would be still around when we arrived for summer training.'

Clubmate Ted Baverstock recalls the new track was made from domestic ash, sifted and recovered from the local municipal tip: 'This worked successfully but there was a curious outcome as the surface was littered with thousands of small rusty nails. This was because the local residents had chopped up wooden boxes for kindling, meaning the nails from the boxes ended up in their fireplace ash. Luckily I never heard of any injuries resulting from this, which was down to the good work of the groundsman.'

The end of the 1951 track season was marked by the BAAB announcing a list of 'possibles' for the 1952 Olympic squad in Helsinki, made up of 79 men and 22 women. Unsurprisingly, Jim was first name listed for the marathon, along with Cox, Iden and Richards. Around a quarter of all the 101 named had also competed in the 1948 London Games, but this was a list thought to have much higher medal potential. The announcement of the names caused some controversy behind the scenes, with Harold Abrahams in particular feeling that by naming athletes so far ahead there was a risk some might mistakenly feel they'd already done enough to win their place in the team – while those not listed might be discouraged and go into their winter training in a negative frame of mind. It was a fair point, but as far as Jim was concerned, a winter of heavy mileage lay ahead and he would be tackling it with 100 per cent commitment, come what may.

CHAPTER 12

Goodbye to Proper Lunches

Within just a few weeks Jim Peters' athletic life had been transformed. In mid-June 1951 he'd been a marathon nobody, just another moderate six-miler ready to try his luck at the longer distance. But by the end of July he was national marathon champion and the fastest Briton in history.

After his months of sweat and toil, much of it in splendid isolation, all of a sudden an indifferent world wanted to know all about Jim Peters. Were the rumours true about his intense training methods? How often did he run? How fast? For how long?

Affable Jim was perfectly happy to reveal his 'secrets' when the press came calling. In the case of *Athletics Weekly*, he even agreed to write a lengthy article about it all, in addition to answering a detailed question-naire, the two items published side by side in an October issue of the magazine.

The sporting public wanted to know how he'd come from nowhere to hit the top of the rankings, seeing off the masterful Holden into the bar-gain. The traditionalists were in for a surprise and many will have gasped in disbelief at what Jim revealed in the article. He said he didn't believe in the conventional even-paced, slow and steady training runs that other marathon men usually went in for. He never ran more than twenty miles in a single outing. Every single run he did was at a pace quicker than six-minutes-per-mile, and some were as fast as 5:15. He ran frequently and at a good speed. If it were possible he would happily run nine times a week, he said, but because of work commitments could only usually manage six. It was remarkable stuff, very different from the established beliefs.

Unlike many of his contemporaries, Jim was clearly not a disciple of Arthur Newton, the distance running sage whose home in Ruislip had in recent years become something of a Mecca for marathoners. On Sundays in particular, Newton would hold court in his suburban living room, dis-pensing advice and copious amounts of tea and biscuits to all the runners who routinely visited him from far and wide for advice about their train-ing, and to listen to tales of how the old man broke 50 and 100-mile records during his younger days in South Africa, Canada, USA and on the London-Brighton and London-Bath roads.

Jim confessed that until the age of 30 he was one of the many who believed faithfully in the Arthur Newton/Joe Binks creed that slow 'jog trotting' was the best way to slowly build stamina and get legs and lungs used to long-distance work. Newton and Binks believed that running hard, and speedwork of any sort, should be largely avoided by marathoners, thus minimising the risk of injury, and keeping them fresh for races. Basically they were saying a runner didn't need to be fast to win a marathon, simply able to keep going at a steady pace. It was a philosophy that had worked for Newton between the wars, for he was the ultimate plodder, bereft of basic speed but who could keep going, literally, for days on end.

But Jim and his coach now recognised that times had changed since Newton's heyday and felt the elderly Binks was also living in the past. Only recently (summer 1951), the highly respected Binks had insisted to Jim that he needn't work on speed, explaining that: 'Once a fellow is fit he can pull his big race out any day.'

These views, however, were no longer acceptable to Jim and Johnny, for they represented an attitude to training that had never, to Jim's knowledge, produced any athletes of the standard now required to win world titles in the 1950s. He was determined to go his own way, and, given the evidence of his first two attempts at the marathon, who could argue with him?

'I am convinced it is now necessary to do 2:25.00 to win the Olympic marathon and my thesis is that if you can do the pace in training you can do it in the race. All that is required is that you have to hold the pace longer,' he wrote. To achieve 2:25.00 with even-paced running, it would require 26.2 miles of five-and-a-half minutes each, and if you never ran that sort of pace in training you surely had no chance in a race.

'All my training is based on speed work. The stamina comes by an accumulation of work. As soon as spring comes and the evenings get light enough, I run 2½ miles to Hainault Forest and do five or seven, or even nine miles, and then run back, fartlek being done in the forest. I do not go for these 20 or 30-mile jogs that most of the boys seem to build up on … Where most of the boys go wrong is that they race too often. Races should be planned, say one year ahead, with the help of your adviser. I believe it is possible to run two races at peak in one season. All others are just building up for the big day.'

Jim pointed out that over the previous year he trained 224 times and covered 1,736 miles, all at a fast lick. He planned to top this ahead of his 1952 marathons by completing 300 runs and more than 2,000 miles. The only outings where he took things easy were Sunday morning walks pushing Robin in his pram, he quipped: 'This keeps my dear wife in a good mood and gives me time to breathe in the good country air.'

The quality and intensity of Jim's training will have shocked some people, and the revelations provided a fascinating contrast to the outlook of up-and-coming miler Roger Bannister. The Oxford medical student had come in for criticism for what was called 'haphazard' low-key training, and the runner himself fuelled this fire, perhaps unwittingly, when he answered *Athletics Weekly*'s questionnaire with great brevity and precious little detail about his training. This led to more accusations that Bannister, and others of similar background, were far too casual about their athletics compared to highly committed working-class men like Jim Peters and the American Fred Wilt. The sporting public always preferred a trier to a gifted enigma, it seems.

Having told the world how he trained, Jim got down to business at the start of the 1951-52 winter cross-country season with a modified plan for the nine-month build-up to the summer Olympics in Helsinki. He and Johnny cooked up a plan that would see him step up his training even further during this period. It meant that on most midweek days – often four out of the five – he would go running twice a day, the first outing at lunchtime on *The News of the World* sports ground track near his Mitcham workplace, and the second after he arrived home in the evenings.

Looking back on the decision to run more often, Jim recalled: 'It meant I had to give up having a proper lunch and have sandwiches, but I was quite prepared to do this if it was going to make me a better marathon runner.' He admitted pangs of jealousy when hearing about elite athletes in certain other countries who were given special dispensations so they could train properly and without difficulty: 'How different it all was in England. If an athlete wanted to do a lot of training, or none at all, that was his look-out.'

Running twice a day, both efforts at a good speed, during a long working day, meant he was piling the pressure on himself, and although it won him the admiration of clubmates, not everyone felt it was a wise way for a busy family man to carry on with his life. South African distance runner Jackie Mekler would interview Jim years later about this and other matters, and Mekler passed me his notes from that meeting: they show that Jim's wife was 'annoyed with him' and that even workhorse Jack Holden warned him to 'take it easy'. To prove he stood by his beliefs, Jim gave Mekler a book that day, inscribed with the mantra 'Train little, hard and often'.

Jim's pals at Essex Beagles, especially the younger members, found his regime awe-inspiring and something they could aspire to, and certainly wouldn't have advised him to ease up. Sixty years on, George Knight, now based in Liverpool, told me: 'I am pretty sure Jim's approach back then informed our belief that you had to run every day to reach a good standard. But there was a general attitude among the older members that you had to be careful not to burn yourself out.'

Beagle Colin Young concurs: 'Jim was inspiring to us young lads, always hammering it every session after working a nine or ten-hour day. He always gave it his all, whether training or racing and young fellow-members such as George Knight, Ted Baverstock, Bernie Hames, Dickie Douglas and myself adopted the same attitude and gained success through his inspiration.'

It is clear that fellow runners, particularly the Essex crowd who saw Peters in action at close quarters, were charmed by his down-to-earth personality and awed by his incredible guts and ability to focus. The way he soaked up heavy training loads using his capacity to ignore discomfort and pain became legendary. Many must have asked themselves how on earth could this workhorse with such an ungainly style, and violently bobbing head, run six miles in around 30 minutes and a marathon in 2:30? The answer appeared to be his unique training regime, allied to a body that coped far better than it appeared to. And it's probably true to say his lack of elegance gained him extra admiration in this cultish world of distance running, for he was viewed as a devotee whose rewards were coming from hard work and not simply from having inherited the right genes. Typical of Jim's admirers, initially from afar but later as a friend, was Len Jones of Southend-on-Sea AC, an enthusiast who converted from football to running fairly late in life. A family man who lived in a humble prefab opposite Southend Airport, Jones said a whole new world opened up for him when sharing a changing room with 'ordinary local blokes' who were serious about athletics – Jim Peters being the prime example. He recalled:

'Jim's very intensive type of training worked in his case because of his make-up of tremendous guts and quite a fair amount of athletic talent. My own efforts were puny in comparison. In the main it was the companionship of my clubmates that was holding my interest, [but] my mates started to have a go at me to do more training. This sort of thing was going on all over the country. In Essex it was Jim Peters who had lit the torch. Jim's performances inspired others who wanted to emulate him, and in my case, I had clubmates who felt we could do a lot better if only we could do more training like Jim. I loved the sport and enjoyed the camaraderie, but when confronted with training twice a day, and in Jim Peters' case sometimes three times a day, that was just too much.'

Jones recalled a chat with Jim about running in middle-age. Instead of advising Jones to ease up, as he had expected, Jim's advice was to have a serious tilt at the marathon – and to run the thirteen-mile round trip to and from work each day as training. Jones was 'horrified and scared' of such a commitment, but was won over by Jim's enthusiasm and confidence, and eventually did exactly what was suggested. Thus Jim's advice kick-started a late blossoming career that saw Jones achieve top-class times at distances ranging from three to 50 miles, and made him a well-known name in veteran circles.

Jim's influence on other runners would be acknowledged later on by the experts. Perhaps the most succinct summary of how his marathon training regime set new standards and influenced others would come in Dr Timothy Noakes' revered tome *Lore of Running* (first edition 1985). Noakes showed that before Jim emerged in 1951, all marathons were won by athletes who, like Arthur Newton, simply ran longer distances in training than anyone else. The marathon had been a race for survivors and the winners were those better prepared to survive long distance races run relatively slowly, because that was exactly what they trained for. But Jim changed things by being the first to train by running fast most of the time, getting close to five-minute-mile pace, achieving this intensity by running frequently, eventually up to a dozen times a week.

Training twice a day wasn't completely unheard of in the early 1950s, for the top Finnish runners had tried it with success, dominating distance running between the two world wars. Paavo Nurmi and his coach Lauri Pihkala were among the first to apply scientific principles to training, recognising the relationship between work and rest. Swedish national coach Gosta Holmer studied Nurmi's methods and adapted them to produce fartlek training in the early 1930s, a session that involved bursts of speed at varying intensities and distances (50 up to 3,000 metres) that would be injected into a run. Fartlek helped develop great speed endurance and led to Swedes Haag, Strand and Andersson setting numerous world records. Fartlek was an invigorating and exhilarating way to run in forested areas, and Jim adopted it with relish on his regular sorties into Hainault Forest.

Many British runners, even the ambitious ones, were unable to copy Jim's training ideas because of work and domestic time limitations, but there was one man determined to do whatever he could to at least get close to a similar workload. This was Stan Cox of Southgate Harriers, fellow candidate for the British team at Helsinki. As mentioned earlier, Cox had secretly intensified his training, but unlike Jim wasn't able to do as much as he wanted and when he wanted. To help out, Cox's club stepped in on his behalf in late 1951 and approached Johnny Johnston to see if he would be interested in coaching their man in addition to looking after

Jim. Johnny consulted Jim, who had no objection, and the arrangement was agreed. Cox lived a fair distance away, so didn't train alongside Jim, but it did mean the nation's top two marathon prospects now belonged to the same 'stable'. It was a big responsibility for Johnny, and he took it very seriously, promising both men he would never 'play one off against the other' as he put it. Both reassured him he had their fullest confidence.

Despite upping his mileage to new levels in the autumn of 1951, Jim maintained his commitment to the Beagles most Saturdays. The midweek runs – some alone, some with training partner Robins – were his bread and butter, but Saturday races with the boys were the icing on the cake. The best club day out of all, the London to Brighton relay, was staged in early October and deemed to be a 'southern qualifier' for a national final in the spring of 1952. This new format didn't meet with universal approval, but the event remained hugely popular with runners. There was great fun and banter as the teams arrived in their single-decker Commer, Bedford and Leyland coaches and parked up on Mitcham Common in the autumnal sunshine.

Jim and his Beagles clubmates hadn't been invited to the relay six months earlier, so were keen to make an impression this time. Unfortunately they got off to the worst possible start, an out-of-form Jim Culver coming in last on the opening leg from Mitcham. It was a blow from which Beagles would never really recover, even though the rest of the team ran well. On the second stage Jim partially recovered the situation by running a blinder to take Beagles up to twelfth, smashing the stage record by 32 seconds. Reg Robins was quickest of all the seventh stage runners, while George Knight and Tom Hosking ran superbly in the latter stages into Brighton, leaving Beagles ninth overall by the end. It would prove just enough to get the club invited to the subsequent national final.

A few days later the AAA announced its annual awards and Jim won the Jackson Memorial Trophy as the outstanding UK athlete of the year, in recognition of his two summer marathon victories. It was a proud moment, one he could tell the grandchildren about, regardless of what fate might have in store for the rest of his career.

To celebrate, he promptly smashed another course record, this at the annual twenty-mile relay promoted by Chelmsford AC, over six legs of 3.3 miles each. Beagles could only finish third behind winners Belgrave Harriers, the same positions as a year earlier, but, in excellent conditions for road running, Jim clocked 15:22 to beat the old record by thirteen seconds. Frank Sando, the talented lab assistant from Maidstone, ran him close with 15:27 and Ken Cook of Hadleigh (15:29) and Charlie Walker of Belgrave (15:33) also beat the old record. Heading off from Chelmsford's Rainsford Road school in Fox Crescent, Knight, Hunt and Culver kept Beagles in the top four over the first three legs, before Jim moved them up to third, passing Southend's man and establishing a good lead that Robins and Baverstock were able to maintain. Belgrave's winning time of 1:34.43 was another record after a great day's racing and Beagles were only 83 seconds behind them.

Training partner Robins turned the tables on Jim when they raced together for the Beagles against Ipswich Harriers in November in the annual match on the roads of the Suffolk county town. Robins was a six-mile specialist with a good turn of speed, whose presence often brought the best out of Jim. In a great finish Robins took the individual prize, pipping Jim by two seconds in 22:24 over the hilly 4½-mile course. The home side had the last laugh by winning the match, however.

A week later, Jim opted out of the North of Thames cross-country championships at Chigwell, but was delighted to see his club rise to the occasion without him and take the team prize. It won them the Lambert Cup for the best aggregate score by the best eight from each team. Conditions were very tricky over this wet weekend, with flooding in many areas, and it was reported that in Devon a teenage cross-country runner had fallen into the swollen River Teign and drowned.

Chigwell was also the venue on the first day in December for Essex Beagles' 7½-miles annual cross-country, and Jim returned to action in style, giving his own course record a good beating (by 42 seconds) with 39:28. In this handicap race, Jim's was by far the fastest run of the day, gaining revenge for the Ipswich defeat by Robins, who was second in 40:08.

All things considered, it had been a wonderful year for Jim, and his progress mirrored the improvements seen generally in English athletics. Over the year, some thirteen English native track and field records had been broken in eleven different events, which included Jim's marathon heroics, of course. The list of the top ten marathon performances of the year showed his Polytechnic victory was by far and away the best, nearly five minutes quicker than any other run by a Briton (next was Charlie Busby's 2:34.06 win at Peterborough in August, setting a Blackheath Harriers club record).

It had also proved a landmark year for athletics in Essex too, and the county's officials, suitably encouraged, set up various weekend coaching courses. They declared their aim of seeking to establish a 'County Loughborough' set-up. One of their courses for throwers, staged in the village of Wicken Bonhunt, got off to an uncertain start, however, when instructor Dennis Cullum gave a demonstration of hammer throwing, only to see his implement fly into the upper branches of a tall tree and get stuck. A local youth centre warden strolled by with his shotgun to save the day. To the athletes' delight, the warden's first shot hit the correct branch, and down came the hammer to great cheers. In recent times there had been various unfortunate accidents involving stray hammers and javelins, but nobody had ever heard of a hammer having to be shot back to earth!

As the calendar year drew to a close, Jim's Olympic prospects remained bright as he continued to go from strength to strength in training and races. Not everyone was as fortunate: the talented AAA 440 yards champion Derek Pugh, a 25-year-old south Londoner who had won double gold at the European championships a year earlier, was struck down by polio and had to quit the sport shortly before Christmas. Pugh's short career had certainly been incident-packed. Before the polio diagnosis he had survived being hit by a stray javelin which appeared to impale itself in his head during a track run. In fact it had freakishly lodged itself between his ear and skull and he escaped with minor injuries. The careless thrower was reportedly more upset by the incident than Pugh himself. Subsequently the unlucky Pugh would turn to the safer occupation of geology, emigrating to Canada, but lived into his eighties.

The loss of gold medal prospect Pugh notwithstanding, British athletics fans were relishing the arrival of Olympic year 1952. An extra mouth-watering ingredient was the announcement from Moscow over the Christmas period that the Soviet Union would be sending a team to Helsinki, their first appearance at an Olympiad for 40 years, since the creation of the Soviet state.

The Olympics were certainly on Jim's mind too, and when asked about his immediate ambitions, he confirmed he was desperate to make the GB squad again, and in Helsinki would aim to run the best race of his life: 'I'm particularly anxious to have a crack at Paavo Nurmi's unofficial record for the full marathon course [2:26.57],' he said.

Asked by *Athletics Weekly* to list his best performances to date at the standard distances, he gave the following data: 440 yards – 0:55, 880 yards – 2:02, 1 mile – 4:28, 3 miles – 14:30, six miles – 30:07, ten miles – 52:23, fifteen miles – 1:22.00, twenty miles – 1:49.03, marathon – 2:29.24 (GB record).

He told his interviewer that coaching had been 50 per cent responsible for his success so far, the rest being down to his own hard work: 'Johnny Johnston was an inspiration to me in 1948 and is still my friend and senior adviser. Reg Robins is my race and routine training companion. Without both of them it would be impossible for me to carry on [training] night after night.'

Expanding to broader topics, he added: 'I'd like to see larger dressing rooms and many more toilets available at cross-country meetings. I think it would be a good idea if our cross-country championships were held on the same racecourse each year, better accommodation could then be made available.' He also issued an appeal to youngsters and novices coming into the sport to do as he did, and support their local athletics club, however humble: 'Join your local club and help put it on the map instead of queuing to join a big one. Read, listen and watch – then decide things for yourself. Pick a coach who was good at your distance himself, turn to him for help when you are down but be capable of knowing yourself. Aim high and if at first you don't succeed try, try, try again.'

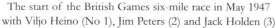

An Essex Beagles minute book from 1936 reveals that youngster James Henry Peters
has joined the club and paid his subs

The start of the British Games six-mile race in May 1947
with Viljo Heino (No 1), Jim Peters (2) and Jack Holden (3)

Jim receives the baton for Essex Beagles during a Chelmsford road relay

Jim leading the Mitcham 15-mile road race, just ahead of close friend Bob Pape

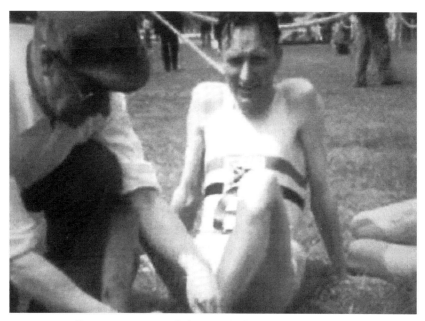

Jim gets some expert help at trackside to treat blistered feet

Jim is seen breaking a stage record during the London to Brighton relay

Jim in typical action on the roads – strong and purposeful, if not smooth and elegant

Jim and fellow Poly Marathon runners meet a young Princess Margaret at the Windsor start

Jim's main ambition when he started was an international vest. Here he gives it an airing on a misty Saturday afternoon

A national newspaper shows the world Jim's favourite training route near his home

Hitting the finish-line at
the 1952 Poly Marathon
and Jim has a new world
record in the bag

Wife Frieda and son Robin
wish Jim luck before his
departure to the 1952
Helsinki Olympics

A wet opening ceremony in Helsinki's Olympic Stadium in 1952

Jim starts to fall behind Emil Zatopek and Gustaf Jansson
during the 1952 Olympic marathon

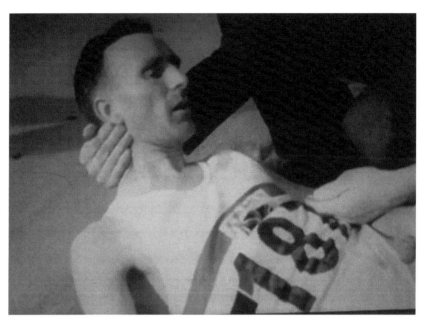

A spectator at the roadside comes to Jim's aid after his collapse
in the 1952 Olympic marathon

Ted Baverstock (left) says his head jolted back in shock when Jim unexpectedly drew
alongside in this cross-country thriller at Chelmsford in 1953

All smiles as Jim races into Chiswick Stadium for a magnificent new world best of 2:18.40 at the 1953 Poly Marathon

Lord Goddard presents Jim with the enormous Sporting Life Trophy for winning the 1953 'Poly'

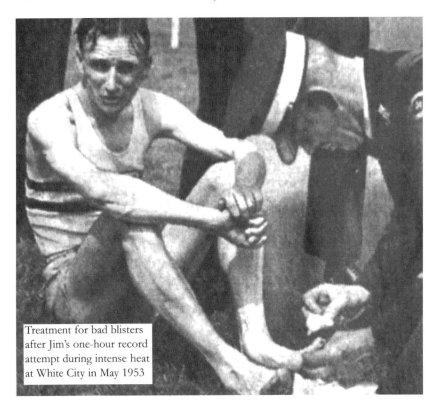

Treatment for bad blisters after Jim's one-hour record attempt during intense heat at White City in May 1953

Jim (61) and Stan Cox (62) share the lead during the Enschede Marathon in Holland, September 1953

Finishing the 1953 Enschede Marathon in a superb 2:19.22,
the fastest ever run on an 'out-and-back' course

Jim chases early leader Ian Binnie during the Morpeth-to-Newcastle race on
New Year's Day 1954, going on to win in a new course record

Jim and Veikko Karvonen share the lead
during the 1954 Boston Marathon

Huge crowds in sweltering downtown Boston greet Jim as he finishes
the annual marathon in second place

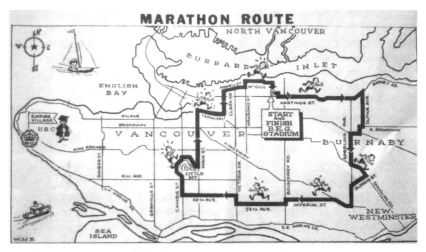

The route is announced for the 1954 British Empire and Commonwealth Games
Marathon in Vancouver

Joe McGhee (697), Stan Cox (335) and Jim Peters in the early stages of
the 1954 Vancouver race

Jim returns to the stadium at Vancouver in a state of obvious distress. The finish line is within sight

Jim crashes to the ground yards from the finish, one of 12 falls during this horrendous finale to his career

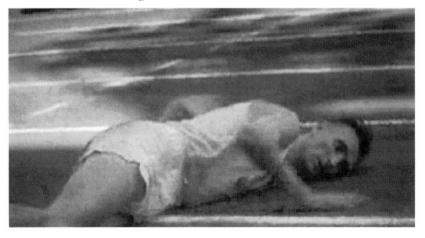

Jim rises again and staggers a few more yards, but it's no use . . .

He falls into the arms of England
masseur Mick Mays, still some way
short of the finish line

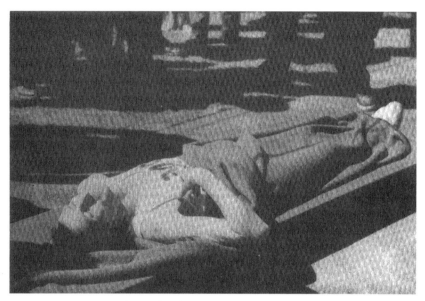

Unconscious, disqualified from the race and carried off to hospital,
Jim Peters' marathon career ends in disaster

Scotland's Joe McGhee,
second man to enter the
stadium, but worthy winner
of the gold medal

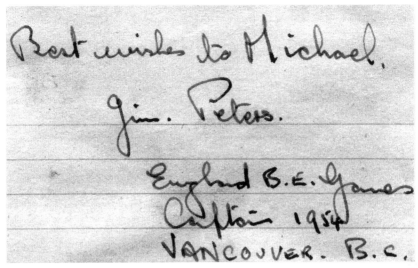

An autograph from the captain of the England team –
signed shortly before his ordeal in Vancouver

Roger Bannister's triumph and Peters' disaster shared the front pages all over the globe

Mile champion Dr Roger Bannister escorts Jim on the plane home from Vancouver

The pair receive a warm welcome outside Jim's home after a
much-delayed journey back to London

The people of Chadwell Heath, Essex, show Jim Peters he's still a winner in their eyes

A year after Vancouver and retirement, Jim, his coach and an associate produced this story of his career

In 1959 Jim joined forces with a
co-writer to publish a novel about a
schoolboy athlete-turned-detective

Jim operates the stopwatch during an attack on the world two-hour record,
led by Gordon Pirie, on the Walton-on-Thames track, October 1955

Jim was the cover star of
World Sports magazine's
September 1953 issue

Hard at work in his other guise:
a dispensing optician at Mitcham
and Chadwell Heath

A bust of Jim by sculptor
Wilfred Dudeney, now on
display at the Valence House
Museum in Dagenham

The final finish line . . . Sutton Road cemetery in Southend-on-Sea, Essex

JAMES HENRY
PETERS

JIM PETERS - MARATHON MAN

BELOVED HUSBAND, FATHER
AND GRANDFATHER

✦24TH OCTOBER 1918

✦9TH JANUARY 1999

REQUIESCANT
IN
PACE

31391

CHAPTER 13

Twin Peaks Revisited

A curious side-effect of Jim Peters' success by the start of 1952 was the increasingly acute space problem at his semi-detached home in Chadwell Heath. He was winning so many trophies that wife Frieda had to impose a ban on him bringing any more home.

The organisers of the annual Morpeth to Newcastle road race were stunned when Jim made a round trip of 560 miles to become the first southerner to win their popular New Year's Day race, only to sheepishly reveal he couldn't possibly take their cup home with him. *The Newcastle Journal*, understandably a little miffed, having stumped up the cash for the impressive trophy, reported incredulously that Jim's wife had forbidden him to bring more silverware into their house as she had quite enough to clean and polish already. Jim told the paper apologetically: 'I simply can't go on taking more home. I decided some time ago that there was no point in accepting any more.'

Jim was one of four men from Essex Beagles to make the long train journey north in bad weather for his first tilt at this 13¾-mile Tyneside classic, staged annually since 1904. Buses were laid on from Newcastle Central Station at midday to take runners out to Morpeth for the early afternoon start. A strong field of 105 had entered, although more than 25 of these failed to show, no doubt put off by the thick snow and slush on the roads, and the high winds and rain forecast for later. The one good thing about the horrendous weather was that it deterred many of the cyclists who normally followed the progress of the race, invariably causing congestion for everyone involved.

Nowadays weighing under ten stones and promising he would be even lighter by the Olympics, Jim looked in great shape at the start, accompanied by his shadow Reg Robins. Both men were highly fancied to do well today, the local press tipping Jim for a course record if the weather abated. Robins, running despite a head cold, led the field up the early hill to Morpeth Golf Club, and as Jim pulled alongside, the contrast in styles was clear, Robins the more smooth, but Peters full of power. Their early pace shocked 45-year-old Bert Hemsley of Gosforth Harriers, the local favourite who knew the course intimately and was the Essex men's main challenger. Scot Charlie Robertson, who, like Jim, often tried to kill off opposition early on, found himself fighting to merely keep in touch.

Jim, wearing No 17 on his vest, accelerated out of Morpeth and proceeded to dominate the race. At one point he led by as much as half a mile and as he passed Gosforth Park Gates he was inside the course record by nine seconds, and looked very relaxed as he waved happily at the crowds when passing through Seaton Burn. As he powered towards the finish in Newcastle's Clayton Road, he eased up slightly in the difficult latter stages. He won with impressive ease considering the wet, slushy roads which saw runners splashed up to their shoulders. There was also a cruel wind in their faces and heavy showers. He won in 1:11.45, missing Jack Holden's course record of 1950 (run in better conditions) by just 21 seconds, and behind him a marvellous battle was won by Robins (1:13.07). Jim's wartime friend Bob Pape, representing *HMS Ceres*, a supply and secretariat training school at Wetherby, and only just back from a Mediterranean posting, was a surprise packet in fifth. The Beagles narrowly pipped local side Bridlington Harriers to the team prize, and their quartet, by now wrapped in overcoats and scarves, accepted their trophies inside the Northern Counties School for the Deaf building, from Robert Clough, editor of *The Newcastle Journal.*

Three days was enough to recover sufficiently for Jim to regain his Essex cross-country crown, romping to victory by a 30-second margin over the 7½ mile course at Woodford Green the following Saturday. His time of 42:56 was too hot for runner-up Ken Cook of Hadleigh, with the holder Philip Morgan a disappointed fifth and complaining that a visit to the dentist's had left him feeling under par on this chilly day. It was a day of unprecedented success for the Beagles, who took senior and junior team prizes, and filled the first three junior positions. Harold Abrahams presented the prizes and paid warm tribute to Jim's current good form. Down in Surrey another Olympic hope, Gordon Pirie, also lifted his county title, winning by a margin of two and a half minutes.

The Olympics were still more than six months away, but it was already clear the expansion of media influence and growth of TV meant Helsinki would be a Games open to more exposure than ever before. The medical profession announced research that proved British children were now healthier than ever before and showing a greater interest in athletics. But nothing changed at the British Amateur Athletic Board it seemed, with the sport's governing body still desperate to prevent the stench of professionalism invading its hallowed walls or tainting Olympic ideals. During January they issued a reminder that anyone caught writing, lecturing or broadcasting about athletics for payment, without prior permission, would lose their amateur status and be barred from competition. Jim, meanwhile, was basing his Olympic build-up around the idea of repeating his twin marathon success of the previous summer. If all went according to plan he would make a second 'double assault' on the marathon in the summer of 1952. First would be the Polytechnic race on 14 June (incorporating the AAA marathon championship) and then the Olympic version in Helsinki on 23 July, with key stepping stones being the Finchley and Essex twenty-mile road races in April and May respectively. In the meantime, his increased training load would be spiced up by cross-country fixtures at weekends.

He clocked up more train miles in mid-January, heading north to York to lead the Essex team in the inter-counties championships, being run from the Rowntree Cocoa Works Sports Ground in Haxby Road. It was Jim's first run against the Coulsdon bank clerk, Gordon Pirie, who showed just why his name was on everybody's lips just now, dominating the seven-mile race from the start to win in 41:07. Jim looked warmer than the rest, choosing a t-shirt rather than a singlet, and was happy with his own run, finishing eleventh in 42:41. Lanky Pirie, a confident and fearless young buck, streaked away after 200 yards and won untroubled against a field of well over 200. Lancashire took the team title, Essex eighth.

The next few weeks for Jim were dominated by training rather than racing, while for the nation as a whole it was a time of mourning following the death of King George VI on Wednesday, 6 February, his daughter Elizabeth proclaimed Queen the following day. Respects were paid at sporting and other events over subsequent days, including at the North of the Thames cross-country championships, staged over a seven-mile flat and dry course at Felsted in Essex. Jim appears to have opted out of this one, thus missing the controversy when William Lennie of Chelmsford AC was declared ineligible just before the start, but defiantly ran anyway, starting behind the 240-strong pack and passing all but seven. Harry Hicks of Hampstead took the title.

Jim tested his own form again at the Southern Counties championships over the downs at Hadleigh, in Essex, overlooking the Thames estuary. Pirie won again in 48:27 with Jim seventh, two minutes down on the soft and sticky terrain. A fortnight later the nation's top distance men gathered for a battle royal at the English National, over a ten-mile course at Perry Barr, Birmingham, on a fine March afternoon. The race was built up as a showdown between holder Walter Hesketh and rising star Pirie. Their magnificent duel lived up to its billing, meaning many failed to notice Jim recording his best placing in a 'national' – fourth in a field of around 400. 'Undoubtedly my best-ever cross-country run, and I finished fairly fast and quite fresh,' was his verdict.

On the hilly but dry Birmingham course, Hesketh was in great form after some superb time-trials on the track and won impressively in 55:32. Pirie had shot off, doing the first mile in only 4:20, but picked up a foot problem and Hesketh overtook him just before the seven-mile point. The rather stony course led to a number of injuries, Pirie's included, but Jim finished strongly, and was given the same time as fifth-placed Frank Sando, a great run by the twenty-year-old, after a late sprint for the line. Sando told me he remembers this race clearly, as it was his first appearance in the senior event, and he was ecstatic at not only matching Jim Peters, but beating Frank Aaron, upon whom he'd based his training.

The race featured a classic 'Hollywood moment' when leader Hesketh slowed at the top of a hill, turned and looked back at the mass below desperately chasing him, but clearly on a hopeless mission. It was a moment for the Manchester man to savour. Among the pack below was his 25-year-old training partner David Coleman, later to find fame as a BBC sports commentator, who finished 89th. Coleman was a useful runner, but an injury this spring would foil his hopes of reaching the 1952 Olympics. Instead of kicking his heels, he offered his services to the BBC to help with athletics coverage; they accepted, and it proved the start of a celebrated career in broadcasting.

Brimming with confidence at the knowledge he was now in the form of his life, Jim led the Beagles in great style at the Round Ilford Relay in mid-March sunshine. There was a strong entry of 34 teams and as they clattered around the 3¾-mile town-centre course, scattering shoppers and pedestrians in their wake, an exciting contest ensued with the lead regularly changing hands. On the seventh stage, Scotsman Andy Ferguson of Highgate broke the lap record of 18:09 by a single second, but didn't have long to celebrate, for on the eighth stage Jim shot off for Beagles and recorded a remarkable 17:54. Sadly, even this brilliant run couldn't hoist his club into a winning position and they ended sixth, Belgrave Harriers victorious.

A day or two later there was interesting news from the Far East that a sensational marathon time had been posted in Korea. In Pusan, 23-year-old Yoon-Chil Choi was said to have run 2:26:07, nearly four minutes quicker than Jim's British record. It wasn't far short of the recognised world best by fellow Korean Suh Yun-Bok (2:25.39) at the 1947 Boston Marathon. The Korean War was by now nine months old, and communication with Korea had never been good in sporting matters anyway, meaning it was difficult for sceptical westerners to assess the validity of Yoon-Chil Choi's new mark. Because of this lack of clarity, and the possibility in some minds that Boston was downhill, or short (or both), it meant the 1936 Olympic winning time of 2:29.19 (by Kitei Son, another Korean) would remain in pole position in many people's view.

Jim's fourth place at the English National earlier had won him a place on the England team for the international championships on Saturday, 22 March, staged at Hamilton racecourse, Glasgow, the site of the inaugural champs half-a-century earlier. Pulling on the white vest was a proud moment and he generously dedicated the achievement to Johnny's training methods, and marvelled at how he'd attained this international status almost accidentally while working through his long-term training plan. Travelling to the event by train from Euston, along with two England teammates and the entire Spanish team, Jim checked into his hotel and immersed himself in the big-race atmosphere.

The cream of Europe's runners awoke in Scotland the next morning to do battle with a nine-mile course across rough grass, battered by relentless drizzle and strong winds (conditions were 'dreich' according to their hosts). The English title-holders were soundly beaten by a fine French display. England packed well and got their six scorers in the first fifteen to finish, but the French did even better, with six in the first ten. Jim was fifteenth overall in 50:25, well behind champion Alain Mimoun, who romped home in 48:19. Summing up for the excellent magazine *Scots Athlete*, former international John Emmet Farrell concluded: 'I can't help feeling that Jim Peters' brilliant record-breaking effort in the Ilford relay the week previous had deprived him of much of his sparkle. I feel convinced that some virtue had gone out of him and instead of gaining over the later stages he was hard put to maintain his position.'

Johnny was relieved to see Jim emerge from the end of the cross-country season unscathed and in good form, having worried that he might have invested a little too much effort and energy in these tough events. He constantly reminded Jim to focus solely on the marathon and only use cross-country as a stepping stone, and not fall between two stools. Most of his winter training was on the roads, and seeing him transfer to hazardous muddy fields for races was a matter of concern to Johnny.

But Jim had been confident and ploughed on with the demanding schedule, simultaneously inspired and intimidated by press speculation that he was not only a certainty for the Olympic team, but favourite for marathon gold. He pointed out: 'Whilst these sort of comments are often a great incentive to training, they can be … a nightmare to an athlete, for to go into a race knowing that you are expected to win may possibly tend to make you overreach yourself in trying to achieve the target that everyone is convinced is easily within your reach.'

On the first Saturday in April the Beagles suffered the type of disaster rarely experienced since their resurgence of recent times. In their first appearance at the national final of *The News of the World* London-to-Brighton relay, they came twentieth and last, their time of 4:15.02 around fourteen minutes slower than they'd produced in the qualifiers. Jim led the side, and the up and coming George Knight was also there, but otherwise Beagles were not at full-strength, and it showed. Historian Wilf Morgan has studied the road relays of the 1950s and is mystified over why Beagles flopped on this rainy afternoon. Surviving members of the club cannot recall the reason, but Wilf says: 'There must be a story here. Perhaps somebody got married that day and everybody but Jim and George got invited!'

What was significant about the occasion was the way Jim Peters took over on the seventh and longest stage (Handcross to Hickstead), with Beagles a long way back in last place, and refused to accept defeat. He ran furiously to record the fastest time on that stage, even though the cause was hopeless. He caught Scotsman Alec Forbes of Victoria Park, a cross-country and three-mile specialist who was a commercial traveller in the radio industry, to put Beagles momentarily into nineteenth place, but after he handed over they slipped back to the wooden spoon position. The event was in ten stages over a 45½ mile route from Mitcham to Brighton and traffic congestion was appalling throughout, partly due to roadworks but mainly to hordes of supporters and clubmates crawling along behind their runners. The police were not happy.

The relay had been a good 'sharpener', but the Finchley 20 a fortnight later would be a truer test of Jim's readiness for the marathon challenges ahead. As runners gathered at the Ruislip start on the hottest day of the year so far, it became clear the conditions had put many off. Nearly 200 had entered but fewer than 150 toed the line, and dozens more would quit before the end. This nineteen-year-old annual event developed into a four-man contest, Jim quickly away at the gun, Stan Cox, Geoff Iden and Exley of Southgate hot on his heels. At the end of the first five-mile lap, Jim had opened a lead in 26:46, and when Ken Cook picked up an injury and was collected by car, the leaders were able to consolidate their advantage. Jim led through halfway, his second lap a little quicker than the first, passing ten miles in 53:30 and raising the distinct possibility a course record was on the cards. Jack Holden's best of 1:50.48 had been set only a year earlier and was itself three minutes better than any other run on this course, which illustrates just how strong Jim's running was.

Cox began falling off the back of the leading pack but hung on gamely, Jim taking them through fifteen miles in 1:20.03. By now, Billy

McMinnis of Sutton Harriers was in the first four and Exley was gone. There was a huge gap between these and the rest, with many men falling by the wayside in the heat. Unbeknown to him, Jim's task on the final lap was to run five miles in half an hour to achieve a course record. This was straightforward in view of his recent form, but he was in no mood to ease up and stayed focused on a fast time and big winning margin.

When he careered over the line in 1:49.39, nearly four minutes ahead of runner-up Iden and 69 seconds inside the record, he could hardly have laid down a more emphatic marker as regards his intentions for the summer. Iden clocked 1:52.18, McMinnis 1:55.05 and Cox 1:56.50. Only 75 others kept going to the bitter end and the first of these was a massive 5:08 behind the pale, exhausted Cox. It was widely hailed as a brilliant run by Jim, his pace quicker than eleven miles an hour, equating to a world best over the marathon distance. He'd even obliterated the long-standing twenty-mile best on a track (1:51.54), set by George Crosland at Stamford Bridge in 1894. Among the other stats that Jim and Johnny chewed over later was the fact that he shed seven pounds in body weight during the race, plummeting from ten stones to 9st 7lbs.

The loss of bodily fluid seemed to have no adverse effect, however, and he certainly felt more comfortable at the end than poor Cox, who complained about 'my dinner coming back on me' during the run, nearly causing him to quit. It was only stern instructions from Johnny at the roadside that kept Cox going, Johnny explaining later he didn't want one of his men getting into the habit of dropping out of long races the moment they felt unwell. All in all, things had gone perfectly for Jim, however, his only anxious moment coming at the very end, when an official's car swerved momentarily in front of him as he was about to breast the tape. It took an atypical and deft body-swerve to avoid disaster, the incident blamed later on the car having jammed its gears.

Athletics Weekly hailed Jim's great performance and marvelled at his recent form and fitness, labelling him the nation's best ever marathon prospect ahead of a major championship. Aware of his hefty mileage and race commitments, they added the sincere hope that he didn't spoil it all by overdoing things.

The titles and personal bests were piling up, and Jim duly annexed his twelfth county championship on Saturday, 26 April on his return to track racing, winning the Essex six miles crown in a new PB of 29:56.6 at Mayesbrook Park. It was the first time he'd dipped under the 30-minute mark and he beat his own championship record by more than ten seconds, breasting the tape 500 yards ahead of Ilford's Alan Perkins, with clubmate Ted Baverstock a further 40 yards back. Just as Johnny had anticipated, Jim's marathon training was helping him achieve great things at shorter distances, a consequence that evidently surprised and delighted the runner himself.

Jim was making considerable sacrifices, more than ever before, to achieve success as a runner, so will have found it hard to fathom the decision by Kent star Roy Beckett to suddenly give up the sport this month, while still in his prime. Twenty-four-year-old Beckett, a wine and spirits storekeeper, who was one of the best three-milers in Europe, quit in the build-up to the Olympics, telling the press he was not prepared to become a slave to running, and had chosen not to make all the sacrifices necessary to stay at the top.

What Jim regarded as 'my final tune-up' for the Poly Marathon was the Essex twenty-miler on Saturday, 10 May in Chelmsford, at which he was bidding for a hat-trick of victories. Like Finchley, it was four laps of a five-mile route, thus presenting a perfect canvas on which to practise the art of even-paced running. Steaming into an early lead and leaving the field to contest a separate race among themselves, Jim churned out laps of 26:12, 27:04, 27:23, 27:54 to win with ease in a course record of 1:48.33. He announced he felt fine afterwards, with just a slight ache in his legs. The winning margin was a huge twelve minutes and 42 seconds.

The emphatic nature of the victory took the limelight away from runner-up Jock Duffy of Hadleigh, who pipped Dennis Horrocks of Chelmsford for second place in 2:01.15. Duffy was a Scots-born bricklayer quietly making his own preparations for a marathon debut at the forthcoming Poly. During wartime Duffy had been a Sherman tank driver in the Eighth Army under Field Marshal Montgomery, but now fought his battles on the roads of Essex. He got to know Jim well and would later put forward the opinion that, although a brilliant runner, he felt Jim was his own worst enemy for always running flat out regardless of conditions. But he admitted to envying Jim's ability to train long and hard, feeling disadvantaged himself because his bricklaying was more physically demanding than the occupation of most of his opponents: 'I was the only one doing a hard day's work,' he recalled with a smile.

Mr and Mrs Peters would certainly have disagreed with Jock's tongue-in-cheek assessment, for Jim's recent training was testing not only his own resilience but that of his wife. Extra washing and the darning of umpteen worn running socks were regular chores for his long-suffering spouse, not to mention the extra food he needed. The food parcels prior to the previous Olympics weren't available this time round, even though rationing of certain products was still in force. It was fortunate that Jim was never a fussy eater, and he was happy to consume extra bread and potatoes instead of whatever was missing from a normal diet, thus ensuring he never went hungry. This was an era when distance runners would find a balanced diet near-impossible to achieve; the pasta and electrolyte drinks beloved of future generations would have seemed light years away. In the midst of coping with his unconventional lifestyle, Jim and Frieda were bringing up young Robin, meaning there would inevitably be disturbed sleep patterns to cope with. Jim's club colleague Ted Baverstock remembers clearly how tough it must have been: 'Bearing in mind the prodigious training schedule, for a man in his thirties Jim was incredible. He had to combine his achievements with responsibilities as a family man. I know he was often roused from his night's rest to comfort his infant son when the boy was unwell or restless.'

With the Poly Marathon around three weeks away, Jim called a halt to his weekend racing, but didn't put the brakes on his training regime. On the first Sunday in June, a fortnight before the race, he was away from home in Staffordshire and took the opportunity to fit in two training runs, of fourteen and ten miles, the former at a faster pace (1:15.55). Next day came another swift thirteen miles, before he headed back to London and work. A run at lunchtime on the Mitcham track was followed by a twelve-miler in the evening, during which he felt worryingly stiff. On the Thursday he confined himself to a fast ten-miler in the evening, resuming twice-a-day running the following day. The penultimate week before the big race therefore saw a tally of 108 miles chalked up, the vast majority of it run hard. Three times that week he jotted in his training log that he felt stiff, and on one occasion reported painful feet, but none of this affected the volume of work.

In the six days prior to Saturday's marathon he decided to run just once a day, five of these over his familiar ten-mile route to Hainault Forest and back, and the final run an easy five in Mitcham during his Friday lunchtime. Each of the ten-milers was run fast, the Wednesday and Thursday efforts both sub-55 minutes and marked as 'records' in his log. The latter was run in the white Dunlop canvas plimsolls from Woolworths, which he called his 'racing slippers' and which he would use in Saturday's race. Weather conditions, for June, had been poor in that final week, but his training log shows that everything else went to plan.

He'd run 322 times since this phase of training began nine months earlier, and the volume and quality of the mileage was surely unprecedented. It had all gone well and any injuries or illnesses were mercifully minor. His form had improved and he seemed to be peaking at the right time. Even before his head hit the pillow on the night of Friday, 13 June, Jim Peters was already dreaming of a world record the next day.

CHAPTER 14

The Greatest Marathon Ever Run

JUNE – JULY 1952

A lightly boiled egg, two slices of bread and butter, and two cups of tea. It may not sound like the breakfast of champions, but it suited Jim Peters well. Three hours later, mindful his marathon was not until mid-afternoon, he indulged in another cuppa and two more slices of bread – this time spread with honey. That would be sufficient for the day, he decided. Even in these austere times it seemed rather skimpy fare considering the physical ordeal facing him later. Jim was well aware this was not typical for a distance runner – but it worked for him, and that was all that mattered: 'It doesn't sound very much and probably precious little on which to run just over 26 miles – but I had found by experience that with such a diet I never had any stomach pains whatsoever during a race.'

No doubt Prince Philip enjoyed a rather more substantial lunch before he emerged from Windsor Castle to meet Jim and the other runners loosening up in the grounds outside before the start of the 1952 Polytechnic and AAA championship marathon. His Royal Highness had celebrated his 31st birthday a few days earlier, and looked slim and handsome in a light-coloured suit as he mingled with the scruffy, grinning little runners, who were twitching hyperactively and desperate for the long-winded formalities to end so they could get on their way.

The Prince, consort to the Queen since her accession four months earlier, was not here just as a token VIP – he had a genuine interest in athletics, and had recently been installed as the first President of the British Amateur Athletics Board (BAAB). When he spoke with Jim he recalled the debut victory of a year earlier, and wished him luck this time out.

Smiling broadly, Jim clasped his hands politely behind his back, dressed in his all-white kit with a No 1 pinned proudly on his chest. He looked a good six inches shorter than the Prince, who chatted amiably before taking the starting pistol. He seemed to enjoy the job of firing it, yanking his arm skywards very enthusiastically, and shouting the instruction to depart loudly with a big grin. Some of the runners appeared not quite ready for the big moment, for some still had arms folded at this point, and few were leaning forward in the normal 'go' position.

Jim was hot favourite to win, with only three or four others from the 170 entrants looking serious challengers if something went wrong. The Dutch champion Janus van de Zande was a threat, but Jim's most serious private worries surrounded Stan Cox, who had already let Jim know he had three ambitions this summer: to make the Olympic team, to go under 2:30.00, and to beat Jim. Both men were going into the race aiming to run 5:30 miles throughout, very ambitious in view of the fact that even 5:40 miling would give either of them a UK best time. After the gun sounded, Jim, Cox, Iden, Van de Zande and Charlie Robertson from Scotland featured prominently. The runners streamed out of Windsor Great Park into the crowded streets in near perfect conditions for marathon running in June. It was dry, pleasantly cool and there was a following wind.

Newsreel clips show Jim running smoothly, and pulling clear early with Cox in pursuit. After a mile he was 30 yards clear and by five miles this had increased to a good 30 seconds. Iden was alone in third and the group behind him seemed to be slowing slightly, allowing the first three to get established. As they headed through leafy Buckinghamshire villages, near the eight-mile mark, there was a close shave when a car driver seemed to misjudge Jim's position and speed and nearly hit him. The shock temporarily disturbed Jim's rhythm and breathing, but then, just as he felt recovered, he had to stop to a juddering halt on a street corner when two cars arrived simultaneously from opposite directions and nearly sandwiched him. He hared off quickly again, worried that Cox was still near enough behind to pose a real threat.

There was more unexpected trouble just before ten miles. Steaming along alone and concentrating hard on the job in hand, he passed a small group of vaguely familiar faces at the roadside. These included Arthur Newton and an animated, elderly figure dressed in running kit and yelling a lot. This was Newton's house guest from Australia, the maverick coach Percy Cerutty. As Jim powered past them, Cerutty sprang into action, brazenly attempting to settle into stride beside him, only to quickly find he was being left behind. Surprised by the pace, he began screaming at Jim to slow down. According to Cerutty's biographer, Graem Sims, he cried: 'Give it away – you can't do it! You'll kill yourself!'

Cerutty explained himself later: 'Peters was hurtling himself along the road in what seemed to me a preposterous effort to do or die. He seemed to be positively lurching along, head on one side, with an uneven stride that maintained a tremendous length, as the uneven beat, so little understood, tends to do. However, I was not used to this fellow's type, or characteristics.' Cerutty, currently in London en route to the Olympics, had never seen Jim in action before and was genuinely shocked to see a marathon man working so hard, so early in a race.

Jim was perhaps too polite and forgiving to make a fuss later, but the interruption annoyed him at the time, and only served to make him drive forward even harder. His tactics and style went completely against the grain as far as Cerutty was concerned, and the coach refused to let the matter lie. When word of his heckling later reached the press, he was interviewed and refused to accept Jim's performance as valid, alleging that the course must be short of 26.2 miles.

Having shaken off the noisy Cerutty, but still worried Cox might be hovering behind, Jim passed the ten-mile point in a superb 51:35, a time so good that when telephoned through to officials at the Chiswick finish, they needed several minutes' consideration before announcing it to the crowd gathered there. By halfway Jim had built a good lead of around two minutes, and was filmed accepting a wet sponge to cool the back of his neck. He ran with head down and shoulders hunched, but was moving very well. He looked to have a good long stride for a small man, not elegant above the waist, but smooth below it.

By fifteen miles the gap between Jim (1:17.23) and Cox hadn't lengthened further, but Iden seemed to be losing touch, albeit still well ahead of the chasing pack. The first three Britons home were virtually guaranteed selection for the Olympic team, and the matter looked cut and dried already – barring unforeseen disasters. Jim's running was relentless, and he hit twenty miles at close to 1:45:00, an almost unbelievable time considering his record at the recent Finchley 20 had been far slower. At this point his legs began to ache and a lead that had grown to three minutes was slowly reduced. Cox ploughed on behind, his running more evenly-paced than Jim's. News that the leader had passed 22 miles in around 1:57.00 was telephoned to Chiswick, once again met by disbelieving ears. Iden was by now battling gamely to hang on to third, his feet giving him trouble, and Robertson looked a decent bet to overhaul him. By the 23-mile point, Cox had cut Jim's lead from three minutes to 90 seconds in less than the space of three miles. Jim would remark later: 'In the last three miles I felt tired and was mentally a little despondent too, for I was convinced my time was not going to be so fast as I had anticipated. My legs were aching, and aching legs meant a slowing of the pace. I knew of course that Stan was behind me but I didn't realise just how close he was for, by this time, [coach] Johnny had gone on ahead to be at Chiswick when we finished.'

Suffering both mentally and physically, but still moving strongly, he pushed on down the Great West Road, past Kew Bridge and down narrow twisting roads that led to the Polytechnic Stadium. He admitted later that the misery of these closing miles caused negative thoughts to cross his mind, including a questioning of why he did this sport, how much he was hating it, and how this would surely be his final race.

All the negativity disappeared as he clattered down the narrow pathway beside the main stand, out under the crowd leaning over to catch a glimpse of him, and on to the blessed relief of the track. The crowd erupted as he swept into view. It brought a smile to his face and he picked up the pace a little to run the final yards on the track, round the final bend and past officials clustered and concentrating hard on their timepieces at their desk beside the finish line. The crowd roared its approval, but as he had no wristwatch, and there were no electronic clocks on view, Jim didn't have a clue how fast he'd run. He was simply desperate to get over the line, stop running and end the pain. He would worry about his time – which he suspected might be a little under 2:30.00 – a little later.

Moments before he hit the tape, the crowd's cheers rose again as Cox entered the stadium, ran smoothly around the track and finished exactly a minute behind. The pair knew they'd secured their Olympic places, barring catastrophe or controversy, and the next question was how fast they'd gone. Jim, exhausted, went over to welcome Cox, shaking his hand warmly and noticing how his friend appeared the fresher of the two. As they lingered on the grass infield, the announcement finally came. Jim had won in 2:20:42 and Cox was second in 2:21.42: 'There was pandemonium, and neither Stan nor I could believe our ears,' he recalled.

By a good margin both men had smashed the previous world best, set in Boston in 1947, as well as the Olympic record set sixteen years earlier. In addition, unratified times of around 2:25.00 set by Koreans had also been rendered irrelevant. Jim had beaten his sensational debut of a year earlier by nearly nine minutes, an achievement so stunning that inevitably there were calls for the course to be re-measured, including from the outspoken Percy Cerutty. Amid all the fuss, few noticed that Iden, in third place, had also beaten the old GB record by a sizable chunk with his 2:26.53 – and had done it despite two stops to rid his shoes of chippings from the newly tarred roads.

Britain not only had a marathon trio to compete with the best, it had three of the fastest men on the planet, ever. The trio were the only runners to break the 2:30.00 barrier at Chiswick, while a further 26 went under 2:45. Debutant Jock Duffy ran well in eighth (2:36.35) to win the Lalande Trophy for the fastest newcomer. The rest of the Kinnaird Trophy meeting, being staged at the stadium simultaneously, was completely overshadowed as reporters and photographers scurried about sending the news back to Fleet Street. After a suitable interval, Jim stepped forward to accept the winners' trophy, by now smartly dressed in collar and tie, the only clue that he'd just run the fastest marathon in history being his slightly ruffled hair.

When he arrived home, tired and triumphant, telegrams and a constantly ringing telephone awaited him. The fuss continued into the next morning, with his face prominent on both front and back pages of the Sunday papers, and dozens of pressmen descending on sleepy Havering Gardens in Chadwell Heath.

'It was the greatest marathon ever run – excepting the historic original,' declared *The Times* in exuberant fashion, while others added a cautionary note, hoping that Peters and Cox had not 'shot their bolt' with this phenomenal display coming so soon (43 days) before the Olympic showdown. The McWhirter twins calculated that Jim had run the first 11mph marathon in history, while Sam Ferris wrote that he'd had the privilege of witnessing the most amazing marathon of all time and doubted if we should ever witness its like again. 'It was more like a chapter from an H G Wells novel,' wrote Ferris. 'These three Britishers made the rest of the world look second-raters.' Jimmy Green of *Athletics Weekly* said he'd always thought the long-distance records could be cut to ribbons by anyone choosing to train seriously, but never expected Jim Peters to prove the point so convincingly.

As well as accusations the course might be short, some reckoned the following wind had been a major help, the latter view scoffed at by coach Johnny, who said: 'Jim's records in the Finchley and Essex twenty-milers, on circular courses and on calm days this year after a record cross-country season, led me to believe that the harder training and extra running – a mere 800 miles – were the main reasons. I thought the rest of the [Poly] field's general improvement was due to the fact they too had taken heed of the reasons for Jim's phenomenal rise to fame as a marathon runner last year and were working harder and learning to run faster.'

The truth about the course's length was clarified soon afterwards when an official re-measurement produced an amazing verdict that made the winning performances even more laudable. The course was certainly not short of the required 26 miles and 385 yards – it was actually 260 yards too long!

The other worrying issue – that the first three men had over-exerted themselves so close to the Olympics – was dismissed by the runners themselves, with Jim reporting that he felt fine and within 24 hours of leaving Chiswick had resumed normal training. A doctor had taken his pulse very shortly after the race and confirmed it was much lower than that of an average man his age.

Jim's winning time reverberated around the athletics world, and from the status of serious medal prospect he rocketed to hot favourite for Olympic gold. Even news from Czechoslovakia that the brilliant Emil

Zatopek was considering running the marathon, as well as the 5,000 and 10,000 metres, failed to put a dampener on British optimism.

Humble dispensing optician Jim Peters found he was now public property. The invitations to attend events and make public appearances piled on the pressure during the six-week spell in which he would have preferred to quietly prepare alone for his date with destiny. He was even summoned to meet the Queen and Princess Margaret. It was all very flattering and exciting, but Jim and Johnny were both conscious of overdoing the non-athletic side of things. One request that he was pleased to grant, however, was to present trophies at the London Federation of Boys Clubs championships at the Polytechnic Stadium. Boys Club events had got him into athletics in the first place, so he could hardly refuse.

The weekend after the Poly saw Jim in smart blazer and flannels attending the AAA track and field championships at White City, along with training partner Reg Robins and a 50,000 crowd. But it was certainly no quiet afternoon watching the athletics. He was feted by well-wishers, had long chats with other athletes and, to cap it all, as reigning AAA marathon champion, was invited onto the in-field to line up and meet the Queen and Princess Margaret. Prince Philip had cried off this event with 'a chill', but his wife and sister-in-law were both well briefed and chatted with Jim about his run the previous week from outside their Windsor home.

At this point Jim was Britain's most talked-about athlete, Gordon Pirie joining him in the spotlight with a sensational White City performance in the six miles, where he won the AAA title and smashed the British all-comers record (28:55.6) after a great battle with Walter Hesketh. At one point the Mancunian appeared to hamper Pirie's progress with barging and use of the elbow, but Pirie gave some back, and the pair ended up in a tangle in lane four. The track referee stepped forward to issue a clear verbal warning as they passed. Given this interruption, Pirie's time looked even better and ensured the Olympic selectors would want him for the 10,000 metres to challenge Zatopek, even though many experts reckoned he should stick to the 5,000 metres.

During the meeting Jim had a long chat with Australian Les Perry, who was planning to do the 5,000-10,000 double at Helsinki. The pair were approached by miler John Landy and coach Percy Cerutty, with the latter now showing a new respect for Jim's running following their bizarre encounter earlier. Cerutty impressed Jim with a detailed breakdown of all the hard work currently being undertaken by a clutch of talented Australian three and six-milers, from whom great things were expected in the 1950s. Jim was growing to like the open, friendly manner of Aussie sportsmen, and he enjoyed the encounter. Being the antithesis of a 'stuck-up Pommie', they also warmed to Jim.

All the talk was of the Olympics, but it wasn't until Monday, 23 June, nine days after his greatest run, that Jim received the letter he desperately wanted, signed by the BAAB president at his Buckingham Palace desk:

'Dear Mr Peters, As President of the British Amateur Athletic Board, I am writing to you on its behalf to inform you that you have been selected to represent Great Britain and Northern Ireland at the Olympic Games, Helsinki, in the Marathon. I send you my congratulations and best wishes for your personal success and for that of the whole team.'

PHILIP (President).

The team was formally announced at a press conference the following day and featured 50 men and sixteen women. Britain looked strong in all the running events, with Bannister and Nankeville competing at 1,500 metres, Disley in the 3,000 steeplechase, Chataway and Pirie at 5,000 and Pirie, Sando and Norris in the 10,000. The press were unanimous that it was the strongest-ever GB team, and much was expected of marathon trio Peters, Cox and Iden. *The Times* talked up Jim's chances and referred to him as 'that remarkable experimenter', praised him for not only covering the distance faster than anyone before him, but for revolutionising the whole idea of how to prepare for the race. They marvelled at how he'd put into practice the beliefs of the great Paavo Nurmi, who had said before the war that the marathon could be speeded up if runners stopped concentrating on nursing their stamina, and prepared rigorously for an appreciably faster tempo. Jim had proved him correct.

Athletics Weekly reckoned potential marathon debutant Zatopek was capable of beating Jim, but lacked the tactical know-how that comes from experience. *AW* then sprang a surprise by tipping Stan Cox to win gold, suggesting that Jim's monumental effort at the Poly may have drained him and spoiled his chances. They reckoned Cox, always the classier runner in the duo's early days, could be a dark horse.

Jim had no worries over being too tired, but was quietly concerned his Poly performance had alerted the world to his tactics. He suspected the opposition might realise their best chance was to box him in and slow him early on. Others could see no reason for such caution – athlete Chris Brasher, for example, would say: 'Peters was the absolute clear favourite for the marathon. He was way ahead of everybody else in the world.'

Carrying the nation's hopes must have been quite a burden for Jim, for in the past many of his best performances had been as a clear underdog, where he had sprung a surprise and exceeded general expectations. Moreover, everybody was painfully aware that Britain had failed to win a single gold medal in track or field at the 1948 games, and now the nation was demanding a much better harvest from the team.

The final weeks before Helsinki were a mad rush in the Peters household. Jim didn't enjoy the stress, but remained determined not to skimp on training during this period. He had big decisions to make about logistical issues, including whether or not his wife and/or coach would accompany him to the Games. A local garage proprietor instigated a subscription fund, publicised by the local press, that would pay for Frieda to travel, but after much discussion she generously conceded that her presence would be of little help, and that it would be better for coach Johnny to go instead. This was a smart move for all concerned, as it meant Johnny could advise both Jim and Stan Cox in those final nervous days before the race, supervising their routine and ensuring they didn't succumb to the distractions and sociable atmosphere of the athletes' village.

Johnny decided it would be better to arrive in Helsinki around three days before the marathon, and not nine days in advance along with the majority of the British team. Careful negotiations were needed with team official Jack Crump to get this rubber-stamped, for he was initially not agreeable. Arrangements were made for Jim and Stan to fly separately on the Thursday before their Sunday race, alongside the GB cycling team, almost a week later than everybody else. This would prove a decision with significant consequences.

The later flight gave Jim and Stan more time in which to prepare in familiar surroundings, although they were still required to attend a reception at Buckingham Palace for the official 'send-off' from the Queen and Prince Philip. Once again the Prince chatted to Jim, this time introducing him to Charlie Fuller, the captain of the Olympic football team and his former schoolmate from Dagenham. Charlie and Jim hadn't seen each other in nineteen years and told the Prince how they'd once been sports-mad kids sitting in adjacent desks at Grafton Road school, dreaming of moments like this. Their mentor, schoolmaster E J Kingdon, heard about the Palace reunion, and called it the proudest moment of his career.

Shortly after this, the rest of the team headed for Helsinki from RAF Bovingdon airfield near Hemel Hempstead, aboard a chartered plane upon which the Olympic insignia and British team name was inscribed. The jingoistic branding turned out to be fortuitous, because the aircraft was later buzzed by Soviet planes who believed it to be contravening airspace regulations en route to Finland. Apparently, only the clear Olympic identification symbols prevented a diplomatic incident.

A number of journals discussed the detail of Jim's training regime in the build-up to the Games. One or two published extracts from his diary and revealed he'd run around 3,000 miles between the end of the 1951 summer season (27 August) and July 1952, in more than 350 outings on road and country. He had missed only three days' training over those twelve months: once on Boxing Day in deference to a plea from his wife (although he did run on Christmas Day) and twice because of travel commitments. Fairly typical of his recent weekly routine was the 111 miles chalked up between 21 and 27 June, the week of the Olympic team announcement. That seven-day period featured thirteen separate good-quality runs, none longer than twelve miles, three of them at six in the morning, four at lunchtime, and six in the early evening. The hardest day was the Thursday: ten miles at breakfast time and twelve in the evening.

Other stats to get a public airing included his daily allocation of time on a typical midweek day. A day in the life of Jim Peters involved 8½ hours sleeping, 3½ hours commuting to work, seven hours working, 2½ hours training and 2½ hours of washing, shaving, eating, dressing and dealing with correspondence. This was a disgrace, reckoned Pat Reekie of *The Sunday Dispatch*, who said surely no other nation would expect, and accept, that its chief Olympic hope, running in the most gruelling race of all, should prepare on one main meal a day plus sandwiches. Reekie said Jim's biggest threat, Zatopek, certainly wouldn't be training in odd moments between his army duties, or living on drab sandwiches which he nibbled during quiet moments at work. Harold Palmer of *The Evening Standard* was also sympathetic, and described how the Peters family had for years gone without trips to the cinema, seaside, theatre or countryside – all because of Jim's running.

Norris McWhirter much admired Jim and his 'back-up team' (i.e. Johnny, Reg Robins, Frieda and son Robin) who, he said, were part of the most decisive comeback in athletics history following Jim's 1949 retirement. McWhirter thought Jim's bid to end Britain's twenty years of near misses in Olympic marathons was threatened most by 25-year-old Finn Veikko Karvonen, the three strong Koreans, and the Argentine fireman and current champion Delfo Cabrera. But because Jim had no illusions about the task in front of him, McWhirter rated his chances highly.

Meanwhile, for his part, Johnny was keen to leave no stone unturned in order to smooth Jim's passage to a gold medal. As well as all the arrangements to arrive 'late' in Helsinki, he spent time collecting suitable bottles which he could place around the marathon course containing refreshment. So that Jim would see them clearly, he obtained a set of small Union Jacks on sticks which would be placed in them.

Johnny then launched a personal investigation into the state of the Finnish water supply, writing various letters in an attempt to ensure Jim would not be taking on fluid likely to upset his stomach. He had always discouraged Jim from drinking copious amounts anyway (before, during and after a race), but what little he did swallow must be clean, he determined. Rumours of dysentery outbreaks in Finland had prompted this angst. He obtained a chemical analysis of the Helsinki mains water, but, unable to make head nor tail of the detailed results, appealed to the chief chemist at the South Essex Water Company for a translation into layman's language. He was told the water on offer at the Olympics would probably be 'fairly soft and satisfactory' and there were no serious risks, although bottled Vichy water would be safest of all, as long as Jim found this palatable, which many Britons apparently didn't.

While the world's top two marathon men mulled over this sort of minutiae back in Essex, the Games themselves opened on Saturday, 19 July amid the usual pomp and ceremony. The Olympic torch had arrived earlier, having been flown from Athens to Denmark, with traditional ground-level transportation not possible because of the Iron Curtain. Excitement was at fever pitch in proud, sports-mad Finland. As *The Times* reported: 'Finland has been scarred by the incursion of Europe's warring factions. She has been all but deafened by their threatening cries. Yet now, standing stoutly free on the rim of the eastern and western camps with the Iron Curtain itself as a frontier, she makes open house for all the athletes of the world.'

The opening ceremony was marred by the unscheduled appearance of a woman in long white robes who was forcibly removed after attempting to commandeer a microphone on the main rostrum to make an appeal for world peace. Heavy rain soaked the athletes standing around during the ceremony. The track was badly damaged but nothing could stop Emil Zatopek the following day as he broke his own Olympic record to win 10,000 metres gold in 29:17.00. Britain's Frank Sando did well to cling on to fifth place and create a new GB record of 29:51.8 despite losing a shoe, while the great young hope Pirie was a disappointed seventh.

By not arriving until the sixth day of proceedings, Jim missed what the press called the greatest day of athletics on record. On the Wednesday new records were set in all seven of that day's events, watched by a thrilled 60,000. Instead of being at trackside, Jim and Johnny, along with Stan Cox and Sam Ferris, were gathered at the Eccleston Hotel in London, enjoying a farewell dinner party with their wives. Johnny and Sam were booked on a BEA Viking flight going via Copenhagen, while the two runners would join the cycling team to fly direct on a more roomy, but less comfortable, Avro York freight plane. It was the first time Jim had ever flown, and it would not prove a happy experience.

CHAPTER 15

Nightmare in Helsinki

JULY – AUGUST 1952

If Jim Peters and Stan Cox were hoping for a relaxing, trouble-free flight to Helsinki they were in for a rude awakening. As their ageing, wartime plane heaved itself off British tarmac, carrying them towards an Olympic marathon just 72 hours away, their problems were only just beginning.

An hour or two later, high above the Baltic, first-time flier Jim was feeling seriously unwell. He was sick several times, felt stiff and cold, and had a violent headache. On his left, Stan, wrapped in blankets, was complaining of a nasty pain down his left side. To cap it all, the plane was then struck by lightning and plummeted sharply from 7,000 to 3,000 feet before the pilot got clear of trouble. The two runners had rarely felt as miserable and fearful. Was this any way for the world's best marathoners to prepare for the biggest day of their athletic lives?

Jim recounted the horrific scenario later: 'Stan and I were given seats near the door. This was done with the utmost of good intentions as at this spot in the aircraft there was a reasonable amount of room, and it was felt we would be able to stretch our legs. Unfortunately there was something wrong with the door and a howling icy cold draught almost froze us solid. The stewardess, who was very concerned about our comfort, gave us blankets, some of which we wrapped round us and with the others tried to stuff up the cracks round the faulty door. But it was no use.'

Once the pilot was aware the two men were suffering badly, he arranged for the cycling team's equipment to be moved so they could try a different position near the front. By then the plane had been airborne for five hours and although it was a welcome respite, the damage had been done. It would have been no consolation for the runners to be told this plane – a British transporter derived from the Lancaster heavy bomber – was of the same type custom-built as personal transport for Winston Churchill, the Duke of Gloucester and Lord Mountbatten. Presumably that trio made sure they sat well clear of the doors.

After arrival at the Olympic village, white-faced Jim and Stan had a meal and retired to bed, neither sleeping very well. They linked up with Johnny the next morning, who noticed their subdued demeanour and spent the day fussing and fretting over them. A car journey over the marathon course may have improved their mood, as they found a gently undulating route with no serious hills and an excellent road surface. Johnny told *The Evening Standard* he would have preferred the course to be a little tougher as his men performed better in tricky conditions. He told the paper he didn't like the arrangement at the halfway point, where runners would have to execute a 180-degree turn around a stone in the middle of the road to begin their return journey to the stadium. He quipped: 'They really need to erect a pole there, so runners can grab it as they swing around.'

After the drive the two men did some gentle training and were filmed by a BBC cameraman as they ran from the athletes' village to the stadium in the Toolo district. They were by now feeling a little better and turned down Johnny's suggestion they get examined by a doctor to check all was well. Resting, light training and lengthy chats about the upcoming marathon took up the next couple of days, a major topic being Zatopek's decision to go for a third goal medal in Sunday's race. He'd won the 10,000 metres earlier in the week, the 5,000 on the day of their arrival, and had now confirmed he was to run the marathon too. He joked that his reason was to make it 3-1 in a gold medal contest with wife Dana, the recently crowned javelin champion.

The Czech had set a new Olympic record of 14:06.6, when just pipping Alain Mimoun in the 5,000, with Gordon Pirie finishing utterly spent in fourth and Chris Chataway hampered by a late fall. Surely a third gold in the most gruelling race of all was beyond even Zatopek, especially on his debut at the distance? Jim and Johnny speculated he might only be running to help other runners from Iron Curtain countries and didn't seriously expect to win himself. But they knew it would be foolish to underestimate him, whatever his intentions.

By the morning of the marathon, Britain had yet to win gold and all hopes were now pinned on Jim and Stan. John Disley had been beaten in the steeplechase, McDonald Bailey in the sprints and Roger Bannister in the 1,500 metres. For the second Olympics in succession, no gold medals had been won in track and field. This situation didn't help the two marathon men. The pressure saw them begin to get on each other's nerves and at one point they deliberately stopped training together to ease the tension. Jim was completely wound up and irritable, convincing himself that other runners would be out to 'nobble' him in the early part of the race. Jim and Johnny also disagreed on tactics, the former convinced he should go hell for leather and grab an early lead as they left the stadium, but Johnny urging caution over the first ten miles to enable a weighing up of the opposition. Rather than argue, Johnny left Jim to make his own decisions on the day.

On race day a good breakfast was followed by a poached egg at lunchtime – a vast improvement on Jim's normal pre-race fare back in England. A few formalities had to be carried out, such as getting approval for the contents of Jim's drinks bottles adorned with Union Jacks. They contained a concoction of blackcurrant juice and salt, and the Finnish authorities gave the go ahead, also agreeing that water-soaked sponges and buckets of water would be made available. Then came a problem, the pre-race medical checks passing Jim as fit to run, but not Stan, who was found to have a resting pulse rate of 120 beats per minute.

The doctor ordered a cardiogram to confirm his findings and this told the same story, indicating Stan was suffering from hypertension. To his horror he was instructed not to run. Fortunately, an American medic intervened, convincing his Finnish counterpart it was merely 'nervous excitement' and not uncommon, and Stan was reprieved. It was the first time Cox's health and fitness had been questioned in this way, and it left him feeling worried at the very time he needed to be relaxed.

Meticulous Johnny checked the inside of their socks and shoes for anything that might cause blisters and, after they were taken to the stadium by car, he and Sam Ferris ventured out on the course to monitor their runners' progress from a number of vantage points. This pair would not be the only welcome British faces at the roadside, for Frank Sando's Aylesford Paper Mills club had sent a party of supporters and the GB cycling team were also out there, in addition to a large group of sailors from the vessel which brought Prince Philip over.

Under a warm afternoon sun, 66 nervous figures, representing 32 nations, assembled on the start-line in four rows. Zatopek made a point of seeking Jim out and shaking his hand. He had already decided to shadow Jim in the first half of the race, and needed to get a close look to be sure he would be following the right man. A number of other runners shook hands and wished each other luck, while others quietly kept their own counsel. The pack set off in somewhat unruly fashion, a Pakistani runner bizarrely choosing to sprint for a short distance. Jim decided to trust his own judgement above that of Johnny's and surged into an early lead. After two and a half laps of the track out they went into the streets of Helsinki, Jim building a lead of about 40 seconds by the five-kilometre mark, Cox, Zatopek and the Swede Gustaf Jansson in a cluster behind.

Wearing No 187 on his bright all-white GB kit, Jim looked in good shape and seemed to be moving well. Little changed until he reached the nine-mile mark in a speedy time of just over 45 minutes. Then, seemingly all of a sudden, Zatopek and Jansson had closed the gap and drawn alongside. For a spell, probably around two miles, the trio ploughed on together, nobody saying a word.

Then came a key moment, often referred to later, possibly exaggerated and embellished, but which surely changed the course of the whole race.

As Jim recalled it, Zatopek seemed to point to Jansson before asking Jim if they were running at the correct pace. Jim, by now not feeling anything like as strong or positive as he had in previous marathons, was keen to disguise his discomfort and pretended they were not going fast enough. Later he explained his strange reaction: 'True to my Cockney tradition, and although I was absolutely shagged and knackered, I told him it was too slow.' Zatopek expressed surprise at the answer, but remained, in Jim's eyes, 'as calm and unruffled as if he were sitting down at a picnic instead of having run twelve fast miles.' The Czech then asked if Jim was absolutely sure they were going too slow, and on getting a reply in the affirmative, responded with a shrug of the shoulders. Jim's bluff had been a big mistake. Zatopek took him at his word and was off.

He surged forward, followed closely by Jansson, and they quickly opened a gap of ten yards, Jim unable to respond. Zatopek casually turned his head to check Jim's reaction, a gesture that said everything about the likely destination of the gold medal that day. Here was Jim, shattered and unable to change pace, and there was the Czech, happy to talk, able to look around without breaking stride and accelerating as and when he felt the need.

They reached the halfway turning point with Jim still ten yards adrift but by now nursing optimistic thoughts of getting through his bad spell and giving chase. There was a cooling breeze in their faces now, and this provided a modicum of encouragement. But, suddenly, he felt cramp in his left leg, and a feeling that his strength was being slowly sapped away. As he passed the rest of the field yet to reach halfway, Jim waved weakly at Stan Cox, but saw that his pal was also suffering, unable to get ahead of Britain's third man Geoff Iden, who was living up to his pre-race promise of running at a perfectly even pace. By fifteen miles Zatopek and Jansson had opened the gap to 150 yards and Jim knew deep down his chance of gold was gone, but was determined to struggle on in the chase for a minor medal. It was a vain hope. Over the next few miles the cramp in his leg worsened and soon he was reduced to little more than a pained hobble.

Somewhere near the twenty-mile mark the game was up. Just as he spotted Sam Ferris at the roadside, he tottered and virtually collapsed in his arms. Ferris, having just seen Zatopek go past and mistaking the

Czech's ungainly style for pain and discomfort, urged Jim to press on in the hope of catching him. Jim responded briefly but had managed to limp barely 200 yards before he crumpled again, falling alarmingly on his back at the roadside, with a spectator's kindly hand cradling his neck in time to prevent further damage. Clearly this was more than merely cramp, for he looked entirely spent. His eyes appeared to close momentarily, but when a cameraman loomed close, Jim despairingly flicked an angry look at him and flailed an arm. For a second or two it appeared his dented pride was going to get him on his feet again. Even in severe distress he was desperate not to let his country down by being filmed in a state of collapse. But it was no use, his energy had gone and his race was over.

He recalled later this moment at the roadside had been one of 'complete despair and feeling thoroughly ill'. Before long, a press vehicle containing British journalists arrived and scooped up his despondent frame. At almost exactly the same moment, some three miles further back, Stan Cox was experiencing his own personal catastrophe. By now in major discomfort all down his left side, he was left behind by the passing Iden moments before suddenly blacking out, collapsing in the road and subsequently carted off by ambulance.

Poor Johnny Johnston, meanwhile, was waiting patiently further along the course, silently hoping the first runners to come into view would be his two brave boys. From his vantage point he could overhear radio reports in Finnish, but couldn't understand them, and was dismayed to see the first man coming around the bend towards him was Zatopek. Rolling and heaving in his usual manner, the Czech was flying along while regularly pulling up his vest to rub vigorously at his chest. This unorthodox style was by now becoming familiar, and it didn't indicate he was in any particular distress – as if to prove it, he continued to chat amiably every so often with policemen, cyclists or spectators.

After Zatopek passed Johnny, then came Jansson, six others, and eventually Geoff Iden, running efficiently in ninth place. Johnny was mortified, still having no clue what had happened to Jim and Stan. He hurried away to try and find out.

Zatopek never let up as he approached the stadium, with its distinctive tall tower, sweeping inside and crossing the finish line in an Olympic record of 2:23.03. His unique treble inspired wonderful scenes, the cheering 70,000 spectators treating him as one of their own. The great man barely paused before signing autographs, posing for pictures and allowing some Jamaican sprinters to hoist him shoulder high. He then dashed back to the finish line to greet runner-up Reinaldo Gorno (Argentina) and third man Jansson with slices of orange. The first seven home all beat the previous Olympic best, but Jim Peters' Poly time remained the fastest on the record books.

The Brits were eventually reunited at the athletes' village, Cox already tucked up in bed and being cared for by a nurse by the time Johnny arrived. Jim was gently escorted in later on. Both runners were exhausted, apparently not seriously harmed, but still incapacitated enough for a baffled Johnny to demand medical examinations of both. He was finding it hard to accept that their discomforts on the plane could be the only reason for such a spectacular collapse. Pole vaulter Tim Anderson, a qualified doctor, did a reassuring preliminary examination before the official medical officer rolled up hours later to dispense sleeping tablets and comforting words. The two runners' despondency was momentarily lifted when Prince Philip suddenly strolled into the room to offer his commiserations, urging them to have another bash in four years' time.

Johnny had to fly home the following day, and he departed still in a state of puzzlement over what exactly had caused his duo to fail so dramatically on a course that had not been fraught with obvious difficulty. One fear that plagued him was that he might have driven the pair too hard in training. He determined to have them examined again by experts once they had returned to England.

Immediately after arriving back in London, Johnny wrote a long letter to the AAA asking for their medical people to carry out a full investigation, explaining that he wanted to be sure his 'severe training methods' weren't to blame for the problems experienced by Peters and Cox. He even offered to hand over the training records of the pair. He told the AAA that both men had been badly hit in the race by ailments on the left side of their bodies, which fitted the theory that the severe draught on the plane to Finland was at least partly to blame.

Meanwhile, the two runners soon felt a little better and Jim was well enough to be one of fifteen athletes attending a post-Games reception at the British Embassy in Helsinki. Their flight home was again on a utilitarian Avro York, but was this time a much more comfortable affair. The team as a whole departed Finland with tail firmly between legs, again no gold medals in track and field, and only saved from complete ignominy by the final-day equestrian victory of Captain Harry Llewellyn and his steed Foxhunter.

Less than 24 hours after the closing ceremony at Helsinki, a British Empire versus USA match was staged at White City in front of a bank holiday crowd of 50,000. It wasn't quite the glorious homecoming of conquering heroes that had been hoped for, but was a success nevertheless, with three world records and ten GB/Empire records broken.

Naturally the inquests in the sporting press had begun long before the Olympians arrived back on UK soil. In *Athletics Weekly*, editor Jimmy Green said he'd been vindicated in his belief that the heat and effort of the Poly run in June had been to blame for Jim and Stan's problems. *The Sunday Express* called for flags to be flown at half mast, while *The People* accused the GB contingent of being too big and cumbersome and cluttered with 'flash athletes who never had a celluloid cat's chance in this flame-seared festival'. *The Daily Mirror* reckoned the can, full of dirty water, must be carried by the blazered-officials at the AAA. Eventually the backlash got so bad that the athletics fraternity retaliated by urging the public not to read 'all the garbage in the sensationalist press' and to concentrate on the more considered verdicts of the full-time, serious sports reporters.

Philip Noel-Baker, Commandant of the GB Olympic team, said the only people who had expected a cluster of gold medals had been the critics themselves. The chairman of the National Union of Journalists was outraged by this, and said team-manager Jack Crump of the AAA had been the one predicting glory. Noel-Baker pointed out that six GB athletes had beaten previous Olympic records, and the squad had representatives in sixteen different finals. He said it should not be forgotten that British athletes laboured under huge disadvantages, including a woeful lack of running tracks around the country, and a shortage of good coaches. There were only 75 cinder tracks for 40 million people – the majority of which were privately owned and concentrated in the London area.

For his part, Crump was keen to defend Jim Peters from criticism: '[Jim] deserved an Olympic gold and was unfortunate this year to come up against the wonder man Zatopek … if Jim had been content to run for a second place he could have gained it easily, but rightly, in my view, he went all out for the winner's medal and paid the penalty. If Zatopek had not been competing, I believe Jim would have adopted better and winning tactics.' Split times recorded at the Helsinki roadside were:

Peters: 5k 15.43; 10k 31.55; 15k 47.58; 20k 64.27; 25k 81.58; 30k 99.53; 35k retired.

Zatopek 5k 16.02; 10k 32.12; 15k 48.00; 20k 64.37; 25k 81.30; 30k 98.42; 35k 116.50.

During August, once the dust had settled, and before they got down to any detailed planning of training and races to come, Johnny pushed ahead with his plan to have his two runners thoroughly examined by medics. The AAA advised him there was little point, as they had by now fully recovered from their ordeal and it was unlikely a detailed medical would find any reason for their Olympic failures. But Johnny was not to be put off and organised things himself. According to one report, Jim and Stan were examined by both Sir Adolphe Abrahams and by the Queen's surgeon Sir Arthur Porritt. Nothing untoward was found with either runner, and the doctors seemed to agree with the theory that the dreadful plane journey had been to blame.

Jim was happy to accept this verdict and he and Stan showed they had lost none of their fighting spirit, deciding between them their only response would be to get back into proper training and work even harder. It was becoming crystal clear that the marathon was an event that would advance quickly during the 1950s and that the plodders of yester-year had no chance of Olympic medals any longer. Jim and Stan had shown once in 1952 how to prepare and run a fast marathon, but they had failed badly in an attempt to quickly duplicate their achievement. Now they had to re-group, re-think and start all over again.

CHAPTER 16

Back in the Groove Again

Two Olympic Games; two failures. But was Jim Peters downhearted? Not likely. His reaction on arriving home was to start planning how he could cram in yet more training. He wanted to work even harder, and began dreaming up weekly regimes within which he could go running at least twelve times. He also vowed that the quality and high tempo of each run would not be compromised either.

To some it looked like madness, old hand Harold Abrahams among them. Hadn't recent events proved Jim Peters was already overdoing things, without increasing his workload further? The crash-and-burn scenario at the Helsinki Olympics had surely been down to attempting two marathons just six weeks apart?

They were wasting their breath. Jim was convinced he knew what he was doing and Johnny backed him to the hilt. As perhaps the more eloquent of the two, Johnny stepped forward to publicly defend his man's methods. One onlooker had a theory that Jim's harsh training schedule would destroy, certainly in most mortals, the very qualities which the noble sport of cross-country builds up in a man. It was an interesting, if quaint, proposition, and Johnny responded: 'The daily run is [Jim's] chosen way of enjoying a few leisure hours and is his way of enjoying his game, in the same way as the cricketer, footballer, tennis player or golfer taking exercise with his game. The marathon man has always spent his hours training and in fact many today spend far more hours per week than Jim in pounding the roads, but if they found life irksome they wouldn't do it surely?'

If Jim had any lingering feelings of anti-climax after the Helsinki debacle, he was doing a great job disguising them. He launched into winter training with his now customary gusto, and even found time to help coach the younger runners at Essex Beagles, grooming them specifically for a serious crack at the next national junior cross-country championships. He was following Johnny's mantra 'The more you put in, the more you get out', and doing it with more zeal than ever. From the beginning of September to the end of 1952, he would fit in 164 runs, totalling more than 1,200 miles (an average of 70 miles in ten runs per week).

He felt very fit and there had been no after-effects from the hectic summer. He told *Athletics Weekly* that 'jogging runs' were basically a waste of time: 'You should have a go on every run, and not finish distressed but feel that you have been out for a run and not a picnic.' He expected in 1953 to run at least 500 times, he said, including 25 or more races of all types, with a grand total of around 4,000 miles for the year. By the middle of the 1952-53 winter he would be running at least ten times a week and this would increase in the spring of 1953. He described a typical winter week:

Saturday: Race, or 10-14 miles training off-road.

Sunday: 10-12 miles on road (morning).

Monday: 6 miles on track/fields (lunchtime), 6 miles road (evening).

Tuesday: 6 miles track (lunchtime), 8½ miles road (evening).

Wednesday: 6 miles track/fields (lunchtime), 8½ miles road (evening).

Thursday: 6-10 miles road (evening).

Friday: 4-6 miles road (if racing next day) or 8½ miles road (evening).

(Week's total: approximately 80 miles in ten sessions).

Working equally hard many hundreds of miles away was, of course, the indefatigable Zatopek. Prague Radio announced that Zatopek's Olympic feats had won him promotion from army captain to major, plus selection as a delegate to a major peace congress in Vienna in December. Furthermore, they added, he celebrated his increasing involvement in politics by visiting the track in Houstka, northern Bohemia, to knock off 'exhibition' world records at fifteen miles, 25km and 30km (1:16.26.4, 1:19.21.8 and 1:35.23.8, respectively). But if this news was slightly dispiriting for Jim, it would be quickly followed by a morale boost, the AAA awarding him the Harvey Memorial Trophy to recognise the best championship feat of 1952, i.e. his Poly win in June.

So what exactly did Jim expect to accrue from all the increased training? He hinted that in the New Year he may make an attempt at both the one and two-hour track records, and run some six-milers on the track, as his marathon training had 'accidentally' led to improvements at this distance, even though it was no longer his specialism. Longer term, he had his eyes firmly on marathons at the Empire Games and European Championships of 1954, and the Melbourne Olympics of 1956, by which time he would be nearly 38.

He made eight race appearances before the end of the calendar year, the first the now annual London-Brighton Relay for southern clubs in October. It proved a pulsating affair in which Beagles nearly caused a major upset, failing by seconds to beat big guns Belgrave and Thames Valley Harriers. It was a cool day, mainly sunny, with a light following breeze – perfect conditions as the first-leg runners lined up in Park Place, Mitcham. Forty-five miles and 478 yards later, outside the Brighton

Aquarium, fourteen of the twenty competing teams came home inside the four-hour barrier, various runners having smashed an amazing nine out of the ten stage records en route.

Ted Baverstock was fourth quickest on Stage 1 for Beagles, handing over to George Knight, whose fine effort took the Cinderella club into a lead of around two minutes. Dickie Douglas, followed by Reg Robins and A Street, all ran well to keep Beagles ahead, although the lead was whittled away a little. Jim ran a scintillating 29:18 to crack the record for Stage 7 by fourteen seconds (previous holder Corporal Palmer of the Essex Regiment), which took Beagles into a commanding lead. Stan Robins did his best to maintain momentum, the lead down to 62 seconds when handed to Bernie Hames. On Stage 9 the advantage was down to a handful of seconds and it took remarkable runs by Ken Norris (TVH) and Alec Olney (Belgrave) to pip Beagles in the closing stages. Olney roared past the final Beagles runner just 100 yards from the Promenade finish.

A week later, Saturday, 18 October, Beagles made no mistake by knocking a hefty three minutes off the twenty-mile course record to win the Sidney C Taylor road relays in Chelmsford. Jim underlined his great form, clocking 15:03 on the 3.3 mile loop to beat his own course record by nineteen seconds, but had to concede the limelight to a sensational run by Frank Sando, who ran 14:50. Sando's effort took Aylesford Paper Mills from seventh to second, but Beagles clung to the lead throughout.

Jim claimed a hat-trick of records the following month when Beagles beat Ipswich Harriers at the annual Ipswich 4½-mile road race. He beat the course best by nineteen seconds with 22:05, some 29 seconds clear of teammate Knight, with Reg Robins third in 22:53. Jim maintained a killing pace in the fine weather in his characteristic 'loose style', reported *The Evening Star*. He had grabbed an early lead on the uphill stretch of Tuddenham Road after the race started late, and after passing Westerfield Church and turning homewards, increased it. When Valley Road was crossed, he was a comfortable 150 yards to the good, but accelerated down to the finish amid a huge ovation.

His dislike of awkward obstacles in cross-country has already been discussed, and this probably contributed to an end to his winning streak at the Beagles' 7½-mile cross-country at Chigwell Row. He lost by a mere 30 yards to Ted Baverstock, whose 38:19 beat Jim's twelve-month-old course record into the bargain. Jim also went inside the old mark, but had the handicap of starting off scratch, while Baverstock had been given a fifteen-second advantage.

As the worst of the winter set in during December 1952, good eyesight was of more benefit than running speed. Over the first weekend of

the month a 'great smog' descended on Greater London, leading directly and indirectly to the death of more than 4,000 people. It would later
be labelled the greatest mass killer of the 20th century. Hundreds of
Essex folk in Jim's area lost their lives as a result of the foul four-day
event. 'A genuine Victorian pea-souper is on the way,' BBC radio had
warned on the Friday, and the ensuing days saw chaos in the capital and
its suburbs. The fog contained pockets of sulphur dioxide and other
industrial gases and Jim's local paper, *The Ilford Guardian*, reported that
many coal deliveries hadn't taken place because merchants simply could-
n't travel. Many families therefore had to abandon their firesides and go
to bed early to escape the misery. Dagenham dockers who made it into
work couldn't even see their own feet, it was reported.

Conditions were marginally better if you could escape the urban areas,
and that's just what Beagles did on the Saturday afternoon. Taking on
Chelmsford AC at foggy and freezing Chigwell Row, the run was a matter of mere survival for most, but Jim had no qualms about the appalling
weather, and powered to victory in 37:13, steam coming off him like a
racehorse. It was a brilliant run in humble surroundings that earned little
publicity, but served as a precursor to an even better one the following
weekend.

Frank Sando caught a cold and told the authorities at short notice he
was unavailable for the England team travelling to the 4½-miles cross-
country international at Aycaguer, near the French city of Lyons on
Sunday, 14 December. Jim was asked to stand in and, knowing he was in
the form of his life, stole the show with a surprise victory by a big margin. One report described it as a magnificent display by our boys, and
doubtful if Jim had ever run better. He beat Jacques Vernier by around
75 yards with the fastest time ever seen on this course (21:49.8) and
shocked the locals. It was all the more impressive as the English had a
laborious journey from London to Lyons with little time to acclimatise.
Ray Hatton and Ted Hardy backed Jim up by finishing in the top six, and
England took the team prize.

Although Jim hadn't planned to race frequently during the winter of
1952-53 his form was so consistently good it was hard to resist the
opportunity, and he turned out again the following week to help Beagles
easily beat Victoria Park at Riggs Retreat, Buckhurst Hill. He won with
impressive ease in 47:17, 26 seconds clear of teammate Reg Robins with
fellow Olympian Geoff Iden fifth.

Knowing he was off to Tyneside for New Year's Day, Jim kept racing
to a minimum over Christmas, but still managed an 80-mile week, granting his family the concession of a zero-mileage Christmas Day. He also

missed the mayhem when thick fog returned at the Friendship Cup race held by Grafton AC at Chingford on Saturday, 27 December. He took one look at the fog and decided a thirteen-mile solo training run would be a better option. Those who toughed it out at Chingford went badly off course due to the poor visibility, one report stating that 200 men ran across Chingford Plain into Epping Forest, but only 130 emerged. Officials said that as so many had taken wrong turns, there was no point trying to adjust the final results. Beagles had five in the first ten and thus lifted the cup, one of the rare occasions they achieved glory without Jim playing a part.

In the first 1953 edition of a newly revamped *Athletics Weekly*, Jim put his name to a two-page article on training, the first of a short series attributed to him. He told readers he had by now competed at everything between 440 yards and the marathon, with the exception of the steeplechase, of which he was 'scared stiff'. He reiterated his philosophy that training must be rigorous, unflinching and a long-term commitment. He sang the praises of fartlek training in wooded areas, wishing he'd discovered it for himself earlier in his career.

His national fame was of course well established, but he showed no signs of neglecting his duties as a good club man, and supported Beagles events and helped less able colleagues whenever possible. He wasn't the type to put on airs and graces and remained modest and approachable despite his constant high profile in newspapers and periodicals. The club newsletter was edited at the time by Dave Green, who recalls those days well: 'I remember Jim as a gentleman, who would always help anyone interested in athletics and who had a good attitude towards other athletes. He also remained good humoured in his outlook at all times.'

Judging by the shape he was in and the results produced over the autumn and early winter of 1952, there seemed a real chance 1953 would be Jim's best year yet if he could steer clear of injury. He certainly started it with a bang, signalling his intent with a new record when retaining the coveted Morpeth-to-Newcastle crown on New Year's Day.

This time there was none of the snow and slush of a year earlier, the district escaping blizzards that struck elsewhere that day. Around 80 had entered, Jim and clubmate Bernie Hames representing southern England, but fewer made it to the start-line. A big crowd jostled around the start area, despite the counter-attraction of the Newcastle v WBA football match at Tynecastle (48,930 attended) and Sunderland v Aston Villa at Roker (42,000). Onlookers were able to keep in touch with the race's progress thanks to what *The Newcastle Journal* called 'special radio telephony' on board a vehicle which followed the leaders.

Jim, wearing No 67 on his singlet, and old friend Bob Pape, a master-in-arms in the Navy, set off fast, and within a mile Jim had pulled away, amazing the roadside helpers working out split times at Blagdon Gates, Seaton Burn and Gosforth. He delivered the predicted course record in style, untroubled by opposition, virtually sprinting by the end, having covered the 13¾ miles in 1:07.06. One awe-struck reporter described the time as 'impossible'. The first three were all inside the old record, but 'Peters blasted it to high heaven'. Jack Holden's mark was beaten by four minutes and eighteen seconds, although Bedlington salvaged a little local pride by taking the team award.

Mindful he had to catch a train back south as quickly as possible to prepare for another event in less than 48 hours' time, Jim quickly changed into his GB blazer and tie for post-race formalities in the nearby school for the deaf. He accepted the cup from the redoubtable fur-coated Mrs Violet Grantham, who had recently become Newcastle's first female mayor and sheriff.

Jim kept his promise to Beagles to make up a team of six for the Essex cross-country championships at Chelmsford, even though it was only two days after the long Morpeth race. It proved a real thriller, and its dramatic finale after 7½ miles lives on in the memory of winner Ted Baverstock nearly 60 years later. He takes up the story: 'I have vivid memories of this race. It was a mild day after night rain, and around halfway Jim and I were clear of the field and stayed together until the finish was in sight. It was then I started to inch ahead and thought I was clear. I had not allowed for Jim's guts and tenacity. With perhaps 50 yards left – it was difficult to be sure as officials had neglected to put up a finishing tape – I was shocked to suddenly see out of the corner of my eye that Jim had drawn level. This was sufficient to jolt me into a final spurt and I won by a tiny margin. Though delighted, I later reflected that my victory was perhaps a little hollow as Jim had won the Morpeth-to-Newcastle just 48 hours earlier and wasn't fully recovered from that. A photo of our sprint finish shows perfectly the moment my head jolted back in shock when Jim unexpectedly pulled level.'

Baverstock was given the verdict in 44:14, a second ahead of Jim, and Beagles, the holders, retained their team trophy. Alan Perkins of Ilford was more than a minute behind the duelling clubmates in third.

By now Jim's employer Douglas Wingate's personal athletic ambitions had been thwarted by back trouble, but he maintained a close interest in the sport and in Jim's career, and in January 1953 donated 'The Jim Peters Trophy' for the winning team at the annual 15½-mile road race staged near their workplace in Mitcham. Free from club commitments, Jim turned out for the race on Saturday, 10 January dressed in his all-white GB Olympics kit, aiming to crack a course record held by Stan Cox.

He again proved untouchable. Drawing away early on, he had Cox and Pape in close pursuit, those positions unchanging for ten miles. Jim hit five miles in 24:10, ten in 49.00 and then went seemingly effortlessly into overdrive, pulling well clear to finish in a new course record of 1:19.21, a massive 4:46 inside Cox's old mark. The victory margin was 700 yards but Cox and Pape also beat the old record as they finished in Jim's wake. Blackheath won the Peters Trophy and promptly filled it with champagne, which they quaffed happily.

Hitting such a rich vein of form in mid-winter meant Jim was currently Britain's number one athlete, and readers of *Athletics Weekly* were eager to devour more of his 'training secrets'. Over two more editions of the magazine, he advocated running off-road all year round to save jarring of the joints, although acknowledged that many working men would only be able to do so at weekends because of dark winter evenings. He recommended using heavier shoes for training than for racing, perhaps with extra rubber or sponge inserted to combat the jarring of road running. He acknowledged that Zatopek had been successful with his famous changes of pace, but endorsed the views of the coach Charlie Smart that runners should strive for even pace and always attack hills in order to achieve this. Jim added that a serious marathoner had to get used to 'bread and butter training' on 350 days per year, although admitted his wife was looking over his shoulder as he wrote, and was insisting they would be having a proper holiday in August, regardless of his training plans.

In mid-January, for the first time since the Olympics, things didn't quite go according to plan. Suffering from what he described as a mild form of bronchitis, Jim failed to set off at his usual lick in the inter-counties cross-country at Kettering, and found himself in unfamiliar territory well down the field after a mile, constantly having to claw back ground after that. He completed the 7¼-mile course in Wickstead Park in 41:53, looking rather subdued in seventeenth place, *The Times* commenting that 'he always seemed to be tired'. The route featured an awkward gate or two, which may have been partly to blame. English champion Walter Hesketh ran with a head cold and came in an unhappy eleventh. Len Eyre of Yorkshire was the popular individual winner, having finished third and second in previous years, and this civil servant from Leeds led his county to the main title.

Any unhappy memories from Kettering were banished seven days later as Jim roared around the Beagles ten-mile cross-country course to win the club championship in 54:24, a new record and nearly three minutes faster than nearest challenger, Don Corney. If he did have bronchitis it was evidently not a serious dose.

At the end of January 1953, normal life was put on hold in much of Essex after the most catastrophic British weather event of the century. A storm surge driven by hurricane-force winds whipped the waters of the North Sea into massive tidal levels which then smashed through east-coast sea walls, breaching more than 1,200 sites in all. Around 1,000 miles of coastline were flooded and more than 300 died. Nearly 50,000 acres of Essex were under water and thousands were evacuated from their homes. With their Chadwell Heath house not far from the northern banks of the Thames, it was a worrying time for the Peters family, but their district was spared the most serious effects.

Within a few weeks Jim had turned his attention to the winter's biggest cross-country races, three of them within a six-week period: the Southern Counties, the National and the International championships. He didn't feel particularly sharp when taking fourth place in the Southern ten-miler at Aylesford, clocking 55:10, some 40 seconds behind third man Doug Holden of Cambridge Harriers. Gordon Pirie took the title after a ding-dong battle with Frank Sando. Jim complained afterwards he was still suffering from the bronchitis symptoms he'd first noticed around six weeks earlier. There was some consolation when the Beagles youngsters, coached by him, lifted the junior title, however.

A fortnight on, the big names at Aylesford assembled again to contest the English title with their Northern and Midlands rivals. The setting was Caversham Park, Reading, the grounds of a Victorian stately home which formerly housed the Oratory School and was requisitioned in wartime as a BBC World monitoring station. Over a fast but quite hilly 9.6-mile course in ideal conditions, Pirie took advantage of the absence of title-holder Hesketh to go one better than his runner-up spot of a year earlier. Looking fresh throughout, he spread-eagled the field and won by nearly 400 yards from Sando in 49:15. Jim worked hard to secure ninth place in 51:01, a performance that won him a place in the England team for the forthcoming international race in France. The Beagles' youngsters again won the junior prize, as targeted by Jim many months earlier, and he had further cause to celebrate when the England selectors invited him to captain the senior team in France.

The honour caught him by surprise: 'Five years [ago] I achieved my one great ambition in getting my international vest – but never did I aspire to being selected to captain a British team. I was thrilled and proud to feel that I was considered a worthy athlete to fill this coveted position.'

The selectors confirmed their team just before the runners departed from Caversham Park, and they gathered for photographers, beaming proudly, looking for all the world like mild-mannered bank clerks in their macintoshes, collars and ties.

The new England captain returned to the back-slapping and congratulatory bosom of his club, ready to lead them into action at the Ilford Road Relays a week later. Staged from Gordon Road in the town centre, it proved a triumphant day, Jim equalling his own course record of 17:54 for the 3¾-mile loop as Beagles won the team prize in 3:07.28, beating a fourteen-year-old course record. Jim's effort took them into second spot on the seventh leg, with the next runner, Ted Baverstock, moving them into the lead, a position never relinquished, the nearest opponent adrift by 74 seconds by the end.

Relay wins were a special treat, but even this couldn't match the pride Jim felt when leading his country into action at the Paris Vincennes racecourse in front of 20,000 spectators a week later on Saturday, 21 March. It was the golden jubilee 50th staging of the International championships (later renamed the World Champs) and ten nations were represented. On a warm afternoon, it was anyone's race until the eighth of ten miles when Yugoslavia's Franjo Mihalic pulled clear of the leading pack and opened a significant gap. England lost Bill Boak, the bespectacled Elswick Harrier, when he collapsed on the last lap with heat exhaustion, to be carried away on a stretcher. He was one of thirteen of the 89 starters who failed to finish. Pirie found the going hard, claiming afterwards he'd been misled about the course and had worn spikes that were unsuitable for the cobbled sections; he'd been forced to stop and remove the shoes, leaving them on someone's doorstep. Sando attempted to pursue Mihalic in the closing stages but was suffering from stitch and did well to hang on to second. Behind him, Fred Norris (5th), Bill Gray (6th), Jim (11th), Pirie (19th) and Pat Ranger (21st) did enough to overcome the strong home side, winning the title by a twenty-point margin. It proved one of the few times Jim would ever finish ahead of Pirie, but leading his country to success overshadowed all other considerations and the team returned across the Channel in high spirits.

They may have appointed him England captain, but Jim was in no mood to defer to the sport's big-wigs shortly afterwards. Word leaked out that an invitation for him to run in Germany had arrived at AAA HQ, but somebody in a position of power had turned it down without even consulting him. Jim and Johnny were both livid to discover that organisers of the 'Round Berlin Race' had been told Jim couldn't run as he had 'too many commitments'. In the 1950s athletes needed official approval to compete abroad, and would be accompanied on any trips by an AAA-appointed manager. Jim and Johnny knew this, but objected strongly to not being consulted about Berlin, and the episode led to an angry exchange of letters.

Upon the arrival of spring 1953, a good winter's training behind him, Jim focused on sharpening his speed. He enjoyed this period, and was pleased, not to mention surprised, to find himself chalking up the best track times of his life some five years after 'retiring' as a track athlete. With speedwork in mind, he targeted two six-milers in April and also tackled a two-miler on the track, clocking a lifetime best of 9:15. At Barking he ran a three-mile personal record, his 14:13.6 beating the visiting Australian champion Geoff Warren into second place.

That guest runner from Down Under, speaking to me nearly 60 years later, remembers the occasion well: 'I had just arrived in England from four weeks on board ship from Australia, where I trained by running thousands of short repetitions on the decks. I was invited to compete in the Essex Beagles three miles club championship where my main opponent was Jim Peters. I remember that struggling style of Jim's right from the start. He beat me clearly, but what I most remember was the feeling of vastness of the track and how fearfully far it seemed to get around it. During that trip I'd watched Jim win the Windsor-Chiswick marathon and saw how drained he appeared after the finish and believe this was common for him. My impression of Jim was that he was quite unpretentious, down to earth and friendly. Determined yet modest, as probably typifies most champions and serious marathoners who suffer for their sport. He seemed to have the ability to push himself to the limit in a race. He had a struggling, battling style and was forward-leaning and intense looking. He was always pretty excitable but if he felt nervousness before a race, and who doesn't, it didn't seem to affect his amiability. That head and arm movement lacked fluidity of motion, yet the whole impression was of working hard and showing it. Zatopek was also described as having an ugly style, but there is a kind of grace and beauty in a style that directs utmost energy to keeping those all-important running legs bowling along beneath. It was how they both applied their stamina and power and it made them impressive in motion.'

Having run well as a team in the London-to-Brighton southern qualifier the previous autumn, Jim and the Beagles looked forward immensely to the national final of the relays, even though they were weakened by the absence of Ted Baverstock, who was busy with botany exams. The event featured twenty teams and proved a real thriller throughout. George Knight gave Beagles a brief early lead on the road to Purley, but was passed before handing over to Andrews, who also lost a number of places. Dickie Douglas rescued things a little on Stage 3 and by the time Jim took over later the club were still in contention. Stage 7 (six miles, 206 yards) was an all-star show with Jim up against Pirie and Olney, the latter pair dead-heating in a stage record 29:05, thus beating Jim's 1952 record by thirteen seconds. In a headwind Jim ran an impressive 29:28 to bring Beagles up from tenth to sixth, a position they maintained to the end on Brighton sea-front, Thames Valley Harriers winning the 45-mile contest in 3:52.16.

The race created horrendous traffic problems, roads throughout clogged by support vehicles. One reporter was so outraged by the behaviour of the drivers he even published the registration number of what he called the worst offender, the South London Harriers team bus. This, inevitably, created a new storm, and SLH were quick to deny any bad behaviour. They admitted 'crawling' along the road for long periods, but only because they were caught up in traffic themselves.

Jim's display in the relays proved he was in great shape and on his return to track action a week later was delighted to post a personal best for six miles. It was a fine achievement at the age of 34, some eight years after first tackling the event seriously, and it came in front of a big White City crowd at the Southern Championships. The track was clogged by a huge field of 38 men, but Jim's 29:01.8 saw him clear in second place, with Pirie grabbing all the headlines with a magnificent 28:47.3, chopping eight seconds off his own GB record. Jim was the only runner to seriously press Pirie, but was shaken off at about halfway. Pirie went on to lap everybody except Jim at least once. Elsewhere on the same afternoon, Jim's event record at the Finchley 20 (1:49.39 in 1952) was given a good hiding on a slightly amended route by Billy McMinnis, the RAF PE instructor running for the St Helens club Sutton Harriers, who clocked 1:47.44.

News of Jim's Finchley record being consigned to history was followed 48 hours later by even more disturbing developments. It was reported that the tiny figure of Japan's Keizo Yamada had apparently beaten Jim's marathon best, running 2:18.51 at the annual Boston race in the USA. It was an astonishing time and was initially put down to help from a strong following wind, on a point-to-point course that drops from 220 feet to sea level.

The real reason would not be revealed until several years later, however – for the course would be found to be a shocking 1,183 yards short of the full distance. This explained everything, of course, but at the time nobody questioned the distance, and Jim and the rest of the world had to accept that Yamada and runner-up Karvonen had both beaten his 1952 Poly record. Jim would recall later: 'Far from being despondent about losing my record, this merely spurred me on to do more training and endeavour to be in the absolute peak of condition for the 1953 Poly, which was not far away.'

With perfect timing in terms of his marathon build-up, Jim could now turn his attentions to twenty-mile racing, a distance that suited him well, with the inaugural Southern Counties twenty-mile road championship being incorporated into the annual Mitcham 20 in early May. On familiar territory, Jim stormed off and led a field of 71 men after just 200 yards. In good conditions he tore round the three-lap course, building a big lead of 95 seconds over Geoff Iden by the five-mile point. He was in no mood to relax and at ten miles the astonished time-keepers declared he'd gone even quicker than the British best for a track ten. If this was hard to digest, there was more to come: at fifteen miles his time was reportedly better than the world track record for that distance. There was uncertainty over these stats, but what was never in doubt was that the athlete wearing No 103 was running like a man possessed and was on course for a sensational time. This was no easy course either, for the steep incline at Rose Hill had to be tackled three times.

He ultimately came home in 1:45.23, just over six minutes and one mile ahead of Iden, a time declared to be an unofficial world best for twenty miles. Ted Hefford of Woodford Green finished third, nearly twelve minutes behind. It was a fabulous time, and inevitably led to calls for the course to be re-measured. This was duly done and it was found to be 460 yards too long.

Jim and Johnny were naturally delighted, but annoyed over the inaccurate course: 'Here was a case where I had run an unofficial world's best time for twenty miles – and yet had had to run twenty and a quarter miles to do it. We both wondered just how track athletes would have felt and acted if their runs were inaccurate? If, for instance, McDonald Bailey had to run 105 yards every time he did the 100 yards sprint, or Roger Bannister was called on to race over one mile and ten yards – and then have their official times for the correct distances recorded as the one they had actually done over the longer ones.'

Bannister, incidentally, also enjoyed success that day, beating the 1937 mark of Sydney Wooderson to create a British all-comers mile record of 4:03.6 on the Iffley Road track in Oxford. It was Bannister's first serious attempt to run four even-paced laps and the outcome encouraged him that the world's first sub-four-minute mile was not out of his reach. It also galvanised the sporting press, who piled the pressure on the young doctor to get the job done soon. Give the British public an occasion that will never be forgotten, they demanded.

Noting Jim's recent good form, long-distance expert Arthur Newton suggested he should attempt a new one-hour record. Newton reckoned it was high time new figures were set for an event that involved running as far as possible in 60 minutes, using a standard 440-yard track. Although Zatopek had set a world best (twelve miles, 809 yards) in Czechoslovakia in 1951, the native English record was 69 years old, and the British all-comers mark 49 years old – set by Walter George (at Stamford Bridge) and Alf Shrubb (at Ibrox Park), respectively. Agreement was duly reached and *The News of the World* made arrangements for Jim's attempt to be staged on the White City track at 1pm on the second day of the British Games at the end of May. What nobody had bargained for was blazing hot weather that proved totally unsuitable for distance running.

Seven talented runners, including Walter Hesketh and Jim's training partner Robins, all looked distinctly uncomfortable as they lined up for the lunchtime start, the Whit Monday temperatures soaring unexpectedly to around 90 degrees Fahrenheit. Live BBC TV coverage of the meeting would commence at 1.50 so the nation could tune in and see how Jim was faring in the latter stages. This, combined with the expectations of a big excited crowd, meant Jim was under pressure to go ahead with the record attempt, even though conditions suggested it would be fruitless.

To his credit he gave it everything, the sun beating down mercilessly as he beetled around for lap after lap. A sympathetic groundsman took it upon himself to spray Jim with a hosepipe every time he passed, a well-meaning gesture, but one that might have led to disqualification later on, for the rules dictated no 'assistance' should be given to runners. Although he remained fully committed and never took his foot off the gas, Jim knew from early on that his plan to run five-minute-miles throughout could not succeed in these conditions: 'We couldn't have chosen a worse day for the record attempt … after the first mile I knew I never had a chance.'

Jim had roared off to complete the first mile in only 4:20.2, closely followed by Hesketh, and the average pace remained slightly under five-minute-miling for something like 27 laps. By this time Norris and McCooke had dropped out due to the heat, but Hesketh and Robins seemed determined to stick it out and keep Jim company. Hesketh began fading shortly after seven miles, just as the clock showed that Jim was falling behind the pace required to achieve twelve miles within the hour. Robins also lost ground, but rallied late on in an effort to help keep Jim going. Even knowing he couldn't beat Zatopek's mark, Jim ploughed on regardless, believing the domestic records were still within reach, trying to ignore discomfort from blisters that were getting more and more painful in the heat.

When the signal came that the hour was up, Jim knew he'd run somewhere between eleven and twelve miles, so kept running in order to record a time for twelve miles. Officials rushed over to mark his position when 60 minutes was reached. They announced eleven miles and 986 yards, which beat George's English native record by just 54 yards, but fell short of Shrubb's Glasgow effort by 151 yards. Jim ran on for the remaining 774 yards to record an English native record for twelve miles (62:02.2). Hesketh, Gray, Pape and Robins all finished the ordeal, but all fell short of completing eleven miles. Jim's split times were as follows:

1 mile – 4:20.2, 2 miles – 9:49.2, 3 miles – 14:48.2, 4 miles – 19:49.6, 5 miles – 24:58.2, 6 miles – 30:12.6, 7 miles – 35:29.2, 8 miles – 40:49.2, 9 miles – 46:13.6, 10 miles – 51:37.6, 11 miles – 57:02.8, 12 miles – 62:02.2.

While a parade of athletes entertained the crowd, Jim was grateful to sink exhausted on to the infield grass. Johnny and the St John ambulancemen quickly attended to his painful feet, removal of his shoes revealing spectacular blisters and red-raw skin. Jim was horrified to see the damage, for the Poly Marathon was only nineteen days away. His anxiety increased as he found his thigh muscles becoming stiff and very sore. The blisters were patched up and he hobbled to the changing rooms, later emerging to accept his winner's trophy from Mrs Jean Emsley Carr, wife of *The News of the World* chairman William.

He headed for home that evening in despondent mood, convinced he'd never recover fully in time for an optimum performance at the Poly. He even went as far as tipping McMinnis, Cox and Iden to take the first three places, pointing to their excellent form at the Finchley 20, where they'd all beaten his own course record.

The following day, his battered feet and legs forced him to miss a scheduled day's training for the first time in many months. The gloom deepened as he pondered on how he'd lost both his marathon world best (erroneous as it would turn out), as well as the Finchley record.

Had he made a disastrous error in agreeing to the White City one-hour run? If only he'd stuck to road work and woodland fartlek, these injuries would never have happened. If only the hour run had been in the cool of the evening and not at lunchtime. If only, if only …

CHAPTER 17

No Sex Please, I'm a Marathon Runner!

JUNE – DECEMBER 1953

Bad blisters, a thigh strain and the loss of his world record. Early June 1953 was not one of Jim Peters' happiest periods. But never for a moment did he seriously consider postponing his forthcoming marathon. Caution had never been among his watchwords.

Most runners would have rested, recovered and delayed any come-back until later in the summer. But the idea of interrupting his training programme and giving up his Poly Marathon crown was anathema to Jim. However unwise it might have seemed to outsiders, he vowed to get through the discomfort and be on that Windsor start-line, come what may. He wanted to complete a hat-trick of wins in this annual event, and another good time for his CV. His plan was to run four good-quality marathons in less than four months (113 days), and his stubborn nature refused to countenance any changes to that target.

The damage inflicted by 48 laps of the sun-baked White City track had been considerable, but just two days later he headed gingerly out of the optician's in Mitcham at lunchtime to complete six painful miles. Later that evening he dragged himself over to Hainault Forest and hobbled a slow and rather desperate ten miles. The punishment continued with identical runs over the next two days. To a non-runner, such behaviour would have seemed obsessive and bizarre. To Jim, there was grim satisfaction from fulfilling his training obligations and not falling behind schedule.

Training didn't even stop for the Queen's coronation on Tuesday, 2 June, a day which saw most of normal British life come to a grinding halt. Streets were deserted and silent, clusters of cars parked outside the houses where an 'H'-shaped TV aerial had drawn neighbours and friends inside. It was the greatest day of viewing in television's short history, but it didn't stop Jim Peters heading out from Havering Gardens for his daily mileage.

Albeit slowly, his injuries from White City began to heal a little, but did not entirely disappear. By Friday, 12 June, nearly three weeks after the twelve-miler, and only 24 hours before the Poly, Jim was still far from happy and not running with his usual freedom. It didn't help that his phone rang continually, mostly reporters checking his progress and asking if he would still run the Poly. On the eve of the race he retired to bed at 9pm, the phone covered in a sound barrier of cushions. He tossed and turned, worried sick that the following day would yield a sub-standard performance. His week of so-called 'easing down' had involved 70 miles, run at a good pace.

Marathon day was bright and cool. These ideal conditions meant the 119 runners streaming out of Windsor Great Park bound for Chiswick knew they couldn't blame the weather for any calamities that might befall them on the journey ahead. Uncharacteristically, Jim set off at a relatively sedate pace, his sore body giving him no other choice, but ironically running in the conservative fashion his critics had always urged.

It would take around seven miles before his early discomfort began to fade and his impatience ran out. Here he opened the throttle and soon pulled well clear of Stan Cox, a stunning three minutes ahead, just a few miles later. He was still a little behind record pace, but now moving nicely and perhaps with more in the tank due to the steady start. McMinnis, the sensation at the Finchley 20, couldn't reproduce his previous heroics and was having a bad day. Cox and Iden were running consistently, but a long way short of posing a serious challenge.

Between ten and twenty miles Jim's pace increased further, his thigh still a little stiff but the blistered feet no longer a problem, and the lead was extended to five minutes. It was becoming clear this was another very special performance as he motored through twenty in 1:45.05 – even faster than his stunning Finchley 20 win. Victory was no longer in any doubt, merely by how much. He duly rattled off the closing miles in style, hurtling into Chiswick Stadium and through the tape wreathed in smiles. He knew it had gone superbly over the last twenty miles, but, as before, had no idea of his time.

After a short wait, the formal announcement surprised all and sundry – not least Jim himself – revealing a new world best of 2:18.40. It was 84 seconds better than his own record, and 10.8 seconds better than Yamada's Boston effort (later to be discredited anyway). As happened a year ago, mayhem prevailed. Pressmen all wanted a piece of him, Jim anxious to satisfy them all but also to shake the hands of the runners who followed him in. Cox and Iden again posted fine runs (2:25.19 and 2:26.39) but found themselves well beaten, followed in by a steady stream, 68 men clocking under three hours.

The first four posed for photographers with Jim looking rather ill-at-ease clutching the spoils of victory in two boxes and wearing a bulky jacket over his shorts and singlet. Cox was wearing a dark, heavy tracksuit, while the others had only just crossed the line and were still in running kit. Once changed and making his exit from the stadium, Jim stopped

briefly to encourage the tailenders, generously acknowledging his respect
for these brave stalwarts. The era of the fun-run was still a long way off,
and the sight of slow, elderly runners on British roads was not common-
place in 1953. Jim was impressed: 'I have actually known men of 60 years
of age complete the course. They take as long as four hours sometimes,
but I have great admiration for their courage and perseverance … more
often than not they are the backbone of their clubs, always turning out,
always willing to make up a team and have a go.'

A small number of runners didn't make it as far as Chiswick, one of
these being German journalist Willy Wange, who had earlier irritated
British enthusiasts by casting doubts on the length of the Poly course and
therefore, by inference, discredited the best GB performances. Wange, by
now sounding a little more humble, explained he had come over to run
the course for himself, but was thwarted by stomach problems which
forced him out at halfway. He blamed this on the 'fried whale flesh' he
was fed by his English hosts before the race, a result of the general shortage of good meat over here.

Wange's first sight of Jim Peters in action provided an interesting perspective: 'He has a peculiar running style,' he wrote. 'He continuously
moves his body to and fro. He does not appear in any way cramped and,
on the contrary, has wonderful free and easy style. He runs not only with
his legs, but forces himself forward with the body.'

The British press reported that, thanks purely to Jim Peters, the
marathon had become the undisputed highlight of the annual Kinnaird
Trophy meeting at Chiswick. One reporter said Jim's latest display was
impossible to describe until somebody invented some new superlatives.
Typically, Jim took it all in his stride and didn't feel the need to use
superlatives; the remarks in his training log made it seem like just another race: 'Hung around for 6½ miles, then flogged it to 15, then pushed to
20. Felt OK except legs stiff.' As well as a master marathoner, he was
clearly a master of understatement too.

Johnny Johnston was not quite so calm. He condemned the fact that
here was another course found to be inaccurate (remeasurement showed
it was 156 yards too long), and reckoned his man should be given a time
around 28 seconds faster. *Athletics Weekly*, apparently unaware of Jim's ailments, said how pleasing it had been to see him taking it easier than usual
in the early stages instead of trying to run opposition into the ground. He
had now proved he was capable of piling on pace at any stage of a race,
they added.

It was a fascinating situation. Left to his own devices Jim employed
high-risk and seemingly irresponsible tactics – often succeeding superbly,

occasionally meeting with disaster. But now that he'd been forced to run in the way the experts advised, he'd produced a new world record in spite of carrying minor injuries. Geoff Dyson, the AAA national coach, entered the debate, saying it was significant that training methods had 'merged' in recent times, with Jim owing his success to lunchtime runs on a track and evenings on the road, whereas Gordon Pirie's track success was based on off-road work on Coulsdon Downs. It was indeed intriguing that Peters and Pirie, and one or two others, were reaping the rewards of high intensity training, whereas the 'Oxbridge types' (i.e. Bannister, Chataway, Brasher *et al*) were also excelling, but on very little training. Shortly after the Poly marathon, Pirie smashed the GB record at three miles (13:41.8), while Bannister ran the third-fastest mile of all time (4:02.2) at Motspur Park. Both young men were in terrific form, but in terms of philosophical outlook and *modus operandi*, could hardly have been more different.

Pirie's spectacular summer continued when he set a world record at six miles in the AAA championships on a cloudy Friday evening in July, his 28:19.4 making Jim's excellent 29:07.4 in fourth place look almost pedestrian. This run was part of Jim's preparations for his second marathon of the summer, the AAA championship event from Maindy Stadium in Cardiff. The time pleased him, showing there was plenty of speed in his legs despite the relentless workload that had seen 450 sessions completed over the past nine months. After finishing behind Pirie he went straight to congratulate him, the two men reassuring each other that their respective times would be sure to make the great Zatopek sit up and take notice.

A fortnight later Jim was collected by Johnny after finishing work in Mitcham and they set off by car for South Wales, planning to find overnight accommodation en route before the following day's AAA marathon. Johnny felt this was the best way to travel, avoiding a long rail journey, but by the time they reached the Welsh border area, things had started to go badly wrong.

After several fruitless hours calling at hotels and boarding houses that were full or closed, they finally secured a room in a small village on the crest of a hill and beside a main road. What they hadn't bargained for was continual heavy traffic creeping past through the night as it headed into England from Welsh steelworks. Jim recalled ruefully: 'As we lay in bed we could hear the whine of the engines getting louder and louder as they crawled up the steep incline. As they came nearer, their headlamps lit up the room and then, time and time again, the drivers crashed their gears in their eagerness to get back into top, and underneath our window was the place they chose to do it. By first light I don't think either of us had more than a few minutes sleep.' After dawn the steel lorries were supplemented by a fleet of military vehicles out on manoeuvres. It was hardly ideal preparation for a marathon, and Jim's mood didn't improve when this boarding house could only provide a meagre excuse for a breakfast.

Race day, Saturday, 25 July, saw torrential rain in the Cardiff area, and the track at the Maindy Stadium was partially flooded. Bearing in mind these conditions, the inappropriate build-up, and the fact he had two more tough marathons to face in the coming months, Jim and Johnny agreed he should take the first ten miles 'as easy as the opposition would let me'. It led to the unfamiliar sight of Jim tucking in behind the leading pack once the race got underway. A field of only 29 men set off on the journey around Roath Park and on to Tredegar Park, along the coast road, through St Bride's and Peterstone to Rumney, with the final few miles through Penylan and then back to the track via the main gates of the stadium. It was not a very hilly route, considering this was Wales, but the bad weather made up for this by giving runners a real buffeting.

Johnny, positioned at the roadside, urged Jim to continue running steadily when he passed by early on, but the pace felt so pedestrian Jim soon gave in to the urge to accelerate and create daylight between himself and the rest. Johnny worked hard trying to give Jim useful updates, but was hampered by mile markers apparently wrongly placed. It must have dawned on Jim that any information or estimates of his speed that he could glean, either from Johnny or other well-meaning spectators, was all mere guesswork.

At around halfway he was a long way clear, but found it hard going once directed off the main Cardiff-Newport road on to the narrow, winding coast road back to the stadium. There was a powerful headwind and most of the partisan spectators were shouting for Welshman Tom Richards, but just as Jim was coming to terms with these irritations, he hit a much more serious problem for a visiting Londoner – a herd of cows was blocking the road just around a blind bend.

'A great black-and-white cow suddenly loomed up in front of me and stood still, right in my path,' he reflected later. 'By this time, of course, I had covered nearly seventeen miles, was just about out on my feet and running almost mechanically. I don't think at that moment I could have swerved. I ran straight at her and pushed with my hand ... To me, who up to that moment had never touched a cow in my life, it was a horrifying experience.'

Shaken by this encounter with rural life, he pressed on, passing a second collection of cows in the road, and continued a bitter struggle with the powerful wind. Exhaustion was setting in, and, discounting his capitulation at Helsinki, this turned into his toughest marathon to date. A 400-yard incline in the closing stages proved a real problem, and Jim would admit here he suffered 'acute strain and distress' unlike anything in previous races.

Into the stadium he chugged, to an enthusiastic welcome from a small crowd, crossing the line in 2:22.29, which was well short of his best, but a magnificent effort in the circumstances, and a massive seven minutes faster than runner-up Alan Lawton of Leeds Harehills AC. The tenth man home, Ron Hopcroft (TVH), would be an incredible 22 minutes slower. Johnny would later call this, Jim's sixth attempt at the marathon, his greatest of them all, given the difficulties posed by the conditions.

His distress after crossing the line was immediately obvious and he had to be hustled away to deal with a sudden attack of diarrhoea. Lying on his back in the changing rooms, Jim was clearly unwell, and Johnny refused to allow him back outside to receive the AAA championship trophy. As usual he craved fluid, but was unable to keep even small amounts down. He presented a pitiful sight, and the youngsters who crept in to ask for autographs must have been shocked by what they saw.

After a while he felt a little stronger, but it was a white-faced and frail-looking champion who was helped away to the home of a nearby army friend who was to put him up for the night: 'He and his wife were convinced they had a very sick man on their hands and it would be a miracle if I were alive in the morning,' recalled Jim.

Survive the night he did, and a hearty breakfast saw normal service resumed. Jim reassured all well-wishers he was fine, and that his coach's 'commando-style' training methods gave him remarkable powers of recovery as well as helping his running. Within a few days he was in full training again and even accepted an invitation to run for Britain against France at White City – just nine days after the Cardiff marathon. Considering how unwell and drained he'd been on the evening of 25 July, to run a world-class track race on 3 August seemed at best unwise, and at worst reckless. But Jim was never the type to turn down an invitation to run for Queen and country, and his main concern was not his own well-being, but not letting the nation down.

He was answering an SOS to race against France, for Gordon Pirie, Walter Hesketh and Scotsman Ian Binnic had all withdrawn from the six miles. Officials were in a state of panic until he agreed to partner Frank Sando against the French pair Alain Mimoun and Alain Soucours. On a fine day, 3,000 were in the stands for Day Two of the match, and they saw Jim take the race by the scruff of the neck, running as fast as he ever had on a track early on. Sando matched him for a while before fading, but then the classy Mimoun eased past to record a fine victory in 28:37.6, Jim's strong 29:06.6 gaining him second. Afterwards, fellow athletes expressed disbelief that he'd run so well so soon after Cardiff, and he told them: 'It's the constant hard training. I had trained for speed and basically it didn't matter whether the speed was required over six or 26 miles.'

Wife Frieda wasn't quite as impressed as his contemporaries. She wisely ordered him to ease back immediately and insisted it was time for their first summer holiday in five years. Jim always struggled with the concept of taking life easy, and admitted his avoidance of holidays was due to his inability to relax. Most of all, he hated the idea of interrupting his training, particularly as he had agreed to run marathons in Holland and Finland during the autumn. But even Johnny agreed with Frieda and eventually the family packed their bags and headed for the beaches of Scarborough in mid-August. Jim craftily sneaked some training kit into his suitcase, just in case an opportunity to run presented itself.

On the very first day of the trip he had to slip away to Driffield where he'd agreed to present prizes at a club event, and then endured six days without any running at all. But Frieda relented midway through the holiday and granted the concession of pre-breakfast runs from their boarding house. It was quite a relief for her hyperactive husband, and suddenly the whole idea of a holiday didn't seem quite so bad after all.

It probably didn't help Jim's state of mind while away to read in the papers about 23-year-old Ian Binnie's performance at a twelve-mile track race at the Cowal Highland Games in Dunoon. The Scot ran eleven miles and 1,571 yards in 60 minutes, succeeding where Jim had failed by beating Alf Shrubb's ancient British record.

Binnie was a prodigious trainer in the Peters mould, who was gaining a reputation as a lively and rebellious character. Fellow runners would tell the story of how he once persuaded a small boy on a bike to carry his baton for him during a relay race. Angry officials amended the rules afterwards to state: 'The baton must be carried.' Undaunted, Binnie then had a pocket sewn into his vest to stow batons until hand-over time. The rules again had to be amended: 'The baton must be carried … in the hand.'

On another occasion Binnie is said to have been phoned by the AAA who wanted him to run for Britain: 'Binnie old boy, we want you to run at the White City in the 5,000 metres. England needs you,' announced the well-spoken official, unaware of his fatal error. The reply was abrupt: 'I'm Scottish and my mince and tatties are getting cold. Goodbye.'

Upon Jim's return from the seaside he had barely a fortnight to prepare for the Enschede Marathon on Saturday, 12 September. But once again, his anxiety not to let people down saw him agree to help out Essex Beagles at the Louis Trophy meeting at Mayesbrook Park, Barking just seven days before the marathon. Risking blisters by wearing flimsy track spikes on a warm day, he turned out and helped Beagles to victory, winning his three-mile race with ease in a routine 14:25, lapping all but three men in a big field of 27. Fortunately the feet suffered no undue damage. He felt fit and well for the Dutch adventure and met fellow invitee Stan Cox and their appointed 'team manager' Jack Crump at London Airport for the flight over the North Sea. The trio were put up in a small boarding house, given a sumptuous meal and retired just after midnight. There was just one bedroom and Crump's loud snoring only served to exacerbate the two runners' irritation at having to travel with an athletics official, rather than with their own coach, which would have been far more beneficial. It hardly helped when they were then woken in the early hours by the noise of Crump struggling to replace a partition wall which had somehow collapsed beside his bed.

Arriving at Enschede by train the next day, they were greeted by news that their two strongest opponents – Corno of Argentina and Karvonen of Finland – had both withdrawn, weakening the field considerably. But Jim still felt motivated to post a top-class time, if only to silence the sceptics among the continental sporting press, who seemed to believe Britain's marathon courses were short or 'easy'. Nevertheless, as had sometimes happened in the past, he approached the race feeling nervous and pessimistic – not entirely sure if his sluggishness was down to a lack of sleep, or to general tiredness from recent high mileage.

After light rain ceased, a variety of nations were represented by the 55 or so who set off on this flat course, beginning with two laps of a grass track. Dutch champion Janus Van de Zande accompanied Jim and Stan at the front early on, going through ten kilometres together in 32:57. Although they were setting a cracking pace, Jim was again deliberately curbing his instinct to get ahead and clear of the pack. Was he growing older and wiser perhaps?

At around thirteen kilometres the leaders began splitting up, Jim opening a gap of 30 yards on Stan, with the Dutchman falling back. Twenty kilometres saw Jim clock a nifty 65:01, by now virtually a minute in the clear, the rest beginning to look out of contention. Positions remained unaltered as he passed halfway in an impressive 68:00, a statistic that apparently engendered disbelief among the continental press corps. Having turned for home, a strong headwind added a new dimension to the battle and at one point Stan appeared in difficulties, but after rubbing his leg and taking a drink, he pressed on strongly.

Looking untroubled, Jim sped back alone into the stadium in good shape, smiling broadly as his reappearance was greeted by a trumpet fanfare and a roar from the big crowd. The clock showed 2:19.22, meaning it was the fastest marathon ever run on an out-and-back course. He was delighted to have gone so close (41.8 seconds) to his own world record – particularly on continental soil – and had easily beaten the course record held by Karvonen, in addition to Zatopek's Olympic best. Those who had questioned Britain's recent achievements in the marathon would have to eat their words. Jim felt so pumped he even found the energy to run over and cheer in runner-up Stan, whose 2:24.38 was more than five minutes adrift, but still eleven ahead of third-placed Viktor Olsen of Norway. Stan had lost out to Jim yet again, but at least he could reflect on the best 1953 marathon time by any Englishman apart from his nemesis.

The two Brits enjoyed the presentation ceremony, a drawn-out affair during which the national anthem was played and flowers and trophies handed out: 'We felt we had struck quite a powerful blow for English long-distance running,' said Jim. News emerged that fourth finisher Van de Zande had been spotted having a massage at twenty miles, but after much discussion nobody bothered to register a protest. Later the trophy winners were whisked off to what Jim described as a 'barn dance', where he was presented with an enormous cake. With great regret he had to refuse it, explaining it wouldn't have fitted inside the plane home. On the journey back to the airport, the two runners and their manager stopped off at an Amsterdam restaurant for a rare treat involving lashings of grilled chicken and trimmings, which cost the BAAB the equivalent of 28 shillings a head. It was the type of luxury Jim and Stan never even dreamed about in austere post-war England. The occasion was rather spoiled, however, when Jack Crump gave them gifts from the BAAB for their wives. Recalls Stan: 'He produced two little carrier bags from under the table and inside each was half-a-piece of Edam cheese worth a few pence!'

Jim's fourth and final marathon of what was turning into a vintage year would be in Turku, Finland, the following month. Jim was desperate to post another top-class time, for he regarded this nation as the scene of his greatest failure (in the 1952 Olympics). His target was to win well here, and then return to the Continent a year hence and lift the 1954 European title in Berne. It had been announced that the Berne marathon would be staged early on the timetable, a consequence of which was that Zatopek was unlikely to run, instead sticking to 5,000 and 10,000 metres track events. So Jim knew if he could maintain current form for another year, the path was wide open to his becoming European champion.

Essex Beagles were proud to hear the good news from Enschede, and at their annual meeting soon afterwards – in the Beaulah Hall, Church Road, Barking – the secretary pronounced the season just ending a momentous one in the history of their club: 'In the words of Jim Peters we have turned the corner and can look with pride on the fact that this club has returned to its former glories. We have ceased to be a Cinderella club and in every sense of the word we are a force to be reckoned with'. He added that the finest attributes of 'the wearers of the black-and-amber vest' was their gentlemanliness and sportsmanship.

Jim was aware that his final marathon commitment of the year – coming just three weeks after Enschede – was a little too close for comfort even for him, and admitted publicly that his training and racing programme had been 'extremely strenuous' in 1953. He said he was treating the whole exercise as an experiment, to see if he could pull off two fast times in a short period.

Sponsored by daily newspaper *Turun Sanomat*, the Turku race toured the birthplace of Paavo Nurmi, and showcased this historic city on the Gulf of Bothnia in its attractive setting at the mouth of the Aurajoki, sheltered by a number of larger islands and a swarm of skerries. It was an eye opener for the British visitors to discover Turku had no fewer than seventeen cinder running tracks within its boundaries, which was seventeen more than most British towns of comparable size. At this point, Britain could only boast 93 tracks in total, and half of these were not for public use. A new, cheaper way of laying tracks had recently been proposed to deal with this problem.

With the Finnish athletic authorities unable to afford the expense of hosting a British team manager, it had been grudgingly agreed for Jim to travel to Scandinavia alone – as long as he went directly to Finland and met an appointed chaperone after arrival. The rest of the foreign entrants would have a more restful trip, stopping over in Stockholm *en route*.

On the Wednesday before the race Jim awoke early, went for a ten-mile spin in Hainault Forest (a nippy 56:20), had breakfast and headed for the airport. A delay-plagued trip followed, and he confessed later the stress of it all led to a sleepless first night in Finland, his mind spinning with paranoia about being so close to the Russian border. Immediately after arrival he had amazed his hosts by heading off for a training run instead of accepting a welcoming meal. He also politely declined what was apparently a serious enquiry over whether he required female company for the night.

An escort wasn't required, but Jim did accept a huge steak dinner. It was an unfamiliar pre-race feast which later hampered his attempts to sleep and made him violently sick. It was not the first time he would be tackling a marathon on the back of less-than-ideal preparations the night before.

Around 50 runners assembled next day in good weather conditions, ready to tackle a figure-of-eight course over bumpy cobbled roads early on, followed by pleasant forest scenery. Each runner was accompanied by a young Finnish soldier on a bicycle, equipped with water, sponges and other aids. Jim established an early lead, baffling his cyclist by constantly turning down offers of assistance until after halfway when he finally took a sponge. By this time he was well clear of Veikko Karvonen, the home favourite, and the only other man in the race with any form to speak of. The second half of proceedings were on improved surfaces, encouraging Jim to accelerate and reel off a 'negative split', his second thirteen miles quicker than the first. He was in a class of his own, Karvonen a long way adrift.

Returning to the stadium more than a mile in the clear, he found the final stages involved no fewer than twelve laps to be run around the outside of the track, in front of a crowd delirious at the prospect of seeing a world record. Although he didn't feel excessively tired at first, having to circle the track so many times at the end of a long road run soon turned into torture: 'There must have been something psychological about my physical reaction to those twelve laps ... for the first I felt fine, but the other eleven were sheer agony,' he revealed afterwards.

With around five of the circuits done, second-placed Karvonen entered stage left. He was a massive seven minutes behind, but his mere presence seemed to increase the pressure on Jim, who was struggling hard to maintain form, and not fully aware how close he was to a world record. During the final agonising 200 yards somebody ran across and placed an enormous wreath around his neck, which cannot have helped, and he loped heavy-footed across the line in a new world best of 2:18.34.8.

The time was a mere 5.4 seconds inside his own record, and the first of his three world bests to be set outside London. As a fierce patriot, doing the job abroad was particularly pleasing, and the race officials seemed equally excited by the outcome. For Jim, the crowning moment of the entire trip came shortly afterwards when their spokesman announced he'd been 'an excellent ambassador for England'. This modest working-class hero felt prouder than ever as these words were translated to him.

As far as the big picture was concerned, Jim's achievement had been monumental. Not only had he created another world best, he had run four marathons in the space of eighteen weeks at an average of around 2:19.00 each, a speed that had never been bettered in a single run by any other Briton to that point. His one regret was that this sensational form had come a year too late for Olympic glory. Four major marathon victories in one season was an unprecedented achievement, and conquering Enschede and Turku so close together convinced him it would be possible to run both championship marathons the following year (Vancouver and Berne, 25 days apart), no matter how much the experts advised against it. And, what was more, he also had a fancy for running the Boston Marathon a month or two earlier in 1954.

'Now I need never hold my head low before a Finn again,' he commented to a British reporter, revealing the extent of his 1952 Olympic hurt. 'My only regret is that Zatopek wasn't here [in Turku], as I was in the mood to beat him.'

Runner-up Karvonen, perhaps affected by exhaustion and his well-known shyness, posed briefly for pictures alongside Jim, but didn't attempt conversation and quickly vanished, telling local reporters he'd been humiliated in front of his own people, and vowing one day he would turn the tables on Jim Peters.

After sending a reassuring telegram to his wife, who would be worrying about him back in Chadwell Heath, Jim retired to bed in a Helsinki hotel late that night, flying home early the next morning. Expecting to be treated as a returning hero and met by excited pressmen and an athletics official or two, he was disappointed to find no familiar faces at all – apart from coach Johnny, who had taken the morning off work to meet him: 'I didn't actually want any fuss, but I do admit I thought it would have been a nice gesture for just one other person to have been there. I was the official British representative in the race and had managed a new record,' he wrote ruefully afterwards. One newspaper agreed with this wholeheartedly, pointing out that had Jim been a New Yorker he'd have been given a ticker-tape welcome on Broadway, and if he had been Zatopek, there would have been traffic jams and vast crowds in Prague to greet him.

It may have been a low-key return, but at least the AAA's records committee acknowledged Jim's efforts, confirming that 25 new English native records had just been ratified, nine of them credited to Gordon Pirie and four to Jim (his eleven and twelve mile marks at the one-hour event, plus two marathon times).

Normal training resumed for Jim 48 hours after the marathon, but his plan to enjoy a quiet week without competition quickly went by the board. His club persuaded him to make up the numbers at the London-to-Brighton relay on Saturday, 10 October, and he agreed on condition he was given 'an easy stage' that would pit him against the weakest runners of opposition teams. Superb runs by the Beagles early runners – George Knight, Don Corney, Dick Douglas, Johnny Mercer, Reg Robins and Alan Murray-Carter – kept Beagles in the top three before Ted Baverstock took them up to second behind Polytechnic Harriers. As Jim grabbed the baton, the lead was down to a matter of seconds. This was like a red rag to a bull. Beagles had never won this relay final before and Jim forgot about any lingering tiredness from Finland and belted after the Polytechnic man Tillotson on the eighth stage. He got past him within a mile and took Beagles into a big lead, clocking a 19:34 record for this four miles and 82 yards stage. Bernie Hames and then Terry Learmouth saw the Essex boys into Brighton with their noses still in front, winning by 400 yards to lift *The News of the World* trophy. The ice cream on the Prom had never tasted so good.

Just a week or two earlier, the remarkable South African Wally Hayward had run all the way from London to Brighton on his own, pulverising the individual record with a time of 5:29.40. Hayward and his runner-up Jackie Mekler were later introduced to Jim at a South London Harriers dinner and amazed to hear the Englishman claim he could comfortably beat Hayward's new record, had he the inclination to try for it. According to Mekler: 'Jim Peters reasoned that as he was now running 26-milers in 2:18, he could comfortably string two together at say 2:30 each, add about ten minutes, and that would give him 5:10 for London to Brighton. We couldn't believe he was serious and none of us accepted this logic, but it gave me an insight into Jim's mental approach to distance running.'

During the same trip to the UK, Wally Hayward would also annexe the 100-mile record on the Bath-to-London route (12:20.28), plus the 24-hour track record, covering a mammoth 159 miles and 562 yards. To circle the Motspur Park track 637 times in the allotted 24 hours, 45-year-old Hayward needed to scoff two pounds of sugar, a pint of tomato soup, a pint of milk, sixteen eggs and several oranges.

With no apparent ill-effects from his incredible season, Jim raced frequently for the Beagles during the autumn and closing weeks of 1953. His club was in better shape than ever and followed its Brighton relay success with victory at the Essex equivalent, the Sidney C Taylor relays at Chelmsford, staged from the Rainsford Secondary school. The six Beagles covered the eighteen miles in 1:33.11 to win by nearly three minutes, Jim chalking up the quickest time of the day. Then, a week after his 35th birthday, he shrugged off a midweek foot problem and headed into

Suffolk to beat his own record at the annual road match with Ipswich Harriers, covering the 4½ miles in 21:56.5.

In mid-November he was one of a three-man England team at the 4½-mile international cross-country in Antwerp, staged by Royal Beerschot AC. At the head of a large field, Van de Wattyne of AS Reinax led for much of the race but Jim remained handily placed and with 900 yards left burst past to win by 26 seconds in 22:36. Teammate Dennis Holden of Cambridge Harriers put up a good show further back, but this would prove to be one of his last races before being ordered to quit after x-rays revealed a shadow on his lung.

A month after Antwerp there was more international action when Jim returned to the Aycaguer event at Lyons, coming second in a field of 300 behind teammate Bill Boak. Soon after the start Jim felt a sharp pain from his heel, which caused him to drift out of the top ten, but the discomfort wore off and he battled back and held off Frenchman Soucours by the width of his vest to claim second. It was back to muddy Chingford a few days later where Grafton AC, the club for Jewish athletes, staged their eighteenth annual Friendship Cup contest and Jim again had to settle for second spot, beaten by Hampstead insurance broker Harry Hicks by 100 yards. Ted Baverstock and George Knight came in close behind, meaning Beagles retained the cup to end the year in celebratory style.

And so another high mileage year ended, this a real vintage twelve months for Jim Peters, now firmly established as the world's top marathoner, and no longer hurting quite so much about his Olympic disaster of 1952.

'Jim is planning another three years of punishment', reported one national paper, although admitting he hadn't confirmed his definite intent to aim for the 1956 Olympics in Melbourne. The final three months of 1953 had seen Jim cover a phenomenal 1,350 miles in training and racing, and he planned a further 3,650 in the first eight months of 1954 – taking him up to the European Championships. He told the paper he wanted to increase his weekly mileage from 100 to around 140 during 1954, in order to be training on a par with Zatopek.

The England football team had just been humiliated 3-6 by Hungary at Wembley, but sports fans could take comfort from the knowledge that by the end of 1953 the nation's best athletes were developing into genuine world-beaters. And their marathon hero was certainly not letting the grass grow, planning yet more records and even bigger victories.

CHAPTER 18

'Train Till Your Eyeballs Fall Out'

CHRISTMAS 1953

'Vintage' doesn't really begin to describe it. The year of 1953 had gone like a dream for Jim Peters. His marathon exploits between the June and October are regarded more than half a century later as the most remarkable sequence of results by a single individual in the event's history. And to cap it all, he also made the history books by becoming the first Englishman to win international vests for road, track and cross-country all in the one year.

He was so busy racing and setting records that the year had flashed by, with little opportunity for reflection on what he'd achieved. So how did he regard this golden period with the benefit of hindsight? Years later he would tell the American newspaper *Stars and Stripes*:

'There was no mucking around. I was [training] 80 to 120 miles a week, broken down into 11 to 13 timed sessions. I was running [them] at a 5:00 or 5:15 pace. And I always ran shorter distance club-level races. You see, jogging will never make a champion. I had a terrible rolling-gait style – they used to say "If he's rolling he's all right" – and my head went back and forth. But I'll tell you what – Johnny Johnston took a film of my leg action and said don't be fooled by anything above the legs. Apparently my power was all in my legs and I never used to raise them much off the ground. The other secret was deep breathing. Once I got into an even pattern of running, I'd take a deep breath and hold it as long as I could. I'd do this over and over for five minutes or so, and that increased the size of my lungs.'

'When I used to line up I'd give myself a psychological examination. I'd say: "Have you done your training? Been living a good honest life? Been behaving like a monk?" If you can answer yes to those questions then you've just got to be a man, take your punishment and go out there and win your race.'

Both Jim and his coach had become aware of the importance of getting his mind in good shape as well as his body. He was a relentless marathon machine, but he wasn't the brainless automaton that some critics seemed to believe. He told *World Sports* magazine in late 1953: 'All the training in the world will alone not make a champion. He must have determination, the ability to fight and take punishment, and still come up smiling. He must also have a racing brain and mind of his own … must have boldness and a sense of purpose to know just what he can do in one season.'

Although he wasn't the type to crave praise, there remains an oft-held view that Jim rarely got the acclaim he deserved following his unprecedented achievements of 1953 and beyond. Marathoner Don Macgregor, a 1972 Olympian, says: 'While his place in running history is secure, I feel Jim didn't receive the acclaim that would surround him nowadays, where second-rate footballers are treated as superstars and money is the measure of so much. This is due partly to the zeitgeist which back then regarded sport as recreational, which it should be, and partly to Jim's own reticent character. His achievements over his peak years were stupendous. I also suspect he didn't get the write-ups he might have because of class distinction. The Achilles dominance of international UK teams was coming to an end then, but there was still an attitude of *de haut en bas* snobbery towards "lower-class or other ranks" athletes, especially distance runners, which is clear, whether expressed or not, in contemporary adulatory articles about the golden boys of that era. Peters was older than most of the other athletes in these teams, being born in 1918, so had little in common with the twenty-somethings in the more glamorous events.'

The class divide was evident in athletics in the 1950s in a number of ways. Runners from working class backgrounds firmly believed those who 'moved in the right circles' would always get on better in the sport. The 'us and them' syndrome was fundamentally based on a competitor's social and educational background, but geography was also a factor. Among those carrying a chip on his shoulder about all this was Bill Gray, the Midlands cross-country champion, who spoke for many based north of London when he said southern athletes were favoured by the authorities. He said athletes like Gordon Pirie moved in the right circles, and therefore benefited when it came to selection issues and matters such as obtaining time off work. Mancunian Walter Hesketh told Pirie's biographer Dick Booth the pro-southern attitude in the 1950s was part of a selection bias that had several layers: 'A northerner would have to run themselves into the team, because they would always pick a southerner in preference. And we believed that they would always choose a university man over a non-university man, and the people from Oxford and Cambridge over the rest.'

For the most part, marathon running didn't appeal to Oxbridge types in the post-war era, for there still remained an element of the attitude that 'gentleman amateurs' ran purely for enjoyment and it was not the done thing to be seen training hard. This mentality was changing, but only slowly. Athletics was still being administered largely by old-school types and Jim Peters had his fair share of run-ins with them, although it was not in his nature to make enemies or court controversy. A speech he made at the Sports Writers Association did stir things up in late 1953 (see below), however, but generally he rubbed along quite well with officials like Jack Crump. Often if there was a protest or a complaint to be made, it would be left to coach Johnny to speak up on his behalf.

The athletics authorities contributed little or nothing towards Jim's development as a distance runner, for he devised his own training and simply got on with it, but of course they were able to bask in the success he was now having on the international stage. According to distance-running historian Andy Milroy, Britain's sudden emergence as a world marathon force at this time had its roots in the war years. He says: 'What is interesting is that in Britain, you actually had new distance races on the road starting up during the war years – for example the Dundee-to-Perth 22-miler, the SLH 30-miler – as well as the Poly Marathon being contested right through the war. This was done as much for morale as sporting reasons, I suspect. However it did have the effect of giving British marathon running in the early 1950s a flying start compared with the rest of the world.'

The way Jim had steered British marathon running to a new level with his original ideas on training and preparation had by now become a matter of endless fascination to the sporting media. Over the 1953 Christmas period he was visited by Alan Hoby of *The Sunday Express*, who wanted to find out what domestic life was like in a household occupied by such an extraordinary individual. Witnessing Jim heading out for a run on a bleak and bitter December night, Hoby would wax lyrical about 'one of the most murderous training schedules drawn up by man'.

Rising to the occasion, Jim provided the type of sound-bite he knew journalists loved: 'You've got to train until your eyeballs fall out,' he announced, revealing to his astonished visitor that he'd clocked up 30 miles of running in three outings on Christmas day itself. This had been largely possible because services pal Bob Pape and family were staying at his Chadwell Heath house for the holiday, meaning the two men could slip out to run without complaint from wives and children.

During the one week of the year in which normal people put their feet up to enjoy plum pudding, mistletoe and wine, Jim Peters was cramming in 120 miles through bog, fog, snow, hail, sleet, rain, wind and thunderstorm.

Hoby was awestruck by it all, adding: 'Falls are common. When he returned from one particular run I noticed his legs were covered with scratches. He came loping out of the darkness, head rolling, vest saturated, breath rasping. Then suddenly he let out a shrill whistle and inside the Peters house his wife – who had been timing the run, her nightly chore – shut off the stopwatch. The front door opened, Peters ran upstairs. Next moment he was relaxing in the hot bath which his wife had drawn ready for him.'

Jim expounded his personal training theories that same week in an *Athletics Weekly* column, saying it had been a fine year for English runners, but nobody should reach for their carpet slippers and relax over winter 1953-54, for other countries, notably Australia and Scotland, were making great progress too. He said all the publicity about his 'blood, sweat and tears' training had produced a diverse mailbag, some of the letter-writers extremely critical of his methods, while others admired his courage and determination.

Jim's uncompromising methods, plus those of Zatopek in Czechoslovakia, were slowly winning friends and influencing people across the globe. After his European tour of earlier and that infamous close encounter with Jim Peters, coach Percy Cerutty returned to Australia to preach the gospel of hard work and 100 per cent commitment in the manner of an American evangelist. The miler John Landy recalls: 'Cerutty's basic message at that time was right. You could train consistently and in fact just get stronger. In this he anticipated the theories of people like Hans Selye, which shows that the body can adapt to repeated stresses.' Landy told author Len Johnson: 'You have to see Cerutty in the context of a time when coaches were greatly concerned about over-training, about becoming stale, muscle-bound or even being burnt out by doing too much. Two or three days a week of about an hour or so for each session was about the limit.'

Nevertheless, it is fascinating to look back and see that Jim's critics were not silenced, even by the unprecedented success he enjoyed in 1953. Harold Abrahams, for one, remained convinced Jim's great results had come about despite his heavy training, and not because of it. Abrahams had earlier suggested that, with no major international championships in 1953, Jim should reduce his mileage and workload to see how he would fare with less training. This proposition, inevitably, fell on deaf ears, and Jim felt such views were blasted out of the water by the tremendous victories he enjoyed. But still Abrahams refused to concede ground: 'The trouble is that what Jim has done doesn't really prove him right and me wrong. All it does prove is that he can produce these magnificent results this way. It does not prove that he could not have produced the same, or even better results another way.'

The ubiquitous Abrahams, a double Olympic medallist, administrator, journalist and BBC commentator, didn't even seem particularly impressed by the rallying call Jim issued when speaking at the Sports Writers Association's annual dinner in London. Jim warned the distinguished audience that an immense task lay before British sport if it was to avoid complete annihilation by Iron Curtain countries, whose morale had just been boosted by the Hungarian football success at Wembley.

'We must train till our eyeballs pop out. We have the men to do it, but the time has come when we amateurs must have help [from the authorities]. We have the guts, but the other countries have the facilities,' he said. With his audience wilting under the intense heat of TV lights, Jim tackled his speech like a marathon and ploughed on with startling passion and conviction, even raising the thorny topic of 'shamateurism'. He pointed out: 'It is no use arguing with the Iron Curtain countries about amateurism. We will never get anywhere if we just say we won't compete with them because they are not proper amateurs. I don't agree with the system, but we must face the facts.'

At this time, the AAA still vigorously enforced the code of amateurism, coming down hard on anybody who 'in any way exploits his athletic ability for profit'. However, standards of performance were improving dramatically around the globe, which inevitably meant athletes needed to devote more time and effort to training. In Britain it wasn't going unnoticed that many opponents from abroad were assisted by their athletics authorities, and were able to prepare for competition in conditions much more favourable. Yet leading GB talents like Jim Peters were expected to abide by strict rules, but left to their own devices over matters such as training and preparation. No wonder there was growing tension.

Warming to his theme at the SWA dinner, Jim said: 'Zatopek does his twenty miles a day comfortably while working as an Army officer. But I am a professional man and have to travel 25 miles to and from my work every day, and my training is done mostly in the evening. I have put up some of my best times on a Saturday afternoon after doing a morning's work and then dashing straight off to Windsor or wherever I have to race. But there are only 24 hours in the day and in addition to my job and my training I must have ten hours sleep.'

His call for better support for GB athletes and for investment in better facilities was warmly received by the audience, one newspaper the next morning calling it a 'brilliant speech straight from the heart'. It was certainly the main talking point from an event where other famous speakers included Alec Bedser (cricket) and Mike Hawthorn (motor racing), and the most distinguished guest had been none other than Lord Burghley, President of the AAA itself.

The speech underlined that Jim was no longer the shrinking violet of yesteryear and that he was coming to terms with his nationwide fame. He understood the curiosity of complete strangers about his training and his lifestyle, and was only too happy to dish out advice and tips. One topic that would recur in this respect was his choice of footwear. What on earth did a man running 120 miles a week put on his feet? Did he have access to special footwear to cope with the pounding he was giving his lower legs?

The answer to the latter question was, of course, in the negative. This was an era long before athletes could sign shoe sponsorship deals and, even though he was the world's fastest marathoner, Jim Peters still had to go down to his local Woolworths store and buy his running shoes there. To most folk, they weren't even running shoes at all. They were simple rubber-soled gym or tennis shoes, widely known as 'plimsolls' and usually made by Dunlop. He would pick out a fairly stout pair for training needs, and keep two or three pairs on the go simultaneously, as a means of reducing wear and to enable them to be 'worn in' gradually. A lighter-weight version would be used for races and he would also create small sponge inserts that would act as shock absorbers and lessen the jarring to his joints from all the road miles. These shoes usually lasted several hundred miles each. Runners liked them, for compared to normal leather walking shoes they felt comfortable and flexible due to their canvas uppers, which were also seen to absorb perspiration. In addition, Jim would generally run in woollen socks, with a minimum of darning and seams, plus a few smears of Vaseline at the toes and soles to minimise the risk of blisters.

He confessed that occasionally he would switch his left and right plimsolls in order to extend their usefulness during heavy training periods: 'It was bloody uncomfortable, but you got extra wear,' he explained. In one interview he reckoned he never paid more than ten shillings for a pair (converts to approximately £10 in 2011 terms), and fellow marathon man Jack Fitzgerald of Mitcham confirms that in the early 1950s the majority of club runners also bought their plimsolls from 'Woolies' and paid around 8s 11d (44p) a pair.

South African ultra champion Jackie Mekler ran against Jim a number of times, and recalls the shoes they wore: 'I believe it was Arthur Newton who first worked out that these shoes needed extra in the heel, and he glued on a piece of crepe rubber to serve this purpose. The heel usually wore out first, but this could easily be replaced. I kept one special well worn-in pair for racing, cutting off any surplus material to keep it as light as possible. Some models had a thin rubber insole, but a cheaper version was also available. We found the Koreans were using a leather version with a separate compartment for the big toe which they believed gave a better gripping action, while the other toes merely acted as stabilisers. Jim Peters always used socks, which we South Africans never did. We merely rubbed soap inside our shoes to create a sliding rather than rubbing action.'

This type of shoe had first appeared in the 19th century, designed mainly for beachwear, and acquired the nickname plimsoll because the coloured horizontal band joining the upper to the sole resembled the plimsoll line on a ship's hull. They became standard kit for school PE lessons and over the years acquired different names according to region. In Northern Ireland and central Scotland they were 'gutties', in parts of the West Country and Wales they were 'daps' (an acronym of Dunlop Athletic Plimsolls), Australians called them 'sandshoes', South Africans knew them as 'tackies', in the USA they were 'sneakers' and in India 'Keds'.

The Keds shoe company had begun selling them in America on a mass scale after the 1914-18 war, by which time specialist running spikes for track use had already been around for several years. British company Foster & Sons (later to become Reebok) developed the earliest running shoes with spiked soles, while in the inter-war years the German Adi Dassler created shoes with hand-forged spikes, with different models for different distances, using state-of-the-art materials to make them as light as possible. It wouldn't be until the 1960s that shoe technology began to boom, with podiatrists and other boffins taking serious account of how humans ran, and the effect of impact on the joints.

In the early 1950s Jim Peters and his cronies rarely grew frustrated or concerned about their primitive training shoes, simply because they'd never known anything better.

CHAPTER 19

On the Floor in Boston

JANUARY – JUNE 1954

As if he didn't have enough on his plate, the important double championship year of 1954 opened for Jim Peters with an eccentric Scotsman noisily predicting his downfall.

Jim headed north to defend his New Year's Day Morpeth-Newcastle title, aware there were people baying for his blood and claiming they had just the man to give this Sassenach a good hiding. Duncan McLeod ('Dunky') Wright, Olympic marathoner and seven times winner of the Morpeth race, was regarded as the father of Scottish athletics, so when he spoke people tended to take notice – north of the border at least. Dunky was of the firm opinion that the young Scot Ian Binnie would give Jim Peters a beating on New Year's Day, probably by as much as 300 yards.

Wright, who had only quit racing himself a few years earlier aged 50, had seen Binnie break Shrubb's long-standing one-hour record, and knew the 24-year-old was currently in the form of his life. Tynesiders took up the cudgel and rooted for Binnie to beat the southern invader Peters. National pride was at stake in addition to prizes valued at around £50, and *The Newcastle Journal* cup. What Wright probably didn't realise, however, was that when it came to running for the honour of his country, Jim Peters was as patriotic as the most fervent of Scots.

Jim lined up wearing No 98 on his dark Essex vest, while Binnie, in hooped singlet, wore 87. Their only concern was beating each other, for neither had clubmates participating, meaning the team contest was an irrelevance. There was an eleven-year age gap between them, a huge gulf in experience, but their capabilities over today's distance looked similar. Everyone had heard of Jim, but few down south knew much about Binnie. Hugh Barrow, former Scottish international, says: 'Binnie spoke to many and listened to nobody. He certainly would not have rated Jim Peters over thirteen miles – he would have called him a padder!'

Aside from this fascinating double-header, a further 103 men had registered for the race. Jim was aiming for a hat-trick of Morpeth victories, and noted that conditions were considerably better than the slush of 1952 and the rain and wind of 1953. He will have secretly nursed the notion of cracking his own course record. He felt very fit, the Christmas period training having bought his weight down to its lowest in years – just

8st 12lbs. He told *The Journal* his best time for twelve miles was slower than Binnie's which should make for 'an interesting contest'.

One man missing at the start was Bob Poxon of Bedlington, who had last year persuaded Jim to hand over his vest after winning, hoping the garment would endow him with some extra stamina and speed. He was grateful for Jim's generosity, but found the vest didn't bring him luck, for a knee injury meant he couldn't even take part.

The runners were accompanied by a radio car, a black Austin 16, with a timekeeper protruding through its sunroof ready to send news of the leaders by two-way radio to officials at the finish. As the field set off, Binnie showed his hand immediately, flying away to take the lead up the early hill, Jim giving chase, then came the Austin 16 and then a big gap to the rest. Binnie was at one point 100 yards to the good, but wasn't allowed to get completely away and when he hit the crest of the hill on the run towards Clifton, Jim hauled him back in, and then spurted ahead. At the foot of Blagdon Bank, Binnie had planned to 'have a real go' at his famous rival, but the reverse happened with Jim turning on the heat and pulling away. By the time they'd hit Stannington, with less than four miles done, Jim had a significant lead. *The Journal*'s photographer captured the moment here when a well-dressed woman in a coat and hat leaped forward from the crowd to give Jim encouragement. His elbow passed dangerously close to her flailing handbag and they nearly both came a cropper, but there was a big smile on his face.

The rest of the race became a procession, Jim maintaining a blistering pace and Binnie, although no longer able to see him, gamely battling on. Jim passed twelve miles in under 59 minutes, which was faster than his ill-fated one-hour effort at White City in 1953. By the end there was 700 yards between them and Jim's 1:06.08 was another course record. The young Scot conceded he'd been beaten by superior stamina and experience. Dunky Wright could barely believe what he'd witnessed, saying Jim's acceleration going uphill had been simply staggering: 'Ian has never met anything quite like this before and no wonder he couldn't cope.'

The Journal's correspondent called it a colossal achievement, and was fascinated by the 'lolloping, head swinging running action' of the winner. Jim told him: 'The trouble is, I can't get anybody to run with me,' referring to his cavalier front-running and presumably not meaning to sound boastful. By the time Newcastle United footballer Ivor Broadis handed over the prizes, Jim had already made a hasty exit, anxious to catch his train back to London, where he had to be back at work the next morning. This would prove the last time a southerner would win the Morpeth race for 38 years (until Paul Evans of Belgrave in 1992).

Jim would tackle plenty of road and cross-country over the next few months, but his main focus of 1954 remained the twin late summer marathons at the Empire Games in Vancouver and European Championships in Berne. He wanted to build up to these by running at both the Poly and the Boston Marathon, although he knew the latter could prove devilishly difficult to organise. He was aware the authorities were unlikely to pay for him to go to the USA as they were fully stretched by ground-breaking trips behind the Iron Curtain (Poland and Romania) in addition to the two championships in Canada and Switzerland.

It was left to Johnny Johnston to try and set up the April visit to Boston. Transatlantic communiqués revealed that race director Jock Semple would be very keen to have Jim in his race, and *The Boston Globe* newspaper would provide funds to get him there. An official invitation from Semple then had to go through the bureaucratic AAA channels, but was blocked by the ruling that Jim could only go if a team manager accompanied him – and that would require more funds from somewhere. On top of this, the British officials were unhappy to see Jim apparently over-doing things again and felt he ought to be saving himself for the summer marathons anyway. Jim and Johnny were furious at this, but eventually *The News of the World* was persuaded to step in and clear up a messy situation. The paper would cover the cost of AAA Hon Sec Jack Crump accompanying Jim to Boston, thus complying with the rules, and although Jim would much rather have had coach Johnny with him, this was a decent compromise.

While all the negotiating and back-biting was going on, life in the fast lane continued for Jim, victorious at the annual Mitcham fifteen-mile road race in January in a swift 1:20.11. It was a bitterly cold day, with some of the roads dangerous and slippery. A record field of over 200 started from the Three Kings Hotel, Jim beating off a stiff challenge from Bob Pape to win an anonymously donated 75 guineas trophy, while the 'Jim Peters Trophy' went to winning team Coventry Godiva. This was followed by a welcome retreat to the warmer and more convivial sur-roundings of the Chelmsford AC annual dinner, to which Jim had been invited as guest of honour, along with hurdler and long-jumper Jean Desforges and West Ham footballer Alan Dick.

The going was soft at the inter-counties cross-country on Epsom Downs, Jim coming in ninth (7¼ miles in 41:02), more than a minute behind winner Ken Norris of Middlesex, and suffering from a bruised ankle and swollen knee after being clattered by others. Norris would also prove top-dog at the Southern champs on Parliament Hill Fields, winning in 57:29 on a real quagmire of a course, Jim a solid fifth in 59:13. Victory followed in Essex Beagles' annual winter ten-miler over the country, Jim's 53:51 leaving Ted Baverstock behind by three minutes and setting a new club record. A week later, Jim was sixth at an international meet in Hannut, Belgium, covering a six-mile course in 33:33, the race dominated by the English.

It was a hectic period, and Jim hinted at how tough and exhausting life had become in a letter he wrote one evening in February: 'Training very, very hard. All my available time is devoted to it. Would spend even more but my job does not permit it.' After finishing this letter, he revealed, he would be off for a ten-mile spin, his 268th run in less than six months, the mileage totaling 2,553. This compared to 236 runs and 1,675 miles over the same period of 1952-53, 159 runs and 1,229 miles over 1951-52, and 102 runs and 504 miles over 1950-51. The fact that such data was apparently close at hand and easy to call upon illustrates the care and seriousness with which Jim recorded his training. Some might even call it obsessive. 'So there you are,' he wrote. 'Sometimes it's heartbreaking, but I try my hardest to stick to it.'

Into March 1954, and the massed ranks of the English National championships provided the racing highlight of the month, the ECCU caravan this year pitching up in Arrowe Park, Birkenhead. A huge crowd turned out to watch, and due to various organisational problems the Union's president Fred Ireland and his good wife were seen standing at the main gates, taking money and tearing tickets. Their headaches increased further after scenes of near-chaos at the end caused by a finish funnel that was far too short. Gordon Pirie, having earlier announced he was abandoning cross-country for the year, did a U-turn and turned up to defend his title successfully in 50:55 (9.6 miles). In good weather on a relatively flat course, Jim featured near the front for spells, but eventually came in twelfth, a minute behind runner-up Ken Norris. Bill Gray of Small Heath ran a strong fourth, but shortly afterwards was found to be suffering from pleurisy, leading to hospitalisation, and was told to rest for at least twelve months.

Jim's arrangements to participate at Boston were by now finalised and he warmed up the weekend before his trip with a great run at the national final of the London-Brighton relays. Most clubs put their best men on Stage 8, the six miles and 206 yards between pubs at Handcross and Hickstead, and this produced a fine tussle between Jim (28:42) and Philip Driver of South London Harriers, the former winning by ten seconds, but both dipping under the previous stage record. Jim was one of many who thrived on the special pressures of a team relay, but not everybody could cope with the responsibility – a Shettleston runner, for example, mysteriously collapsed on the ninth leg and his team had to drop out. Down the years there had been several cases of runners folding under the pressure, becoming physical and emotional wrecks, with the press usually told they were injured in order to save face.

On this day, South London Harriers, helped by Pirie, were first to reach the seaside in a record 4:31.37, the route having reverted to a Westminster start and now over 54 miles long. Jim's efforts helped secure third place for Beagles, cheered on by around 100 travelling supporters to their best-ever finish in 4:31.37. It was the first time all teams had to carry a baton, in addition to the special baton that was traditionally passed down the line containing a message from the Lord Mayor of London to his Brighton counterpart.

Returning from Brighton, Jim now had a few days to prepare for Boston, and tried to detach himself from the controversy brewing over his AAA chaperone Jack Crump, accused in the press of being a 'free-loader' who was depriving Britain's best runner of the vital presence of his coach. Crump would defend himself robustly, saying they'd allowed Jim to go to Boston because his 'desperation to run' had won them over, and as Crump had to go to the USA anyway for talks about a British Games fixture, *The News of the World* had consented to pay his expenses. Crump would also point out that it was he who had secured the time off work that Jim needed: 'I think it was my personal assurance that I would get Jim back to his work as quickly as possible and my personal friendship with [his employer] Mr Wingate that secured the necessary leave of absence.'

The flight was delayed twelve hours at Glasgow Prestwick and later had an unscheduled stop at Goose Bay, Labrador. Crump pointed out: 'We had a most trying journey going out, for we had to overfly Boston because of fog and over New York were told that it was impossible to land there and that we should have to go on to Philadelphia. However our pilot, not disinterested in Jim Peters' mission [to beat the Yanks in their own back yard] flew back to Boston and when no one expected it – least of all ground control at Boston – made a good landing and we arrived several hours late.'

They were besieged by pressmen at the airport, but a weary Jim was dissuaded from chatting to them and whisked straight to the Lennox Hotel to rest. This annoyed race director Jock Semple who had promised the waiting media interviews with the big star from England. Later, worried that he had a jet-lagged runner on his hands, Semple personally massaged Jim's legs and took him out for a meal. The race was on Monday, 19 April, Paul Revere Day, which commemorated the man who warned locals of the coming of the British red-coats in the War of Independence. It seemed rather appropriate in view of Jim's status as an invading force from the old country.

His main opposition, notably Veikko Karvonen, had been in town for some time by now, but Jim had barely 48 hours to acclimatise and inspect the course. Typically, his main request was for a demanding training run, and due to the heavy rain was taken to Boston Garden, an indoor venue, where he ran between rows of seats to complete 74 laps of the tiny arena in one hour. Onlookers thought he'd gone mad, but Jim was glad to be running anywhere in order to stretch his legs. The local press, who made him hot favourite, was full of stories about how he was desperate to win well because, in America, Boston was considered the unofficial world championship. While wandering around, Jim encountered a group of Japanese runners, who politely invited him to run their local marathon later in the year: poor Jim didn't quite know how to respond, visiting such a destination so soon after the war seemed unthinkable, although he appreciated their gesture of goodwill. For the sake of diplomacy, he avoided the question and ended up cracking a joke instead.

Nearly 200 men lined up at the Hopkinton start for this point-to-point contest, and were set on their way by a revolver from a policeman's holster, after the starter's pistol failed to work. By now the rain had disappeared and it was becoming a very warm day. Jim was amazed to see thousands of spectators lining the entire route, an invigorating change from most of his races, normally run mostly in splendid isolation. He was prominent in a lead pack, some of whom looked determined to cling to his heels come what may. After around six miles of little decisive action, Jim and Karvonen slowly pulled clear and would have each other's company for the best part of fifteen miles, although never a word was exchanged.

The temperature rose and Jim felt uncomfortably hot, his anxiety hardly helped when a small dog ran out from the crowd and got tangled in his feet, knocking him off his stride and almost to a halt. Around now Karvonen also had troubles, his stomach complaining about his pre-race drinks of blueberry juice and coffee. On one particularly hilly stretch he failed to respond when Jim forced the pace, but the break was temporary and by the top of Heartbreak Hill the Finn was back on terms, the ache in his belly replaced by a fierce desire for revenge after what Jim had done to him in Turku.

The notorious Newton Hills area felt hot and hostile and Jim realised to his horror he could no longer hold on to Karvonen, who was now running smoothly, while he seemed to be lurching along uncomfortably.

As on the odd occasion this sort of thing had happened before, his mind became crowded with negative thoughts of how he was letting down his country, his wife, his coach, Jock Semple, and any number of others. In his torment, he even began thinking he would have to quit altogether.

Karvonen pulled well clear and Jim knew the game was up. As they went down sun-baked Beacon Street and towards Boston's busy downtown district, the crowd roared them on, Jim hunched and miserable, but now willing himself to at least complete the job. He crossed the line in Exeter Street two minutes behind Karvonen in 2:22.40 and nearly two minutes ahead of the Finn Puloakka in third. The winner was shattered and fell limply into the arms of the Mayor of Boston as the laurel wreath was placed over his head, but Jim managed to top even this, collapsing into the embrace of Jock Semple, sending the two of them tumbling to the ground, where Jim banged his head and bruised his hip. It was the first time in eight marathons that he had finished without winning.

The heat had proved a major factor, a groggy Karvonen unable to recall anything about the closing miles, his last memory being the rasping sounds of Jim's breath, a noise that had convinced him he would win. The other runners stumbled over the finish line in Exeter Street, many of them collapsing in the nearby changing rooms which resembled a hospital casualty department. Jim needed three hours to recover before he was taken for a light meal and some gentle sightseeing to avoid the pack of reporters, and then to his hotel room where he could nurse his blisters and get some sleep.

Despite the various excuses or mitigation that he could have offered (major travel difficulties, no acclimatisation, the heat, etc, etc), Jim simply told the press: 'The better man won on the day,' a gesture which impressed *The Boston Herald* in particular, whose Bill Cunningham wrote: 'That is sportsmanship, dearly beloved, and serves to be retrieved from the bottom of the typographical pile, duly buffed until its true colours are gleaming and then safely enshrined in the temple where such things are kept.'

The long flight home was again interrupted and delayed, this time by stops at New York and Goose Bay. Johnny met him at London Airport, but due to the hold-ups was unable to escort him all the way home, meaning Jim found himself hobbling around the London Underground all alone, journeying from Liverpool Street to Newbury Park, complete with painful blisters, stiff legs, a heavy suitcase and huge silver trophy.

'I couldn't help feeling it might have been nice if some car or taxi had been laid on – that wouldn't have made me professional,' he said, ruefully reflecting on how the world's fastest marathoner had helped attract a

250,000 crowd in the USA, but was coming home alone and £5 out of pocket. On the other hand, the knowledge that race promoter Jock Semple had spent a large sum of his own money looking after Jim meant he was hardly likely to complain too much.

Within a day or so of his return Jim appeared on BBC TV's *Sports Report* to talk about his adventure, and received a number of letters and telegrams of congratulations. One was from Crump, praising him 'for putting up a very good show for Britain'. This made him feel better.

With hindsight Crump would admit it had been 'an ill-considered decision' to allow Jim to run at Boston, but said he was willing to take the blame, because he had become fond of 'this enthusiastic, great-hearted runner, who made so much personal sacrifice for his sport and was prepared to run himself into the ground for the honour of his country. He was a fine chap to travel with, but I felt afterwards that his invitation to the Boston Marathon [should have been] delayed a year.'

Crump was an influential official representing the very body which Jim and fellow runners constantly had cause to complain about, but the two men developed a mutual respect all the same. Crump had first become involved in running athletics in his twenties after injury curtailed his own ambitions, organising races at a flower show before rising to senior officialdom in Surrey, and then appointments at national level before the war. He was now a very influential figure at the top of the sport, writing columns in many national papers and magazines and thus able to justify some of the controversial team selections he made himself.

As a postscript to the Boston episode, the course used for the race between 1951 and 1957 would later be discovered to be considerably short of the full marathon distance, due to various construction works that took place during that period. Re-measurement and correction would finally be carried out after Antti Viskari of Finland won the 1956 race in an unbelievable 2:14.14.

Jim saw his next major target as defence of his AAA title in his fourth appearance at the annual Poly Marathon two months hence. Crump winced at this, and tipped him the wink that it wasn't necessary to run to gain selection for the Vancouver/Berne squads, but Jim wanted to appear anyway. In the meantime, he ignored a nasty cough to rattle off an even-paced 29:07.4 to give Essex third place in the inter-counties six miler at White City. A lively party at the Dorchester Hotel followed ('One of my very rare late nights').

The last few weeks before the Poly was a busy period, distractions including the fact his wife was due to give birth to their second child, and Roger Bannister making athletics history by being the first man to run a mile in under four minutes. Bannister's 3:59.4 sent shock waves around the sporting world from windy Iffley Road in Oxford on Thursday 6 May. It signalled a new era in athletics and even superseded Jim's marathon feat of being the first man on the planet to go under 2:20.00. Then, three weeks later, Zatopek chalked up his ninth world record by running 5,000 metres in Paris in 13:57.2. This prompted Jim to publicly acknowledge that at nearly 36 he no longer had the raw speed or the motivation for shorter races any more, even though that summer he achieved his own lifetime bests at three miles (14:09.8) and six miles (28:57.8).

Early to mid-June 1954 saw Jim feeling 'a little off-colour' which may have been partly down to the exhausting Boston experience, and partly to the worry and turmoil surrounding the arrival of a child. Daughter Jennifer entered the world during a violent thunderstorm on Saturday, 12 June – a momentous event that even caused Jim to miss a day's training, a very rare occurrence in recent times. He resumed normal service in the fortnight leading to the Poly Marathon, but most of the runs in his training log were accompanied by rather irritable remarks ('Didn't want to run, but plugged away,' etc). Then a bad stomach ache on the Tuesday before the race forced another rare day off.

Elsewhere that week, Bannister's new mile record was blasted out of the water by John Landy, his 3:58.0 in Turku coming on the same day England named its team for the Empire Games in Vancouver. Thirty athletes got the nod, Jim immensely proud when it was confirmed he would be team captain. The line-up for the European Championships, a few weeks after Vancouver, was also announced and Jim's intention to run in both marathons was endorsed by the selectors. Not such good news was the absence of his Essex running pal Jock Duffy from the Scotland squad going to Vancouver. The Scottish selectors only deemed one runner worth taking (Joe McGhee) amid rumours that Duffy's face simply didn't fit. Jim sent them a letter, pleading them to reconsider, but there was no U-turn for the Hadleigh Olympiads runner.

Jim's own club, meanwhile, were involved in a scheme to raise funds for a testimonial for him. Essex AAA wrote to the Beagles asking them to approve and assist, but after *The Daily Express* declined to get involved the matter seems to have fizzled out. But the Beagles were desperate to honour Jim in some way, and an alternative proposal was to name their proposed new clubhouse in Mayesbrook Park as 'The Jim Peters HQ'. This idea was welcomed at a committee meeting and there was further excitement when members were told that among the club's new recruits that month was an 'R Bannister'. Sadly it turned out not to be the four-minute miler, but fifteen-year-old Roy Bannister of 842 Dagenham Road.

CHAPTER 20

Take That, Zatopek!

Don't go flat out, Jim! It was a strict instruction from a deadly serious Johnny Johnston, and one that even headstrong Jim couldn't afford to ignore.

Here he was, for the second successive summer, attempting a series of major marathons in a relatively short period – and expecting to run seriously fast times in all of them. He'd pulled the trick off in style in 1953, running four of them in sixteen weeks (average time 2:19.00). Could he possibly do it again in 1954, with this year's quartet scheduled for a twenty-week period?

Many people had their doubts, but single-minded Jim wasn't a man easily put off. Jack Crump and fellow AAA official Les Truelove were top of the list of those convinced it was wrong for Jim to expect to win at both Vancouver and then Berne just three weeks later. Jim didn't agree, and to emphasise his point, he was now about to tackle the Poly Marathon too, just a month before Vancouver. No wonder Johnny had pleaded with him to take it easy.

The two AAA men agreed that, ideally, Stan Cox should have been allocated the Vancouver race and Jim be earmarked for Berne. That would surely produce double gold for England, but, as Crump wrote later: 'Jim and his coach were certain that Peters could run and win both, and in an amateur sport the athlete's personal wishes must not be disregarded.'

Nobody had ever tackled marathons and their build-up periods in the same bullish fashion as Jim, and in his eight attempts to the end of 1953 he'd achieved seven astonishing times and had just the one disaster. So who was in a position to tell him he was doing things wrongly?

Jim believed he knew his own capabilities better than anyone, and the negativity from the outside world didn't seem to fluster him. He listened respectfully when Johnny pleaded for a more calm, conservative approach, but that was as far as it went. He was nearly 36, he might have two years left in the sport if all went well, so what was the point of dithering around and being overly cautious?

The re-measurement of the previous year's Poly course, which revealed the stunning news that it was too long, had led to the 1954 event being made 150 yards shorter, a fact that instantly set tongues wagging

about another possible record for Jim. Curiously, the news that their journey would be slightly shorter didn't please Stan Cox, and he wrote to
Athletics Weekly to complain that the new finish arrangements – involving
two laps of the track - would only cause potential confusion for runners,
officials and spectators alike. He cited the case of the Wigmore fifteen-
mile race in 1951, which had ended in mayhem as runners came in and
joined others already on the track, nobody sure who'd done the required
laps and who should be carrying on. Cox queried the purpose behind trying to achieve the precise distance of 26 miles and 385 yards when
marathon courses varied so much in nature, and the event was not formally recognised for record purposes anyway?

Nearly 200 men registered for the Poly, one of the highest entries in
its 45-year history – 181 would actually start from Windsor Castle, some
42 of these being 'marathon virgins' and, it was noted, the average age of
the field appeared to be much younger than in the past. Marathons were
clearly no longer the territory of the elderly plodder, and the main reason
for this was Peters, the man in the all-white kit, his singlet bearing No 1
and the three seaxes of the crest of Essex.

Proceedings began at the hottest part of a hot day, just after 3.30 in
the afternoon, when Lord Burghley, AAA President, fired the starting
pistol. The heat would be a factor, although, thankfully, it wasn't especially humid and there was a nice following breeze too. It looked
inevitable that Jim and Stan Cox would dominate proceedings again,
although there was much discussion over whether 33-year-old Jack
Braughton of Blackheath Harriers could live up to recent reports that he
was 'out to do big things' today. A 1948 Olympian at 5,000 meters,
Braughton was said to be ready to achieve around 2:25.00, which, if true,
would make him a real and unexpected threat. The rumours were not dis-
pelled in the early stages through Eton, Chalvey and Slough, for
Braughton followed Jim and Stan closely and the trio passed the five-mile
point in a brisk 26:40, nearly 100 yards clear of the chasing pack.

The roads were busy and the added race traffic led to a number of
hold-ups. The timekeepers had been waylaid in the Eton area, for example, where an important cricket match had added to local congestion.
Running largely side by side, Jim and Stan began dropping Braughton in
the Uxbridge area after around eight miles. They recorded 52:53 at the
ten-mile point, some 27 seconds ahead of the Grimsby-born interloper.
The news from this part of the race was relayed to those waiting at the
Chiswick finish, who were said to have become highly excited when told
Cox was slightly ahead. Had they known this was only by a mere stride or
two, the hubbub might have been reduced. The chasing group, including

the consistent Geoff Iden, were by now well adrift. The next few miles, past Iver Church and West Drayton, proved decisive for Jim, who was running strongly in the suburban sunshine. He opened a gap on Stan which quickly grew to 60 seconds' worth, a remarkable feat considering Stan still looked to be running as well as ever.

With less than ten miles left of this route he now knew so well, Jim could have been forgiven for easing up slightly, but there was no evidence of this at all. If anything he dug deeper as he strode relentlessly on. He passed through Heston and Osterley to hit the twenty-mile point in an excellent 1:44.25, nearly 500 yards to the good, and looking on course for another world best. He would reveal later he was well aware throughout the race of the wisdom of not over-doing things in this early part of the summer, but as usual was running on instinct, felt good and saw no reason to slow. In the critical closing miles along the Great West Road his pace barely wavered at all, while those behind began to fade alarmingly quickly.

After 22 miles the lead had widened to four minutes, which was the final statistic to be relayed to the finish, meaning the crowd had to wait on tenterhooks until the leader would burst into view on the sun-baked track. Jim beetled purposefully on through Strand-on-the-Green, alongside the Thames and left into Grove Park Road, right into Bolton Road and across the Polytechnic sports ground to the stadium. The clocks showed 5.45pm when the great moment arrived, Jim quickly down the tunnel and into the stadium, raising his left arm to acknowledge the huge roars that went up. If anyone could cope with a soul-destroying two-lap finish it was him, and, sure enough, he even raised a gallop to cross the line looking as strong as ever. All those worries over recent sluggish training runs had been emphatically banished.

He'd done it again. A fourth successive Poly triumph and the last three were all world best times. His record of a year earlier had been trashed today by 60.8 seconds, the time confirmed as 2:17.39.4. The rest of the world would gasp when the news came their way. Take that, Zatopek!

It was a truly stunning effort, appearing all the better when Cox arrived in an admirable 2:23.08 only to find himself beaten by a massive five and a half minutes. Eric Smith of Leeds Harehills kept the crowd waiting for another four minutes before coming in third. While all around were losing their heads with excitement, one man remained cool as a cucumber: the winner himself. His satisfaction at this latest 'miracle run' was deepened by how strong he'd felt throughout and how quickly he'd recovered : 'Except for a slight nagging pain in one of the muscles in my left leg, I really had no trouble at all, which made me convinced that a marathon can still be run considerably faster … without wishing to detract in any way whatsoever from the performance of the other competitors, I did have a little bit in hand throughout the race.'

The press marvelled at Peters' feat, *The Times* reckoning he now had this course 'down to a nicety', and had learned to run it like a young businessmen who knows how much time he has to run from his house to the railway station every morning. The paper acknowledged Jim's undeniable status as the world's fastest marathon man, but said to the untrained eye it still looked as if he 'has to flog himself' to achieve these astonishing times. Runners and athletics followers keen for a detailed account of the race in *Athletics Weekly* were left disappointed, for the editor had been on holiday and the reporter appointed in his place had at short notice been unable to attend. Former Poly winner Sam Ferris came to the rescue with a retrospective look at the race in a later issue. The Poly was now distance running's 'event of the year' said Ferris, paying tribute to the work behind the scenes of Arthur 'Mr Meticulous' Winter.

The following day saw photographers make their now annual pilgrimage to Jim's Chadwell Heath home. He kept them happy by posing in the sunshine in the garden, alongside son Robin and pet dachshund Mitzi. He was also asked to hold up the family tortoise Charlie, which may or may not have been a reference to the old tortoise-and-hare legend. Jim wasn't intending to spend the entire day with his feet up on the lawn, however, for there was training to do. To the astonishment of those who appreciated what he'd achieved the previous day, he took off for a run of 10½ miles in Hainault Forest. He conceded his legs felt stiff and two toes were blistered, but the stopwatch nevertheless revealed a highly respectable time of 58:40.

There were now less than seven weeks until the British Empire Games marathon, but Jim felt this was sufficient to fit in one more serious competitive fixture. He put his name down for the AAA six-mile championship race on Friday, 9 July at White City. He knew he was likely to be up against a powerful field, but was convinced he could achieve a time better, or very close to his own best, and that such a run would benefit his training for Vancouver and Berne.

On the evening of the race it was cool and overcast, British record holder Gordon Pirie testing a foot injury behind the stands at White City and declaring himself fit to run just twenty minutes before the start. It proved a strange and eventful contest, the early rhythm disrupted by the presence of a barefoot Kenyan teenager, Lazaro Chepkwony, who was determined to shadow the race leader, no matter how fast they went. Pirie, Ken Norris, Frank Sando and Ian Binnie all hit the front at various points, all finding Chepkwony bounding along on their heels. His awkward, unbalanced style unsettled the others until he suddenly pulled up and fell to the ground with a knee problem. The big, partisan home crowd seemed sorry to see him go. He and teammate Nyandiki Maiyoro, a Tisii tribesman, were among the first top-class runners to emerge from black Africa and their uninhibited barefoot running on the cinders endeared them to the spectators.

Jim had got into his stride early and was running strongly, if somewhat overshadowed by the shenanigans ahead of him. Not long after Chris Chataway quit the race, Jim and Binnie were dropped by the lead pack, but the real turning point came with barely half a mile left, when young Peter Driver passed clubmate Pirie and the latter reacted by stepping off the track, his foot injury presumably the main cause. Sando and Driver took advantage and had a rare battle in the closing lap, the latter coming out on top by twenty yards in 28:34.8, a fast time, but short of Pirie's GB best and Zatopek's world mark. Jim came in fourth, delighted to have beaten his lifetime best by a good margin, going under 29 minutes for the very first time (28:57.8).

'I don't think anyone else in the world at my age, nearly 36, had recorded such a fast time for six miles on the track,' he glowed afterwards. He saw this result as further vindication of his heavy training: a runner of nearly twenty years' experience who achieves a PB at both marathon and six miles within a fortnight must be doing something right, he reasoned. And so, without a second thought, the following seven days saw him step things up again, cramming in no fewer than eleven training runs totalling 132 miles.

Then, in mid-July, the flight to Vancouver just days away, came the type of unlucky break that plagues most ordinary runners, but for some reason Jim usually avoided. During a routine run through Hainault Forest he banged his heel on a semi-hidden tree root. The pain was only bad momentarily, and he was able to continue on his way, but soon afterwards it flared up and become so sore it kept him indoors completely on Wednesday, 21 July. For Jim Peters to cancel a day's training, this had to be something serious.

FOOTNOTE: Jim's winning time of 2:17.39 in the June 1954 Polytechnic Marathon would survive as a recognised world best time for four years until the tiny Russian Sergey Popov lowered it in Stockholm in 1958 (2:15.17) at the European Championships. On that day Popov also matched Jim's feat at the Poly of winning a major marathon by the huge margin of five minutes-plus.

CHAPTER 21

Pillow Fights Over the Atlantic

July – August 1954

Lotions, potions, manipulation and massage. They all failed to make Jim's heel problem disappear before the trip to the Empire Games in Canada. But through gritted teeth, his only concession was to curtail his final two day's training to one long run per day.

He found the heel didn't complain too much while running, only afterwards did it become seriously sore again. It was a major concern, but he was England captain and it would take more than this to make him stand down.

The flight from London Airport (now Heathrow) to Canada on a Lockheed Constellation proved a lively affair. The party of 30 athletes looked smart in their blazers, striped ties and Panama hats as they waved farewell on the steps into the propeller-driven plane. The two marathon men Jim and Stan Cox found themselves seated at the back, alongside the Oxbridge set (Bannister, Chataway, Brasher, *et al*) affectionately known by their working-class teammates as 'the Royal Family'.

Prominent in the ensuing fun and games, which featured pillow fights and the like, was Jim's vice-captain, the burly thrower 'Little John' Savidge, and the teenage diver from Ilford, Ann Long (who was almost literally half Savidge's size). 'Quite a lot of good-humoured ragging took place,' was Jim's rather discreet description of events.

Strong headwinds forced a stop at Goose Bay, Labrador, something Jim was now familiar with, and a group of athletes spent this idle time marching up and down the airfield's small compound, simply to stretch their legs and relieve the boredom. Then came an overnight stop at Montreal. Here they enjoyed a highly popular 'All-you-can-eat' self-service breakfast, but spirits were dampened when a group, led by Jim, went for a long walk only to become stranded and soaked in a rainstorm. Back on the plane for the final leg of the journey, and once again there were unexpected delays. Jim must have thought he was jinxed when it came to plane journeys.

The skirl of bagpipes and a horde of reporters met the plane at Vancouver and, as team captain, Jim was obliged to step forward and speak for his country. He took the opportunity to publicly deny a recently published story that he didn't rate the chances of teammate Fred Green in the three-mile race. Jim was by now used to dealing with tricky pressmen, but admitted to being much less skilled than the 'loquacious and well-organised' Roger Bannister.

Within hours of arrival at the athletes' quarters at the University of British Columbia, Jim completed a ten-mile training run, while others sought to take things a little easier. On the first night, a Canadian 'mountie' maintained an all-night vigil outside Bannister's room on the orders of the England team's *chef de mission* Sandy Duncan, who didn't want the star miler disturbed after his tiring flight. The good doctor had the 'Mile of the Century' to prepare for, a head-to-head contest with John Landy, the Aussie who had recently snaffled his famous world record. Jim Peters didn't expect such VIP treatment, although he did welcome the arrival of some coconut matting, which was placed in the corridors to deaden the sound of athletes going in and out for after-dark entertainment. Well-behaved Jim, a notoriously light sleeper, had no such plans, and needed peace and quiet.

With his own three-runs-a-day routine soon established, Jim was astonished to see how the likes of teammate Chris Chataway trained only lightly and regarded his running as merely a recreational hobby: 'How on earth [Chataway] produces such results, I don't know … if he wanted a cigarette or a glass of beer he had them, but he never let England down and I'm certain he'll be remembered as one of Britain's best ever athletes.' Jim was able to renew acquaintances with several foreign runners, notably Jackie Mekler of South Africa. Mekler recalls the time clearly: 'We were housed in the grounds of the university, which occupied a peninsula on the Pacific Coast. There were beautiful roads on which to train and the scenery was superb. The students were on vacation so we occupied their quarters, which consisted of log cabins containing about ten rooms for two people per room. The open-plan dining room, with a modern well-equipped kitchen with automatic dish washer, was open virtually around the clock. The selection of food was unbelievable and well prepared. As each of the teams of the competing countries arrived, a ceremony took place in front of the main reception area, where each country's flag was hoisted.'

Mekler chatted with Jim and noticed how he 'greatly cherished' his position as England captain: 'We discussed the forthcoming marathon, our fitness, the course and various other aspects. Jim said he felt the winning time was likely to be in the region of not much under 2:32 due to the high temperatures predicted.

'On another occasion he said he feared the course, predicting this time it would be won in around 2:36 – I didn't take him too seriously! Jim also appeared worried about [my teammate] Jan Barnard's chances of beating him, but I put this down to pre-race nerves, his concern over the weather, or plain gamesmanship.'

Jim enjoyed Mekler's company, but grew particularly fond of the Australian runners. Allan 'Al' Lawrence from Sydney, later an Olympic medallist and well-known coach in the USA, was then a 24-year-old rookie and remembers the Vancouver adventure well: 'My teammate Bryce MacKay, true to his nature, soon made friends with the working class members of the English team. This special group consisted of Jim Peters, Stan Cox, John Savidge, Harry Kane and Fred Green. This group, plus Macca [MacKay] and myself usually had breakfast together, while a small group that included Roger Bannister, Chris Chataway, Chris Brasher and several other Oxford boys, sat together. Our group referred to them as "The Cads".

'There was never any personal enmity between members of either group and a lot of good-natured joshing occurred when each group left the cafeteria, but it wasn't difficult to sense the "line of demarcation" between the groups. Jim Peters seemed to like the Australian distance runners immensely, and Macca was his favourite. Macca was a natural mimic and able to speak several dialects of the English language and was also an expert in cow-cocky [Australian outback lingo]. Jim particularly liked Macca to read selected snippets of Empire Games news from the local newspapers with an upper-crust English accent. One one occasion Jim asked me one day after breakfast if my family had emigrated to Australia from England, like Macca's. I told him my grandfather had, and he said: "Now I know why I like you Aussie lads".'

Lawrence also points out: 'Jim really was a delightful man. He had a way of building you up and down-grading his own ability – and even though you knew you weren't nearly as good as Jim made you out to be, you appreciated his recognition and his kindness. I suppose the best way to describe Jim was as a true English gentlemen who could run like the wind. But there was no doubt about it, as an athlete he was biomechanically ugly and as a young runner who truly believed that form was the secret to success, I was shocked that anybody like Jim or Zatopek could be as successful as they were. It created the notion for a period of time that it wasn't style but mileage that counted. Australian runners of my era would say Jim was crazy for the way he ran most of his races. This was perhaps the greatest compliment that an Australian could give to another runner – for it actually meant "respect" and "wonderment".'

Jim and Stan's first task during these championships – newly renamed 'The British Empire and Commonwealth Games' in an attempt to move with the times – was to tackle the six-mile event on the opening day,

Saturday, 31 July. The marathon was scheduled for the final day, Saturday 7 August, meaning the two races were conveniently well apart. Both Englishmen were treating the 'six' as little more than a warm-up for the longer race, although with no Zatopek and no Scandinavians involved, there was a realistic chance of gaining a medal.

With this year's Vancouver summer proving a very hot one, it was inevitable there would be criticism over this decision to 'double up'. But as Jim pointed out: 'Many critics said Stan and I ought not to run in the [six-mile] race – but it was quite obvious they didn't know our training methods. I liked to do some speedwork a week or so before a marathon and there was really nothing better than a race for producing the required result. The only danger, of course, was getting blisters from wearing spikes.' He sounded convincing, but it was noticeable that the only other runner doubling up in this way was the relatively inexperienced Australian Lawrence.

Jim's final training sessions before the Games began were generally off-road, on a nearby golf course and track, to protect the heel injury that was still proving an irritation. Stan, on the other hand, preferred to run up and down the marathon route itself, to familiarise himself with the ordeal ahead. Their preparations would include one pleasant interlude when invited to the home of the Lane family, London expats living in West Vancouver, who laid on roast beef and Yorkshire pudding to make them feel at home.

More than 250 athletes from 23 countries were in town for the fifth staging of these Games, meaning it had taken almost 25 years to achieve a true ethnic mix of the Empire. Only twelve nations had made it to Auckland last time out, but this time the likes of India, Kenya, Nigeria, Pakistan and Uganda were making their first appearances.

The opening ceremony on Friday, 30 July was attended by a shirt-sleeved crowd of 25,000 and Field Marshal the Earl Alexander of Tunis, currently Minister of Defence in Churchill's government, and a former Governor General of Canada, delivered a message from the Queen. Jim and the other six-milers were greeted by another bright and hot day when competition got underway less than 24 hours later. A disappointing crowd of less than 11,500 was in the stadium for day one, reportedly a reaction to the high ticket prices.

The soaring temperatures prompted Jim to limit his warming-up routine to five minutes or so in the shade outside the arena, although his England teammates Peter Driver and Frank Sando risked a 30-minute jog in the sun. There were fifteen in the race and all seemed somewhat cowed by conditions, barring, that is, the young Kenyan Chepkwony, apparently fully recovered from his White City tumble. A track that felt soft to the British contingent, plus the effects of the heat, meant the race was relatively slow early on. To his surprise, Jim found himself leading for long periods even though he was planning not to over-exert himself seven days before the marathon. He regarded himself as one of best dozen six-milers in the world and therefore a medal contender, but didn't want to flog himself hard and then find himself out-sprinted by the fast finishers Driver and Sando.

Doug Kyle (Canada) and Neil Robbins (Australia) dropped out altogether and with around a mile left, Aussie Geoff Warren and New Zealander Laurie King, along with Stan, all looked out of contention. There was a degree of confusion over the displaying of lap-count boards, but Peters, Sando and Driver knew where they stood, and with 600 yards to go, Jim called to the other two that they were 'hanging around too much' and putting themselves in danger of being beaten by 'the old man' (i.e. himself). It may have been coincidence, but at this point the pair suddenly surged away for a spectacular final lap, Driver's blazing time of 58.6 giving him victory and a Games record of 29:09.4. Sando was just six-tenths of a second behind at the line, and a further ten seconds behind was Jim, who claimed the bronze medal and completed a clean sweep for England.

There was great relief for Jim and Stan at getting through unscathed and with respectable times. For Jim, the medal was a big bonus, and he reflected: 'When they hoisted three flags of St George and the band played "Land of Hope and Glory", I was a very proud captain. Stan Cox rumbled in a very happy fifth and quite fresh. Indeed, we were so comfortable that later that evening we did contemplate going out to do some more training, but common sense prevailed and we didn't.'

A clean sweep of the medals was indeed a rarity. Sir Arthur Porritt, the Empire and Commonwealth Games Federation chairman, reckoned it was the greatest athletic sight he'd ever seen when the three flags of St George were hoisted together in the sunshine, accompanied by Elgar's stirring music. This was quite something coming from a man born and raised in New Zealand. The scenario would be repeated a few days later when England also dominated the three-mile race, via Messrs Chataway, Green and Sando.

Turning their full attention to the marathon, Jim and Stan encountered a problem that initially troubled them deeply, Jim in particular. During training runs, and after a full inspection from inside a courtesy car, they became convinced the marathon route was too long. They commandeered different courtesy cars from the athletes' village and repeated the journey, and on each occasion the speedometers indicated it was around 27 miles. Although aware measurement by a car would not necessarily produce pin-point accuracy, it did seem as if they were being asked to run at least one kilometre over the normal distance.

Did it matter? After all, every runner would have to tackle the same route, whether or not it was accurate. Jim agonized over this, but eventually decided they should make a fuss, for having to run unnecessary extra distance in the heat would not benefit anybody, and he had another marathon planned in less than three weeks' time. Moreover, all his training was geared towards getting the best out of himself over 26.2 miles, not 27. Why should he accept this basic error without speaking up?

The marathon was just a few days away, but England team manager Les Truelove was approached, who in turn contacted Alex Frew, Games administrator and race referee. A surprised but co-operative Frew agreed to accompany them on another car trip around the official route. Off they headed from the stadium, eastwards down East Hastings Street towards the Burnaby district. A sharp turn down Duthie Avenue led to a steep hill and then they headed westwards along 54th and 49th Avenues. A steady incline along the side of 'Little Mountain' was followed by a downhill stretch of Main Street and then another climb to Clark Drive, up Powell Street and another fairly steep climb, on to McGill Street and back to the stadium via Cassiar Street.

Adding on the distance that would be covered inside the stadium, calculations were made and Frew was shocked to be told it added up to close on 27 miles. According to Jim, Frew said this was 'ridiculous' and said car speedometers could not be relied upon. The car was driven over an official police-measured mile in the city to check its reliability, and appeared to be giving accurate readings. The runners thus felt vindicated, but Frew – polite yet obstinate – seemed determined not to shorten the course. His final concession was a promise to go around it again with the local civil engineer who had measured it in the first place.

His final verdict was that the course was only around 80 yards too long. Jim recalled: 'We just laughed at this and were still unconvinced – and said so.' The original measurement had reportedly been done tight along the kerbs of the city streets, whereas the re-measurements were carried out in heavy traffic nearer the middle of the road. This possibly explained discrepancies, but didn't solve the immediate problem. Frew finally agreed they would knock 250 feet off the length of the course by re-siting the finish line. It was all very unsatisfactory and certainly not the first time that doubts over a road race course had led to bad feeling and disputes. Within a few years the issue would be addressed definitively by

John Jewell in London, whose calibrated bicycle and seminal 1961 paper on road measuring established new standards of accuracy.

Al Lawrence recalls that Jim asked him to get the Australian team manager to measure the Vancouver course and join the English protest, but because of a lack of courtesy cars [only their general manager got one, a sore point in the Aussie camp], this wasn't done. The English runners and officials also made a fuss about the start-time being in the heat of the day and made a fruitless request for a switch to 6pm, says Lawrence.

The controversy lasted three or four days and provided a good story for the international press corps. Jim had to be philosophical, let the matter lie and get back to his training. But had he known what would happen in those final crucial yards on race-day, he might have not have been quite so accommodating.

Before one of his last training runs out of the university camp, he was able to have a brief chat with Earl Alexander, who was representing the Queen at the Games. The much-decorated VIP visitor regaled him with an eye-witness account of the Italian runner Dorando finishing the 1908 Olympic marathon in a state of collapse, and getting disqualified when helped over the line.

Their topic of discussion was highly interesting in view of what was about to happen some 46 years later here in Vancouver. Perhaps Earl Alexander had heard the weather forecast for race-day, and was issuing some sort of veiled warning to Jim?

CHAPTER 22

Women Wept, Strong Men Lost Their Lunch

SATURDAY 7 AUGUST, 1954

As the world's fastest marathoner, it seemed perfectly reasonable for Jim Peters to have two simple requests when he lined up on the final day of the Empire Games in sun-soaked Vancouver.

Firstly, he wanted a sponge soaked in cool water to be provided at the feeding stations. Secondly, towards the end of the race he would be grateful for an update or two on how far ahead or behind he was. They were basic requirements, the sort of thing normally accommodated with ease at a major marathon, and perfectly within the rules. Not too much to ask, surely?

Incredibly, both requirements failed to materialise, and the English champion was left to fend for himself in the unforgiving heat. And, as it turned out, the lack of cooling sponges and race information didn't merely hinder his progress, it nearly killed him.

Officials and helpers, it seems, were too busy watching the much-anticipated mile race inside the stadium. The four-lap showdown between Roger Bannister and John Landy was billed 'The Mile of the Century', and, clearly, was a far more enthralling prospect than waiting around for marathon men to go struggling past on the roads outside.

Unlike at the Poly, and others Jim had completed, there would be no Johnny Johnston popping up around this course, armed with sponges and crucial information about his position in the race. There had been no funds to pay for Johnny to fly over, and the English team officials had little marathon experience and were inadequate substitutes. Vice-captain John Savidge, understanding Jim's anxiety, volunteered to go out on the course and help, but Jim knew Savidge would really rather watch the Mile with everyone else, and turned down the kind offer. Quietly Jim cursed the English authorities for not including somebody in their party who could cater for the special needs of marathon runners.

He and teammate Stan Cox spent the hours before the start fussing and fretting about minor matters such as headgear and neckerchiefs, all the while suspecting they were about to run the toughest race of their lives without proper help and support.

Jim always went to a start-line worrying about something, and today, as he recalled, his biggest concern was roommate Stan. Jim had tossed and turned in bed the previous night, while Stan slept soundly a couple of feet away: 'I knew Stan was absolutely determined, perhaps as never before, to do his utmost to win the marathon, and consequently I began to fear him more than I had ever done.' The sound of a dripping tap nearby also hindered his efforts to get to sleep.

Sixteen men, six representing the host nation, assembled at the stadium for the 12.30 start, their prize being the Empire marathon crown currently worn by England's Jack Holden. Despite his worries, Jim, wearing No 349, was overwhelming favourite. His best time was a full fifteen minutes quicker than the event record.

Much of the nervous chatter among the runners was about the continuing heatwave. Stan opted to wear a large handkerchief tied around his neck, an idea Jim had abandoned after nearly choking himself when trying one on earlier. Jim also decided against using the peaked baseball cap he'd obtained earlier for a dollar, partly because it felt too heavy for running, and partly because he was worried it would fall off because of the way his head wagged about when he ran fast. He tried it on backwards but it still felt wrong. Before leaving his room he found he'd mislaid it anyway, so the decision was made for him. Joe McGhee of Scotland had purchased the same type of hat, and would end up discarding his at the roadside.

The sixteen runners had been told sponges and drinks could only be provided at the official feed stations, and not by helpers along the route. No vehicles containing helpers would be allowed to follow runners as their exhaust fumes would annoy other competitors.

Jim and Stan arrived at the stadium at about 11am and the nervous wait to get started seemed like a lifetime. It was noticeable how everybody, even the marathoners themselves, were discussing the much-anticipated mile race, which would take place shortly before the marathon finished in the stadium. Jim remembered the last-minute advice he got from England team manager Les Truelove: 'No records today Jimmy, look at that sun, just go steady.'

England's star turn in the mile, Roger Bannister, recalled the glorious scene that lunchtime: 'The stadium was filled with one of the most enthusiastic crowds I've ever seen, the setting was perfect, the newly built stadium lay there in the sunshine, the flags of the competing countries silhouetted against the mountains of Vancouver Island.'

Outside the stadium were dozens of ticket touts (known locally as 'scalpers') who were asking more than 100 dollars a ticket. The Duke of Edinburgh would turn up in good time for the Mile in a fuschia-coloured limo, having descended from his eighteenth floor suite at the nearby Hotel Vancouver. It was rumoured that one of the main reasons the marathon couldn't be switched to a cooler time of day was because it had to finish at a time when the Duke was present in the stadium.

South African entrant Jackie Mekler, No 744, has clear memories of waking that morning and getting ready to run: 'The sun was soon up in a clear, bright blue sky, with all the indications of a warm day ahead. Breakfast was taken early to allow it to settle before we strolled across to the medical centre in the university grounds for our check-up. Race numbers were only handed out after passing the medical examination. We then went to our cabins to lay down in an attempt to rest before making our way across the city to the stadium by courtesy car. A new bridge linking the peninsula to the mainland had just been opened. We made certain of arriving in plenty of time. On arrival, we tried to rest on benches in the changing rooms after putting on our running gear. It was difficult to relax or to take one's mind off what lay ahead. I was pleased when we were finally called out to the track for the 12.30 start. The temperature was said to be 28 degrees C, with clear sunny skies. There was a light-hearted moment when an unofficial runner tried to line up with us, and this helped ease our pre-race anxiety. He was a bit of a crackpot, and was soon hustled off the track.'

Al Lawrence, No 235 from Australia, also remembers the 'crackpot'. Speaking from his adopted home in the USA some 57 years later, Lawrence says: 'A man in a white singlet and red shorts elbowed his way between Peters and Cox. He didn't have a race number, and both English runners, obviously annoyed and nervous, stepped off the starting line and called out to the starter and other officials to remove him to his proper starting position. Officials quickly intervened and attempted to find out what country he represented. They soon discovered he didn't speak English and was not even an official entrant for the race, for he indicated by sign language he'd come out of the stands! Incredible as it might seem, some of the Canadian officials initially thought it would do no harm to let him start the race as "He would soon get tired and drop out". Jim Peters would have none of it and kept appealing "Remove this madman" and after several minutes of bedlam and academy award theatrics, the race was ready to start without the mysterious madman. I'd never thought of Jim being a particularly nervous athlete, but when the imposter crashed the start I was surprised how upset he became.'

When the pistol sounded and they finally set off, Jim seemed to be following orders, and common sense, by not rushing into an early lead, and in his own words was 'virtually last out of the stadium'.

Al Lawrence isn't quite so sure: 'Whether the gate-crasher incident had a significant upsetting effect on Peters and Cox, I can't say, but they both took off at the starting gun as though pursued by a fast-running axe murderer.'

As the runners left the stadium and headed down the wide expanse of East Hastings Street, the first three miles or so would prove mostly uphill and tough going. After about twenty minutes of running Jim recalled being very surprised to find the Australian and South African opposition were already nowhere to be seen, and he and Stan were leading with only McGhee for company. Little changed as they headed south through the streets of the Burnaby area and with the ten-mile point fast approaching Jim recalled he and Stan glanced at each other and, without needing to speak, simultaneously accelerated to open a gap on McGhee.

Meanwhile, Mekler, well used to distance running in intense heat, was keen to take things steady in the first half. He recalls: 'Three Canadians had led the field out of the stadium, one of whom was veteran Gerard Cote, followed by Peters, Cox and McGhee. Those three soon passed the Canadians and went into the lead and stayed there until about ten miles, at which point Peters and Cox dropped McGhee. Because of the heat I was determined not to be tempted into anything foolish, but rather to start easily and to run as relaxed as I could. Carefully I kept count of the runners ahead of me. Strangely, I found it difficult to get into an easy rhythm as my legs were sore right from the start, but couldn't figure out the reason. I felt I was battling at ten miles. By fifteen miles I guessed I was lying ninth and felt I had to now move up the field.'

By now everyone was finding the hills and the heat gruelling, and Jim was a little surprised to find himself pulling slightly ahead of Stan. At around halfway he took a good look round and estimated Stan was some 300 yards adrift. Far from being encouraged, however, he recalled this as a disturbing discovery, for it seemed too close for comfort and forced him into a decision on whether or not to apply pressure to make the gap bigger. Characteristically, this was a no-brainer and he soon piled on the pressure even though it felt wrong to be working so hard with so many miles still to go. 'I was by no means going all out [but] the heat by now was almost overwhelming,' he recalled.

Jim admitted to 'dearly wanting a wet sponge' to cool down his burning head and neck but knew he would have to wait for them at the official feed stations later on – and even then he might be disappointed, for already he'd only been offered sponges that were virtually bone dry and didn't do the job properly. Being unable to cool himself down, and being unaware how far behind second-placed Stan was, combined to annoy him greatly. Up yet another slope, the centrally located 'Little Mountain', he felt himself grunting and groaning more than usual. At this point he was a full mile ahead of struggling Stan, and had nearly completed twenty miles, but in his mind imagined the lead was probably no more than 500 yards. This false picture of his position created unnecessary pressure and anxiety.

An official vehicle with loudspeakers blaring out was travelling around the course, but never positioned itself quite near enough for Jim to be able to make out the messages. He certainly never heard anything about how substantial his lead had become. If only Johnny had been there to call out the true picture.

Unbeknown to Jim, fellow runners were dropping like flies as he plugged on along Powell Street towards the closing stages. The final feeding station was between the 25 and 26-mile points, and when he struggled to it he still believed Stan was well within challenging distance, and he refused to let himself relax or consciously lower his pace. Had he known the truth, he could have stopped, dropped into a nearby house for a shower and a drink, and still emerged with a healthy lead.

Second-placed Stan had not only been a long way behind, he had actually collapsed near the 24-mile mark with sunstroke after a nasty collision with a telegraph pole. He was out of the race. Running steadily much further back down the course was Joe McGhee, the schoolmaster from Stirling, now unknowingly in second spot. With less than 1,200 yards to run, the astonishing truth was that Jim now held a massive lead of more than three miles – roughly seventeen minutes – but was completely ignorant of the fact.

'If only I had known that, I could have stopped at the last feeding station, had a good sponge down and trotted in slowly,' he would write ruefully later. Al Lawrence dropped out at 22 miles himself, and confirms that Stan's exit came on the climb up Powell Street at nearly 25 miles, an ambulance ferrying him quickly to hospital: 'Stan was told at that point that Roger Bannister had just won the Mile and he assumed Jim Peters had won the marathon by then too.'

Mistakenly convinced Stan was looming up behind, Jim became aware of massive fatigue and over-heating in these final stages, but was scared stiff at the thought of slowing down and being caught. He reckoned he reached the stadium environs in around 2:20, a superb time in the circumstances, which had been exactly what he had planned earlier. Having felt in shape to run a 2:15, he had added five minutes to allow for the severe conditions and another three for the suspect length of the course – giving a total of 2:23. Had he continued to the finish line without further problems, 2:23 would have been close to his final time. He'd been convinced 2:23 would be good enough to beat Stan [and therefore everybody else too], and had never dreamed of going for records, intending just to win, then recover to face Karvonen in Berne eighteen days later.

As Jim battled with the final few grim furlongs, further back Mekler was also completely unaware of his current standing and that of anybody else. He says: 'From fifteen until about 22 miles I didn't see a soul. I felt extremely dejected as I knew I wasn't running well. I was given my drinks at most of the official feeding stations, but no official offered any indication as to position or what was happening up ahead or behind, which was remarkable. My South African teammate Jan Barnard was looking most uncomfortable and struggling as I passed him at 23 miles on a lonely stretch in an industrial area. All I could offer in support was to say "Go on, keep going". There was still no one else in sight, and all I could assume was that I was probably lying ninth. We turned into Dundas Street, a short, sharp incline. From the bottom of the hill I could make out a runner about 300 yards ahead.'

Mekler goes on: 'A loudspeaker at the final feeding station at 25 miles, at the top of the hill, was blaring forth. I strained every sinew to try and pick up any information on the placings, but couldn't make out anything intelligible. Going up this hill I noticed definite signs of water splashed in the middle of the road so I assumed someone had received attention at an unauthorised point in spite of the strict rules. By the time I reached the top of the hill the mobile loudspeakers had moved off altogether along with any information they might have been broadcasting. On reaching the feeding station, I called for a sponge from which to suck water and splash over my head, as was my usual custom, but was handed a dry towel. My drink couldn't be found, causing me to lose valuable time on the runner in front of me, who was by then only 50 yards ahead. I couldn't waste time so I pushed on without drink or sponge. I still had no idea what my position was, or where the other competitors were.'

Meanwhile, the crowd of nearly 33,000 inside the stadium was in uproar after witnessing the so-called Mile of the Century live up to its name. Bannister and Landy served up a wonderful contest, the Englishman winning and both men dipping well under the magical four-minute barrier. Up in the commentary box were the McWhirter twins from London, Norris assisting Rex Alston of the BBC, and Ross working for the Canadian Broadcasting Corporation. After the Mile finished, a message came through that ABC of Australia wanted to take a broadcast feed for a further hour, so Ross found himself instructed to keep talking for another 60 minutes. He knew the marathon leaders would soon be arriving, but couldn't imagine how he would fill an hour describing this, especially as there were likely to be less than a dozen finishers.

What McWhirter did not anticipate was the scale of the awful drama about to be played out in front of him. In the words of a fellow media scribe, what was about to occur 'Would make women weep and grown men lose their lunch'.

Jim's own description of the subsequent events would emerge in full via various interviews and in his book *In the Long Run*, published a year later. He would recall how, just outside the stadium, he tried to work out if somebody had just told him Stan Cox had collapsed, or whether his exhausted mind had simply imagined it. 'Did that spectator really say that, or was it wishful thinking? You are being a coward, you're just imagining he's out of the race. Get on with it, you coward, finish it!' Had his coach been present there would have been none of this turmoil, and he would have been told to stop and cool himself down. 'When I came into the stadium I thought "What are you working so hard for?" but then thought I should get on with it and get around that wretched last lap. But as I ran on to the cinder it seemed like quicksand.'

He recalled that as he went uphill on the approaches to the stadium he felt himself wobbling a little, which surprised him, and then into the gates of the stadium came a rather untimely steep ramp. As he approached the top he recalled wobbling again but says it still didn't concern him for he knew he was desperately tired but would soon be finished. He went on: 'Now I never did like looking down from a height. When I was young even to look down from Tower Bridge at the water used to make me feel giddy, and still does. On top of that ramp I had a similar feeling for a moment, but still didn't think too much was amiss and went down on to the track. I then had about 380 yards to go.'

At this point he recalled wondering whether he ought to wave to the crowd as he usually did at the finish of the Poly, but decided against it: 'You're really tired, don't kid them, just do those final 380 yards … [then] suddenly I fell to the track. I just couldn't understand what had happened. For a moment I was completely bewildered. Then I made my mind up I was going to finish. I didn't want to disgrace my wife and kiddies. I thought of them at that moment and said to myself I'm going on, there's a tape you've got to break, you don't stop till you hit that tape.'

Jim's painful progress might have been seen as the denouement of the mythical tortoise-and-hare scenario, with him playing the part of a seriously distressed hare. By now he was evidently slipping in and out of consciousness, so for the most revealing views of the unfolding drama we have to turn to the recollections of eye-witnesses. Better placed than most was Australian runner Geoff Warren, who earlier in the week had come fourth in the six-mile race and sixth in the three-miler. Warren saw

Jim at close quarters both outside and inside the stadium and what happened is etched deeply in his memory. He says:

'Initially I was up in the stands, sharing the intense excitement over the mile race, and sharing the deep disappointment of Landy's defeat, many of our Aussie party in tears at what we felt was an inappropriate defeat of a much-admired teammate. With the buzz of the mile still going on, I ran out the back entrance of the stadium and up the road outside to meet the marathon leaders and find out how that race was going.

'I recollect the road was deserted, no spectators or officials, no such thing as lead cars back then. Jim had just about reached the fence of the stadium. The only person in sight was him. I met him between 300 and 400 metres from the back entrance to the stadium and he was weaving from side to side of the road. I spoke to him. His face had a fixed staring expression and though he appeared to look straight at me he showed no sign of recognition and went on weaving down the road even colliding with a lamp post beside the road. He was still running, but slowly, so I followed and saw him directed into the back stadium gate.

'He gained some impetus down the slope inside leading to the track, but on the track he started this long, horrible slow-motion run. It was actually more like a walk, with his arms grasping in the air in front, his legs also reaching forward like a puppet and his head mostly tilted back. And, every few steps he would fall over backwards, turn over, and climb to his feet again and continue his awful progress. There had been a roar from the crowd at the first sight of Jim arriving on the track, but it was now replaced by a horrified silence.'

Warren goes on: 'By now I had crossed the field and was again close to Jim. England's vice-captain, the giant shot-put champion John Savidge, was also close to him and repeatedly imploring "Give up Jim". This was later reported as him saying "Get up Jim!" but that was not as I heard it. Nobody would touch Jim, no doubt aware that this would have him disqualified, for they were hoping he could somehow still reach the line. He eventually did and was gathered up in someone's arms and carried to receive medical help. The realisation soon spread that this was not actually the finish line for the marathon, which was 200 metres further on at the end of the back straight. This was a shock to all of us, who thought we'd seen an incredible win. But there was no way Jim could have gone any further.'

Horrified England teammate Chris Brasher was also close by: 'Jim was suffering from dehydration, salt deficiently and overheating and his balance was gone. He came down the ramp on to the track swaying all over the place, collapsed, got up and collapsed all over again. It was a hell of a scene and one of the most horrific in athletic history. I was on the side of the track and saw it all. They took his temperature right there and his brain temperature was about 107 or 108 degrees. It is something that would be absolutely unbelievable in medical circles. He was on the verge of cooking his brain.'

Skip Rusk of *The Vancouver Sun* noted how the drama started on the steep gravel slope leading to the north-east entrance of the stadium, Jim having turned off Casslar Street to descend what should have been 'a slope to glory': 'His thin legs wobbled, his arms hung from beat shoulders. His glassy eyes stared straight ahead and his mouth hung open. He fell twice on the concrete entrance to the stadium, landing hard on his back the second time. He pushed himself up with his hands, crawled on to the track backwards, looking up into the blazing sun. Confusion and pathos mounted. Someone was heard to call out to Roger Bannister: "Roger, this is murder!" and the shocked miler replied: "this is like feeding Christians to the lions".'

Bannister would write later: 'No one who saw the tragic gallantry of his futile attempts to reach the finish wanted the painful exhibition to continue, yet no one seemed to have the authority to remove him from the race. He crossed the same finish line as Landy and myself. He did not know his own finish was some 200 yards further on.'

During his painful and extended stagger, Jim had at one point veered towards a shaded area of the track under the main grandstand. Here he lay on the track for what some estimated as nearly five full minutes before clambering back to his feet and attempting to go on. This took place close to where Prince Philip was sitting. Roy Moor of *The News Chronicle* pointed out: 'Children sitting in front of the Duke were told to hide their faces to shut out the pitiful sight. And if I thought such a scene was likely to be repeated I would clamour for the abolition of marathon racing. Men and women turned their heads away as Peters continually fell, sometimes lying spread out on the cinders for several seconds. Twelve times he went down.'

New Zealander Murray Halberg, who earlier finished fifth in the Mile, observed: 'There was a stark, shocked silence in the crowd and I felt like being sick. I wished someone would stop this agony. It was beyond everything that is sport to see that stricken man, all alone before thousands of horrified spectators, lurching in virtual collapse. When a boxer is punched into that condition the referee stops the fight. Peters should have been stopped. He was no longer responsible for himself … that deathly silence was in stunning contrast to the uproar at the end of the magic mile, it was unreal and something I'd like to forget, but I'll never forget it … We New

Zealanders felt particularly bad about Jim Peters because he had been so friendly and helpful to us earlier.'

Another Australian, 400 yards gold medallist Kevan Gosper, had just finished warming up for the 4x110 relay when Jim first appeared. 'Someone with a while singlet and shorts came down the ramp into the stadium in almost eerie fashion. He wasn't running, he wasn't walking, he looked as if he was in a trance. There was a sudden hush as the crowd immediately recognised something was seriously wrong. I completely forgot my race and moved into the centre of the field to see what was happening. It was very distressing. His mouth was open and his eyes vacant and staring into space, his limbs didn't seem to be coordinating and I was worried he might collapse and die. The crowd alternated between being hushed when it was worried about him, and then cheering him on each time he managed to lift himself forward. It was a pitiful sight.'

Gosper, who in later years would become a senior International Olympic Committee (IOC) member, had been on the infield alongside fellow countryman John Landy, the valiant loser in the Mile. Landy was equally horrified and dismayed at what was unfolding and says he still feels sad about the *faux pas* over the finish-line location. He says he liked Jim, found him a real gentleman who always gave his all, and who didn't deserve such a disaster, for he wasn't reckless, but as well-prepared as anybody running the marathon that day.

Celebrated sportswriter Frank Keating would put his own evocative slant on the scene: 'The acclaim that greeted Jim Peters froze to a horrified silence as the traditional victory parade of a single 400-metre circuit of the track turned into a grotesquely hideous ballet ... a pitifully tottering dance of death. Instinct and a misbegotten willpower under the merciless sun had Peters keeling over onto the cinder track again and again like a drunken vaudeville tumbler. Each time he hauled himself up once more to stagger on in a groggy, futile nobility. When some from the grandstands, unable to bear it, began to shout for a stop, the stadium announcer crassly called for order and "respect for sportsmanship".' High in the pressbox, Peter Wilson of *The Daily Mirror* fed another sheet into his typewriter to convey his horror at 'the nauseous spectacle of a semi-conscious man being allowed to destroy himself while no one had the power or gumption to intervene'.

One paper reported that experienced Calgary newsman Gordon Hunter was physically sick while watching Jim, and hard-bitten *Life* magazine photographer Ralph Morse was in floods of tears. Morse had been leaving the stadium with pictures of the Mile but when he saw the new drama, quickly returned. Many women wept and averted their eyes, and the Duke of Edinburgh was also seen to turn away from the scene several times, a grim expression on his face.

Al Lawrence is still amazed some 47 years later that the English management didn't know, or hadn't been properly informed, that the marathon finish-line was 220 yards further on – knowledge that would surely have seen them pull Jim out of the race earlier to prevent this gruesome spectacle. Lawrence points out: 'Canadian officials had repeated this to us Australian runners several times when we checked in and lined up for the race, but it was pretty obvious that many of the other team managers might be still at the Village assembling their teams or still in transit. Whatever, it was taking a dangerous risk announcing something this important on such a brutal day, to the runners only. And I cannot believe there were no Canadian officials around at the end to inform the English people where the line actually was.'

The grotesque sight of Jim collapsing and getting up again lasted around eleven awful minutes before he reached the painted line many apparently believed was the finish. Here he was caught by English trainer and masseur Mick Mays and the official Ernest Clynes, just before he toppled for a thirteenth time. But as he was still half-a-lap short of the appointed finish, Games officials had no alternative but to disqualify him, announcing the fact as he was being borne away on a stretcher.

Wrote George Whiting of *The Evening Standard*: 'Who can ever forget the convulsions of those skinny limbs over the sides of the stretcher as they bore him away like a wide-mouthed fish that has fought and lost?' Like thousands of other onlookers, Whiting had struggled to comprehend why England officials restrained a blue-shirted doctor who was trying to bring succour to the zigzagging Peters when he first arrived. He was later named as Dr Craig Arnold, who, like his medical colleagues on duty, had never attended athletics before, and was unfamiliar with procedures.

Beleaguered team manager Truelove tried to fend off the criticism: 'Yes, had I known when Peters entered the stadium that he'd been expected to run nearly a whole lap more, I would have ordered him to be taken out immediately.' Mick Mays had been in the same boat, assuming the 'normal' finish-line where they were waiting was the correct one for Jim to head for. There had been no early intervention from the English because they thought their man was very close to finishing, and didn't want a repeat of the 1908 disqualification controversy surrounding Dorando (Jim would later state his firm belief that when Mays grabbed him, he genuinely thought he had finished and therefore won the race). There was booing from the crowd when the disqualification was announced, but the people gathered alongside Jim's stretcher had by now become more concerned about whether he would live rather than his fate on the results sheet. He was whisked away to the Shaughnessey War Veterans hospital in Oaks Street, put in an oxygen tent, given a saline drip and a knotty cramp was rubbed from one of his legs.

Geoff Warren takes up the story again: 'Poor old Joe McGhee came into the stadium a fair while later and seemed to be hardly noticed, his win an anti-climax after the Peters drama. Jim was criticised by some for not making allowances for the heat, but I argued at the time that this wasn't so. He had discussed it beforehand and I know he lowered his planned pace and schedule to allow for the effects of the heat. The huge lead he had through the middle of the race had caused people to jump to their conclusion. His judgement was pretty close to spot-on accurate for, after all, had the finish had been a quarter-mile closer, it would have been a glorious victory. I got to know Jim pretty well and liked him a lot. The Aussies who visited him in his rooms at the Village got on especially well with him and our little tough-nut marathoner, Bryce MacKay, formed a particular bond.'

The crowd held its breath when McGhee finally arrived, expecting to see another hapless figure struggling to stay on his feet. The relief was palpable when the Shettlestone Harrier ran in smoothly and untroubled to win in 2:39.36. Jackie Mekler came in, amazed to find himself second in 2:40.57, his compatriot Jan Barnard a weary and blistered third in 2:51.50. Only six of the sixteen starters finished the ordeal.

Mekler recalls with a smile: 'When I finally ran into the stadium I was told by excited spectators I was about to finish second, but I couldn't believe it. Only when Vic Dreyer, who'd just finished second in the hammer, dashed across the track and yelled at me "Jackie, you are lying second!" did I think it might be true. Suddenly I no longer felt distressed and sprinted that last lap on the track. I was so relieved I felt I had just woken from a bad dream.

'McGhee, Barnard and I were led to the podium after a while and I suddenly realised I hadn't practised what to do next. Not being a ra-ra fist-throwing person, I thought "just be yourself" and waved a limp arm and stood looking vague while the strains of the Scottish anthem wafted across the stadium. What an incredible race-cum-fiasco!' McGhee and Mekler felt good, but poor Barnard had painfully raw and blistered feet and had to be supported on the podium by McGhee and two boy scouts.

In terms of medals, England had been the best-performing nation at the Games, with Bannister's marvellous mile the triumph to savour, but inevitably it was the Jim Peters drama that preoccupied most of those in the pressbox. They had a field day dissecting the remains of Jim's grisly defeat.

Frank Rostron of *The Daily Express* wrote: 'I cannot recall anything in sport quite so shocking as the spectacle of the poor, semi-conscious Peters … if you think I exaggerate, I can only say that over a score of women fainted at the dreadful sight of the three-parts unconscious Peters, staggering and falling, staggering and falling, getting up, crawling, pawing the air and stumbling blindly like some maimed animal. Red Cross men carried women out on stretchers. Thousands of others averted their eyes. Strong men either bit their lips or screamed "Get a doctor"!' *The Daily Mirror's* Peter Wilson said: 'I never want to see another marathon in which someone cannot step in and say "This is no longer sport" … Sport can be heroic or routine, you can thrill to it or yawn through it, but it should never revolt you, make you squirm, force you to close your eyes and feel dirty and ashamed, as though you had paid a black market price to be a privileged spectator at a public execution.'

Dick Beddoes of *The Vancouver Sun* admitted to being sickened yet awe-struck: 'Memory of the Londoner's raw courage in defiance of the comforts of quitting was so vivid as to be nauseating. For his performance was overwhelmingly wonderful yet completely horrible. It was like watching a man die. Each time he fell he grew more wretched, a tormented soul dredging the depths of his resolution. And when nature had exacted its terrible toll he collapsed into the mercy of oblivion. The tragedy was compounded when he stumbled blind to the cinders, the finish line mocking him 185 yards away. What happened before unconsciousness set in caused women to weep and strong men to lose their lunch. One such was a veteran newsman, a good one and a tough one. He went under the stands and was revoltingly sick by himself.'

The Canadian public was horrified and wrote to local papers in droves, some calling for marathon running to be outlawed. 'We nearly had a tragedy on our conscience,' wrote one. Another condemned as 'indecent and disrespectful of a hero' the description by local columnist Jack Wasserman who had said Jim 'flopped around like a gutted salmon'.

In 2011, Jackie Mekler reflects: 'What happened at Vancouver did not surprise me, but the manner and severity of it certainly did. Peters was no doubt a very fast marathon runner, but needed ideal conditions to perform to his best ability. In South Africa we were well aware that both he and Cox dropped out of the 1952 Olympic marathon. Being mindful of the expected warm weather conditions, Johannes Coleman, winner of the 1938 Empire Marathon, and ultra record holder Wally Hayward openly predicted Peters would fail at Vancouver. Should the event have been

staged at a cooler time of the day? I would generally agree, but not totally so. I was delighted that it wasn't, because I was used to 54-mile
Comrades Marathon distances, as well as running in races under the conditions to be expected in Vancouver, and always relished hard, tough conditions. Is a marathon race not supposed to be a test of endurance as well
as speed? Should a top marathon runner not be able to adjust to all conditions?

'While Peters was doing his short, sharp training runs, I was out doing
50-milers in the heat of the day. To me, one of the most lingering memories of Vancouver was the fact that there were strict instructions that
runners' attendants or managers were not allowed on the course, no
intermediate times were given by officials, and certainly at the final feeding station, shambles reigned. There were no officials present to ensure
that their ludicrous rules were carried out.'

And so as the dust settled on Vancouver that Saturday night, the nurs-
es at Shaughnessey Hospital kept a close eye on their pale and limp star
visitors from England, Peters and Cox. Six-mile runners Frank Sando and
Peter Driver were among the anxious faces in the waiting room, hoping
to get an update on their teammates' progress, as was thrower John
Savidge. Newsmen were largely kept at bay by the medics. Jim's new
Australian friends were among the countless others deeply concerned for
him, and at one point the following morning, they were stunned to hear
strong rumours that Jim had actually died during the night. Geoff Warren
recalls this episode:

'The following morning I went rowing with a friend in a boat on
Vancouver Lake and we passed a couple picnicking on the shore. They
had one of those huge heavy portable radios of the time and we heard
clearly a news broadcast to the effect that sadly Jim Peters had died in
hospital. The shock of this news put an immediate end to our outing and
we returned gloomily to the Village, only to hear thankfully the reports
were untrue.'

FOOTNOTE: BRITISH EMPIRE & COMMONWEALTH GAMES MARATHON,
VANCOUVER BC, CANADA, SATURDAY, 7 AUGUST 1954:

1 Joe McGhee (Scotland) 2:39.36.0; 2 Jackie Mekler (S Africa)
2:40.57.0; 3 Jan Barnard (S Africa) 2:51.49.8; 4 Barry Lush (Canada)
2:52.47.4; 5 George Hillier (Canada) 2:58.43.4; 6 Bob Crossan (N Ireland)
3:00.12.2. Only six finished.

DID NOT FINISH: Gerard Cote (Canada), Stan Cox (England), Keith
Dunnett (Canada), Rowland Guy (Australia), John Kay (N Rhodesia),
Allan Lawrence (Australia), Bryce MacKay (Australia), George Norman
(Canada), Jim Peters (England), Les Stokell (Canada). Sixteen started.

CHAPTER 23

The Inquest Opens

8 AUGUST – 31 AUGUST 1954

According to which of the various reports you believe, Jim Peters' first words on regaining consciousness in hospital were either 'Did I finish?' or 'Did I win?' A kindly nurse is said to have quickly come up with a diplomatic answer: 'You did very well, dear.'

Jim would admit that upon waking he immediately had the strong feeling he hadn't been victorious in Vancouver; his memories of the previous day were hazy and he had no recollection of breaking a tape. When news of his disqualification was eventually broken to him, he was bitterly disappointed, remaining convinced his collapse had come many yards after completing the regulation distance of 26.2 miles.

He would later tell *Stars and Stripes* newspaper: 'The first bloody bloke I see [after waking] is Stan Cox in the next bed. So I look at him and say what the bloody hell are you doing here? And when he said he'd collapsed I realised I hadn't imagined it all, and that I hadn't been a coward either. With the heat and exhaustion Stan had even run head first into a telegraph pole. I said, you didn't win then? And he said no, so I said, who the hell did then? And he didn't know.' Laying there dazed and confused, the two runners watched as a sympathetic surgeon's wife came in and placed a pink rose from her garden on Jim's bedside table.

Jim would recount how a specialist had likened his condition to a man exposed to the sun in an open boat for two weeks, and that they estimated he'd been unconscious for about two hours in all. He cleared up the mystery of why he kept veering to the right on the track, saying it was not really a lack of control, but more a desire to head for the shade. More than 32,000 people had seen him fall twelve times, but he could only remember three of these. After one of the tumbles it had suddenly occurred to him that it would be cooler if he could reach the shade of the main grandstand in which the Duke of Edinburgh was sitting.

One of the few reporters to gain access to his hospital room would be Jack Oaten of *The London Evening News*, who Jim knew well and who wormed his way in by promising to get a message to Jim's worried wife back home. Frieda was staying with runner Bob Pape and his wife Dinah, whose Southsea home was not on the telephone. Oaten's plan was to phone his own exclusive story through to his newsdesk late on the Saturday night after the race, and then get a message relayed to Jim's coach Johnny Johnston, who could then track down the Peters family members.

The news that Jim had recovered consciousness and was in no immediate danger was passed first to his father-in-law in Chadwell Heath, and then to Southsea police. An officer of the Hants constabulary tracked down the Pape household early on the Sunday and poor, fretting Frieda was finally given the good news.

As he slowly recovered his senses during the Sunday, Jim was fascinated to find that for the first time in his marathon career he didn't have stiff muscles the day after a race, putting this down to the effect of the saline injections they'd given him. By the Monday he'd had time to take stock of his running career, and although he knew that running Berne in late August was now out of the question, he initially felt he might still be capable of giving the 1956 Olympics a shot. However, as he revealed in his 1955 book, this idea soon paled when it dawned on him the Vancouver experience had badly scarred him, mentally if not physically: 'I knew that I would never be able to fight again as I had often had to do in my races in the past.' The thought that he had gone close to dying meant he might never again be able to call on his peculiar ability to push himself to extremes in a race. It was time to stop, and even stubborn Jim Peters knew it.

Other factors supporting retirement were his age and the fact he was not happy with 'my position in life', a reference to a lack of advancement in his career due to his preoccupation with running. He had a wife, two young children and a smart home to support, and felt that if he could put the same energy and enthusiasm he'd put into running into his business affairs, he would do well. And, of course, how much better it would be to retire at the top, before the younger bucks started overtaking?

As he lay in hospital mulling this over, back home his horrific experience dominated both front and back pages. The story of his gallant failure was seen as bigger news even than Labour leader Clement Attlee's visit to the Soviet Union, a flood disaster in China and a major riot in Morocco. The papers also announced that his place in the team for the forthcoming European Championships would be filled by Geoff Iden and there was news that Melbourne officials had promised not to stage their Olympic marathon of 1956 any earlier than 3pm, having noted what happened to Jim.

On Jim's fourth bed-ridden day, *The Daily Express* organised a transatlantic phone call to the hospital involving Frieda, but team manager Les Truelove stepped in and banned it, saying that because a newspaper was involved it constituted an interview and these must wait until he was fully recovered. Jim was remarkably forgiving in the circumstances, saying: 'Although this decision may have seemed a hard one, it must have been very difficult for him at such long range to differentiate between what was perhaps a genuine effort to help Frieda, and what was just journalistic strategy.'

On the Wednesday evening he was finally permitted to speak to his wife, unbeknown to her from the confines of his wheelchair, and he assured her he was fine and that he'd decided not to run any more marathons. Arrangements were then made for his delayed homecoming, and Jim was deeply touched to find that not only had Truelove waited on in Vancouver to take him home, but so had Mile hero Roger Bannister. The latter had only recently qualified as a doctor and felt Jim might need assistance on the long flight. He had acquainted himself with the details of Jim's case and would know how to react if he became unwell again.

Sir Roger recalls how he handled one of the very first patients in what would be a long and distinguished career: 'I went to see him in hospital on the evening of the race – I saw to it that he had the best of care. He was in good spirits when I accompanied him from Vancouver and back to his home. I don't know the details of his training, but it was clearly effective for him generally, except in Vancouver when the environmental conditions required a change of fluid and salt intake. In retrospect he didn't adapt well to the heat conditions and allowed himself to be water and salt depleted, leading to his collapse.' Asked if Jim had been unwise to also run the six-miles earlier, Sir Roger adds: 'In my view it is better to concentrate on only one race in a championships.'

The London Evening Standard ran a dramatic piece about the scenes at the hospital in the wake of Jim's arrival there, although by the time it appeared in print he was, of course, well on the way to recovery. It must have nevertheless been quite disturbing for friends and family to read George Whiting's graphic tale of 'two tiny rooms with bare concrete walls' at the Shaughnessey Hospital thousands of miles away.

'These rooms,' wrote Whiting, 'will stay in my memory forever. This was where I saw the aftermath of possibly the greatest triumph and possibly the greatest tragedy in the whole panorama of athletic sport.' He described a grim iron bed, blanketed in grey, upon which Jim Peters was 'whimpering like a wounded animal, his arms jerking convulsively, his plimsolled feet twitching a ghastly kind of tattoo on the wall, his knees cinder-scratched, his pores oozing perspiration, saliva drooling from his colourless lips.'

This was the room of tragedy, whereas the other room had the whiff of triumph, for it contained Bannister, speaking quietly yet incisively as he took his small media audience step by step through his great Mile victory, bringing the so-called 'interview' to a halt by putting on his Panama hat and dark glasses and briskly exiting through a private door with a policeman.

Meanwhile, other papers broke the news that Jim's efforts would see him presented with a special gallantry-in-sport medal from the Helms Athletic Foundation of Los Angeles. In addition, the Duke of Edinburgh had also expressed a wish to make a 'small personal presentation' later in the year, in recognition of Jim's gallant attempt to win a gold medal. Prince Philip's personal secretary confirmed this, just as the royal party set off on their own quest for gold, flying from Vancouver to Whitehorse in Yukon, where they were shown relics of the fabulous 'gold rush' days. After the best part of a week in hospital, Jim was declared fit to travel and, looking frail but smiling shyly, he left Vancouver to a warm farewell. The Canadian public had taken him to their hearts and he received a testimonial message from the Mayor on behalf of the city. He was also touched to be asked to lend his name to two trophies that would be competed for by young local runners, in recognition of the courageous and dedicated example he'd set.

His Constellation airliner's laborious journey eastwards involved stops at various Canadian cities. At Montreal the Scotland team's plane was spotted just departing, prompting Jim to quip that they should hurry so that he could finally catch up with Joe McGhee. Having crossed the Atlantic, the journey had lasted almost fifteen hours by the time they were told there was serious fog across England and they were being diverted from London Airport to Manston aerodrome in Kent. This was bad news for the reception committee at the airport, which had included Alderman Aubrey Headley, Mayor of Ilford, and Jim's family.

The fog was merely one of a series of difficulties, for the plane experienced trouble with its undercarriage when preparing to land, and there would follow more delays getting through customs at Manston, followed by considerable traffic congestion as they headed by hire car across London. A weary Jim finally arrived home many hours late to find the patient reception committee had by now decamped to his front garden. The fog had gone and a BBC film crew was among the hordes of reporters, neighbours and council dignitaries wilting underneath coloured bunting in the sunshine. Having seen his 'patient' safely home, albeit much more slowly than anticipated, Roger Bannister was now free to depart for his own homecoming ceremony at Harrow.

'For he's a jolly good fellow' they sang, as Jim, limping, his pale face adorned with a badly blistered lip and his tie hanging loose, embraced

Frieda and gleeful son Robin, and then held baby Jennifer. Within an hour or two he was tucked up in bed, sound asleep while the rest of Britain gasped in horror at their first sight of his ordeal on the TV news that evening. According to *The News Chronicle*, newsreel film showing ten minutes of Jim repeatedly collapsing had been edited down to a mere 43 seconds, so distressing was the content. Jim had lost control of several bodily functions, it seems, and the footage of his twitching, traumatised body had to be treated with care; it was shown on the mid-evening news and sensitive viewers couldn't retreat to another channel (ITV would launch in 1955, a year later). At least the mood would be lightened immediately afterwards when music hall act Bransby Williams and the feature film *Train to Auburn* took over.

Over the next few days, seemingly everybody wanted a piece of exhausted Jim, youngsters arriving on the doorstep for autographs, the phone constantly ringing and mail arriving by the sackful, some from sympathetic well wishers, others inviting him to functions here, there and everywhere. Eventually, it all became too much and the family beat a hasty retreat to an old Army friend's remote cottage in South Wales, a haven of peace and quiet where they were almost completely unreachable. After six days of complete relaxation here, the time came to 'pay' for the holiday, Jim attending a series of functions in the neighbourhood, where he was feted like a hero, shaking hands and signing autographs for hours on end.

By now he'd convinced his wife he was definitely quitting competitive running, even though she worried that she'd heard this all before. This time was different recalled Jim: 'For the first time for many years I had lost a lot of my enthusiasm – and what is more, I felt that I had lost my killer instinct, which I apparently always previously had the moment I toed the line for a race. Where it had come from I don't know, for with all modesty I think most people have always considered me quite a kind-hearted sort of person – until I ran a marathon, then it was "kill or be killed".'

A chat with coach Johnny sealed the matter once and for all, the pair of them agreeing he should quit now, while he was about a mile quicker than any other marathoner in the world – a situation that would not exist by the time of the next Olympics in two years. The Russians and Finns, in particular, were now training on the same lines as he had, and would be considerably quicker by 1956, whereas Jim, by then approaching his 39th birthday, would surely have slowed somewhat. It felt right to get out while he was still top of the tree, but they agreed not to announce it publicly for a week or two.

It was clear Jim would badly miss the camaraderie and buzz of competition, but he consoled himself by planning a brand new lifestyle. He would run gently and occasionally to keep fit, continue his involvement with the sport via coaching and writing, and channel most of his energy into setting up and launching his own optician's business.

He may have privately declared his career over, but the inquest into what happened in Vancouver would carry on for months. He was quite happy to give his side of the story when asked, for a sense of injustice still burned within him about certain aspects of the race. He reiterated to *Scots Athlete* magazine about the scandalous lack of support and information out on the course: 'I will not comment on the English officials in this respect, but this I do know: the Scottish team manager, to his undying glory, had the interest and foresight to get out on that sun-baked road to help Joe McGhee. How he managed it, or how much he followed Joe, I am in no position to say or judge as I was away out in front. But I will say this, I bear no malice and if I had been the team manager of Joe I would most certainly have done all I possibly could to help my boy too. I do not consider it breaking any rules and I furthermore consider that [organiser] Alex Frew was much too severe in laying the rule down that managers must not follow in cars.'

Meanwhile, the American magazine *Track and Field News* supported Jim's claims that the race had been considerably over distance and gave officials heavy stick over this and other issues. But Alex Frew defended himself in a lengthy statement in which he said: 'Every preparation for the race was properly carried out.' He said that six feeding stations spread out after the ten-mile point had been manned by an average of six officials and the exact requirements of every runner were supplied. Frew also pointed out: 'It has been stated in the press that English officials were not permitted on the course. This is not true. They were told they would not be allowed to accompany their runners in a car. I wanted as few cars as possible on the course for the simple reason I wanted to keep exhaust fumes away from the runners. English officials and all other officials were told they could station themselves at feeding stations to keep an eye on their runners. The English did not take advantage of this opportunity which was open to all, [whereas] I personally saw Scotland's coaches at five different spots around the course.' He added, significantly: 'All runners were shown at the start of the race the exact finish line.'

Silver-medallist Jackie Mekler points out that some people did feel Jim's troubles had been largely self-inflicted: 'Several highly respected British athletics critics went on record condemning Peters' judgement. Joe Binks and James Audsley both claimed that Peters' pace under the prevailing conditions was suicidal, and that he should have adjusted his speed to the conditions.' British official Jack Crump also raised a fair point: 'While I yield to no one in my admiration for the courage of Peters and Cox … I cannot understand why this pair, great friends as well as great rivals, trained by the same coach and running for the same country, felt it necessary to run each other into the ground rather than run together for 25 miles and fight out the last mile and 385 yards. I am sure England would have then been first with Peters and second with Cox.'

Binks was scathing: 'Peters crumbled from exhaustion because he thinks mainly of speed and records in a marathon. It is suicide and Peters knows it. It took him only 28 and a half minutes to run the first five miles, but fifteen minutes to painfully crawl or stumble 200 yards to what he thought was the finish line.'

The other main criticism levelled at Jim concerned his decision to run a hot six-mile track race seven days before tackling the marathon. But six-mile runner-up Frank Sando told me this hadn't been significant: 'I was not surprised he chose to double up, but the six miles was probably more of a hard training run for him. In fact he ran it very well, as it happened. I did witness his upsetting collapse at the end of the marathon and remember visiting the hospital in the evening with Peter Driver to find out about him. Seeing both him and Stan Cox in beds attached to drips convinced me that marathons were not going to be my scene later in my own career.'

The controversy rumbled on for weeks in the athletics press, with one side condemning Jim's uncompromising and reckless approach to racing and training in all conditions, and the other praising his courage and great record. Perhaps the most entertaining contribution would come from his friend Bob Pape, who told *Athletics Weekly* that Jim was 'the greatest marathon specialist of all time, with all due respect to the gallant plodders of yesteryear'. He said Jim's methods had taken him to the top and 'bashing it' was the only way he could run. He said he'd even seen Jim run a fast ten miles shortly after a huge Christmas dinner one year. Pape concluded: 'Any man who contemplates a "jellyfish" approach to training and racing over long distances may as well go home and play tiddlywinks.'

Generally, any criticism of Jim was washed away by a tsunami of sympathy and admiration, and prominent was *Athletics Weekly*'s clarion call: 'Don't feel you have let the old country down, Jim. We think as much of you now as we should have done if you'd won in world record time, and on a course of such severity this would have been next to impossible. No one could have put up a better show of British guts and we're proud of you!'

Even his critics had sympathy, with runner-up Mekler telling me: 'One does have to spare a thought for Peters. If only someone had told him at that last feeding station how great his lead was, he could have walked the rest of the way and still won. The anticipation and excitement [of the mile race] definitely impacted negatively on the marathon as many officials became caught up in the frenzy surrounding that.'

Although there had been no live TV coverage, Jim's Vancouver adventure had been relayed back to his friends and family via BBC radio. Clubmate Colin Young recalls: 'I heard about it all on the radio back home – that was our only media connection with live athletics in those days – via the voices of Harold Abrahams, Norris McWhirter and Rex Alston. As I listened I knew it was typical of Jim to stumble on and on – for he would never have wanted to repeat what he considered the worst day of his athletic life at the Helsinki games. When I and a couple of the Beagles lads saw the finish on TV a couple of days later we knew exactly why he had staggered on – Jim simply never knew any other way.'

Ted Baverstock told me: 'I was living in Barking at the time and clearly remember the cinema newsreel footage of it, for I couldn't afford a TV at the time. Like many other athletes, along with the general public, I was shocked by Jim's physical distress. We were in awe of his determination and courage to finish and his struggles to rise to his feet. If it's true the actual distance of that race was far in excess of the standard 26.2, then he was robbed of an amazing triumph through official incompetence. Quite tragic.'

In the hours, days and then years after the race, a number of half-truths and myths grew about what exactly had happened to eventual winner Joe McGhee during the race. There had been reports he'd stopped running altogether on five occasions, in one incident had fallen into a ditch, and that he had quit more than once, only to be persuaded to carry on. The general impression grew up that McGhee had been a somewhat 'lucky' winner, stumbling along haplessly for many miles, and only able to pull himself together when news reached him of Jim Peters' collapse up ahead.

This was clearly nonsense and McGhee came away from Vancouver with less credit than he surely deserved. He went on to become Head of Applied Linguistics at Aberdeen College of Education and an English lecturer at the University of Aberdeen, and told author Peter Lovesey in 1980 that because he had been disgusted by the 'ballyhoo' surrounding Vancouver he had resolutely avoided entering all the debates afterwards. In fact, it would be 50 years before he gave a detailed account of his side of the story, thus finally putting to bed the various misunderstandings.

This was in an interview with *Scotland on Sunday* in 1994 when he revealed his plan had been to latch on to the leaders until their pace felt too hot and then simply concentrate on finishing. He stayed with Jim until nine miles, when the English champion 'launched himself into a tremendous spurt' on a hilly section, a move he did not follow. At ten miles the unbearable heat saw him toss aside his peaked hat which had become an annoyance. For the next eight miles he ran alone before Al Lawrence overtook, a bad moment that provoked a personal crisis in which he began to believe he wouldn't even finish.

He then re-passed Lawrence, who had quit at the roadside, and then saw Scottish team manager Willie Carmichael up ahead, recalling: 'I was determined not to drop out, but was hoping desperately that Willie would be merciful, take the decision for me and pull me out. His response was simply to scowl and gruffly urge me on. I swerved, half twisted to glare back at him, and found myself running into a high, jaggy hedge. The prickles and my resentment of Willie stung me into a short-lived burst of speed.'

A mile or so later McGhee says he was told Stan Cox had been carted off by ambulance, meaning he was now second with less than five miles left. A very difficult period followed, including a heavy trip on a kerbstone, plus realisation that two South African runners were closing from behind. 'It was at that very moment my own personal miracle occurred, demonstrating the power of the mind over the body. I suddenly realised I was going to finish these last three miles and my energies and my racing instincts came surging back.'

By trying to 'hide' from the South Africans by running close to the crowded pavement, he then suffered a nasty collision with a group of spectators, but recovered to settle into a comfortable steady pace. Determination had by now replaced exhaustion and the prospect of a silver medal dragged him onward, and he tried to ignore excited messages that the man ahead (Jim Peters) was in poor shape. At the hill outside the stadium he was told of Jim's collapse and admitted his reaction was panic, not joy. He looked back but the two Springboks were nowhere to be seen: 'I knew then I could not be beaten and I never felt better in any race. The hill held no terrors for me now ... into the stadium and I was struck by the deathly hush. The crowd had been shocked into silence by Peters' collapse. "What is the next man going to be like?" was the question uppermost in everyone's mind.'

Framed in the opening to the track he saw the track-suited figure of Dr Euan Douglas, Scottish team captain, initially shocked but then ecstatic to see a Scot leading. Added McGhee: 'I have never received such a reception. The crowd's reaction must have been one of immense relief that this runner was not in a state of collapse. My ears were literally popping with the din as I raced around the track towards the tape to become at 25 the youngest marathon winner in the history of the Games.'

McGhee then summed up the reasons for Jim's failure with perhaps the most concise and perceptive verdict that anyone had so far come up with. It had taken 50 years, but it seemed the nail had finally been hit firmly on the head. McGhee said: 'England should have won the gold and silver medals comfortably, and it is not enough to point to the weather conditions and the hilly nature of the course to explain why they did not. After all, these were the same for everyone and, when you race you are competing not only against the other runners, but the elements and the course as well. You have to adapt accordingly. I personally ran half a minute slower per mile than I was capable of. Peters obviously did not. A world record time was simply out of the question that day. The whole point of the exercise surely was to win the medal and each of us was chosen by our respective countries to do just that. I managed to do so, Peters did not. A "glorious failure" is all very well but it does not disguise the fact that Jim Peters, the best and most experienced marathon runner in the world at the time, lost because he ran an unintelligent race.'

CHAPTER 24

Time to Call a Halt

Six weeks after his Vancouver ordeal, Jim was examined for a second time by the AAA's medical adviser, the distinguished physician Sir Adolphe Abrahams. He was pronounced fully recovered, but instead of going out for a celebratory run, the patient sprang a surprise by promptly making a formal public announcement that he was quitting.

Some had by now suspected Jim would never be seen on a marathon course again, but many who knew him fancied he would return to the roads after a rest, and were stunned by his announcement. It was certainly a big disappointment to organisers of an all-star marathon planned for Tokyo, who had been hoping to set up 'the greatest marathon of all time' featuring Peters, Zatopek, Cabrera and Karvonen.

Jim said he was retiring to concentrate on his business career, and was proud to be stepping aside while still the fastest man in history. A factor in his decision was the likelihood that the next Olympic marathon, in Melbourne, would be another hot one. He told one reporter: 'If I ran in Melbourne I wouldn't be able to hold back. I told John Landy that if it was hot there, I'd only go and tear the floor down, just like I did before.' Right to the very end of his career, Jim knew he could really only run one way, and that was 'eyeballs out'. Although he was now older and wiser after Vancouver, it would still be a dangerous move to let him attack the marathon distance in hot conditions, and now he could see that.

He was retiring at the top, with four of the six best marathon times ever run under his belt. It was a status that more than 50 years later would see at least one expert describe him as the greatest marathoner of all time. He was hanging up his racing shoes with a stash of more than 200 cups, medals and plaques, a long list of international, national, county and club records, not to mention nearly twenty years of great memories. He'd run eleven marathons in three glorious years, winning eight of them, one second place, two failures to finish, and four 'world bests' into the bargain. Moreover, he'd dragged the event into a new era. It was the unparalleled record of a man totally immersed in his chosen sport, and many of his acquaintances refused to believe he could just walk away from competitive running like this.

The Barking Advertiser's sports columnist was one of them. He reckoned he had it on good authority Jim had been out running in his old

Essex haunts, although no longer doing so on a daily basis. He was doing 'light training spins in the region of ten miles', in the company of Vancouver opponent Bryce MacKay, who was in Europe for the championships in Berne, it was stated. Essex Beagles had been stunned by Jim's retirement announcement, but felt that although he'd steer clear of marathons, he would continue to run for them at club level. So certain were they that he would reappear in the gold-and-black hooped vest that they named him in their London-to-Brighton relay team. Jim may have been tempted, but he stuck to his word and there would be no comebacks.

Undaunted, the Beagles offered Jim a place on their general committee in addition to his position as an honorary life member, but he declined, saying he was simply too busy these days. The club was disappointed and, at their AGM, members heard an impassioned plea from coach Dave Green urging them to start showing a little more club spirit. In the new era without star performer Jim Peters, he said the members must forget their recent obsession with 'pot-hunting' and think more of the good of the club.

Jim told them he was keen to coach the club's juniors in his spare time, but nothing more. His new life was becoming hectic, for he was making plans to take charge of his own business and was accepting various writing commissions from the national press and starting work on an autobiography, for which he'd even bought himself a typewriter. On top of this, he had a list of 28 functions to attend between October and Christmas 1954. Importantly, he added, he was also getting back to life as a normal family man 'for the first time in eight years', helping plan the christening of daughter Jennifer at St Chad's Church and making time to play football with son Robin. In between all this, he was still running, albeit relatively gently, three times a week.

At this point, as well as renewing his friendship with Bryce MacKay, Jim also bumped into Aussie runners John Landy, Geoff Warren and Don Macmillan, who were staying nearby during their world tour. They trained at the Beagles' summer HQ at Mayesbrook Park and were impressed with the facilities. Landy told the local paper: 'It's one of the best tracks I've ever run on. I'm hoping I'll manage to have a track built on the same lines back in Australia.' He said there were no cinder tracks in his home state of Victoria and he was planning to take home a sample of the composite cinder and clay surface to show people.

Meanwhile, the tributes to Jim continued unabated. There was one from Dagenham Trades Council which supported a resolution to have Dagenham Council confer the freedom of the borough on Jim, whose home in Havering Gardens was marginally over the border with Ilford, but who had spent most of his life in their territory. Then, during the Louis Trophy athletics meeting at Woodford, presentations were made to Jim and Frieda, the latter accepting a gold wrist watch and a brush set from Barking councillor W Sugden, who called her 'the courageous wife of a very courageous man'. Jim took the microphone, explaining Frieda was too shy to do so, and spent a few moments reminiscing about his early days with the Beagles: 'I was so keen to run that as soon as I was old enough I saved up a whole month's pocket money – one and sixpence – to pay my first subscription. It was money well spent!'

Like it or not, Jim was now a real 'celebrity' and some of the public appearances he was urged to make had little or nothing to do with sport. On one fine Thursday in September he took Frieda and Robin to the cavernous Olympia exhibition hall in London where they had to clamber onto a platform and declare open the Handicrafts, Homecrafts and Hobbies exhibition. For the umpteenth time he was asked to regale a big audience with a summary of his collapse in Vancouver. As he did so, two teenage girls a few yards away were incongruously demonstrating the art of wallpapering.

One function he found particularly enjoyable was a Poly Marathon Reunion Evening, at which he was guest speaker, and which featured a lengthy film of his June 1954 'world best' run between Windsor and Chiswick. Produced by enthusiasts from the Heston Community Centre Cine Club, the film delighted its VIP audience by featuring a dubbed 'running commentary' from Jim himself. Particularly well received were Jim's self-effacing remarks about how nervous he'd always been before races, especially during that 'awful moment' many runners experience when collecting a competitor's number beforehand.

He was becoming quite adept at charming an audience with his unpretentious cockney accent and modest manner and, now that he'd opted out of competitive running, found himself free to speak out on various thorny issues without the fear of upsetting administrators to his own disadvantage. He made an impassioned plea for promising youngsters (as he had been in the 1930s) to be awarded athletics scholarships to help their development, and for elite performers to be given work that would allow them to train properly. He told the reunion:

'The old diehards won't like this, but the standard of world sport has reached such a peak that unless an athlete is given a job where he can give sport top priority we shall not win any more gold medals at Melbourne in 1956 than we did in Helsinki in 1952. I know I could have done better for Britain but for the fact that coming between me and the job of reaching perfect fitness was the more important task of providing for my family. Therefore I condemn the system that forces part-time athletes to struggle against the subsidised might of America, the millions behind the Iron Curtain and, let's face it, the whole continent of Europe. I condemn the men who are preventing Britain from leading the world in sport.'

In a newspaper article, Jim criticised the training methods of English professional footballers in the wake of Arsenal's feeble 0-5 defeat at the hands of Moscow Dynamo in an October friendly match. His remarks coincided with his idea of giving training/fitness lectures to clubs outside of athletics, with his local club West Ham United being one of the first takers. He believed footballers could learn a lot from the way athletes trained, but his opinions outraged England wing wizard Stanley Matthews, who said distance running and football were poles apart and Jim ought not to pontificate on something he knew nothing about. 'Football is much harder than athletics,' hit back Stan, currently still starring for Blackpool at the age of 39.

Towards the end of 1954 plans were underway towards Jim opening his own optician's business. He subsequently leased premises in Western Road on Fairgreen, Mitcham and before long 'J H Peters, Dispensing Optician' was up and running. Later he would open a second shop at 192 High Road, Chadwell Heath, a short distance from his home, the latter premises carrying his name long after his eventual retirement.

With characteristic energy and commitment Jim threw himself into making his business a success, and the time he spent on athletics matters diminished even further. He admitted he was still keen to take on a coaching role in some form or other, but because he found himself 'comparatively poor' knew it was more important to give priority to the business venture. In late 1954 he'd still been unable to afford a car, although the family did by now have mod cons such as a washing machine, television and fridge at home. Within a month or two of launching the business he was barely doing any running at all, and after the manuscript of his book was finished, the athletics writing work fizzled out too.

His Mitcham premises were only a short distance from his previous employers in Monarch Parade, meaning that when the Melson Wingate directors were confronted by their new competition they were more than a little miffed. Nigel Wingate told me: 'My father [Douglas Wingate, the former runner] had certainly enabled Jim Peters to take considerable time off work in order to compete. There were only two weeks' holiday in those days. So what my father found very upsetting was that having given him all that support, Jim then opened up his own optician's shop in direct competition.'

At a Mitcham Rotary Club luncheon at the White Hart Hotel, Jim appeared as guest speaker, sitting alongside Mick Mays, the man who caught his limp body at the climax of the Vancouver marathon. No doubt aware of the importance of making well-connected friends in the Mitcham business community, Jim gave his rapt audience good value for money with a lengthy address. He told them that initially he'd thought 'life was finished' when he gave up his running, but had since discovered it was only just beginning.

As if to underline his point, just a few days later he would experience what he called 'the greatest moment of my career in the world of sport'. A handful of Christmas parcels arrived in the post at his home and the postmark and insignia on one indicated it had come from Buckingham Palace. Inside was a large gold Empire Games medal, set in a thick perspex stand, bearing the message: 'This gold medal was given to HRH The Duke of Edinburgh at Vancouver and presented by him to J Peters as a token of admiration for a most gallant marathon runner.'

For once, Jim Peters was almost speechless.

CHAPTER 25

'A Hell of a Bloke'

1955 – 2011

Jim hardly had the time to contemplate how much he was missing running, such was the busy nature of his new post-1954 life. Inevitably his waistline did miss the daily mileage though, and underwent its own expansion programme. By the end of the 1950s he admitted to being several stones heavier than during his heyday.

Annual cross-country events, twenty-milers and marathons came and went without his cheery presence, which initially felt strange to all the other stalwarts, but there was no danger yet of Jim Peters' name being forgotten.

A 216-page book, *In The Long Run*, was published by Cassell in 1955, a recap of his first 36 years as told to Joseph Edmundson, a part-time author better known as organiser of physical education at London Polytechnic. The foreword was contributed by politician and diplomat Philip Noel-Baker, a former mile champion and Olympian, a great admirer of Jim's, and a former cabinet minister who in 1959 would win the Nobel Peace Prize for campaigning for an international arms control treaty. Noel-Baker reckoned Jim's life represented the moving story of a modest man who overcame the greatest of difficulties with courage, sacrifice and resolution.

Having summarized his story on paper, Jim's physical likeness was then crafted for posterity by Wilfred Dudeney at the well-known sculptor's studio in Putney. By 2011 this bust had come 'home' to Dagenham, put on prominent display within the oak-panelled rooms of the impressive Valence House Museum in Becontree Avenue, just yards from where Jim grew up.

In April 1955 Jim received an illuminated address and engraved medal, paid for by public subscription, from the Mayor of Dagenham, and there was further recognition a few weeks later when Woodford Green AC staged its inaugural inter-club match for the Vancouver Trophy. This competition had been instigated by club president Bertie Campbell and friends, who purchased the trophy to honour Jim's gallant efforts in Vancouver. Then it was off to the London HQ of the National Playing Fields Association, where Jim received a Helms Foundation Medal from the USA from the Duke of Edinburgh, the NPFA's president.

During the summer of 1955 the Poly Marathon was won for the first time in five years by someone other than Jim Peters, Flight Sergeant Billy McMinnis's winning time of 2:26.22 some nine minutes slower than Jim's of twelve months earlier. It was followed a month later by the AAA championship marathon in Reading, where Lancastrian McMinnis won again, and Jim watched from the roadside in horror as various of his old friends wilted in exceptional heat and humidity. He helped rescue runner-up Geoff Iden at the finish, who collapsed and had to be taken away on a stretcher. From an original entry of 70-plus, only sixteen men finished, half-a-dozen ending up in hospital. It reignited the Vancouver debate over marathons being run on hot afternoons. Jim called it madness and folly, and warned that one day soon a runner would die, but the counter argument was raised that runners ought to learn to adapt and go slower. Jim was invited to serve as president of the relatively new Road Runners Club, taking over in 1955 from Sam Ferris, and was also invited that summer to Gateshead to perform the opening ceremony at a new stadium with cinder running track. The decline of industry on the south bank of the Tyne had freed up the land in question, but twelve inches of top spoil had to be laid to render the arsenic contamination safe. Within a few years the site would be staging international meetings and witnessing world record attempts.

Jim's influence could be seen around the country in the immediate years after his retirement. Fred Norris was one example, a Lancashire coalminer of similar build and height to Jim, who trained for around one hour, six nights a week, after emerging from his day's work underground. Norris twice broke the British record for the one-hour track run, exceeding the twelve-mile mark each time.

Despite all the fears over staging another major marathon in the heat, the 1956 Olympic event in Melbourne took place on a cloudy day featuring rain and strong winds. It had been so chilly, in fact, that one newspaper even ran a cartoon of a runner swallowing cough mixture and declaring: 'I told you it was dangerous to hold marathons in the afternoon – I've probably caught pneumonia!' Leading Englishman that day was Harry Hicks of Hampstead, who came fifteenth in 2:39.55, a colossal 22 minutes slower than Jim's best time.

By the summer of 1957 Jim had put his name to a second book, a coaching manual again written in conjunction with Joseph Edmundson and Johnny Johnston, this entitled *Modern Middle and Long Distance Running* and aimed at serious runners willing to train hard all year round. 1957 was also a year in which Jim took the opportunity to return to Canada, appearing on TV in Toronto and assuring viewers that he didn't regard his 1954 race as a failure. Once back home he watched with delight as his young Beagles protege of years gone by, George Knight, ripped ten seconds off Gordon Pirie's British 10,000 metres record to post the fastest time in the world that year (29:06.4).

In 1958 Jim's name was finally erased from the world record lists after six years, when tiny Sergei Popov of the Soviet Union clocked 2:15.17 at the European Championships marathon in Stockholm. Popov's mark would last two years, beaten by a single second by barefoot Abebe Bikila at the 1960 Rome Olympics.

By the end of the decade that had made him world famous, Jim's business was doing well enough to enable purchase of a new home, in leafy Townswood Road, Chigwell – appropriately entitled 'Endeavour' – close to his training haunts in Hainault Forest.

Teaming up with author Robert Hoare, Jim tried his hand in 1959 at writing a children's novel, which they called *Spiked Shoes* and told the tale of a schoolboy runner who turns detective when his athletics club HQ is mysteriously burned down. The book would later receive critical acclaim as 'the most authentic insight into modern running' since the 1927 Jackson Scholtz classic *Tales of the Cinder Path*. Roger Robinson's *Running in Literature* compendium commends Hoare and Peters' book as convincing in terms of its racing and training sequences and its depiction of the social context of an English athletic club.

Public appearances were becoming less frequent by now for Jim, but he joined Chris Chataway at the opening of Essex Beagles' new clubhouse in Chigwell Row in September 1959. He was then a vice-president of the club and would also serve as its president, in addition to a later stint (in 1972) as president of the Essex AAA. According to stalwart member Colin Young: 'Jim had put all his energy and drive into his business following Vancouver. I remember vividly standing with him watching the Ilford Road Relays when he said that he would soon be a richer man because he planned to work even harder and put in more hours than he had into his training.'

At the start of the 1960s the all-time British marathon list was still led by Jim, with his 2:17.39 nearly three minutes faster than the best of the rest. He went along to watch 39-year-old Arthur Keily (Derby & County) win the 1960 Poly in 2:19.06, *The Times* correspondent rather unkindly noting that Jim looked 'a deal stouter' than in his competitive days. At this point he also still held the records for the Essex and Southern Counties twenty-milers and the Morpeth-to-Newcastle event. His Poly course record would finally tumble in 1963, when the American Leonard 'Buddy' Edelen, a schoolteacher based in Essex, won the 50th staging of the race in a stunning 2:14.28, thus creating a new British all-comers and world best.

Jim's times were now being bettered internationally, but his name remained revered in British running throughout the 1960s. Colin Kirkham, at the time an emerging talent based at Durham University, recalls meeting him at a Romford race and painted me an evocative picture of road-running during that era: 'There were very few road races of distance in the North East, so I entered races down south. At the Romford half-marathon, Jim Peters presented the prizes. I came first and Jim handed over a goat-skin rug as my prize! I was broke, only had my grant, and mum and dad were Yorkshire mill workers and not well paid. So I used to write to the clubs staging races to ask if anyone would put me up. If not, I'd sleep rough. I spent many a happy hour on the embankment in London, where the tramps were surprisingly kind. We all used the catering van under Waterloo Bridge for breakfast. If I could afford the luxury of milk-train travel, I would sleep on Leeds Station instead.'

In the mid-1970s, with retirement not too far away, Jim's Mitcham business was bought out by his former employers Melson Wingate. After a spell based at his Chadwell Heath premises, Jim decided to retire aged 60 and in 1979 he moved from Chigwell to the seaside at Thorpe Bay, a short distance along the Thames estuary from Southend-on-Sea, where he would be nearer daughter Jennifer and her family. To keep himself busy he accepted the opportunity to become president of Dagenham Rotary Club in 1981, and the same year was elected president of Southend-on-Sea Athletics Club, a post he would hold for six years.

During the 1990s, his 80th birthday not far away, Jim and his family received the awful news that he had bladder cancer. Athletics writer Doug Gillon wrote that this had been regarded as untreatable as it was feared Jim wouldn't be able to tolerate the side effects of chemotherapy. According to Gillon, Jim met the challenge with typical forthrightness: 'I told them I had been a marathon runner – and told them to get on with it!'

He underwent treatment and in 1996 was feted, along with Vancouver winner Joe McGhee, by the London Marathon organisers at an emotional reunion event. From that day the two runners would stay in contact, Jim referring to McGhee as 'The Prof', a reference to his position as a lecturer in applied linguistics. Jim was admired for bravely making light of his health problems, telling Gillon: 'I still really enjoy myself, though chemotherapy has curtailed my sex life'. Cruelly, Jim suffered further grief when his running trophies were stolen from his home – barring, that is, his beloved gallantry medal from Prince Philip which had been on loan to an exhibition at the time.

In 1998 he was said to have suffered a heart attack and was hospitalised after celebrations to mark his 80th birthday. By now he was the figurehead president of the local Vestall Virgins running club, who took him for a birthday breakfast at Southend Leisure Centre, their chairman Noel Kelleway commenting: 'He is an inspiration to us all, and still well remembered and respected by British athletics as a whole.'

On Saturday, 9 January 1999, after battling the cancer for around six years, Jim passed away at the Fair Havens Hospice, a few yards from Westcliff seafront. He was buried in Southend's Sutton Road cemetery, plot NN, grave number 31391. Following a private funeral for close family, a few weeks later a memorial service at the St Margaret Lothbury parish church in the City of London was conducted by Rev Tom Farrell. There were readings by London Marathon chief Dave Bedford, fellow marathoner Stan Cox, by now also 80 and living on the Suffolk coast, and runners Doug Wilson and Richard Nerurkar.

National newspapers carried substantial obituaries and tributes flooded in from across the globe. Jim Alder, an orphan from the Glasgow Gorbals who became an international marathon star, said he'd been inspired to take up the sport by the sight of the plimsolled Peters smashing the Morpeth course record in 1953: 'He was ahead of his time, that man – a hell of a bloke.' Dave Bedford pointed out: 'Jim was a class runner when marathon running, unlike today, was unfashionable. Few athletes these days push themselves to such exhaustion as Jim did at Vancouver.' Simon Turnbull of *The Independent* called Jim 'one of the giants of 20th Century sport, the man who transformed marathon running from a plodding battle of endurance into a high speed race against the clock'.

Jim's son-in-law Barry Wadley-Smith recalled the remarkable sight of young African runners besieging Jim for him to sign their tatty coaching manuals on a trip abroad. From New Zealand, Jim Valli wrote that Jim's valiant struggle for gold in Vancouver had made an indelible impression around the world, and it seemed remarkable he'd survived another 45 years after that dreadful collapse under the unforgiving sun.

A few weeks after his memorial service, Jim's passing meant the annual dinner of a club known as 'The Notable 19' had to be staged in sad circumstances, its ranks now reduced to eighteen. Membership was exclusive to Britons who had held world records or medals from major marathon championships. The age range of their membership was between 43 and 92, reflecting the poor state of GB marathoning. 'Quite frankly, I don't know what has happened to British distance running. It's a disaster,' admitted Chris Brasher, co-founder of the London Marathon. 'The marathon isn't just about physical strength but mental toughness. Too few Britons now have that toughness.'

The group would return to its full complement of nineteen when it belatedly inducted Dale Greig from Paisley, acknowledged as having set a women's world marathon best of 3:27.45 on the Isle of Wight in 1964, with an ambulance following close behind in case of mishap.

By way of tribute to Jim, the London Marathon created the Jim Peters Trophy in 1999, to be awarded to the first British runner to finish each London race. Nearer home, the annual Southend-on-Sea half-marathon followed suit and renamed itself the 'Jim Peters Half-Marathon' and, some six months after his death, its runners were asked to observe a minute's silence before setting off on a route which, appropriately, passed close to Jim's grave. There were strong winds and torrential rain that day, meaning the passing runners had to work furiously as they battled past the cemetery. Jim would have approved. At the end of the run, his widow Frieda presented a special cup to the first Essex-based finisher.

In 2008, the *South African Medical Journal* (SAMJ) published a paper investigating the circumstances of Jim's collapse at Vancouver, written by Dr Tim Noakes, Discovery Health Professor of Exercise and Sports Science at Cape Town University, Jackie Mekler, and London Marathon Medical Director Dr Dan Tunstall Pedoe.

The trio were unable to pinpoint a clear proven cause of Jim's collapse, but concluded that the combined effects of a moderately severe hyperthermia (overheating), hypertonic hypernatraemia (reduced fluid/electrolyes), associated with a possible hypoglycaemia (low blood sugar) might have combined to cause a transient encephalopathy (brain disorder). They emphasised, however, that this conclusion, 54 years after the event, was 'speculative' only.

Medical records retrieved from Vancouver showed that some myocardial (muscular tissue of the heart) changes had taken place during the episode, which were responsible for inconsistent heart readings, but Jim had not suffered a heart attack that day. The SAMJ report also made public a letter by Sir Adolphe Abrahams following Jim's return to London, in which he said Jim's appearance at the end of the race had given the impression of a much more serious condition than his 'subjective sensation', which made it extremely alarming for onlookers. Abrahams said salt depletion and low blood sugar had not played a part and he didn't attach any importance to ECG readings as 'queer conditions may occur in any athlete after exercise'.

Noakes and his collaborators said that Jim's decision not to drink during the marathon had been used as anecdotal proof that he must have developed heatstroke. Yet, they pointed out, Mekler and Jan Barnard also drank little and they didn't collapse. The extent to which an athlete drank during exercise did not predict their post-exercise body temperature, nor apparently their risk of developing heatstroke, they said.

Nevertheless, Jim's habit of not taking on fluids seems remarkably foolish and almost suicidal when viewed through the eyes of modern day distance runners. In 1984, quizzed by Jackie Mekler, Jim himself admitted he'd been wrong not to drink more, but offered a number of excuses: 'I always wanted to get the agony over, so I never used to stop and drink. When I did drink I used to get diarrhoea. My bowels were always very open. My mother always said if anything was wrong, always pour down the Senna pods. As a young runner I always got sick. Fluid used to go straight through me. Buddy Edelen was another – when he did his 2:14 in the 1963 Poly he went to the toilet six times. All my Poly world records came after doing a morning's work, then eating two or three slices of brown bread, with nothing extra to drink. I'd carry two acid drops or mints in my pocket and after fifteen miles maybe suck one of those. I made plenty of mistakes, but by the time I retired aged 35, I knew more about it all. I didn't drink at all at Vancouver. I'd managed to get a couple of sponges earlier but they were nearly dry. At that last feeding station if only I'd had a drink, or a bucket in which to soak a hankie! But all I had was my two acid drops.'

Jim always acknowledged that running made him thirsty, but rarely did he deal with it in the normal way. This was partly down to the beliefs of his coach, who wrote in 1953: 'It should be possible to run up to twenty miles without the need for liquid or solid refreshment, but to relieve the parched feeling a drink of your liking may be used in small quantities, but usually a rinse of the mouth with sugared water or tea suffices. Jim takes no solid food or concentrates, a drink will be taken as a rinse and the sponge is always taken, when offered, for the neck, face and mouth to be wiped. For emergency a blackcurrant juice drink with salt added is available at the permitted points [in a marathon] from nineteen miles onward, namely 22 and 25 miles (the rules don't allow you to collapse anywhere else!) and I have yet to be at a marathon where a 25-mile feeding station operates. After the race it is impossible for several hours to satisfy the craving for liquid and first of all a strong fruit and salt drink is given – this is found fairly palatable – long drinks are refused, but frequent sips and small drinks given, the salt content finally is nil. This in time replaces the salt and liquid lost from the body during the race – and as a matter of interest, Jim loses 7 to 8lbs – it all depends on the temperatures of the day.'

Experienced international Donald Macgregor confirms from his own experience that even as late as the 1960s, elite marathon men were still not drinking fluids during a race. The International Amateur Athletic Federation (IAAF) had, until the 1970s, stipulated no drinks stations until at least eleven kilometres (6.6 miles) and allowed a maximum of around six after that. But by the late 1990s the thinking had changed, and suddenly runners were being urged to take plenty of fluids on board – before, during and afterwards. The New York City Marathon certainly saw the light, providing as many as 30 water stops.

Notwithstanding all his self-confessed mistakes about fluids and pace judgement, Jim Peters certainly made an indelible mark on marathon running and the size of his achievements can be gauged from the fact that even 60 years after he first took up the sport, a depressingly low number of British men can beat his best time of 2:17.39.

Hardly surprising then, that in 2011 Jim should be one of seven athletes nominated on a short-list for induction into England Athletics' Hall of Fame, to stand alongside the likes of Seb Coe, Daley Thompson and Jonathan Edwards. Most folk who remember Jim at all, only do so for having seen his spectacular and sickening Vancouver collapse on the Pathe newsreel, but his 2011 nomination means his superb achievements before that dreadful day are at last receiving the recognition they richly deserve.

The unprepossessing town of Dagenham has produced more than its share of celebrated names – Alf Ramsey, Jimmy Greaves, The Tremeloes, Sandie Shaw, Dudley Moore and Terry Venables to name a few. But its first and original famous son was undoubtedly James Henry Peters (1918-99), a modest maestro of the marathon.

PROGRESSION OF THE WORLD MARATHON RECORD:

2:55:18	Johnny Hayes - USA	July 24, 1908	London
2:52:45	Robert Fowler - USA	Jan 1, 1909	Yonkers, USA
2:46:52	James Clark - USA	Feb 12, 1909	New York City
2:46:04	Albert Raines - USA	May 8, 1909	New York City
2:42:31	Henry Barrett - UK	May 26, 1909	Polytechnic, London
2:40:34	Thure Johansson - Sweden	August 31, 1909	Stockholm
2:38:16	Harry Green - UK	May 12, 1913	Polytechnic, London
2:36:06	Alexis Ahlgren - Sweden	May 31, 1913	Polytechnic, London
2:32:35	Hannes Kolehmainen - Fin	August 22, 1920	Antwerp
2:29:01	Albert Michelsen - USA	Oct 12, 1925	Port Chester, USA
2:27:49	Fusashige Suzuki - E Japan	March 31, 1935	Tokyo
2:26:44	Yasuo Ikenaka - E Japan	April 3, 1935	Tokyo
2:26:42	Son Kitei - E Japan	Nov 3, 1935	Tokyo
2:25:39	Suh Yun-bok - S Korea	April 19, 1947	Boston
2:20:42	Jim Peters - UK	June 14, 1952	Polytechnic, London
2:18:40	Jim Peters - UK	June 13, 1953	Polytechnic. London
2:18:34	Jim Peters - UK	Oct 4, 1953	Turku, Finland
2:17:39	Jim Peters - UK	June 26, 1954	Polytechnic, London
2:15:17	Sergei Popov - Soviet Union	August 24, 1958	Stockholm
2:15:16	Abebe Bikila - Ethiopia	Sept 10, 1960	Rome
2:15:15	Toru Terasawa - Japan	Feb 17, 1963	Beppu-Oita, Japan
2:14:28	'Buddy' Edelen - USA	June 15, 1963	Polytechnic, London
2:13:55	Basil Heatley - UK	June 13, 1964	Polytechnic, London
2:12:12	Abebe Bikila - Ethiopia	Oct 21, 1964	Tokyo
2:12:00	Morio Shigematsu - Japan	June 12, 1965	Polytechnic, London
2:09:36	Derek Clayton - Australia	Dec 3, 1967	Fukuoka, Japan
2:08:33	Derek Clayton - Australia	May 30, 1969	Antwerp
2:08:18	Rob de Castella - Australia	Dec 6, 1981	Fukuoka, Japan
2:08:05	Steve Jones - UK	Oct 21, 1984	Chicago
2:07:12	Carlos Lopes - Portugal	April 20, 1985	Rotterdam
2:06:50	Belayneh Dinsamo - Ethiopia	April 17, 1988	Rotterdam
2:06:05	Ronaldo da Costa - Brazil	Sept 20, 1998	Berlin
2:05:42	Khalid Khannouchi - Moroc	Oct 24, 1999	Chicago
2:05:38	Khalid Khannouchi - USA	April 14, 2002	London
2:04:55	Paul Tergat - Kenya	Sept 28, 2003	Berlin
2:04:26	Haile Gebrselassie - Ethiopia	Sept 30, 2007	Berlin
2:03:59	Haile Gebrselassie - Ethiopia	Sept 28, 2008	Berlin
2:03:38	Patrick Makau - Kenya	Sept 25, 2011	Berlin

Printed in Great Britain
by Amazon

14390575R10157

DREAMING OF BABYLON

The Life and Times of
Ralph Hodgson

DREAMING OF BABYLON

The Life and Times of
Ralph Hodgson

John Harding

GREENWICH EXCHANGE
LONDON

Greenwich Exchange, London

DREAMING OF BABYLON
The Life and Times of Ralph Hodgson
© John Harding 2008

First published in Great Britain in 2008
All rights reserved

Printed and bound by Q3 Digital/Litho, Loughborough
Tel: 01509 213456
Typesetting and layout by Albion Associates, London
Tel: 020 8852 4646
Cover design by December Publications, Belfast
Tel: 028 90286559

Greenwich Exchange Website: www.greenex.co.uk

Cataloguing in Publication Data is available from the British Library

ISBN-13: 978-1-906075-00-2
ISBN-10: 1-906075-00-X

Contents

Ralph Hodgson's Book-Plate 1894

ACKNOWLEDGEMENTS

I must first give thanks to Bryn Mawr College for permission to use materials from their extensive Ralph Hodgson collection at the Mariam Coffin Canaday Library. I initially made contact with the library concerning the Collection in March 1994, when I stayed on campus while looking at the library's papers and letters, many of which had been deposited there by Seymour Adelman, who befriended and assisted the Hodgsons when they came to settle in America in 1939. I met James Tanis, then Director of Libraries, and he kindly gave me permission to consult and copy material for use in the biography. I made three further visits to the library in 1995, 1996 and 1997, working closely with the then Head of Manuscripts, Leo Dolensky, and helped by Lorett Treece and Kathy Whalen as well as other members of the library staff at that time. Since then I have received encouragement and practical help from Eric Pumroy, Director of Library Collections, and Seymour Adelman, Head of Special Collections, Barbara Ward Grubb, Visual Collections Specialist, and many more at Bryn Mawr, including Mary S. Leahy. Ammon G. Kershner Jr., wrote an invaluable dissertation on Hodgson back in the 1950s, and I was privileged to meet him in 1996, when he and his wife entertained me in their Philadelphia home.

Philip Milito (Berg Collection, New York Public Library), Vincent Giroud (Curator of Modern Books and Manuscripts, Beinecke Library, Yale) and Terrance Keenan (Special Collections Librarian at Syracuse University, New York) have also lent practical support.

Dr Wesley Duaine Sweetser's bibliography was invaluable, of course. I'd also like to mention Marcia Allentuck, Professor Emerita of English and Comparative Literature at City College, City University of New York, and Brook Ellen Egglestone, who researched Hodgson's links with the American poet Olive Dargon.

Where primary research in England is concerned, I must go back in time a long way and start by expressing my heartfelt thanks to the late Bob Hodgson. Ably assisted by his partner Betty Beesley, Bob spent decades searching for his uncle's ancestors and history. Bob's sister, the late Sybil Hodgson, was also of great assistance both to Bob and later to me. Since then, Betty has proved a stalwart friend and I wouldn't have progressed as far as I have without her encouragement. Shirley Colquhoun, Hodgson's niece, has always been supportive and extremely kind, sharing her memories of her uncle 'Rafe' and his first wife, Dolly. Colin Fenton, Hodgson's last editor, had already passed away when I first started work on the book, but his widow, Mrs S.Y. Fenton, kindly allowed me access to her late husband's private collection of papers. I later accessed his papers at the Bodleian Library, where a great deal of his primary research, including some valuable interviews from the 1960s, is stored.

Genealogical researcher extraordinary Sue Liddle, along with her good friend Margaret Pitt (a great-niece of Ralph Hodgson's), have provided invaluable material concerning the Hodgson family tree and Margaret's grandfather, Herbert. Wendy Kemp, another Hodgson great-niece, has also been very helpful.

In Japan, Prof. John Hatcher, of Fukuoka University has allowed me to quote from an excellent article he wrote some years ago on Hodgson. Thanks, too, to Kimiko Hirohashi of Keio University, Tokyo, Prof Ineko Kondo, Tuda Women's College, Tokyo and Kazuhisa Takahashi, English Literary Society of Japan for helping me with memories and material concerning Hodgson and his life at Sendai University between the wars. Thank you, too, to Mavis Pilbeam, a Japanese specialist, who translated various documents from Japanese.

The poet James Kirkup has been a champion of Ralph Hodgson's work for many years and gave me some very useful pointers. Poet and novelist Robert Nye also read the manuscript and pointed out a variety of errors to me in no uncertain terms! The late Ian Hamilton read an earlier manuscript and was very supportive at a time when I needed encouragement. I must also thank comic historian Denis Gifford who helped enormously where Ralph's cartooning days were concerned. Others who have lent a helping hand are Julia Abel Smith of the Royal Society of Literature, Nigel Miskin of the Hurlingham Club, Prof. Gary Day at De Montfort University, Cecil Woolf and Jean Moorcroft Wilson, plus Graham Moss of Incline Press.

In Hodgson's last home town, Roger Bartley of Minerva, Ohio, whose knowledge of and interest in Hodgson goes back decades, has been a good friend and constant help, providing much insight into Hodgson's last years. I must also mention Seth and Suzanne Glasser in New York, whose New City home was an essential and welcoming base on many American trips.

James Hodgson of Greenwich Exchange must, of course, be sincerely congratulated. There are too few publishers today courageous enough to take the leap of faith involved in producing a book such as this. He has been ably supported by Peter Randall, plus editors Henry Maas, Rosalyn and Janet Davidson. At Q3, Ryan Tomkins has been an enormous help. However, especial thanks must go to Sue Albion, who has worked tirelessly and well beyond the call of duty to get the book into such good shape.

Finally, I must thank Janet Unwin for all her hard work on this project. It really would not have been possible without her.

> In the depths of the sea
> May lie buried the silver gem,
> And the wind blows
> And stirs up an angry sea,
> Yet I will not rest till I've got
> The gem
>
> Man'yōshū

Prologue

Mr Ralph Hodgson, Minerva, Ohio. Birds watched and bull terriers taken in free of charge. Pugilism. Snooker. Poetry. Dog Fancier. Telegrams. 'Cruftitude'.
(Calling card made by Siegfried Sassoon for Ralph Hodgson)

In 1956, John Betjeman wrote: "Even literary gents, and I suppose I must call myself one, have their literary heroes. To me these are those who never go to parties nor are seen on television nor are heard on the wireless, but are just names on printed pages. They never even publish portraits and biographies of themselves on their dust-wrappers. I have sought and found a few. I knew Anthony Hope, I have met Ralph Hodgson ..."

Ralph Hodgson would have been an extremely difficult man to find, let alone meet, in the 1950s. In fact, when he was awarded the Queen's Gold Medal for Poetry in 1954, many friends and acquaintances were surprised to learn he was still alive. Having left England after the First World War at the height of his fame to teach at Sendai University in Japan, he had returned home only for brief periods and moved to the United States in 1939, eventually settling in Ohio on a remote farm some six miles from the small hamlet of Minerva. No more than a score of local people ever set eyes on him during the years he lived there until his death in 1962, aged 91.

For a man so profoundly English, it may seem strange that he chose to live his last 20 years so far from the society and the people he knew best. His love for the country of his birth is very evident in the long letters which he wrote home to friends in England. Its countryside and country pursuits, London in all its vibrancy and the wry eccentricities of the English people rang profoundly through his poetry all his life.

In Japan, for instance, he dressed and ate like an Englishman, never taking to Japanese food. As Professor John Hatcher of Fukuoka University has written:

> Unlike Blunden, Plomer, Empson or even Binyon, who had spent only two months in the country, he wrote no poems about Japan. We have no record of his encounters with Noh, kabuki, the tea ceremony or Zen poetry (although one of his successors at Sendai,

James Kirkup, suggested that some of the terse, one-line poems Hodgson wrote after he left Japan such as 'Who shall paraphrase a tear?' are reminiscent of *senryu* or Zen parables). The things that moved him most – birds, dogs, the personalities of individual Japanese, the colleagues, students and townsfolk he grew to love – were things he could have found anywhere, things endemic to nature and human nature.

He remained similarly disengaged from American society. Once, when asked why he chose Minerva in particular, he observed, "The birds seemed just as interesting as in England, and I'd never seen a humming-bird. It took my mind."

As usual with Hodgson, however, things were not quite as simple as they appeared. Whether he could have survived all those years without the support of his much younger, cheerful, Ohio-born wife, Aurelia, who worked as a clerk in the local wax-paper factory to support them both, is questionable. His rarity value in a country that has always made much of eccentric 'characters' was something, however, that he could (and did) manipulate and manage. But to what end? What was he doing out there all those years? Dreaming a great deal (or "time travelling" as he once described it), working on his long, unfinished poem 'The Muse and the Mastiff' and writing reams of letters to fellow poets, writers, academics, friends, ex-students and distant members of his long-abandoned family.

One thing he did not write, however, was his memoirs. In fact, Hodgson never published an autobiography and was so antagonistic to the very idea of anyone *else* writing the story of his life that he would often plant false information into the minds of those making even the most discreet of enquiries as to his forebears. However, he was never rude to enquirers. The occasional student, journalist, academic or even fellow poet who arrived at his door in search of enlightenment would be genially rebuffed or engaged in long, entertaining but totally tangential conversations. Having been fed and beguiled, he would then be sent on his way none the wiser.

Even when it might have been beneficial to his and Aurelia's always meagre personal finances, Hodgson steadfastly refused to produce memoirs or portraits of those he had met and worked with in his long life. What tales he might have told of that giant of modern journalism, Lord Northcliffe, who gave him his first significant job; or of legendary black-and-white illustrators such as Phil May, Tom Browne and Roland Hill, alongside whom he worked throughout the 1890s. There was the stage designer and artist Claud Lovat Fraser, with whom Hodgson produced revolutionary 'chapbooks' in 1913, not to mention a score or more of poets including Edmund Blunden, Edward Thomas and Ezra Pound, T.S. Eliot, Walter de la Mare and W.H. Davies. With these and many, many more he talked and argued and scrapped across café tables for 20 years or longer. And yet he refused to speculate, reveal or reminisce. He respected the privacy of others as fiercely as his own.

It is true that he had always shown a disinclination, at times bordering on the obsessive, towards writing anything that might interfere with the business of producing poetry. However, he eventually explained his personal reticence to a close friend thus: he wanted his poetry to speak for itself. If *it* didn't survive, then what purpose would there be in knowing anything more about him?

Hodgson's poetry has survived, of course, and sometimes in surprising fashion. From the very first, his verse appealed to musicians who found in his spare but powerful lines the perfect basis upon which to build vast choral pieces or craft compellingly direct folk ballads. 'Time, You Old Gypsy Man' and 'The Hammers', for instance, dealing with the ephemeral place of man in the remorseless and ultimately destructive march of time, have been set to music by an eclectic mix of musicians from classical artists such as Arthur Bliss through to contemporary jazz legends John Dankworth and Cleo Laine. 'The Mystery', 'Eve' and 'The Song of Honour' and many more have also found their way into contemporary compilations – 'Eve' can be heard today on folk singer Peter Michael Rowan's MySpace site.

This should not be a surprise. His simple but fervent poems of protest at man's inhumanity to animals such as 'The Bells of Heaven' and his sardonic observations on the catastrophic destruction of the environment such as 'Stupidity Street' remain as fresh and relevant today as when they first appeared almost a century ago.

Indeed, Hodgson's work transcends time and place, as did Hodgson himself. A product of Victorian England living happily in the wilds of Ohio, dreaming of distant civilisations, while watching humming-birds in the trees beyond his porch. It's certainly time his story was told.

1

Childhood

I woke to hear the song that early rang
My boyhood on from Spring to fairer Spring …
('Holiday')

He was born Ralph Edwin Hodgson at 2 Garden Street, Darlington in the county of Durham on 9th September 1871. He was the eighth child of eleven (seven boys and four girls – two of whom died young) born to parents Ralph and Mary. He occasionally hinted that a distant uncle of his was William Bewick, the portrait and history painter, but the link has never been established. It appears to be based on fanciful stories told by Hodgson's father, who had worked his way up to something approaching prosperity from relatively humble beginnings.

Ralph senior's mother, Hannah Walker, was born in the small town of Romaldkirk, Yorkshire in 1806 where she married John Hodgson, a butcher from Middleton, Co. Durham in 1825. They lived in West Auckland all their lives and produced seven children. By 1871, when the children had left home, they were still in West Auckland but by then John owned a farm of some 57 acres and employed a labourer. Hannah died aged 70 in 1876, and John in 1883, aged 77.

Mary Hodgson's parents, Joseph and Mary Graham, were strict Wesleyan Methodists from Middridge, not far from West Auckland. Joseph Graham was one of eight children born at the Red House, a large detached house in the village, and, though little is known of his parents, they must have been comfortably off. He became a master joiner and builder and was so influential in chapel and village affairs that he was dubbed The Bishop. He was a man of many talents. In 1881, he was listed as both a draper and a grocer. In later years, he taught himself Greek and was very well educated in mathematics and English.

Ralph senior entered the coal business in 1851 with the help of relatives, starting as a clerk with a local company. By the age of 26 he was a manager for a collier called Stobart. By 1865, he was running his own coal 'factoring' business and owned a fine house at 47 Northgate,

Darlington. In 1871, the year of Ralph junior's birth, he moved with his wife, Mary, to No 2, Garden Street, and local directories suggest he owned a coal and lime depot at Bank Top Station, Darlington, complete with his own rolling stock.

'Coal' Hodgson was an outgoing, ebullient character, a good talker and an avid Charles Dickens reader. Sadly, his business rapidly and dramatically collapsed for reasons unknown. Whether his reputed drinking was the cause or the consequence of his financial ruin is also uncertain. The removal of the family from the relative opulence of Garden Street to a small, claustrophobic dwelling in Station Terrace, opposite Bank Top Station, did not, however, appear to dim a natural, if ill-founded, optimism. When not working as a checker on the nearby Bank Top Coal Depot, Coal turned his hand to producing various medical potions and medicines which he hoped to sell at local fairs. John Henry, his eldest son, who at the time was a chemistry student, recalled:

> He had great hopes for the future and spent much of his time in the washhouse at Station Terrace, working on his inventions. The washhouse was a cupboard-like extension to the scullery only used for its original purpose once a month on a Monday. His desk was a copper, above which ran a shelf loaded with his books, bottles, pots and pestles. Apart from his beloved Dickens, the books were largely on 'leech-lore' and pharmacy, and the bottles and pots contained balms of various sorts. From the ceiling he had hung bunches of drying herbs.

The tradition of herbal cures was a long and honourable one among the Hodgson family – and among farming folk in general. Coal, however, was interested in a particular cure-all balm to relieve toothache, backache, burns, sore throat and various spots and blemishes. It could also be applied to cattle, horses and dogs and was apparently invaluable in curing canker in cats' ears. Perhaps, not surprisingly, it had an acrid odour. John Henry explained:

> Coal's experiments were aimed at introducing into the balm a lavender scent, reckoning that he could then sell the concoction to women. They, in turn, might use it as a cheap form of perfume, having bought it under a respectable medicinal guise. It was marketed as 'Hodgson's Cure-All Aromatic Balm for the Use of Women'.

The balm seems to have made little difference to the family's fortunes and in 1882 they moved from Darlington to Newcastle upon Tyne, to 62 Grove Street, where Hodgson's mother, Mary, had plans to open a small school along similar lines to one successfully established by her father and sisters back in Darlington.

Coal continued experimenting with his medicinal compounds, but within two years of the Newcastle move he was dead. At the time of his death in 1884, aged 50, only his eldest son Harry was present in the house as the rest of the family were on a weekend trip to the Hodgson cousins' farm in Eppleby. When they returned, all traces of their father – his pipes, his extravagant waistcoats and his workshop clutter – had been removed.

Ralph Hodgson said nothing of note about his father other than the cryptic comment, "My father was a gentleman." The suspicion remains, however, that Coal's agnosticism and social habits caused some friction between his and Mary's parents. No one from the Graham family attended their marriage ceremony held at Eppleby, but Coal's business collapse appears to have been instrumental in bringing the families back together again.

The 1881 Census reveals Ralph Hodgson staying with his maternal grandfather, Joseph, in Middridge while his sister Amy was lodging with her mother's sisters Hannah and Eliza Graham, schoolteachers in Darlington. In later years, all the Hodgson children spent holidays with their formidable maternal grandfather. Ralph even told an occasional affectionate anecdote about the old patriarch.

In sharp contrast to Coal, Ralph's mother Mary was certainly a formidable woman, inheriting her father's determination and resolve. She it was who set the tenor of the Hodgson household. Children were never allowed an idle moment and followed a strict routine from dawn till dusk. Passages from improving books like *The Pilgrim's Progress* and Matthew Arnold's poetry were memorised; good manners and deportment were insisted upon; a high degree of self-control in all things emotional was demanded.

Prayers were said each evening at home with seats arranged as in a chapel and Methodist hymnals supplied. Censorship of newspapers was rigidly enforced, and books were scrutinised and edited for religious correctness. There was plenty of fun to be had, however, despite the monastic overtones. According to Walker, Ralph's elder brother by some seven years, the Hodgson children spent their childhoods roaming the local countryside searching for ancient fossils, clambering over Saxon earthworks or picnicking amid the ruins of medieval castles.

Family entertainment at home consisted of playlets written and performed, spelling tests and singing – usually hymns – but not exclusively. Even the sudden descent into the abyss of the Darlington slums failed to interrupt the pattern. Walker recalled:

> The house in Station Terrace was very much smaller than our old home in Garden Street and not all the family could be

accommodated there. Some of us lodged nearby but we always foregathered on Sunday evenings at No 17, Station Terrace, and because of mother's insistence that certain standards should be maintained, our lives changed only in a material way. At Station Terrace an even stricter discipline was demanded. No matter how busy mother might be she would stop her work on hearing one of us make a grammatical mistake or if she detected the slightest sound of a local accent in our voices. Because of the constant shower of smut from the adjacent railway, daily washing and whitening of the doorstep was necessary. No 17 was respectable ...

The fact that Mary Hodgson ran a school would explain the high level of literacy and artistic ability among the children. Its prospectus included the inevitable reading, writing and arithmetic along with pianoforte and art, as well as a course in playing the mandolin – a speciality of her daughter May's.

The question as to how Ralph Hodgson and his brothers and sisters were formally educated remains unanswered. No school cards or records exist for any of them, although it is thought that, for a time until Coal's fortunes declined, the eldest boys attended a Wesleyan Methodist establishment, Walworth House Collegiate School close by Garden Street, Darlington.

There is no doubt they all did extremely well, however. The eldest son – John Henry (b.1860) – qualified as a chemist, while Walker trained as an engraver and illustrator. Herbert, born in 1865, also received a scientific training and worked for many years as a chemical analyst for the chocolate makers Fry's in Stockton, eventually becoming a County Councillor of long-standing in the town. Amy, born in 1876, became a teacher of English in France, while Walter (b.1870), Ralph (b.1871) and Frank (b.1874) all followed careers in graphic art: illustration, art-editing, etc. The remaining daughters, May and Josey, became teachers in their mother's school.

As far as one can gather, after Walworth House, Ralph Hodgson's formal education was rudimentary at best, completed by sporadic attendance at what he called the Dames' School run by his aunts in Darlington where he was taught to draw. He never attended university and never trained for a profession.

Indeed, by the age of 15 he was, by his own account, roaming the Northumberland and Durham countryside with fairground folk, striking tents, tending animals and performing in boxing booths. At about 18, he claimed he travelled on a merchant ship to the USA where he eked out a living scene-painting in a New York theatre and labouring in Canada. He eventually returned to Europe and London in 1889 where the rest of his family had just settled.

Hodgson produced no evidence for his American trip except occasional teasing anecdotes about Cherokee Indians and a cryptic reference to his

4

days in America in a letter to his first wife. It's possible, however, that he travelled by courtesy of his brother Walter, who had left the family home around 1888 to serve as a purser on a tramp steamer called the *Creole*. This sailed around Europe through the Mediterranean and across the Atlantic fetching and carrying a motley collection of cargoes: coke, coal, tinplate, etc. In later years Walter's tales from a decade at sea were written up as short stories by a close friend and boys' fiction writer, Stacey Blake, under the title *The Blue Highway*.

Walter's relationship with his younger brother was close and supportive, often to Walter's financial detriment. A family legend has it that their mother, sensing that she could not control the wayward Ralph and realising that he would regularly find himself in difficulties placed an injunction on Walter to "watch over Eddie" – as Ralph was known in the family. Walter thus became an increasingly regular source of advice and practical help as later Ralph drifted away from gainful employment.

As a youth, therefore, Ralph Hodgson appeared free to please himself with little heed to possible consequences. An uncomplicated, indolent but resourceful character, he inhabited a private world of his own. Trips to Thomas Bewick's home by bicycle, bird spotting, billiards and boxing occupied him most. There was one passion in particular, however, that remained with him all his life. As he told a friend in later years, "I was a stamp collector once in the 1880s, but bull-terriers knocked all that sort of nonsense and a great deal more of sound and valuable sense out of my head."

For a teenager, growing up in Durham and later in Newcastle, the fashionable side of dog-breeding was a world away. When Hodgson came to know the bull-terrier breed in the late 1880s, dogfights were still very much part of an underground working-class culture, and the dog had to be acquired surreptitiously; one had to know someone or somewhere – a pub or a yard – where breeders met and traded.

His interest began by chance: his oft-told anecdote had it thus:

> I saw an old man with a strange-looking, short-bodied, flat-headed animal on straight, sturdy legs having little dark eyes set close together and a good-natured expression, running beside him. Day after day I looked out for the dog and his old master. At last I determined to ask him what sort of dog his companion might be. I must have been about the most disappointed boy in England after I had stopped him with many apologies and put my question and got for my answer: 'Twenty minutes past four, my lad.' The old man was stone deaf!

However, the young Hodgson was bitten by the bug and, soon determined to have one for his own:

It was not long afterwards when I met a man who owned a great, thick-headed, brindled fighting dog – a dog bred and trained solely to fight other dogs, to make sport, and I asked if he could give me the like of it. He said he could and he said he wouldn't and I had better not think any more about it. But, of course, I was all the more determined to have a fighting dog when he insisted that what I wanted was a show dog – 'a gentleman's dog'. Night after night, drawn by an irresistible fascination, bit hard by the bull-terrier passion, I would go and sit with my friend – he kept a small barbershop – until eventually I made the barber sell me a bull-terrier pup for seven shillings and sixpence.

Hodgson's youth would appear to have been dominated by these dogs. As he explained:

When a man takes up bull-terriers – if once he grows keen – this love will never fail, no matter whether he drifts along the paths of fascination that lead to the grand passion, or whether he falls in headlong, head over heels. Once in, he never comes out. Myself, I fell into the passion – love at first sight.

He had a succession of dogs: "After Herc(ules) there were Piper and Yorick and Baby, Queen of Clubs and little Folly – twenty or twenty-five dogs I owned at different times ..."

According to Count Hollander, a later friend and Kennel Club man: "In his youth he practically starved in order to possess a bull-terrier. Having acquired it, he walked all the way from Stafford to Newcastle sustaining himself with berries and anything else he could find. His dog, as usual, was well fed."

A secretive boy, the nether-world of dogs and their breeders clearly acted as an alternative universe, into and out of which he could slip at will. He shared an esoteric knowledge and language the public at large was unaware of, in a world hidden away behind fashionable facades such as he found in later years in working class Pimlico: "for there in the backyards of small tradesmen's houses, in sheds, spotlessly clean, perfectly sweet, on beds of fine straw, they know how to keep their dogs those Pimlico breeders."

But it was a paradox – loving dogs that were bred principally to kill, either one another or other animals. Whether Hodgson as a young man ever frequented dog-fights is hard to tell. He certainly condemned the sport in print, calling it a loathsome, brutish business, but he conceded that he owed a debt of gratitude to the men who had knitted together the foundation of the breed whose first condition was, over all breeds, courage. At the same time he hoped, "it was no mere love of blood and sensation that called them to their bad holidays. They followed an ideal, darkly enough, we may not doubt, of courage," but, "they themselves practised the same stiff lessons of give and take they laid upon their maimed and stricken victims."

His great friend and fellow poet Siegfried Sassoon noted this contradiction in him: his great compassion for animals and their suffering, yet his tolerance of and lack of bitterness towards humans who, perhaps unintentionally, caused such suffering. This ambivalence could stem from his days on the road as a youth in the 1880s when he claimed he followed the travelling fairs, mixing with a quasi-gypsy crowd who traditionally showed little compassion for their beasts of burden. Travelling people were hard but not gratuitously cruel.

But the carefree dog days were to end in 1889. Mary and her younger children left Newcastle and moved to London to join her sons John Henry and Walker who had moved down some years previously. They took lodgings in Chalcot Crescent, Primrose Hill where Mary set about establishing another private school to support the family. It was an almost total break. Only Herbert remained in the North. In years to come their only contact with the family past would be occasional holidays with the Hodgson farming cousins in Eppleby. Over the next 75 years or so, Hodgson himself made no more than half a dozen trips back to the town of his birth.

from 'Bull Terrier Talk' by Marcus Woodward for Pearson's Magazine, Illustrated by Ralph Hodgson (Yorick) October 1904

2

Cartooning

'You can't drive a bent nail home'
'Twas Noah who first made that remark
At the building of the Ark,
Waggling a bloody thumb
And his delighted children's mirth
That gave the Comic Spirit birth ...
                    (*Flying Scroll* No.5)

Walker, the second eldest of the five Hodgson brothers, had been one of the first to make the break from Newcastle and take on the wider world. His career as an illustrator, however, had begun locally: at 19 years of age he was talented enough to be employed on Darlington's *Northern Echo* newspaper.

In 1885, the *Echo*, attempting to broaden its appeal, launched an evening edition which was more downmarket and chatty in style than its daily parent. Because newspaper photography was still some way off, illustrations, pocket cartoons and line-drawings were introduced to liven up the paper's visual image. These were to be the sole responsibility of Walker.

His light, somewhat fragile style gave 'colour' to articles about local politicians, visiting royalty and sensational murder trials. He also made trips to outlying villages to interview the oldest inhabitants, cover dog shows and election hustings – the local journalist's smorgasbord of duties, in fact.

Walker had ambitions beyond Darlington, however, and within a few months had set off for London to make his fortune in Fleet Street. Here he worked first as an engraver's artist, but found time to produce a book of original cartoons to commemorate Queen Victoria's Golden Jubilee (1887) and then to write and illustrate a children's comic-book guide to the London Zoo. He also secured commissions to work on illustrated journals published by Cassell & Co. a publishing business that aimed to provide good literature for the working classes. A special feature of Cassell's popular books were the illustrations, and Walker's work was prominently featured in *Cassell's Magazine* for many years. At around this time (1892) he commenced a series of drawings and engravings from life of the prominent artists of the day: Sir Frederic Leighton, Edward Burne-Jones, G.F. Watts and Lawrence Alma-Tadema were among his sitters and many of them would become his friends.

So much in demand was he that in 1892 Jerome K. Jerome asked him to work on his new weekly, *To-Day*, sister paper to the already successful *The Idler*. Jerome was then riding high on the success of his novel *Three Men in a Boat*, and his new magazine would draw on work from Thomas Hardy, Arthur Conan Doyle, Israel Zangwill and Rudyard Kipling. It also included much escapist literature of the Bret Hart/*Tales of the Klondyke* variety. It appealed to that great constituency of clerks then filling the counting-houses and insurance offices of London and other provincial cities, those "single men in rented rooms" who craved a diet of cycling, photography, hobbies and pretty 'tararaboomdeaaaay' girls.

Walker's first commission on the paper was a prestigious one – to illustrate Robert Louis Stevenson's last novel, *Ebb Tide*, serialised in numerous episodes throughout 1893. Walker ruefully conceded many years later that it hadn't been his best work; Stevenson clearly agreed. Writing to his agent in England the following year to complain about the general standard of illustration of his work, Stevenson said, "and the same remarks apply to that unhung ruffian who made a public ass of himself in *Today* or whatever it is called ... "

Whether Walker ever learned of the great man's disparaging comments is unknown; he continued to work on *To-Day* for another year, however, before setting off in 1896 for Australia with the explorer/writer/goldmine investor A.F. Calvert. It was Calvert's fourth expedition to the west of Australia, then still very dangerous, uncharted territory – he had lost two companions on the previous trip.

Walker was the party's artist and became something of a celebrity. Calvert wrote:

> Hodgson was throughout, the lion of our party. Journalists, photographers and mining engineers were not new, even in the bush, but a real artist with a sketchbook and the power of filling it with familiar objects, was a man to be made much of. Several times it was necessary to rescue him almost by force from a crowd of demonstrative admirers and I am convinced that he could travel from Roebourne to Marble Bar and from Marble Bar to Coolgardie and never have to put his hands in his pocket for his bodily nourishment.

Subsequently, Walker both illustrated and contributed to a lavish book by Calvert about the expedition entitled *My Fourth Tour in Western*

Australia. It is one of the most magnificent books on the Western Australian goldfields and the bush and was reprinted in 1989.

In spite of his considerable success as an illustrator, however, Walker's career now began to falter. He was undoubtedly talented, but he did not have the strength of character to sustain his success. By the turn of the century his professional life had all but ended; he was still obtaining occasional commissions from his brother Walter, then art editor of the *Captain* magazine in Fleet Street, for drawings or running errands, but his erratic lifestyle – disappearing for long 'tramps' north for weeks on end, not to mention occasional stays in psychiatric hospitals – suggests that he could no longer hold down a regular job.

He had already shown himself something of an eccentric. Before he left for his Australian trip he delivered to the family home an odd overmantel, a monumental mahogany structure upon which were affixed, in coffin-like frames, the signatures of "one hundred great artists". Above two small bookshelves was an engraving of a stern-looking Tennyson "glaring across the centrepiece at a benign Emerson". Beneath the centrepiece, a carved oak panel announced that "Great Art is Nature's Priest of Fervent Love", and all over the mantel's mahogany surface were quotations in gilt letters taken from Walker's writings. The centrepiece was a bas-relief of Walker himself under convex glass.

His eccentricity grew as the years went by, a process almost certainly exacerbated by drink. (Hodgson's one and only reference to his brother has him stumbling upstairs in the family home in Darlington "drunk and vomiting …")

The possible alcoholic addiction may well explain the fact that there is hardly a single mention of Walker in surviving letters, reminiscences and recollections by Hodgson and family, and hardly any of Hodgson's purely literary colleagues seemed to have been aware of Walker's existence.

Nevertheless, it was undoubtedly Walker's connections that played a major role in gaining Ralph and his brothers an entrée into the world of book and newspaper illustration. For Ralph, the breakthrough would come in comic papers – at that time a burgeoning branch of popular publishing.

In his autobiography in 1934, the novelist John Cowper Powys, writing of his schooldays in the late 1880s, spoke of "that fantastical publication known as *Ally Sloper*". Though the comic portions of it were abhorrent to him, he confessed that the

> daintily-sketched outlines of the feminine form contained within were most perfectly suited to my exacting senses. These *Ally Sloper* ladies I would cut out with trembling hands and carry about with me in my pocket. What matter if these enchanting figures … were torn from the ridiculous and vulgar pages of *Ally Sloper*?

Powys was referring to a periodical called *Ally Sloper's Half Holiday*. Originally called *Judy*, it had been bought by the respected wood-engravers and quality printers, the Dalzeil Brothers, who employed an artist called W.G. Baxter to transform its central character, Ally Sloper. Sloper – an often inebriated, often dubiously-employed rogue – was a working-class anti-hero with clumsy lower-middle-class aspirations. His adventures, part-satirical comment, part-parody of middle-class mores and manners, shocked those of a prim, conservative outlook, but he was a hero not only to hundreds of thousands of working men and women but also to members of upper Bohemia such as William Morris, Edward Burne-Jones and later H.G. Wells and G.K. Chesterton. What's more, Ally Sloper's bawdy, irreverent humour and revolutionary comic techniques set the standard for a boom in comic papers during the 1890s.

Ralph Hodgson was a close contemporary of Powys and shared his taste for innocent Victorian pin-ups. He continued to collect examples of the genre until well into old age, but he would have parted company with Powys where the rest of the comic was concerned – the 'vulgar' Ally Sloper cartoon character, in particular. As an artistically-inclined teenager, Hodgson copied out the work of Ally's creator, W.G. Baxter, collecting examples of his hero's artwork and at the same time developing a comic line and style all his own.

However, humorous journals and 'comic' papers such as *Punch* and *Judy* had not been aimed specifically at young readers. The content had featured little original, home-grown artwork, with much of the inspiration and cartoon material coming from abroad – France, Germany and the USA. However, with the passing of the 1870 Education Act and the spread of basic literacy among working-class people, rapid changes began.

James Henderson was one of the first of a new breed of publishers to create products specifically attuned to the tastes, not to mention the attention span, of working-class men and women. He also specialised in juvenile literature, beginning a weekly *Young Folks Budget* in 1871 and a juvenile comic called *Funny Folks* in 1874, which he published in offices in Red Lion Court just off Fleet Street. His success engendered competition and, as the 1880s progressed, he was fiercely challenged by two young men who would feature prominently in Ralph Hodgson's own pressman career – George Newnes and Alfred Harmsworth (later to become Lord Northcliffe).

In 1881, Manchester-born Newnes devised the hugely popular *Tit-Bits*. This was a scrapbook style weekly – not a comic, but a light-hearted, informative gathering of 'human interest' snippets, short stories and even full-length fiction serials, which spawned many imitations: *Funny Bits*, *Pic 'n' Bits* and others. By the mid-1880s *Tit-Bits* was selling 900,000 copies a month.

In 1888 Alfred Harmsworth, the Dublin-born son of an English barrister, decided to join his brother Harold in publishing a similar type of magazine called *Answers to Correspondents*. He told his readers that every question sent in would be answered by post, and the letters of general interest would be answered in the magazine. *Answers to Correspondents* was a great success, and within four years he was selling over a million copies a week.

Ever the innovator, as the 1890s began, Harmsworth decided to develop a comic specially for children, as he felt that the magazines known as 'penny dreadfuls' – of which *Sloper* was the prime example, with its shocking images and foul language – were a bad influence on younger readers. Thus the halfpenny *Comic Cuts* appeared in July 1890, introducing a completely new genre: innocent, pure fun with comic strips and characters continuing from week to week. A comic 'war' between publishers now began in earnest and during the next six to seven years, scores of titles appeared and disappeared, colour was introduced, sizes were altered and fortunes made.

The rapid expansion brought a demand for original artists, illustrators and joke merchants, as there was a limit to how much could be plundered from abroad. Ralph Hodgson who in his late teens had contributed cartoon strips to omnibus comics such as *Illustrated Bits* (the 'Largest Penny Illustrated in the World') now landed a job with what would be the principal competitor to *Comic Cuts*: *Funny Cuts*. This was a product of the Dalzeil Brothers and, being published in Red Lion Court in the heart of what had become 'comic land', it was in direct line of descent from W.G. Baxter and *Ally Sloper*. Baxter had died of alcoholic poisoning in 1888 but his successor on *Sloper*, W.F. Thomas, was a close friend of Ralph's brother Walker.

Ralph Hodgson was now working in distinguished company, as his fellow cartoonists on *Cuts*, Alfred Gray and Gordon Hood, had also worked on *Judy* many years before. *Funny Cuts* was an almost immediate success. Published each Monday, by late 1890 it was featuring pieces by Hodgson of a 'roving reporter' kind, uncannily similar to his brother Walker's work for the *Darlington Echo*, such as trips to the Crystal Palace dog show or horse-racing notes from Tattersalls, etc. By 1891 he was being allotted whole pages, and his name was prominently displayed on the comic's masthead, while his distinctive, free-flowing style stood out from the more staid, composed traditional tableaux that usually served to illustrate a music hall-style joke or punchline.

The full page entitled 'When We Were Young' in April 1891 demonstrates not only his ability to blend various aspects of current affairs (General Booth, Randolph Churchill, Gladstone and the Prince of Wales were featured along with prominent sportsmen) but also his almost casual, swirling, throwaway style of composition. His cartoon world was an anarchic mix of sporting slang, animals, vignette-style fillers, all held together by plays on words and puns, a far cry from the sharp, poignant observations of a Phil May or a Harry Furniss, yet perfect for the juvenile market for whom he was operating.

Funny Cuts ran for 30 years but Hodgson disappeared from its pages after just 18 months. Having spotted his potential, Alfred Harmsworth decided to poach him for an enterprise of an entirely different stamp.

Having made a considerable fortune with lightweight publications such as *Answers* and *Comic Cuts*, Harmsworth turned his attention to Fleet Street. In 1894 he bought the loss-making *Evening News* for £25,000 and set about revamping and relaunching it in a newer, brasher, more popular mode modelled on American methods. Harmsworth had been to New York and been impressed by Joseph Pulitzer's campaigning, radical, populist paper the *New York World*. He would use the *Evening News* as a dummy run before turning his attention to the daily press.

With the help of the editor Kennedy Jones, he dramatically changed the paper. Although he retained the traditional seven-column layout, advertisements were now reduced to a single column on the left. Six columns of news were presented in a crisper style with eye-catching headlines such as *Was it Suicide or Apoplexy?*, *Another Battersea Scandal*, *Bones in Bishopgate*, *Hypnotism and Lunacy* and *Killed by a Grindstone*. A new journalism of short, snappy, sensational paragraphs, popular interviews and sports results would be developed to attract, as Harmsworth put it, the "tens of millions who were conventional without being cultivated and who were demanding more and more to be amused".

Dashingly bold in appearance, and now visually attractive, the paper also used illustrations in a way not attempted before, in particular in a form of large, arresting cartoons, something for which the *New York World* had long been famous. The cartoonist whom Harmsworth engaged to produce the new front-page look was Ralph Hodgson, from now on known under the pen-name Yorick.

Hodgson's drawings had appeared gradually, at first in the shape of small illustrations to accompany the visit of a foreign celebrity or a court case or a crime. They were later used on a series of articles on well-known *Men Who Have Earned Success*, the first of whom was the tycoon-founder of the Piece Coffee Stalls. This was followed by profiles of household and furniture manufacturers, artists and music hall entertainers, all of whom had risen from nothing to become rich and influential. The series was based on a new American 'interview' format. The interviewer, Stanley Warren Bell, was a good friend of Hodgson's who worked under the pseudonym Tantalus. Bell would later work in similar fashion with Hodgson's brother Walter.

A full page of Ralph Hodgson's work for *Funny Cuts* August 1891
(with Hodgson and his dog in the bottom left-hand corner)

Together, 'Yorick' and 'Tantalus' criss-crossed London during 1894, hurrying in and out of courtrooms and coffee shops, great mansions and music halls, meeting and profiling the successful lower middle classes so beloved of Northcliffe. Gradually, Hodgson's contributions developed. In October 1894 he produced a three-column-wide illustration to accompany the paper's tongue-in-cheek coverage of the social reformer Mrs Ormiston Chant's campaign to close dance halls that she suspected were being used by prostitutes to pick up clients, and later that month he illustrated the dramatic trial of a man accused of murdering his pregnant fiancée. A boxing fatality received extensive visual coverage, followed by exposés of East End anarchists, and in January 1895, the Socialist MP John Burns was attacked by the paper for accepting favours from a rich industrialist – lavish illustrations accompanied this story for weeks.

It would be political matters that saw Hodgson employed to most dramatic effect. January brought the start of campaigning for the London County Council elections in which Harmsworth threw his weight behind Liberal reformers against the incumbent Conservative administration.

A bitterly cold winter, resulting in death and distress for thousands of London's poor and destitute, presented the *Evening News* with a perfect excuse to pillory local councillors and others whom it held responsible for the capital's poor, as well as to promote its own 'Feed the Poor' campaign. Hodgson's pen was kept fully occupied producing pictures of political demonstrations; the suffering, needy poor; and pompous, ineffectual politicians. There was one enormous cartoon showing the Progressive Party with a muck-rake cleansing London of an oddly assorted mixture of evils while promoting pure water, cheap gas and reduced rates.

Hodgson's stint as a political/current affairs illustrator came to a dramatic climax at the Old Bailey when he was present to sketch the climactic event of the *fin de siècle* decade, the trial (or rather trials) of Oscar Wilde. Hodgson's spare, swift illustrations captured Wilde at his most vulnerable. Many years later he recalled: "I can still see Wilde's full, supercilious but good-natured and very handsome face, thick, dark-brown hair worn parted in the middle and rather long but trim behind, as if it were but yesterday …", and of Wilde's subsequent conviction he wrote, "The gloom of that hour over London and particularly over the literary and art side can never be described – it discoloured and darkened life everywhere."

Hodgson was now an established character in Fleet Street, and a colleague at the time recalled:

> I can see him in his white shirt-sleeves, standing before a sloping drawing-board drawing pictures with humorous captions for the *Evening News* under the nom de plume 'Yorick'. He smoked Black Cat Cavendish tobacco out of a well-covered clay pipe and was continually wiping his pen on his shirt sleeves which were covered in ink.

Within four months, however, Hodgson's work ceased appearing in the *Evening News* and he was replaced by Raven Hill. A couple of months later, his work appeared in *The Idler* – Jerome K. Jerome's successful men's magazine – alongside that of artists such as Phil May and Max Beerbohm. He illustrated articles by Mrs Humphry Ward (the granddaughter of Thomas Arnold) who was a champion of both London's poor and women's education. He also produced Phil May-style cartoons featuring glamorous young ladies.

By early 1896 he had moved again, this time to an independent magazine called *The Minster*, joining such luminaries of the illustrating world as the Beggarstaff Brothers, Sydney Sime, Max Cowper and Dudley Hardy. The enterprise claimed as its aim to make *The Minster* "the first English magazine, not merely in the excellence of its literary and artistic matters but also in its reproduction and printing". Work by J.M. Barrie, Rudyard Kipling and Conan Doyle was promised, but it ran for just two editions before closing. The following year Hodgson followed his elder brother Walker, and joined the Pearson Publishing Company, working briefly on *Pearson's Magazine* before teaming up with the cartoonist Tom Browne to help launch Pearson's hugely successful children's comic *The Big Budget*.

Why he moved about so frequently and why he left Harmsworth when he appeared to be in such a promising position, poses questions to which there are no clear-cut answers. He himself certainly didn't see his sudden departure from the *Evening News* as a failure. It was, he claimed, the result of a clash of personalities. He once commented, "Northcliffe liked me. I kept a dog and a bird in a cage in my office. No one else dared to. He saw me fighting in the street. 'What a way to act out of office,' he said. I left the paper because his brother and I couldn't agree." Northcliffe's brother Harold was a notoriously hard driver of men and it was said that you were no one if you had not been fired by him.

Hodgson once recorded that Northcliffe had predicted a great future for him, and Hodgson himself was said to have been devoted to Northcliffe for many years until the latter became too powerful for his liking. Proof that there was no animosity between the two men came a couple of years after Hodgson and Harmsworth had gone their separate ways when Harmsworth attended Hodgson's wedding, and presented him and his wife with a large cheque as a present.

3

Marriage and *Big Budget*

*My Dear Darling Doll, I feel so lonely here without you, it makes
me feel absolutely how much you have become to me.*
(Hodgson to Dolly Chatteris, 1896)

In 1898, just a couple of years after the Hodgsons had left Chalcot Crescent,
the social reformer Charles Booth passed by on one of his famous London
walks and deemed it a "lodgings" street, inhabited mostly by clerks and
shop assistants, hardly salubrious. A street or so away, opposite Regent's
Park and overlooking the London Zoo, is St Mark's Square where one
finds large, well-proportioned houses, inhabited then and now by wealthy
members of the middle class. It was here that Ralph Hodgson's future wife,
Janet 'Dolly' Chatteris lived with her parents and sisters.

Hubert Chatteris was an advertising agent, a profession just then
starting to become respectable and immensely profitable thanks, in part,
to men like Harmsworth and their million-selling popular newspapers.
The Chatteris household was decidedly middle class. When Janet was
seven they had lived in fashionable Sloane Street, the family of six having
a nurse, housemaid and cook to tend to their needs.

How Ralph and Dolly first met, given the wide disparity of their social
spheres, is unknown. It's been suggested that Hodgson first made the
acquaintance of Hubert at a dog show and was introduced to the family a
little later. It was also rumoured that Dolly was already engaged and that
Hodgson had persuaded her to break the engagement. He could certainly
be persuasive once he settled on a female target.

The wedding ceremony took place at St Mark's Church, Regent's Park
on 6th February 1896 and was sufficiently noteworthy in social terms to
receive a full-length report in *The Gentlewoman* the following month,
where it was described as "very bright and dainty". Dr William Sparrow-
Simpson, a high churchman and one of the most learned clerics of his day,
conducted the ceremony. According to the *Gentlewoman*'s report, none of
Hodgson's family attended, even though they were now living no more than
a mile away in Lawford Road, Kentish Town. Hodgson's best man was one
of Janet's male friends and the guests were almost all of the bride's family

and friends. It was a gathering of bankers and musicians, ambassadors and artists, and the wedding gifts suggested a level of wealth far beyond Hodgson's humble, North County origins: Dresden china, bangles inlaid with rubies, gold and enamel brooches, silver egg-stands.

Hodgson's guests were exclusively Fleet Street orientated. They included the novelist and playwright, Stanley Warren Bell, the artist and cartoonist Jack Yeats, the Harmsworth journalist William (Henry) Maas, who would remain a lifelong friend, and Hodgson's erstwhile employer himself, Alfred Harmsworth. The couple left for Skindles Hotel, a smart new establishment in the fashionable Thames riverside resort of Maidenhead, and later spent some days in Brighton at the Hotel Metropole, a luxury facility that had been completed as recently as 1890.

They were to be an apparently blissfully happy couple. Janet herself was a small, pretty woman, delicately featured; she suited her sobriquet 'Dolly' to perfection. A frequent guest at the Hodgson household in the early years of their marriage recalled somewhat disparagingly: "She was a quiet little thing whom, I suppose, because so quiet and withdrawn, I remember not at all." Yet she wasn't, as another of Hodgson's female friends wrote, "a patient Griselda". She was resilient and witty, had studied at Girton College and soon became a favourite of Hodgson's mother and spinster sisters despite their apparent absence from the marriage ceremony – so much so that she would be buried in the family grave in East Finchley. Mary, one suspects, admired Dolly for her ability to cope with the one son she herself had never managed to control but upon whom she clearly doted. She was recalled by another lifelong friend of Hodgson's many years later:

> Dolly was tiny and reminded one of some exquisite Persian miniature. Her dark hair, parted in the middle, was worn in two smooth, gently folded wings. This classical style was in marked contrast to the convoluted exuberance of most women of her age. She dressed, as a rule, in simple, dark, woollen coats and skirts, their wide hems just touching her in-step and a belt of the same material clasped with a silver buckle held them firmly round her waist. Her white linen blouses were so neat one wondered how she got into them. One never saw her with a hair out of place, even when the bull-terriers dragged her about on their leads; indeed, this somehow made their behaviour all the more outrageous in our eyes! We admired her enormously and her innate and timeless elegance must have filled other women with despair. He had made her give up furs and feathers when she married him, thus, in some way, creating her true image.

Dolly's resilience would be sorely tested over the years. The Hodgsons moved house almost every year for the first six years of their marriage.

Amersham, Pinner, Micheldever, Great Bookham, Fleet, West Byfleet –
they had homes in each of these picturesque Home County villages, and
in each, Hodgson's dogs would have pride of place.

Elizabeth Crutwell, then a child living close by the Hodgsons at Great
Bookham, recalled:

> Their drawing room, with French windows opening onto the garden,
> had been given over to bull-terriers Jim and Dulcie. It was largely
> unfurnished; I do not remember a table or a rug. Without being
> sentimental, Hodgson had a Franciscan attitude towards Jim and
> Dulcie. That they played merry hell with Dolly when Hodgson
> left her alone with them when he went up to town, he preferred to
> ignore. He expected her to exercise them when he wasn't there.
> Dragging her down the lane one day by their leads they succeeded
> in wrapping her round a tree, and my brother and I flew to her rescue
> ... we were disappointed when she asked us not to mention it to
> Hodgson. It was quite beyond his comprehension that others might
> not share his enthusiasm for these exuberant animals.

Despite such anecdotes, Dolly appeared as keen on the dogs as
Hodgson, and was also happy to keep home while Hodgson came and
went as he pleased.

Once Hodgson established himself as art editor at *Big Budget*, his life
settled into a routine that would be sustained for a decade or more, one
that suited his outwardly indolent character. In 1904, his editor informed
Big Budget readers: "The quiet, peaceful Hampshire Downs are Yorick's
haunts now, and though he spends two to three days at the office, his
magnificent front page is invariably produced at his country home ...",
which at that point was a comfortable country cottage called St Ivels in
Great Bookham (Surrey, not Hampshire).

Working for Arthur Pearson – a philanthropist and educator at heart
– also seemed to suit Hodgson's philosophical outlook rather better than
the frantic, cut-throat world of Grub Street. His pen-name symbolises
that attitude.

Adopting a pen-name is not unusual in the cartooning world today, but
back then it wasn't quite as common. Indeed, Hodgson had, along with all
the other contributors to *Funny Cuts*, begun his comic career signing his
work with his full name. It even adorned the *Funny Cuts* masthead. But
throughout the rest of his Fleet Street career, before the First World War,
'Yorick' was all the public had to go on by way of identification.

It is easy to see why he chose it. Yorick is both the name of the dead
jester in Shakespeare's *Hamlet* and also of Laurence Sterne's parson in
Tristram Shandy. Little is said of Shakespeare's character, but Sterne's
Yorick is an oddly humorous man, with many idiosyncrasies whose

unfortunate wit makes many foes. He is a jocular character, who dislikes gravity and mocks serious individuals. It's clear that Hodgson saw something of himself in Sterne's character.

Adams Gowan Whyte, a journalist colleague who was working his way up through the Pearson publishing company, confirms this, recalling:

> Hodgson treated me openly as a curiosity; he would sit cross-legged on my desk, puffing clouds of shag smoke and quizzing me as he might a fish out of water yet miraculously trying to live. I had happened to write for an ethical journal an article with the august title: 'Will Ceremonial Survive?' and he would stare at me intently and murmur the title over and over again in a tone of awe and bewilderment. His nickname for me was 'Ethical Bill', which fully expressed his opinion of people who worried to argue 'about it and about', while there were larks to listen to and bull-terriers to train.

It must not be thought that being art editor of a boys' comic meant there would be no opportunity to create or build a lucrative reputation. Black-and-white artists, as cartoonist/illustrators were known in the thirty years preceding the First World War, were often celebrities on a par with music hall stars, many earning small fortunes. In fact, *Big Budget* consolidated the fame of his colleague Tom Browne, who left two years after the comic started in order to pursue a flourishing publishing business and artistic career. Browne eventually bought himself a large studio in Blackheath where he produced work that led to his election to the Royal Academy, and he also founded a lucrative picture postcard and advertising business. Perhaps to make Hodgson's point, however, Browne died early, largely through overwork.

Throughout his long association with *Big Budget*, Hodgson remained securely behind his *nom de plume* almost to the point of complete anonymity. Only once in the ten years or more that he worked on the paper did a photo of him appear in its pages, when he can be seen standing among a group of contributors and editors posing by the River Thames on a staff outing, a raffish boater tilted at an angle, pipe in mouth.

For the rest, he was content to appear as a fleeting cartoon character, one that he had been refining and developing almost from the beginning of his press career. In 1891, when Hodgson was almost twenty, we catch a glimpse of him scurrying across the foot of the page of *Funny Cuts* cartoons dressed in almost Pollyanna-style American garb: short-waisted jacket, gaiters, broad-brimmed banded hat, clutching a long stick and being dragged along by a bull-terrier on a lead. Ten years on, he strolls across the pages of *Big Budget*, the stick – now a formal walking stick – tucked beneath his arm, trademark bowler hat clamped on his head, wearing a three-quarter-length Crombie-style overcoat, a high Edwardian collar

The Evening News.

SPECIAL EDITION.

LONDON: MONDAY, FEBRUARY 18, 1895.

WAITING OUTSIDE ONE OF OUR SOUP DEPOTS.

Ralph Hodgson cartoon depicting London's poor
during the LCC elections of February 1895

completing the picture. A pipe now juts from between his teeth; the bull-terrier is still tugging on his lead.

And while other staff members posed for pocket photos for a Christmas number, Yorick appears as a cartoon sketch, clay pipe in place, a bulbous nose adding to the caricature. When the editor revealed that poor old Yorick had had a real accident while out cycling, Hodgson provided another caricature of himself accompanied by a fantastically rearranged bicycle that could well have leapt out of an episode from the hugely popular front-page strip 'Airey Alf and Bouncing Billy'.

Big Budget rapidly became the best-selling boys' comic in Britain. Founded in 1897, it was Arthur Pearson's main thrust in the 'comic war' and it set standards in home-grown comic production that would serve as an inspiration for succeeding generations of comic artists and writers. Its main front-page comic-strip characters, Airey Alf and Bouncing Billy, originally created by Tom Browne but produced exclusively by Hodgson from 1899 on, were among the first of countless such partnerships that would be the staple diet for children through the coming century.

Hodgson's work on *Big Budget* was distinctive and he was to originate many successful strip-cartoon series such as the Badlots, the Stoneybrokes,

21

Sunny Jim and Dismal David, the Poll Poll Family, Honeysweet the Dog plus the Big Budget Kid. This character bore a close resemblance to the *New York World*'s Yellow Kid, evidence that Hodgson was closely in touch with developments across the Atlantic and that he may even have travelled to New York with Harmsworth back in the early 1890s to study the methods of American cartoonists.

In fact, in the history of comic papers, he played a significant role in moving the genre forward. The late Denis Gifford, cartoon historian, wrote:

> Yorick was the first to flirt with actual speech in the frame; he helped consolidate the style that by 1900 was becoming the standard: clean, neat, open line-work, spotted with well-balanced blacks plus plenty of action. Action, simple slap-stick in pictures, this was the compelling new thing the humorous magazines lacked … the gist of a joke in no more than the flick of an eye-ball.

Hodgson's work on *Big Budget* was not restricted to mere slapstick, either. The comic established itself as a market leader during the Boer War, when it devoted much space to real-life heroes such as Baden-Powell and dramatic incidents such as the siege of Ladysmith. The comic was stridently imperialist in its views. It carried stories entitled 'Empire's Great Peril' or 'A World in Arms', boasting square-jawed heroes such as

Ralph Hodgson's illustrations for the London Evening News' court report of Oscar Wilde's first trial at the Old Bailey in May 1895

Graydon Garth cutting swathes through the Boers' front lines. Graydon Garth, created by a colleague of Hodgson's, Sidney Drew, was described in the *Big Budget* publicity as a "Statesman, Empire Builder, and Leader of Men", a staunch patriot who (like all the penny dreadful characters) unthinkingly believed in the superiority and moral righteousness of the British cause.

Hodgson wasn't far behind in the 'tub-thumping' stakes. His principal contribution would be to produce enormous double-page spreads caricaturing the main butt of British contempt, the Boer leader General Kruger. 'Kruger Takes a Bath', 'Kruger as an Exploding Frog', 'Kruger Takes a Midnight Flit' – all these personifications were enormously popular. Readers could order prints of them for 6d and they were also issued as postcards. Images of them were even flashed up, to great effect, on a screen at a number of West End music halls. Alongside this he produced cartoons with a definitely satirical edge lampooning the War Office as blunderingly out of date, and poking fun at amateur war critics, including his former employers Harmsworth and J.K. Jerome. He even created an incompetent war correspondent called Bounderby Bounce.

In fact, Hodgson was so influential as a comic creator that in 1903 Pearson turned to him to produce, almost single-handedly, a spin-off comic – *Funny Pips* – which was to accompany a new paper called *The Boys' Leader*. The *Leader* was to be the standard-bearer of a new organisation called the National Brotherhood, which was a precursor of the Scout Movement, but in early 1904, Yorick was reported to be unwell. *Pips* was dropped and its main strip character, Sunny Jim, inspired by a breakfast cereal character advertising Force Flakes, was eventually discontinued. *The Boys' Leader* was soon swallowed up by *Big Budget* which then moved away from being a comic fun production. Hodgson's heyday had passed, and the subsequent decision of Pearson to turn away from *Big Budget* completely and put all his resources into producing *The Scout* for Baden-Powell marked the end of Hodgson's children's comic career.

One senses that he wasn't unhappy about this, although at thirty-seven years old, his immediate future looked uncertain. What is clear is that he was rapidly coming to the conclusion that journalism as a trade was incompatible with the writing of serious verse, an activity that would soon come to dominate his life. To deal in words and images as purely saleable commodities in order to earn a living would, he considered, inevitably damage the poetic sensibility.

Frank, his brother, recalled seeing him in the *Big Budget* offices one day working on Weary Willie and Tired Tim. Hodgson commented, biting his nails, "This may be comedy for some but it's tragedy for me."

A journalist/illustrator works in a transitory world, producing scores of images each week, hundreds, perhaps thousands each year, all to be 'consumed' and then forgotten. To someone like Hodgson – who would prove to be an obsessive perfectionist where his verse was involved, and a man wedded to the idea of the sanctity and importance of the 'artist' – this increasingly superficial process became ever more frustrating.

And yet, as he moved away from cartooning and the day-to-day Fleet Street routine, it is clear that he took with him certain technical skills that would influence his verse. He would not be alone in this. With the rapid expansion of newspaper media in the late 19th and early 20th centuries, many more young men and women were being trained to use language in a rapid, easy-to-consume form, a process that could not help but have an effect on literature in general.

The critic, Cyril Connolly has written of this period in *Enemies of Promise*:

> The idiom (of our time) is journalism and the secret of journalism is to write the way people talk. There can be no delayed impact in journalism, no subtlety, no embellishments, no assumption of a luxury reader. And since the pace of journalism waxed faster than that of literature, literature found itself in a predicament.

According to his analysis, literature in general either competed or retreated into the ivory tower. Prose writers competed; hence the success of the Edwardian novel. On the whole, poetry, however

> ran away and so we find from the 1890s to the First World War desolate stretches with no poets able to make a living and few receiving attention from the public. The stage is held by the journalist poets like Kipling and Masefield.

Interestingly, John Masefield was making a name for himself in the early years of the century when Hodgson was first tentatively offering samples of his verse to the *Saturday Review* and, although the two men were not to meet until 1914, their lives followed oddly similar routes.

Like Hodgson, Masefield had had a restless, unsettled childhood. Brought up by his grandparents, at the age of 12 he joined HMS *Conway* – a training ship – and from there went to sea. Like Hodgson, Masefield found himself in the USA in his teens but, unlike Hodgson, he channelled his experiences at sea into a volume of verse entitled *Salt-Water Ballads*.

Masefield ultimately became a journalist and in 1899 moved to London where he came to know W.B. Yeats, J.M. Synge and many other late 1890s poets. His early verse borrowed heavily from the aesthetics of Synge, Laurence Binyon and Swinburne, but by 1909 he was producing narrative, vernacular-based pieces, aimed at appealing to as many people as possible, with the emphasis on verse that could be spoken aloud and easily understood. He dealt with subjects that had wide appeal – boxing, village life, fox-hunting, etc. – and his long poem, *The Everlasting Mercy*, published in 1911, was a breakthrough event, selling in thousands and inaugurating the 'Georgian' period.

Ralph Hodgson, like Masefield, had a Fleet Street career, although as a cartoonist rather than a writer. Thus he differed from Masefield in significant ways. The latter's strength lay in narrative and an identifiable place as context for much of his work. As a comic-strip expert, Hodgson was less committed to a conventional storyline, and thus his verse inclined to the episodic, the abstract – even, at times, the fantastic: a Dodo gathering wool upon a hillside; a Baghdad Barber kicking a beau called McHaroun, and laughing children with feathered heels.

Ralph Hodgson's front page of Airy Alf and Bouncing Billy
in *Big Budget* January 1901

4

First Poems

Go little book; fear not thy fate;
Though men deride and rail
And pass thee by, yet Truth is great,
By Jove! and will prevail.

('Farewell')

Hodgson's first published poem appeared in April 1904 in *The Saturday Review,* a weekly periodical whose main concerns were things political, educational and social as seen from a 'constructive Tory' point of view. The poem was entitled 'The Missel Thrush' and was, according to George Allen, who would soon publish a collection of Hodgson's work, Hodgson's first serious effort at verse.

However, according to George Hutchinson, a colleague of Hodgson's on *Big Budget,* Hodgson had been writing poetry for some years before the acceptance of 'The Missel Thrush'. Hutchinson was a regular visitor to Hodgson's various homes along with another colleague from the Pearson publishing house, the playwright Rudolf Besier. Hutchinson recalled:

> Besier and I went to weekends with him in his (then) rural wild more than once. Lighting was by lamps and candles, shopping by the local Cripp's the Carrier. After every meal we played billiards on a do-it-yourself table, tightly-strung canvas bands for the cushions, screwed-in pockets and lighting by innumerable candles stuck wherever they would go and renewed at intervals.

Once the billiards was over, however

> Besier and I were more than ready for bed by that time but, 'and now we'll *talk!*' Hodgson would cry – and did, Besier nodding off and awakening with a start at intervals. [Hodgson] suffered badly at times from haemorrhoids. I remember one time when we went down [to visit] finding him stretched out on a sofa with the wretched trouble and I think no billiards that time but, non-stop *talk.*

Rudolf Besier was, at that time, making a name for himself as a playwright in London's West End. Hodgson had first met him when Besier was editing the *Royal Magazine* for Pearson's and they discovered they had mutual interests – dogs, birds and verse. Hodgson later recalled Besier as, "a tall, slender young man with a pale intellectual fineness about his handsome face. No one with eyes ever mistook Besier for other than he was, the eternal devotee of poetry for sheer love of beauty."

Besier recalled in a letter to Hodgson almost forty years later, that their friendship had started uncertainly:

> We had quarrelled about Lloyd George, whom I'd called a cad. You spat out a withering remark and went out, slamming the door behind you (I think you were sorely tempted to land me one on the jaw – you were pretty handy with your fists in those days!). For weeks you avoided my room and if by chance we passed each other, well, I simply wasn't there. Then one day we met on the stairs. I said, 'Hod, they've taken my play!' Your whole face lit up with delight as only your face can – and that cad Lloyd George was forgotten!

Besier's first play, *The Virgin Goddess*, was produced at the Adelphi in late 1906. Written entirely in blank verse with chanting choruses, it was compared favourably with work produced that year by Maurice Hewlett, Laurence Binyon, Thomas Sturge Moore and Arthur Symons, all well-known poets who had turned to verse drama following W.B. Yeats' lead. Even Swinburne's dramatised *Atalanta in Calydon* was placed by the *Stage* critic below Besier's work.

It was followed by *Don*, a portrait of an eccentric but kind-hearted poet, which earned him more praise setting him on the road to success and considerable fortune. Later he collaborated with H.G. Wells on a dramatised *Kipps*, wrote a successful verse drama for Mrs Patrick Campbell and crowned his career in 1930 with *The Barretts of Wimpole Street*.

The success of Besier's work rested on simplicity of construction and bringing colour to stage dialogue. In fact, he declared, he was more interested in words than plot and character – a characteristic that impressed Hodgson who clearly respected Besier's judgement and taste. Many years later Hodgson wrote:

> I think Besier drew more downright enjoyment from poetry apart from his own dramatic work than any man I have known. When he laid aside whatever play he was busy with, it was to roll himself in Shakespeare, Blake, Coleridge or Wordsworth for sheer refreshment. He was the best reader of poetry I have ever known: his judgement of poetry was equal to any man in my experience.

It's no surprise, then, that Hodgson accepted Besier's advice where his own verse was concerned. According to Hutchinson:

> Hodgson used to bring poems up for Besier to see. I well remember the day when Besier saw in one [of the poems] so much that he directed it should be submitted to the *Saturday Review*. The poem was submitted and to the high thrill of the three of us was immediately accepted. Besier's association with those early verses was (his delight in them apart) occasional vetting of their punctuation and, I seem to remember, suggesting sometimes a different word. Hodgson gladly accepted the punctuation and, as often as not I daresay, the better word.

The Saturday Review's editor, Harold Hodge, a social reformer who left the job in 1913 to work for the poor in the East End of London, was also a keen fan of Hodgson's verse and encouraged the reluctant poet to send in "as much of it as will come", attracted perhaps by the fiercely ecological zeal running through many of the early pieces. "Your work gives me life," he wrote to Hodgson, "amid so much mediocre stuff."

With such an ardent advocate, Hodgson became, for a time, almost the *Review*'s 'house-poet', his work being both a welcome diversion for readers weary of the world of current affairs, yet at the same time powerful enough to stir their conscience.

There were many other *Review* poets but few of high quality: Arthur Symons, Thomas Sturge Moore, Ford Madox Hueffer were the only ones that have lasted. The young James Joyce did, however, manage to get a poem published just a couple of months before Hodgson's first in April 1904.

In 1907, Hodgson was persuaded to gather together enough work to form his first collection. Entitled *The Last Blackbird*, it was published in April by George Allen and Co., had a dull red cover, was priced 7s/6d and was dedicated to "a close friend", G.B. Dewar. Sadly, the world at large didn't share Hodgson's friends' high regard for his verse.

The Last Blackbird

This first collection revealed Hodgson as a poet possessing a vision shot through with bizarre humour and agonised loss, with a compulsion to sing with joy yet at the same time also to wash himself and the world clean of a great sin, to escape from sterile failure into an almost wordless, ecstatic dream. All this would be underpinned by a darkness hinted at by both Dewar and Edward Thomas in their reviews when they identified echoes of Coleridge's ambiguous and troubled narrative poem, 'Christabel' in reviewing Hodgson's work.

The Last Blackbird falls, perhaps quite unintentionally, into two distinct sections. There is an opening sequence of ten poems whose mood-swings alternate from rushes of joy to dark and violent depths, the poetic self growing more and more exhausted. In the second half of the collection, the Hodgson poetic persona alternates between bookish musings, mild burlesque, semi-comic ramblings on his creative processes, and ends in epigrammatic quips and jests.

The collection opens with a short statement – *Lines*. This provides the motif for the book: that nothing in the world is too small for consideration and human compassion.

In 'The Treasure Box' (inspired perhaps by William Blake's 'Crystal Cabinet') Hodgson casts a wondering, quizzical eye at rainbows over the sea, icy patterns on windowpanes, river bubbles, the pinprick images of stars at night, winter roses and gnats weaving "mad magic" in the sky. He cocks an equally acute ear to blackbirds singing at twilight, ocean maids calling, church bells at harvest time and June birdsong. Sounds and images are wondered and guessed at, questioned and speculated upon with a barely suppressed gladness and joy as well as some puzzlement.

'St Athelstan' marks the first change of mood. In a windswept medieval wood, a father searches for a lost shepherd-boy son who is terrified by a mysterious, threatening animal. He then watches as a guardian angel is slaughtered by a grey wolf. The bloodstained grass is afterwards washed clean by rain and the demented boy, now rescued, is carried away.

In 'The Sedgewarbler' Hodgson wanders in early summer moonlight to listen to the bird of the title singing its "old, old ballad new beside the mill". He watches a bat zigzag around an elm followed by a fern-owl, and the sounds detected become tinier and tinier: a beetle's drone, a leaf unfurling, a bloom bursting open and filling the air with incense. A lizard scurries by, and the poet, mesmerised, falls asleep to be woken at dawn by "the babel of the summer day".

An underlying threat of violence materialises in 'The Missel Thrush'. The defiant bird sings as winds swirl and thunder roars and "heavens bleed flame". "The grey clouds burst, I saw it spill/Black floods as skiey seas fell whole …" Lightning splits the bough of a tree before the storm passes and plovers rise, "ten score as one, and ribboned in the East".

'The Last Blackbird' sees Hodgson, weary now, stumbling, "to a place where linnets drink / And lizards go in ferny loveliness". Lulled to sleep by a blackbird, he wakes to face questions from a deity in angel guise. He answers that mankind has felled the woodlands, nature has fled along with beauty and most animals have been killed – save the blackbird, whose feathers will be used the next day to decorate a woman's hat. Nature, enraged by what she hears, summons a flood "to wash my world", upon which the poet wakes, "a dizzy man", to find a storm brewing.

Before it arrives, he wanders across 'The Down by Moonlight', sensing time "old as the dark". Here, emotions are like physical disturbances, even thought itself being overloud.

In 'Holiday', childhood memories flood over the poet: birdsong and familiar sounds that he will hear when he is dead and buried in some "moist cradle" in the soil. In 'The Linnet' he rejects cynics who try to tell him that life is reducible and relative. Instead, he poses the insoluble riddle of the bird's very existence in a hedgerow.

But then, as if to negate his hopes, 'The Winds' return to roar and stun; to bruise and scream. They whirl everything away into a decadent vision of dead mists, mildewed flowers, "tumour blooms", poisoned sweets and dead, cold air.

Hodgson's principal medium in these ten poems is birds. For a poet starting out – particularly a lyric poet concerned with the 'music' of verse – birds and birdsong are perfect material. They provide images of freedom, of spirits soaring, of nature untrammelled. In addition, the traditional catalogue of ornithological symbols and sounds establishes an instant rapport with a reading public primed to accept and understand such literary devices. It is significant, though, that the novelist and critic Ford Madox Hueffer castigated the 'Georgians', a loose poetic movement into whose ranks Hodgson would soon be co-opted, for their overuse of such traditional tropes: "The song of birds, moonlight – these the poet playing for safety and the critic trying to find something to praise will deem the sure cards of the poetic pack. They seem the safe things to sentimentalise over and it is taken for granted that sentimentality is the business of poetry."

Hodgson's use of birds is anything but sentimental, however. He was a keen ornithologist, and Dewar commented at one point in his review: "There's no catching him out in birds." The sedgewarbler, for instance, would be found only in the secluded spot described in the poem bearing its name. The missel thrush was a bold, fearless bird that *would* continue singing into the teeth of a storm.

Friends who recalled Hodgson in the early years of the century attest to this aspect of his personality. The poet Maud Slessor wrote: "His knowledge of the comings and goings of birds was remarkable and in a rather charming, naive way he took it for granted that other people were as interested in their doings as he." His Fleet Street colleague Adams Gowan Whyte recalled: "One room in his house was virtually an aviary and it is characteristic of him that although he found endless delight in his lively and vocal collection, he gave it up completely under an emotional reaction against the practice of keeping any sort of wild animal in captivity."

The remaining 16 poems in *The Last Blackbird* present an uneven mix of mood and method, and in the years to come Hodgson would hardly stray beyond the confines of their subject matter. All his major preoccupations are here: time and its passing, books, love and inspiration, and the Muse, that Romantic concept so crucial to Hodgson's relationship with versification.

During much of his life, Hodgson would remain fascinated by Julian Huxley's theory of the evolution of the human mind; its mental and social rather than simply organic evolution. Hodgson was convinced that mankind evolves emotionally and that poetry is an important part of that evolution, a vital form of communication down through history. The psychologist Carl Jung's theory of latent race memory played a part here. This is the idea that we recapitulate at our deepest levels the whole history of the race, thus explaining the universal validity of certain archetypal images. For example, Jung commented on the effectiveness of mythological imagery in poetry long after we have ceased to believe in myths.

Robert Graves shared some of these views, feeling that poetry defied logical explanation, that the inspiration to write poetry shared common features with dreams and, like Jung, that poetry related culturally to older anthropological memories. Graves would be one of the few 20th-century poets to explore the idea of the Muse at length, and he saw 'her' as Hodgson did – the inspiration of all true poetry and possessing three faces: creative, lovely and fatal. The essence of poetry, he believed, was an unconscious conspiracy on the part of all true poets to carry this ancient female-divinity idea on into a post-matriarchal society.

Hodgson was thus certainly not alone in thinking the way he did. He believed that poetry defied easy, conventional explanations, and that it was almost akin to a life force, sacred and not to be defiled in any way. Where Hodgson may have diverged from Graves is in how he saw the role of the poet in the process of writing – or rather of *receiving* – poetry. Graves could not simply accept the passive approach that poetry would come on a whim and the poet simply had to wait. His understanding of the process involved a more studied, active, intellectual role. For Hodgson, such effort was of no value: poetry was mysterious, and to receive it one needed an almost spiritual connection to its source, with the Muse.

In various of his poems in *The Last Blackbird*, we can glimpse some of these ideas at work. In 'Beauty Sprite', Hodgson is enamoured of a ghostly female entity he calls Beauty, which inspires him

> Sometimes to hear a song,
> Sometimes to seize a hand,
> I even yours

when the world seems dark and filled with distress. The poet and Beauty seem 'wedded':

> Go with me till the sun
> Mine be and yours,
> Star and companion,
> Ours, even ours.

In 'An Erring Muse', his relations with the source of his poetic inspiration are described with defensive humour. Lots of mock-Elizabethan terms such as "raff", "pother", "ogles" and "bogles" abound, but he still writes a compelling stanza:

> She weeps, she only weeps nor heeds nor hears me.
> At every turn I face ill-fortune's prong
> Yet know not whether most her weeping tears me,
> Or I am torn with anger at my wrong.

'An Elegy' is a long poem about a poetic miscarriage, the source of much pain and sorrow, which describes his mental travels with Imagination across the world, across time, even down into himself:

> E'vn in the dim recesses of my own mind
> I've dared to look; held inquisitions there,
> Strange riddles solved and mysteries divined,
> Nigh laid the secret of my being bare;

While in 'The Night' he tells his Muse to sleep and conjures up in two short stanzas an image of peace, rest and love:

> The wall of night is up; around, across,
> Above nor sound nor sense of day remains;
> Comes only now the fitful drive and toss
> Of moths upon the yellow window-panes.

(This last line is echoed in Eliot's 'Prufrock'.)

Despite the angst and pain contained in much of his verse, Hodgson was always sustained by a sense of good humour. It would run like a silver vein through both his life and his work. It was a peculiar brand of humour, too, as demonstrated in two or three of *The Last Blackbird* poems, in particular 'The Vanity of Human Ambition and Big Behaviour', in which Arabian Nights-style characters place bets on the Sherbert Stakes at Scanderoon, and the doomed and joyless Mameluke Githar fatally pelts his murderous uncle with a bar of soap while the latter takes a bath. Characters such as Mac the Barber of Baghdad Town, and Tegg the Potboy become involved in long, rambling discussions about the exact name of an ancient warrior who broke a lance fighting a mythical swordfish. Many of the names mentioned suggest that the piece is well-grounded in ancient research.

There are even one or two mock-academic footnotes.

Modelled perhaps on Samuel Johnson's 'The Vanity of Human Wishes', this almost indecipherable ramble contains little that can be found in the literature of the Arab world, whether history or of legend and mythology. Byron's 'The Giaour: A Fragment of a Turkish Tale' and George Meredith's 'The Shaving of Shagpat, An Arabian Tale' could well have been inspirations, but the poem remains a puzzle.

The Last Blackbird sold no more than half a dozen copies; it was reviewed only by Dewar in the *Saturday Review* and Edward Thomas in the *Daily Chronicle* – and nowhere else. Hodgson, Thomas said, possessed a particular quality which he called the "emotional picturesque". "Few others living could equal him in that," Thomas wrote, suggesting that the book had the mark, "not merely of a class or a school but of an individual, singular, unique, whom we cannot mistake for someone else".

Even such a close friend as Dewar was slightly unsettled by what seemed an ambivalence in the relentless jesting. Hodgson's poetry, he thought, certainly had a "strange, haunting beauty", but he had a suspicion, "that the author is partly jesting, tickled at the reader being touched by the pathos he does not feel himself".

Dewar was more familiar with Hodgson's work, having been a close friend since the early 1890s. Significantly, he emphasised what Hodgson's poetry was *not*:

> It is mercy that Mr Hodgson has not been tempted by the example of half a dozen of the more talked-about, most printed and most rising bards of today, to go in for Empire, and the Veldt; and Our Lady of the Snow; or The Great White Queen; or Red Russia, or Purple Turkey – of which he would probably, like all the others, make a hash …

Dewar was also pleased that Hodgson had not tried "that other fashion that pays in poetry today, the swooning love business".

Though no Futurist, Dewar, like many middle-class intellectuals, thought that popular taste was lacking in discrimination and that, while there existed a large reading public, "quite honest and in many matters by no means unintelligent", they had no way of telling good verse from bad. As a consequence, he feared that Hodgson would not, as he put it, "take on", because he refused to deal with popular topics, the "poetic stock-in-trade". Those many thousands of readers who consumed the works of Marie Corelli and Hall Caine, Stephen Phillips, George Meredith, Alfred Lord Tennyson and Thomas Hardy would, Dewar was certain, fail to detect in Hodgson anything more than a "little" amateur poet: "Amateur, unimportant and unambitious, probably – that is what Mr Hodgson will be taken for."

Whatever his poetic intentions, Hodgson certainly felt the failure of his first volume keenly. In fact, his poetic career, begun diffidently because he doubted his powers of expression, almost ended with *The Last Blackbird.* Once the book had appeared and just as rapidly disappeared, his poetic output, sparse at the best of times, dwindled down to almost nothing. So scathing was his self-criticism that he would attempt to suppress the book in the coming years, referring to it, if he had to, as "that miserable thing".

It did, however, mark a turning point in his life. Within a few years he would be relying almost totally on his poetry to feed himself, Dolly and their various dogs and, for a man approaching 40 years old, as Hodgson was in 1908, this was a considerable gamble. In the process, he sacrificed everything he had built: a Fleet Street career of almost 20 years' duration, a comfortable house in the country and financial security.

5

Amongst Poets

In its infancy, the Georgian movement was uncharacterised by evidence of design, that is, it did not, like other schools, preach or practise a special dogma of poetic art. It was fortuitous and informal.

(Harold Monro)

In the years following the publication of *The Last Blackbird* in 1907, Hodgson began to move in more overtly poetic circles. He recalled:

> I became one of a group of men who used to meet at St George's Restaurant in St Martin's Lane. On a Tuesday morning, Edward Thomas used to come up from Steep and, after having got through his visits to the offices of various journals he reviewed for, he was free for the rest of the day …

It was Thomas who invited Hodgson along to the "little gathering of bards … literary people, the stage and chess". It suited Hodgson perfectly as St George's was clearly not an intense intellectual gathering:

> Through the little door on the right, up two flights of brass-bound stairs, through the door with 'Smoking' on it to the chess-room where he [Thomas] presided over a gathering at tea. The place was a refuge for artists, writers and painters; the waitresses were jolly and expected no tips.

Thomas usually arrived at St George's after lunch with the Square Club at the Mont Blanc restaurant, an altogether more cerebral affair organised by Edward Garnett with such luminaries as John Masefield, John Galsworthy, Hilaire Belloc and W.H. Hudson discussing, "with grave solemnity the social problems of the day, not to say continental literature, etc." There is no evidence that Hodgson was invited on a regular basis to the Mont Blanc, although he would come to know many of the men attending Garnett's gathering.

Hodgson had met Thomas via mutual Fleet Street connections, Thomas being a hard-working reviewer and writer of hack books on the English countryside as well as the author of a number of respectable biographies. Hodgson indeed became a regular visitor to the Thomas household in the years before the First World War. Thomas' wife recalled:

> He used to spend many weekends or longer with us at Petersfield high up above the hanging beech trees. We all loved him. He looked in those days rather like one of the prize fighters he loved to talk about. He was the most indolent man I have ever met. He used to sit in our living-room with his feet on the mantelpiece smoking his pipe of shag which he kept in an enormous india-rubber pouch.

He rarely joined Thomas on the latter's long tramps across the countryside, and one senses that the melancholy, reflective Thomas would not have proved ideal company for the more voluble, chatterbox Hodgson. Hodgson certainly enjoyed the family atmosphere and became a firm favourite with the children. His expertise with dogs and his ability to tell and illustrate a story made him the perfect 'uncle'. In fact, he was such an accepted part of the family that he could tease Thomas when the latter expressed disapproval at Hodgson's cuddling of his daughter, Bronwen. "Damn it, man! She's only seven. It's nothing to what I'd do if she were seventeen!" Hodgson is said to have retorted, to Thomas' grudging amusement.

Their poetry would be as different as their personalities, however, in both style and subject-matter. Thomas' concerns with the connection between the ancient past and the immediate present would have been appreciated by Hodgson, but, unlike Thomas, Hodgson made very little use of actual places in his work except in the most general of ways. He was not writing about England, or even Britain, as Thomas often did. Thomas, in turn, admired Hodgson's work more for its exuberance and oddity than for anything Hodgson said. As a friend put it: "He liked Hodgson's poetry but not excessively." In 1913, however, Thomas would vote for Hodgson's 'The Song of Honour' over Rupert Brooke's 'Grantchester' for a *Poetry Review* prize.

Thomas, of course, was not writing poetry during the years Hodgson knew him well, at least, not overtly so. His poetic awakening would come in a brief period between 1914 and 1917 when the two men were estranged, and Hodgson played no part in either encouraging or recognising Thomas' talent. He was, however, instrumental in providing the key that unlocked Thomas' latent genius when he introduced him to Robert Frost.

A largely unknown young American poet, Frost was brought along to the St George's tea table by Hodgson. He was an admirer of Hodgson's verse, having come across it in an odd way when he spotted sections of one of his first successful poems, 'Eve', on a scrap of newspaper on the floor of a railway carriage. Wilfrid Gibson then introduced the two men and Frost showed one of his own poems, 'The Death of a Hired Hand', to Hodgson. Hodgson wrote to him in September 1913:

> I very much like it and imagine it must be unique in American poetry; it is like nothing I have seen from your country and I foresee a welcome for it in ours.

A few months later, Hodgson arranged for himself and Frost to visit Ezra Pound, but Pound had already left for Paris when the two men arrived at his rooms in Hampstead, and Hodgson took Frost on to meet Thomas. Hodgson later wrote:

> It is everywhere known today that Robert Frost's personal magic burst the iron gates that had imprisoned up Thomas's lyric gift; it came about at Ryton, a village in Gloucestershire where Frost did the trick, earning the thanks of endless lovers of poetry the wide world over.

Oddly enough, in later years Frost did not credit Hodgson with the hospitality and encouragement he showed him at the time, writing instead of his London years: "The only fast friend I won was Edward Thomas and his melancholy was our cement." Everyone else, he claimed, looked "quizzically askance" at him.

Nevertheless, it was around the St George's tea table that Hodgson came to meet poets such as Walter de la Mare, Gordon Bottomley, John Freeman, Charles Dalmon and W.H. Davies. One must be careful about the term 'to meet', however, as it might suggest that these disparate talents came together consciously to establish an agenda or a programme, as the Futurists or the Imagists did. This was not the case, even though most of the St George's crowd ultimately featured in the Georgian anthologies (named after the reigning monarch rather than the restaurant) compiled by Edward Marsh, and eventually came to be regarded, whether they liked it or not, as a 'movement' of sorts.

Like Hodgson, most of them were approaching middle age, and were established in professions of some kind such as journalism or business. They were hardly young men carried away with the romance of being poets or poetic revolutionaries. Like de la Mare, they may once in their youth have been 'dandies' in dress and behaviour, but they were now more respectable and even conservative when viewed from the perspective of someone like Ezra Pound, who'd burst upon the London scene in 1909 looking like a throwback to the 1890s decadence with his weird hairstyle, his cloak and his extravagant shirts.

The St George's group were, by contrast, experienced, often much-travelled men. Davies had been a bona fide down-and-out for a number of years; Hodgson had roughed it in America as a young man and was now a Fleet Street veteran of some twenty years; John Freeman had given up a successful career in insurance to write full-time; Walter de la Mare worked in the statistics department of the London office of Standard Oil. For them, poetry was no youthful, bohemian enterprise, and their gatherings were, in fact, much more social occasions than artistic ones. Poetry as a profession was rarely talked about, certainly not in terms of technique and purpose. Thomas had not yet started writing verse; Hodgson preferred chatting about dogs, boxers and billiards; de la Mare was usually too shy and reticent to discuss working methods; and Davies was too naive or cunning to "talk poesy", fearing that others might steal his ideas.

Although de la Mare was the first published poet Hodgson came to know well, it was Davies who became his closest poetic friend during the years 1908 to 1912. Davies, the famous 'tramp' poet, had first come to public notice in 1905 when a book of his poems had caused a stir in literary circles. Hodgson himself had first come across him

> one morning when I was reading a paragraph in the *Daily Mail*. In those days early in the century new poets did not come along by the dozen. This account of the discovery of a brand new poet, a real one, set all London talking. He was, according to the reporter, a short stumpy man in his early thirties with a ruddy face and a wooden leg. He had not been discovered in the scented, cowslip meadows of Sussex or under the shady beeches of Buckinghamshire, but in a common lodging-house in a squalid corner of south London; what was more he was a confirmed habitué of such places – a tramp and a beggar! One or two other good poets were coming along at that time but as none of them had a wooden leg, they and their poetry were not news ...

Edward Thomas brought the two men together a couple of years later in typically casual style. Hodgson recalled:

> Thomas one afternoon asked me to come to the corner of Ludgate Hill and Fleet Street; here, leaning against a lamppost, was Davies – a short man, not a little man; there was a lot of him from the hips up. He was plainly and cheaply dressed in dark clothes and a cap and carried a thick walking stick. Unless my impression of him is strangely out, he wore a small short-clipped moustache. We had no more than a word or two together at that time; on the following Wednesday afternoon we met again at the St George's Restaurant.

By now, Davies was approaching the peak of his fame via his

Autobiography of a Super-Tramp, much trumpeted by George Bernard Shaw and much assisted by Edward Thomas (who found him a house in the country and bought him a new wooden leg). Thomas clearly thought that Hodgson and Davies had much in common, and he was right. Davies recalled:

> Hodgson was a man to my own mind for we both preferred to talk of dogs and prize-fighters instead of poets and poetry ... [and] there was another strong bond between us which was that he smoked the same common strong tobacco as I did. For that reason we could help each other out in case one of us ran short.

Born within months of one another in 1871, both men had led unconventional early lives in both England and the USA. This provided them with a common and almost exclusive topic of conversation, not to mention Hodgson's brother, Walker, who by now was wandering the roads of England as a semi-vagrant. Neither man had benefited from a formal education beyond junior-school level. Hodgson said of Davies, " [he] was the least complicated man I have known among men of genius."

Davies was a curious mixture of childishness and suspicion, with firm views about his own importance. Unlike Hodgson, he enjoyed fame while at the same time being very impressionable. In fact, he was a notoriously difficult man to gain the confidence of, and was known to harbour ungenerous suspicions of his fellow poets, whom he often saw as competitors or simply as objects of envy. He seems never to have turned against Hodgson, however, perhaps because Hodgson was so clearly unambitious and hardly a competitor.

In many ways Davies was the perfect foil for the more thoughtful, broadly based Hodgson, who possessed a kindly but mischievous tendency to tease. Thomas recalled ruefully an occasion when, invited to a ladies' club, the two men were told they could smoke:

> Hodgson, however, knowing the strong odour of his tobacco and mine said, 'Don't mind Davies' tobacco, it is awfully strong'. This remark, of course, acted as a restraint on my smoking and I had to puff too gently for my full enjoyment. Whereas Hodgson, who usually puffed enough smoke for two men, had his courage increased by my timidity and made enough smoke for three. The only satisfaction I could take was to break up the party by leaving early, knowing that Hodgson must follow before the truth came out as to which smoker caused the most annoyance.

Hodgson, for his part, was honest enough to acknowledge his teasing of Davies. His favourite tale concerned Davies' legendary susceptibility where small animals were concerned. Visiting him one evening in his rooms in Great Russell Street, he saw Davies preparing a mousetrap. Hodgson proceeded to concoct a sad tale of a homeless mouse travelling all the way from the East End of London and happening upon Davies' lodgings, tired and hungry, just as the trap was being set: "Davies' eyes had grown wider and wider ... then he pitched forward in his chair and stomped into his bedroom and I heard his heavy boot come down smash on the mouse-trap. He brought it over and threw it onto his sitting-room fire, saying, 'That's settled, Ralph!'"

Davies was not a total innocent, of course: a heavy drinker and womaniser, he sometimes viewed Hodgson from a quizzical vantage point that demonstrated great insight:

> On one occasion we dined with one of Hodgson's best friends who was also a great friend of mine. As Hodgson was a strict teetotaller, while we were drinking men, his friend and I began to wonder how Hodgson would be affected by drink. Seeing that Ralph was such a furious and loud talker and always gave the impression that he was intoxicated, we came to the conclusion that drink would make him a melancholy whiner and not the jolly, laughing man we saw at our side ...

The connections between their respective poetic works were few, and though they shared certain broad themes, their sensibilities were in total contrast. Though Davies protested against the stupidity of suffering, his poetry being suffused with the sordid atmosphere of the slums and their mindless violence, he seemed unable to do more than watch blankly and passively, possessing no fund of rage ("What is this life if, full of care/ We have no time to stand and stare".)

Claiming not to understand complex social forces, he insisted that as a poet he should be "a singer not a seer". The poet and critic Harold Monro agreed: Davies, he said, seemed out of place in London:

> that simple man, a natural innocent, unable to see reality except that it interrupted him when he stood and stared – still in childhood and wondering. He talked artlessly as though in an effort at shrewdness and cunning, as if all were new around and his eyes opened last Monday which, of course, they had not.

Hodgson, on the other hand, knew exactly what he was looking at, and his treatment of animals, dogs especially, would be combined with a teacher's skill and compassion. He looked on and wondered, but he also judged – man in particular – harshly. Indeed, he gave the impression in both his poetry and his conversation that he was forever on the brink of leaping up to declaim and denounce.

Unschooled and largely self-taught, Hodgson would always remain somehow apart from the middle-class, urban intellectual elite among whom he increasingly moved. To some extent his specialised knowledge of dogs, especially his unsentimental understanding of them, set him apart and gave him a language and an originality of his own which none of his poet friends could match.

James Stephens, poet and close friend of James Joyce, once complained of Hodgson that his sympathies were not quite human, adding, "He is only happy when he has a dog around ... it was Jim when I knew him – a bull-terrier with a mouth like a coal-scuttle and the savagery of a rabbit."

Hodgson's deep love of dogs would not for many years translate itself into poetry. His first published attempt to make it do so – 'Ode to Dulcina' – was not a success. But he had no need to write about dogs, for they embodied some of the fundamental qualities and concepts that he never ceased writing about. Courage, loyalty, evolution of character – these were some of the great ideas that would always engross him. In spite of an often gregarious nature, he was basically an intensely private person, and his dogs guarded both physically and symbolically the interior world in which he spent most of his time. They were the defenders of both his hearth and his inner self.

Stephens' recollections mirror those of many writers encountering Hodgson in the years around the First World War. The dogs' names might change but the breed and image remained constant. Maud Slessor, poet and neighbour of Hodgson's in Great Bookham in 1910, remembered him as "an uncouth, untidy man with strong blazing eyes and a shock of hair invariably escorted on his walks abroad by a retinue of six to seven huge bull-terriers who, like their master, were less fierce than they looked".

John Cournos, then a young poet at the start of his career, who first encountered Hodgson deep in conversation with Ezra Pound in a pub just off the Strand, was struck by Hodgson's obsession with things canine:

> He was often seen in the streets of London or in a restaurant accompanied by a bull-pup on a lead. He had a passionate fondness for dogs, seemed to understand them; even when he joined a conversation on some subject quite alien to the subject of dogs, he could readily attribute an illustration from the dog world; there was scarcely anything that he did not know about the breeding of dogs, the ways and feelings of dogs. It seemed to come naturally and did not, as far as I know, bore his brother poets.

As one of Hodgson's long-term friends, L.A.G. Strong, recalled, Hodgson often stressed the connection between dog-breeding and poetry:

Ralph felt that all criticism of literature should be as expert and objectively technical as the summing up of the points of a bull-terrier. He told me with fury one day of a lady who had professed great admiration for his work, and turned out to know nothing about it. 'Damn it, woman, *prove* your right to admire!' and he inveighed on the arrogance of those who praised or dispraised what they were not qualified to understand. Where bull-terriers were concerned, there were few people alive who could match his knowledge and expertise.

In fact, Hodgson's knowledge of these dogs, their breeding and showing, intrigued many fellow writers, if only because, in his company, they caught a glimpse of a world many had not the least inkling of. The poet, Richard Church wrote

> A walk down Lambeth Cut with RH was a perambulation liable to be frequently interrupted by greetings and knowing taps on the shoulder from coves wearing cutaway coats and choker-handkerchiefs …

L.A.G. Strong recalled:

> There had been a series of bull-terriers, each a resplendent example of its tribe. He was a great connoisseur of these animals and had many friends in the East End: pub-keepers, bookies, boxers and the like, who shared his enthusiasm. Sometimes, catching sight of the splendid animal with him, such fanciers would stop him in the street and technical discussions of immense complexity would follow.

The connection with this netherworld, a predominantly working-class world of dog-fanciers and 'sports', added a touch of mystery to Hodgson that he was never shy of exploiting. It went with his mode of dress, unchanging and just a little 'racy'. Maud Slessor noted his "sportsman's" appearance: "clean-shaven, with the long upper-lip of a Puritan bigot, a bowler-hat, a clay-pipe and short, tightly-cut trousers, he looked a regular billiard-room habitué."

The clay pipe was another essential component of the 'look'. It was usually packed with some extremely strong shag tobacco and was as offensive to some people as the dogs were. It gave off an odour that, Hodgson admitted (one suspects with no little pride), was very popular in the docks and tannery districts of Bermondsey and Southwark, but not in South Kensington and St James's or even Chelsea. "I have, however, smelled it at Hampstead on Bank Holidays."

The evil-smelling tobacco, the powerful dogs straining at the leash, the 'cockney cove' apparel – all suggested something rougher and tougher than what was really the case. Richard Church was certain he saw qualities in Hodgson akin to those possessed by his 'fighting dogs':

> It is said that you may know a man by his dog. I would say it of RH. He was an impressive figure physically; not tall but in shape like an isosceles triangle, the sharp angle consisting of his feet and the broad ones denoting his shoulders. From that massive hanger, which carried a neat, sardonic head, the body diminished downward through a narrow waist. There was an indication of speed, of streamlining. As for his features, I have always felt that if that large mouth, backed by the nervous, muscular jaws, once fastened on an idea – then, like dog like master. His eyes were dark and watchful; not benevolent but ready for any emergency.

There were times, however, despite Cournos' assertion to the contrary, that Hodgson's insistence on talking dogs rather than literature could irritate: Hodgson once told Siegfried Sassoon, "The last great Black and Tan I remember belonged to Arthur Quiller-Couch, at his home in Cornwall thirty years ago. I was told later that he was annoyed by my wanting to talk about Black and Tan terriers instead of poetry, but his Black and Tan is poetry!"

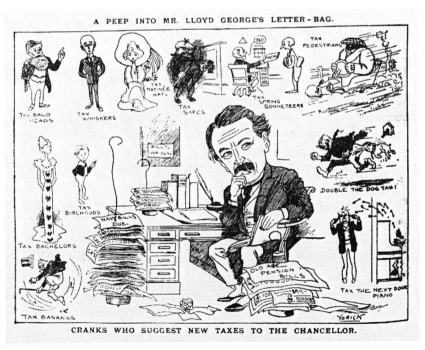

Ralph Hodgson's topical cartoon for *Tit-Bits*, April 1909

6

Weaving Wings

*I see a good deal now of Ralph Hodgson. You would like him, such
a vigorous and simple nature, careless, generous and in some
ways unfortunate – did you read his 'To Deck a Woman' I think it
his best ...*

(Edward Thomas to Gordon Bottomley, November 1910)

During 1908 and 1909, Hodgson's poetic output stalled. Following the
publication of *The Last Blackbird* he produced only three more poems in
1907, two in 1908, while in 1909, a year of change and personal turmoil
for him, he managed just one. All were constructed around birds: 'The
Late Last Rook', 'The Weaving of the Wing', 'To a Linnet', 'Wood Song'.
'The Journeyman' and 'The Beggar' dealt with another issue close to his
heart; man's *treatment* of birds.

'To a Linnet' could almost be said to be autobiographical in that it
was written during a time when he was suffering from an extended bout
of ill health. The *Big Budget* editor reported to readers in late 1907 that
Yorick was ill and it wouldn't be until February or March of the following
year that he returned to work. 'To a Linnet' examines his fears, his lack
of courage when contemplating "malign" fate and the "dread assault" he
was facing (" ... for I fear that I cannot stay the poisoned whip ..."). He
seeks out the linnet in order to learn – "a near and heavy need" – to "sing"
and "put away a craven lip".

For Hodgson, physical pain would eventually come to dominate his life.
Haemorrhoids – a legacy of years of watching birds in damp meadows and
unsuccessfully operated upon five or six times over the next forty years –
would cause him extended discomfort. The linnet was a favourite bird of
Hodgson's. He had already cited it for its courage and endurance, and as
a symbol of the mystery that remained for him at the heart of existence:
that despite the relentless march of science, the natural world remained
a sanctuary and an inexplicable source of hope.

'The Late Last Rook' and 'Woodsong' both concern nightingales, a
bird whose cries represent a renewal of hope, of life and springtime. 'The

Late Last Rook' carried overtones of sado-masochism in the mingling of pain and pleasure, the bird's cry fierce and clear, a torn wail that was "sweet to wounding". It also contains images, apparently casually drawn, that demonstrate Hodgson's splendid visual clarity: "The old gilt vane and spire receive/The last beam eastward striking." Crows dream of flapping "beside a spectral team", which ploughs the land stalked by "ghostly scarecrows". The poem as a whole presents a surreal landscape of dream and reminiscence. It also demonstrates Hodgson's ability to move easily from the large-scale to the small, deftly linking everything, this time by means of colour: "Now day is sinking and the West/Is redder than a linnet's breast."

'Woodsong', originally entitled 'For a Child' is a small piece paying homage to the 17th-century poet Robert Herrick's 'Going a Maying' with its lines "Now one and all you Roses/Wake up you lie too long!" Its reference to "Slug-a-beds and Simples" demonstrates the palpable sense of affection the poet has for children and flowers: "Each from its olive chamber/His babies one by one/This very morning clamber/ Into the shining sun."

No such joy and laughter fills 'The Journeyman', evidence that the highs and lows of his poetic world would continue to oscillate wildly. 'The Journeyman' concerns man's blind destructiveness and slaughter of all things natural, in this case, birds. The message was bleak: "It may be late, it may be very late/Too late for blaming then …" In fact, 'The Journeyman' looks ahead to 'To Deck a Woman' – the culmination of Hodgson's angry denunciations of the plumage trade. Yet there is still time for mystery and wonder: the ecstatic 'The Weaving of the Wing' is a celebration of nature, the poet stumbling upon creation at work in gorse and furze. The poem is suffused with light: "He brought a hundred strands, sun yellow, to her hands", "the flaming whin [gorse]", "wild bursts of bloom" – everything held together by the use of a simple narrative line:

> As down the wild I came,
> This day, the crown of Spring,
> I tapped a knotted spray
> Above a whin aflame,
> And saw a ribboned wing,
> Sun-yellow slip away
> And hand and eye confessed
> A young-forsaken nest.

When he looks closer he sees the

> … silk of sun,
> Her loom and weavers plain,

And heard a muffled din
And knew a web begun –

He thus rejoices, knowing that

An aeon and a day
From this, the crown of Spring,

he'll once again tap the knotted spray "And stir a yellow wing!" the
Universal Voice telling him: "The work is done ..."

This beautiful, simple, haunting piece, skilfully recycling and
rearranging short, powerful lines, introduced the universal voice for the
first time: a pantheistic/quasi-religious Being with whom Hodgson was
wont to commune, and who would re-emerge some years later in his most
influential and praised work, 'The Song of Honour'.

In 1910, when Hodgson was trying to change the direction of his life,
only two poems were published – 'The Skylark' in February and 'To
Deck a Woman' in September. The latter would help to make his name
and bring him influential friends, although the poem's overall quality
was questionable. "Monotonous and of a Tennysonian finish, perhaps",
according to Edward Thomas, "but most interestingly wrought".

Published in a supplement to the *Saturday Review* it was, in fact,
a polemical piece, "propaganda raised to rhapsody" according to the
American academic Cornelius Weygandt. Its target was the plumage trade,
and its inspiration was the bill before Parliament restricting the import
into Britain of a whole variety of birds' feathers. This was by no means
the first or the last attempt to regulate or abolish what to many appeared
a barbaric, destructive industry in birds' feathers.

In a sense, the intense social reaction to the wearing of feathers and the
plumage industry in general was part of a growing interest in the wider
natural environment, particularly the denuding of the landscape of animal
life. Birds were perfect symbols for such concerns, and Hodgson's poem
'To Deck a Woman' was shot through with sentiments then widespread
and growing in influence: anger, scorn and a foreboding for mankind's
threatened future if such behaviour was not checked.

The Field magazine reported in 1890 that a London dealer received in
a single consignment 32,000 dead humming-birds, 80,000 aquatic birds
and 800,000 miscellaneous pairs of wings. W.H. Hudson, the naturalist,
described in a pamphlet a "purple day" at the Commercial Sale Rooms in
the City of London. There was, he wrote, a consignment of 125,000 Indian
parrots which would have covered a large portion of Trafalgar Square with,
" a gay, grass-green carpet, flecked with vivid purple, rose and scarlet".

Another pamphleteer, the Revd. H.C. Ricketts, quoted the American Council of Ornithology: "England alone imports 25 million slaughtered birds a year; Europe as a whole takes 300 million and all are made into articles of personal adornment. A single London dealer receives annually 400,000 humming-birds."

It was clear to many, therefore, that certain bird species were threatened. The question of cruelty also became central to the debate as wider humanitarian arguments were introduced and protests began on several different levels.

In 1889 the Royal Society for the Protection of Birds was formed. *Punch* then began to publish cartoons lampooning women who wore birds' feathers in hats, and probably no newspaper campaigned more strongly against the plumage traffic than *The Times*. It accused women of "wholesale, wanton and hideous cruelty", of dishonouring their sex, of "robbing nature of her beauty without adding to their own".

More significantly, news photography was increasingly used in the campaign to halt the trade. In 1906 the wholescale destruction of the breeding grounds of egrets in New Zealand caused an international outcry because the report was accompanied by graphic illustrations: " a shambles of dead adults, starving moribund nestlings ..."

The idea of the world stripped bare of beauty and natural species by voracious mankind was by no means an original one in 1910. For much of the preceding half-century on both sides of the Atlantic, ecological awareness had been growing and making its voice heard. Hodgson's poetry would thus form part of a growing chorus of protest and warning of an ecological doomsday.

'To Deck a Woman' is a long, perhaps overlong, poem of some 436 lines divided into 23 sections. As a piece of propaganda, it touched many but created no uproar. In some ways, it is a confused piece of work and Hodgson himself admitted as much when he wrote to a critic: "As a whole it is a long and unequal poem", to which Maud Slessor added that its inequality marred both its execution and its conception.

Edward Thomas, in a review for *Poetry and Drama* wrote that it was, "a passionate, an astonishing poetic pamphlet addressed to men and angels, on the matter of plumage as head-gear ... of such disproportionate length for a weekly as to draw attention to the poet and to an editor's confidence ...", while James Stephens, in recommending the work to Edward Marsh, considered it, "astonishing in spite of many inequalities. At times and through long stretches the verse is of the most amazing technical excellence, full of passionate lyricism, an extraordinary emotional and impulsive rhythm."

As with everything Hodgson wrote, the structure is simple and tightly controlled, the narrative straightforward and undemanding. The poet/

narrator wanders to one of the poet's secret idyllic bowers and falls asleep. He dreams of two women, one pretty, the other angry. Reversing the pattern of Coleridge's 'Christabel', it is the angry, mysterious woman who is the 'heroine'. She is, in fact, Mother Nature, a goddess, who upbraids the pretty woman and all the other vain members of her sex whose insatiable demands for beauty products (feathers especially) have led to the destruction of animal species across the globe.

The goddess describes her Eden when first created, then recounts how, on returning from tasks elsewhere she senses something is wrong: birdsong is dwindling; *insects* are making more noise. She soon realises why. Man is to blame. She then travels across the world, witnessing the destruction, the atrocities carried out by mankind, happening upon the slaughterer going about his business:

> A widowed fox with smothered bark
> Foretold his foot, and hid in fear,
> A bird uneasy in the dark
> Declared him come or crouching near.
>
> I saw him bowed beneath a load
> Of carrion heads and eyes and wings,
> And down his breast and shoulders flowed
> The blood of doves and dying things.

As in 'The Journeyman' the male is depicted in almost neutral fashion: "the dull utilitarianism of man"; his "endless craft and patience"; his "tireless foot", his "ready eye", his "learned art of hook and spike". These are morally neutral descriptions except for the powerful line, "the charnel place that was his soul".

It is the female of the species who comes in for most of the opprobrium. As the title implies, woman is the cause of all the pain, and when nature turns on her, the vocabulary alters immediately:

> His consort and familiar
>
> Who, lapped in lewdness viler made
> By plenteous grace of lip and limb,
> Crept sanctuaried in his shade
> And ever closer attended him
>
> Whose avid "More!" and "More! Yet more!"
> Urged every bout of shame and blood,
> Or lovesick hern he ravaged for
> The tassels of its lustihood.

Now the horrors commence. Finches and larks are "broken", seals "flayed" and flung to crimson waters still crying, terns are "humbled", foxes "trepanned":

> Some forest thing with frightened eyes
> Across the pool at night he slew.
>
> A thousand homes of seal and stoat,
> Of mew and tern rejoiced his reins –
> A thousand sweets to glut the throat
> Of Bloodwant shrill for Beauty's veins.

It is in her "dread name" that blood is shed and the weaving of soft female images ("With thine own fingers white and fair") with the language of disgust ("Blandished beauty to the snare/With love calls made by thy red mouth", "foul'd savannahs", "vile", "lewd delights and carrion lusts") leaves an uneasy impression, a mingling of masochism and aggression that perhaps goes a little too far in its misogyny.

Although 'To Deck a Woman' was not the last of Hodgson's bird poems, from now on he produced work of a more accessible nature. He broadened and developed themes from that epic poem, in particular exotic animal life, the mysterious hymn of creation, the 'Garden of Eden', the swift movement of time. His bird poems from now on took the form of warnings, 'Stupidity Street' being the classic example. Short and ostensibly simple, he wrote it to be used by the RSPB in a protest against the sale of larks for human consumption and as songbirds in cruel competition:

> I saw with open eyes
> Singing birds sweet
> Sold in the shops
> For the people to eat
> Sold in the shops of
> Stupidity Street
>
> I saw in vision
> The worm in the wheat,
> And in the shops nothing
> For people to eat;
> Nothing for sale in
> Stupidity Street.

The symbolic significance of birds would now be abandoned. 'The Skylark', written early in 1910, was Hodgson's final foray into this traditionally English genre. It contained the germ of his Schopenhauerian conviction that some sort of Universal Will, hidden behind appearance, linked all sentient beings. Birds, the poem suggests, seem more attuned to the existence of this Will. The poet's optimism stems from the belief that human beings will surely one day hear the birds' music ("Suns will break for us in time"):

> And lit within we'll stand among
> The corn at last receiving
> The secret of our skylark's song,
> And more we go believing.

That optimism, that 'tuning in' to the music of creation and the universe, would continue to be the keynote, not an original note, certainly, but developed with such intensity and passion, that it deeply impressed a generation still looking to lyric poetry for such purity of vision.

" Larks are cheap to-day "

A. THORBURN

STUPIDITY STREET.

I saw with open eyes
Singing birds sweet
Sold in the shops
For the people to eat,
Sold in the shops of
Stupidity Street.

I saw in a vision
The worm in the wheat,
And in the shops nothing
For people to eat;
Nothing for sale in
Stupidity Street.

Ralph Hodgson.

If every Fellow, Member, and Associate of the Royal Society for the Protection of Birds and all other bird-lovers will refuse to deal with any poulterer or with the game department of any store where Larks and other song-birds are offered for sale, those stores and those poulterers will quickly find that it is not a paying business to provide them.

Royal Society for the Protection of Birds postcard campaigning against the sale of songbirds to eat c.1910

1. 'Coal' Hodgson with sons John
(back left), Herbert (right) and Walker
(seated front), c.1873

2. Ralph Hodgson aged about 10

3 & 4. 'Dolly' Chatteris and Hodgson as they appeared in the *Gentlewoman*
announcement of their marriage in 1896

5. Rudolf Besier in 1911

6. Ralph Hodgson sketch of
Walter de la Mare, 1913

7. Hodgson's mother Mary with
sisters Josey (right) and May in East
Finchley, 1913

8. Walter Hodgson in the Byron
Studios, c.1918

7

Dewar and Salt

About his bird touches is a sort of magic ... perhaps birds have long been in this poet's family. Bewick was his ancestor.
(G.B. Dewar, *The Book of the Seasons*, 1910)

The years 1908/9 saw Hodgson's connections with Fleet Street loosen significantly. Following his prolonged illness in late 1907 and early 1908, his name ceased to appear on the *Big Budget* masthead as art editor and, though his contributions gradually picked up, the heyday of this particular comic had passed.

Its nature had altered from the time when it was predominantly a cartoon comic, filled with strips and pages of zany, anarchic and very juvenile jokes. It had grown up with its original readership and by 1907 was filled with long-running, wordy serials about spies and adventurers as well as real-life boxers and music hall artists telling the secrets of their trade. Yorick would now be employed on illustrating humorous stories or embellishing the editor's homilies on thrift, self-improvement and resourcefulness, the importance of family life and getting a good steady job. The days when Hodgson used his substantial gifts across both front and back pages, as well as producing middle-page spreads lampooning the likes of Kruger in *Ally Sloper*-style magnificence, were long gone. By late 1908, in fact, close observation of the paper reveals that Yorick had left and his pen-name soon starts appearing beneath work in *Tit-Bits* and *Fry's Sporting Magazine* – productions owned by Pearson's arch-rival, George Newnes. Hodgson was at a crossroads in his life. In 1909 he was working exclusively on *Tit-Bits*, producing half-page adult cartoons every other week. *Tit-Bits*, a chatty, phenomenally successful but ultimately trivial paper, had no tradition of visual humour; indeed, Hodgson's cartoons were a striking departure from his normal work. He produced a series of tamely humorous digs at various aspects of modern metropolitan life: fads and fashions such as the new shopping craze sparked by Oxford Street's expansion and the creation of up-market emporiums such as Selfridges; the endless inconvenience caused to travellers by the electrification of railways and the laying of tramways; the construction of the new Embankment, the opening of the Rotherhithe Tunnel and the development of The Strand. There was much silly fun to be had at the expense of suffragettes and the new pensions and unemployment offices as well as the plethora of new technological inventions: powered flight, submarines, the motor car, not to mention new crazes such as roller-skating.

It was regular but hardly lucrative employment, and suggested that Hodgson was drifting. His old friend G.B. Dewar wrote to him, "You really will have to see Harmsworth when he comes back and begin working for their papers ... Please think it over."

During the pivotal year of 1910, with Hodgson turning his back on cartooning, moving closer to London to a smaller house and searching for work, Dewar's friendship was significant. Although he could not persuade Hodgson's publisher, George Allen, to take more of Hodgson's poetry (although they would have been pleased to consider "other schemes of publication or plan in which you would co-operate"), Dewar prevailed upon Hodgson to review a volume of Swift's poetry for the *Saturday Review*.

He also sent a copy of *The Last Blackbird* to Thomas Hardy. Hardy enjoyed the book, and endorsed its sentiments, commenting: "It appealed to me because I hate blood sports and because many years ago I wrote some verse with similar feelings."

Most important, perhaps, Dewar included three of Hodgson's poems in an anthology he was editing called *The Book of the Seasons*. Hodgson thus appeared alongside Keats, Carew, Browning, Wordsworth, Shelley and Chaucer and in the introduction Dewar revealed that Hodgson's first published poem – 'The Missel Thrush' – had been written at Weston in Hampshire, which happened to be where Dewar lived.

The two men's friendship had begun back in the 1890s and was close, although, on the surface, unlikely. Dewar, some ten years Hodgson's senior, came from landed gentry/military stock. He was Oxford-educated and, having found no amenable position in the usual professions of law and church, he turned to politics and journalism. After ten years serving as parliamentary private secretary to a Conservative MP he became, as he put it, a full-time "chartered libertine" of Fleet Street: columnist, feature-writer, ornithologist, and an expert on country matters in general.

Holbrook Jackson wrote of him:

> In all his books, and they are several and delightful, one feels the English pulse, one feels the English note. The very titles suggest the English idea: *Wild Life in Hampshire Highlands, The Birds in Our Wood, The Faery Year, The South Country Trout Streams, Young England Library, Isaac Walton's Complete Angler* as well as collections of short stories, recorded in a simple and gracious English which is an attraction in itself in an age of peacock phrases and strident epithet.

Wild Life in Hampshire Highlands, published in 1899, contained a number of illustrations by Hodgson.

For many years, Dewar and Hodgson cycled and rambled together across southern England, spotting birds, examining earthworks, visiting churches and arguing. In the late 1920s Dewar recalled:

> All sorts of things and most names have gone out of my memory and will not return; but you remain in my memory in virtually every cycle ride we had together. Turner's Temperance Inn where we stayed together at Winchester has ended for many years; but sundry other places where we stayed still exist and they move me when I see them.

Hodgson, although devoted to the same flora and fauna of the English landscape, shared none of Dewar's educational or family advantages and had grown up in an entirely different environment. In literary terms, Dewar was a devotee of Lamb, Johnson, Bacon and Shelley and possessed, according to Hodgson, a "rare facility of arousing interest in his own sympathies, be they with dogs, birds, horses or country folk and of increasing your vision as you see with him". Dewar succeeded in smoothing some of Hodgson's rougher edges, broadening his horizons and opening his eyes. It is also clear that Dewar's humanitarian ideals, in particular his campaigns against the ill-treatment of animals and birds (he wrote, amongst other things, articles condemning the cropping of bull-terriers' ears and tails), made an impression on Hodgson. He also was persuaded by Dewar that it was cruel to keep birds in cages, until then one of his principal hobbies.

At a certain point, however, the two men began to differ, in particular over the question of animal rights and how far to go in promoting them. Dewar felt that Hodgson was not a man to stand on a soap-box and declaim. In 1913 he wrote:

> We remember seeing a letter from a poet to a publisher in which the writer said he aspired to ride in high on the crest of the great wave which brought in the Radicals and the new humanity in 1906. No such a mount for Mr Hodgson. He makes not the least sign of hurling himself in rhythm at the 'great vital questions of the hour, sir.' His total inability to hit the public running is now quite plain. If his friends ever looked for great feats from him in such matters, they had better give him up at once and search elsewhere. He cannot, he will never, 'Do it, Do It Now'.

However, when Hodgson became editor of *New Fry's Magazine* in 1911, he specifically commissioned articles calling for "shabby blood-sports" to be banned, and his direct involvement in attempts to reform the law relating to animal treatment suggests a more radical approach than that of his long-time colleague. Hodgson saw the campaign for a Plumage Act as part of a wider humanitarian programme to reform the behaviour and attitudes of society in general. Dewar, on the other hand, felt that mass slaughter for industrial purposes was unacceptable but stopped short of condemning all killing of "lower creatures".

'To Deck a Woman' certainly brought Hodgson into contact with animal rights activists, particularly those concerned with the Plumage Act, which was being debated in Parliament in 1910. Attempts to pass a bill had begun in earnest in 1908, when Lord Avebury had introduced a measure in the House of Lords, and continued through to 1914 when the outbreak of war ended such attempts for the time being. Supporters of the pro-plummage trade argued and lobbied long and hard, claiming that unemployment would result from a ban and that Britain would lose out to the Continent. There was much debate about the extent and nature of the trade, with committed campaigners such as the New Zealander James Buckland playing a pivotal role in obtaining evidence to place before parliamentary committees. Raids on warehouses were mounted to obtain specimens, and it was on the occasion of one such incident that Hodgson recalled meeting Buckland. He wrote:

> The occasion and its details are unforgettable. I had become acquainted with James Buckland when he and his wife were trying to get a Plumage Bill through Parliament. Some written or spoken statement of theirs in connection with the importation of tropical bird feathers had been contradicted by the trade supporters, whereupon Mrs Buckland, with considerable ingenuity and tact had gone for her facts to the London docks and managed to get a box of skins as they were put up for auction there; this she brought to their flat in St Thomas' Mansions just across Westminster Bridge. On the afternoon of my visit it lay open on their kitchen table, crammed full of West Indian and South American species, mostly humming-birds, with parrots, parakeets and other species stuffed into the corners; lying on top was the receipted bill from the auctioneers, 'One crate Humming', with the price – something under £10.

Buckland was something of an adventurer and explorer, who mysteriously disappeared from Britain in 1918 after the death of his wife. Hodgson had published an article by Buckland in *New Fry's Magazine* in 1911 entitled, 'The Shambles of the Forest' – headed by extracts from 'To Deck a Woman'. It was a restatement of the horror stories of 1906 of the slaughter of egrets in New South Wales, complete with photos and a reiteration of the 'natural imbalance' argument: without birds, the insects they controlled would multiply and endanger agriculture.

Hodgson remembered Buckland as being:

> a civil engineer by profession … a fairly thick-set man of middle
> height, apparently in his early fifties. He had thick, dark brown
> hair, dark burning eyes and a dark bristly beard to his ears, turning
> grey and trimmed short; he had a plain, direct manner of speech: a
> masculine, rather unsmiling and not 'clever' man … The Bucklands'
> other guest was Henry Salt. Later he and I walked over the bridge
> to the Underground railway where we parted …

If Buckland was not clever, Henry Salt, founder of the Humanitarian
League, in Hodgson's opinion certainly was and his admiration for the
older man became immense. By the time Hodgson got to know him
well, Salt's political influence was on the wane. Honorary Secretary
of the Humanitarian League from 1891 until 1920, he was part of the
radical movement of the 1880s that included Sidney and Beatrice Webb,
William Morris, G.B. Shaw (who helped him with his autobiography)
and John Burns. This formed the basis of what was to become the
Social Democratic Federation from which the Independent Labour Party
eventually emerged.

Salt, though of the left, was less a political radical than a spiritual one.
A revolution in *feelings* for both men and animals was needed, he believed
to bring about fundamental change in society. This approach led him in
a variety of directions at once: the reform of slaughterhouses as well as
prisons; an end to blood sports as well as capital punishment; pacifism;
workers' rights. A radical approach to sex was also part of his programme.
He was a lifelong friend of Edward Carpenter, whose pioneering book on
sex and marriage called *Love's Coming-of-Age* and a collection of essays in
1908 entitled *The Intermediate Sex*, which was the first generally available
book in English that portrayed homosexuality in a positive light rather than
as purely a medical or moral problem, caused controversy and unease at
a time not many years after the Oscar Wilde trial.

Proclaiming a comprehensive humane doctrine to be applied to all
sentient beings, Salt hoped to give shape to newer and more advanced
humanitarian feelings. This was an altogether different thing from old-
fashioned philanthropy on the one hand, and kindness to animals on the
other. According to Salt, men and animals were equal – all had rights. Salt
advocated his view in his 1894 book *Animal Rights*, while his Humanitarian
League continually produced pamphlets attacking rabbit coursing, the
extermination of birds and other forms of animal cruelty.

He was, however, more than just a campaigner for causes. A classical
scholar, he translated the *Aeneid* into English verse, wrote biographies
of Thomas De Quincey, James Thomson ('B.V.'), Shelley and Tennyson
and was an enthusiastic champion of Walt Whitman, Thoreau and W.H.

Hudson.

Hodgson revelled in Salt's company and held him in the highest esteem:

> I liked him not only for his abundance and the freshness he brought to bygone times and peoples, but also for his sharp interest in later times up to the latest, and his speculations on times to come, and also for his general ripeness, wittiness and in a souring world, for his sunny disposition. His presence before my eyes ... was a guarantee of human future ...

He likened Salt to bygone reformers, known and unknown:

> Those who got rid of the Bankside and Hockley bear-pits and bullrings up and down the country everywhere, with their followers and forerunners, all divine nuisances to numbers of people in their day as Salt was in his, and continues to be. He was that rarity, a man of sovereign parts without personal ambition or ends of his own to serve ...

To what extent Hodgson aligned himself with all of Salt's opinions is hard to say. It's clear they had differences. Hodgson's popular, anti-Kruger cartoons that appeared in *Big Budget* during the Boer War suggest that pacifism and anti-colonialism in general did not find favour with him. Hodgson's love of boxing (a human blood sport) would also have run up against Salt's dislike for violence of any kind. But his profound admiration was very much for the nature of the man and what he represented in human terms. Besides, Hodgson enjoyed an argument, especially with friends, though the intensity of his advocacy sometimes shocked even the closest of colleagues.

H.J. Massingham, the journalist and naturalist who would use Hodgson's poems after the First World War as propaganda for his own successful campaign to pass a Plumage Bill in 1921, remembered how *their* friendship ended:

> Hodgson believed in his own ideas as a volcano [does] in its fires and his own dynamic eloquence so reinforced his convictions that opposition he could not brook. His friendship hung upon your chiming with his mind. When I published a book deriving the cornerstone of our first civilisation from the Mediterranean, his Nordic passion could not put up with it. We went our opposite ways and never met again. For years I missed the beauty and even the dogmas of his wine-dark mind ...

With Salt, no such eruptions occurred in a friendship that lasted until the old humanitarian's death in 1939. His friendship with Salt was the closest Hodgson came to involvement in radical politics of either the right or the left.

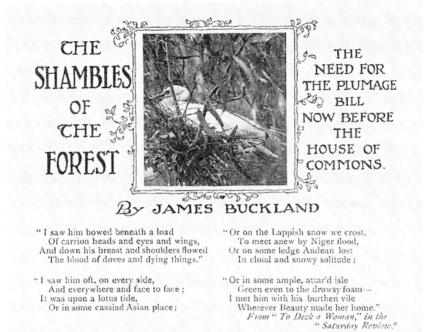

THE SHAMBLES OF THE FOREST

By JAMES BUCKLAND

THE NEED FOR THE PLUMAGE BILL NOW BEFORE THE HOUSE OF COMMONS.

" I saw him bowed beneath a load
    Of carrion heads and eyes and wings,
And down his breast and shoulders flowed
    The blood of doves and dying things."

" I saw him oft, on every side,
    And everywhere and face to face ;
It was upon a lotus tide,
    Or in some cassiad Asian place ;

" Or on the Lappish snow we crost,
    To meet anew by Niger flood,
Or on some ledge Andean lost
    In cloud and snowy solitude ;

" Or in some ample, attar'd isle
    Green even to the drowsy foam—
I met him with his burthen vile
    Wherever Beauty made her home."
    From " To Deck a Woman," in the
    " Saturday Review."

The heading for Buckland's article on birds in *New Fry's Magazine*, 1911

8

New Fry's Magazine

Confronted one afternoon with the need to fill a blank eighth of a page, he inserted a small half-tone block of a rabbit, more or less in the air, with the astonishing under-line, 'An evening nibble'. There was no evidence that the rabbit was eating or to be eaten, nor was there any hint of evening. Nevertheless, this small item was a major success ...

(C.B. Fry)

In 1910, Hodgson consolidated his move from the publisher Arthur Pearson to George Newnes by producing a series of articles on dogs for the latter's *C.B. Fry's Magazine*, an outdoor, sporting publication edited by Fry himself, one of England's great sportsmen. The move resulted in Hodgson working for a magazine that could hardly have been more closely attuned to his personal and social interests and enthusiasms. He also cemented a friendship with C.B. Fry himself that would endure for decades.

Fry was one of the great all-rounders. He was an Oxford Blue at athletics, an amateur soccer player with professional Southampton (with whom he played in a Cup Final) and a supreme cricketer: he scored over 30,000 runs in a career equalling that of W.G. Grace in influence and legend.

He was also a Classics scholar at Oxford and a fine journalist, and began a regular association with George Newnes in 1899 when he started contributing to the boys' magazine *The Captain*, whose art editor was Ralph Hodgson's brother Walter.

In 1904, Newnes had suggested to Fry that he launch a magazine bearing his own name devoted entirely to sport. Thus *C.B. Fry's Magazine* was born – but not in quite the way Newnes had in mind. Fry objected to being typecast as a sportsman: "I identified myself rather with the world where field games occur as an incident, a world of a much more general kind." Though the magazine would always contain a preponderance of sporting features, especially on football, tennis and cricket, its remit would be the whole world of recreation, including spare time, holidays and leisure. It was to become the forerunner of the 'man's' magazine, similar in many respects to Jerome K. Jerome's *To-Day* and *The Idler* of the 1890s, but broader in concept, less rakish and flippant. For one thing, it contained articles for women on such things as self-defence, swimming and hockey. Being a Newnes publication, it also served as a 'How-to' magazine, a consumers' guide reflecting the preoccupations of a prosperous lower-middle-class readership spending its money and free time pursuing active hobbies.

Being of a restless nature, and also in great demand at Lords and the Oval, Fry's involvement in the magazine waxed and waned. Added to this, in 1908 he established a training ship for young men keen to enter the merchant navy, an enterprise very close to his heart, which he and his wife would run for the next 40 years. It was situated in Birkenhead, and for long stretches of time, Fry was away from London. The magazine would thus be produced by a hard core of Newnes' seasoned journalists, prominent among them Hodgson's elder brothers, Walter and Walker, plus a long-term friend and colleague of Hodgson's from his early Fleet Street days, R.S. Warren Bell.

Bell had been the *Evening News* roving reporter 'Tantalus' back in the early 1890s who, with Ralph Hodgson as illustrator 'Yorick', had scurried across London plunging into the maelstrom of politics and controversy. Bell was now editor-in-chief of *The Captain*, and he also oversaw *Fry's* for a number of years, all of Newnes' magazines being edited from the firm's Southampton Street office just off The Strand.

C.B. Fry's Magazine, in its heyday, sold over 10,000 copies a month, making it one of the top-selling monthlies in the country, but its circulation gradually declined, owing partly to Fry's regular periods of absence from the front office. Newnes himself fell ill, and in 1910 he let go of editorial control to the new owner, Lord Riddell, who decided that the magazine needed a revamp. Fry disagreed: "He wanted to run it. So did I. And I saw it first. So the magazine went away as a separate concern." Having secured alternative financial backing, Fry set about producing the magazine independently, aided principally by Ralph Hodgson.

For the first time in his life, Hodgson found himself in a position of authority and not a little power. The power would increase almost immediately as Fry opted to play a minimal part in the magazine after the two opening issues, the first of which was substantially put together in a room Fry had taken at the Waldorf Hotel in the Aldwych. By the time the first issue emerged in April 1911, editorial offices had been found at Effingham House by The Strand and it was from here that Hodgson enjoyed a year or so as sole, untrammelled editor of a national magazine.

The nature of *New Fry's*, as it became known, is worth considering briefly, for Hodgson wrote some of his most accessible poems when he was editing the magazine, poems in many ways utterly different from those thus far produced. The *New Fry's* 'world' certainly suited him, especially its concern with the countryside, with rambling holidays in gypsy caravans or on canal boats, with the flora and fauna of England, and, most importantly, sport. By its very nature, it was not an intellectual magazine. Politics was hardly discussed except in terms of individuals whom Fry wanted to profile to promote his personal fads like 'national fitness'. Of literature there was no discussion at all. Hodgson could hardly have cared less. He only wrote one piece of poetic criticism in his whole life, his dismissive article on Swift's poetry in the *Saturday Review*.

That *Fry's* was dominated by sport, its technique and its governance, would once again have proved no difficulty for Hodgson. In many respects, he was a sportsman himself, and he had no reservations about physical competition, unlike so many literary men of his and later generations. The link between sport and deeper themes in his life and work alike was spotted by Harold Monro, who commented that Hodgson's poetic language "has a curious sporting ring. We come upon (and not usually for any reason inherent in the poems where they occur) phrases that belong to the vocabulary of dog breeding, prize-fighting, hunting, coaching and the other native pastimes of England." Monro then cited: "Turn upon the cur", "Now to get even", "The song of pretty fighters", "Tighten your rein", "Alert from top to toe", "At odds with life and limb" and concluded, "It cannot be doubted that his sporting phraseology is contributive, in a way, to the popularity of Hodgson's poetry."

Hodgson was particularly drawn to various individual sports. Tennis attracted him (he was known to play the game in a rather wild fashion), and one of his closest pre-war friends was Tony Wilding, Wimbledon champion for a number of years before the First World War. Hodgson later wrote of him: "Of all the citizens of the world I have known, about the choicest and most unfading in a long life, would be Tony Wilding." He encouraged Wilding to write articles on the game for *New Fry's*, and the gallant New Zealander's death during the Great War caused Hodgson great anguish.

Billiards was almost an obsession with Hodgson. He played daily in various halls off The Strand such as the Bodega and the '45 Club, and was extremely good at the game. He possessed a table of his own, and counted some of the top billiards players as his friends.

Boxing, however, was the sport he seemed most drawn to on a number of levels, both as a spectator and as a participant (though his youthful stint in the boxing booths may have been apocryphal). He was certainly a regular visitor to boxing halls in the East End such as Wonderland and Premierland as well as higher-class venues such as the National Sporting Club in Covent Garden, where he first saw the 'Mighty Atom' Jimmy Wilde. Other favourites were Joe Bowker, Bombardier Wells and Freddie Welsh, all of whom were then making their way up the ladder to fame, and all of whom won Lonsdale Belts, first instituted in 1909 by the National Sporting Club as emblematic of a British championship. This trophy played an important part in the modernisation of the sport as it shed its gory, bare-knuckle image, something one feels Hodgson rather regretted, for he was a keen student of the old prize ring. He liked to tell of an occasion in 1895 when, in a pub discussing the bloodline of a particular dog, he had his first sight of the great old-time champion, Jem Mace ("a moment to cherish!").

He went to great lengths to extol the qualities which boxing developed and called for: "Nothing adds a lustre to courage like magnanimity in victory and dignity under defeat; and those things are the common possession of boxers." Boxing, he felt, was the supreme competition:

> in developing and strengthening habits of fair play, modesty, perseverance, fun, good-nature, self-control and temperance in all things. Boxing is the equal of any paid calling of our time. May boxing flourish! May there be no more of that silly outcry against it which made so much noise a season or two ago! I couldn't despise the boxer without despising the panther, too! If Welsh is not a masterwork of his creator then for me Blake's Tiger is a lie!

Boxers, (like dogs, perhaps) were, according to Hodgson, "a breed worth nourishing" although, as a humanist, he was interested in their welfare. The Boxers' Union was attempting to establish itself during these years and Hodgson invited Desmond Shaw, its secretary, to contribute articles to *New Fry's*. Interestingly, in the immediate pre-war years, boxing was increasingly being taken up by the military authorities as a perfect method of entertaining men and inculcating good habits of fitness and discipline. Whether Hodgson made the connection between sporting prowess and military efficiency is doubtful. There is no doubt that C.B. Fry did, however, as the first issue of *New Fry's Magazine* was dominated by his anxiety for the 'health' of the nation. The very first article he commissioned was from Robert Blatchford, the editor of *The Clarion*, an early socialist proselytiser and, according to Fry, "one of the finest friends I ever made".

Under the title 'Universal Military Training and the National Physique' Blatchford wrote: "It is the duty of every citizen to fit himself to take part in the defence of his country", and, "I believe that the national safety depends upon the military training of the whole male population." Such training, he felt, would "infuse into the people the spirit of collectivism … " as "a trained nation has a national soul."

As time went by, however, once Fry had retired into the background, Hodgson assumed more control and it soon became noticeable that the magazine was shifting its emphasis in a number of crucial areas. Straight sports articles became fewer in number, while visual imagery such as cartoons and illustrations increased dramatically. Articles on dogs, billiards and boxing also increased, and though the amount of poetry included declined, the poets featured, such as Walter de la Mare, John Freeman and others, were mainstream writers rather than rhymesters employed to fill a space.

Articles on motoring and, surprisingly, cricket, were cut back and a definite 'holiday' tendency appeared. Articles entitled 'Camping on the Thames', 'Holidays on the Broads' and 'Sailing for Pleasure' all conjured up and promoted a suburban dream world of sun-dappled riverbanks, winding country lanes and painted caravans – a touch bohemian and comfortably escapist.

The most dramatic change from the old style, however, was the attitude the magazine now took towards animals. Hodgson commissioned James Buckland, his old animal rights colleague, to contribute an article entitled 'The Shambles of the Forest' about bird destruction and the Plumage Bill, while Hodgson himself penned an article on 'Shabby Blood Sports Worth Ending'. In addition, there were many pieces extolling the beauty of animals, their strength, their natural ways, rather than on how to kill them. Though grouse shooting, and shooting in general, were not criticised, "woodland barbarities" such as trapping and snaring were. Column space was also devoted to the treatment of animal illness with articles like 'First Aid for Dogs'. There were also articles on 'Dogs' Homes', 'Horses' Rest Homes' and 'The Hospital at the Zoo'. All this from a magazine once inclined to print eulogistic pieces about big-game hunting and the barbarous working-class sport of lark-singing contests!

Hodgson also brought in his own friends and acquaintances to produce articles. Desmond Shaw of the Boxers' Union; Arthur Brook, Hodgson's old editor on *Big Budget* contributed on birds; William Maas, ex-editor of *Big Budget* and a friend from the Harmsworth days wrote a piece on bare-knuckle boxing; Henry Leach, another lifelong friend, produced articles on golf. Leach had once written: "In so many English sports, something flying or running has to be killed or injured; golf calls for no drop of blood from any living creature."

Count Vivian Hollander, famous in the Cruft's Dog Show world, became a regular contributor. Edward Thomas wrote on Goodwood Races and Hilaire Belloc and E.V. Lucas were featured prominently. The novelist Edgar Wallace contributed *Sanders of the River* as the magazine's first serial. There was even a long piece on Rudolf Besier and his new play for Mrs Patrick Campbell.

The paper also suited Hodgson's essentially indolent nature perfectly. He found that the production routine, held together by various 'office boys' who were, in fact, experienced sub-editors, accommodated all his foibles. His daily round, once the magazine had acquired a momentum of its own, was almost gentlemanly. He would arrive at the office in Effingham House at around 10 a.m., usually accompanied by his two dogs, Dulcie and Jim, Mooster having passed away. He wore, according to Bill Clarry, a long-time employee of George Newnes, large spotted ties and a short overcoat. He would draw near the window, smoke and attend to various office matters before leaving for lunch at about 12 noon. He would return around mid-afternoon for an hour or so, and then go off to play billiards in The Strand or to Eustace Miles' vegetarian restaurant near Leicester Square, where he now had his own table.

However, being Hodgson, the *New Fry's* editorial post was effectively over within 18 months of his assuming it. In late 1912 he was succeeded by one Burton Bawdry for reasons that must remain speculative, though his lack of complete dedication to the job and the magazine's falling circulation must have played a part. Gradually, his financial situation had deteriorated. He and Dolly, plus dogs, moved to rooms in Poulton Square close to King's Road, Chelsea, in those days an 'artistic' quarter. (Hodgson once recalled seeing Isadora Duncan walking by with her son each morning.)

They were not destitute: Hodgson continued for a time working on *Fry's*, and whenever money was desperately needed he could always obtain commissions from his brother Walter who was still working on *The Captain*. But from now on, poetry became Hodgson's abiding obsession and his dedication to his moods of inspiration would appear more marked. When he was working on a poem, all else fell away and nothing was allowed to interrupt or divert him, least of all the irksome business of earning a living.

Janet 'Dolly' Hodgson's drawing of Mooster, c.1908

9

Eustace Miles

The lunches with Sickert gradually gave way to lunching at Eustace Miles' Vegetarian Restaurant somewhere near Leicester Square. Here Ralph Hodgson was permanent king of a special table.

(Enid Bagnold)

Ralph Hodgson's literary relationship with the poet Edward Thomas was principally one of poet to critic rather than poet to poet. With Walter de la Mare the relationship was more complicated. When they met in 1911, de la Mare was just beginning to make his name and in fact he was awarded the Polignac Prize for his novel *The Return* during that year. Although, according to Siegfried Sassoon, his "diffident personality paled beside Hodgson's", their friendship would be a lifelong one.

De la Mare, according to his biographer Teresa Whistler, "felt more intense admiration for RH's work than for any other poetry of his contemporaries". Hodgson best epitomised what chiefly fascinated de la Mare in life and literature alike:

> flavour, character, gusto, and unexpectedness. His knowledgeable love of the inexhaustible mysteries of Nature was brilliantly contrasted by his idealism and a passion for beauty.

Nevertheless, they were never to be as close as Thomas and de la Mare would become, perhaps because of Hodgson's innate introversion and his desire for personal privacy.

Aged 40 in 1911 and, despite having been a married man for 15 years, Hodgson seemed unattached to the humdrum everyday affairs that so beset his poet friends. For example, de la Mare, although receiving a Civil List pension secured for him by Henry Newbolt, still worked long and hard, like Thomas, producing books and articles, reviews and poetry in order to support a growing family.

Hodgson, on the other hand, had no children (although, intriguingly, he once made a serious offer to adopt one of de la Mare's sons, Colin). His wife, Dolly, appeared content (or perhaps resigned) to seeing him disappear for days, even weeks, on end, while she tended to the dogs and whichever house they happened to be living in at the time. Thus he was set apart from the usual concerns and worries of middle-aged, married men, and his ability to breeze through life (even his editorship of *New Fry's Magazine* seemed somehow semi-detached) must have appeared 'gypsy-like' to his colleagues and friends. This, combined with his tendency to avoid talking about his own life, his past and his family, closed down avenues for discussion that might have led to shared confidences. Indeed, although Hodgson's conversation, according to Teresa Whistler, "was his greatest creative gift – full of intransigent opinion, poetry and a strong, inborn Puritanism – hot, denunciatory and imaginative", it was hardly the stuff of which close friendships are forged.

Where de la Mare and Hodgson's *work* was concerned, there was a general assumption that they shared a philosophy or purpose. The critic Conrad Aiken wrote in 1919 that the two men's overall attitude "predicated poetry as something separate from our tortuous lives, a something additional, perfect in itself; a something to turn to for delight, which shall take us not deeper into ourselves but away from ourselves". This seems more accurate where de la Mare is concerned, his poetry and stories being aimed sometimes at children and evoking a world of dreams, fantasy, entrancement and nightmare. Hodgson's work was less easy to categorise in content and style, and certainly was never consciously aimed at anyone other than an adult.

The two men's work, however, did share certain superficial qualities. The delicate fancies and rhythms of some of Hodgson's verse, its occasional apparent whimsy, seemed to partake of some elements of de la Mare's world. But Aiken was surely wrong to suggest that Hodgson never or seldom spoke in his own voice or developed psychologically any personal or dramatic viewpoint or that

> the darker chords of intellectual and emotional frustration which
> shake the centre of individuality itself and which in the past have
> given us our greatest poetry are here untroubled.

Hodgson was certainly a serious poet, but his subject matter would rarely satisfy those in search of deeper significance, those who considered *what* you wrote about as being almost as important as *why* you wrote. Hodgson never touched upon social or political issues, nor did he overly concern himself with the feelings and experiences of individuals. However, his yearning for emotional and physical freedom would now produce one of his most approachable poems, 'The Gypsy Girl', which appeared in June 1911.

Opening with a piece of simple dialogue: "'Come, try your skill, kind gentlemen, / A penny for three tries …'", the five-stanza poem relates a single incident, a fleeting observation. A gypsy girl at a fair calls to a man who then insults her. She doesn't respond in kind ("not blush as Saxons do") but merely repeats her cry ("sweet gentleman"). However, the poet observes a "den of wild things in / The darkness of her eyes".

Nothing more happens, the substance of the poem being the poet's own observations, his attraction to the girl, his keen eye for the details that stir him: "She was a tawny gypsy girl, / A girl of twenty years," he says, and notes her gold earrings, her flaring yellow scarf, her velvet coat. And yet, Hodgson is still not too far removed from his obsession with the animal world. The girl is barely human, she fawns and whines and, Hodgson notes, when insulted did not "turn upon the cur". In the last verse, omitted in subsequent reprinting, the poet confesses, "The tameless savage of her soul/Was like a wolf to see," and that it was this, "more than the pretty rags and riches", that so captivated him.

'The Gypsy Girl' is a study in social defiance but shares in a contemporary romantic interest in gypsy life and the open road which was strengthened by cheap reprints of the mid-19th-century writings of George Borrow – and a new biography of Borrow by Edward Thomas. In fact, it is possible that Hodgson owed the genesis of the poem to his good friend Thomas. In the same month as the 'The Gypsy Girl' was published, Thomas produced an article for *New Fry's Magazine* describing a day at Goodwood Races – a popular venue for gypsy fairs and hucksters. He, too, seems to have had half an eye on the gypsy girls: 'the bony-faced women from neighbouring tents, their brown faces newly washed, their black hair combed and evenly parted, their eyes bright as with a little quicksilver and their lips smiling as they bent down holding buckets at a pump worked by their men-folk'.

Another of Hodgson's colleagues on *New Fry's Magazine*, the American journalist Ralph D. Paine, had also produced a piece on gypsies some years before. In this, the intriguing legend of the gypsy girl's *glance* had been outlined:

> Through hop-picking time in Kent the gypsies gather in force and there you may see some of the lithe and tawny belles of the old English families of the Romany, and learn that with good reason our term 'mash' or 'mashing' means 'to fascinate or take in by the eyes' for there are the wild beauties 'who sealed their souls into the corners of their eyes by many generations of shafts sent sidewise and wantonly … '

Thomas' article was accompanied by a sketch of a gypsy girl "at the booths" – tall, striking, beshawled and proud – and there was much there to suggest a certain male escapism. Hodgson, as we have seen, claimed that he was no stranger to fairs and fairground life, having run away as a teenager to work with a travelling fair. His close friend G.B. Dewar certainly felt that Hodgson's work was, "suffused with the gypsy character of the poet himself; real gypsy, not the faked-up romantic stuff that is palmed off as gypsy".

Hodgson returned to the gypsy theme later in 1911 when 'Time, You Old Gypsy Man' was published in the *Saturday Review*. This time it served as a vehicle for a much more important and intangible idea, that of the fleeting, inevitable estranging touch of time. It is a theme that usually weights and sobers poetry, but Hodgson handles it with swift good-humoured strokes to achieve a slight, blithe pathos:

> Last week in Babylon,
> Last night in Rome,
> Morning, and in the crush
> Under Paul's Dome;
> Under Paul's dial
> You tighten your rein –
> Only a moment,
> And off once again;

'Time, You Old Gypsy Man' has a compelling and maddeningly addictive opening line (one parodied and adapted many times down the years). In 1961, the critic Naomi Lewis tried to pigeonhole it by deeming it what she termed an 'anthology' poem:

> To have the anthology touch is a special gift; many poets never achieve it at all. Whatever its level, the anthology poem is always bold, direct and memorable, preferably not difficult in thought since the impact must be immediate, not delayed. 'Time, You Old Gypsy Man' is in no way a profound or valuable statement in itself. Really the thing is no more than a single puffed-out image and not at all a tenable one at that. Yet it is and will be remembered with horrific persistence.

In fact, it is a perfect juxtaposition of ideas. The eternal gypsy, as Dewar noted, the epitome of time suspended: "on Micheldever Down, a bit of scarlet cloak, a tethered pony cropping the close turf, a wisp of smoke from the camp-fire ..." yet linked to onrushing history:

> Off to some city
> Now blind in the womb,
> Off to another
> Ere that's in the tomb.

This last line is redolent of Hodgson's 'The Hammers' (*Saturday Review*, March 1907) tapping into an underlying anxiety at the swiftness of change at the turn of the century. His newer poems of 1911 borrowed much of the economy of effort exhibited in 'The Hammers'. Critics and admirers of his work were now using terms such as "concentrated intensity", "quick", "clear, light and rapid", suggesting that he achieved his effects with an "absence of verbiage" – qualities rapidly becoming the touchstones of merit in the second decade of the century. As Harold Monro commented, "His phraseology resembles the careless offhand language of the ordinary man" and while most poets gleaned their vocabulary "from poetry itself, [Hodgson] gathers his, as it were, raw from life."

Not quite as raw as some, such as John Masefield and Rupert Brooke, both of whom were that very year producing groundbreaking and popular verse. But still, according to Monro, Hodgson spoke "a language of his own and with such natural purity does he use this tongue he knows so well, that he never utters a word of it in a wrong sense, nor fails to make himself clearly understood".

Hodgson's subject matter, however, though changing, still remained at several removes from everyday life, and the ill-conceived charge that, like Walter de la Mare, he wrote for children, persisted. 'Ghoul Care' (*Saturday Review*, July 1911), for instance, with its injunction to the devil to retreat because he, the poet, possesses "Three charms against disaster" namely a lizard's eye, a droning bee and a singing goldfinch, seems calculated to charm and intrigue a clever child, a poem to recite to a young person at bedtime or round a campfire:

> Say, 'In the greenwood of his soul
> There was a goldfinch singing,
> A pretty goldfinch singing.'

But such a poem has many levels, not least the prophetic, perhaps even the mystical. Maisie Spens, an Anglican contemplative writer, wrote in 1929:

> Hodgson is nothing if he is not a dreamer, for he is continually
> visited both by waking and by sleeping dreams which are born of
> an imagination keen as a child's but quite the reverse of childish ...
> His imagination, kept under superb control, is never fanciful, never
> allowed to run riot and is therefore amazingly creative.

Thus, with 'Ghoul Care':

> the simpler his verse becomes, the more doggedly he sticks to
> certain fundamental truths. The sights and sounds of nature are

good insurance against any evil that may beset one; the lizard's eye sees and watches; the bees drone which works and soothes at the same time; and the gold-finch's song that fills the day with music and the psalm that lifts the heart in gratitude for life …

Spens continued:

There is nothing naïve in this, or even childish. It is the full and complete faith and gospel of a man active and imaginative, rather than reflective. Of a man, too, who knows what 'Ghoul Care' is and means, defying the sour fiend and all his 'glooms and smuts' to do their worst. And the three charms? Mysterious meeting places, greetings between ourselves and the all. When more than half the commerce between the living of this world is fear, how can it be saved? Even to see beauty, to wake to wonder, is an act of virtue as real as charity. Because it means that for a moment one is the thing one loves and pities.

Thus, according to Miss Spens,

the real Hodgson emerges from his poems a childlike personality. The child attribute of wonder is his in over-flowing measure and is, indeed, the dominant note in all his work …

It is ironic, in the light of this analysis, that the great Georgian patron and editor, Edward Marsh (who had a great bearing on Hodgson's subsequent reputation and public reception), when finally setting eyes on Hodgson's verse ('Eve', *Saturday Review*, February 1912) should, with a lack of perception, comment: "Hodgson's poem 'Eve' is very disappointing. It turns out to be a nursery rhyme, in the exact style of 'Little Miss Muffett'. As such it has a certain charm but I can't think it's an appropriate manner for the subject."

The subject of 'Eve' is the Fall from Paradise, or rather, Eve's seduction by the serpent. Hodgson depicts her as a cross between a simple country girl and an Isadora Duncan-style sylph:

Picture that orchard sprite,
Eve, with her body white,
Supple and smooth to her
Slim finger tips,

The snake tumbles from the tree whispering her name, leading her, "Down the dark path to/The Blasphemous Tree". The animals in the wood express their contempt for the snake/devil and pity Eve, who is left crying outside the orchard with, "no dish of sweet/Berries and plums to eat".

Oh what a clatter when
Titmouse and Jenny Wren
Saw him successful and
Taking his leave!
How the birds rated him,
How they all hated him!
How they all pitied
Poor motherless Eve!

The mixture of rustic innocence and sexual initiation though presented in sing-song style, nevertheless carries an erotic charge rare in Hodgson's work and largely unremarked on by those who read and reviewed it when it first appeared.

According to Harold Monro in *Poetry Review*, "In a jaded world of Futurists, Vorticists and Unrealists generally sounded the enchanting flute notes of Hodgson's 'Eve'." Hodgson was not afraid of "pithy, vigorous words", according to Mary Sturgeon. He was praised for his, "absolute sincerity of feeling: not fantasy, nor subtle, nor whimsical; but imaginative power firmly controlled by a sense of fact", following as he did the Bible narrative closely. However, Eve was "no longer a remote Mother of us all but a living woman of today", according to Louis Untermeyer. "In his [Hodgson's] candid lines, Eve was any young English country girl filling her basket, regarding the world and the serpent with a frank and childlike wonder."

Some critics dwelt on the beauty of the poem – "a creature of exquisite fancy"; "the eternal stuff of beauty, of tears, of faery" – while others thought it possessed "consummate delicacy", was "heavenly music" and was a "thrilling tour de force of melody and imagination". "The most fascinating poem of our time," according to E.V. Lucas, "the most musical, most tender, most strange", while, in sharp contrast to Edward Marsh, he added: "One is not left with a sense of inadequacy, or triviality; instead, a tragedy seen from a bravely sympathetic attitude."

Perhaps the true charm of the poem lies partly in the transposing of a grand theme into locally familiar and miniature terms, and partly in its naive speaker, who tells the story with open and full-hearted sympathy for the victim, as though he were watching a stage melodrama. By doing so, he keeps the reader at an emotional distance, following and responding to the story and yet appreciating the artist's control. The poem is deliberately minor and playful, yet has pathos and horror. It is witty, poised, controlled, artificial and evasive – evasive in that it would be impossible to say what Hodgson personally feels.

Not everyone praised the poem, however. The Imagist John Gould Fletcher dismissed 'Eve' as "a pretty picture – a miniature, doubtless, but still a pretty picture", and a poor imitation of the "artificial pastoral" of

Robert Herrick, one of the 17th-century cavalier poets. The *Times Literary Supplement* reviewer, while feeling it was, "a thing of truly original loveliness and pathos", regretted that owing to the exigencies of metre, Eve's name had been altered to Eva on occasions.

Perhaps the most surprising note of dissent would come from Hodgson's elder brother Walker – who occasionally liked to make mischievous fun at his more famous brother's expense. In a ditty composed some years afterwards he wrote:

> Eve indeed was gypsy tawny
> A different tone – quite new
> Eve was not a William Etty
> Nor a Monsieur Bouguereau
> Not at all a pale-face pretty
> Such as these fine painters show.

Such minor criticisms, however, serve to illuminate an important aspect of the poem and its possible genesis. It has an up-to-date feel, the Bible in modern dress, as it were. As one critic said, Eve was, "a living woman of today", and Harold Monro suggested that "All trustful beauty that has ever been betrayed finds an echo of its grief there ..."

In fact, 'Eve' is one of the few Hodgson poems directly linked in inspiration to a real person, in this case Enid Bagnold, although Hodgson never confirmed this. In the year he composed the piece, 1912, he was presiding over a gathering at Eustace Miles' vegetarian restaurant in Chandos Street near Leicester Square. He recalled: "We met daily, except Saturday and Sunday, at one o'clock and usually sat for a couple of hours."

One of Hodgson's young devotees at the table, Bagnold, was then a would-be poet and art student. She was extremely attractive, inquisitive and impatient with the constraints of her middle-class home in Blackheath, and, together with a friend, she took a small flat in London in order to explore 'artistic' London social life.

For young middle-class women, the pre-war London art world was an exhilarating prospect, and Bagnold moved swiftly through various guises. She modelled for both Walter Sickert and Gaudier-Brzeska, then tried her hand, unsuccessfully, at painting. She adopted the guise of the *ingénue* poet but eventually settled for the role of a lady journalist. She worked for the writer and editor Frank Harris on two doomed papers before he went briefly to prison in 1914 for contempt of court.

She appeared at times rather fey and not particularly serious. Referring to Sickert, she wrote: "I didn't fall in love with him. Or hardly." She was thus quickly assessed and dismissed by women writers such as Katherine Mansfield. Men, however, responded to her beauty and whimsicality. W.H.

Davies offered to marry her, H.G. Wells made propositions in a teashop and Hodgson took both her and her poetry just a bit too seriously.

Nevertheless, Bagnold was no fool, possessing a sharp eye and a nose for detail. She recalled the Eustace Miles days and Hodgson, in particular:

> When I first knew him he was editor of *C.B. Fry's Magazine*. How he squared that with the hours spent from lunch into a vague teatime when he brooded tipping back his chair at that table, I don't know. Hodgson was older than most of us gathered at the table, had a wife and went home at night. But Eustace Miles. We were none of us vegetarians. The restaurant was chosen by Hodgson because the management allowed his Staffordshire bull-terrier to sit on a chair beside him ...

The gatherings were run very much according to Hodgson's rules. Bagnold continued:

> RH dictated that no one should join our table except the Pure. He had a very special meaning to this. I knew what he meant but I disregarded it. I wasn't so mad about the Pure. He knew what he meant but didn't trouble to explain. If one possessed a gift, one was only Pure if one lived like a hermit hungry for God. All petty pleasures must be forgone; especially if the gifted creature was a girl ... Pure was compounded, too, of a little jealousy.

The "tyrannical Puritan", according to Bagnold, regularly argued with her, particularly when she introduced her boyfriends to the Eustace Miles table:

> I met a man at a dance. His name was Slattery. He wrote me a note signed: 'Yours without flattery, Sincerely, Slattery.' I asked him to lunch. 'You think that funny?' said RH savagely when I showed him the note. Then suddenly, 'You haven't *asked* him?' I had ... Throughout the meal RH's long-lipped lantern face hung like a lit turnip at Xmas in terrible silence. The guest hour was hideous ... 'Never do that again!' thundered the turnip. Oh God! He was an unrelenting man! He stood aloof as the picture says. But he was close as a husband to those he loved; in the sense that one has to study a husband and mind his whims.

Bagnold's liaison with Frank Harris, however, broke all the taboos:

> I introduced him to the friends I had made. They couldn't bear him. RH wouldn't speak to me while I knew him. I was cut off from Eustace Miles and isolated ... In his anger and sorrow, RH wrote

his poem, 'Deep in the bells and grass' ['Eve'] about it ... When I was finally forgiven, RH gave it to me with an inscription.

Bagnold was notoriously erratic and vague in both her life and her recollections, and it would seem the poem was published in the *Saturday Review* well before she had plunged deeply into Frank Harris' murky world. But one can see what she meant, as the poem certainly contains elements that suggest the sort of male triumph at a virgin's seduction that a notorious womaniser like Harris would indulge in, the final lines running:

> Picture the lewd delight,
> Under the hill tonight –
> 'Eva!' the toast goes round,
> 'Eva!' again!

As the critic Arthur Waugh put it: "The degrading toast of her shame goes round the table." The change of name from Eve to Eva also sounds right, suggesting a crude familiarity, and hinting that she was fair game for anyone who might like to try his hand. The reference to "under the hill" is also intriguing, being the title of Aubrey Beardsley's unfinished 1890s novel, and harking back to a period of sexual decadence with which Frank Harris was more than familiar. One can almost see what sort of job Beardsley would have made of illustrating the poem, a phallic snake no doubt representing the "sinister daintiness" of the poem.

Whether Hodgson knew Harris or not is unclear. He referred only once to him in later years: "It was at Eustace Miles, though not at our table, that I first came into contact with that Chinese Puzzle, Frank Harris." In a curious way, Harris – some fifteen years older than Hodgson – circled Hodgson's working life. He edited the *Evening News* some years before Hodgson joined it, edited the *Saturday Review* a couple of years before Hodgson's poems appeared in it, and later edited *Pearson's Magazine* some years after Hodgson had first contributed to it. For a year, 1911-12, he ran a magazine called *Home and Hearth*, financed by the father of Hodgson's collaborator-to-be, Lovat Fraser.

It was during this time that Enid Bagnold entered Harris' life, acting as an unpaid dogsbody on this and a subsequent journalistic venture, *Modern Society*, which folded when Harris was jailed. By then he had seduced her and she only discovered some time later that he was simultaneously involved with another woman. Yet still she contemplated posing for nude photos so that she could earn some much-needed cash. In 1914 she realised she had been made a fool of and fled back home.

Whether Hodgson was, as hinted by Bagnold, a little jealous of Harris or any of her suitors is hard to say. His emotions, where women he cared for were concerned, could certainly be dramatic, as happened a decade or so later when he remarried after Dolly's death. His attitude to Bagnold, however was symptomatic of a duality, a contradiction in his nature. On the one hand he could appear harsh and puritanical, unforgiving of ill discipline, of breaches of trust and faith, but on the other he exhibited a hot-blooded passion for the ultra-feminine.

Walter de la Mare's biographer, Teresa Whistler, described him thus:

> He had a horror of drink and would only touch ginger beer himself and he thought dancing immoral. Yet at the same time he disapproved when Helen Thomas' friend, little, sparkling Janet Hooten, wore sensible, emancipated suffragist clothes. He tried to reconvert her to silk underwear instead of serge and had a weakness for the frilly femininity of waitresses.

His struggle with his young sister-in-law, Vere Chatteris, underlined the problem. Bagnold explains:

> Hodgson contributed a small sum so that she could live in one room in London (and pursue her career as an artist). But this was to the end that she should draw. When Hodgson found out she was going to dances, he arranged a wardship with her landlady. When her goings-on were reported, he blew up in a series of rows and denied her the ordinary pleasures of a girl. She also should 'sit waiting on her gift' as he did. She rebelled.

Hodgson had clearly not adopted an 1890s aesthete's liberal approach to sexual matters. The illustrator Claud Lovat Fraser recalled Hodgson exclaiming:

> Walter Pater is responsible for a great amount of sloppy, silly sentimentality that gave a pretext to all those foul vices of sodomy and the like that pervaded the 1890s.

For many men brought up in the 1870s and 1880s, the sexual politics of turn-of-the-century London were unsettling and confusing. Violent suffragism, which involved bombs, physical attacks on prominent men and public demonstrations, were clearly a threat. One reading of 'Eve' demonstrates Hodgson's underlying fears. He suspected that 'liberated' women were vulnerable, naive and heading for the sort of catastrophe Enid Bagnold had encountered at the hands of Frank Harris which had so angered Hodgson. Odd, therefore, that Hodgson chose Eustace Miles' restaurant as a base, where radical suffragists would regularly gather to have breakfast after being released from Holloway prison!

His friendship with Bagnold would endure, however, and Hodgson penned her some extravagant letters on her attempts at poetry:

> The thing that is most like your poetry is Dürer's 'Melancholia' –
> 'The Melancholia that treasures all wit', or James Thomson's 'City
> of Dreadful Night' – though don't read that poem for ten years. I've
> not seen the picture for a long time but your writing brings it back
> vividly to me. You are wonderful, passing up and down among the
> crowds with a head reeling with glooms and spaces and smoking
> stars, and few people guessing at you …

Though not a genuine poet, Enid Bagnold became a successful novelist and playwright. She wrote a successful diary during the First World War based on her experiences as a Red Cross nurse, which Hodgson helped edit. Her observations of Hodgson, therefore, though missing the point where his poetry was concerned, are illuminating, being both affectionate and tongue-in-cheek:

> Long after we had gone from lunch RH would sit on, hour after hour
> talking to friends who dropped in to see him, or silent, smoking his
> pipe, the back legs of his chair creaking under him – waiting his gift.
> When the poetry didn't come he stayed at the door in attendance.
> He suffered greatly from piles. They made him miserable and often
> short-tempered. When he asked us to his home he lay on a sofa while
> we discussed over his body whether it was safe to abandon life on
> the chance of inspiration. Once he sat up suddenly and said: 'You
> can only write poetry on a breath. And if it stops you mustn't pad.
> If you keep waiting and waiting the breath gets longer.'

Whatever he may have meant (if these are indeed his words), the impression created by Bagnold is slightly misleading. His poetry did not simply 'arrive' fully formed. He was a meticulous reworker of material once the overall concept had been established, and a relentless destroyer of work he felt had failed. One gets the feeling that Bagnold was rather out of her depth with Hodgson. As she later admitted: "I liked to talk of writing with RH [but] it didn't happen often, and it didn't do an injury. He talked in pointers and always stopped before being precise."

Whatever his attitude to the young people frequenting his table at Eustace Miles', it was a milieu very much to his liking and one that was repeated in various forms in the years to come. The keynote was youth: men and women sometimes half his age. "None of them had won the Golden Spurs for services to the muse yet, but they all did, in one field or another in the years that followed," he wrote. It's clear that Hodgson felt happiest among younger people, not necessarily because of any hero-worship he might receive, though possibly the absence of a challenge or a confrontation that might have come from his more accomplished peers was an attraction. Though Hodgson liked to talk, he often baulked at opposition.

The very existence of the Eustace Miles 'table' among so many more prestigious literary gatherings springing up across London, is evidence of the rapidly changing atmosphere in literary terms that characterised the capital in 1911. Excitement was certainly rife as a more fluid scene emerged, with new magazines and new poets starting to claim attention. For the first time in a decade people were beginning to talk of poetry in the same way that the novel and drama had been discussed during the Edwardian period. In this year, the critic Middleton Murry began *Rhythm*, Ezra Pound brought out *Canzoni*, and Walter de la Mare won the Polignac Prize. At the same time, two poets, John Masefield and Rupert Brooke, succeeded in causing a stir and selling copies of their work in significant numbers. The principal attraction of their poems would be the *language* they used.

In Masefield this was evident in *The Everlasting Mercy* which dealt with the activities of a village poacher, Saul Kane. According to Harold Monro: "the rapid free doggerel of 'The Everlasting Mercy', its modernity, its bald colloquialism and its narrative interest awakened the curiosity of the public in 1911 and a revival in the dormant interest in poetry was at once assured." The misadventures of the poem's protagonist ("I drunk, I fought, I poached, I whored"), its sentimental liberalism, its depiction of the radical sinner coming home to roost, were compelling, but what struck the average reader was the *manner* in which the tale was told. Including mild oaths and profanity, it was verse which the general reader, "could appreciate without straining his intellect", according to Monro.

Brooke's contribution, though less immediately popular but equally significant, appeared in his first published collection of poems. In 'Channel Passage' he describes a young man aboard a Channel steamer who suffers simultaneously from seasickness and lovesickness, and the former is described in some detail. Such verse was considered "brutal" and "ugly" by some reviewers, but Brooke was an undoubted 'star' and had an influential patron in Edward Marsh. Hodgson knew Brooke from the very beginning as a regular at Edward Thomas' table at the St George's Restaurant. Hodgson recalled:

> Rupert Brooke used to come when in London; he was still at Cambridge then, 'The young Apollo, golden-haired' was exactly as Mrs Cornford described him. He made a sensation wherever he appeared; it is quite true, it took one's breath away to look at him, to use a homely phrase, he was as good as he was good-looking. He was quite simple and unspoilt – really so – and the world was already doing its best to spoil him. The world, however, sometimes finds hard nuts to crack and Brooke was one of them.

The new 'brutalism' or 'realism' would seem to have little in common with 'Eve'. Its exotic, jungle-like setting (cinnamon trees next to plum trees, cobras and Jenny Wren) and the almost cartoon-like quality of the narrative, remove it from the urgent here and now. However, other creatures than fallen damsels were stirring in Hodgson's jungle and would soon propel him to the forefront of the new poetry.

Claud Lovat Fraser's *Flying Fame*
illustration for *Eve* c.1913

10

Georgians

In its infancy, the Georgian movement was uncharacterised by evidence of design, that is, it did not, like other schools, preach or practise a special dogma of poetic art. It was fortuitous and informal.

(Harold Monro, 1923)

Apart from Davies and de la Mare, Hodgson remained, for many years, unacquainted with figures in mainstream poetry. His friendships and working relationships were with journalists such as Edward Thomas, William Maas, Henry Leach and the Morrow brothers, illustrators like Lovat Fraser and Tom Browne, playwrights such as Rudolf Besier and Enid Bagnold and others gathered around the Eustace Miles table. In a way, this could help explain his lack of 'visibility' at crucial moments. Arthur Quiller-Couch, compiling a compendium of Victorian Verse in 1912, which included, unusually, contemporary poets such as Rupert Brooke, John Drinkwater, Lascelles Abercrombie and Walter de la Mare, failed to spot Hodgson.

The omission was pointed out by a man who had known Hodgson for under a year but who would soon become a close friend and colleague, the journalist and author Holbrook Jackson. Jackson wrote in *T.P.'s Weekly*: "In my opinion, the most serious of all omissions from the [Quiller-Couch] anthology purporting to represent modern lyric verse … is that of Ralph Hodgson, one of the most original and powerful of the younger generation of poets."

Another more significant omission came that same year when Edward Marsh, art connoisseur and patron of new ideas in art and literature, was compiling the first *Georgian Poetry*, a seminal collection of verse by poets produced within the previous two years. Like Quiller-Couch, Marsh had never read or even heard of Hodgson. Marsh compiled the collection with the help of Rupert Brooke, whom he'd befriended when Brooke was still an undergraduate at Cambridge. The collection was consciously intended to reflect the new 'Georgian' age, being a poetic breath of fresh air, a sweeping-away of Victorian and Edwardian poetic styles and preoccupations. The epithet 'Georgian' was initially considered quite radical if not exactly avant-garde. Plain speech and realism were its keynotes, the collection being intended to prove that verse in England was healthy and grappling with contemporary life. Crucially, it maintained that poetry could be as popular and widely read as novels and plays were, a belief that would set it apart from Modernism after the war.

Georgian poets never set out to form an exclusive, ideologically narrow clique or movement such as those involved in Futurism, Acmeism or Imagism. Thus Edward Marsh initially excluded no one of note. Even Ezra Pound and T.E. Hulme were interested and submitted poems. However, the very existence of the collection helped all involved in verse to define their own positions more accurately. Within a few years, Georgian poetry would be seen as representative of a specific sensibility or lyrical outlook, best summed up by the words of James Stephens, who wrote: "The duty of the lyric poet is not to express or explain, it is to intensify life and its essence."

Ultimately, however, and particularly after the First World War, the term 'Georgian' came to signify something much less, poetry that was conservative in technique, nostalgic and whimsical in spirit and content. Whether in its earlier, more appealing form, or its later degenerate state, the Modernism of T.S. Eliot, Ezra Pound and W.H. Auden would be anathema to it. Nevertheless, *Georgian Poetry's* appearance in January 1912, coinciding with the opening some months later of the Poetry Bookshop in London by the poet Harold Monro, certainly helped create a feeling of excitement, of movement and heady awareness in poetic circles, particularly as it sold in amazing numbers.

As Hodgson had missed being included in the first anthology, Holbrook Jackson took up his cause with enthusiasm. In April 1912, Jackson penned an article in *T.P.'s Weekly* concerning the treatment of the month of April as a subject by English poets. This he led with a quotation from Hodgson's 'To Deck a Woman'. In May he went much further and wrote a full-page article on Hodgson entitled 'A New Poet':

> I know for certain that I am not the only one who watches the pages of the *Saturday Review* for the appearance of the same writer. His work bears the mark of one who sings a more or less unpremeditated song, in which artistry happens, as it were, like a happy chance born of a natural gift, rather than strenuous literary polishing.

Like Enid Bagnold, Jackson rather mistook Hodgson's method, but it pleased him to think of Hodgson's verse as having simply 'happened' – just as it pleased him to know, with rather more justification, that Hodgson wrote "with almost entire disregard of literary opinion and he himself is entirely lacking in the literary habit". Hodgson's studied indifference to fame was a reassurance to Jackson: "Such an attitude is healthy and natural and we should have a great deal more good poetry if our poets would cease to be literary *specialists* and live for something else besides the writing of poems."

The 'amateur' in Hodgson thus appealed to Jackson just as it had done to Dewar, although the two men, as befitted their different origins, had different visions of the artistic world to which Hodgson was seen as a throwback. Not only did Hodgson appeal to Jackson for what he *was*, he was also attractive for what he wrote about. He was a 'natural' poet whose subject was 'nature' or 'naturalness'. Jackson placed Hodgson in the mainstream of British lyric poetry which " ... in the last resort stood or fell by its power to interpret feelings associated by contact with nature". No nation, he said, "had produced nature lyrics that could approach the passion, the insight and the imaginative splendour of our own poets".

Nature was important because, for Jackson and many of his contemporaries, buffeted and confused by bewildering physical, social and philosophical changes, nature was eternally there. It was a consolation and an inspiration. When all else failed, nature would provide a firm handle to grasp hold of, to reflect upon, to anchor one's imaginative consciousness and inner self to. Added to this, Hodgson's contempt and scorn for modern man's mechanical slaughter of wildlife also appealed to Jackson's sensibilities. He concluded:

> Hodgson approaches nature from another side. He approves of wild animals and one couldn't imagine him treating them with cruelty. Those who have observed the eyes of animals and dreamt themselves into the dreams they have seen there could not but feel that Mr Hodgson had got nearer to their thoughts than might be imagined possible by the casual observer.

Jackson was referring indirectly to a long poem called 'The Bull'. It was published in *The Saturday Review* in January 1912 and was, in Jackson's words, "so superb in conception and fine in execution that it is superfluous to praise its self-evident beauty and strength". 'The Bull' describes the animal, approaching the end of its life and defeated by a younger pretender to leadership of the herd, standing alone, waiting to die, abandoned and bleeding. As it waits, it drifts in and out of dreams of its childhood, its days of pomp and grandeur, while above, vultures hover, waiting to feast on its flesh.

> Bravely by his fall he came:
> One he led, a bull of blood
> Newly come to lustihood,

Fought and put his prince to shame,
Snuffed and pawed the prostrate head
Tameless even while it bled.

There they left him, every one,
Left him there without a lick,
Left him for the birds to pick,
Left him there for carrion,
Vilely from their bosom cast
Wisdom, worth and love at last.

Jackson wrote, "In spite of it all, the old bull is undaunted and the tragedy of it is that the hope within him is not yet dead." Just how Hodgson intended the reader to feel about the bull itself is, however, unclear, for the poem's tone hovers between sympathy and indifference, an ambiguity reflected in much of the subsequent critical comment on it.

The American literary critic William Phelps wrote: "We resent being made to feel such ardent sympathy for the poor old bull, yet [he] absolutely compels our pity for the bull", and Henry Newbolt thought the tale was, "told with an intensity of sympathetic feeling such as is seldom found even in tales of human life".

Hodgson's fellow poet James Stephens, was also impressed by this leap of imagination: "His bull has, I think, true imaginative observation and is a real piece of psychological delving." The critic W.H. Chesson certainly judged that Hodgson had a definite purpose in all this:

Severely simple in its horror, 'The Bull' raises to heroic dignity a creature that more than any other is the butt of man's facetious carnivorousness. I have not much time for psychic experiments but I think the results might be rather interesting if a dozen ordinary adults, picked at random, were asked which, on reflection, they found more powerful – the pictorial humour advertising a beef extract or the images evoked by Mr Hodgson's grim poem, 'The Bull'. One thing is clear: anything which tends to exclude laughter from the shambles deserves praise, because Mr Hodgson enables us to see the life of a bull as a conscious continuity dominated by passion and competitive courage, he makes it more difficult to snigger at the transformation of Taurus into tabloids or his migration into tiny bottles.

But Hodgson's 'The Bull' was, of course, far more than a piece of animal rights propaganda. For the most part the tale is told in a simple unsentimental, matter-of-fact style:

Pity him, this fallen chief,
All his splendour, all his strength,
All his body's breadth and length
Dwindled down with shame and grief,
Half the bull he was before,
Bones and leather, nothing more.

See him standing dewlap-deep
In the rushes at the lake,
Surly, stupid, half asleep,
Waiting for his heart to break
And the birds to join the flies
Feasting at his bloodshot eyes, –

The prevailing literary taste for 'realism' and straightforward 'unadorned language' appeared to have been satisfied here, though criticising it for its "repellent", "repugnant" images, as some readers did, seems exaggerated. Apart from the bull's mouth running "slaver red" and flies "feasting at his bloodshot eyes" there is no gore or violence. But the picture Hodgson paints is a bleak one because he is dealing directly and unambiguously with death. Not necessarily what it *means*, rather that it inevitably arrives.

Samuel Beckett, much later in the century, also concerned himself with human decay and that stretch of time spent waiting and half-dreaming, half-aware of the end, contemplating earlier, happier delusions amid the ugly, uncomfortable present. Lessons to be learnt are few; there is only a stoical, stubborn persistence in being.

In April 1912 Hodgson published a small poem entitled ' The Moor'. It serves as a pendant to 'The Bull', but in human terms:

The world's gone forward to its latest fair
And dropt an old man done with by the way,
To sit alone among the bats and stare
At miles and miles and miles of moor-land bare
Lit only with last shreds of dying day.

On this bleak, Beckett-like landscape, no one comes except the inevitable Journeyman, Death, who offers the old man a hand. To which the man responds resignedly, "Unbody me – I'm tired – and get me home." Death is also imminent throughout and at the close of 'The Bull':

And the dreamer turns away
From his visionary herds
And his splendid yesterday,
Turns to meet the loathly birds
Flocking round him from the skies,
Waiting for the flesh that dies.

Searching for antecedents and precursors is an abiding habit of critics, and Hodgson's 'The Bull', because of its impact and success, found many anxious to exhibit their literary knowledge. Some thought his inspiration came from William Blake, some from the Victorian poet Thomas Gordon Hake. Cornelius Weygandt, was much closer to the mark when he suggested that the poem's genesis could be traced to Hodgson's youthful admiration for the work of Thomas Bewick. 'The Bull', Weygandt said, appeared to spring almost fully formed from Bewick's monumental *History of Quadrupeds* published in 1789, in particular, the Chillingham Bull, of which Bewick has much to say in his autobiography, a book known to have been read in the Hodgson household.

The animal in question was part of a herd of wild cattle, the last in Britain it was thought, and kept in the grounds of Chillingham Castle. To sketch them necessitated a dangerous journey on foot into woodland, the danger stemming from the fact that the animals had a reputation for turning on trespassers. Therefore Bewick had been obliged to see one that had been conquered by a rival and driven to seek shelter alone in the quarry-holes and woods. Hodgson's bull, however, is not a British bull. The exotic setting, including cranes, parrots, monkeys, serpents, lions, leopards and green savannahs, takes the reader far from bleak Northumberland, where Bewick's animals lived. In fact, we are transported into a world of dreams:

> Cranes and gaudy parrots go
> Up and down the burning sky;
> Tree-top cats purr drowsily
> In the dim-day green below;
> And troops of monkeys, nutting, some
> All disputing, go and come;

Rather like the setting of 'Eve', there is something oddly unreal about the picture constructed in 'The Bull'. As we have seen, some poets of this period turned to the natural and even exotic worlds for inspiration, and were eventually criticised for doing so. To turn to nature was surely quite justifiable, but in order to avoid nature itself being categorised and simplistically defined by modern readers, some poets transformed it. They made it exotic and mysterious, and so placed it beyond the reach of the empirically minded scientific world.

But use of the exotic is not necessarily a deliberate evasion. The jungle, wherever it may actually be, is a primitive, non-social, even non-human setting, ideal for portraying truths stripped bare of contingency. Hodgson's achievement in 'The Bull' matches that of the primitive painter Douanier Rousseau, whose direct, simple, haunting visions of picturesque exotic subjects were so popular and influential at the time.

Primitivism in art consists of a sense of pure, formal beauty naturally combined with a feeling for the pristine, magical quality of the subject. It was this, and not the actual visual form, that the Primitives and Hodgson distilled from the visible. They did not paint or depict their subject in its unique accidental context but presented instead the objective idea which they had formed of it. They brought their image into conformity with their own realisation. Reality thus took on a much more significant meaning.

As John Masefield said when presenting Hodgson with the Polignac Prize in 1914 for both 'The Song of Honour' and 'The Bull', " 'The Bull' ... provides the fancy with a means of escape into the ideal region where things are so much more real, the light so much deeper and the adventures so rare ..."

In purely literary terms, the successful manipulation of a single manageable object, according to J.C. Squire, linked Hodgson with the Imagists. But, though Pound, Richard Aldington and the poetess H.D. (Hilda Doolittle) were friends of his, Hodgson was no Imagist. His extended narrative form, his 'lapses' into sentiment and characterisation, his regular and simple rhythms – all were anathema to Pound's clique with their strict code of poetic conduct and their missionary zeal. Furthermore Hodgson's method of composition would have seemed to Imagists and later Modernists far too reliant on pure inspiration to be acceptable.

As Hodgson himself explained to American undergraduates in 1942, when talking about how he came to write 'The Bull',

> Suddenly this picture became a reality before my inside eyes. Nothing would do but to give that picture in the form of a poem, and I wrote 'The Bull' ... I was so excited that nothing in this world had any value until I had written that poem. Pictures seen with the inside eyes are different from those seen with visible eyes. It took a long time to finish the poem because the proper words did not come right off. I was a young man at the time and felt I could not finish it. I soon learned it's no good labouring, no good working. If it's there and your conscious mind has grappled with it and you have sent down this sort of furious prayer to your subconscious mind, you can feel it's all right and sometime later it will come to you. There's no mistaking inside you what you want, but you may have to wait, so it is best to stop thinking and it will come to you when you are thinking of something entirely different.

Just like Rousseau, Hodgson was mistakenly regarded by some as an amateur. He had previously been accused of being an occasional versifier, someone who did not take poetry seriously enough. 'The Bull', however, was his first truly major achievement and the first piece to be extensively written about. It placed Hodgson squarely in the public eye and it made him, whether he wanted to be or not, a Georgian poet.

11

Flying Fame

Morris dances have been revived: it was about time somebody revived broadsides and chapbooks.

(Arthur Waugh, 1913)

In March 1911, while in the *New Fry's Magazine* editorial seat, Hodgson received a letter from a young artist called Claud Lovat Fraser, enquiring whether the magazine could use any of his illustrations or caricatures. Hodgson, after some delay, replied that he would talk to Fry. Fraser was dubious, writing to his mother: "I don't think there is anything in the *Fry's* correspondence. My work is absolutely unsuited for an athletic periodical."

Undaunted, however, he eventually took his work along to show to Hodgson, who was impressed but later admitted: "I wasn't the first to recognise Lovat Fraser's genius. The credit of that belongs to Haldane McFall: he beat me by about a week."

Fraser was then only 20 and on the brink of giving up his training in law to become a full-time artist. Hodgson later recalled:

> When I first met Fraser, he hadn't yet left his father's office where he was articled to the law. He still wore a bowler-hat. One afternoon that very week, however, after much discussion with his father, Lovat laid aside the law and his bowler together for good: he bought the widest-brimmed desperado hat in London that afternoon and joined the art class at Walter Sickert's school next morning: there he studied for only a week or two ...

Hodgson had met a young man whose inclinations and talents would reflect and complement his own to an uncanny degree, even though Fraser's background and education were utterly different. Solidly middle class, his father the founder of a City law firm, Fraser was educated at private schools and Charterhouse, which he left in 1907. He became an articled clerk in 1908 in his father's office, but in the third year it became clear he had neither the taste nor the aptitude for law – and, as Hodgson recounted, he left.

With the financial backing of his parents he was able to set himself up in his own studio in Roland Gardens, West Kensington in late 1912, where he pursued his own, very individual, direction. Fraser, as Holbrook Jackson put it,

> was not docketable as an artist … In the fullest sense of the word he was a designer. Art for him was a bringing together of various materials for a pleasing and useful but not necessarily utilitarian purpose. He had no views, only tastes. He belonged to no 'movement', only his own which is inimitable and ends with him. Haldane McFall, the first critic to recognise his genius, labelled him 'mass impressionist'.

Hodgson suggested his genius lay, "in mass, colour, and a feeling for blithe decoration that was his own discovery". Among the affinities and influences of his own period were the illustrators Jack B. Yeats, Gordon Craig and Max Beerbohm. Yet he seemed always to be looking back to earlier centuries, the 18th in particular, researching costume and stage design and early book illustrations. It was, in fact, difficult to pin him down. Ultimately he would gravitate to the theatre, designing stage costumes, settings and whole productions of opera and Shakespeare in the end of the First World War before his early death in 1921.

For now, however, he was busy producing highly individual paintings, caricatures and illustrations, and it was his keen interest in early book production that led him into fruitful collaboration with Hodgson. In fact, Hodgson's new-found friendship with Lovat Fraser would be crucial. Fraser's studio in Roland Gardens was just a short walk from Hodgson's new quarters in Chelsea, and within months of the two getting acquainted Hodgson was using it regularly, although whether sharing the rental is extremely doubtful.

Fraser, though a private person and usually preferring his own company, nevertheless seems to have taken to Hodgson, and for the next two to three years their friendship and collaboration would be the focal point of both their lives. Fraser's diaries document a happy, carefree, extremely convivial association built around mutual respect and admiration, close enough for Hodgson to give Fraser his first corrected copy of 'The Bull', just a month or so after first meeting him.

Hodgson's long career in Fleet Street, his knowledge of legendary black-and-white artists such as the Beggarstaff Brothers and Tom Browne fascinated Fraser. Where Hodgson was concerned, Fraser's personality and company were a great stimulation. He would always recall Fraser's

> endless bubble of conversation – he had enormous mental vitality; was a big lad, with a round most mobile and amusing face and a

passion for riding in hansom cabs; he rarely walked a hundred yards – it was a waste of time and he had none to spare: I believe that this was really so: he was not the first young genius to have bodeful premonitions.

His humour, lack of pretension and self-deprecation clearly attracted Hodgson because Fraser's whimsical, cheerful and amusing demeanour seemed essentially childlike and innocent. Enid Bagnold was a close friend, unfortunately too close for Fraser, whose father was inveigled by Bagnold's lover, Frank Harris, into lending over £1,000 for a doomed magazine, money that was never repaid. As young, middle-class aspiring 'artists', Bagnold and Fraser explored London together. Bagnold wrote:

> Lovat's family were comfortably off and lived in Kensington. He loved and protected his mother's old-fashioned paintings in gold frames on the drawing-room walls. Why not? He had no ferocity and needed no rebellion. He was loved and adored by his family and his own character was sweet to the core. He had a studio then in Roland Gardens with a gallery round the top. Here he was busy decorating everything, every bit of paper, every letter; even the menus as we ate … Everything that came from his white, indefinite hands (not the hands of a painter in oils) had a fascination and, perhaps, too limiting a perfection. He made his talent like a round 'O' that you couldn't break. He was sunny, gay and a wonderful companion. I wandered about London with him. I had never had its freedom; it was like a city abroad. He loved evening expeditions after his day's painting. 'Let's go and see the tarts in Leicester Square,' I said. I had never been sure I'd seen one and wanted a man's corroboration. We ended up hanging over a blow-hole on Ebury Bridge while Lovat drew the girders, the engines, the bonfire-ish station from the top …

Fraser's progress was, in terms of an artist's career, haphazard and intermittent. His friendship with the art critic, Haldane McFall, led to his illustrating the latter's long-running series *The Splendid Wayfarer* for over a year, and he succeeded in placing caricatures and illustrations in such publications as *T.P.'s Weekly*, *The Onlooker* and *The Illustrated London News*. He helped design toys with friends; he attended art school and started oil-painting in his studio, where he had an exhibition in February 1912, well supported by wealthy friends.

Nevertheless, although he had met Gordon Craig, an influential theatre theorist and later a very good friend, and had made the acquaintance of the equally youthful Gaudier-Brzeska, Fraser had, by late 1912, established no artistic identity or firm direction. It was then that the idea occurred that would bring him into direct collaboration with Hodgson.

It was Haldane McFall who claimed the credit for putting the idea of *Flying Fame* into Lovat Fraser's head. In Dan Ryder's bookshop, he had introduced Fraser to the work of the 18th-century woodcut artist Joseph Crawhall and the chapbook publisher Jeremy Catnach. Chapbooks were small softback booklets of pocket size, usually no more than fifteen to twenty pages long. A broadside was a single sheet, usually decorated, and printed on one side. They once provided a cheap and effective method of distributing not only verse but religious homilies and examples, ballads, tales, extracts from longer works, lampoons and satirical squibs. They were aimed at the general public and were often extremely bawdy.

Fraser was so impressed that McFall suggested he produce something in the Crawhall style, "to give some of the younger poets their hearing ..." Ralph Hodgson remembered how Fraser later introduced the idea of an artistic collaboration:

> One afternoon, early in our acquaintance, Lovat and I were having tea together in Essex Street off The Strand; he had taken me into his confidence and I had responded by taking him into mine and shown him my verse; now he asked me to let him make some decorations to one or two pieces and produce a little chapbook from his studio. I agreed that it was a jolly idea; in that way our private press, *Flying Fame* came into existence.

There was, however, a third member of the *Flying Fame* project, the early champion of Ralph Hodgson's poetry but also a keen bookman – Holbrook Jackson. Jackson remembered the beginning of this famous venture as, "a game – almost an incident". According to Jackson, all *three* were in the coffee shop at the time and "decided to pool the sum of five pounds each plus certain pieces of poetry and prose for the purpose of the adventure".

The establishing of *Flying Fame* stemmed from a very modern, very Georgian impulse – to provide ordinary people with accessible, enjoyable poetry. Fraser wrote:

> Many 18th-century chapbooks were published for as low as half a penny. Ours are 6d and our broadsides are 2d and 4d. Our idea is to produce good books cheaply in a convenient form, enabling men to slip them into their pockets and women to carry them in their handbags. They are aimed at all classes but it is surprising the number of working men who have bought our books. This has pleased us very much as we were very anxious to place good books within the reach of people who have a desire for the beautiful in literature without the money to buy it. For one working man who can afford a shilling there are thousands who can only spend 6d. It seems to me that most people seriously underestimate the literary and artistic taste of the average working man.

The success of the series in purely commercial terms owed much to the opening of the Poetry Bookshop, close to the British Museum, by Harold Monro. It stocked all the chapbooks and broadsides, took orders and placed advertisements in the literary press – although Hodgson always maintained that neither he nor Fraser nor Jackson paid for the advertisements. Joy Grant, biographer of Harold Monro, called it a "startling idea for its time – in that there were no cheap paperback editions of poetry available before the First World War". Thus the chapbooks were, as Harold Monro himself put it, "something between the periodical and the collected volume".

The *Flying Fames* certainly appeared at a fortunate time. The first of the influential *Georgian Poetry* volumes edited by Edward Marsh was then leading the poetry field in marketing terms, and two prominent Georgians, James Stephens and Walter de la Mare, were *Flying Fame* contributors. The main contributor, however, was Hodgson, and whether the growing popularity of *Flying Fame* was due to the overall concept or the growing popularity of Hodgson's verse is hard to say. It certainly provided an opportunity to buy Hodgson's verse in printed form for the first time since the publication of *The Last Blackbird* in 1907.

In all, between May and November 1913, some 21 of his poems appeared in four chapbooks and six broadsides. Though nine poems were new, four were no more than three to four lines long, while major new poems – 'Eve', 'Time, You Old Gypsy Man', 'The Bull', plus all those published since 1911 – appeared. To cap it all, his most important poem of the pre-war period, 'The Song of Honour', which earned him entry into *Georgian Poetry 2* and the award of the Polignac Prize appeared in chapbook form.

They sold well and by 1919 they were collectors' items, much sought after and expensive. The critical reception of the *Flying Flame* chapbooks was also generally favourable, if limited in extent and generally devoted to the *idea* of the chapbooks rather then their content. Friends like Haldane McFall in *Hearth and Home*, Edward Thomas and Walter de la Mare gave them a warm response, while Holbrook Jackson saw to it that the *Fames* generally received extensive coverage in *T.P.'s Weekly*.

One influential reviewer wrote: "The broad humour of the 18th century has been transformed into a flying and fanciful wittiness, the light sword of satire has taken the place of the heavy bludgeon of pietistic moralising; while poetry of spirituality and beauty now prevails in place of the coarseness of a less sensitive age."

Not everyone thought the idea worth pursuing, however. The reviewer for the *The Athenaeum* was moved to protest: "An age that will not rely on its own resources betrays its lack of inspiration." He was clearly irritated by what seemed the pointlessness of the whole enterprise: "What possible aesthetic ideal purpose is served by this reproduction of a convention happily adaptable to the atmosphere and conditions of Elizabethan literature, but fallen into merited desuetude in the 18th?"

He insisted that modern lyrics, illustrations and production methods didn't suit the original style which had been attractive because of its rough-and-readiness. "There is nothing 'old world' about their modern broadsides, chapbooks and garlands any more than there is about [Horace] Walpole's Gothic castle at Strawberry Hill. They are purely and simply an affectation, a modish exercise in the sham antique."

This rather missed the point, and tended to dump *Flying Fame* into the same bin into which much of Georgian poetry was once tipped and for much the same reason. There was a misunderstanding of both intention and achievement and a mistaken assumption that the predominant preoccupation was with nostalgia.

Fraser would always insist that *Flying Fame* was not simply an exercise in imitation:

> [Though] we have tried to keep the robustness (a rare quality nowadays) and the comeliness of the 18th century, some people imagine we are reprinting the actual chapbooks and broadsides of 100 years ago. But, of course, all those published at the *Flying Fame* are written by modern poets and authors and have little in common with the older chapbooks but their quaintness and small size.

Haldane McFall, agreed: "Lovat avoided the stupid mistake of trying to revive dead things and producing antique fakes. He just drew modern decorations in an 18th-century spirit." He still had reservations however. The chapbooks, he wrote, were

> by no means on a level with Fraser's finest achievements and the decorations lacked something of the vigour of handling of his work with the reed pen which raised his superb decoration of the *Splendid Wayfarer* to so remarkable a height. But it was all charmingly done in its smaller way.

McFall's damning praise may well have been influenced by his dislike of Holbrook Jackson, mingled with some jealousy that he had not been brought into the *Flying Fame* project.

There has, however, continued to be a misunderstanding concerning Fraser's visual contributions to the *Flying Fame* productions: as Haldane McFall commented, Fraser *decorated* rather than illustrated and the images he produced were often unconnected directly with the text. His 'Eve', for instance, has no basket when she's "deep in the bells and grass".

Though on occasions appearing slight, Fraser's work, was highly original in a number of ways, and responded to contemporary themes

90

and preoccupations. The creative use of light, shape and colour created atmosphere rather than depicting realistic detail. It is clear, for instance, how affected he was by the contemporary cult of the oriental and the exotic as seen in modern theatre and ballet. He saw and learned from Bakst's 1910 sets for *Scheherezade*, with its eastern costumes, and likewise from the theatre director Max Reinhardt's lavish spectacles, also popular in 1911/12. In addition, his work was characterised by a spontaneity and freedom that contributed to its freshness.

As his later work in the theatre testified, when his 'futuristic' designs for *As You Like It* were booed and considered the product of "sophisticated modernism" (when in fact he had created 13th-century costumes from illuminated missals which he guessed Shakespeare himself might have used when writing the play), he was very much a part of his age, though keen to improve its aesthetic taste. He was unafraid to draw freely on the past for inspiration, and the range of his commercial artwork for the *Daily Herald*, Heal's department store, Fripp's Olive Oil, MacFisheries, Eno's Fruit Salts, posters for the Lyric Theatre, Hammersmith, not to mention calendars, menu cards and toy design, is testimony to his involvement in the 20th century.

If Fraser's work for *Flying Fame* was controversial, then Hodgson's poetry surely gained from being presented in such a way. Free from the constraints of a formal publisher, he was able to group and relate his poems as he liked. He had total control and no outside interference. It was the ideal situation, unconcerned as he was with commercial success, positively loathing the modern world of celebrity and fame, yet at the same time wanting an audience and to feel part of the literary tradition.

Of the four chapbooks devoted to his work, two contained a single poem each: 'The Bull' and 'The Song of Honour'. 'The Bull' ran to 20 pages, 'The Song of Honour' to 24. The two remaining chapbooks, *Eve* and *The Mystery*, contained selections. 'Eve' was 23 pages long and was grouped with 'Time, You Old Gypsy Man' plus three epigrams: 'Reason Has Moons', 'Babylon' and 'God Loves an Idle Rainbow'. Its cover was mustard-yellow and it was dedicated to Rudolf Besier. Decorated front and back with Fraser illustrations it was a best-seller for Hodgson, and it is easy to understand why, for it is quite clearly escapist, the poems evoking a timeless dreamland.

The main poem, 'Eve', was followed by the gentle plea in 'Time, You Old Gypsy Man' for time itself to slow down. The poem was adorned with Babylonian domes and the gypsy man himself was seated, hansom cab-driver style, dozing on his seat. These two were followed by three haiku-style poems:

Babylon – where I go dreaming
When I weary of today,
Weary of a world grown gray

was the first. The second,

God loves an idle rainbow
No less than labouring seas

emphasises the desire not to strive but to contemplate, while

Reason has moons, but moons not hers
Lie mirror'd on her sea,
Confounding her astronomers,
But O! delighting me!

confirms the anti-rational mood, the pleasure that results when reason is rebuffed, when answers are not forthcoming, when mystery triumphs. The whole booklet is curiously static: Eve should not have bothered seeking knowledge; if only time would stand still; God's happy with beauty alone; there exists another realm of reality, that of the world of sleep and dreams. It was just the antidote for busy, harassed commuters, heading home for the suburbs, weary of the ever-changing world of work.

The Mystery, the fourth chapbook in the series, is 20 pages long containing four poems, 'The Mystery', 'After', 'A Wood Song' and 'Swallow'. It had the drawing of a rose on the front cover and a herald's face on the back. The tone differs from 'Eve', being slightly more sombre, concerned with death, pain and the afterlife. There is also a form of devotion that suggests a belief in God, yet which could easily be translated into something less clear-cut. As William Phelps wrote, "To him each bird, each flower appears as a form of worship." 'The Mystery' itself certainly suggests a religious experience:

He came and took me by the hand
  Up to a red rose tree,
He kept His meaning to Himself
  But gave a rose to me.

The poem goes on to suggest that the poet did not ask for an explanation: he was simply content to smell the rose and see "His" face. Once again, Hodgson's inclination is to accept, not to question, to celebrate rather than seek to change or understand. According to Phelps,

he faces life with steady composure. But it is not the composure either of stoicism or of despair. He finds it so wonderful just as it is that he is thankful that he has eyes to see the beauty, ears to hear its melodies.

It was a theme continued in 'After' where the dead poet, asked what life was like when he was alive, replies, "'Oh well enough'", and then describes what he *saw*:

'I saw blue flowers and the merlin's flight
  And the rime on the wintry tree,
Blue doves I saw and summer light
  On the wings of the cinnamon bee.'

while in 'A Wood Song' he encourages all of nature to hurry up and rejoice in the thrill of existence:

Now one and all, you Roses,
Wake up, you lie too long!

The only poem that suggests anything approaching ambiguity or anxiety is a small piece entitled 'The Swallow', and it is interesting for a number of reasons. The poem concerns not the swallow itself, but a woman and her baby:

The morning that my baby came
They found a baby swallow dead,
And saw a something, hard to name,
Flit moth-like over baby's bed.

The narrative concludes:

My joy, my flower, my baby dear
Sleep on my bosom well, but Oh!
If in the Autumn of the year
When swallows gather round and go –

and thus it ends, the suggestion being that the child will suffer or even die when swallows migrate. It's an oddly poignant poem, based in fact on an ancient legend. In Roman times it was said that the swallow was sacred to the household gods. It was lucky if you had one in your house but to injure one would bring the wrath of the gods on you and your family. There is also a link with the rose figured in 'The Mystery', in that it was said to be the swallow that flew above the cross crying "Svala, Svala" ("Console, Console") – hence the swallow as a symbol of consolation, raising the intriguing question whether Hodgson – by linking the rose and the cross in the same booklet – was making an indirect reference to Rosicrucians, that legendary and secretive 15th-century order generally associated with the symbol of the Red Rose.

Sixteen Broadsides were issued intermittently over the period that *Flying Fame* was in operation, seven of them featuring Hodgson's work. They display a feeling of open-air, sweeping country-side with a touch of the bizarre and the surreal. Typical of the work included is 'Song', the first of two child-centred verses. It is concerned with mood, moment and echoing sound than straight narrative. The second poem, 'Playmates', however, is about two children playing but meeting with disaster. A branch falls on them, killing the girl and leaving the boy, permanently crazed:

> '... And though it's all so very long ago
> He's never left the wood a single day
> I've often met him peeping through the leaves
> and chuckling to himself, an old man grey ...'

Here we are in a world of secrets and sinister woodland worlds, a throwback to 'St Athelstan' when a boy is driven mad by the slaughter of an angel, and a complement to 'The Birdcatcher', where we encounter yet more 'fancies in his head', this time a bird-catcher who sets out to trap birds with clap-net and decoy, lurking:

> ... among the thickets
> of the heart where they are bred
> and catch the twittering beauties as
> they fly into my head.

From heart to head – from free, liberating heart to destructive limiting intellect – Hodgson's tendency would always be to trust the heart rather than the head, a feeling shared by many who were now tasting poetic success, in particular the Irish poet James Stephens. It was Stephens who urged Edward Marsh to consider Hodgson for *Georgian Poetry 2*.

In a letter, Stephens strongly pressed the claims of 'The Bull' for inclusion in the anthology but he also mentioned an even longer poem that appeared in 1913 in the *Saturday Review* and was entitled 'The Song of Honour'. Of this Stephens wrote, "it is one of the most sustained and beautiful things I know ..."

9. Claud Lovat Fraser in his Roland
Gardens studio, 1913

10. Front cover of Flying Fame 'Eve'

11. Holbrook Jackson in 1917

12. Roland Gardens Studios, Pimlico

13. Enid Bagnold, c.1915

14. Ralph Hodgson in Royal Artillery
uniform, c.1917

15. Aurelia Bolliger in Japan in 1928

16. Ralph Hodgson and T.S. Eliot,
plus puppies, 1932

12

James Stephens

I love that Bull. I think if Hodgson can stick it he will produce
a book at least which Englishmen may be proud of and which
Irishmen may envy them.

(James Stephens to Edward Marsh, October 1915)

Stephens had known Hodgson since 1911 having been introduced by
Arthur Morrow, one of four Irish brothers working in Fleet Street as
illustrators and editors. Rather like Hodgson, Stephens was a late developer
in poetry. He left school at fourteen without going on to university; instead
he worked in an office and wrote in his spare time. He first submitted his
poems to the Irish Nationalist newspaper *Sinn Féin*, where they came to
the notice of AE (George William Russell, poet and journalist). Russell
became something of a literary godfather to Stephens, encouraging and
promoting him during a crucial time for Irish letters and politics.

Insurrections, Stephens' first collection of poems in 1909, was a
considerable success, and his second, *The Hill of Vision* in 1912, even more
so. Two poems from the book were included in *Georgian Poetry I*. They
concerned God in search of a mate. Henry Newbolt wrote: "They could
only be read – and couldn't quite be read – in one breathless rapture."

Stephens himself commented some years later on these poems:

> The God of that poem is too anthropomorphic even for poetry. But
> in those days I did not expect nor suspect an Absolute and was
> willing to credit deity with my own desires and very generously to
> confer these on him. Well, I suppose I am the only poet that ever
> married God the Father. It was well meant.

Despite the two men's many affinities, Stephens' rather whimsical,
self-indulgent approach to verse would eventually cause something of
a breach with Hodgson. It would also bring to the fore Hodgson's strict
poetic code, his insistence on perfection in anything he wrote – and his
demand for such perfection in others.

Walter de la Mare had spotted flaws in Stephens' work very early on,
suggesting that his verse occasionally fell into the florid and rhetorical.

Lacking discipline, he thought, Stephens often confused profligacy with creativity. Interestingly, Stephens' admiration for Hodgson's verse would be tempered by Hodgson's apparent reluctance to produce large quantities of work. "'The Bull' and 'The Song of Honour'," Stephens wrote to Marsh

> have both ecstasy and passion ... in some parts [they] soar and flash. Unfortunately, and this is the case with practically every good man who is working at the present time, his lode is thin and one must not expect from him that amplitude of matter and treatment which is the unfailing mark of a really great man.

Stephens erred in the opposite direction.

The two men met just twice before the war, in 1911 and 1914, when Hodgson was initially charmed by Stephens' unworldliness. He wrote many years later:

> No Englishman had ever seen a leprechaun until Stephens came from Dublin to London in 1911; the sight of him removed a great deal of scepticism about Irish myths and folklore.

Hodgson continued with an anecdote about how Stephens boarded a London bus in Bloomsbury one morning and travelled back and forth from the East End to Richmond all day because he had lost his boarding house address and was frightened he would get lost. His wife eventually spotted him on the top of the bus close to midnight as it headed back east to the depot.

However, Hodgson also revealed to Lovat Fraser his exasperation and impatience with things Irish, finding the pre-occupation with fairies and the like tedious, and Ireland's whole literary output overrated. Fraser recalled in his journal Hodgson saying:

> Do you know that I don't think Ireland will produce a really great poet. Yeats is a genius and Oliver Goldsmith is in a place by himself and even Tommy Moore didn't write twenty-five poems a week, but a Milton, a Shakespeare, a Shelley or a Wordsworth – it has left England to produce.

And as for Ireland's "wailing":

> A poor country that has no future and I believe never had a past. Its past, save for a moment in the 6th Century when it was an important mission base, was but a sadly parochial affair.

Such attitudes, if he ever expressed them to Stephens, would have caused an irrevocable breach, as Stephens was forever lauding his country's culture and literature, commenting to a friend, "Hodgson is, or may be, the best *Englishman* in English poetry. Russell and Yeats are the *best* things in English poetry."

Hodgson grew even more impatient with all things Irish in 1916 when the Easter Rising occurred, and Stephens wrote ruefully to Lovat Fraser: "I expect RH will never forgive me because the boys went onto the roof. It had to be done or this country would have died of shame and stagnation."

Hodgson was no Empire Loyalist or Unionist; he deplored the military garrison in Ireland and had long-standing friendships with Jack Yeats, the Morrows, and numerous other Irish men and women working in Fleet Street. Perhaps it was something about Stephens himself that elicited the ungenerous comments Hodgson made during this period, for Stephens eventually also disappointed him in his poetry.

In 1913, however, the two men seemed to have formed a mutual admiration society. Five Stephens poems were produced as a *Flying Fame* chapbook, the only poet other than Hodgson to be so honoured. Stephens was also an excellent writer of prose – a mixture of ironic wit, nonsense, fantasy and philosophy, and his book *The Crock of Gold* won him the Polignac Prize for 1913.

To commemorate his success, Hodgson dedicated a section of his important poem, 'The Song of Honour' to Stephens later that same year. It was now that the problems began. Stephens felt obliged to pen a poetic reply. As he wrote to Stephen McKenna the novelist, "Well, he has sung about a hill and I have parried him with a mountain. I want to call my poem Ben Bulben (Sacred Mountain of Ireland and all the rest of it)." It took Stephens just two nights to write his poem, which was eventually titled 'A Tune on a Reed'. He later claimed he'd not written much recently and had had to gear himself up for it. Embarrassingly, however, he could at first find no one willing to publish it.

"I sent it to the *Saturday Review* people, but the dogs returned it. They wouldn't even take my stuff as a gift," he wrote to a friend. After trying unsuccessfully to interest Harold Monro, editor of *Poetry and Drama,* Stephens finally placed it. He wrote to Edward Marsh:

> By the way, isn't Harold Monro a friend of yours? My heavy curse on him. He has just returned to me the best poem I have ever written with the statement that it isn't up to his standard. Clement Shorter has accepted it, however, for the *Sphere* and he will give me real gold for it. Do keep an eye on next week's *Sphere* and tell me do you agree with Monro's judgement. If you don't, I beg you to murder the man for me.

This was but a prelude, however, to a longer saga. In January 1914, Stephens sent a batch of poems to Marsh seeking advice on selection and arrangement, as Macmillan was about to publish them. "A regular tornado of poetry has overtaken me," he wrote to a friend, and to Marsh: "For the last two weeks I have bathed in verse, 12 poems in two days is my average … I get my harvest and then for months together I am dumb."

Marsh called on Hodgson for help, but when the latter read the poems he was shocked at how poor they were. In fact, he had not liked 'A Tune on a Reed', but the proposed collection he considered even worse. He claimed he wasn't alone, telling Lovat Fraser that Edward Marsh had tears in his eyes when reading them: "A child of six wouldn't be proud of them," Marsh is supposed to have said.

Fraser recorded Hodgson's dilemma in his diary. On 21st February 1914:

> RH came into the studio today very worried, indeed almost distracted about JS. He and Edward Marsh have been going through a book of verse of JS's that he wanted their opinion of. I gather that the poems are very bad. RH says that they are rubbish and together they wrote back a joint letter strongly urging him not to print them, only to receive the answer that the book was already in the publisher's hands. RH went on to say, 'three months ago I would have backed JS for immortality against any man at present writing but since reading these poems I should be loath to do so. They were rubbish, absolute rubbish. He has lost his moorings and away from AE [Russell] he is helpless. He has no sense of discrimination. He has an untrained lust for always writing. He writes when he isn't inspired and the consequence is merely a flux of bad, useless meaningless work. He has made a reputation with *The Crock* and he is merely throwing it away. Reputation qua reputation, you know, I don't care in the slightest degree about, but he is a man with a family and reputation is bread and butter to him. Much as I like JS I would consider myself but a poor friend did I not judge his work by the harshest criterion as harsh and as stern as I use towards my own.'

He continued:

> It was a bad day for JS when he left the office. When he was there he was occupied with his duty and only wrote when he could or wanted to. He is in a very bad way and I am terribly distressed at it. So terrible do I find it I only hope that this is merely a nightmare and I shall awake to find it all nothing and JS unblemished as ever he was.

Hodgson felt that the pain he had inflicted on Stephens had taught himself a great lesson and revealed:

98

I have broken a rule that I promised myself I would never break, that I would never interfere with a man and his work.

Fraser interjected:

But you know that you would do it again and again and again – you surely rate your honesty higher than a friend's wounded feelings? It had to be done.

To which Hodgson replied:

Yes, it had to be done, but I have taught him doubt. Doubt of himself and I am sorry that I have done so. JS has genius and nothing else. He lacks all those virtues that belong to talent, such as judgement, sense of balance, discrimination, self-criticism and the like. He lacks all these.

After taking further advice from AE, Stephens postponed publication, and the book entitled, *Songs from the Clay* eventually came out in 1915 to no great acclaim. Stephens' poetic reputation then began a slow decline, and he turned with much greater success, to prose and journalism. Stephens rewrote many of the offending poems, taking a much more relaxed view of the situation than Hodgson. He wrote to him some weeks later:

Why did you distress yourself about that honourable and friendly letter you sent me? I am surely obliged to you and Marsh for it and when I remember that, but for you I might have published the abortions, I burn with horror.

Their different responses – at least in public – underlined Hodgson's conviction that poetic politics did not pay; and his antipathy towards too close contact with other poets was clear. He was demanding of himself to a severe degree and resented literary talk.

Fraser recorded an evening in March 1914 when Hodgson had been to Walter de la Mare's house

and had a rather dreary time of it ... He met Noguchi there who, I fear, got on his nerves rather. 'I am not a literary man,' said RH, 'and I don't enjoy their company. It is a misery to me to know that every word I say is being weighed up and measured. I have no interest in watching the poetry of other men if it does not appeal to me. There is no jolly humanity about them. No, give me the honest, honourable Philistine in preference to them and the bull-terrier breeder above them both! Noguchi was a clever, much-travelled Jap with a raucous voice and it was an ominous sign but he admired that fellow Hulme.

In fact, Hodgson regularly absented himself from serious poetry gatherings, as another Fraser diary entry attests:

> Jan 6, 1914. Eventually to Pecorini's in Soho, Frith Street, where Monro had collected some 20-odd poets of various degrees to dinner. A mournful, dismal affair. RH, however, made our end of the table uproarious. Monro, de la Mare, Thomas and self were quite cheerful but even then things were chilly despite RH's earnest entreaties to Thomas to recite 'The Boy Stood on the Burning Decadent'.

A proposal was made to move across to what Fraser described as

> a strange dimly-lit place where a T.E. Hulme-inspired gathering was taking place (Epstein, a beastly-looking fellow, God Help us! And there were many belly-less – not my word for it but apt – beings, like unhealthy exhalations from Beardsley's mind … all a little odd, weird, like a horrible dream … ugh!').

Hodgson managed to escape with Monro to spend the rest of the evening playing billiards.

This antipathy to the 'business' of poetry, however, eventually left Hodgson creatively isolated. Though not 'a literary man' he was now very much a recognised poet, and it is clear he was beginning to rue not having a sympathetic figure like AE to confer with about his writing. He confirmed this one evening to Fraser, when talking about his previous letter to Stephens:

> I wish I had had a friend to write a similar letter to me when I published that wretched *Last Blackbird*. I had not, and I have paid very dearly for it. It has taught me humility and what a poor thing, beneath all contempt I was when I wrote it. There is not one line in it worth the writing.

To Fraser's retort of "nonsense", Hodgson continued:

> There is not one line in it worth the writing – it has taught me a bitter lesson, that book. I have paid for it in cash. You know that I get a good many letters now full of praise for my work. Well, today I got one from a man saying, 'You are rich, sir, you are rich!' and I could not tell you what a curious sensation it roused in me. I thought, if only that man knew to what a small poor thing he was writing – and do you know, it made me feel almost like a fraud?

Whether Hodgson would have listened to criticism from someone else is open to doubt. G.B. Dewar had been free with comments about his work in the early days, as had Rudolf Besier, but obviously Hodgson needed someone he respected as a poet rather than simply a friend.

Although he was not interested in success of the kind Stephens sought, it was not long before he inadvertently followed in his footsteps. The poem Stephens so admired and was so adamant that Marsh should include in his next collection, 'The Song of Honour', established Hodgson as a poetic force. It also earned him money and recognition, something he was typically adamant a poet could do without.

However, talking one evening about Francis Thompson and John Davidson, two 1890s poets who had suffered ignominious ends, he declared to Fraser that he had no sympathy for such "dolorous men". Acknowledging that they had suffered, he continued:

> But they needn't whine about it and the lack of 'recognition'. No artist can care and afford to trouble about such things. I hate all this pity lavished by a foolish world on a poet who is 'unrecognised'. He is by far the happiest being on earth, why should he be pitied?

The period during which *Flying Fame* was in full flow, from mid-1913 to the end of 1914, was certainly one of Hodgson's happiest. His days were filled with dogs, billiards and endless conversations with Fraser in the Roland Gardens studio, which Hodgson now used almost as a second home. Fraser's diary records their camaraderie in detail:

> We had a great talk on the old civilisations which so attract him, Babylon is magic to him. Nothing fascinates him more than the birth of man's first intelligence and the endeavour to form the evolution of the social code …
>
> Find him in bed with a terrific cold reading a book on African travel – Addis Ababa – this time for ethnology and travel. He had indeed a voracious maw. He reads the old spirit of adventure into it and the early race-riddles: 'Where do we come from? Where are we going?'

They discuss the merits of Greek statuary as against that of Rodin. They talk about 17th/18th-century costume drama. ("He knows more than I do about them and I am interested," Fraser confesses.) They discuss Pablo Picasso's work, and visit the painter, David Bomberg's, latest exhibition: ("RH says that a new sort of man is being born into the world with sympathies that are not born into us who will understand all this sort of work. It seems a sane view.") They look over Fraser's collection of street literature, and have fun destroying Frank Harris' books. After all, as Fraser ruefully noted: "He took father's money for *Hearth and Home* – £1,000 or so. He has seduced – to the best of my knowledge – poor old Enid whom

I had, trusting in friendship, introduced to him. Enid was a fool in some matters but that was no excuse."

They read to one another constantly from favourite authors such as Dickens and Gray and they write spoof books. They have great fun composing letters of rejection to hopefuls who have submitted poetry for *Flying Fame* while Hodgson takes typical delight in playing tricks on Fraser when he can ("He shouted with malign glee at my expression of woe when he tells me that he has accepted on my behalf an invitation to de la Mare's to dinner. Heavens! A solitary journey in the dusk to Penge. I shudder ..."). They lunch at the Cottage Tea Rooms, the Electric Restaurant, the Strand Palace, Pecorino's, take tea at the poetess Alice Meynell's and Haldane McFall's, while vigorously dissecting other writers and their ideas.

Throughout all this Fraser was the perfect audience (and diarist) for Hodgson as the latter poured forth his views and enthusiasms: for Darrell Figgis, the Irish poet and politician, who (Hodgson predicted) would sweep all before him; for his desire to "look at men and women through eyes that are not prejudiced by my own views"; for his observations on people's habits in the street and the conversation of English girls ("They talk nowadays of Oscar Wilde and that affair with the utmost freedom"); and for the little gems of cockney witticisms that he would assiduously jot down in a notebook.

With a base in Roland Gardens, and the publicity garnered by *Flying Fame*, Hodgson was now meeting or renewing acquaintance with people of all kinds and callings: Alice and Wilfrid Meynell; the actor Rudge Harding who had appeared in Rudolf Besier's first plays ("As soon as I heard who he was I rushed downstairs and told RH who I knew wanted to meet him. They screamed at one another happily for an hour of their reminiscences and both liked the other hugely"); E. V. Lucas ("who says the 'The Song of Honour' is one of the greatest poems of modern times ...") and who discovered in Hodgson a fellow billiards player; Jack Yeats ("He is a queer, dry, quaint fellow ... I like him," Fraser observed); Middleton Murry ("Looking awful – I suppose that is the fruits of Katherine Mansfield – we live to learn, but poor fellow!"); all these and John Masefield, Gordon Craig, John Cournos found their way to the studio in search of *Flying Fame.*

Hodgson moved rooms during this period and Fraser lent a hand: "They are very comfortable-seeming. I gave Mrs RH a hand in trying to force a shilling into the gas meter, which I couldn't."

Fraser later visits Hodgson and

> find him in bed, all muffled up with jacket and whatnot, till he looked like an arctic explorer ... bad but cheerful and lively. I advised him to sit close to the fire in the other room. He wouldn't have the doctor, silly ass. 'I shall be alright in a day or so,' says he. He might be alright at once had there been a doctor.

And always there would be the dogs:

> Visited Mrs RH to tea. She is still upset about Jim ... and when
> I get to see them both it is a household of woe. Poor Jim, the
> bull-terrier, has fractured his back leg and has had to go off to the
> hospital today. It is all due to his weight, his legs not being able
> to hold up his 60lbs. See him safely into his 'ward'. Mrs RH is
> grieving badly for Jim.

Fraser's diaries end in August 1914. A few days previously James
Stephens had visited London with his family and together with Fraser and
Hodgson they went to Selfridges for lunch. Fraser recorded:

> Afterwards go onto the roof-garden where one gets a magnificent
> view of London. Hodgson and Stephens are engrossed throughout
> in a vast discussion on metaphysics and 'inner circles'. RH will
> have none of it, JS *will* be interested in it. The result, many, many
> words, some great. Then, still talking of Madame Blavatsky and
> metaphysics I get them into a taxi ...

The next day, "RH comes in and is suffering from liver, so we make
a grand pair ... war seems to hang over London like an ominous threat
..."

13

Polignac Prize

It is absurd to prophesy these things; but a posterity that forgets
'The Song of Honour' will do this generation an injustice.
(*The Nation*, 2nd June 1917)

The poem 'The Song of Honour' has long been considered Hodgson's finest achievement. However, the history of its reception at the time and its meaning for those who read it when it first appeared, is complicated and overshadowed by the fact of war.

First published in the *Saturday Review* in late 1913 and as a *Flying Fame* in 1914, it went on to be awarded the Polignac Prize by the Royal Society of Literature in the same year. In 1915 it was accepted along with 'The Bull' for inclusion in *Georgian Poetry 2* and reprinted by the Poetry Bookshop. In 1917 it was included in Hodgson's successful *Collected Poems*. Thus 'The Song of Honour', a paean of praise for existence, for life itself, would be widely read, discussed, lauded and criticised against the backdrop of the most shocking and destructive event in British history.

Quite simply, the poem concerns a moment when the poet stands on a hill at dusk and, as the stars come out, he begins to hear song, music, a mounting chorus of sound ringing up from the earth in praise of God and creation. Thus, not celestial music from on high but music emanating from below:

> I climbed a hill as light fell short,
> And rooks came home in scramble sort,
> And filled the trees and flapped and fought
> And sang themselves to sleep;
> An owl from nowhere with no sound
> Swung by and soon was nowhere found,
> I heard him calling half-way round,
> Halloing loud and deep;
> A pair of stars, faint pins of light,
> Then many a star, sailed into sight,
> And all the stars, the flower of night,
> Were round me at a leap;

To tell how still the valleys lay
I heard a watchdog miles away ...
And bells of distant sheep.

I heard no more of bird or bell,
The mastiff in a slumber fell,
I stared into the sky,
As wondering men have always done
Since beauty and the stars were one,
Though none so hard as I.

It seemed, so still the valleys were,
As if the whole world knelt in prayer,
Save me and me alone;
So pure and wide that silence was
I feared to bend a blade of grass,
And there I stood like stone.

He realises, however, that he is hearing sounds from much further
afield:

The babble-wren and nightingale
Sang in the Abyssinian vale
That season of the year!
Yet, true enough, I heard them plain,
I heard them both again, again,
As sharp and sweet and clear
As if the Abyssinian tree
Had thrust a bough across the sea,
Had thrust a bough across to me
With music for my ear!

It is then he grasps that he is listening to all the sounds that ever
were:

I heard them both, and oh! I heard
The song of every singing bird
That sings beneath the sky,
And with the song of lark and wren
The song of mountains, moths and men
And seas and rainbows vie!

I heard the universal choir
The Sons of Light exalt their Sire
With universal song,
Earth's lowliest and loudest notes,
Her million times ten million throats

Exalt Him loud and long,
And lips and lungs and tongues of Grace
From every part and every place
Within the shining of His face,
The universal throng.

Not just animals, however:

I heard the hymn of being sound
From every well of honour found
In human sense and soul

There are painters and poets, philosophers, beggars and kings, soldiers and sailors:

The song of lovers – who knows how
Twitched up from place and time
Upon a sigh, a blush, a vow,
A curve or hue of cheek or brow,
Borne up and off from here and now
Into the void sublime!

It is a poem built of images and references that would be familiar to Hodgson readers stretching back to 'The Last Blackbird'. Birds are myriad: rooks, sparrows, nightingales, wrens, owls and larks. There are the beggars who feed them; exotica from Africa as well as mice; there are fighters, boxers and children playing; the idle rainbow and the rose, even the Bells of Heaven. It is, in fact, Hodgson's cast of thousands called on stage to deliver a rousing finale. No wonder Walter de la Mare, reviewing it in the *Edinburgh Review*, declared it "a breathless and universal Benedicite".

Hodgson is said to have written the 215-line, 26-stanza poem in one creative rush that left him exhausted, and it feels that way when read. It is an exhausting poem because it attempts to sustain a high lyric note with hardly a breath, and one can feel sympathy for him when he concludes:

I heard it all, and then although
I caught my flying senses, Oh,
A dizzy man was I!

The poet, Laurence Whistler, wrote in 1950:

In November 1938 I stayed with Siegfried Sassoon and Hester
Sassoon at Heytesbury to meet RH who was there for a week or
so. He told me that 'The Song of Honour' was written in Surrey
a year or so before the War, but that the experience of the poem
came to him many years before when he was staying with his

wife at Wendover one winter, and the hill is the outpost of the Chilterns immediately above Wendover in the direction of Princes Risborough. From that hill the wide view is across the Vale of Aylesbury to the low hills at Oving and Whitchurch. RH said that his visit to Wendover had been of great importance to him ever since – that he lived then in a high state of poetic exaltation which afterwards bore fruit.

'The Song of Honour' would become the most talked about of Hodgson's poems during the inter-war period. Critics concerned themselves largely with its spirituality, its possible religious/mystical qualities as well as its antecedents, works by John Clare and Christopher Smart, in particular. During the war, however, it was viewed in a different light, one that came close to associating it with Britain's struggle against Germany. While not seen as open propaganda, it was considered to represent, in poetic form, certain values that Britain was defending. It also adopted an attitude to life and death that appeared to some to be utterly appropriate for the struggle in hand.

Hodgson's own view on the war was fairly straightforward. Though an opponent of state interference, an anti-militarist and an enthusiast for humanistic causes in general, nevertheless he had no qualms about joining up when the call came. He encouraged his friends to do the same, writing to Marsh that the conflict was to be welcomed as it would get certain things "out of the system – cleverness, sham, mountebanking ..."

But his poem was not about the war (written as it was in 1912/13) and, though it contained certain prescient verses like:

> The song of courage, heart and will
> And gladness in a fight,
> Of men who face a hopeless hill
> With sparking and delight

along with verses referring to "armies bleeding white" and "mighty ships ten thousand ton/Go down like lumps of lead", it must have irked him to read a reviewer in *The Englishwoman* in 1916 commenting:

> The chapbooks lay in many a young officer's pocket until they crumpled ... 'The Song of Honour' has given us eyes to see the heart of our own land and our own people. It is fitting that he should be now in the ranks of this inarticulate army of the single aim; to whom what he calls 'the old kind tales of pity' mean more than martial ardours do.

His old paper, *The Saturday Review*, in 1916 also took the line that came very close to aligning his work with king and country:

The whole motive of this poem is praise for a wonderful world. There is no sickness here or complaint that it is not the millennium. There is no suggestion of a universe awry where animals are milled and eaten and where there are capitalists as well as caterpillars. There is, instead, a robust certainty that even sparrows sing.

Noting that although he believes in life he "cannot omit from his chorus the note of war", the reviewer continues:

> If this song rings pertinent today it is because 'The Song of Honour' is complete and sane ... Therefore, it will never be out of fashion, indeed, it is hoped more such poetry will be written in the days to come.

And it is this trait, this celebration of endurance and courage rather than protest and rejection, that so appealed to the reviewer in *The Times Literary Supplement* in 1915 in a long assessment of Hodgson's work which Edward Marsh considered excellent. "It really gives you your place," he wrote to Hodgson, then serving on an anti-aircraft post somewhere in Essex.

Poetry, the *TLS* reviewer says, is not a luxury in wartime but a necessity. In these "dark and anxious days" for many it had proved a true encouragement and consolation. The year of 1915 was indeed dark – one of the lowest. Following the retreat from Mons, the destruction of the original British Expeditionary Force at the two battles of Ypres, the introduction of poison gas, and looming conscription, attrition had become a key word: endurance, with no end in sight.

The reviewer continued:

> The spirit of the *Flying Fame* now floats over an English camp and if there is one thing clear in Mr Hodgson's verse, it is his delight in 'a pretty fighter'. The phrase is purest English.

The 'Song of Honour' was thus "a vehement breathless hymn of praise" to God and to "The Great Compassion", for a world of men who "in the service of beauty or love or wisdom or of pity or who in sheer stubborn resistance against circumstance are at odds with fortune night and day, 'fight the good fight'".

Death, the reviewer continued, must come to us all, "life is a conflict that has one inevitable end", and if we continue to regard death as something awful rather than, "an undressing, an unbodying, a getting of the tired home ... we shall never free imagination from the entanglement of the mind". That, he felt, was what was good about Hodgson's poetry. Hodgson *accepted*, "he didn't argue or dissect or try to do anybody any good." The effect of his poetry was as direct as a punch on the nose: "As open as sunlight, as star-shine, it has few fine shades and little of what is generally meant by atmosphere." It was concerned almost exclusively with things in themselves rather than with causes.

But to those who first read the poem in the immediate pre-war days, its importance lay beyond a recommendation to buckle down and accept the horrors of war as a necessary inconvenience in the drive for military victory. A characteristic feature of 'Georgianism' was, to quote D.H. Lawrence, "a proclamation of faith in the vastness of life's wealth, an exultation in the vast freedoms that human beings possessed". This was where its real importance lay.

The war, unique as it was, had merely accelerated processes – technological, mechanical, organisational – that were rapidly transforming Western urban society. There was also a corresponding loss of faith in God, in science and in the community. It was against these destructive forces that Georgianism had reacted by defiantly exulting in the spiritual and the individual by means of ecstasy.

As E.V. Lucas put it " 'The Song of Honour' was a psalm of exultation in the joy and splendour and reality of life …", and Sir Henry Newbolt wrote that 'The Song of Honour' presented "life as one great act of sympathetic happiness within the reach of everyman". Mary Sturgeon wrote of it: "It was suggestive of the most vital current of modern thought … for it takes its stand upon the solid earth, embracing reality."

Hodgson certainly looked within the world of observable experience seeking an eternal and creditable truth, a truth he saw consistent with the human spirit and its aspirations. He also hoped for a reunion with the senses and instincts of the animal kingdom. His pantheistic search was shared by many 19th- and early 20th-century writers. W.H. Hudson and Richard Jefferies in England, Ralph Waldo Emerson, Henry Thoreau, Walt Whitman and John Burroughs in America, all looked to nature for salvation and illumination.

Jefferies, in his autobiography *The Story of My Heart* (1883), has a moment of ecstatic illumination rather like that of the narrator in 'The Song of Honour':

> I looked at the hills, at the dewy grass and then up through the elm branches to the sky. In a moment all that was behind me, the house, the people, the sounds, seemed to disappear and to leave me alone. Involuntarily, I drew a long breath then I breathed slowly. My thought or inner consciousness went up through the illumined sky and I was lost in a moment of exaltation … while it lasted there was no formulated wish. I was absorbed: I drank the beauty of the morning; I was exalted.

And, similarly, Abel in W.H. Hudson's *Green Mansions*, who hears the note of the bell bird and is "swept to a sense of the impersonal, all-comprehending One who is in me and I in him, flesh of his flesh, soul of his soul. The sounds ceased but I was still in that exalted mood and, like a person in a trance, stared fixedly before me ..."

Others saw its possible limitations. The poet and academic G.S. Fraser, writing in the 1960s, recalled:

> Like Sir Herbert Read I was bowled over as a schoolboy by 'The Song of Honour' and then a year or two later found that the drug or enchantment no longer worked. In a perfectly sincere way, 'The Song of Honour' expands and dilutes the ecstatic nature mysticism of Shelley in 'The West Wind' or Keats in 'The Nightingale'. It leaves out the under-note of exhaustion or darkness, the drag of the death wish. It is, therefore, a very suitable poem for introducing schoolboys painlessly to that phase of romanticism. The verse moves at a tremendous, confident and exhilarating gallop:
>
>> ... the sky was lit,
>> The sky was stars all over it,
>> I stood, I knew not why,
>> Without a wish, without a will,

It was just such versification that prompted D.H. Lawrence to absent himself from the ranks of 'Song of Honour' admirers. Lawrence, in 1913, was concerned at the poem's loose technique, complaining to Edward Marsh: "No one should say, 'I stood, I knew not why', anymore. It is as meaningless as 'Yours truly' at the end of a letter."

Perhaps, as the children's writer Naomi Lewis said in the 1960s, though the verse was "quick, sharp stuff, all of it and acrobatic, too, in a sense", yet "it was not demanding that inward leap of the mind we expect to make today; the impact is brought to the top; the statement itself is enough; the fact is never an image for a deeper battle beneath. These were not the values of Mr Hodgson's time."

Thus it was that Sir Henry Newbolt, very much of Hodgson's time, could suggest, countering Lawrence, that Hodgson

> had no need to spend time on the invention of a new material form. He wanted a simple instrument fitted for a swift and sustained movement. Thus he chose the one Christopher Smart had used, confident that a measure will always be a new measure when it expresses a new man ...

'The Song of Honour' may well have had limitations as verse, but its optimism and its compelling idiosyncratic assault on the senses won for it widespread admiration and poetic acclaim. In November 1914, the

Academic Committee of the Royal Society of Literature composed of eminences such as Shaw, Yeats, Newbolt, Sturge Moore, Masefield, W.H. Hudson, Edmund Gosse and John Galsworthy, selected this poem (along with 'The Bull') to win the Polignac Prize, an award "intended to be an encouragement of pure letters and given each year to the most distinguished new work published in the preceding twelve months."

John Masefield, presenting the prize to Hodgson, said of 'The Song of Honour' that it was, "a means of escape to a more glittering world than this, a world delight and strangeness". Hodgson had achieved this, according to Masefield, by using his "starry power with a lovely fresh abandon like a man in ecstasy".

The prize had been offered by the Princesse Edmond de Polignac (born the heiress Winnaretta Singer of New York, later a great patron of music) for an experimental period of five years in memory of her husband. Political in-fighting and squabbles had, predictably, been a feature of the award in previous years. Newbolt manoeuvred to get Walter de la Mare the prize in 1911; Yeats achieved the same trick for James Stephens in 1913. No record of the discussions or voting for 1914 survive to indicate with whom Hodgson might have been competing and who voted for him, although he knew various academic committee members such as Alice Meynell, while John Galsworthy and J.M. Barrie, among others, had expressed open admiration for his work. John Masefield, in his address declared: "Mr Hodgson writes verse because it is, like music, a finer kind of speech to be used where the common kind fails."

The year of 1914 would, in fact, be the last that the prize was awarded. Suspended during the war, the endowment was not renewed in 1919. As a result the Polignac Prize celebrated the Georgian canon at its finest. The four winners: Masefield, de la Mare, Stephens and Hodgson represented the best of all aspects of that disparate pre-war movement. The Great War, like a cultural Big Bang, would then shatter all certainties and replace Hodgson's full-throated exultant 'Song of Honour' with Eliot's ambiguous, puzzling 'Love Song of J. Alfred Prufrock'.

For Hodgson, however, who confessed to Edward Marsh in November 1914, to being surprised by his success, the prize would bring some much-needed cash and firmly establish his poetic reputation.

14

The First World War

*Have not seen RH for months. Suppose he is busy keeping Zeppelins
off London. Which is not nearly such useful work as writing
poetry.*

(Holbrook Jackson to Lovat Fraser, October 1915)

Hodgson wrote little verse during the First World War. In fact, he would
not write poetry seriously again until the mid-1930s apart from a couple
of smaller pieces in 1921. As he commented to Edward Marsh about
Edward Thomas: "It's remarkable that he is stimulated to writing these
days – I'm dead."

Aged 43 in 1914, Hodgson did not serve at the front, although he tried
to. He wrote to Fraser in 1915: "I volunteered for foreign service but the
doctor turned me down, naturally enough. So I am fated to stay on home
shore." As Fraser confided to Jackson "It was very plucky of him all the
same, especially as he still has trouble with his old complaint." In fact,
Hodgson needed an operation for his haemorrhoids before he could take
up his chosen role as a chief petty officer in the Royal Naval Volunteer
Reserve, which he joined in May 1915. He did not go to sea, however.

Zeppelin attacks on London began in May with a bombardment on East
London, followed by an attack on the West End; until then, air defences
had been poor and uncoordinated. In late 1915, the army took them over
and Hodgson was transferred in July 1916 to the Royal Garrison Artillery,
Middlesex Regiment.

He seems to have buckled down to the boring, repetitive military life
quite well. Holbrook Jackson wrote to Lovat Fraser in October 1915 that
Hodgson, "looked more like a brigand or a beachcomber than ever!" while
Hodgson wrote to Fraser:

> *It's drill, drill, drill, etc. all sorts of drill ... I've been all over the
> countryside and know more geography than I did but have not
> gained much more ...*

Later, from Bacton-on-Sea, Norfolk, he wrote:

Had a harsh spell, but fit. Looking at birds, blue-throats, fieldfare, warblers, wheatears …

and in August 1915:

Life with me is odder than ever. I'm camp cook. From 6.30-9.00 in the evening. I'm in a little corrugated-iron kitchen, roasting and stewing and learning. Haven't been out of my clothes for a fortnight. My bed has been a sack of straw for a month. Today I've bought a portable bed. No time to oneself is about the worst of it – that and the weather. Yet somehow it is quite satisfying – that is the most puzzling thing.

And to Edward Marsh he wrote:

It is an odd sort of existence but glad to have a job of any sort and am more or less satisfied …

Then he added, "Sometimes I wish I could meet myself alone for an hour again."

He would end the war as a lieutenant in the Labour Corps. An army acquaintance, Alan Biddell, remembered him as,

never being much of a gunner. His mind was not on it and he was rather a dreamer. One day when attending a gunnery lecture, the instructor noticed he was away and apparently not paying any attention so dropped on him suddenly. He was explaining the breech action of an AA gun and the safety catch and said, 'Mr Hodgson, I don't think you are listening to me.' 'Yes Sir,' replied Ralph. 'Safety catch! What a wonderful name for a bull terrier.' Unfortunately, our Colonel, Cyril Hankey (a brother of Sir Maurice Hankey, Secretary to the War Cabinet) was not satisfied with him and, after interrogating him on a rather hair-raising drive back to Chatham, decided he wasn't suitable for the RA and recommended his transfer to the RASC or the Labour Corps. Shortly after he was ordered away.

Hodgson had been an enthusiast for the war – that is he had taken an aggressively anti-German line and felt everyone should "do their bit". It had brought him into conflict with Edward Thomas, who preferred to adopt a more ambivalent line than Hodgson could tolerate. Thomas hated what he called the "newspaper patriotism", the lies, the propaganda and deception of the press. Thomas had, in fact, quarrelled with his father when he asserted that the Germans were as brave as the English and that cold steel would bring fear to any man's heart. According to a mutual friend, "In a London restaurant, Thomas expressed his views to a few of his friends. Among them was Hodgson who promptly called him a Teuton, rose in great wrath, kicked over tables and chairs, left the place, and never spoke to Thomas again."

Whether the scene was quite as dramatic as all that, the two men agreed not to speak to one another until the war was over – but kept in touch with one another's movements through friends. When Thomas enlisted in July 1915 in the Artist's Rifles, he is said to have telephoned his wife, then gone to the Poetry Bookshop where he met Mrs Harold Monro. "Tell Hodgson I've enlisted," he said to her over his shoulder as he went upstairs. When Hodgson heard the news he wrote to Fraser: "Heard about Thomas? I feel pleased about it – it is the rummest thing."

Thomas was to die at Arras in April 1917. Hodgson, who had earlier heard that Thomas had started writing poetry, wrote to Marsh:

> Did you hear poor Thomas was killed? He had written some good verse recently.

And to John Freeman:

> I was shocked to hear of poor Thomas' end, and can hardly believe it. It just numbs one, leaving nothing to say. I can well believe what you tell me of his fretting to be as near to danger as possible – it was what he went for, poor Thomas. Hope someone will publish his 'fresh' work – the verse – in a book by itself ...

Ironically, Thomas' first collection would appear, to indifferent notices, in 1917, simultaneously with Hodgson's next publishing venture, his *Collected Poems*.

There had been no such quarrels with Lovat Fraser, however, who, reluctant though he was to fire a rifle, and not exactly the fittest of men, had volunteered early in October 1914.

Fraser found army life tedious and bewildering by turns, but he received a commission and went to France in early 1916. Hodgson had been full of admiration, writing:

> You've done the gallant thing, Lovat, and when you come back the act will go into every stroke of your brush. Never doubt it. All the trials you have borne and bear will flower in the work and your future ...

To Lovat Fraser's father Hodgson wrote: "Lovat's lived right up to his own standards. I'm very proud of him," and when Fraser wrote to say that he'd lost his copy of 'The Song of Honour', Hodgson sent him a replacement, pledging his devoted friendship: "I often meet you at '45, in the evening ... " At this point, Hodgson was full of what they would do when the war ended:

You will come back and we will fall to again, we two, on chapbooks! This I have told one or two folk who have recently asked me to collaborate and it is my dearest hope and wish. For I'm very proud of the work you've done with me.

Fraser had an event-filled war. He was one of few British officers to survive the battle of Loos in late 1915. In December that year, Fraser's battalion was the first to withstand a German gas attack. In the excitement and confusion of the event, he neglected to put on his gas mask until he had emerged from his bunker, and was dispatched to England for a short sick leave. Fraser was promoted to captain in January 1916, but by late February he was home on leave again, suffering from the effects of gas and shellshock after a battle at the Ypres Salient. Successive Medical Board Reviews continued to pronounce him unfit for battle through to the end of the war. Instead he served the army as a clerk upon the completion of his sick leave in August 1916. He then worked in the War Office on visual propaganda from October 1916 till late April 1917 and at the Army Record Office at Hounslow to his discharge in March 1919.

When Fraser had gone into battle at Ypres, Hodgson wrote again talking of the work they would do when the war had ended:

All my hopes are now that you have good luck with you and that we renew our old attack on dullness and our old praise of beauty together in chapbook form at the earliest moment fate permits … Goodbye, old boy, I'd like to wake up and find old Robinson bringing in the tea and you in your old painting coat at the other side of the stove … well, one day. In the meantime, God Bless You.

In March 1916, with Fraser home and suffering shellshock, Hodgson wrote from his barracks on the east coast in March: "I hope you are yourself again after your terrible trial." He then added, almost as an aside, that he did not want *Flying Fame* to continue.

From then on, his communications with Fraser began to peter out, though he congratulated him on his marriage announcement in October 1916. In February the next year he would apologise for not having been able to attend the wedding. (He wrote to Holbrook Jackson somewhat casually, "saw Lovat was married the other day … were you there?")

When he began putting his collected poems together in mid-1917, however, it is clear that Fraser had to glean information from Holbrook Jackson on what was going on with Hodgson. By 1918, he was confiding to his diary that he was hurt and puzzled.

I shall never really understand why RH has drifted off from me in this way and I shall never find another such friend. However, if it is his will to do so, I shan't press myself upon him.

The two men never spoke to one another again, as Fraser was to die at the early age of 31 in 1921. Why Hodgson reacted in this way remains a mystery. A close friend of Hodgson's, the painter Sylvia Baker, once commented that he was liable to be unforgiving when his friends failed him in any way. But it is difficult to see how Fraser could have done such a thing. There may have been some growing jealousy on Hodgson's part at the increasingly smooth development of Fraser's life. His new wife, Grace Crawford, was the daughter of a wealthy mine owner, and within months of the marriage a baby was expected. Fraser was offered prestigious commissions in the theatre and continued working with the Poetry Bookshop throughout the war. Indeed, he was hardly idle for a day from his demobilisation to the day of his death. The contrast in their fortunes during the war could not have been starker. Throughout this time, Hodgson was condemned to years of tedious garrison life on the North Sea coast, patrolling petrol wharves or chasing sightings of Zeppelins.

However, his strange reaction may well have been exacerbated by a deeply distressing trouble in his own life. A debilitating nervous condition had begun to attack his wife Dolly, and would eventually lead to her death in early 1920. Dolly's collapse in 1916 has been attributed to an accident or to the effect of working in a munitions factory, or simply the accumulation of stress as her life alone in rooms on the King's Road stretched on year after year with little contact with Hodgson. Fraser himself records seeing her in May 1918 when she claimed not to have heard from Hodgson for almost two months.

She suffered, according to one letter from Hodgson, from "neuritis". He wrote to Fraser in 1916 that she had been having "electric massage from a friendly hospital nurse" and had made "a fine recovery".

> She is going along happily and they say they can make her a really healthy woman entirely free of her nervous trouble. They have been splendid at the hospital – I don't know how many specialists they had for her, they are very much interested in her case and lecture students on her.

However, she seems to have struggled along, suffering relapses for the next four years.

By 1918 she had entered Camberwell House in South London, a long established psychiatric hospital, and was under the care of Dr Hubert Norman, a respected specialist and author of a standard work on mental disorders. In 1918 Hodgson wrote to Marsh: "Wife broken down with terrible illness – mental – haven't written anything in army and mind's not been my own since." In February 1920 Dolly died. It is clear from comments made by Hodgson's sister and others that Dolly's last days were painful and frightening (" ... thankful that poor little Dolly has been spared more suffering ... her poor little face at that awful Camberwell ... " wrote one of her closest friends). James Stephens wrote to Marsh: "Given all the circumstances, it is better that an intolerable state of things should end somehow." For Hodgson, the four years of Dolly's illness, compounded by the deaths of his eldest brother (in South Africa) and his mother in 1919, plus the breakdown of his sister Josey, were grim ones, and the good fortune of others must have seemed bitter indeed.

If Fraser failed to extend enough of a helping hand that may have been Hodgson's justification to himself for dropping his *Flying Fame* collaborator so surprisingly, although it seems unlikely. Fraser was an open-hearted, kindly man, and appears bewildered by Hodgson's reactions. There could be no cynicism or laughing off the breach. In 1920 he wrote in his diary, "It was a privilege to have known him and, coming as it did in the most critical days of my life, his friendship was of infinite value in forming high ideals and noble tastes." Fraser had, if not worshipped Hodgson, then regarded him with deep affection and admiration. Once, on holiday in Italy, he had scattered the ashes of a 'Song of Honour' chapbook in the gardens where Shelley had written 'Ode to the West Wind' – "a piece of unmitigated sentimentality. RH called me an ass for doing it but was quite pleased nevertheless." From now on, however, for whatever reason, Fraser's only contact with Hodgson would be via the third member of the *Flying Fame* trio, Holbrook Jackson.

By this time Jackson had successfully overseen Hodgson's *Collected Poems* into print. It would seem that Hodgson began thinking of putting all his published poems together in book form some time in 1915, a factor, perhaps, in his decision to abandon *Flying Fame*. The idea of a collection was not particularly welcome to him, but he wanted to ensure that no one, Americans in particular, pirated any of his pieces.

Throughout his life he would be obsessed with controlling his copyright and, possessing no business sense at all, he was unsure of contractual procedures and disliked contact with publishing houses. Requests would come in for his work and he would remain anxious about what granting permission actually implied. Hodgson therefore enlisted Holbrook Jackson, then preparing to relaunch his paper *T.P.'s Weekly* as *Today*, to act as editor and agent.

By October 1916 Hodgson was writing, "It is damned good of you, old boy, to take all this trouble," and sending him copies of the new poems that would complete the collection. In fact it was hardly a new collection at all. Apart from 'The Bride' (1915), 'The Royal Mails' (1914), 'Babylon' (1914), and 'The House across the Way' (1914) all 21 poems had appeared in *The Saturday Review* or *Flying Fame* (or both) in the years before the war.

It cannot be said that Jackson was overwhelmed with publishing offers. Macmillan in London showed some interest in late 1915 but stalled. Yale University Press seemed keen, and Methuen Press, following an exchange of letters with Holbrook Jackson, thought they had a formal agreement. E.V. Lucas was on the Methuen board and was a close friend of Hodgson's. He already had most of the poems in draft form and had talked to Hodgson at length about the project, but Jackson disliked the terms offered and, not without some acrimony, took up an offer from Macmillan in New York instead. They were keener, for some reason, than their British counterparts but once the Americans had signed a contract, the British also came on board.

The terms Jackson was able to secure were poor, however. Rejecting a request for a bigger percentage, Macmillan in New York wrote in November 1916: "Twenty percent is not only the highest rate we pay even to any of the poets on our list as, for example, Mr Masefield, but it is the highest rate of royalty we pay even to the most popular novelists whose books we publish in very large editions." Hodgson would thus get ten percent, and an advance of £20. "While we hope to do very well with Mr Hodgson's poems, you will realise that he is as yet almost totally unknown to our public."

Hodgson, writing from an anti-aircraft gun station somewhere in Essex and unable to get leave, complained of the "paltry advance" but acquiesced. "And you might ask them at least to send half a dozen copies to me with their regards. Oh Jackson, Jackson, my heart is breaking!"

When the *Poems* appeared in 1917, however, he had some reason to rejoice if he was in a mood to do so, which is doubtful. The collection quickly went through three editions in as many months and was reviewed and praised in *The Times,* the *Daily News, The Sphere*, and many more. The *Daily News* reviewer wrote of the collection: "It is a little book of delights which fully justifies his reputation. He has humour, fancy, a heart of goodness and a sense of the serious world." Lovat Fraser commented, "I am overjoyed to see such magnificent tributes to the muse of RH. I don't expect that they interest him personally at all, but we who have watched him all these years feel almost the reflected glory of it."

Hodgson's *Collected Poems* appeared in a year crowded with poetic milestones. Collections from Robert Nichols, Siegfried Sassoon, Robert Graves and Edward Thomas were also published in 1917. It was also the year in which Ezra Pound made moves to promote T.S. Eliot ('The Love Song of J. Alfred Prufrock' was published in a limited edition). Pound also promoted Wyndham Lewis, James Joyce and himself with articles in *The Egoist* and the *Little Review*. Attacks were mounted against 'rival' British journals and magazines; the poetic battle lines were becoming clearer, the criticism sharper and more personal.

Hodgson's collection received a great deal of attention, most of it laudatory as perhaps might have been expected. As a respected Georgian, his work appeared in *Georgian Poetry 3*, which came out in November 1917, where it attracted praise from poetic traditionalists who held most of the posts of critical authority. These included Henry Newbolt, Arthur Waugh, Nancy Royd Smith, Edmund Gosse, Holbrook Jackson and William Maas, one of the best of his old Fleet Street friends. He also attracted attention from a number of American editors in *The Nation*, the *Boston Evening Post*, *The Dial* – although the latter publication, though not noted for its 'radical' stance, would carry two of the most critical reviews Hodgson would ever receive.

For those who welcomed Hodgson's collection, such as Waugh, one of its most appealing characteristics was that it represented a bridge between poetic old and new. As Waugh put it, Hodgson was neither a "plunging slap-dash Georgian" nor one of the "Cockney" school. Instead, he was an artist working with three main themes: the pathetic passage of time, the tragedy of human sacrifice and melancholy resignation at growing old.

The 'younger school' wanted no truck with the past, Waugh asserted, "but Mr Hodgson's 'Muse' is more than half in love with it and hates to see its stones disturbed." He refers to 'Babylon' and 'Time, You Old Gypsy Man' and makes the point:

> The metrical beauty of the poem is indisputable, the refrain haunts the memory and yet the effect is obtained without the least concession to the jingling melodies of a cheap popularity. Idea and expression are indissolubly wedded and at the same moment the old and the new schools of thought are brought into a swift spiritual alliance.

The Times Literary Supplement – always a Hodgson champion – was equally convinced of his importance and relevance. He was a Georgian and thus modern, but

> he avoids the worst pitfalls of ultra-modernism, handling his common materials so that the result never strikes us as merely tame or flat or merely startling or repulsive. His measures are never ugly or tuneless; they are never even so much as rhymeless in obedience to one prevailing fashion of the day. In matters of form, Mr Hodgson does not so much avoid or break with tradition as impose upon traditional modes of verse a new and personal spirit which varies and reanimates them,

while at times his work moved close to plain prose.

The critical comment in other journals played variously on these themes. It emphasised his skill, his dexterity within traditional forms, his assertions of courage, health and high instincts. He was not 'defiant', preferring to try and make the most of an imperfect world. In that sense, he was reassuring, and he seemed to prove a number of points both ideological and popular which those then under the cosh of Pound and the emerging Modernists wished to see proved. As the *Athenaeum* critic wrote: "His work is withdrawn from the emulation of the intellect and the warfare of the coteries." And the *Observer* critic went so far as to claim that Hodgson's poems were "the most remarkable poetic achievement since the publication of Mr Yeats' early volume, immensely superior to Imagists, Vorticists, Futurists – as well as Gibson, Drinkwater, Abercrombie and Brooke ... "

The reaction to all this praise, if reaction is the correct word to use, came via two pieces written by Conrad Aiken and John Gould Fletcher respectively in the American *Dial* magazine. Both men were poets, both American and both had strong contacts with the newer, radical movement centred on the Imagists. Aiken had actually introduced T.S. Eliot to Ezra Pound and would be concerned to promote a more subjective, psychological approach to verse, the 'stream of consciousness' method. Fletcher was older, an exile from Arkansas with money to support himself. He was an original Imagist but had developed a dislike of Ezra Pound, who had manipulated and upset him.

Both men saw Hodgson as a representative of things redundant in verse, and they used their reviews of his collection to make broader points. Aiken was concerned with the essential difference between American and English poetry, and his piece also included a consideration of Walter de la Mare and Harold Monro. There was much to admire about Hodgson, he felt, although his was a "limited range", a "single tone", a "simple melody", aligned with a gift for modulation "to carry him over inversions that to others would have proved fatal". Turning to what Hodgson had to say, rather than how he had chosen to say it, Aiken again remained general. Hodgson's mood was clear, nothing was wasted, a "cool magic" was woven through it all, "plus a twinkle of whim". Hodgson was vigorous, naïve, honest and matter-of-fact, but what he lacked was a "personal or psychological standpoint". He never, according to Aiken, spoke in his own voice and the "greater part of human experience remained unexpressed". Hodgson's poetry was "not a window to see through, but a picture on the wall ... He never strikes us through our emotions."

Fletcher, devoting a whole piece to Hodgson's verse some months later, took up the baton and carried it to the finishing line. To Fletcher's mind, Hodgson was simply a "conscientious, painstaking writer who believes he is following the true path", but all he was doing, consciously or unconsciously, was aping earlier, greater works. 'Eve' was simply a derivative of Robert Herrick; 'The Bull' of William Blake; and 'The Song of Honour' a transcription of Christopher Smart's 'The Song to David'. 'The Royal Mails', one of the few new poems in the collection, was "a poem of Wordsworth's, but out of time". He hastened to add that he was not impugning Hodgson's honesty but insisted that Hodgson was just a typical example of one tendency in present-day English poetry, a "refusal to grow, to move on", a tendency that "no longer draws its nourishment out of life but out of libraries".

It was probably the hardest attack on Hodgson in print and, amid the general chorus of praise, hardly noticed. It was significant, given the two critics' sympathies and allegiances to certain 'progressive' groups. Neither critic dealt with, or seemed interested in *what* Hodgson was actually saying, only with *how* he said things and, by implication, what he *didn't* or perhaps couldn't say.

By then, in 1917, most of Hodgson's work was from an earlier time with the exception of four new poems. Attractive and interesting as these were, they added little to the canon. 'The Royal Mails', an allegory set in a medieval wood, tells of a messenger (an artist) who allows himself to be robbed of his mails/message (inspiration) by robbers (fame and fortune). Hodgson told Fraser it was about an artist's failure of nerve, but he admitted that he wasn't really sure of its merits. 'The House across the Way' is much better: at its centre a shattered human being, who admits that

> In a gambol
> I took my soul astray,
> But tomorrow I'll drag it back from danger,

but dies before he can do so, slumped at a table, the principal image being
> … the leaves stared in at the window
> Like the people at a play.

'Babylon' is an extension of his little three-liner from *Flying Fame*: "Babylon where I go dreaming". In this piece, he pleads with archaeologists to leave the sunken city where it is and not disturb its remains, not to "catalogue and pigeonhole" but to "leave the dead men's dust alone". 'The Bride' betrays one of Hodgson's hobbies, that of looking at old photograph albums and allowing his imagination free reign to wonder at the faces that stare out and imagine who they actually were. He was fascinated by genealogy and ancestry, by racial memory and its growth. 'The Bride' in question he sees quite suddenly ("I never stopped so startled/Inside a book before") and is instantly drawn towards her musing on her life and her courtship ("The hugging in the barn/You brazens both of you!/I nearly burst out crying/With thinking of you two").

The *Collected Poems* propelled Hodgson into a limelight he both disliked and yet, one suspects, secretly revelled in. The ensuing interest in his personal affairs, however, he really could *not* understand, even raising objections when Holbrook Jackson asked him for his place of birth, wondering why on earth anyone would want to know it. Nevertheless, he found himself increasingly in the company of literary and artistic celebrities of all kinds: Nigel Playfair, the producer, wanted Hodgson to write songs for a review, and John Galsworthy wrote to express his "unequalled, unparalleled admiration for your poems". They met for dinner with their wives, and Galsworthy later commiserated with Hodgson over Dolly's "neuritis" which, he revealed, troubled his wife too. Edward Marsh asked him if he'd like to come to a "reading of poets and their work" at Elizabeth Asquith's (daughter of the former prime minister) who had specially asked for Hodgson, though Marsh added, "I don't suppose you would care about it." Princess Beatrice, and aunt of the king, invited him to the Palace for a private reading of his verse, and, most bizarrely of all, he was contacted by Olive Custance, poetess and wife of Lord Alfred Douglas ('Bosie'), Oscar Wilde's fateful lover.

She wrote to invite him to her home, complaining as she did so about her husband: "It's not been possible to please him; yet I seem to please so many other people." She wanted to know all about Hodgson and "to ask all sorts of things children ask of their new friends", his birthday, what he looked like, whether he was married … At home, she revealed, "I dance, and laugh and dream and read books. Cry, tie a blue bow in my hair and laugh again!" Hodgson replied to her many letters, but whether he took Lady Alfred up on her offer of a visit is unknown.

Perhaps, after all, it was fortunate that he had 'lost contact' with Lovat Fraser by this time: Fraser noted in his diary for 1920:

> Mrs Spencer Watson, Holland Park Road, some sort of concert. A strange woman dressed in what seemed to be overalls with green pigs all over them. Thin and gawky as a ramrod. Then a woman dressed improbably sang with a voice like a corn-crake 'Holiness' by Drinkwater and RH's 'With Love among the Haycocks'. They had cut his last two lines and inserted whatever they thought fit – a perfectly senseless sort of 'Yo Heave Ho!' chorus. The result was too comic for words. With love among the haycocks, we played at hide and seek (Gone away O! gone away O!). Children sort of 'sensed' (the correct word I'm sure) the poem by jumping about in front of the singer … How RH would have writhed to see it!

15

Cast Adrift

You have lost the bravest, most faithful friend a man could have.
(Edie Hodgson, Ralph Hodgson's sister to Ralph Hodgson, February 1920)

Dolly's death in February 1920 more or less completed the dismantling of Hodgson's world as he had understood it before the War. Aged forty-eight, he now had no job, no permanent home (all his furniture and his vast library were in store), and with no one to act as guardian of the dogs and hearth, he drifted disconsolately among friends and relatives. Hodgson had by then moved out of the King's Road flat he and Dolly had occupied since 1914 and lived in a bachelor room lent to him by a friend at the Adelphi Gallery, close by Cleopatra's Needle on the Victoria Embankment. This was really no more than a series of garrets in a small grid of streets designed in the 1780s by the Adam brothers. It was close to Hodgson's working haunts in Fleet Street and a short walk from the Constitutional Club, where an old wartime colleague, Tom Stephenson, worked as doorman. Close by were the offices of Holbrook Jackson's literary paper *Today*. Thus Hodgson was easily found by friends, colleagues and the many ladies ready to lend a hand. Harold Monro's wife, Alida, cooked him meals; Enid Bagnold coaxed him out to restaurants "for consolation and laughter"; the poetess Nancy Royd Smith invited him for tea and talk of dogs. When he took a short holiday in Christchurch in late 1920 he was accompanied by a doting young art-student and ultimately lifelong friend, Sylvia Baker.

Eventually he left the Adelphi for rooms in Richmond and then for lodgings in Hampstead in the house of J. Douglas Young, a lawyer, prospective Parliamentary candidate and future High Court judge in India. The two men had met through the revived Plumage Group Campaign instituted by H.J. Massingham in 1921. Young's house in Middleton Avenue, Golders Green on the fringe of the fast developing Hampstead Garden Suburb was a complete contrast to his bachelor 'digs'.

Here he led the life of a favourite uncle amid Young's young family, befriending their friends, including a dashing young tennis-player called Christabel Hardie, the "Elsie Glee" of her day as Hodgson once described her. Thus there followed a summer of tennis tournaments at the Hurlingham Club, trips to their holiday cottage in Finchley and rambles across the Heath in a highbrow, middle-class milieu. It served as a healing time and a counter to his depressive, introspective tendency.

Two other good friends were important to him at this time. Firstly, Edward Marsh was on hand to offer words of comfort both before and after Dolly's illness, and he also provided much-needed money by way of royalties from *Georgian Poetry 2* and *3*. He introduced Hodgson to stimulating characters like the famous society hostess Sybil Colefax, the painter Paul Nash and, in October 1919, to T.E. Lawrence (of Arabia).

Marsh wrote: "You will like [Lawrence] enormously. Will you dine on Thursday, 20th at the Ivy Restaurant opposite the Ambassadors?" For some six weeks or so before Lawrence left London, he and Hodgson met to talk and laugh and spend money. One day Lawrence called on him at the Adelphi saying he was "stinking with money" and wanted Hodgson's help to spend it. Lawrence's aversion to fame, and his personal secrecy must have appealed to Hodgson. Lawrence's later conduct – joining the RAF as a lowly aircraftsman – was described by Hodgson to a friend as "backing into the limelight". In fact, they got on famously, and Lawrence pressed Ezra Pound to include some of Hodgson's work in a magazine he was putting together. Pound expressed a liking for Hodgson himself, but found his poems boring.

Hodgson's second good friend during this trying time was the ever-loyal Holbrook Jackson who continued to handle Hodgson's finances and publishing affairs. Jackson played a large part in the new Plumage Campaign, and he urged Hodgson to write a poetic oddity, a curious diatribe called 'A Hymn to Moloch' that Jackson published privately in a limited edition in 1921. But it would be Jackson's paper *Today* that offered the main means by which Hodgson kept in touch with literary affairs and, tentatively, with his own faint poetic muse.

His specific literary activity will be considered presently. His main activity during these years, was talking, and Jackson's bringing together of Hodgson and the young Australian poet and music critic W.J. Turner was inspirational. Turner was making a name for himself in the early 1920s and knew many of the younger poets, like Siegfried Sassoon and Robert Graves. In fact, Sassoon had rooms in Turner's Tufton Street home in Westminster, and it was here that Hodgson would first meet the controversial war poet whose temperament and poetic vision so perfectly chimed with his own.

Hodgson greatly admired Turner's poetry and urged Jackson to publish as much of it as he could, Turner being "the real thing": "Get Turner to contribute liberally – poems, not poetical exercises which are abominable things and have no connection with t'other, or little. I admire him beyond any of the men writing – the newer men, I mean."

Turner was a great talker and Hodgson swiftly established a routine, visiting Turner's house each Friday evening without fail. Sassoon recorded in his journal that Hodgson, over a three-year period from 1921 to 1924 "would have been here 150 times and have smoked at least 1,000 pipes on our premises". Hodgson remarked that the visits were "something in my life which nothing could have replaced". They were, in fact, a precursor of the famous gathering dubbed the "Thursdayers". This was a group of like-minded, garrulous male intellectuals who met in restaurants and homes during the 1920s and 1930s, membership of which august circle Hodgson prized highly.

Hodgson was adamant, however, that his poetic 'muse' had fled, and although he was present at the Adelphi Buildings in 1919 at a dinner hosted by Marsh to mark the publication of Rupert Brooke's *Collected Poems* as well as to 're-establish' the Georgian fraternity, he was not an active player in the ensuing poetic squabbles. His lack of output meant he would not be included in any subsequent Georgian anthologies and would thus escape the opprobrium heaped upon the other contributors' heads by modernist critics.

He was, in fact, by this time admired and respected in many normally antagonistic corners. Robert Graves was keen on his work. 'The Bull', he thought, epitomised the true strengths of the pre-war Georgian movement. A succession of young poets including Edmund Blunden, John Drinkwater, John Freeman and Siegfried Sassoon looked to him for advice and approbation; and requests for his work to appear in anthologies and collections continued to arrive steadily.

Perhaps Hodgson's attachment to *Today* was understandable, given that Holbrook Jackson's paper probably veered more towards the Georgians than any other group. *Today* in fact was be the last English journal to publish a new poem by Hodgson. Apart from 'A Hymn to Moloch', Hodgson submitted 'Silver Wedding', his lament for Dolly, which appeared in June 1921 on the twenty-fifth anniversary of their marriage. It is short and simple. The poet hears his wife talking in her sleep saying:

> 'Want me and take me
> For the woman that I am
> And not for her that died,
> The lovely chit nineteen
> I one time was,
> And am no more.'

In his remorse, the poet realises that hers was, "a heart he'd never searched, / Nay hardly seen inside ..."

Apart from that, his only contribution to *Today*'s columns was a small collection of snatches of cockney conversations overheard in the street. One of his abiding interests ever since his cartooning days, was a technique of recording conversation borrowed from Phil May, who was a past master at capturing amusing malapropisms to which he would provide brilliant illustrations. But even about these small pieces Hodgson wrote to Jackson, "When you use those little street conversations, don't use my name."

However, if Hodgson's creative output had ground almost to a halt, other aspects of his life were starting to revive. In November 1920 at a gathering at Alida Monro's flat just nine months after Dolly's death, Hodgson met Muriel Fraser, a Canadian by birth, who had been brought up in the United States. A friend of the Turners and of the artist and Royal College of Art principal William Rothenstein, she was dark-haired, in her mid-thirties, well educated, artistically inclined and by all accounts, strikingly attractive.

The following Monday they lunched together in Chelsea and Hodgson admitted to her, "You have me in the grips and I cannot get away". In December, Muriel travelled home to Canada to see her family and did not return until the following May. Hodgson wrote a series of letters to her, often as regularly as five times a week, passionate, urgent letters that clearly impressed her. They were married on 1st June 1921 at Holy Trinity Church, Brompton.

Curiously, that other Fraser in Hodgson's life, his ex-colleague Lovat, died only a few weeks later, on 18th June. A well-attended service at St Mary, The Boltons in South Kensington was held on 24th June but there is no evidence that Hodgson was there. In fact, by then he was on honeymoon with his new wife, oblivious to the world.

From the testimony of friends we know that Muriel was independent-minded and, by her own admission, perhaps a little vain. Despite being in awe of Hodgson as a writer, however, she would come to understand almost nothing about him as a man. An inkling of the trouble ahead can be spotted in correspondence passing between H.J. Massingham, who knew Muriel socially, and Holbrook Jackson. Massingham wonders whether Muriel will be able to cope with Hodgson. In 1921, he writes to Jackson from Cornwall where the Hodgsons were on what turned out to be an extra-long honeymoon of almost three months:

> They are perfectly happy but there's an end to all wifely ambition. 'Hog' [as Hodgson was known to friends] has won hand and fist; the master of the field and surpasses even himself in laziness. As for Muriel, I can't detect any regrets at her defeat; she's evidently one of your learners and is content to be dominated by the masterly inactivity of RH.

Massingham wasn't quite so sanguine some months later when he again wrote to Jackson asking for his help with a poem he'd hoped Hodgson would allow him to use in an anthology of bird poems. Hodgson had worked himself up into a state bordering on hysteria over the poem's copyright and the possible 'stealing' of rights. He'd at first agreed, then changed his mind, thus upsetting Massingham, who regarded Hodgson's verse as the centrepiece of his anthology ("There is no pretending that 'To Deck a Woman' isn't the text and point and essence and consummation of the whole").

Muriel had been dragged into the dispute as letter-writer, and Massingham commented, "Poor Muriel, she's got a bit of a handful with RH", at the same time adding, "it is about time RH ended his honeymoon and that the pair of them got a breath of the real world again ..."

When the Hodgsons finally returned to London, the problem of money quickly raised its head, for neither of them had a job, Hodgson because he didn't really want one and Muriel because Hodgson didn't want her to have one. At fifty, Hodgson remained determined not to have to earn a living from journalism or writing prose. However, in his hour of financial need, he turned to his hard-working and resourceful brother Walter, whose commercial art business, the Byron Studios, near Farringdon Road, employed a score of commercial artists and illustrators to supply Fleet Street with cartoon strips and art work of all kinds.

A great deal of Hodgson's days during this time appeared to have been spent, somewhat to his chagrin, working in and around the Studios. Walter even rented him a little room above a teashop nearby where he could be alone. Hodgson's nephew Clive and elder brother Walker would then scour the streets in search of wood or boxes to burn in his small grate. Thus Hodgson's habit of disappearing to escape into some private secure space as he used to do at Fraser's studio in Kensington before the war, continued.

Walter also lent Hodgson small sums of money when he could; he was, in fact, already paying for the storage of most of Hodgson's original household effects. In return, Hodgson made various attempts to devise schemes that might make the Studios some money. There was a projected cartoon series involving the Grenadier Guards: Hodgson seems to have spent some weeks watching them parade outside St James's Palace, but the idea refused to take off. He then proposed a cartoon double act similar to those found in *Big Budget*, a detective duo called 'Tec and Towser'. The idea, involving a lovable dog, seemed so promising that Walter felt it might translate onto the screen as a film cartoon of the kind becoming increasingly popular in the fast-growing cinema industry.

In order to develop this, the two brothers transferred operations to East Finchley, to Dunoon, their mother's private school, still in operation but run now by the two spinster sisters, Josey and May. Close by Dunoon, Walter rented an empty house with a big enough bathroom to house a large wooden tread wheel to wash the finished film. He also recruited a team of unemployed artists to produce the hundreds of sketches needed. It was a suburban cottage industry that grew and grew but ultimately collapsed through lack of finance. Walter simply ran out of money and, according to his son Barrie, "the enterprise finished in a gigantic pyre of artwork, miles of film, drawing-boards, drying drums ..."

By 1923, however, Hodgson could avoid the call of Fleet Street no longer. Whether as a favour to Walter, or under pressure from Muriel, he took a job as a parliamentary sketcher for Newnes *Westminster Gazette*, adopting the pseudonym of Edward Southe when applying for a press pass. Thus, through the early months of 1923, Ralph Hodgson sat in the Press Gallery of the House of Commons drawing the prominent and the not-so-prominent political actors of the day. Herbert Asquith and Oswald Mosley, William Joynson-Hicks and Ramsay MacDonald, Philip Snowden and Lloyd George himself.

It was an interlude in his life that he wanted no one of significance to know about. In fact, he reacted furiously on one occasion when Massingham innocently asked him in company if he was still working for the *Gazette*. After three months, he refused to sign the contract tying him to the job for a couple of years – and he returned to the days of idleness and contemplation.

It's clear, however, that despite his protestations that he was content to await his Muse while avoiding the corrosive influence of Fleet Street drudgery, he was increasingly unhappy with his situation. He was intermittently scraping a living at the Byron Studios and at the same being welcomed into the houses and exclusive circles of literary and artistic

Ralph Hodgson's Parliamentary Gallery sketch, 2nd March 1923

London. There were, however, moments of sublime consolation, as when he received an invitation to spend a few days with the poet laureate, Robert Bridges, a man he admired immensely.

Bridges had written in July 1923 to invite him to his home at Boar's Hill, Oxford: "No entertainment but the countryside is pleasant," he wrote. It was fine weather when Bridges met Hodgson at the station and the two of them walked to Bridges' home across the fields. It was a visit that thrilled Hodgson. As he told Siegfried Sassoon a few days later, "The day went like lightning" and to students some twenty years later he revealed that he had felt himself to be "in the presence of history":

> To have known such a man was worth a lifetime on this hazardous planet; nothing small or meagre physically or mentally or spiritually, one of the truest of poets and a grand human being: a tremendous discoverer and enjoyer of beauty in life: as simple-hearted as William Davies himself.

Entering his fifty-third year, Hodgson was facing painful choices. Then, quite by chance, an opportunity arose. In June 1923, Saito, a visiting professor of English from Tokyo University, came to London and Siegfried Sassoon took him to lunch at the Reform Club. Takeshi Saito was familiar with Hodgson's poetry, and when they met later that evening at W.J. Turner's Tufton Street home, he revealed that he had translated 'Time, You Old Gypsy Man' into Japanese. Saito would subsequently spend many happy hours at the Baker Street flat Hodgson and Muriel were then renting and found him a "master-mind of versatile knowledge … and an extraordinarily brilliant talker".

Saito was at that point on the look-out for someone to replace Robert Nichols as professor of English at the University of Tokyo. Hodgson recommended Edmund Blunden and brought the two men together one evening.

Hodgson and Blunden had got to know one another soon after the First World War when Blunden's poetry had been included in *Georgian Poetry 5*. As early as 1920 Hodgson had been advising him on his verse. Blunden wrote to him in August of that year, enclosing a collection of verse entitled *The Waggoner* that would establish Blunden's reputation: "I owe you a long score – for encouragement and for setting my feet (like the Psalmist) in a large room."

The two men had a lot in common. Blunden was then working on the recently discovered papers of John Clare and had clearly learnt much from Hodgson about the poet. In 1921, for instance, he asked Hodgson to write an article for the *Athenaeum* on Clare. The two men were soon close enough friends to indulge in a private world of 'in-jokes'. They also shared a bookish, antiquarian relish for obscure and overlooked detail, their imaginations drifting along similar byways. In 1922, when Blunden was working on a history of Christ's Hospital, his old school, the two men earnestly discussed and reflected on the records Blunden had discovered of Charles II's Mathematical School, which detailed the destinations and subsequent fates of pupils bound to ships as midshipmen and cabin boys. Finally Hodgson contributed an endpaper illustration to Blunden's book *The Bonaventure*, a record of the latter's recuperative trip on a tramp steamer to Argentina.

Blunden's emotional life during the early 1920s was in turmoil as his marriage was difficult and increasingly troubled. Hodgson became a confidant of both Blunden and his wife Mary, and helped them find lodgings in Cricklewood, in northwest London, when they were evicted from their Northampton home. In 1922 both were frequent supper guests at Hodgson's flat in Baker Street, where Blunden studied Hodgson's library. Blunden wrote:

> It was an education. The out-of-the-way books which contained some genuine idea or information, had been seized upon by him with radiance. It was to him another clue to the past, the present, the future, on all of which he would sometimes talk with prophetic power past midnight.

While Blunden pondered on the Japanese job offer, a colleague of Saito's, Kochi Doi, professor of the newly-established Department of English at Tohoku University in Sendai in northern Japan, asked Saito to help in finding a visiting professor for *his* university. Saito suggested Hodgson, who at first turned the idea down, explaining that he wasn't an academic, he was "simply a poet, and for a poet a crow in the sky is more than a pile of books, which a professor ought to peruse whether he likes them or not." Both Doi and Saito emphasised that they were not looking for academics ("Professor Dry-as-Dusts" as they termed it). Rather, they were after people who might ignite in their students a passion for literature. Within a month, after being given assurances by Doi that he would be allowed much greater freedom from academic formalities than normal, he reconsidered. In fact, he turned to Blunden, declaring that he would take up the post in Sendai if Blunden agreed to go to Tokyo. As Blunden later put it, "He didn't want to go without some literary companion and he just decided that we got on well." Blunden, anxious for personal reasons to change his circumstances, also agreed to take the plunge.

Hodgson's departure was quite an event, dominated by his nervous, bewildered, preoccupied state. When Siegfried Sassoon arrived at Waterloo Station to bid him farewell on the boat train, he encountered Walter de la Mare also looking anxiously for Hodgson. He and Hodgson had been having a vehement discussion about religion, but when it was discovered that there had been a mistake about Hodgson's carriage (he'd paid for first class and been put in a third), Hodgson had rushed off to the booking office to get a refund.

Sassoon, de la Mare, Holbrook Jackson, Mrs Rothenstein and her daughter, Professor Saito, W.J. Turner and his wife Delphine, along with Hodgson's brother Walter with his children – all waited anxiously for Hodgson to reappear. Sassoon recalled:

> ... at the carriage door, Mrs Hodgson leant out, holding a small bunch of red rambler roses. Whistles blew. Doors slammed. Fifty seconds before the start RH appeared at a shambling trot, and as he appeared I felt protective and pitying; he looked so middle-aged and ill and rattled. 'Don't hurry, don't hurry,' I exclaimed putting my hands on his shoulders and steering him toward his carriage door. Then he was up and inside and leaning out and everyone was shaking his hand and ejaculating good wishes ... The train drew slowly out and we waved him away to Japan with our hats. Turner and I and de la Mare walked sedately down the platform. 'How funny, old Hoddy going off like that,' remarked de la Mare.

Ironically, in view of what was to come, one of the last things that Sassoon and de la Mare heard from Hodgson as the train pulled away was a defiant parting shot from the carriage window, Hodgson snapping his fingers and calling, "I don't care *that* for your old thug Jehovah!"

16

Japanese Ordeal

Never go to Japan, Jack, it's only an ugly gimcrack place, all volcanoes and bamboo hat-stands. I hate bamboo and Japanese novels and cunning Japanese faces.

(John Freeman, 1927)

In 1924 Sendai was a small city of some 150,000 inhabitants, capital of Tohoku region, 300 kilometres north of Tokyo on Japan's main island. 'The City of Trees' as it was known, lay in the centre of Miyagi Province, an agricultural region concentrating chiefly on forestry, fishing, beef and rice. Bounded on three sides by mountain ranges and on the fourth by the Pacific ocean, it had very hot summers and very cold winters. Tohoku University had been founded in 1907, the English department as recently as 1923, so that Hodgson was the faculty's first 'visiting professor'. The couple arrived at the end of August to be greeted at Kobe port by Professor Kochi Doi.

They travelled by train to Tokyo where Edmund Blunden was waiting, having arrived some three months earlier. A few days later they entrained again for the trip north to Sendai, Hodgson's luggage consisting of ten boxes of books and Joseph, a crippled magpie that he had nursed back to health and could not bear to leave in England. Despite the warm welcome, it must have been a severe culture shock when the couple finally settled in Sendai. Even Doi admitted that the town itself consisted of

> an army division, schools and colleges and a university plus a settlement of American missionaries. These latter lived by themselves, building their houses in the American style, baking their bread in their own way and living as if they were in their homeland. The soldiers formed their own colony but the university members, who were the newest residents in Sendai, could not form their own society and they still felt themselves to be strangers to the city and to themselves.

The Hodgsons were billeted temporarily with an American missionary couple while their own house was being prepared. A woman student called

Mrs O'Hara, who encountered them soon after they arrived, recorded her thoughts in a diary:

> It was three o'clock in the afternoon and raining heavily. Hodgson, when I first met him, looked very gentle and soft and old, though with strong muscular features ... his features were not those of a handsome man like Robert Nichols; he looked somewhat like a monkey but his big expressive eyes were very impressive. He received me very warmly. He was not moody at all, but very kind and cheerful.
>
> He never put his pipe aside even for a moment. Mrs Hodgson offered me cigarettes and lit one for herself. When she started to complain, 'I only smoke three cigarettes a day. The cigarettes we could buy at seven yen in England cost fifty yen in Japan with a luxury tax ...' Hodgson said, 'Will you stop such gloomy talk on a rainy day like this?' and changed the topic. A famous bird-lover, he said, 'Mrs O'Hara, do you know anything about the songbirds in Sendai?'
>
> In due time Mr Kanaya suggested we leave and I hurriedly stood up in case he left without me, as it was raining. Mr Hodgson offered to get a jinrikisha but I declined and when I walked out of the door I felt relieved. In less than two minutes I heard Mr Hodgson calling, 'Mrs O'Hara!' Looking back, good gracious, I found him running after us in the pouring rain with his raincoat on but no hat, swinging over his head the handbag I had left behind, saying, 'I'm sorry! I'm sorry!' He ran in the pouring rain leaning forward, smiling and repeating, 'I'm sorry!' I was so confused and could only repeat, 'Thank you,' again and again. I was so sorry for him that I wished I could hide somewhere ...

As Kochi Doi observed, though Hodgson never learned Japanese

> He had the wonderful art of making himself understood by any Japanese [person] with his charming gestures and, when driven by necessity, he drew pictures very quickly. He refused to think of himself as living in a stranger's land or of himself as a stranger. He talked quite honestly and unreservedly with anyone, expressing his anxiety about the increasing militarism of nations, or discussing such problems as fundamentalism, etc. In contrast to her husband, Mrs Hodgson could not feel so at home. She could find no congenial friends and seemed to suffer from the dreariness of life. She missed the cordial society of London and it was soon feared that she would become neurotic if she stayed in Sendai ...

Doi's remarks tell only part of the story. Both Hodgson and Muriel were struggling to cope with the strange new campus life in Japan, a struggle exacerbated by a language neither could understand and a people who, though polite and kind, were also distant and not a little bemused by Western ways. Muriel, in fact, always felt she was like an insect beneath a magnifying glass, watched by countless unseen eyes.

Hodgson began to suffer badly from his perennial complaint of haemorrhoids, for which he'd been operated on just before leaving England. He, therefore, refused to sightsee or travel when not teaching. Muriel found herself cooped up in the faculty house day after day with nothing but back numbers of *Vogue* to flip through, a gramophone and some records to play, cigarettes to smoke and the odd servant boy to chat to – and all the while the rain poured down outside.

Thus stranded, the couple's always unlikely relationship began to unravel. In Sendai, there was nowhere to go and no one to talk to. Hodgson, one of nature's loners, was capable of enduring what others might consider to be social isolation; he had his own interior world into which he could retreat when not in the classroom. As Hugh Massingham had suspected much earlier, Hodgson demanded from his wife a reciprocal devotion to personal privacy, along with a merging of personalities and almost total adaptation to his attitudes and tastes. He had assumed she would share his need for seclusion as well as his rather odd sense of what he termed "contamination" when coming into contact with people and ideas he disliked. Not surprisingly, the notion that Muriel would not only retreat with him, accept his world view and adopt his patterns of behaviour, but would also work to provide a comfortable situation for him, soon proved unacceptable to her.

There had been earlier warnings of Hodgson's jealousy when emotionally committed to someone, in this case his new wife. His passionate declarations of love and devotion poured into letters written to Muriel during an earlier trip home to Canada were prized by her, but one is inclined to think she did not fully understand their import. She once commented to a friend that Hodgson had threatened to kill or "mark" anyone who made overtures to her. She regarded such declarations as flattery.

But Muriel had no resources of her own with which to cope with the situation in which they found themselves. She reacted to his outbursts of anger and deepening mental distress by mocking him and goading him into rages. Her tactics were a disaster.

There were increasingly violent arguments late into the night, the drama rendered almost tragi-comic by the presence in their midst of the manic magpie, Joseph, in an enormous cage placed in the centre of the living-room, According to a Japanese student, Joseph was

> neither pretty nor interesting nor had it a beautiful singing voice. Instead it squawked incomprehensible greetings day and night

and bit anyone foolish enough to reach into the cage and touch it. One mad midnight it succeeded in tearing a piece of flesh from Hodgson's finger when he was feeding it; Hodgson ran about the house in a fury, waving the bloodied index at Muriel in glee and pain.

Edmund Blunden, meanwhile, though hardly in the best of emotional states, had gradually built a tolerable life for himself in Tokyo. He had found a job for the poet William Plomer, who had been passing through Tokyo and who would provide intellectual companionship. He started a literary journal and he buckled down to the task of teaching English literature to largely uncomprehending pupils. He also started to write poems as well as large portions of what would turn out to be a classic memoir, *Undertones of War*.

Inevitably, however, he would be drawn into the maelstrom of the Hodgsons' chaotic life in Sendai just a couple of hour's train ride to the north. He made regular trips to see Hodgson to talk about poetry and books and to reminisce about England, but he increasingly found himself acting as a referee and go-between in the marital rows. Muriel frequently fled to Tokyo where she would pour out her worries and complaints to Blunden. So often was she in his company that Blunden's wife in England, Mary, suspected he was having an affair. Unfortunately for Mary, he *was* having an affair, but not with Muriel.

In March 1926 Hodgson was still ill and suffering from nervous exhaustion while Muriel was facing a trip back to Canada to see her ailing mother. Blunden was prevailed upon to stay and nurse Hodgson. Muriel left Sendai in April after just eighteen months; she would never return. She went first to Winnipeg, where she found that her mother had died; she then travelled to New York and got a job in Brentano's Bookshop. Intriguingly, Louis Untermeyer, later a great champion of Hodgson's verse, remembered being served by her there.

In May Hodgson sent her some money and condolences over her mother, but it wasn't until later in the year that he wrote anything at length. He then suggested that they might attempt to rebuild their lives together somewhere in Canada where, as he put it, Muriel's "undoubted gift for dress" could be used to help the "spread of fashion". He meanwhile could work in a school helping to advance "the aesthetic life" of young people. He advised her not think about living in a big city and not to consider returning to London.

Muriel, however, replied that she had no intentions of burying herself in some small town "somewhere between Ottawa and Montreal". At that point, the tone of Hodgson's letters changed, and though he mixed his harsher remarks with gestures of concern and compassion, it was clear that his mind was made up: they would not be reconciled, there would be no going back. He wrote to her: "For me, our separation of the last ten months has been a period of peace from a contentious, unteachable, relentless woman. I feel ten years younger for it."

Muriel had been cut adrift. In August 1927, Hodgson and Blunden, at this point still the best of friends, having finished their contracts, returned to England. Neither of them was alone, however. Blunden brought with him a Japanese woman, Miss Hayashi, with whom he had become emotionally entangled, who acted as his secretary and researcher. He would eventually leave her somewhat stranded. He returned to his wife, but when, some years later they divorced, he married someone else entirely.

Hodgson was also accompanied by a woman, a young American missionary teacher called Aurelia Bolliger whom he and Blunden had befriended in 1926. She was *en route* back to the USA where she was to study for a master's degree before returning to her religious work in Sendai. She stayed in Britain for three months, during which time Hodgson showed her London, introduced her to his friends and family and took her on sightseeing tours.

Muriel, having by now returned from America in order to discover exactly where she stood with Hodgson, would not learn about the mysterious Miss Bolliger until some years later. It was Edmund Blunden who suffered as unwitting buffer between the warring couple. Muriel, staying with the Rothensteins, bombarded Blunden with letters and threats. Blunden wrote to Hodgson:

> Mrs H has written to me two or three times but I do not know what I can say that would be of any benefit to either you or her. She says she is without support from you, but I imagine that can only be if you are yourself without means. She expresses the desire that you would let her have Joseph which I was pleased with, as it might lead to some better expression between you both …

Hodgson however, was clearly angry at Blunden's attempts at reconciliation. Blunden replied: "You mistake me when you feel I am trying to sound you re Muriel." However, Muriel was threatening to call him in evidence in a court case she was contemplating in order to win financial assistance from Hodgson. Furthermore she had letters in which Blunden had mentioned his Japanese companion, Miss Hayashi, "which she proposes to use, no doubt replies to her own letters but still the obvious means of dragging out much sad fact".

Blunden, in communicating Muriel's material demands (a list that included rugs, household linen such as pillows, a large lacquered tray, some silver that had been her mother's and, somewhat poignantly, Joseph the magpie), made it clear how upset he was at having been dragged in, suffering as he was from the strain of his *own* marital troubles: "I would stay altogether out of the question and would pay for the privilege if I could."

Eventually, Muriel fell ill and Hodgson relented. Visiting her at her Radcliffe Gardens flat, he told her that though they might remain friends, they would never live together again and that he was planning to return to Japan. They kept in touch over the next few months and, when Muriel went into hospital for an operation, he visited her daily until they quarrelled – according to Muriel because he had taken the love letters he'd written her and refused to return them. It was the last time they wrote or communicated until Muriel penned a final letter some thirty years later. The marriage eventually ended in 1933 when Muriel filed for divorce citing a woman called Phyllis Howe, with whom Hodgson, for the convenience of the letter of the law, was supposed to have spent a night at the Charing Cross Hotel.

Muriel eventually obtained a post with the Royal College of Art. Oddly, she became good friends with Sylvia Baker, a devotee of Hodgson's from the First World War. Sylvia would write to Hodgson in the 1950s suggesting he write to Muriel, who was then going blind. Hodgson declined to do so. Muriel never married again and retained her married name until her death in 1961. Hodgson's final rebuff (he never returned her precious letters) was to let Joseph free in Siegfried Sassoon's garden in Wiltshire. The bird lived happily for a year before falling out of the sky dead from what Sassoon guessed was a heart attack, Hodgson commenting, "a splendid death for that bird."

It was not only Muriel who would find herself cut out of Hodgson's world. When he eventually returned to Japan in September 1928 he did not bother to tell Blunden, who remained in England. He wrote to Takeshi Saito: "RH has disappeared from my world like a rocket. He kept his return very mysterious. He is offended with me but my conscience is clear. He likes, or rather his nature requires, to find offence where only goodness and service was intended. I bless him all the same." They could have been the words of Lovat Fraser. Years later, Blunden recalled Hodgson in verse with wry affection:

'The Last of the Fancy!' In Sendai!
Tales of John Roberts and C.B. Fry,
Pictures of Cruft's from knur and spell
To hunting the rare book! Hours speed well
When that enchanter pointed his pipe
At the visions of time, and enjoyed each type
He had gathered out of the nineties, he
The prize of them all to you and me.
Bull-terriers, boxing and poetry
Gallery and studio, zoology,

'Man's miry past,' and what will be,
All the birds in the world – all fantasy.
'The Last of the Fancy' – surely he charms
Still a few of his kind, with dogs under their arms.

Viewed from the outside, it seemed strange to many of his friends that Hodgson had, almost without hesitation, signed up for another three years in Japan. Few academics came away liking the life there. Robert Nichols, who had preceded Blunden in Tokyo, likened the experience to his time in the trenches during the war, while Peter Quennell and William Plomer would also write of their experiences in less than enthusiastic terms. Yet here was Hodgson eagerly packing crate after crate with books he had bought, borrowed or retrieved from storage, stocking up with tobacco, not to mention a motley collection of ointments, salves and balms for his haemorrhoids (for which he had been operated upon yet again in November 1927). In fact, it seemed he could not get back fast enough, and this after an extremely eventful year's sabbatical filled with friends and conversation.

In December 1927 after leaving hospital, he'd embarked on a round of visits, book hunts and cultural trips as only he could. With W.J. Turner and John Drinkwater he went to the theatre where they saw *Macbeth* in modern dress, the *Masque of Venice* by George Gribble, and *Outward Bound* by Sutton Vane. He had dinner with the pianist Artur Schnabel after one of his performances. He caught up with old friends such as Henry Salt in Brighton and Enid Bagnold in her splendid Rottingdean home (she had married the head of Reuters), where he met Arnold Bennett and Logan Pearsall Smith. He went to Cruft's Dog Show and the Kennel Club Show, where he reacquainted himself with the champion dog breeder and long-time friend Tom Gannaway. He went north to visit Henry Leach, an old Fleet Street friend living in Yorkshire. He followed this up by touring Darlington and family haunts with his brother Walter, after which he went round Sussex bookshops with the Turners and made a hurried visit, with Siegfried Sassoon to see Walter de la Mare, who was recovering after an operation.

Gratifyingly, there were many people interested in his work. The Russian translator S.S. Koteliansky was keen to set up a literary magazine with him; Louis Untermeyer wrote from the States offering him a lecture tour; a composer wanted to put 'Time, You Old Gypsy Man' to music.

All this activity was punctuated by regular Wednesday and Thursday gatherings for tea and supper with a group of friends who would assume mythical status in Hodgson's subsequent years of exile abroad. The 'Thursdayers' and the gatherings at Ridgeway's tearooms in Regent Street were a continuation of his pre-war teatime marathons at the Eustace

Miles and St George's restaurants and the post-war Friday evenings at W.J. Turner's Tufton Street house where he had first met Sassoon. Talking, listening and arguing had always been the essence of Hodgson's friendships, preferably in a London tearoom where time would hang suspended, evenings would draw in, and the last bus home loomed.

The establishment of the 'Thursdayers' crowd stemmed from the painter Mark Gertler's friendship with W.J. Turner and S.S. Koteliansky. The three had first met at Ottoline Morrell's London home and, when Gertler established himself in the mid-1920s in a studio in Worsley Road, Hampstead, he practised a strict weekly meetings routine: Saturday evenings at Koteliansky's; Wednesday afternoons at Ridgeway's; Thursdays at Worsley Road. This soon drew in a number of other middle-aged men who shared his cultural and artistic tastes and outlook.

The group embraced a mix of characters drawn together by their love of conversation, mutual admiration and empathy. Gertler, Koteliansky and W.J. Turner; J.W.N. Sullivan, a scientist and musicologist and expert on Beethoven; John Mavrogordato, professor of Modern Greek at Oxford; T.A. Levy, professor of Jurisprudence at University College, Aberystwyth; James Stephens, now happily reunited with Hodgson after years of silence; Herbert Milne, classical scholar at the British Museum, and his housemate, Professor A.S. Fulton, keeper of Oriental Books at the same museum. Through Koteliansky there came Marjorie Wells, daughter-in-law of H.G. Wells, plus Peggy Nunn, a young nurse. This odd assortment formed an almost mystical society, each member bringing something unique to the long evenings of endless conversation.

Gertler was a particular friend of Hodgson's, who warmed to the artist's "mental traveller" approach to life and was totally sympathetic to Gertler's insistence on an ordered, almost ceremonious daily routine. Koteliansky was another whom Hodgson admired very much. A Russian Jew, he had come to England in 1910 and worked for the Russian Law Bureau in High Holborn. He was a man of striking appearance: "His head was large with masses of thick hair above a pale, rather sensitive face with thick lips and dark eloquent eyes." He worked on translations that brought him into the ambit of Bloomsbury writers: Gilbert Cannan, D.H. Lawrence, Katherine Mansfield and Leonard Woolf, among others. He befriended Lawrence before the war and became involved in his schemes for a utopian society. Hodgson took to Koteliansky immediately, loving his 'patriarchal' image which others, including Katherine Mansfield, were more than suspicious of. Mansfield wrote, "He is an old fraud; he always pretends he is a humble person but in his heart he thinks he is very great."

Leonard Woolf, on the other hand, wrote: "Kot's passionate approval of what he thought good, particularly in people; his intense hatred of what he thought bad; the directness and vehemence of his speech; his inability to tell a lie – all this appealed strongly to Lawrence." Such qualities were everything Hodgson admired and he remained a faithful friend, writing to him consistently until Kotelliansky's death in the 1950s.

The camaraderie and closeness of the group lasted long after the regular teatime meetings ceased sometime in the early 1930s. Kot kept the spirit of it going via letters to Hodgson in Japan, and to Stephens in America, but once Gertler had married and various others died, it would be alive only in reminiscence.

Far off in Japan, Hodgson would retain a vivid picture of those afternoons and evenings, invoking in his own letters to Kot a nostalgic world where time stood still in the London of the 1920s. At a certain dwindling hour

> Stephens is giving up his ticket at Piccadilly Underground, Kot is coming down Regent Street on his bus, Turner is paying the billiards' marker and Sullivan, in his favourite restaurant is saying, 'That is excellent whitebait, waiter, give me another pot of ale ...' Miss Sutton is dressing her table, Gertie is dressing her ringlets and Doris – Doris is looking like a rose, saying something behind her menu-card ... Keep the pot going, we'll join you all. Geography never really counts.

In 1928, with the group in its heyday, with his family and friends close at hand, his ever-expanding circle of literary acquaintances a constant delight, Hodgson had plenty to cause him to linger in London rather than hurry across the globe to lonely Sendai. But none of them could deflect him from his goal, a goal few of his friends were even aware of. In March he wrote to Aurelia Bolliger:

> London is very pleasant. I appreciate the warmth and kindness of my many friends and I don't stint myself of pleasure in them. But it all vanishes in a moment. You are the keystone of my arch and I am that of yours. I have an idea that it will be years before I come back to England and am well able to say what that means to me. I love this place but if I could board the ship that might take me to you, and though I might never set foot in London again – and knew it – I should be the first passenger on board. You are my country, my love, my life, in the deepest sense, my all.

17

Aurelia

How can we see the world alike, when our preliminary impressions of childhood are so different, when we enter different experience worlds? I don't care about the letter of the law, or even law itself. (We differ on that, don't we.) ... If my association with Ralph Hodgson troubles some people, I am sorry for them. I will not change.

(Aurelia Bolliger, writing to her parents in 1929)

Aurelia Bolliger was 28 years old when Hodgson first met her in late 1926. A teacher of English and Bible Studies at Miyagi Girls' School, she was a member of the American Reformed Church Mission and had been working for the Church in Japan since 1922. Her "decision to serve" had been the inevitable result of her upbringing. Her parents, the children of first-generation European immigrants, had met at the religious Calvin College in Cleveland, Ohio in 1890 where her father, Theodore, the son of a Swiss preacher, was himself studying for the ministry. He graduated in 1897, obtained a post in the town of Wilkes Barre, Pennsylvania and married Elizabeth Mohr the same year. Aurelia was born a year later.

Thus, Aurelia's whole life would be spent in a God-fearing, hard-working household, her father proudly announcing on the birth of his third daughter in 1909: "These will be my three missionaries – one for China, one for Africa and one for Japan!" Aurelia did not disappoint him. She worked diligently at school and at Heidelberg College, Tiffin, Ohio. When the family moved to Wisconsin she taught at River Falls before making the decision, apparently unprompted, to apply to the Board of Foreign Missions and become an English teacher in Sendai, Japan.

She had lived, by her own admission, a quiet, sheltered life allowing herself little free time. When studying for a degree at the University of Wisconsin she had no boyfriends and rarely attended social events, preferring to help her mother at home with the younger children, or to work voluntarily in the local church. She was shy, untalkative and ill at ease in the company of men. Somewhat starved of love by her busy, imperceptive parents, she remembered always wanting to be older and always wanting children.

Her father's ambition to have three missionary daughters seemed well on the way to fruition when Aurelia was joined in Sendai by her sister Louise, two years her junior. In February 1925, however, Louise died of pneumonia, a blow from which Aurelia took a long time to recover. She dreamed of Louise for years afterwards, and regularly spent time by her grave. No member of the family came out to help her cope. Some months later, however, a school friend from Ohio joined her as a room-mate and the humdrum life of the American mission continued undisturbed.

When Hodgson entered her life in late 1926, Aurelia was a valued member of the mission, being a popular teacher and a representative member of the Mission board. She checked the accounts and ledgers and taught a regular school schedule, led chapel services, preached sermons and otherwise amused herself as best she could in the somewhat straitened little society that was the Reform Church Mission. When not working, life consisted of bridge sessions interspersed with regular tea parties and suppers with married couples (the Gerhards, the Fausts, the Nosses, the Sieples: names betraying the origins of the ethnic community from which the church had sprung). There were polite social evenings with Japanese teachers and pupils and long hikes in the countryside. It was a small, claustrophobic community which fed on gossip and personality clashes and silent feuds. The climate was uncomfortable and the inevitable threat of illness such as Louise had suffered hung grimly over it all.

Thus the Aurelia Bolliger whom Hodgson first saw in the audience of one of his lectures, and had later met in person at a social evening back in November 1926, was no severe, evangelical zealot. She was a small and slightly plump twenty-eight-year-old woman who wore unflattering spectacles but had lustrous blonde hair which she coiled over her head in plaits. By her own admission she was docile and highly impressionable.

Initially, the unlikely couple made no overt assignations. They might meet by chance at the post office or in the college grounds. Then there were books borrowed and returned, followed by awkward tête-à-têtes at various teatime gatherings with students and staff. Hodgson intrigued Aurelia from the very start. Muriel had recently left for Canada and he was living alone in his house. Hodgson's apparent vulnerability, his mesmeric talk, his startling insights into her likes and dislikes, intrigued her. She read his poetry and wrote that it "revealed his soul". There was also a sense of danger about him, exacerbated by the close judgemental scrutiny of the academic and church communities of Sendai. Many a church career had been blighted by scandal, 'incorrect' liaisons invariably being the cause. Nothing was missed; each nuance was spotted. The growing mutual interest they felt in each other was certain to set tongues wagging.

In early 1927, she was preparing for a year's sabbatical back at the University of Wisconsin. The journey was intended to include a sightseeing tour of Rome, something she had dreamed of for years. When it became known, however, that Hodgson and Blunden would be returning home on the ship taking her to Europe, she commented, "people will say he is eloping with me."

In fact, the planning for the impending European trip soon became the means by which Aurelia, Hodgson and Blunden became thoroughly familiar, and her diary entries begin to sound like the confessions of a lovesick teenager: In early May Aurelia admits: "He looks wonderfully tall and broad in his street clothes. No wonder I am crazy about him." And then, "That I am in love cannot be hidden much longer. He, no doubt, knows it. He is partly also ... it is a powerful emotion. Therefore, I would rather not see him often."

On 23rd June 1927, they are alone after dinner in his flat, and she notes breathlessly, "Our world upset. The dark stairway started it in part, but it has been developing. Then he took down my hair and fussed over it time and again ... then his kisses ... You must be careful. Yes. This is playing with fire ... I am curiously apathetic, nearer to tears than ecstasy ..."

Hodgson would inevitably be heavily criticised for his role in developing the affair, the "lawless love" as he rather dramatically dubbed it. He was an experienced man and knew exactly what he was doing. That he was also somewhat less than honest with Aurelia about Muriel and his marital status cannot be doubted. She admitted a year later, "There may have been a check [on my part] if before May 1927 he had indicated that he was not free. Avoiding him would have been the method." Even after she was made aware of the complications involving Muriel, they must have been underplayed by Hodgson as Aurelia actually packed "one or two necessities" for the trip to Europe, "in case I should be married en route to America".

The eventual trip to Europe was quite bizarre. Edmund Blunden, accompanied by his Japanese mistress, was ill with overwrought nerves, fearful of his wife's reaction when he arrived home. Hodgson, on the other hand, behaved almost as if tomorrow, and the consequences for *his* marriage, would never arrive. Aurelia had made various resolutions before setting out, as did Hodgson: "He explained why I need never fear his love or his transgressing it, though he seemed to take liberties." Later she admitted, "plans to keep him out of my room a failure obviously."

In fact, the days on board ship travelling across the Indian Ocean through the Suez Canal and into the Mediterranean took on the aspect of a honeymoon, Aurelia all the while being subtly shaped and guided by Hodgson into avenues that suited him. He certainly made her feel important and essential, telling her variously that she was everything a female could be to a man, that he wanted children and had already named them and that in her he found "complete mental, spiritual and physical satisfaction". He had already started referring to her as his wife, and even suggested that one day they would be buried in the same grave.

When it came to her trip to Italy, there was, not surprisingly, a difference of opinion, with Hodgson wanting her to go straight on to England and Aurelia standing her ground and insisting on her trip of a lifetime. Hodgson, inevitably, got his way but in a manner that allowed Aurelia to imagine it was her own decision:

> Ralph took the announcement [that she would make the trip] like a man. While I laundered and packed I thought over what Ralph had said and what he had not said; weighed the individual's freedom and loneliness with what I have now – and decided to go to London as he suggests … It is immoral and cowardly to want great pleasures in life without responsibility or sacrifice. I'll remember that.

Once in England, she was introduced to the Hodgson family; Walter and his teenage children took responsibility for her when Hodgson was elsewhere. She was taken on sightseeing tours, generally where Hodgson wanted her to go. Her father had sent her an itinerary but she declined to follow it. She was, she suggested to herself when musing on the way she slipped her arm into his as they walked, replacing one father with another. One afternoon, however, without telling Hodgson, she went out to look at Hyde Park: On her return she, " … found him ill with terror. Ralph shook terribly … his whole manner was altered. He was trembling with anxiety … Felt in disgrace all evening. I will be good now, for my dear one's sake."

As her journey home to Wisconsin drew closer, he took her out and bought her clothes. She once again acquiesced, noting, "Ralph chose three woollen dresses and two hats for me. If my clothes aren't attractive in the future, it surely won't be his fault." They exchanged rings and made vows, and finally, she sailed away on the SS *Minnekahda*, home to Madison, Wisconsin – leaving her personal diary behind for Hodgson to read.

Her decision to tie herself to him for the rest of her life was ultimately taken after much soul-searching, carried out during her eleven-month sojourn in the USA. Although her parents were kind and generally considerate towards her she had to face their disappointment and disapproval of her relationship with Hodgson. At this point she might have had second thoughts herself, but she did, in fact, resent her parents' attitude:

> … I have at last asserted myself and taken a step consistent with my own standards and beliefs … why did I grow up keeping my own ideas so exclusively to myself that now, years belated, this rupture has come bringing terrible pain?

Throughout this time, Hodgson was writing letter after letter filled with endearments, flattery and an almost suffocating devotion. At the same time, it was clear, he was also attempting to manipulate her into a role suited to his own needs. In February 1928, for instance, he wrote that he was worried that her studies were putting too much of a strain on her:

> Do your best without strain and if that does not please, take a whole term's holiday and give your dear little head up to matters of worthier moment, such as reading novels and poetry and buying pretty hats and clothes and dreaming of the future.

His 'wholesome' suggestions were made for her well-being, he insisted. "Be 'Peg' and not Miss L.A.B. Your happiness doesn't lie in ambition."

He suggested she drop scholarly journals and "study *Vogue* and other fashion papers". She wrote in her diary: "I bought *Vogue* and can dispel his fears to that extent …" but her studies continued. Hodgson's advice, though seemingly given for her benefit, clearly sought to quell any sense of independence on her part. He wanted a helpmate, someone who would play a subservient role in exclusive devotion to the maintenance of his own existence. It was a part Aurelia would eventually assume with great contentment, and it offered her a fulfilment she sensed her current existence could never provide. Paradoxically, marriage to Hodgson promised her a kind of freedom – in particular, mental freedom.

She eventually finished her year's study, and in August 1928, headed back to Sendai and Hodgson who had returned the previous month to start his second three-year contract. Travelling across the USA to San Francisco where she was to embark, Aurelia stopped off to visit her younger sister, Katherine, who was then preparing to marry, and other relatives. These were people she had hardly known, a mixture of farmers, carpenters and electricians. At one stage she joined in a large family picnic and she noted the simple happiness and warmth between them. They kissed one another! Unheard of at home! This contrasted so noticeably with the cold, narrow-minded attitudes of the church communities she was familiar with and in which she had seemed destined to spend the rest of her life.

The next few years were not easy ones. It would be another four to five years before Hodgson managed to obtain a divorce. Back in Sendai, against the inevitable disapproval of the church authorities, she insisted on maintaining the closest of relations with Hodgson. In June 1930, the mission decided to force her hand and offer her a choice: Hodgson or her job. The choice was simple. She found herself lodgings with friends and worked as a secretary at the university. Though the two travelled to England together in 1931/2 and stayed in rooms in Hampstead, their relationship remained chaste. Their "virgin love", as she called it, was her bulwark against the inevitable disapproval of the church authorities, her family and society in general. Aurelia was a firm advocate of marriage and its sanctity. In early 1928 she wrote to Hodgson from Wisconsin asking him to send her details of Bertrand Russell's educational ideas after hearing and disapproving of Dora Russell's views on 'companionate' marriage.

In 1933, however, a telegram arrived at her parents' home from Yokohama announcing: **MARRIED, TWENTY-FOURTH, AURELIA**. Immediately after the marriage, Aurelia moved into Hodgson's university house, and from that point on they would rarely be parted for more than a few weeks at a time until Hodgson's death in 1962. To the outside world, it appeared he had found a meek and dutiful servant: Aurelia certainly took on all household chores and more from the moment they settled into the 'professor's' house on the banks of the Hirose River – a household dominated by dogs and birds, but primarily by Hodgson's writing and working routine. But Aurelia was intensely happy. She had found a life and a purpose that suited her utterly, and one that was by no means docile or passive. She became Hodgson's partner and she took control of him in a physical sense, an almost natural process, given their age difference of almost thirty years.

Their mutual devotion impressed many who met them down the years. One student recalled years later:

> Sometimes students visited him in his house on the river bank in the afternoons when he had no classes. I distinctly remember one such visit. It was just after he was married to Aurelia, his American wife who, in her self-effacing devotion made his later life especially happy and productive. Strangely, the scarlet dress that Mrs Hodgson was wearing then, the sound of her cheerful laughter and Hodgson's peaceful, contented look and also the innumerable canaries which seemed to fill the house, come back to me much more vividly than anything else that happened that afternoon.

18

The Man In White Spats

*Going into the dining-room Ralph was speaking of being transported
in time to another century and asked T.S. Eliot whether he'd like
to go into the future or the past. "Into the past. It's finished." Mrs
Eliot commented, "It's never finished. It always follows us."*
(Aurelia Bolliger's diary, 1932)

Hodgson's trip back to England in 1931/2 (his second twelve-month
sabbatical from Japan) was his last sustained encounter with a world that,
though still familiar to him, was, nevertheless, changing rapidly. In twelve
crowded months he witnessed the deaths of his brother Walter and Harold
Monro of the Poetry Bookshop; he met and befriended T.S. Eliot as well
as cementing his friendship with Siegfried Sassoon; he even entered,
albeit briefly, the Ottoline Morrell circle, encountering Julian and Aldous
Huxley, Leonard Woolf, Lord David Cecil and others. He embarked on
book hunts in the West Country and the North of England and frequented
his beloved tearoom, Ridgeway's, whiling away long afternoons with
Koteliansky, Mark Gertler, W.J. Turner and W.H. Davies. There were old
friends to chase up: Walter de la Mare, Henry Salt, G.B. Dewar, Holbrook
Jackson, William Maas, the Rothensteins; and Edward Marsh introduced
him to Charles Morgan, Duncan Grant, Violet Bonham Carter, Charles
Dalmon and Gilbert Spencer.

For much of the time he had Aurelia with him. She travelled from
Japan via America where she had visited her parents, arriving in London
in October some three months after Hodgson. No longer hidden away in
a Young Women's Christian Association hostel, as she had been in 1927,
she first stayed in Sussex Place with W.J. Turner and his wife, then with
Sylvia Baker and finally, albeit surreptitiously, with Hodgson himself
at Hampstead Square. She met everyone and, as an avid diarist, she
documented the next few months in meticulous detail.

Apart from the sadness caused by the deaths of Walter and Harold
Monro, it was a satisfying and significant year for Hodgson. He was
confident, even excited at the prospect of his life ahead with Aurelia, and
this suffused his every encounter. His first meeting with T.S. Eliot, however,

was a moment when his confidence faltered, however briefly. The literary hostess Lady Ottoline Morrell, intrigued to learn that the two men had never met, thought it might be fun to bring them together.

Hodgson was at first reluctant to take up her invitation, not from any lack of interest in Eliot who was then at the height of his fame but rather from uncertainty whether Eliot would be interested in meeting *him*. Their temperaments, Hodgson felt, were quite different. Nevertheless, in December 1931, at a literary soirée in Ottoline Morrell's Russell Square flat, Hodgson met Eliot for the first time.

As the evening progressed, the two men did find common ground, a process made easier by the presence of Koteliansky. 'Kot' had been one of D.H. Lawrence's old friends, and he berated Eliot loudly for not joining in the struggle for a Lawrentian "new world order". Hodgson's quiet aside that "the future is a mystery and man's only obligation is to find the courage to face it" appeared to strike a chord with Eliot. At the end of the evening, as the coats were being handed out, Eliot said to Hodgson, "Must I wait another 43 years before we meet again?"

Some weeks later, after meeting again at the Morrells', Eliot's wife, Vivienne, sent Hodgson an invitation to dinner at their Clarence Gardens home near Regent's Park. She added, "Bring nice puppy and Miss B. Friday 15th, 7.30."

Though cats eventually figured prominently in the two poets' relationship, it would be puppies that provided the initial common talking point. At the Morrells', Vivienne had been carrying a small Yorkshire terrier called Polly. Aurelia recalled, "When we went into the dining room, she kept it on her lap, saying to me, 'I don't like to have dogs running about the floor in a crowd of people, do you?'"

At the second Morrell gathering, Vivienne had left the terrier in the car, "only to keep on jumping up several times to go out and look at her until Lady Ottoline urged her to bring the dog indoors. We had Pickwick, our mastiff bitch puppy and the two were duly introduced, although Pickles had to stay on our laps."

Thus, when the Hodgsons' arrived at Clarence Gardens, they had Pickwick with them, although Aurelia later confessed to feeling uncomfortable:

> I was conscious of Pickie all the evening and perhaps a little nervous on his account ... The Eliots were very kind towards him. We warned them that he was only three months old and not house-broken. It didn't *matter* to them. It was a genuine indifference to wet spots and their actions were better than their words! It was *such* a relief to me, for Pickie's actions could not be predicted in this respect. Mrs Eliot protested when I kept him quiet on my lap, that it was 'cruel'; when he was playing freely he was certain to

act as tho' he were at home …

Indeed, Mrs Eliot just laughed heartily as the waterfall continued
and got a cloth. Once when he retired to the end of the hall and
made a mess in front of the dining-room door she got the shovel
and paper and cleaned it up herself. She wouldn't ever let me tho'
I felt I ought at least to clean up after him. Mr Eliot just remarked
calmly, 'We're used to it. Sometimes I get down on the floor myself
and scrub away the marks.'

Over the next six months, the two couples met frequently. In fact,
Aurelia was soon 'adopted' by Vivienne as a part-time companion, at
first to spend evenings with her in the Regent's Park flat arranging Eliot's
library or listening to the radio, later to stay whole weeks with the Eliots
while Hodgson was away from London. In the end, Aurelia (or 'Bollie'
as she was nicknamed) left a bundle of belongings in the small bedroom
in the Eliots' flat that she used as her own.

Her position was an awkward one, however, acutely aware as she was
that her relationship with Hodgson remained ambiguous. In fact, in June,
1931 Hodgson set up a bogus 'adulterous encounter' in the Charing Cross
Hotel to provide Muriel with evidence to divorce him, keeping Aurelia's
name out of things.

Vivienne had already commented to friends ("in caustic fashion"
according to one) on the way Hodgson referred to Aurelia as his 'secretary'.
It was hardly a comfortable position for a devout Christian girl who was
still technically a missionary in Japan. To make matters worse, that Easter
Eliot delivered several radio talks on Christian themes. Hodgson and
Aurelia listened to one of them in the company of Vivienne on the Eliots'
radio. Aurelia recalled:

In that last radio address, he stood for Christian marriage. I often
wondered then whether the churchman – or rather the serious
Christian – in him didn't stand in judgement over Ralph and me,
like my father and some of the Sendai (Japanese) community. If
it did, there was never *any* sign of it. On the contrary, there was
evidence that he *understood* the situation without explanation, for
once he said to Ralph: 'It's in your face that you have had great
trouble.'

Aurelia got on well with Eliot, and he treated her with the natural
courtesy other close friends had noted in him. Two American expatriates
together, they chatted easily about English pronunciation, food and Japan.
So easily that it occasionally aroused Vivienne's jealousy:

When he and I were alone we chewed over a matter as long as we
liked. Vivienne would wander into the room with a cigarette and a

pile of bills or letters, catch a phrase and make a comment. Or she might ask, 'What are you two brawling about now?' Sometimes the conversation went on; but sometimes he left the room at once.

On more than one occasion, she found herself being used as a foil in Vivienne's increasingly bitter arguments with Eliot:

> At the table Mrs Eliot inquired something about Japan, and Mr Eliot started to explain some point to her, as to a child. She checked him abruptly with, 'Why do you interrupt me? Here's my chance to hear from someone who *knows!*' and more in the same tone of sharp criticism. He was quite right in what he had been saying and I substantiated it, glancing at his face. I generally avoided looking at him during any episode of this kind. I had no wish to see his embarrassment or to betray my own. This time he was looking at me, with a self-conscious apologetic smile. I met it straight, then looked away.

But Vivienne was genuinely drawn to Aurelia. Over Easter, she allowed herself to be persuaded by Aurelia, against her inclinations, to attend a performance of church music:

> The music was beautiful. Vivienne liked it too and was so glad she had come. As we were leaving the building, we met her mother and aunt in the court and we all returned to the Eliots' together. Mrs Haigh-Wood was happy that Vivienne had got there, and Vivienne explained that she wouldn't have come out but for me. Her mother answered, 'Yes, I see that she's magnetic.'

Vivienne was soon regularly inviting Aurelia to lunch, usually when Eliot was at work at Faber's or lunching with Hodgson at Ridgeway's. It gradually became obvious, however, that Vivienne was not well. According to Aurelia's diary,

> Several times she was still in bed when I got there at 1.30 and I wouldn't see her until 2 or so. Once she felt too wretched to dress and had to stay in bed. I had the choice of eating alone in the dining-room or in the bedroom with her. Of course I preferred the latter. Her lunches were always delicious. She ate little herself, usually passing up meat very lightly, if not altogether.

Vivienne suffered badly from hysteria and was usually in need of company. Her friends were regularly called upon at all times of the day and night. Aurelia was soon one of them, summoned by telephone or telegram, sometimes by Eliot himself:

I couldn't guess what might have occurred. Over the telephone line Mr Eliot partly explained that she had been ill during the night but was now asleep. The [telegram] message was, could I come and see her during the day? It was urgent … When I entered the dim room Vivienne explained the telegram. After we had left on Friday night, she got desperately ill with repeated vomiting. I hadn't mentioned the canaries [a hobby of Aurelia's] lately, how they were or what they were doing. She feared she might have offended me, somehow, so that I had kept silent about them. These thoughts had haunted her during the night so Mrs Eliot sent the telegram … I reassured them both to feel free to telegraph or summons me at any time.

Which Vivienne did, so that at times Aurelia seemed to be acting rather like a lady's companion, putting Vivienne to bed on occasions, tidying the study. She stayed over on some weekends and once, when Hodgson was away, for a whole week. She became part of the household:

I am very happy here. The Eliots are excellent hosts and friends. Last evening was pleasant indeed. Mr Eliot tended the radio; Mrs Eliot did her household accounts and got the laundry ready, chatting much of the time.

It wasn't always sweetness and light, however. After one fraught evening, Vivienne wrote to Aurelia:

Sorry you didn't have a happier evening. I am afraid, my dear girl, that we have come to look upon you as too much one of the family. But that in itself is the greatest compliment, if you could only see it. I feel so much at ease with you that I can write my 19 letters while you are here and Mr Eliot can read and grumble and you can arrange the books. It is all very delightful if you can look upon it in the right way … I hope you do.

Meanwhile, Eliot and Hodgson had formed an equally unlikely friendship, stemming from common personal traits: devotion to a strong mother, an intense regard for personal privacy and a shared sense of humour.

They had taken to exchanging walking sticks whenever they met, a ritual Eliot recalled many years later in a letter to Hodgson:

I hope you remember that long ago I admired your walking stick, the malacca stick with the leather-covered handle. On our next meeting you surprised me by the gift of a walking-stick similar to your own … I should like you to know that it is still my principal walking stick and that I think of you whenever I use it.

The two men met regularly at Ridgeway's tea rooms in Piccadilly, and occasionally Eliot took Hodgson along to other luncheon spots he frequented across the city, where he regularly met friends and fellow writers. In March, one of those good friends, Harold Monro, proprietor of the Poetry Bookshop, died after a long illness. Eliot wrote to Hodgson;

> I do not know whether you saw the notice of Harold Monro's death (which I wrote) in *The Times* today. I am sure it would be a gratification to Alida if you would come on Saturday at 11.30am to the interment at Golders Green Crematorium. There will be very few friends there, only, so far as I know, myself and Frank Flint. 'The poor procession without music goes' [a quotation from the poet Lionel Johnson]. And it would give satisfaction to me if you came.

Eliot was known for his bizarre sense of humour, his tendency to dream up fantasy characters, and to impersonate them in letters to friends. Hodgson, too, having been for over a decade a children's comic artist, was also adept at surreal flights of fancy and even a gentle form of satire. Eliot clearly warmed to this, and together they cooked up ideas for spoof books. Hodgson suggested a billiards book, "where the same anecdote would be repeated in precisely the same words by a number of billiard champs as though original to each – this both to fool and amuse the reader ..."

He also mooted a series of 'shilling guides' to English towns and cities: "a precise book in some ways including the association of famous men with each town and adding many wholly fabricated connections, historical and modern, but omitting the cathedral, say, all in a prosey, matter-of-fact style". Hodgson added, "It would make all the inhabitants furious, mad ... The whole series would be called a mad library!"

Aurelia recalled the two men laughing heartily over their crazy schemes and Vivienne Eliot, catching the mood, pointing to Eliot in delight and shrieking ... "Mad! That's just what he is!"

In many ways, however, the two men were polar opposites. Robert Selincourt, a close friend of Eliot's, noted how Hodgson provided a, "sharp contrast to Eliot's fineness: his [Hodgson's] accent was homely, his figure portly and his manners hearty; but he was a man of acute sensitiveness and wonderful freshness, with a heart of warmest loyalty. All this Tom appreciated."

They were also of different generations and temperaments. Hodgson was 60 and Eliot 43. Eliot drank, sometimes heavily, while Hodgson was teetotal. And while both men enjoyed boxing, there was, according to Ottoline Morrell, something sadistic in Eliot's nature brought out by watching violence: "Eliot says he feels a strong desire when seeing a man down in boxing to trample on him, tear him."

The first six months of 1932 were possibly some of the unhappiest of Eliot's life as he contemplated leaving the increasingly unstable Vivienne. What, one wonders, might Hodgson have been able to say to him over their tea and toast at Ridgeway's? In fact, a great deal. Hodgson's first wife Dolly had died in an insane asylum, a terrible death that still haunted him. It had resulted in a cessation in his writing of poetry except for the one small piece in which he expressed his guilt at the way he had treated her. He had then endured the traumatic two years in Japan with his second wife, Muriel, an ill-conceived union that suited neither of them. He had now found tranquillity with Aurelia, something Eliot may well have envied.

Eliot had many friends and close acquaintances, of course, with whom he was on far more intimate terms than with Hodgson, but there developed between the two men a mutual fascination that, on Eliot's part, was soon commemorated in verse.

Although also in the middle of an unusually long fallow period in the writing of serious poetry, Eliot continued working on smaller pieces, such as 'Lines to a Persian Cat' and 'Lines to a Yorkshire Terrier'.

One evening, Aurelia recalled:

> Vivienne told me he had written the former the day before and after dinner she asked him to read it to me. He found it and said that he would if we both stayed in the room. 'The more people there are, the easier it is to read.' I felt very honoured. When Ralph was present a few days later we asked him to read it again. By then he had the two and he felt that the latter was the better. Ralph said, 'Read them both and we can see.' He did, though after the first, he opened a copy of Blake's poems and read one about three nuns that was remotely suggestive. TSE said, 'A poem is nothing if it isn't unique and this one isn't.'

Within a couple of months of the Hodgsons' departure for Japan, Eliot had penned two more 'Five-Finger Exercises' that he illustrated and sent on to Hodgson. The first, 'Lines to Ralph Hodgson Esqre.' celebrates Hodgson's 'oddness', his love of birds, of dogs and of sitting in restaurants eating gooseberry pie while attended by adoring waitresses.

Certain details in the poems came directly from Eliot's afternoons at Ridgeway's tea rooms in Hodgson's company. The 'adoring' waitresses included, for instance, a certain Doris, who would correspond with Hodgson right up until his death. "He has 999 canaries" is a reference to the birds that Hodgson and Aurelia bred in Japan and about which Aurelia was writing a 'family history' entitled *Consider the Canary*, while the "Baskerville Hound" Eliot mentions comes from an anecdote about Hodgson's own bull-terrier. Aurelia recalled:

It was at Ridgeway's Tea Rooms that Eliot told the story he had heard of Ralph being given five complaints by the police because a maid had one of Ralph's dogs on a Whiteleys' Exerciser instead of on a proper lead and he had gone about attacking people in the park! Though Ralph claimed the story was apocryphal, he later admitted to me that it was true!

The second poem, 'Lines for Cuscuscaraway and Mirza Murad Ali Beg', presents Eliot in stark contrast to Hodgson, someone sour and grim whom no one would wish to meet. Yet, despite their light-hearted nature, these poetic squibs hint at a certain envy of Hodgson's elusive yet fascinating character. It has even been suggested that Eliot hurriedly penned the second poem in an attempt to balance what looked suspiciously like a sly satire of Hodgson.

It was all destined to end in late July, of course, when the Hodgsons returned to Japan. As the date approached, Vivienne became more and more anxious to make appointments with Aurelia, fussing over telegrams, confirming and reconfirming arrangements. She wrote to Hodgson: "Sorry to bother you again, but wrote to remind you she promised to telegram. I have waited for two days. I last saw her on Sunday night. I ask *you* – may she once more go to Hindhead? In the car, for two days as before – to the same hotel where my mother is. Mr Eliot feels too tired to go *unless* she goes (I get little enough fresh air)".

At the very end, Aurelia received a sad note from her: "I heard from T.S. that you and Mr Hodgson have taken tickets and that is bad news for me. I got your postcard this morning about the canaries, etc. so I hoped that would delay you! As you have not telegraphed me I suppose you will not run away without coming to see me again as you *promised.*" Her mother, Mrs Haigh-Wood wrote: "Viv will miss you terribly for you have become quite a sister to her and I wish you could have remained until Tom comes back from the USA but the next best thing is for you to write often and cheer her up."

Eliot left for America soon afterwards and never returned to Vivienne, who eventually entered a psychiatric home.

During the next three to four years, however, Eliot kept in touch with Hodgson, primarily because he had discovered that his friend had begun work on a new long poem. Entitled 'The Muse and the Mastiff', it seemed to have originated in a single line of Coleridge's 'Christabel' ("For what can ail the mastiff bitch?") and was, according to one prominent critic, "as vigorous and strangely charming as it was cranky and incoherent".

Eliot was an admirer of Hodgson's early verse and he now worked hard to persuade Hodgson to let Faber bring out a definitive collected edition of his work, including the new poem.

His first attempt received a bluff, perhaps even rude, response from Hodgson who was notoriously difficult – not to say eccentric – about publishing matters. Eliot replied in mock-severe cockney:

> Now then Mr Hodgson, Sir, I ain't done with you yet though it did take me indeed some time to recover from your letter of August 31st but now I have recovered my Wind and here it Is. I can only suppose this sort of attitude comes from your associating so long with poor little Orientals what you can bully with your Fist but Sir you can't treat big men 6000 miles or more away like that ... always had thought you were a sound decent Englishman but if you are coming out all over Scotch the Lord help you. Don't you realise that if Faber and Faber publish a book and call it POETRY then the public believes that it is poetry we have toiled for ten years to arrive at such a position and it's not for you to question our knowledge and whatever we do we mostly have sound reasons for. So don't you say There You Are to people who know better than you so ... well sir are you going to come back with my stick because I have yours for you but where do you want it? Now I hate to talk like this to a man I used to respect highly when I knew him in the flesh and in his right mind apparently but there is limits to human endurance and every Christian knows ...

Hodgson apologised and cited poor health as a reason for stalling. Eliot soon returned to the fray, brushing aside Hodgson's excuses:

> Well, to return to poetry, it is my ambition to be the best dressed man over 70 in Pall Mall and I shall beat you to it. Well now how long are you going to stand on one leg sucking your thumb? Haven't you realised yet as I have painfully that once you have written and published writings you can't suppress them and that if you don't let your poems be republished properly now somebody is going to come along and do it after you are dead for 50 years or so in a way you won't like as much. I am not talking about your future work knowing what a lazy devil you are there is more hope of that if we deal with the present first and no use worrying about the future till you get back to Ridgeway's and we can fill you up with gooseberry tarts. As for the past now so far as Macmillan is concerned you can leave that to us to see what can be done.

Once again, Hodgson responded unfavourably and Eliot finally withdrew, content to let his fellow editor Frank Morley keep in touch with his friend about publication matters. A decade later, Morley offered to include Hodgson's new (but still unpublished) poem in the same list as Eliot's 'Dry Salvages' but Hodgson remained adamant that he would publish his own work in his own time, which he did – against all professional advice – in the 1950s via a series of plain, single broadsides called *Flying Scroll*.

Before then, in late 1938, the two poets would have their last face-to-face encounter. When Hodgson passed through London *en route* for the USA and the small farmhouse in Canton, Ohio, where he would spend the rest of his life, Eliot invited him to lunch: "I want to have a private conversation with you about CATS and have waited impatiently for some months." For Eliot, remembering Hodgson's cartooning career, had decided he was the artist to illustrate *Old Possum's Book of Practical Cats*.

They met in early September and, a month later, for a second time in the company of Faber directors. Eliot subsequently accompanied Hodgson to a ritual Ridgeway's lunch. Hodgson wrote to Aurelia (now back in the States):

> Eliot was immensely interested to hear about the [new] poem. Solemnly at the door of Ridgeway's we met. He placed my old walking stick in my hand. I his own in his. Then we went upstairs. Eliot has a manuscript of a book of nonsense poems he has written about cats which they insist upon my illustrating. It seems absurd, but there it is.

Hodgson, under some pressure, agreed to do the drawings as long as his name did not appear in the book. Eliot agreed, suggesting Hodgson be referred to only as "The Man in White Spats". Aurelia, however, could sense Hodgson's reluctance and wrote back to him, "Your illustrations for TSE's book quite surprises me. Do you still want a loophole out of that? Here it is. If it means you must have a cat in the house for observation, I veto it. I really don't see how a cat will fit into this menagerie" (the menagerie being various cages full of birds plus two dogs the Hodgsons had already accumulated).

In 1938, Hodgson was 67 years old, his mind still totally absorbed in his "long poem". He was also anxious to rejoin Aurelia in America, and the *Cats* idea was one he felt he couldn't pursue in any practical way. At the same time, that he should dismiss such an idea out of hand was courageous. In 1939, Eliot was the country's pre-eminent poet and the *Cats* idea would have meant a useful fee, the Hodgsons being anything but well off at that stage.

Once in America, however, Hodgson continued to stall and so, in early 1939, Eliot tried one more time. He sent Hodgson a small spoof 'quiz':

> Miscellaneous: How did Mr Magnus amuse his friends? What is the meaning of 'Hole and Corner Puffery?' What do you associate with the sound of a key bugle? With a large laburnum tree? What was Mr Mivkin's greatest weakness? Etc ...

> (To be attempted only by Mr Ralph Hodgson.)

THE
CRITERION
A QUARTERLY REVIEW
EDITED BY T. S. ELIOT

TELEPHONE: MUSEUM 9543
TELEGRAMS: FABBAF, WESTCENT, LONDON

24 RUSSELL SQUARE,
LONDON, W.C.1

28 October 1938.

Respected Towser;

I need the refreshment of your company again as soon as possible. The days fill up quickly; with this or that futility; and you will soon be leaving for Madison. Will you lunch with me say ten days hence? Say Tuesday week? Let me have a provisional reply. Would you be willing to meet one or two carefully hand picked vintage characters who recognise the importance of Mr. R.H., or alternatively lunch alone with your

faithful old

Possum

To
The Man in White Spats;
c/o S.S.Kotelianaky Esqre.,
5, Acacia Road;
S.John's Wood;
N.W.8.

STOP PRESS? Ezra is in town. Address him at 34, Abingdon Court, W.8. His mother-in-law has died, and he is winding up.

Letter from T.S. Eliot to Ralph Hodgson in 1938 concerning 'Cats'

Having in mind the four cats in the wheelbarrow, what are you doing about the Depicting of Cats?"

Hodgson replied:

> I haven't made a start on *Possum's Cats* for many reasons: The chief being that we haven't found a suitable house to settle down in yet ... I believe I have a good enough eye for cats to justify my undertaking this work – but not in my inner consciousness: therefore I must have cats about me to study and proper conscience for their well-being (and for my dogs also, and I want to do a bit of breeding). I trust this isn't as tedious to read as it is unpleasant to write, for I regard it as a high honour to be asked to illustrate *Possum's Immortal Cats*, but after all, the fun of doing it – or attempting to – is the thing and that is only possible with my feet up on the mantelpiece, as the saying is.

Old Possum's Book of Practical Cats went ahead without Ralph Hodgson. On 5th October 1939 an edition of 3005 copies priced at 3/6d appeared with Eliot's own drawings on the front cover and the dust-wrapper. Inside was a small dedication to 'The Man in White Spats'.

Although Eliot visited the United States on a number of occasions after the war, he made no further attempts to see Hodgson on his remote farm in Ohio. As Eliot quipped to a reporter: "It isn't on a map though it is rumoured that a bus from somewhere will take you to it once a day."

Ironically, towards the end of Hodgson's life, cats *would* enter his and Aurelia's menagerie. Strays from surrounding farms in Canton, Ohio, where the Hodgsons eventually settled, would set up residence in his home and he would admit: "Cats begin where dogs leave off." He even managed a small cat poem:

> Kitty and your thimble –
> And all the jungles of Malay
> Between the four corners of your chair.

17. The 'Thursdayers', including Ralph Hodgson, (seated left), Kotelianski (seated right), and Mark Gertler (standing far left), 1927

18. Aurelia and canary in front of Gooseberry Grange, Sendai, Japan, 1934

19. Ralph Hodgson with puppy, Aurelia and Japanese teachers and students at Sendai, Japan, 1934

20. Ralph Hodgson and Seymour
Adelman c.1948

21. Owleacres, Minerva, Ohio, 1948

22. Ralph Hodgson and Aurelia in
Owlacres

23. Ralph and Aurelia Hodgson's
headstone in Pleasant Grove
Cemetery, Carroll County.
The lines are taken from Hodgson's
'The Skylark'

19

Sassoon

*But in the last resort we are lucky, being poets. For poetry cannot
be taken from us and those who serve the muse are the children
of light ...*

(Siegfried Sassoon to Ralph Hodgson, 1954)

In the spring of 1932, with Aurelia staying at the Eliots' arranging the great
man's library and acting as companion to Vivienne, Hodgson was deep in
the English countryside in Wiltshire. Fitz House, in Teffont Magna, was
the home of Siegfried Sassoon from where he wrote to Aurelia: "This is
wonderful, lovely, a sort of rural heaven."

Hodgson's friendship with Siegfried Sassoon was an odd one on the
surface of things. Sassoon was from a wealthy middle-class background
and Hodgson was from the North, a descendant of tradesmen and farmers.
Sassoon, although having recently married and produced a son, was
homosexual. Hodgson eschewed any such leanings. Yet their literary
inclinations, if not their poetic work, chimed perfectly. Neither was
strictly academic. Sassoon finished university without a degree, having
preferred to play cricket and billiards and to hunt. Hodgson left school at
fourteen to idle *his* days away with dogs, fairs and bird watching. Both
liked to search for the forgotten and the obscure in literature; both liked
the contemplative, almost indolent life, sitting by the fireside whiling away
the hours in conversation or silence.

They had been friends since the early 1920s when Sassoon lodged with
W.J. Turner. Indeed Sassoon had once sought Hodgson out before the First
World War. He recalls in *Siegfried's Journey* how on that occasion he had
gone to Hodgson's King's Road lodgings:

> ... one soaking wet afternoon early in June, much hoping that I
> was about to meet the man who had written 'The Song of Honour'.
> For there was a startling freshness in his poetic voice which had
> made his words come to life on the printed page in a way which I
> welcomed without being able to tell myself how the mystery was
> effected. I was eager to see what he was like, but I also wanted to
> thank him for what he had done.

Hodgson had not been at home but when at last Sassoon did meet him after the war, he wasn't disappointed, particularly as Hodgson regarded Sassoon's own poetry with such enthusiasm. Sassoon wrote in his diary: "RH says I am one of the living writers who has an individual vocabulary" while of a poem Sassoon had published in the *New Statesman* in 1923 Hodgson wrote:

> I did like it very much indeed. Its force and carry, so gay and sombre. Savage, too. Most of all for doing what it set out to do with simplicity in spite of some words that ain't no friends of mine, usually …

For Sassoon, Hodgson appeared to be a fascinating character as much for his poetry as for his mind, his conversation and his ideas. Sassoon was then close to the centre of fashionable Bloomsbury society and moving freely among the Morrells, the Huxleys and the Sitwells. Yet references to Hodgson occupy sizeable chunks of his post-war journals as he attempts to pin down Hodgson's views and speculations on the war, the future, television, the cinema, even the impact of the growing welfare state.

Sassoon particularly enjoyed Hodgson's reminiscences of Fleet Street and the black-and-white artists like Baxter and May: "What a book he might have written about them!" He later wrote in his journal: "It seems wicked that he can't put his talk on paper. Perhaps he does but I fear it all goes up in pipe smoke and passes away with the cups of tea."

Sassoon had seen Hodgson off on his first trip to Japan in 1923, and the two had corresponded intermittently during Hodgson's first period at Sendai. In 1927, during Hodgson's first furlough back in England, they had met for a couple of days, when Sassoon was in the throes of finishing the first part of his war trilogy. When Hodgson returned in 1931 for his second break from teaching in Japan, however, the two men rapidly cemented a close and enduring relationship that would last for the next twenty-five years.

By then, the once angry war poet had retreated to the isolation and solitude of the English countryside where in careful, measured prose he worked his way through the trauma of his wartime experiences. He also produced various popular volumes of verse that were, as the poet Jon Silkin has written, "suffused with a knowing melancholy and regret, merged with some pleasure, the whole seeming to stem from a nostalgic memory of the pre-war past".

Sassoon's retreat from the hurly-burly world of letters, made possible by private wealth coincided with his gradual estrangement from Robert Graves, his wartime colleague and fellow poet, whose book of reminiscences, *Goodbye to All That* hurt and angered Sassoon.

Sassoon was easily hurt. As Silkin put it: "His background was not one to prepare him for either war or for strenuous emotional and intellectual activity." Sassoon once admitted that the world at large often baffled him and he had little social awareness. Before the war, he had shown little curiosity about ideas or aesthetics and he had a disinclination to explore or experiment with language. As he wrote to Hodgson: "Thinking in pictures is my natural method of self-expression. I have always been a submissively visual writer." According to Silkin: "This produced immediate but short-term results: directness, clarity and even a ferocious sharpness, but limited his ability and desire to explore his own feelings ..."

Robert Graves was sharp, witty, acerbic and intolerant, and he made no secret of his dislike of Sassoon's post-war work. Of the volume of poetry entitled *The Heart's Journey*, privately printed in 1928, Graves thought, "a book better unwritten: lace-Valentine vulgarity ..." He also made no bones about Sassoon's "emotional shortcomings" and when Sassoon defended himself, Graves pointedly asked, "Who *are* your friends, Siegfried?" Sassoon might well have replied, "Ralph Hodgson for one", whose comments on *Heart's Journey*, indeed on all of Sassoon's poetry, would always be enthusiastic and supportive.

When Sassoon showed Hodgson drafts of his memoirs, Hodgson responded: "It is [human] nature with a pen! A thing of glory!" and he insisted that Sassoon produce many more volumes: "I'm very glad that you now see your way to going on through the War and send you endless wishes for a satisfactory journey."

As for his verse: "The same full warm breath and blood that is in all your poetry and in so precious little elsewhere these days [is] work in which I can and must wholly believe ... things that give me happiness and reassurance in a tipsy world."

Sassoon welcomed Hodgson's support, writing in 1928:

You are one of the very few on whom I still rely ... Oh, Hodgson, the thought of you warms my heart!

Occasionally, very occasionally, they indulged in technical poetic talk. Sassoon wrote to Hodgson:

[Edmund Blunden] had a good look at my poems and gave his expert opinion which was very encouraging. I urged him to pick as many holes as possible and he made a few suggestions (quite tentatively) and I naturally pass them on to the printer: 'The multitudinous dead'. The last two lines seem to me to depart a little. 'Lineaments' perhaps is an image a shade out of consonance with what preceded. The fading out effect was, of course, intentional and I am doubtful about altering it.

There were further references to odd words, the metre of certain lines, at the end of which Sassoon asked, "Do you think I ought to interfere with these poems, which seemed to me pleasantly natural in expression?" To all of which Hodgson replies:

> I think there's some justification for EB's remarks, nothing, however, that gives me concern … I wouldn't suggest altering anything. You are in wonderful form and I hope it lasts long … It's impossible to tell you the enchantment of possessing these imperishable things from your hand.

Hodgson rarely interfered with anyone's work. Having burned his hands way back before the First World War with James Stephens, he was content to let a poet's work emerge as it might. As he once put it to John Freeman, "I'm no critic as you know, always having difficulty in getting into another man's mind and looking out of his windows …" Nevertheless, Sassoon liked to feel that he and Hodgson shared important characteristics as poets:

> You see, RH, more than any man alive, you have been an inspiration to serve the art of poetry faithfully. I know you aren't impeccable, any more than I am, but you have always understood me and had faith in my powers as a writer. Blunden has understood me, too, but yours I think has been a more powerful understanding. Dear EB hasn't always understood the necessity of conserving one's poetic energies. He would like me to be more profusive as a writer. Wrong. I'd be spoilt by over-production, like you.

Ironically, the main difference between Hodgson and Sassoon was that Hodgson never repeated himself, whereas Sassoon continued to write poem after poem very much in the same mood and metre, covering very much the same ground. Hodgson's poem 'The Bride', in fact, is just about the only piece that could in any way be compared with Sassoon's work, either in preoccupation or style. A contemplation of pretty faces in an old photo album, redolent of so many of Sassoon's poems in its preoccupation with looking back in sadness and bitter-sweet melancholy to a 'better' time. Hodgson never wrote another poem like it.

As to Hodgson's verse, Sassoon was quite obviously a great fan. 'The Song of Honour' had been a big influence, but he also liked a great deal from Hodgson's first volume, the 'miserable' *Last Blackbird*. "You will probably frown me away," Sassoon wrote as late as 1953, "but there is a poem in *The Last Blackbird* which haunts and comforts me – 'Beauty Sprite'. I know it isn't one of your best, but it has magic for me. I can't forget it. It plays on my heartstrings." He also expressed admiration for

'The Missel Thrush' and 'Treasure Box' suggesting that "posterity will grab these eagerly."

In some strange way, there are echoes of Hodgson in various Sassoon poems: the boyish enthusiasm at waking to the sound of birdsong (in Hodgson's 'Holiday' and Sassoon's 'Strangeness of Heart'); romantic longing (in Hodgson's 'Fancy Fair' and Sassoon's 'Long Ago'). Hodgson actually wrote a small piece using the phrase "the loved one and the lover" adapted from one of Sassoon's poems in *The Heart's Journey*.

Hodgson's arrival in England from Japan in late 1931, just as Sassoon had finished the second part of his war trilogy, saw the two men cement their alliance. In early November, they set out from the Reform Club in Sassoon's Packard motor car, following an itinerary of bookshops in towns as far north as Scarborough. It was a trip that furnished both men with subject matter for letters for years to come, not to mention droll observations. Sassoon wrote to a friend in 1934: "I lunched at Bridlington on 13th November 1931 when I was motoring RH to Scarborough and back. I never saw a seaside place look so forlorn! The girl who served us with poached eggs said, 'It's enough to make a girl go wrong.'"

Hodgson's interest in books and the collecting of unusual editions was a constant one throughout his life. It was a link with friends such as Edmund Blunden, Holbrook Jackson, Lovat Fraser and others back into the 1890s. In a talk given to students in America in 1940, he explained his bibliophilic tastes, emphasising that he wanted books, "only which give me pleasure to read", rather than merely valuable or rare ones

> I like it too if possible just as it was sold from the shop or came from the bookbinder to the first owner; if it belonged to or carries the name of the author or some other person I know about whose memory I cherish, I like it all the better; and no worse if the flyleaf is blank or if it bears an inscription to or from some person unknown.

He did not hunt for what he termed "pedigree" books – they were usually too expensive. He had a particular liking for editions of certain poets who

> from a shy beginning, have come to lustrous fame: the early Moxon editions of Keats and Shelley published for the general reader and not as poetry is published so frequently nowadays, as educational aids; in those times, people – young people, grown-up and middle-aged and old people – lower-middle class, middle-class, upper-middle and so on – great numbers of them read poetry just because they liked it! Read it, quoted it, talked about it and pondered on it: in fact, did everything they could with poetry except attempt

to write it: one cause of this abstention was a very real reverence for The Muse.

Wordsworth's *Lyrical Ballads* was a favourite. He possessed the second edition published in 1800, "and in the original boards, too, as sold over the counter: it gives me weird and blissful thrills every time I look at it."

But Hodgson was as keen on obscurities as he was on giants like Keats, Coleridge and Wordsworth. He was a literary rag-and-bone man, always searching for the unconsidered trifle, the jewel amid the stones. As someone who had spent his life slipping down literary alleyways in order to avoid confronting the heavyweights, the 'unprofessional' was always a delight to him:

> The great want is biography of the lives of ordinary people. Very naturally it is a weakness in our knowledge that we only know about highly placed or talented people. We go askew and get life wrong. The obscure uncles and grandfathers of England, Scotland, Wales, etc. is the stuff, including aunts and pretty cousins. Also the writers of these books aren't clever, don't pose and often startle you with their ability in putting life into their ghosts – ghosts isn't the right word, they're never that.

On the trip north, for instance, he obtained a copy of Martin Tupper's *Proverbial Philosophy* and an 1851 edition of *Percy's Reliques of Ancient English Poetry*. Hodgson was fascinated by the "over-looked poet, the forgotten and the neglected", and he delighted in discovering a line or a phrase that continued to reverberate. In fact, he planned to collect enough such "gems" to fill a volume, the "big book" that he and Sassoon would compile, the fruits of their "researches into the sublime". It would be called *Without Comment* but, like so many of Hodgson's schemes during these years, never came to fruition.

On one level, the search, the discoveries, the obscurities were part of a conviction shared by both men, but by Sassoon most sharply, that a particular world was disappearing, was being destroyed. The "whiskered sons of plunder", the professional book dealers who were buying up all the treasures represented the wider world of commerce ("Mammon lurked in their features") and were denuding what were once treasure troves of anything worthwhile. This was symbolic of the demise of "old England" – a largely pre-industrial England, of course, one to which Sassoon was drawn emotionally and, with his purchase of Heytesbury Manor in 1933, one that he could actually inhabit.

The house and its substantial estates were, until the end of the 19th century, in the ownership of the Lords Heytesbury, and Sassoon's letters to Hodgson in Japan, following the latter's 1932 furlough were filled with

164

descriptions of his idyllic, almost lord-of-the-manor life in the country. His horse rides, the local characters, the long evenings musing before an open fire, that "prelapsarian world" (before the fall of Adam and Eve) he so much preferred to the real one. He was living in virtual isolation ("Five and a half months and I haven't been away for a night yet!").

Sassoon seemed desperate at times to convince himself and Hodgson that what he saw around him, the world he had immersed himself in, *was* real. Referring to the "old crusted characters" who had worked on the estate all their lives he asked: "Do their honest simplicities mean anything or don't they? Encountering them, in detail, from day to day, I affirm that they mean a lot to me."

They certainly meant more to him than the world beyond Heytesbury with its "fatuous officialdom", its "ugly businessmen", people "poisoned by possessions", a world of growing materialism and militarism. It's ironic that he should write a poem about the *threat* of aeroplanes when, in the newer, harsher poetry of the 1930s (such as that of C. Day Lewis), airmen represented something exciting and glamorous. In that sense, his poetry seemed to him as dated as his politics. Modernism clearly irritated him. He wrote to Hodgson:

> I can't make much of all the new bards at present – especially Auden
> – but as you say, they are there and trying for something fresh.

Later that year he defended himself and his subject matter:

> I repeat that it is still here [traditional England] though I may be living in an oasis. Auden has not yet arrived in Wiltshire. But I suppose he is industrial. I'm afraid I haven't quite accepted these young chaps yet. I read some of Spender's aloud [to Hester, his wife] recently and we felt there was something slightly wrong somewhere ... But how interesting it is to watch the new thing arriving! (Leaving oneself as an obsolete object some way down the road – gradually finding out what it feels like to be Sir William Watson). Good-luck to 'machine-age imagery'. 'Night's last goods train ...' is as much as I can manage so far, but I may be able to work in a petrol pump someday.

His remarks would grow harsher, however, particularly when his published verse was reviewed in less than glowing terms. Then it was the "storm-troopers" who were rubbing in his "obsolescence as a bard". Despite his disavowals, Sassoon worried about his literary fame and position.

Hodgson, by contrast, seemed less anxious – after all, he was now publishing nothing and was far away in Japan, watching events with a wry smile. He did his best to reassure Sassoon, however, suggesting that literary "gangs" come and go quite rapidly: he even penned a ditty about them:

The Old Gang

The Young Men of the 20s
Came crowding on the stage
To turn the Old Gang out
It's often stated;
But the Young Men of the 20s
Are now in middle age
And the Old Gang's still about
Rejuvenated.
The Young Men of the 30s.

As for the literary "storm-troopers" that Sassoon had complained of, Hodgson felt it was, "more and more becoming a matter of age, crop and generation". But then he continued, "what about 'Nae Luck'?" – referring to the phrase "There's Nae Luck about the House", a tale of a sailor's wife and the safe return of her husband from the sea by Jean Adam, an 18th-century Scottish poetess. This had stuck in Hodgson's mind for some months and he thought it "imperishable poetry".

Hodgson's tendency to wander off at such tangents, although no doubt sincere enough, at times smacks of a strategy – to avoid falling into the trap of becoming a literary 'grumpy old man'. He wasn't without opinions: during this period he produced a series of witty cartoons that were never published, lampooning the poetic cliques and literary salons of London. But literary politics had never worried him much and certainly didn't now. As Lewis Bush, a government official and friend of Hodgson's in Japan later wrote:

Never did I hear a harsh criticism of other poets and writers escape his lips; although he believed that poetry had declined so much because it no longer reached the hearts of men and did not move them as had the songs of all the great poets through the ages; but he wondered that perhaps his inability to understand and appreciate some of the modern forms was simply that he was out of touch.

Hodgson, however, was naturally ambivalent about Sassoon's England. He understood that the past was only somewhere to retreat to through his imagination with his books and pictures. He understood that it was his own creation and was no longer grounded in reality. Old books and directories provided him with a series of mental magic carpets:

I gloat over the possession of Rocque's *Plan of London*, published about the same time as *Tom Jones*; similarly I find it rapture to wander about the pages of Harwood's Plan of the great city published 50 years later. Here every house is marked. It is delightful, for instance, to trace William Blake's various habitations; with the aid of a little imagination, I have often seen him coming out of his front door with a parcel of coloured engravings under his arm ...

For a time, somewhat surprisingly, he appeared keen to return to England and retire. Sassoon's Wiltshire seemed to offer the ideal setting and he talked of buying a three-roomed cottage, "up an overgrown sheep-walk lane off the main road a mile or so. Breeding dogs, watching birds, wonderful, wonderful!" He was learning to use a hand-press in order to recreate the *Flying Fame* enterprise and was keen on the idea of his own poetic 'cottage industry'. This would come to pass, but not in England.

It was in 1938 that Hodgson saw Sassoon for the last time. On his way to join Aurelia in the USA, he stayed at Sassoon's Heytesbury Manor, making it his base for the four months he spent in the country. Sassoon had written that Hodgson would find it all almost too perfect and Hodgson was clearly impressed. But his mind was, as ever, set on Aurelia. She was his real world and, from Sassoon's idyllic English setting he wrote to her: "When I get across the Atlantic, back home to you and bliss, I wish it could be in some remote, though not too remote, corner of the state of Wisconsin. (Where I could see more birds than people.)"

He and Sassoon continued to exchange long letters – two reclusive figures, sharing the glimpses of birds, flora and fauna. In the 1950s, Hodgson wrote, not without a slight dig at Sassoon's wealth:

> As you go your rounds from day to day, I go mine, in the morning mainly as the dew dries up and in the evening before it falls, cutting down a bit of growth here and there, snipping off over-hanging boughs much as you do on your acres, though you pay more attention to the dandelions with your wide lawns in mind.

Sassoon for his part never ceased to marvel at their long and fruitful correspondence, and in one of his last letters to Hodgson he wrote:

> How well I remember you being driven away from the front portico (of Heytesbury) singing at the top of your voice and on top of the world. Strange, isn't it, that we've had all that mind-life together since then. Surely it must mean something here and hereafter?

20

Gooseberry Grange

I love England; I keep her customs, but I'll be happy if I am a mere man and belong to no nation. I hope there'll be in the future no national or racial feelings in the world.

(Ralph Hodgson to Professor Saito)

In many ways, the fact that the Japanese were prepared to renew Hodgson's contract in July 1935 after the complications of his relationship with Aurelia and their eventual marriage, is a tribute to the tolerance and dedication of his departmental head, Professor Kochi Doi. Though he was reticent in his memoirs, Doi certainly had to take risks to shield Hodgson from criticism and possible dismissal in an increasingly uncomfortable situation on the campus. He clearly felt Hodgson was worth the effort.

Doi had always wanted someone unorthodox to teach his students, of course. As a colleague, Ineko Kondo, recalled "Doi and myself thought that in our university the usual course of lectures should be offered by academically trained scholars, while special courses of various types could suitably be given by guest professors. Stimulation rather than information for the students should be expected from them. In other words, guest professors of English Literature need not necessarily be professors, scholars deeply immersed in research."

Hodgson's eclectic knowledge, his interest in obscure literature, his skill as a caricaturist and his brilliant talk were the type of qualities desired. In a sense, he was a poet-in-residence rather than a teacher. Indeed he'd glimpsed the possibilities of such a role back in the early 1920s. The Royal College of Art's principal, William Rothenstein, had expressed the desire to "broaden students' education" and after he had painted the portraits of notables such as T.E. Lawrence, Chesterton and Hodgson himself, he would persuade them to give informal talks to students in the Queensgate common room. Hodgson reversed the process. According to Kochi Doi:

> His lectures were very well prepared; he did not write them out or try to memorise, but he visualised them even down to details. On the platform, if he was going to talk about one of his poet friends,

he would first of all draw his portrait on the blackboard very quickly, then read some selected poems and explain them piece by piece and sometimes he would draw other pictures to illustrate the poem just as he had done in the *Broadsides* published by the *Flying Fame*. Those who attended his lectures acquired not only a knowledge but also a very intimate and delightful sensation of the poem, so that they left the classroom carrying an evanescent memory of their having seen the poet face to face and receiving a portion of his poetical vision.

He lectured three times every week on 'The Background of English Literature', 'Contemporary English Poetry' and 'The Infinite Variety of English Poetry'. Doi added, "The last really *was* infinite varieties and he went on for more than ten years never repeating the same topic. I suppose he was secretly determined to act as a cultural minister for England, and he carried out his mission splendidly."

Students could recall the impression he made on them decades later: One wrote:

> It was in the early 1930s when I took courses from Hodgson in Tohoku University. Hodgson must have been over 50, but I could not tell whether he was old or young. Everybody who was in his class will remember that Hodgson, when he entered the room, would remove the pipe from his mouth, greet loudly, "Good Afternoon", and sit heavily down on the big instructor's desk (speech table) on the platform and start the lecture. Saying that a dog thinks, he would imitate a dog in meditation, with the innocent aspect of his character fully exposed. We would often burst out laughing. He might have imitated a dog for the purpose of keeping students awake. For his courses were said to be credited by regular attendance to the class even for those who were dozing all the time – there were some such students.

For women students, however, the thrill lay in Hodgson's attitude towards them. In inter-war Japan, women were struggling hard against a patriarchal system that placed great barriers before them in their education. Ineko Kondo recalled:

> To me, who felt very small in the university whose primary purpose was to educate men, it was an extremely surprising and agreeable sensation to hear him speak so courteously to us women. Sometimes when we were late and entered the lecture room after Hodgson had already begun his talk, he always turned to us and explained what he had been talking about. He never did this for male students so I had secret pleasure, feeling as if I had suddenly moved to the heavenly land of women! How well I remember Mr Hodgson as

he entered the lecture room carrying his stick and his hat. He put them carelessly on the desk, took off his coat and put it also on the desk. He then sat on his coat on the desk for, unlike other lecturers he, instead of sitting on the chair provided for that purpose, sat on the desk on the platform and, dangling his legs, talked to us, often with his beloved pipe in his mouth.

He was, in fact, a teacher ahead of his time in many ways. When asked by the Japanese Education Ministry for suggestions on how to improve the teaching of English literature to foreign students, he drew up a document that emphasised the visual and the inspirational, and the importance of the *sound* of poetry and its delivery. The use of the gramophone was also recommended. In short, he was as far from the conventional academic as it was possible to be. No surprise, perhaps, as Hodgson had never been to a college or university, had never been trained as a teacher and generally disliked academic life.

His devotion to the inspirational and the mood of the moment remained as strong as ever. When Doi asked permission to have a stenographer come in and take down his lectures with a view to publication, he refused. He would only commit to paper what he wanted to *live* in some way and that, for him, could only be poetry – something that was at last gradually returning to him.

Hodgson generally avoided speaking before learned gatherings. When pressed for a lecture by the English Society at Tokyo University in 1928, he replied that he had no interest in lecturing on literature but would be "delighted to talk about dogs". However, in 1930 the Japanese Association of English Literary Studies held their annual meeting at Kyoto and asked Hodgson to give a lecture. He spent a month of his summer vacation preparing a long piece entitled 'Christmas Bells'. Contrary to his usual practice, he wrote it out in full and had Aurelia type it up, all fifty pages if it. In the two and a half hours it took him to read it he impressed upon his audience the meaning of humanism and the dangers of allowing it to be eroded, a process he'd seen begin in the mechanised mass slaughter of the First World War. He feared that the world had all too soon forgotten the horrors of modem warfare and was once again blindly fumbling towards the precipice. He made his own position perfectly clear, quoting John Scott's poem 'Recruiting', which begins:

I hate the drum's discordant sound,
Parading round, and round, and round.

Professor Kochi Doi described it as "a warning to us against the militaristic tendency, and a cry for world peace. I often am reminded of this as the first tolling of the prophetic bell, warning [of] the Second

World War." Sadly, what Doi described as a "very interesting human document" never appeared in the English Literary Society's journal, *Studies in English Literature*, as might have been expected. Perhaps, given the nature of its theme and the prevailing political climate in Japan, it was quietly forgotten.

Hodgson's form of Quaker pacifism would have met with little official sympathy in an increasingly militarised Japan. During the 1930s the country became more and more a semi-fascist state with restrictions on speech, the press and assembly, with sporadic and increasing arrests of those suspected of holding or uttering "dangerous thoughts". Hodgson's open support for the local Jiyu Gakuen (School of Freedom) for girls run by a Mrs Hani would have gone totally against the prevailing grain. Female emancipation has never been a popular cause in Japan, and certainly was not in the 1930s.

However, Hodgson made no more forays into public affairs after the 'Christmas Bells' lecture. Indeed, after 1935 he worked with the Council for the Promotion of Science in Japan, helping with the translation into English of the *Manyoshu*, the oldest anthology of early Japanese poems. Ishii Hakuson and Obata Shigeyoshi were charged with translating 1,000 poems that experts had selected from more than 4,500 in the anthology, and Hodgson, despite the fact that he knew no Japanese, was chosen to give the finishing touch to their work. Kochi Doi explained:

> Every week he read the manuscripts which Hakuson Ishii, the translator, brought to Sendai. He picked out some parts that did not sound well to him, asking the translator questions, and suggesting a more pertinent English expression, but the rest he left for the translator. He did not offer his own translation. Thus the translation of about one thousand poems in the *Manyoshu* was completed.

With their closeness to the natural world, populated by creatures of all kinds, including 37 species of birds, the *Manyoshu* poems must have been congenial to Hodgson. For his work on this project he received, in 1938, an official award – the Order of the Rising Sun.

In many ways, life couldn't have been better for Hodgson during these inter-war years. The university authorities built him his own house (called Gooseberry Grange by the Hodgsons). It was a traditional two-storey Japanese residence with plenty of rooms and a veranda that looked out on to a bank of cherry trees lining the river. Beyond, wooded hills were alive with birds, although with over 40 canaries around the house in various cages, the Hodgsons were never starved of birdsong.

They had three servants: the faithful manservant Otsune San, and two live-in servant girls, Yoshiko and Toyoto. Aurelia's many diaries and notebooks document a happy if frugal existence. Their dogs, Towser and

Bridget (the latter a Japanese Akita Dog), had, as always, an almost free run of the house. Aurelia lamented in a letter to her mother about the shabby sofa covers: "the newest one lost so much colour in the wash that I am not very proud of it for our living room – if only the dogs did not wrestle on it."

Aurelia was responsible for the canaries that filled the house. Her journal, *Consider the Canary*, kept over a number of years, ran into five volumes, and gave a detailed, day-by-day account of the birds' habits, breeding, courtship, singing.

It was a contented, quiet existence, utterly private and unlike any kind of life Hodgson could have organised or afforded anywhere else in the world, let alone England. As he wrote to Rudolf Besier in 1935

> The Japanese are the pleasantest of people. Few know them beyond their own coasts. Tourists least of all. We have a little house near the university, Gooseberry Grange. My wife is a good gardener and grows excellent green peas. Our marriage is an entirely happy one, the Dunmow standard, I may as well say. Her name is Aurelia – Weg for short. She is a jewel, not alone to me but to everybody around her.

She was certainly indispensable to Hodgson. The vegetable and fruit garden that she tended produced gooseberries, currant bushes, thyme, columbine, feverfew, violets, corn stalks and much more. She baked bread, learned how to take photographs and mastered the use of a printing press that Hodgson was hoping to use to print his poetry. She altered and made clothes as well as working on Hodgson's lectures as typist and research assistant. She also catalogued his collection of three thousand books, many of which were stored permanently in boxes and trunks in case of earthquakes, and was thus well equipped to hunt down quotations when he needed them for lectures. She could even translate Japanese on occasion though she knew little of the language.

In many ways, Hodgson was not actually living in Japan at all. John Hatcher, professor of Literature at Fukuoka University in Japan, wrote:

> No one could have been more profoundly English than Ralph Hodgson, yet no one could have been less of a Little Englander. His love for England, especially the countryside and country pursuits but also the vibrancy of London and the wry eccentricities of the English people, rings through his poetry and memoirists, records of his conversation.

To visiting westerners, Hodgson, by contrast, seemed like a relic from the 19th century, his chatter and dress were unchanged from his *Big Budget* days. The American diplomat Lewis Bush wrote:

Ralph liked to describe himself as the 'Last of the Fancy'. There was indeed something of the Beau Brummel about him. The blue, gilt-buttoned jacket [which he wore], the canary-yellow, double-breasted waistcoat, white corduroy trousers, immaculate linen and well-matched necktie [were reminiscent of] London in the Nineties. Wilde, Swinburne, Shaw, his friend who played a one-man band and tootled the horn on the Brighton coach, the musichall and magic names like Albert Chevalier, Dan Leno and the incomparable Marie Lloyd, he spoke of with enthusiasm touched with sadness. He was an inveterate pipe-smoker. He had three hundred and sixty-five pipes made specially for him in Vienna and as he finished a pipe it would be tossed into a box, cleaned carefully by the maid and then placed at the end of the roster.

Some of these visitors were poets and literary men who kept him in touch with Western thinking. William Plomer visited during the early years, along with Laurence Binyon. In 1927 he spent some lively evenings in Tokyo with I.A. Richards; Peter Quennell visited when he was teaching at Tokyo University. William Empson arrived in January 1934 *en route* to ski on Mount Fuji. Aurelia recalled him to a friend as:

the same odd man who came here last year and burned a hole in the yellow pillow top you quilted for me. This year he burned a little hole in the Chinese linen on the dining table. In Cambridge he was in the group of Modernist poets …

The poet Roy Campbell spent time with the Hodgsons and expressed himself a fan of Hodgson's work. Hodgson also befriended the German philosopher Karl Löwith, who later wrote of Hodgson's special ideas on what constituted 'freedom' and personality. Löwith noted Hodgson's "expressive face, well formed with a mighty nose between two prominent eyes, a wide mouth, witty and sensual".

Hodgson's last three-year contract, from September 1935 to August 1938, ended amid much international uncertainty. He was now almost sixty-seven, and with war clouds gathering, the decision was made to leave Japan for good. Most of their household effects were left behind to be auctioned by the servants. However, complain though Hodgson might about being so far away from Ridgeway's tea rooms or being unable to sit around Sassoon's log fire and while away the evenings, he had long since ceased to feel that England offered him anything at all. It would be to the United States that he and Aurelia would now head.

In late 1938, when passing through London on his way to the USA, where Aurelia, having gone on ahead, was already safe at home in

Wisconsin, he wrote of how foreign the city appeared to him, how so little of what he remembered remained:

> Sick and weary of heart, I came away, got on a bus and travelled west, looking at the hordes of people more foreign to me than anything we saw in the East, almost.

It was all "mechanism, make-up and modernism":

> When I leave England, if I do, I'll never come back or wish to. It is as well that I have seen it. I couldn't have pictured it. The young look at least as if they just wanted to finish their jobs and get away and I suppose that is the whole story today – get away out of sight of it, as if it was just a living they got out of it, not the satisfaction of making or doing something they were born fitted to do, poor wretches. I feel sorry for 'em all.

Ralph Hodgson 'doodle' c.1937

21

'The Muse and the Mastiff'

There's nothing I've personally been so thankful for as the return
of my muse – via Weg – these latter most unhappy years!
(Ralph Hodgson to Siegfried Sassoon)

When Hodgson stayed in England *en route* for the USA in 1938, he was uncharacteristically keen to announce to friends and publishers alike that he was in possession of a new long poem, unfinished but clearly very important to him. T.S. Eliot was told and was immediately interested; the publishers Harold Macmillan and his brother were also interested. James Stephens, whom Hodgson met by chance in the street and with whom he spent an hour or so in Oxford Street Lyons Corner House, was also told: "He shook me by the hand solemnly and long – to the wonder of the people about us!" Down at Heytesbury Manor, which Hodgson made his base for his four-month stay, he fulfilled a long-held dream. He read the poem to Sassoon and his wife one evening in front of the fire, and Sassoon commemorated the occasion in verse:

> Said Heytesbury House, "I've mainly been
> A place where nothing strange is seen –
> Or heard – but now, what's the event
> Which fills me with astonishment?
> A man named Hodgson comes to stay
> One sultry hot midsummer's day
> And though I've scarcely got to know him
> Reads a most peculiar poem."

It wasn't the first time 'The Muse and the Mastiff' had been read aloud. Kochi Doi, Hodgson's superior at Sendai University, remembered how, in 1936, after some two years' intermittent work on the piece, Hodgson read the first 700 lines of it to the Japanese English Literary Association. No reactions are recorded, and one imagines the Japanese audience would have made little of it, for it would be Hodgson's most ambitious piece of work and the least understood.

Hodgson seems to have been taken unawares by the poem's 'arrival'. His muse had ceased visiting him years before but, in 1933, soon after his marriage to Aurelia, he wrote to Sassoon: "the oddest thing happened to me" and announced that he had started to work again.

In 1935 he wrote to Rudolf Besier:

> You ask about my verse. It's awful. When I came to, out of the stupefaction of 1914-18, I found my muse still about in a lost sort of way. There was nothing to do but accept it. Something in life was over. It happened to a lot of other people. She wasn't dead – just dumb ...

However

> it seems comic after all this to turn to my verse again. After many years my muse came back last autumn and fairly bowled me over. I had to drop my work at the university. These [university] people are full of understanding in these matters. The students brought me a flowering thorn and a bowl of bulbs. The result was a long poem, longer by a good deal than the others. I'll send it to you one of these days. It's in the bake house now.

It was certainly an inconvenient visitation. Kochi Doi recalls:

> One day I called upon him and he said: 'I had a call from my muse last night.' From that day he was intent on writing the poem. He seemed like a man possessed. He would go to the university on a cold morning without hat and overcoat, or would lose his cane or some other things. The duty of lecturing seemed to be very hard for him in those days and I feared he would break down before he could complete the poem. As the Christmas holidays were near at hand I advised him to put aside his classwork till the poem was completed.

The subsequent work read out to the Literary Association was by no means complete, however. Indeed, there is reason to believe that what Doi heard was substantially altered in the coming years, for when Doi read the published version in the 1950s he didn't recognise it, although this could have been due either to the passage of time or the poem's obscurity. In many ways, given his pleasure in announcing it to all and sundry as well as reading it to various audiences, 'The Muse and the Mastiff' would be Hodgson's most public piece of work, although its genesis was born of that most private of all his relationships, his marriage to Aurelia.

Hodgson's dedication to her at the start of the poem reads: "You witnessed with me the bull-terrier's dream, the origin of 'The Muse and the Mastiff'", and, while in England in 1938, he wrote to her, "'The Muse and the Mastiff' owes its birth – or at least a good deal of its breeding – to your patience, intelligence and quiet apprehension." In the same letter, Hodgson describes how she was crucial in creating the uniquely propitious aromatic and sensual atmosphere that seemed so essential to his work:

> How wonderful those visits (of the muse) in Sendai – what a satisfying trio it was upstairs in that little room. I think your shampoo had something to do with it, and your wide-brimmed hat. Let's have that Herrick record on, the girl's voices – and then such shampoo! You ask me, 'Which dress shall I wear?' 'Oh, the new flowery one.' 'And the white shoes?' 'Good – sit over there, that's right. Darling!' 'Darling! Chair this way a bit – there. My Weg! Stop the gramophone!'

W.H. Auden has said that poets *use* people; that they need them as a focus for the sensations about which they want to write. The 'muse' idea, an ancient concept related to creative inspiration stretching back to the Greeks, is another way of saying the same thing: that a particular person can unlock certain creative powers within an artist. Auden implies that the muse is embodied in a real person. Among Hodgson's poet friends, Walter de la Mare felt that Nancy Royd Smith provided him with his inspiration, while Edward Thomas identified the poet Eleanor Farjeon as similarly influential in his own poetic life. For Hodgson, however, the muse was never that tangible. Aurelia was more of a medium who created an aura, as in a séance, enabling the muse to appear and thus enabling Hodgson to work.

This doesn't mean that Hodgson's muse was something vague and ethereal, however. He had firm ideas as to her age and her nature and, in a long, unpublished opening to 'The Muse and the Mastiff', he makes this clear. The poet in the poem vehemently rejects suggestions that the muse was in some way unsavoury or "loose", that she was a "harpy" or a "houri" or a "hag":

> 'Hag!' A girl like her!
> Forever just turned seventeen!
> I've never heard her slandered so,
> The Heavenly Maid!

In 'The Muse and the Mastiff', the muse would be a blushing, sensitive, ultra-feminine figure, similar to those at the heart of earlier, important poems such as 'The Last Blackbird' and 'To Deck a Woman'. However, although a pure virginal idea is central to Hodgson's muse concept, the muse must bear children in the shape of poems. As he wrote in 1940

The Muse consorts with whom she will
Brought to bear and safe delivered
She rises as the cord is severed
Mother anew and maiden still …

Thus, while young and innocent, there is the *possibility* that the muse can also be a wanton, a "trollop" – on occasions bearing "brats beyond belief". Although not the muse herself, Aurelia shared important characteristics with Hodgson's ideal. First and foremost, when he met her in early 1927 she was still, despite being close to 30 years old, a virgin and she would remain so for at least the first five years of their relationship, possibly longer. Perhaps that was why Hodgson found her so refreshingly "girlish" and why she had not, in his eyes at least, lost the essential innocence which he felt so many young girls in modern society lost unnecessarily early.

In the Hodgsons' physical relationship playing on this girl/woman, virgin/whore dichotomy clearly intrigued him. Photographs taken of Aurelia during the early days in Japan invariably depict her as neatly, if soberly dressed, her hair wound demurely in plaits around her head, the perfect, even angelic, academic wife. There are other photographs, however, taken by Hodgson, in which she is almost unrecognisable. Her hair cascades from beneath a jauntily-tilted French beret, her hands are placed firmly on her hips which are thrust provocatively forward, a mischievous grin on her face. Whether Aurelia was conscious of it or not, Hodgson clearly behaved towards her as Auden suggested poets *will* behave towards significant others in their lives: he enlisted and subordinated her to serve his vocation. As Auden wrote, "the poet's concern [is] with the object to be created, an object which, however much of himself goes into it, must end up as a non-self".

The other important element of the poem, as important to Hodgson in life as in art, was his relationship with dogs. Strangely, despite his obsession with bull-terriers and his relentless championing of them as a breed, he had only once attempted to write about them. In the 'Ode to Dulcina' included in *The Last Blackbird* collection, he had written of his love for the dog. 'The Muse and the Mastiff', however, would be his first major foray into the dog's mind or at least into the dream-world of a dog.

Kochi Doi once recalled Hodgson pointing to his Japanese bull-terrier making faces in its sleep: "He told me the dog was now remembering far-off days when his ancestors were fighting wild bears in the primeval forests of Siberia." 'The Muse and the Mastiff' starts from just such an incident. The owner of a dog tells a poet friend of its troubled dreaming. The poet assumes the dog is being visited by some sort of animal "shade".

178

The Muse appears and the poem begins.

The line from Coleridge's 'Christabel' used as an epigram, ("For what can ail the Mastiff bitch?") is answered: an ancient bear, the last wild one in England or Europe, which has come

> Buffeting his way through time and tide
> A thousand years to threaten yours,
> And mystify the best of men
> And rush the Muse – in all her glow
> And innocence of Ah, how long ago!

Hodgson had long been fascinated by Julian Huxley's theory of inherited memory, of evolution being both social and emotional. Combine this with an interest in spiritualism, and we have the rationale behind his time-travelling bear:

> ... Did we dare assume
> That threatened by approaching doom
> He pierced the veil with second sight?
> Some beasts appear to have the power,
> Why not he at such an hour?

It all makes for a rather jumbled construction. A dog dreams of a bear whose story is told via a muse to a poet, both of whom then recount the tale to a friend who is the owner of the dog. During the recitation the bear itself actually appears in the room where poet and friend are sitting. It is clear that Hodgson struggled to shape the poem satisfactorily. He dropped an opening consisting mainly of dialogue between poet and friend, as well as subsequent dramatic parts of the poem that might have helped make it clearer. Furthermore he published only half the completed poem, and presented it disjointedly, starting with the ending first, so that hardly anyone who had not read it in its original form could make head or tail of it. His motives for this procedure will be discussed later. For now, 'The Muse and the Mastiff' starts in puzzling fashion. We meet a mysterious male animal in the opening line:

> Something of him still comes out
> Of his moorland fog – some hazy, dim,
> Old family death's-head print of him
> In her blood and bones – ...

It is only after some forty lines or so that we can confirm it is a bear, perhaps the last wild bear that England knew. Dead a thousand years, it still troubles the mind of the sleeping mastiff who, it must be said, figures no more in the poem: like Aurelia, this precious animal is no more than a medium. The bear continues:

> Hoisting itself across the wall
> And shuffling a hairy foot about
> The shrubbery and paths at night
> In her sleep: Here, Now: a call

just as he used to descend on moorland villages:

> When he was in his fleshly prime
> And she in hers – as still she is –

Moreover, it is only after ninety lines that we discover the speaker to be the muse present in the room with the poet and his friend. The muse describes how, in later life, the bear sometimes paid such nocturnal visits in search of food, always much bothered by competitors, both birds and beasts. She is just mentioning weasels when she falters in mid-sentence. The room changes rather dramatically and the bear himself materialises and completes the sentence for her:

> Thus the Muse: her troubled tones
> Lifted in the forest gloom
> That hung three-quarters of the room,
> Its briar-trellised wallpaper
> And window-boxes: all at once
> Evoking hiccups, yawns and groans
> And lusty belches in response –
> To make no mystery, from the bear,
> None other than himself: his lair
> The corner-cupboard, blithe and gay
> With rosy Minton till he woke,
> Then a disembowelled oak,
> Between the walnut chiffonier
> And doorpost, also in decay,
> Lichened ruins now, all three –
> And in a husky whisper, low
> But loud enough to bring her glow
> Full flush and halt her by his tree,
> The groan: Those hairy leeches, Lass!
> … Those hairy leeches in the grass –
> She thanked him – making signs to me
> To turn the locked-up cupboard key
> And save ourselves a shower of glass,
> Not before high time – the bear
> Tumbling out of his lichened lair
> Just as I regained my chair,
> Thinking to himself …

But before we get the bear's thoughts, the poet himself, reading aloud, acknowledges that all this must seem far-fetched to his friend but still pleads its plausibility. Returning to the bear and its thoughts, we learn that it is food that brings him out haunting the habitations of men and dogs. The greater part of the poem relates the bear's moody, pungent and sardonic comments on all those in the animal world who compete with him for sustenance: birds, beasts and insects. He talks of wolves and bears, weasels and polecats, finches and crows. He argues with the muse (who throughout the piece is anxious that the bear does not condemn all his fellow creatures) about whether these animals are greedier or smellier than he; whether hedgehogs or wolves behave any better than he. Birds annoy him most, however:

> Birds of prey
> Had been upon his mind all day:
> Incredible amounts they ate;

Indeed, birds would appear to be his worst enemies. In one passage he muses on how good it would be to be a spider:

> The little websters everywhere
> Amazed him by the flies they caught;
> The mystery was, where they managed to stow
> Their plant and stock, so pinched for room
> They seemed in contrast with a bear,
> And how they made their jennies go;
> 'N the summer he gave much time and thought
> To spiders, stopping for hours to stare:
> Not only did it lighten gloom,
> It worked him into such a glow
> Of fancy as their prizes fought
> Against the rigours of the snare,
> Boding worse – all buzz and fume
> Till quieted and trussed up taut,
> That a body of eagles floundered there,
> Knelling each its eyrie's doom;
> In ecstasy his forearm brought
> All but a mash of flies to naught.

Later he dreams of being able to fly and batter the birds in flight! And it is on this fundamental difference of opinion about birds, in particular, between the muse and the bear, that the poem actually turns. The muse, not surprisingly given their significance to her, adores owls:

> Little Christians who indeed
> Outside the letter of the church

They manifestly were ...
Emblems of rue and
Reverie for aeons

The bear had teased her about them, considering them stupid and worthy
to be eaten, but the muse will hear none of it. The last, long section of
the poem concerns her reflections on owls and on her own role through
the ages:

Looking back the ages through
At such variety of scene
On either side her path – how long!
– The circumstance was hardly new;
Listening to herself in song
From whatever source it drew –
Madonna or the Gypsy Queen.

She concedes that her "song" was not always perfect, that in the
springtime it was apt to be "always somewhat over strong", but she
concludes that her concern for owls had never been misplaced, that she
had not made a fool of herself:

Answer was not long delayed
All alive: a family of five
They tumbled up and out that night
In feather for a furlong flight
Blithely, beautifully flown
Up and down the moonlit glade:

If the construction of 'The Muse and the Mastiff' was unresolved and
overly confusing, Hodgson's style in this, his last major work, and the
culmination of his poetic efforts, is sharp, colloquial and wry. The artificial
poetic sound has long-since been abandoned, the language now both
down to earth and, syntax apart, easy on the ear. It is thus able to sustain
several passages of accurate, sweet description such as only a lifelong
close observer of nature could achieve:

So the misselthrush was at their bush
Beyond himself so blithe and gay,
Acting like a bird in wine,
Throwing tendrils out of twine,
Tugging and tearing spray from spray,
Fold from fold, till gaps between
Rendered void – practically destroyed
All that held the sun at bay,
And her owlets cowered from his brazen ray;

Sobersides and Woebetides,
Innocent of gall and spleen,
They looked with little mouths drawn down
Into their chins, like cherubins,
On monuments on marble brown
To persons of antique renown,
A medieval King or Queen ...

But the mood is not sweet for the most part. Fury is aroused as the poet, to the mortification of the muse, remembers bear-baiting:

I spoke of blood-sick Marybone:
The Hockley pit: the Bankside hells:
Of Blackface and old Sackerson,
Scabby hunks and others there,
Week in, week out, year after year
Unhutched amid the yawps and yells
And titters of the ghoulery –
To sweat the brows of God in Heaven,
And start a bead on London's even,
Smelling sin one day in seven –
And waited trembling: as did she,
Scarlet to her scalp for me
And my repellent species: hers,
By adoption, not by blood
She meant it to be clearly understood

The published version of the 'The Muse and the Mastiff' ends inconclusively, almost in mid-story. The remaining unpublished section, which is almost as long, takes the action up with the bear's principal dilemma, that which had awoken him prematurely from his hibernation, the desperate need for food. It explains the risks he takes coming into the village, using all the wiles his mother had taught him. But it seems the villagers are waiting for him. There is a final fight, and we presume the bear dies, although Hodgson leaves this open:

But whether that night he stole away
Red with glory home again ...
Or there and then paid his owings
Who can say? Even your Mastiff now forgets
Or only your mastiff knows today.

Hodgson never worked this last section up into the style and feel of the published piece. It remains one-dimensional and less compelling. What is certain, however, is that as the poem progressed, more and more of his own self emerged, both in the manner of expression, or of his own history.

As his old friend William Maas said, "It is quite the most characteristic piece you have written as it brings you before me as nothing else you have written does – your voice, gestures, and the questioning stare, as much as to say, 'Think differently from me if you dare'."

Though set in ancient times it is recognisably the North-East of England, with its "dothery-grass" and with Hodgson's own Durham accent coming through on occasion ("grass" rhyming with "lass" for instance). There are references to Thomas Bewick, and to old bird books such as *Yarrell's British Birds*. There are outcast bulls; "dizzy young men" sitting down to listen to birdsong; references to times past "when Stonehenge was new". In fact, it is a latter day 'Song of Honour' in many ways, though of an animal rather than human kind, and noticeably less generous in tone.

Hodgson left a note to his final editor concerning the possibilities of his ever finishing the work: "To be continued elsewhere perhaps (but) for good reason not." Perhaps this was a hint that it didn't really matter much because the bear was going to die anyway.

Towards the end of his life he wrote to the same editor: "My hesitation (about completing the poem) came to a head through the creeping fear that some cinema-writer might chance upon it and put it to his own uses, which might be very unlike my own ..." He added that it had been a radio piece by Eric Severaid, an American commentator, about the voracity of TV that had alerted him to the danger.

Whether that was the real reason, or whether his fading mental powers left him unable to work the piece into shape and feel that satisfied him (and he had worked on it almost without a pause for nearly twenty years anyway) is hard to say.

Critical reaction to what Auden called "Surely one of the most extraordinary English poems of this [20th] century ..." is scattered, probably affected by the idiosyncratic way in which it had been published. Hodgson sent excerpts of the poem on a series of broadsides called *Flying Scroll* (his American version of *Flying Fame* broadsides), to friends and people interested in his work, other poets, and academics.

The critic I.A. Richards wrote in October 1942: "I'm still too puzzled by it to comment yet!", though he asked Hodgson if he wanted to read it at Harvard University for $50. Seven years later, having received more fragments of it, he wrote, "it is taking mysterious form though it remains no less a puzzle than ever ..."

When another recipient, the poet and critic Robert Hillyer, replied to Hodgson: "It interests me deeply – haunting, difficult, beneath simplicity, full of ambushes, something to be pondered over and lived in for a while." He also suggested Hodgson read the piece aloud. Hodgson replied:

> Don't study it – it is a personal poem, not in the least by design and intention but as an old friend in London has said in a recent

letter, it might well be subtitled 'For Close Friends Only' – those with a long and intimate acquaintance with my mind and feelings. Others will find it difficult *and they do.* So don't you bother about that poem.

The old friend was William Maas, with whom he'd first worked back in 1893 in Fleet Street. When he received his copy, along with some explanation, he wrote to Hodgson that, for the casual reader, certain 'signposts' might be needed to explain what the poem was about.

In fact, the poem's obscurity prompted Hodgson to write to Edward Marsh:

> I stopped frozen in 1940-41 when I was revising the long poem. I printed some of it in a chapbook a year or two ago and had intended to send you one. I didn't because one or two [people] who saw it found it unintelligible, and, as I dislike unintelligible verse myself, I withdrew it. If I get another push I may complete it when I hope all will be clear enough, but one can't tell.

Edith Sitwell described it as an, "impressive, strange, memorable fragment". She felt, however, that *some* of its difficulty stemmed from its incompleteness, but much more from what she considered perverse punctuation:

> [inserting] a full stop here, a parenthesis marked there, wonderfully reveals its meaning. One senses a certain indifference to the reader – such an indifference as long withdrawal into privacy might promote – and an inclination to write for oneself, that audience to whom all is plain.

Sassoon also felt Hodgson had used:

> a verse shorthand that dodges about with oddities of syntax and whimsical allusions which make it outwardly a difficult poem – [it] takes as a bit of following, in fact, until one gets accustomed to its fascinating and original idiom. Conceived and begun more than 20 years ago, it is an outstanding achievement. Quite unlike anything else he has written, it has an unclassifiable quality and certain lines and passages of rarest magic. No other English poet has produced anything to compare with it in naturalistic wizardry, except Meredith in 'The Woods of Westermain' from which it differs in being devoid of morality and conscious literary artifice.

The critic Naomi Lewis thought it obscure but not complex:

once the scrambled surface is resolved, the underlying motive then is clear. A forceful, and eerily puzzling work in which the muse, the baited Elizabethan bear and the poet all add their thoughts in a jocular, fierce, allusive rhyming tide of four-iambic lines.

She said she could:

> hear the old (i.e. early) Hodgson shout all right. It is the shout itself, the idiosyncratic assault that catches and compels. For energy is Mr Hodgson's unfailing quality. In poetry it can come from a number of sources: loss as well as love; pessimism as much as faith. Mr Hodgson's impetus is usually anger – a thunder of rage on behalf of animals and birds oppressed by men. Oddly untouched by two major wars this special anger continues, through 50 years, to burn.

G.S. Fraser wrote that 'The Muse and the Mastiff' was "the most bizarrely original thing" Hodgson had done, and added: "I believe that Mr Hodgson has genuinely relived the ancestral romantic experience … Like his primeval bear he wanders about our world looking for a kind of ancient nourishment, of which he finds little …"

As Hodgson left England for the last time in late 1938, heading for the United States and Aurelia, he must have known he would never return. (Indeed, he once told Muriel Hodgson that he sensed he would die in the US.) Aged 68, with a world conflict threatening, the United States would become his physical haven. 'The Muse and the Mastiff', however, would be a place of even deeper refuge. As he wrote to Aurelia: "I don't know where I'd be without that poem: it would be a world of loneliness intolerable."

22

Owlacres

*To vegetate
's to live at a terrific rate:
Pinks drudge like slaves:*

*From a bed of phlox in blow
Butterflies work as hard as bees.*
('To Vegetate')

Just a few days after his arrival in America, at the Hotel Atlantic in Chicago, Hodgson was presented with the Japanese insignia of the fifth class of the Order of the Rising Sun – the reward for his work on the Manyoshu poems. The British consul general, Robert Ross, who granted him official permission to wear the insignia, asked, "Is this the same Ralph Hodgson I knew in Brighton when I was a war patient there? Who instilled in me a love of beautiful writing?" Such pleasant surprises would be a feature of Hodgson's reception in the USA. Numerous academics and poets who'd known and admired him from Georgian days reacted with delight at his arrival, some astonished to find him still alive and writing poetry.

Among those to write and welcome him was Louis Untermeyer, professor of Literature at the University of Michigan, who had met Hodgson in the 1920s; Leonard Bacon, professor of English at the University of California who had been captivated by a reading of 'Eve' in 1914; and Robert Hillyer, professor of English at Harvard. There was also Edward Davison, a Scot who had served in the Royal Navy in 1914-18 and was now professor of English at the University of Colorado; Professor Ed Sanders at Ypsilanti University, Michigan, who had been trying for years to get Hodgson to lecture in the States; plus influential older poets such as Witter Bynner and William Rose Benét. Most significant of all, however, was Professor Cornelius Weygandt at Pennsylvania University, Philadelphia, who introduced Hodgson to Seymour Adelman, a man who would play a major role in the publishing of Hodgson's work over the next decade or more.

Inevitably, all were admirers of everything Georgian. Some, like Davison and Hillyer, had had contacts with de la Mare, Bridges and Housman. Hillyer, in particular, was a strong critic of the Modernism of Pound and Eliot. Most were poets in their own right of a decidedly Romantic, traditionally lyrical kind, and all saw Hodgson as a quintessential voice from that distant, golden time, an inspiration and a model in many ways.

There would be no job offers, of course as Hodgson was now 68 years old, but over the next couple of years there would be regular invitations to speak and lecture at poetry conferences. He gave a talk entitled 'Poets Remembered' at Goucher College, Baltimore and he repeated the talk, plus another on collecting books, at a summer school in Boulder, Colorado. He did the same at Ypsilanti, as well as taking part in a question-and-answer session at Pennsylvania State University where he was recorded reciting some of his poems.

The sums of money earned, usually something between $300 to $400 a time, were crucial as the Hodgsons had little, if any, capital. A small legacy had come Hodgson's way in 1938 from a grandfather of Dolly's, and Aurelia had some bonds her father had invested for her during the 1920s and 1930s, but with no wage coming in and nothing saved from Japan, times were hard.

At first they stayed with Aurelia's parents in Madison, Wisconsin, but within six months they had made their way east, to Wilkes Barre where she had been brought up and closer to various contacts and friends. They then rented a flat in Philadelphia while they looked around for somewhere more amenable. This proved to be difficult, and they eventually moved to Canton, Ohio where, in early 1941, they discovered just the place, a small farmhouse a few miles from the Ohio township of Minerva. It was set amidst countryside that delighted Hodgson. He was searching, as ever, for the little cottage he had once suggested he and Muriel might retire to back in the 1920s.

Ever since arriving in America, Hodgson had been sounded out about further publication. Macmillans in New York remained keen to take whatever poetry he might offer but he was suspicious of their motives and eventually fell out with them. Frank Morley, once of Faber, and now with Harcourt Brace in New York, was also pressing him to sign a contract that promised to deliver sufficient money to buy his farmhouse. Morley offered him $1,000 for a book of his thoughts and reminiscences, a sort of diary-cum-autobiography, to be followed up by his new 'long poem' which would bring another $500 advance. They would have appeared in the same list as Eliot's *Four Quartets*. There was also talk of a book on dogs, plus a project close to Hodgson's heart, *Without Comment*, the collection of neglected and obscure verses which he and Sassoon had partly assembled a decade or so before.

Hodgson at first seemed more than amenable. However, he fell ill with flu in February 1941 and, when recovered, he wrote to Morley turning the whole thing down. He was committed, he wrote, to finishing 'The Muse and the Mastiff', and having to write a prose book would simply get in the way. He would, he told Morley, revive the *Flying Fame* instead and publish his verse that way for a time.

Morley was sceptical of the new *Flying Fame* idea, dubbed 'Packington Pound' by Hodgson after a popular Elizabethan ballad. Times had changed from the pre-First World War days, and he thought that Hodgson was doing things the wrong way round. He should publish the verse properly first and then indulge in broadsides.

Others, including Professor Davison at Colorado, were also worried about the potential obscurity of such a project and Edward Marsh cast doubts on Hodgson's motives, recalling Max Beerbohm's observation that Sappho had devoted her life to "polishing the exquisite little poems which with feminine tact she passed off on posterity as the fragments of her complete work ..."

Hodgson's motives in rejecting such promising propositions were the usual mixture of ambivalence about fame and an aversion to the effort needed to secure it. There was also a deeper and genuine concern that his poetry, if published prominently, might fail – the *Last Blackbird* experience still haunted him.

He had written as long ago as 1935 to Professor Sanders:

> I might venture this so far as my own small amount of published verse is concerned: I do not know of any quality in it that is likely to preserve it beyond its day and it is late afternoon now – perhaps evening. I have my publisher's figures. If anything is found alive in the morning, well and good. Somebody will remark the strange occurrence, and curiosity about its author will then be reasonable. I *mean* alive: capable of affecting new people's minds, not merely worthy of inclusion in Period or other anthologies, often graveyards. Put differently, found to be a bit of real mulberry-fed stuff, not the rayon substitute, however intelligent or attractive it might be. Until then I think it not amiss in RH to stand back a little. He may not be wanted. Personally, I cannot know if I have written poetry. I can and do wish to avoid cheapening it.

Later, in 1950, William Maas wrote to Hodgson wondering whether it was worth going on writing his own short stories. Hodgson replied:

> I can answer this if I ask myself the same question with regard to my poems. Since I can't help going on with them when they come, I can only conclude you can't either. Whether it is worthwhile is, of course, the question but it seems to be irrelevant ... we both write for ourselves to satisfy something that demands that kind of satisfaction and I don't suppose that either of us looks for any

other. So far as printing for the public goes, I don't think it *is* worth while going on, but that question arises not at all: I print my poems in Scroll form, not for the public but in order to copyright them and to send as a greeting to a few – very few – people I like and have a reason for believing they like me ... I should add that the Scroll idea is a convenient way of saving up poems for a book form if I should at a future time wish to give it them: for the last few years that has become a dim notion, but it may brighten if Doom-fall should clearly postpone itself and the world again assume something vaguely resembling the planet as we knew it in our ignorant hey-day. I don't expect that, Maas ...

Thus commercial publication, though offered and clearly worthwhile financially, was rejected. He still needed cash, however, both for the farm and for the small chapbooks he was keen on producing. It was now that he rather shrewdly turned to Seymour Adelman, whom he had met a year earlier in Philadelphia in the company of Cornelius Weygandt. The reclusive Adelman was a wealthy young real-estate agent with a passion for collecting books and other items related to what he termed the three Ps: poetry, pugilism and Philadelphia. Shy and retiring, he was self-taught where literature was concerned, having dropped out of university before completing his studies.

He nevertheless would eventually settle into a curator role at Bryn Mawr College near Philadelphia, a post earned largely as a result of his decision to deposit his impressive collection in the college library. This consisted of, among other things, the papers and original manuscripts of A.E. Housman, the illustrations and personal papers of Claud Lovat Fraser and the largest collections of bare-knuckle boxing literature and artwork in the world.

Hodgson was a particular favourite of Adelman's, in fact, as he wrote excitedly to his parents soon after being introduced: "I know you won't believe it – I don't myself, yet it's true. I'm sitting here pinching myself – My God! Ralph Hodgson – it seems a dream, but it's true ... Lordy, am I thrilled!" According to Adelman, Hodgson was "the greatest living poet and one of the greatest in all English literature". For a few weeks in early 1940 Adelman had happily driven Hodgson around the Philadelphia district looking for a place to live – the ostensible reason for their being introduced in the first place. That venture had come to nothing but now, in March 1941, Hodgson was suggesting something even more exciting.

In January of that year, Aurelia had informed Adelman that Hodgson had been gathering a quantity of new material which he wanted to publish privately in chapbook form: "I seem to remember your saying you would like to have a part in such a venture ... the project is ready for a financial godfather ..."

Adelman, needless to say, expressed great enthusiasm, and in March Aurelia wrote again enclosing a list of almost 20 possible chapbook titles as well as outlining certain financial costs entailed in moving to their new home such as paying for a new furnace and a new electric range. She suggested three advances of, say, $250 each.

As collateral, the Hodgsons offered various packets of mint-condition *Flying Fames*, holographs of signed Hodgson poems plus various old rare books that Hodgson had collected over the years. She added, "Of course, we don't want to part with these things, but there they are to reimburse you if anything went wrong or something unforeseen should happen to Mr Hodgson or me."

Selling at 25 cents each in editions of 300-500 with no distribution system or advertising, the project made little commercial sense. Adelman, however, as Hodgson obviously knew, was flattered to be asked. In September 1941, therefore, the first chapbook, entitled *The Silver Wedding*, was printed. It was the first time since 1921 that anything new by Hodgson had seen the light of day, although, as the title poem suggests, this first chapbook contained as much old material as new.

Published by the Boerner Publishing Company of Minerva, Ohio, *The Silver Wedding* was in direct line of descent from *Flying Fame*. A sign reading *Packington Pound* and labelled *Late Flying Fame, London, England*, appeared on the back cover. It was 6 inches by 4 inches, had a yellow cover, was 20 pages long and decorated with small Hodgson pen-drawings. It eventually ran to two editions. A second chapbook, entitled *Selections from The Muse and the Mastiff* appeared in 1942.

After a gap of two years, the first *Flying Scroll* appeared. These would be printed by Adelman himself (the Namleda Company) after difficulties had arisen with Boerner, and consisted of single, unadorned sheets. Eleven in all would appear between 1944 and 1951, when the project came to a halt. In the process, just about everything of any significance that Hodgson had written since 1921, including all he wished made public of 'The Muse and the Mastiff', would be published. There is little evidence that the project made Adelman any money at all.

When the Namleda project ended in 1951, Hodgson was 80 years old and had reached the end of his creative journey. From then on, he spent his days watching birds, tending his animals, rummaging in books and immersing himself in those mental journeys that had long been a substitute for real life. In this latter pursuit he was sometimes joined by Adelman, who had rapidly become more than simply a financial godfather. Adelman shared Hodgson's fascination with books and illustrations, with book hunts and with long searches for the ill-considered trifle, the long-forgotten fact. His passions for particular poets were similar to Hodgson's: Coleridge, Keats, Wordsworth, Shelley and Blake. He also enjoyed indulging in that quintessentially Hodgson pursuit of mental time-travel, particularly to London in the early 19th century. He would draw particular streets in minute detail, indicating famous literary people's abodes, and these Hodgson would pore over with delight.

On a more practical level, he kept Hodgson supplied with newspapers and magazines, hunted down particular tobaccos and paintbrushes that Hodgson was in no position to search for himself and, on occasion, helped out with household finances. Accompanied by his sister, Adelman visited Hodgson several times specifically to record him both in conversation and as he recited poems. He also took many photographs. In fact, he became an invaluable branch of the Hodgson family, fussed over by both Hodgson and Aurelia.

Although quite obviously an unworldly enterprise, the *Packington Pound* and *Flying Scroll* project achieved exactly what Hodgson wanted in practical, everyday terms. Avoiding the effort and drudgery of producing long prose books that might well have earned him sufficient money to survive independently, but which would have occupied all his time, he was able to concentrate his mental energy on his poetry and, in a precarious sort of way, his poetry eventually paid most of the substantial bills.

In 1946, for instance, the American Academy of Letters, awarded Hodgson its annual prize which carried with it a substantial cash award, enough to pay off the mortgage on the farm. In 1954, his work had once again attracted enough attention in Britain for him to be given the Queen's Gold Medal for Poetry. This award brought considerable publicity in its wake and, as we shall see, a further welcome financial subsidy of a considerable kind.

It must not be overlooked, however, that the day-to-day grocery bills, and a great deal more besides, were paid by Aurelia who, in 1944, took a job as a clerk at the Minerva Wax Paper Company. For a number of years until she managed to buy a car, she lived in rooms in Minerva during the week and spent the weekends at Owlacres, as the farm was named, looking after Hodgson. He meanwhile consorted with his muse and prepared the *Flying Scroll* that would carry his poetic message to the world at large.

As we have seen, the *Packington Pound* chapbooks and the *Flying Scroll* format, were principally concerned to introduce 'The Muse and the Mastiff' to Hodgson's friends and admirers. Alongside that mammoth work, however, there appeared numerous smaller pieces, poetic off-cuts almost, referred to by Edward Marsh as "exquisite little poems", a peculiar sub-genre all Hodgson's own. The first *Packington Pound* production, *The Silver Wedding*, though containing extracts from 'To Deck a Woman' as well as the title poem itself, would introduce readers to this new, somewhat baffling body of work.

The poems seemed at times to have no reference point, no identifiable context, though they might have a date, perhaps, or a historical name. Academic friends were frequently puzzled ("What is a 'twite'?," wrote Louis Untermeyer in reference to 'The Shepherd's Warning'), their requests for information usually being rebuffed or grudgingly acceded to by Hodgson. ("I'm not fond of notes regarding poems," he commented after explaining something of the 'The Hever Picnic' to William Rose Benét).

'The Hever Picnic' is a good case in point. It appeared in *Flying Scroll* No 1, and its sixteen-odd lines tell of a certain Anne Bullen's encounter with a gypsy fortune-teller called Luckie Lee who comes dancing round a tree during a picnic. Luckie takes a piece of cake handed to her by Anne, and then dances off again, leaving Anne (and the reader) nonplussed as to what has been foreseen. One would need to know that Hever Castle was where Anne Boleyn once lived, and that Bullen is a version of Boleyn, to make some sense of it all.

Other smaller poems featured Noah hitting his thumb with a hammer as he builds the ark and thus inventing slapstick comedy, or the poet himself encountering Old Testament figures on the road to somewhere, accompanied by a dog, the name of which intrigues him. The jocular tone of many of the smaller poems recalls 'The Vanity of Human Ambition' and 'Big Behaviour' from *The Last Blackbird*, while some pieces could well have formed the basis of a *Big Budget* comic strip:

Queer – Queer

As a face at a bricked-up window,
Or the banging of a door in the desert,
This: 'Poking your nose in everywhere!'
'Me?' 'You – I give you warning:
'F I catch you in my dreams again,
I'll break your neck next morning!'

One can almost see the indignant old gent swinging his walking stick in the air at some cheeky urchin. There are also numerous one/two-liners that could well have run along the foot of a *Tit-Bits* page: "The fish looked bigger in the water"; "The hand-writing on the wall could be a forgery"; "Skunks, the squirrel said, are sent to try us." On a slightly more serious note, some of the pieces were penned during the Second World War and contain clear references to the conflict just past:

The Peace
And now beware the tearful rogue
Who pities the tapeworm, not the dog.

But on the whole, the references to the world at large are either general, gnomic warnings of possible catastrophe or diffident, almost half-hearted recommendations, instantly withdrawn. An example is 'The Pansy':

> I've looked as far as I can see –
> Though that's not far – down into me;
> If you have seen as much of you
> And tell me it's a pretty sight,
> Look again and take a light.
>
> On second thoughts, don't trouble to,
> You may be right –
> And where's my introspection now?
> I missed that pansy in the slough.

It is simply a reference to how pointless it is trying to call others to self-examination, as there are much better things to do with one's time, life being short. The same reluctance to press a particular case is evident in 'To Hang a Man':

> To hang a man:
> To fix the cap,
> And fix the rope,
> And slide the bar,
> And let him drop.
> I know, I know:
> What can you do!
> You have no choice,
> You're driven to;
> You can't be soft –
> A man like that;
> But Oh it seems –
> I don't know what –
> To hang a man!

These sentiments are repeated in 'The Foreman Said', which takes the case of a jury foreman and the difficulty of accepting responsibility for another person's life. Making judgements and the implications thereof was another theme, one where Hodgson reveals compassion for the subject of another's condemnation or praise. 'The Smile' shows close affinities to John Betjeman's 'In a Bath Teashop'. What is interesting, however, is the wide range of his subject matter, the glimpses of what was possible if he could have pressed on further. Instead he made only what appear to be thumbnail sketches – almost throwaway in tone and nature.

His major themes of time and nature were, however, still well represented in these smaller works, in particular, the animal world. 'The Ousel Cock' is a delightful little fable about how cock blackbirds chose the colour black for their feathers. It was really quite simple, the bird explains to the poet:

'Black goes with gold
'In a manner that dizzies
'Our hens to behold
'In the Spring of the year;
'That's why we chose black
'In the ages far back,
'And how we got here,
'If you need to be told.'

'Of Nature, Write' is a Hodgsonian declaration of nature's essential purity:

So write of Her; tell
That all's Eden and well:
No sniggers and smirks
At sight, sound or smell
Affront Her chaste Works;
She never fell.

Later critics, however, chose to concentrate on two poems: 'Time' and 'There is a Lady' both of which stood out as more substantial than the rest, being perhaps reworkings of earlier poems on similar themes. 'To a Linnet' in *The Last Blackbird* had been Hodgson's salute to the brave and tuneful bird who had provided him with a model of courage when he was faced with illness. 'There is a Lady' tells of another, more recent occasion when that same unnamed illness again threatened, but now he finds solace of a kind in singing an old Elizabethan tune to Aurelia:

Which an olden-days Lover
Sang to his Lady;
– Did, and does now
As I sing it to mine
Over and over.

The poem is typical of his new style, stripped of any vestige of flowery language, absolutely matter-of-fact in tone and delivery. Hodgson seems now like an old-timer sitting on a veranda whittling sticks. Each poem has that thin, turned feel, as though carved and shaped and decorated with a casual ease.

'Time' certainly has that quality about it, of delightful, artless caprice, of images conjured up for the sheer fun of the exercise. Adelman recorded Hodgson reading this poem, and his mode of delivery conveyed a sense of mischief, almost, as when he produces this simile/metaphor to convey one of time's qualities:

> Comparing it for sound:
> The wisp of gossamer
> Caught in a squirrel's fur,
> Groans like a ship aground;
> Shadow makes more noise.

The response he seeks is a smile or laughter. There is nothing beyond or behind the poem, although Walter de la Mare felt echoes of his childhood beckoning him as he read it: "The lines about the spinning-tops ... these took me back clean and away to the very moment of contemplating one in this condition – and the exact spot too – though I can't have been more than seven or eight ..."

> Comparing it for poise:
> The tops we spun to sleep,
> Seemingly so deep
> Stockstill, when we were boys,
> No more than stumbled round,
> Boxwoods though they were,
> The best we ever wound
> Or whipped of all such toys.

23

Final Years

*We're all alike, we poets, living in a land which is not our own but
we especially whom they want to discipline until we are all ready
to concede that black is not really black but some other colour of
the rainbow. Stick it out even to the edge of doom.*
(William Carlos Williams to Ralph Hodgson, 1961)

In July 1954 Norman Holmes Pearson, professor of English Literature of
Yale University drove out to Owlacres:

> … weaving my way along the wilderness of black dirt roads which
> twisted up and down hill through really beautiful farmland, rather
> like England in its way, in the soft light of evening. The fields
> of stubble where the wheat had been cut were gold in the sun.
> Finally after the many turns to the right and left I came to a large
> farmhouse, very prosperous, immediately beyond which was a cart
> road which plunged between the trees and curved toward a tiny
> farmhouse which must once have been the farm-helper's cottage.
> There, just emerging from the open barn-door was Mrs Hodgson
> who had only just arrived; and popping up from behind shrub-like
> trees was Hodgson himself, cheerful and smiling, tanned, in a
> loose grey shirt open at the neck and a pair of even looser linen
> trousers, bagged at the waist with the surplus that must earlier have
> accommodated a much ampler figure. They led me by rubbish piles
> along a path to the door of their house which had no yard but only
> a pump, piles of cinders, scattered dishes of food for cats and a
> great triumphant sunflower facing the door. When I sat inside, it
> faced me and Hodgson and I quoted Blake together.

A year earlier Pearson had written to Hodgson telling him of an offer
of financial aid. The writer Bryher (Annie Winifred Ellerman), a close
friend of Pearson's and a companion of the Imagist poet H.D., was a rich
Englishwoman who had helped writers in the past through her foundation,
distributing "Awards for distinction of achievement in letters". Though
the foundation had been dissolved, she now wished to help Hodgson
privately, having admired his poetry from afar since she was a girl ("I
knew Hodgson by heart when I was seventeen".) The offer came out of the

197

blue, and both he and Aurelia were dumbfounded. "You will understand my astonishment at your letter and its contents; I shall not readily recover from it," Hodgson wrote. They were very grateful, as times were becoming increasingly hard.

Whilst acting as the go-between for Bryher, Pearson soon became a valued correspondent and friend. He had never met Hodgson before and knew virtually nothing about his history, only the sparse details known by all. He was therefore a keen observer, and he found the Hodgson household fascinating:

> There were no bull-terriers, only a small, friendly mongrel who lorded it over the cats, pushing them from the food-bowls so that after he had eaten he had to be brought inside while they fed. The bowls were everywhere: a double set. When a filled one was brought out in the evening, the morning's bowls were taken in. The house itself was tiny: two medium-sized rooms and two small ones. That was all. We sat in a crammed combination of kitchen, dining-room, living-room, with a large round old-fashioned dining-room table near the door where we sat down for tea Hodgson himself had prepared and where we continued to sit for supper and continued on during the evening until eleven when I left. In it was a bellied iron stove for heating, a cooking stove, and a couch piled high with belongings: cardboard cartons of books, portfolios of drawings, magazines, a coat or two and capping them was a two-tiered crown: a dirty-white desert helmet with a straw farmer's hat on top. It was very convenient. Hodgson kept his smoking equipment on the couch and had only to reach out to pick it up or reach whatever else was useful to illustrate his point. He had a supply of what looked like opium pipes in which, however, he constantly stuffed a shredded tobacco he smoked.

The money Pearson would regularly forward to Hodgson was considerable: $1,500 a year at first in 1955 but increasing to $2,000 by the start of 1960. It enabled Aurelia to buy a car and eventually move back to stay in the farmhouse rather than the rooms in Minerva during the week. The money also enabled them to refurbish the property by installing storm windows and repairing the antiquated heating system.

Pearson's visit was quite an occasion, for Hodgson rarely entertained. During the war, he had been able and, grudgingly, willing to travel to universities to earn some money talking and taking part in poetry conferences. He was, however, always a reluctant traveller, and after the war he rarely left the farm, not even to accept his award from the American National Institute of Arts and Letters in 1946. Frank Morley stood in for him, and Hodgson wrote: "You did it for the muse's sake and your reward will be in heaven. In the meantime, we have received the cheque."

He was chary of receiving visitors other than Pearson. Only a chosen few made it down the muddy track from the world beyond – a world that was, by the 1950s, beginning to frighten and depress Hodgson. For America was then firmly in the grip of the Cold War and Hodgson, an avid radio listener, had come to fear a nuclear holocaust. He said as much to Pearson:

> He would bang the table with his hand until the tea things rattled and he was so engrossed that he did not stop even when his wife had laid the table for supper and waited for him to carve the meatloaf. Once in a while he would get up and leave the table, going into the other room to calm himself. 'A thousand years of man's development and progress towards what? Now there isn't time any more. There isn't time. If you can't sense it you can't be told it. A mountain of men's bodies slain by the atom bomb. Look at these hills. I can see them in a few years: the people will crowd the highways leaving the cities, and they will march down the country roads, pillaging the fields and slaughtering the cattle. They will come into the cellars of the farmhouse for food and strip the shelves before passing on to somewhere else where there will be more food to pillage. Maybe there will be a few people left in some corner but everything, from one thousand, two, ten thousand years will have been wasted!' One could see that it shook every corner of his life. 'Stop me,' he would say to his wife: 'Stop me when I get this way.' What could one say? But there could be no poetry, he said, where there was no time.

Hodgson not only feared nuclear disaster. He was increasingly suspicious of governmental manipulation and suppression of news, especially about flying saucers and UFOs, which were then highly topical. He claimed he had seen one in 1949 and made a detailed, annotated sketch which he sent to disbelieving friends. In a sense, this fear of ever more pervasive mind and thought control put him in line with various underground writers and poets of the period. He was certainly not drifting off into a rose-tinted old age. He was raging at the dying of the light, and some of his poetic 'squibs' attempted to encapsulate this bitterness at mankind's foolishness:

> This is not a foolish joke: Anno Bombino.
> Only the eskimo
> Staring at his dusty snow,
> Will ever know.

There's no doubt that Hodgson's fears were exacerbated by his self-imposed isolation, his hermit-like existence broken only by a chosen few old friends like Alida Monro and Christabel Hardie – who had settled in America. Certain poets, such as Stephen Spender, Robert Frost and Witter

Bynner, were entertained. There was Pearson, of course, who brought Bryher in 1953. Seymour Adelman visited regularly as well as a few younger people, usually aspiring poets whom he had met and befriended during the poetry conferences he attended during the war.

Queries from students or academics wanting to write theses about him were comprehensively rebuffed. However, one such student, Ammon Kershner, a student of Cornelius Weygandt's at Pennsylvania University, *was* granted an audience, probably in deference to Weygandt, whom Hodgson liked and considered a kindred spirit.

Kershner was treated politely, though not allowed to ask any biographical questions. Hodgson spoke at length about the perfidious influence of literature courses and the education system in general. This theme he would develop over the years and expound whenever he could; it was his Georgian rebuff to academic Modernism. Teachers, he insisted, had no right to indulge in such things as 'literary appreciation'; it was simply a means by which scholars forced their own ideas on young people rather than allowing them to discover literature, of whatever kind, for themselves. For who, said Hodgson, had the right to define what was good or what was bad? "If a person has his thirst for lyric poetry satisfied by a rendition of 'Oh Dear What Can the Matter Be?' who is to say he is wrong?"

Teachers, Hodgson felt, should confine their activities to imbuing basic skills like syntax, spelling and the correct meanings of words. He was also disdainful of 'form' in poetry and art. That, he asserted, was merely the picture frame, not the picture. And he talked of poets' souls having antennae just like TV aerials, which could pick up poetic signals. As for the muse – that was a private realm, not to be discussed in public.

The atom bomb, thought control, UFOs – all were expounded upon at length, leaving Kershner somewhat perplexed: "He speaks in a rather teasing manner, such that the listener can never be quite sure just to what degree he is spoofing and just to what degree he is serious. He seems to fluctuate rapidly between mock seriousness and genuine seriousness."

On one subject, however, Hodgson was extremely serious as it underlay his whole performance. That, according to Kershner, was

> his diligent attempt to dissuade anyone from writing anything about him or letting his work get into the hands of the detested graduate schools. He constantly warns that all his recent work has been copyrighted. On the other hand, he is most willing to read his visitor selections from his own work and from the classics …
> He reads through dark-rimmed spectacles, which he pushes up on his forehead in the manner of an aviator's goggles, when he interrupts his reading to interject comments. He reads poetry in the old rhetorical style of the 19th-century orator. He thunders forth in the tone and manner of the prophet.

Having thus exhausted his intrepid researcher, Hodgson fed him:

> The dinner consisted of an unusual delicacy – marrow balls scraped from the inside of a large beef or 'soup' bone, mixed with bread crumbs, fried in small pellet-like pieces and served buried in a large serving-dish of peas …

before packing him off down the track to Minerva, older but not perhaps very much wiser.

Hodgson's determination to remain *personally* unknown, to leave only his poetry to judgement, might lay him open to criticism that being *so* secretive actually *created* an interest. He was unrelenting, however. In 1959, when he was a sick man and confronted with a student from Princeton on his doorstep asking questions, according to Aurelia, he

> checked the student's desire to write about him. Ralph got out a magazine of the early 1800s and read the names of the verse writers. 'Now if you still want to write your essay in 200 years come around then.'

At the time of Kershner's visit Hodgson was still issuing *Flying Scrolls* and was still, to a large extent, an active poet. Once 'The Muse and the Mastiff' had been committed to the *Scroll*, however, his poetic work tailed away, but he continued to work fitfully each day, transcribing odd lines, usually the result of dreams, onto scraps of paper attached to pegs around his 'cot' or improvised bed. He wrote to Siegfried Sassoon in early 1950:

> My difficulty in writing is just that I can't find a thing to write about now. The one matter at the back of every thought and feeling is not for letters. That the world and everybody in it can and does carry on precisely as it used to is the most confounding fact of all, except the existence of the Horror itself. A maniacal yell from one end to the other is what one might have expected from a world sane enough to give it; that's what I say to myself, and yet I don't know; I hush down my own shriek and go on with my verse whenever I have a little luck as before. Once – I can't fix the date – hazily about the opening of the century – I had a strange reassurance, a feeling, not a thought, arising out of something almost like a spoken voice, that the world would escape by the skin of its teeth – escape what, I had no idea so far as I can remember – there was nothing on the remotest horizon at that time to account for it. I was almost wholly occupied with the future of bull-terriers and such matters. How I wish I could have that feeling or hear that voice 50 years later! Having apparently no future before us, since we are all bent on breaking off relations with Time for good, I find the past, and particularly the past before the opening of the century the best countryside for my mind to wander about in: even the dowdiest

late- and mid-Victorian days are a sort of Paradise to poke about in whenever I can find a column of print factual enough for secure footing upon, or a square inch or two of illustration with point and freshness left; and when those days begin to bore me, as they sometimes do, and I turn to old Regency Directories, London and Provincial, to whet my relish for old surnames and so on, I shove all those books away and regularly turn to my old standby, Robert Chambers, 3 Vols. of *Domestic Annals of Scotland*, with his songs and ballads of Scotland handy at my elbow for tea. After that I ruminate on the pleasing and unpleasing matters of my own memory, or I exchange memories with Weg, many of which I of course share now, or present-day observations with visitors now and then if the state of our byroads allows them to come within five miles of Owlacres.

He also devoted large amounts of time to watching birds, about which he wrote at length to Sassoon, Walter de la Mare, A.S. Fulton and William Maas. Birds were a link with so many of his friends as well as being a conduit to memories which haunted Hodgson almost physically at times: "Occasionally I catch a song I can't identify, leaving me perplexed precisely as the outburst of an unknown warbler once did in a wood at Newdigate forty years ago which troubles me still," he wrote to Sassoon.

Generally, though, the memories were precise and illuminating. When almost eighty he wrote to Walter de la Mare:

I remember getting off my bicycle half a mile north of Amersham to watch and listen to a grasshopper warbler on a furzy patch over a hedge. I think of Homewood beyond Dorking when I mention that bird; the common there was thick with them trilling along for hours on summer nights ... I still see as plainly as you do your spotted flycatcher, my only hooded crow at a spot between Wendover and Aylesbury; hawfinches in a back garden at Wendover, a used nest of gold-crested wrens at Halton ... I have heard and seen – strangely – buntings in Hampshire and can imitate their odd little call to this day ... I once watched with a friend who was going over the golf-course at Hartley Wintney a couple of merlins flying very low and as swiftly as whippets at their fastest ... but I think my best London bird was a heron in broad daylight flapping above Baker Street Station ...

It was a strange existence he led, inhabiting a solitary world of books, letters and birds, with only a radio for company. A sort of Samuel Beckett character shuffling to and fro between obscure volumes and albums, with no one on the horizon once the post boy had passed. With Weg working in Minerva all week, the phone would ring occasionally, the radio would murmur incessantly. Alone with fantasies and memories overlapping and intertwining, of Edwardian London, 19th-century Darlington, England in the 1930s, America in the 1950s. An interior world for which he could have been preparing all his life, for which he seemed perfectly suited and equipped and, as Kershner and Pearson discovered, utterly contented, with age having stripped away whatever minimal social desires or habits he possessed. Not lonely or isolated, his temperament and inclinations were now fully catered for. No responsibilities, no obligations, a sort of grand self-effacement, cocooned, thanks to Aurelia and Adelman and Bryher, *in* the world yet no longer *of* it: a disembodied voice reaching friends and relatives far and wide as if from some parallel world.

Yet it was a contradiction, for he was a man who loved to converse for hours on end. Now he would pour his observations into letters to regular devoted correspondents. There was Sassoon, of course, and Peggy Nunn and Fulton of the Thursdayers; Kot and Alida Monro, now a breeder of dogs; Sylvia Baker who continued to adore him just as she had done when a girl; Vere, Dolly's sister, to whom he remained devoted; even Doris Tibbs, the Ridgeway's waitress, who wrote in the 1950s to tell him that she often read his poems to her neighbours: "They ask, 'How long have you been reading poems, Dot!' says I, 'a very long time ago …'"

These letters reminded him of a world seemingly long since gone, voices that no longer inhabited a world of flesh and blood, although, of course, they *were* flesh and blood. Yet one senses that he did not want to know that; rather, he wanted *their* disembodied voices simply to remind him of his past; he wanted no part of their real world. That, after all, was why he had taken himself away to Japan and then to America. He had never really wanted to live in a cottage just down the road from Sassoon; he wanted to be able to return to Heytesbury or anywhere else whenever he chose to; and leave whenever he felt like it. That had been his way when he was younger, always keeping the world at bay, dipping in and out when it suited him. Now he would do it mentally.

Inevitably, his very longevity brought with it regular painful reminders that even disembodied voices are finite. The years in the USA were punctuated with death notices of friends and family – a world literally disappearing. In 1939 Mark Gertler and Henry Salt passed away, followed during the war years by the Georgians W.H. Davies and Robert Nichols plus Hodgson's old Fleet Street friends Rudolf Besier and Henry Leach. In 1946 came news of the death of his brother Walker, soon followed by that of W.J. Turner. In 1948 it was the turn of Holbrook Jackson, at whose funeral 'The Song of Honour' was read, and in 1950 James Stephens. In 1952 his sister Josey died, the last of the doughty band of relatives who had struggled on in the little school founded back in the 1890s by their mother but doomed once the war ended. The year 1953 saw the passing of Edward Marsh and Edward Shanks; in 1955 Kot died of a heart attack;

the following year Walter de la Mare, his first true poet friend. Each death added to the encroaching gloom – he was approaching ninety and his health was poor. But no death seemed to hit him harder than that of William Maas – his old Fleet Street colleague – for whom Hodgson felt an almost brotherly affection and concern.

Oddly enough, Maas was now also living in America after his daughter had brought him over to stay in a nursing home in Virginia, as he was now suffering from Alzheimer's disease. Hodgson had written to his wife:

> Do please try to make it clear to him that my memories of 60 years ago and 50 and 40 are never more than two minutes away from him: every act or word we shared in those days of long ago seems to me to be as fresh as if it were yesterday, time after time, surprising me, astounding me with the freshness and vividness of all my memories connected with old Maas. Don't trouble him with these things but, if you can convey to him that, in a sense, I am at his side now, at this very present and chatting away to him about Wendover and the hills round about …

When he was told Maas had died, he was unable to write back, dictating instead to Aurelia: "It's the end of an era, the end of a period … the last man who knew Northcliffe. Maas was a unique friend in my life …"

Some optimism, however, was brought into his life in 1958. Yet another devotee of his work, a bibliophile and wine merchant, Colin Fenton, approached him to ask permission to issue all the *Scrolls*, plus everything else that remained unpublished, in a limited edition hardback. Hodgson consented, and Fenton, with the illustrator Reynolds Stone and the Curwen Press, produced *The Skylark*. It was a project after Hodgson's heart, only 350 copies printed, the first 50 signed by Hodgson, and it burst upon the poetry scene in late 1958 to a reception he might only have dreamed of.

Once again, Hodgson had been 'rediscovered': John Betjeman, Siegfried Sassoon, Philip Larkin, Richard Church, among others, reviewed the book. In *The Times* the headline ran: "A Poet Breaks a 40-Year Silence", while others announced, "A Voice from the Past", "An Undiminished Voice", and, inevitably, "Meet Mr Hodgson". Larkin, perhaps inevitably, struck the only sour note, his piece running under the headline, "Down among the Dead Men", although he later included Hodgson's work in his *Oxford Book of Twentieth Century Verse*.

The following year Macmillan reissued it and *The Times Literary Supplement* devoted a front page to a review by Edith Sitwell: 'A Poet's Journey in Time'. There were articles reminiscing about Hodgson, including a piece in *Time* magazine, and three years later, in 1961, Macmillan published the *Collected Poems*, once again edited by Fenton. Hodgson was briefly back in the poetic and literary mainstream.

In that year he was nearing 90, and Professor Pearson contacted a score of poets young and old to compile a *Festschrift* of letters and poems dedicated to him. T.S. Eliot, C. Day-Lewis, W.H. Auden, Stephen Spender, Robert Graves, Marianne Moore, Robert Lowell, Robert Penn Warren and John Masefield, among others, contributed.

Masefield thanked Hodgson for his 'Skylark': "[which] will sing with Shelley's and Hardy's in everlasting sunshine". Robert Lowell wrote:

> You have rung in my ears for 25 years or more. First when I read you aloud to myself and others as an undergraduate. Then when I heard Dylan Thomas read you and finally when I.A. Richards and I spent an evening reading you aloud three or four years ago in Boston. Let me congratulate you on your poems, the ring and shine and humour and lastingness of your poems. Surely you are the oldest true poet alive, but it is you that give distinction to your age, not the other way round.

The small farmhouse at Minerva was flooded with reviews, letters of congratulation, requests for autographs, all of which Aurelia took care of. It was a welcome respite from the ongoing struggles of the previous few years. By 1961 Hodgson was almost completely bedridden and close to being blind. Strokes, spasms and falls had dogged him since 1955, and during the past year he had needed almost constant nursing. Aurelia had coped, as Hodgson had always known she would, although she was increasingly despairing. Hodgson was not an easy patient. He refused all forms of heating, he was scornful of medical help, intolerant of noise or anyone working in the house. His increasingly narrow routine was adhered to religiously.

Aurelia wrote to Pearson in January 1961:

> He is not doing well at all. [He needs] food every two hours, sitting up for a bit, and then back to bed. Can he last to enjoy his birthday 9th September? I don't know. Just a few days ago he said, 'Don't you see I'm a dying man?' He chose this farmhouse twenty years ago but there has been a penalty. He is too isolated from minds he would naturally enjoy.

In July 1961 he had a bad fall: "No harm done by some miracle. Often I lean over him – the breathing feels so very quiet. Several times he has opened his eyes: 'I'm still alive my dear.'" And in August 1961:

> Forgive me, but this summer I've stopped letter-writing ('Lower the blinds now ... A few matches in this box ... It's time for news. Three spoons of sugar ...'). I weep a few tears in the pantry and then back to the kitchen ...You'll understand.

In late October 1961, after another fall and further spasms, Hodgson entered Alliance City hospital, unable to stand. A severe stroke followed and two days later, at 3 a.m. on 3rd November, he died.

After a short service, followed by a reading of 'The Skylark', he was buried in Pleasant Grove cemetery in Brown Township, Carroll County, half a mile from Owlacres. "There, now he lies in the country churchyard just across the field from home, on his hill-top," Aurelia wrote to Seymour Adelman.

Epilogue
by Robert F. Richards

Ralph Hodgson. Poet and Person

From Hodgson's talk and from his poetry, we understood that the bull-terrier had an almost mystical meaning for him, and I dreamed of some day having the kind of dog he constantly praised.

In 1949 this dream was realised when a friend offered us the pick of a litter of bull-terriers sired by his own dog. We picked a tiny bitch and named her Lady Rafe – after Hodgson, of course, an affectionate diminutive of Ralph. We sent Hodgson a picture of Rafe, along with a copy of her pedigree. He wrote in reply that she would "take a lot of living up to, for she is a nailing little puppy".

In 1951 we took her to New York with us, stopping on the way at Owlacres, Hodgson's farmhouse. I well remember crossing the creek beside the road, and walking with Lady Rafe up the path to the farmhouse. Hodgson was coming down to meet us, and Rafe the bull-terrier met Rafe the poet but, more important to him, the poet met her. He said in wonder, "I thought I would never see another bull-terrier."

She occupied his attention from that moment on. He examined her eyes, her lips, her ears. She was a white cavalier, all white with a black spot on one ear and the peculiar slanted dark eyes of the pit bull. He said, "I don't know how they are running now, but in my time she would have been among the best." He reflected that he had personally known many of her ancestors.

As we walked he called me "Richards" and asked me to call him "Hodgson". He called my wife "my deah gel", but Rafe he called "little woman", and offered her titbits of ham. We stayed overnight on that visit. Hodgson and I talked long after my wife went up to the attic bedroom to sleep in the big bed with its high bedboard, under the soft old-fashioned comforters. Hodgson spread a little rug for Rafe near the door, where his own dog had used to sleep. Every once in a while he would look over at her, saying, "I will have nightmares about this."

After we reached New York, he worried about her and wrote that we should be very careful because many people would want to steal her. I did not understand his anxiety until Rafe (the bull-terrier) had died. Then I found myself following the two or three bull-terriers I saw afterwards, as if I were under a spell, and introducing myself to their astounded owners. A year and a half ago I saw a white cavalier on a street corner while I was driving. I could not stop, but I remember the dog standing beside his master, foursquare and confident, pointed ears up, as unreal and familiar as a unicorn.

Rafe the poet and Rafe the bull-terrier died within three months of each other, he in November 1962, she in January 1963. If, as I have been told, one year of a dog's life is equal to seven of a man's, he and she were the same age when they died. It is a coincidence that would have pleased him.

Dulcina, one of Ralph Hodgson's favourite bull-terriers.

Bibliography

Personal papers/collections consulted
Mrs S. Y. Fenton, Mrs Shirley Colquhoun and Ms Betty Beesley (Private papers of Robert Hodgson) plus Silvia Baker's unpublished 'Memories of Ralph Hodgson'

University collections consulted
The Ralph Hodgson Collection, Special Collections Department, Bryn Mawr College Library, Collection Number: M 49, Mariam Coffin Canaday Library, 101 N. Merion Avenue, Bryn Mawr, PA 19010-2899

Claud Lovat Fraser and Grace Crawford Fraser Collection: Manuscripts Special Collections Department, Bryn Mawr College Library, Collection Number: M 25 Mariam Coffin Canaday Library, 101 N. Merion Avenue, Bryn Mawr, PA 19010-2899

Ralph Hodgson Papers Gen Mss 245 Yale University Library, Beinecke Rare Book and Manuscript Library 121 Wall Street New Haven, CT 06511 (incl. Professor Norman Holmes Pearson (Yale Papers) Correspondence and 'Visit to Ralph Hodgson' typescript)

Bodleian Library, Oxford: The Department of Special Collections and Western Manuscripts (misc. corresp. and papers of Colin Fenton) (interviews with Elizabeth Crutwell, Adams Gowan Whyte, Maud Slessor, George Hutchinson) Ammon G. Kershner Jr. Dissertation: *Ralph Hodgson: A Biographical and Critical Study*, University of Pennsylvania, 1952

Unpublished prose by Ralph Hodgson cited
Educational Suggestions for Japanese Students (1936)
The Oddity of English Names (1934)
Old Books (1957)
Memory of a Ghost (1957)

Published prose by Ralph Hodgson cited
'Some Popular Fallacies Concerning Dogs', *C.B. Fry's Magazine*, 1910
'On Buying a Puppy', *C.B. Fry's Magazine*, 1910
'The Bull Terrier, The Policeman of the Hearth', *C.B. Fry's Magazine*, 1910
'The Visits of Ikey', *C.B. Fry's Magazine*, 1910
'England's Disappearing Dogs', *New Fry's Magazine*, 1911
'The Doggerel of Swift', *The Saturday Review*, August 1910
'The Boxers 1913', *The Saturday Review*, June 1913

Poems by Michael McKenna, edited and introduced by Ralph Hodgson
   (Nonesuch Press, London, 1932)
Poets Remembered (Rowfant Club, Cleveland, 1967)

Works of Hodgson from the Japanese cited
The Man'yōshū: One Thousand Poems Selected and Translated from the Japanese (Tokyo: Published for the Nippon Gakujutsu Shinkokai by the Iwanami Shoten, 1940).

Magazines featuring Ralph Hodgson's poetry
Saturday Review, 1904 onwards
To-Day, 1921
Harper's Bazaar, two poems by Ralph Hodgson, May 1960

Magazines, Books, Newspapers and Comic Papers featuring Ralph Hodgson's art-work
Funny Cuts, 1891, *The Minster*, 1895/6 Vols. 1-3, *Big Budget*, 1897–1908
George A.B. Dewar *The Birds in Our Wood* (Lawrence and Bullen, 1902)
E. Harcourt Burrage *A Knowing Dog* (Greening and Co., 1908)
George A.B. Dewar *The Book of the Seasons* (George Allen and Son, 1910)
C.B. Fry's Magazine 1904–10, *Tit-Bits*, 1909, *New Fry's Magazine*, 1911
Edmund Blunden *The Bonadventure: The Random Journey of an Atlantic
   Holiday* (Richard Cobden-Sanderson, London, 1922)
Westminster Gazette 1923.

Magazines and Comic Papers featuring Walter and Walker Hodgson's graphic art-work
Darlington Northern Echo, 1883–6
W.W. Hodgson, *The Victoria Park Jubilee Book of Sketches* (Samain Brothers,
   London, 1887)
W.W. Hodgson, *Zooland* (Ward Lock and Co., London, 1892)
Cassell's Family Magazine, London, 1891/2/3
The Idler, 1895/6
The Windsor Magazine, 1896
A.F. Calvert, *My Fourth Tour in Western Australia* (William Heinemann,
   London, 1897)
The Captain, (Newnes), 1903/4/5
W.E. Hodgson *Some Hints on Magazine Illustration, Press Art School* Special
   Supplement, No. 6, 1912

Periodicals and Reviews containing criticism and comment on Ralph Hodgson's life and poetry cited
English Literary World (Eigo Bungaku Sekai) Vol. 6, No. 6, September 1971
   (Ralph Hodgson Issue)(various authors)
(Anon.) (Marriage Report) *The Gentlewoman and Modern Life*, April 1896
(Anon.) 'Chapbooks of Today', *Daily News and Leader*, 18th December 1913

(Anon.) 'Broadsides, Chapbooks and Garlands', *Athenaeum*, January 1914

(Anon.) 'The Poems of Ralph Hodgson', *Living Age*, 287, December 1915

(Anon.) 'The Poems of Ralph Hodgson', *Times Literary Supplement*, 7th October 1915,

(Anon.) 'The Song of Honour', *The Englishwoman*, 1916

(Anon.) 'Mr Ralph Hodgson in One Volume', *Times Literary Supplement*, 14th June 1917

(Anon.) 'Contented If He Might Enjoy', *Athenaeum*, August 1917

(Anon.) 'A Lyrical Poet', *The Nation*, June 1917

(Anon.) 'A Poet's Journey in Time', *Times Literary Supplement*, 13th February 1959

(Anon.) 'A Sense of Strange Glories', *Times Literary Supplement*, 6th October 1961

Conrad Aiken, 'Three English Poets', *Dial* 63, August 1917

Conrad Aiken, 'The Deterioration of Poets', *Dial* 64, April 1918

John Betjeman, *The Spectator*, December 1956

John Betjeman, 'Elusive Ralph Hodgson' *Daily Telegraph*, March 1959

W.H. Chesson, 'Three Masters of English, I The Poetry of Ralph Hodgson', *Nineteenth Century and After* 88, July 1920

Richard Church, 'A Voice from the Past', *The Listener*, 3rd December 1959

Richard Church, 'A Century Remembered', *Country Life*, December 1971

Walter de la Mare, 'Song of Honour', *Edinburgh Review*, 219, April 1914

Prof. Kochi Doi, 'Ralph Hodgson', *A Century of English Studies in Japan*, 1968

Colin Fenton 'A Poet Breaks 40 Years Silence', *The Times*, 7th November 1958

J.G. Fletcher, 'Poetry of Ralph Hodgson', *Dial*, 19th July and 30th August 1917

O.W. Firkins, 'English Voices', *The Nation*, 24th August 1918

G.S. Fraser, 'I, My Ancester', *New Statesman*, 18th August 1961

Lovat Fraser, 'Popular Ballads and the Broadside', *T.P.'s Weekly*, 25th April 1913

John Fuller, 'Meet Mr Hodgson', *Time*, 30th March 1959

Tom Greenwell, 'The Age of the Clever, Clever', *John O'London's Weekly*, 17th December 1959

The Revd Leslie W. Hayes, 'The Poetry of Ralph Hodgson', *The Methodist Recorder*, October 1948

Holbrook Jackson, (Editorial) *To-day*, May 1917

George Landor, 'Ralph Hodgson's Poems', *The Bookman Gallery*, January 1917

Philip Larkin, 'Down among the Dead Men', *The Spectator*, 18th December 1959

Naomi Lewis, 'An Undiminished Voice', *New Statesman*, 7th February, 1959

E.V. Lucas, 'The Poetry of Ralph Hodgson', *The Nation* 99, 17th September 1914

H.J. Massingham. 'The Wild Birds Protective Act', *Country Life*, 27th October 1923

Haldane McFall, 'Of Broadside and Chapbook', *Hearth and Home*, 19th June 1913

Harold Monro (ed.) *Poetry and Drama* Vol. 1 No. 1, March 1913–1914
Sir Henry John Newbolt, 'The Poems of Ralph Hodgson', *To-Day*, June 1917
William Lyon Phelps, 'The Advance of English Poetry in the Twentieth
    Century', *The Bookman*, January 1918
David. A. Roberston, 'Contemporary English Poets: Ralph Hodgson', *English
    Journal*, 15th February 1926
Takeshi Saito, 'Ralph Hodgson in Japan', *Japan Quarterly*, April–June 1962
Siegfried Sassoon, 'Ralph Hodgson Redivivus', *The Tablet*, December 1958
Edith Sitwell, 'Great Writers Rediscovered, 5: The Poets of Delight: Bottomley
    and Hodgson', *Sunday Times*, 5th May 1957
Maud Slessor, 'Ralph Hodgson', *The American Bookman* 80, April 1931
John Sparrow, 'The Skylark and Other Poems', *The Listener*, 12th March 1959
John Sparrow, 'Ninety Years a Poet', *The Sunday Times*, 13th August 1961
Maisie Spens, 'Ralph Hodgson', *Poetry Review*, 20th July 1929
Edward Thomas, 'A Summer Singer', *Daily Chronicle*, 30th May 1907
Helen Thomas, (Letter) *The Times*, 7th November 1962
Anthony Thwaite, 'Collected Poems of Ralph Hodgson', *The Spectator*,
    1st September 1961
Leonard Woolf, 'Kot', *The New Statesman*, 5th February 1955
Arthur Waugh, 'Flying Fames', *New Statesman*, 28th June 1913
Arthur Waugh, 'The New Poetry', *Quarterly Review* 226, October 1916
Arthur Waugh, 'Mr Ralph Hodgson', The Book of the Week, *The Outlook*,
    17th June 1917
Marcus Woodward, 'Bull Terrier Talk', *Pearson's Magazine*, October 1904

Books cited
Seymour Adelman, *The Moving Pageant* (Sutter House, 1977)
D.J. Adley and W. Lofts, *The Men Behind Boys' Fiction* (Howard Baker, 1970)
Conrad Aiken, *Scepticisms* (Alfred A. Knopf, 1919)
Enid Bagnold, *Enid Bagnold's Autobiography* (Heinemann, 1969)
Clifford Bax, *Some I Knew Well* (Phoenix House, 1951)
Clive Bloom (ed.), *Literature and Culture in Modern Britain 1900–1929*
    (Longman, 1993)
Charles Booth, *Map Descriptive of London Poverty, 1898–9* (London School
    of Economics)
James Buckland, *The Pros and Cons of the Plumage Bill* (Edmund Evans,
    1911)
Lewis Bush, *The Road to Inamura* (Robert Hale, 1960)
John Carswell, *Lives and Letters 1906–1957* (Faber, 1978)
Richard Church, *The Voyage Home* (Reprint Society, 1964)
John Cournos, *Autobiography* (G.P. Putnam's and Sons, 1935)
Gerald Cumberland, *Written In Friendship: A Book of Reminiscences*
    (Grant Richards, 1923)
David Daiches, *Poetry and the Modern World: A Study of Poetry in England
    Between 1900 and 1939* (University of Chicago Press, 1940)
W.H. Davies, *Later Days* (Jonathon Cape, 1925)

Gary Day and Brian Docherty (eds.) *British Poetry 1900–1950: Aspects of Tradition* (St Martin's Press, 1995)

George A.B. Dewar, *A Younger Son* (Grant Richards, 1920)

Robin Doughty, *Feather Fashion and Bird Preservation* (University of California Press, 1975)

(Elizabeth Fagan) (ed.), *From the Wings by 'The Stage Cat'* (W. Collins, 1922)

Eleanor Farjeon, *Edward Thomas: The Last Four Years* (Oxford University Press, 1958)

Penelope Fitzgerald, *Charlotte Mew and her Friends* (Collins, 1984)

G.S. Fraser, *The Modern Writer and His World* (Pelican Books, 1964)

C.B. Fry, *Life Worth Living: An Autobiography* (Eyre & Spottiswoode, 1939)

Mark Gertler, *Selected Letters*, ed. Noel Carrington (Rupert Hart Davis, 1965)

Joy Grant, *Harold Monro and the Poetry Bookshop* (Routledge Kegan Paul, 1967)

Robert Graves, *The Common Asphodel: Collected Essays and Poetry 1922–1949* (Hamish Hamilton, 1949)

(Denis Gifford), *Victorian Comics* (George Allen and Unwin, 1976)

Christopher Hassell, *Edward Marsh, Patron of the Arts* (Faber, 1959)

John Hatcher, *Ralph Hodgson Poet and Artist. Britain & Japan: Biographical Portraits,* ed. Hugh Cortazzi, Vol.V. (Global Oriental, 2005)

Holbrook Jackson, *Unpublished Letters of Holbrook Jackson to Joseph Ishkill* (Oriele Press, 1960)

Richard Jefferies, *The Story of My Heart* (Longmans, Green & Co., 1883)

D.H. Lawrence, *The Letters of D.H. Lawrence, Volume II, June 1913–October 1916*, ed. George J. Zytaruk and James T. Boulton (Cambridge University Press, 1981)

D.H. Lawrence, *Selected Literary Criticism*, ed. Anthony Beal (Heinemann, 1955)

Henry Leach, *Fleet Street from Within* (Arrowsmith's Bristol Library, Vol. 93, 1905)

F.R. Leavis, *New Bearings in English Poetry* (Chatto and Windus, 1932)

John Lester, *Journey Through Despair: Transformations in British Literary History, 1890–1914* (Princeton University Press, 1968)

Haldane McFall, *The Book of Claud Lovat Fraser* (J.M. Dent, London 1923)

Wallace Martin, *The New Age under Orage* (Manchester University Press, 1967)

John Masefield, *'Fourth Award of the Edmund Polignac Prize', Royal Society of Literature: The Academic Committee: Addresses of Reception Nov 27. 1914* (Oxford University Press, 1915)

John Masefield, *So Long to Learn: Chapters of an Autobiography* (Heinemann, 1952)

H.J. Massingham, *London Scene* (Cobden Sanderson, 1933)

Theodore Maynard, *The Last Blackbird Becomes the Phoenix: Our Best Poets, English and American: Hodgson* (Henry Holt, 1922)

Harold Monro, *Some Contemporary Poets* (Leonard Parsons, 1920)

Ottoline Morrell, *Early Memories of Lady Ottoline Morrell*, ed. Robert Gathorne-Hardy (Faber and Faber, 1963)

John Middleton Murry, *Between Two Worlds* (Cape, 1935)

Henry John Newbolt, *The World as in My Time: Memoirs 1862-1932* (Faber and Faber, 1932)

David Perkins, *A History of Modern Poetry, Volume I: From the 1890s to the High Modernist Mode, Part Two: Poetry in Rapport with a Public* (Harvard University Press, 1976)

R. Pound and Lord Harmsworth, *Northcliffe* (Cassell, London, 1959)

John Cowper Powys, *Autobiography* (Macdonald & Co., 1934)

Peter Quennell, *A Superficial Journey Through Tokyo and Peking* (Faber and Faber, 1932)

Alfred Rawlinson, *The Defense of London 1915-1918* (Andrew Melrose, 1923)

James Reeves (ed.), *Georgian Poetry* (Penguin Books, 1962)

Timothy Rogers (ed.), *Georgian Poetry 1911-1922: The Critical Heritage* (Routledge, 1977)

Robert Ross, *The Georgian Revolt 1910-1922: Rise and Fall of a Poetic Ideal* (Faber, 1967)

William Rothenstein, *24 Portraits: Second Series* (Chatto and Windus, 1923)

William Rothenstein, *Men and Memories: Recollections of William Rothenstein 1900-1922* (Faber and Faber, 1931)

Henry Salt, *The Creed of Kinship* (Constable and Co., 1935)

Henry Salt, *Company I Have Kept* (Allen & Unwin, 1930)

Siegfried Sassoon, *Diaries 1920-1922*, ed. and introduced by Rupert Hart-Davis (Faber and Faber, 1985)

George B. Saul, *Withdrawn in Gold: Three Commentaries on Genius* (Mouton, 1970)

Anne Sebba, *Enid Bagnold* (Weidenfeld and Nicolson, 1986)

Robert Selcourt, *T.S. Eliot A Memoir* (Garnstone Press, 1971)

John Silkin, *Out of Battle* (Oxford University Press, 1972)

Stan Smith, *Edward Thomas* (Faber Student Guide, 1986)

C.K. Stead, *The New Poetic* (Penguin Books, 1967)

James Stephens, *Letters*, ed. Richard J. Finneran (Macmillan, 1974)

Robert Louis Stevenson, *Letters, Vol. II (1854-1879)* ed. Bradford Booth and Ernest Mehew (Yale, 1994.)

Richard Stonesifier, *W.H. Davies: A Critical Biography* (Cape, 1963)

L.A.G Strong, *Green Memory* (Methuen, 1961)

Mary Sturgeon, *Studies of Contemporary Poets* (G. G. Harrap and Co., 1920)

Wesley D. Sweetser, *Ralph Hodgson: A Bibliography* (Garland, 1980) (incl. 'Ralph Hodgson, Poet and Person' by Robert Richards)

Allen Tate (ed.), *T.S. Eliot: The Man and His Work* (Pelican Books, 1971)

Edward Thomas, *Letters to Gordon Bottomley*, ed. George R. Thomas (Oxford University Press, 1968)

Helen Thomas, *As It Was and World Without End* (Faber, 1956)

Lawrance Thompson, *Robert Frost: The Early Years 1874–1915* (Cape, 1971)

Louis Untermeyer (ed.), *Modern American and British Poetry* (Harcourt, Brace and Co., 1942)

Barry Webb, *Edmund Blunden: A Biography* (Yale University Press, 1990)

Cornelius Weygandt, *The Time of Yeats* (Russell & Russell, 1969)

Theresa Whistler, *The Life of Walter de la Mare: Imagination of the Heart* (Duckworth, 2004).

Stephen Winsten, *Salt and His Circle* (Hutchinson and Co., 1951)

J. Howard Woolmer, *Poetry Bookshop, 1912-1935: A Bibliography* (Woolmer/Brotherson, 1988)

Index

Photograph credits

GREENWICH EXCHANGE BOOKS

"Some things have to be believed to be seen" (Ralph Hodgson)

Ralph Hodgson's most influential and enduring work appeared just prior to, and during, the First World War. This new selection brings together, for the first time in 40 years, some of the most beautiful and powerful 'hymns to life' in the English language, work imbued with a spiritual passion for the beauty of creation and the mystery of existence.

In 1961, the American poet Robert Lowell wrote to Hodgson, "You have sung in my ears for twenty-five years or more. Let me congratulate you on your poems, the ring and shine and humour and lastingness of them." Poet Laureate John Masefield wrote of Hodgson's poem, 'The Skylark', "It will sing with Shelley's and Hardy's in everlasting sunshine". Stephen Spender remarked after meeting Hodgson in the late fifties: "I was reminded by the gleam in his eye, the sacred devotion with which he spoke old-fashioned about the Muse, that he belonged to a kingdom of poetry in which all who were poets were equal ..."

Enjoy the shine and beauty of Hodgson's poems with this new, collected edition.

'The Last Blackbird' and other poems by Ralph Hodgson edited and introduced by John Harding. 2004 • 70 pages • ISBN 978-871551-81-5

GREENWICH EXCHANGE BOOKS

LITERARY & BIOGRAPHY

Matthew Arnold and 'Thyrsis' *by Patrick Carill Connolly*
2004 • 180 pages • ISBN 978-1-871551-61-7
The Author, the Book and the Reader *by Robert Giddings*
1991 • 220 pages • illustrated • ISBN 978-1-871551-01-3
Norman Cameron *by Warren Hope*
2000 • 226 pages • ISBN 978-1-871551-05-1
Aleister Crowley and the Cult of Pan *by Paul Newman*
2004 • 222 pages • ISBN 978-1-871551-66-2
John Dryden *by Anthony Fowles*
2003 • 292 pages • ISBN 978-1-871551-58-7
The Good That We Do *by John Lucas*
2001 • 214 pages • ISBN 978-1-871551-54-9
D.H. Lawrence: The Nomadic Years, 1919-1930 *by Philip Callow*
2006 • 226 pages • ISBN 978-1-871551-82-2
Liar! Liar!: Jack Kerouac – Novelist *by R.J. Ellis*
1999 • 294 pages • ISBN 978-1-871551-53-2
Musical Offering *by Yolanthe Leigh*
2000 • 56 pages • ISBN: 978-1-871551-46-4
In Pursuit of Lewis Carroll *by Raphael Shaberman*
1994 • 118 pages • illustrated • ISBN 978-1-871551-13-6
**Poetry in Exile: A study of the poetry of W.H. Auden, Joseph Brodsky &
George Szirtes** *by Michael Murphy*
2004 • 266 pages • ISBN 978-1-871551-76-1
Wordsworth and Coleridge: Views from the Meticulous to the Sublime *by
Andrew Keanie*
2007 • 206 pages • ISBN 978-1-871551-87-7 (Hardback)

POETRY

Adam's Thoughts in Winter *by Warren Hope*
2000 • 46 pages • ISBN 978-1-871551-40-2
Baudelaire: Les Fleurs du Mal *Translated by F.W. Leakey*
2001 • 152 pages • ISBN 978-1-871551-10-5
Lines from the Stone Age *by Sean Haldane*
2000 • 52 pages • ISBN 978-1-871551-39-6
Lipstick *by Maggie Butt*
2007 • 72 pages • ISBN 978-1-871551-94-5
Martin Seymour-Smith – Collected Poems *edited by Peter Davies*
2006 • 182 pages • ISBN 978-1-871551-47-1
Shakespeare's Sonnets *by Martin Seymour-Smith*
2001 • 194 pages • ISBN 978-1-871551-38-9

The Rain and the Glass *by Robert Nye*
  2005 • 132 pages • ISBN 978-1-871551-41-9
Wilderness *by Martin Seymour-Smith*
  1994 • 52 pages • ISBN 978-1-871551-08-2

FOCUS SERIES

Emily Brontë's Wuthering Heights by Matt Simpson (10-1)*
T.S. Eliot's The Waste Land by Matt Simpson (09-5)*
Thomas Hardy: Poems of 1912–13 by John Greening (04-0)*
The Poetry of Ted Hughes by John Greening (05-7)*
George Eliot's Middlemarch by John Axon (06-4)*
Michael Frayn's Spies by Angela Topping (08-8)*
James Joyce's A Portrait of the Artist as a Young Man
by Matt Simpson (07-1)*
The Poetry of Tony Harrison by Sean Sheehan (15-6)*
Harold Pinter by Lee Jamieson (16-3)*
Wordsworth and Coleridge: Lyrical Ballads (1798)
by Andrew Keanie (20-0)8*
Edward Thomas by John Greening (28-6)*
William Blake, Songs of Innocence and Experience
by Matt Simpson (26-2)*
F. Scott Fitzgerald's The Great Gatsby by Peter Davies (29-3)*

HISTORICAL FACTION

The Secret Life of Elizabeth I *by Paul Doherty*
  2006 • 210 pages • ISBN 978-1-871551-85-3 (Hardback)
Death of the Red King *by Paul Doherty*
  2006 • 190 pages • ISBN 978-1-871551-92-1 (Hardback)

STUDENT GUIDE LITERARY SERIES

The Greenwich Exchange Student Guide Literary Series is a collection of essays on major or contemporary serious writers in English and selected European languages. The series is for the student, the teacher and 'common readers' and is an ideal resource for libraries. The Times Educational Supplement praised these books, saying, "The style of [this series] has a pressure of meaning behind it. Readers should learn from that ... If art is about selection, perception and taste, then this is it."

(ISBN prefix 978-1-871551 applies unless marked*, when the prefix 978-1-906075 applies.)

Antonin Artaud by Lee Jamieson (98-3)
W.H. Auden by Stephen Wade (36-5)

Honoré de Balzac by Wendy Mercer (48-8)
William Blake by Peter Davies (27-3)
The Brontës by Peter Davies (24-2)
Robert Browning by John Lucas (59-4)
Lord Byron by Andrew Keanie (83-9)
Samuel Taylor Coleridge by Andrew Keanie (64-8)
Joseph Conrad by Martin Seymour-Smith (18-1)
William Cowper by Michael Thorn (25-9)
Charles Dickens by Robert Giddings (26-9)
Emily Dickinson by Marnie Pomeroy (68-6)
John Donne by Sean Haldane (23-5)
Ford Madox Ford by Anthony Fowles (63-1)
The Stagecraft of Brian Friel by David Grant (74-7)
Robert Frost by Warren Hope (70-9)
Patrick Hamilton by John Harding (99-0)
Thomas Hardy by Sean Haldane (33-4)
Seamus Heaney by Warren Hope (37-2)
Joseph Heller by Anthony Fowles (84-6)
Gerard Manley Hopkins by Sean Sheehan (77-3)
James Joyce by Michael Murphy (73-0)
Philip Larkin by Warren Hope (35-8)
Laughter in the Dark – The Plays of Joe Orton by Arthur Burke (56-3)
George Orwell by Warren Hope (42-6)
Sylvia Plath by Marnie Pomeroy (88-4)
Poets of the First World War by John Greening (79-2)
Philip Roth by Paul McDonald (72-3)
Shakespeare's A Midsummer Night's Dream by Matt Simpson (90-7)
Shakespeare's Hamlet by Peter Davies (12-5)*
Shakespeare's King Lear by Peter Davies (95-2)
Shakespeare's Macbeth by Matt Simpson (69-3)
Shakespeare's The Merchant of Venice by Alan Ablewhite (96-9)
Shakespeare's Much Ado About Nothing by Matt Simpson (01-9)
Shakespeare's Non-Dramatic Poetry by Martin Seymour-Smith (22-6)
Shakespeare's Othello by Matt Simpson (71-6)
Shakespeare's Romeo and Juliet by Matt Simpson (17-0)
Shakespeare's Second Tetralogy: Richard II-Henry V by John Lucas (97-6)
Shakespeare's Sonnets by Martin Seymour-Smith (38-9)
Shakespeare's The Tempest by Matt Simpson (75-4)
Shakespeare's Twelfth Night by Matt Simpson (86-0)
Shakespeare's The Winter's Tale by John Lucas (80-3)
Tobias Smollett by Robert Giddings (21-1)
Alfred, Lord Tennyson by Michael Thorn (20-4)
Dylan Thomas by Peter Davies (78-5)
William Wordsworth by Andrew Keanie (57-0)
W.B. Yeats by John Greening (34-1)